D0928152

THE LOEB CLASSICAL LIBRARY

FOUNDED BY JAMES LOEB 1911

EDITED BY

JEFFREY HENDERSON

ARISTOTLE

II

LCL 391

ARISTOTLE

POSTERIOR ANALYTICS

EDITED AND TRANSLATED BY
HUGH TREDENNICK

TOPICA

EDITED AND TRANSLATED BY
E. S. FORSTER

HARVARD UNIVERSITY PRESS
CAMBRIDGE, MASSACHUSETTS
LONDON, ENGLAND

First published 1960
Reprinted 1966, 1976, 1989, 1997, 2004

LOEB CLASSICAL LIBRARY® is a registered trademark
of the President and Fellows of Harvard College

ISBN 0-674-99430-2

Printed and bound by Edwards Brothers, Ann Arbor, Michigan
on acid-free paper made by Glatfelter, Spring Grove, Pennsylvania

CONTENTS

THE TRADITIONAL ORDER of the works of
Aristotle as they appear since the edition of
Immanuel Bekker (Berlin, 1831), and their
division into volumes in this edition

THE TRADITIONAL ORDER

THE TRADITIONAL ORDER

THE TRADITIONAL ORDER

POSTERIOR ANALYTICS

INTRODUCTION

I. The Composition of the Analytics

It is hardly satisfactory to discuss the contents of the *Posterior Analytics* without first considering whether the work is rightly named ; that is, whether (upon the whole) it presupposes and forms a logical sequel to the *Prior Analytics*. Aristotle himself does not distinguish the two ; when, in the course of another treatise, he has occasion to mention either, he refers simply to τὰ Ἀναλυτικά. The division into Prior and Posterior is not certainly earlier than about A.D. 200, when Alexander of Aphrodisias wrote his commentary on *An. Pr.* I ; but it can be traced back with probability to the Alexandrian scholar Hermippus (late third century B.C.). The presumption that the names so assigned correspond to the order of actual composition has been assailed by Professor F. Solmsen (*Die Entwicklung der aristotelischen Logik und Rhetorik*, Berlin, 1929). At the time when I was translating the *Prior Analytics* I was disposed to accept his conclusions ; but I have since changed my mind. It is not possible here to examine Solmsen's ingenious arguments in detail (this has been done sufficiently by Sir David Ross in the introduction to his edition of the *Analytics*) ; but it may be useful to summarize some of the more important and to indicate how they may be met.

Assuming that Aristotle's thought became pro-

2

gressively emancipated from Platonic influence, Solmsen offers (among others) the following grounds for supposing that *An. Post.* is more Platonic, and therefore earlier, than *An. Pr.* :

1. It is preoccupied (especially in Book I) with mathematics.

2. Its theory of ἀρχαί springs from Plato's doctrine of ὑποθέσεις in *Rep.* vi-vii.

3. It contains passages implying acceptance of the Theory of Forms (treatment of points, lines, planes and solids as a " chain of Forms," 73 a 35 ; recognition of a ἓν παρὰ τὰ πολλά, 100 a 7).

4. The word ὅρος, common in *An. Pr.*, rare in *An. Post.*, represents the final stage in the development of Aristotle's thought away from the Platonic εἶδος, by way of καθόλου, to a purely logical conception.

5. In the *Politics*, if we accept Jaeger's conclusions, discussion of the Ideal State precedes consideration of existing imperfect states ; in the same way the doctrine of scientific demonstration by the first figure should precede the examination of indirect or inconclusive methods of reasoning, just as in Aristotle himself Platonic idealism gave place to a scientific interest in observable facts.

More generally, (6) the tentative methods of *An. Post.* provide a significant contrast with the brisk assurance of *An. Pr.*

Ross has shown (I think) very fairly that, however much truth there may be in these arguments, none is conclusive. (1) Mathematics is the only science that can provide examples of pure demonstration. (2) No one doubts that Aristotle's theory of ἀρχαί owes much to its Platonic prototype, but the differences are at least as great as the resemblances.

(3) The passages cited need not and should not be interpreted as evidence for belief in Forms. (4) ὅρος (in the sense of " term ") occurs more often in *An. Post.* than Solmsen apparently realized (fifteen times instead of three ?) ; in any case one would expect to find it more often in a discussion of formal logic ; and it is defined only in *An. Pr.* 24 b 16. (One might add that Aristotle's terminology is so fluid that no argument of this kind can be really cogent.) (5) The argument from analogy (for it is no more than this), though attractive, can hardly be said to prove anything ; and if we are assessing probabilities it may well seem strange that Aristotle, having discovered syllogism in Barbara, should elaborate a whole theory of demonstration before experimenting to see what could be done with other combinations of premisses. (6) Apart from the fact that *An. Pr.* is a more highly finished work, differences of manner and method can be sufficiently explained by differences in the nature and difficulty of the subject-matter.

These counter-arguments weaken but do not destroy Solmsen's thesis. Far more telling is the evidence of direct reference and presupposition. Ross has shown that all the explicit references from one work to the other support the traditional order, and that at least eighteen of the thirty-four chapters of *An. Post.* I contain passages that definitely presuppose a knowledge of *An. Pr.* ; so that, to accommodate the received text to Solmsen's view, we must assume more re-writing than is consistent with reasonable probability.

If, as I hope, this summary gives a fair picture of the facts, we can be moderately confident that the *Prior Analytics* is really the earlier work (apart from a few passages which seem to have been added after the *Posterior Analytics* was written).

II. The Conditions of Scientific Knowledge

In the *Prior Analytics* Aristotle has stated and developed his theory of syllogism, analysed and illustrated the various figures, moods and modes, described the conditions under which syllogism is possible, examined its mechanism and properties, given practical advice for its use, and distinguished it from other methods of reasoning. He now turns to the problem of knowledge : what it is, how it is acquired, how guaranteed to be true, how expanded and systematized.

Knowledge and Demonstration

In the first three chapters we are shown that all reasoned acquisition of knowledge involves a process in which the mind advances from something that is already known. This starting-point may be knowledge of (*a*) fact, or (*b*) meaning, or (*c*) both. It seems clear that Aristotle has already tacitly restricted his survey to ἐπιστήμη proper, because he illustrates (*a*) by a general axiom and (*b*) and (*c*) by mathematical examples ; and he goes on to qualify his original statement by observing that when we draw an inference by syllogism in the first figure, although the major premiss must be known at the outset, the minor may only be grasped at the same time as the conclusion. Thus he shows (1) that some of our previous knowledge may be only potential, (2) that reasoning consists in the actualization of potential knowledge ; and (pointing out in passing the differ-

5

ence between universal and enumerative propositions) prepares us for his explicit account of scientific knowledge (ch. i).

We have unqualified knowledge of a fact only if we (1) attribute it to its true cause and (2) recognize it as necessary. One form of such knowledge is acquired by demonstration through syllogism. The ultimate premisses from which our conclusions are drawn must be (1) true, or the conclusions would not be demonstrable as necessary, (2) primary and immediate, because otherwise they could only be known by demonstration. They must also be causative of the conclusions, prior (as being causative and more fundamental in nature) and better known (*i.e.*, more intelligible in themselves, as being more universal). Finally they must be appropriate, *i.e.*, not borrowed from a different genus.

These ultimate premisses are of two kinds. First there are axioms (ἀξιώματα, κοινά, κοιναὶ ἀρχαί), among which Aristotle reckons not only universal principles such as the Laws of Contradiction and Excluded Middle, but principles such as " equals subtracted from equals leave equal remainders," which are relevant only to quantities. Perhaps it was his failure to distinguish these that made him uncertain about the precise function of the axioms in demonstration ; at any rate he speaks of them sometimes as the source (ἐξ ὧν), sometimes as the means (δι' ὧν). Secondly, there are θέσεις, principles special to individual sciences : these are either ὑποθέσεις, assumptions that the primary subjects of the science exist, or ὁρισμοί, nominal definitions of technical terms. These principles are not demonstrable. If knowledge were only possible through demonstration, then either (1) demonstration would consist in an infinite regress, and we should never reach *first* principles, or (2) if we did reach them they would be themselves indemonstrable and unknowable. Aristotle shows that there is no escape from this difficulty by supposing that everything can be proved by circular demonstration, because this does not prove anything at all (chs. ii-iii). How the first principles *are* known is not explained until the end of Book II.

Demonstration and its Premisses

Scientific knowledge is concerned only with necessary facts ; these can only be known as necessary if they are proved as such ; therefore the premisses from which they are proved must be necessary. They must also be scientific ; and this implies certain relations between predicate and subject. (1) The predicate must be true of *all* the subject. (2) The predicate must be essential to the subject, or the subject to the predicate. (3) The predicate must be true of the subject considered strictly as itself, not as a member of a higher class. Only so will the conclusion state a commensurately universal relation between predicate and subject (Aristotle shows how we may fail in achieving this result) ; and only so will it be known to be necessary (chs. iv-viii).

It follows that the facts of one science cannot be proved from the principles of another, unless the former is in some sense a sub-genus of the latter ; that facts which are not eternal (*viz.* intermittent phenomena) can be proved and known only in so far as they exhibit eternally necessary connexions ; and that the special principles of single sciences cannot be proved from common principles (chs. ix-x). How

7

the common principles can be used (1) by science and (2) by dialectic is briefly indicated in ch. xi.

Faulty conclusions may be reached by (1) the right use of premisses which, though appropriate to the subject-genus, state false connexions ; (2) the wrong use of true and appropriate premisses ; (3) the use (right or wrong) of inappropriate premisses. Further, a logical proof may fall short of scientific demonstration if it fails to show the reason as well as the fact ; e.g., if the premisses are not immediate, or if proof is in the second figure where the middle term does not exhibit the cause. (Fact and explanation may even fall under different sciences, if one is in any sense subordinate to the other.) Only the first figure can satisfy the requirements of science by demonstrating the reason as well as the fact (chs. xii-xiv).

There can be immediate negative as well as affirmative premisses—not if either term belongs to a class which excludes the other (nor, it would seen, if both belong to the same class), but only if both are *summa genera* or categories (ch. xv).

Forms of Error or Ignorance

Error with regard to an immediate proposition may be due either to assuming or to falsely inferring its contrary. Aristotle enumerates the forms that such false inference can take, and then shows how it is possible to infer falsely the contrary of a mediated proposition. Lack of a sense-faculty may hinder one's grasp of a general principle (chs. xvi-xviii).

There can be no infinite chain of Predication

The steps of Aristotle's reasoning are not always

easy to follow, and it may be helpful to set them out in some detail.

How can we be sure that propositions are immediate ? Is it not always possible to interpolate middle terms ? If so, predication will form an infinite chain.

Since there are predicates which cannot be subjects and subjects which cannot be predicates, we can restate our problem in the form : If a chain of predication in which the predicate (or subject) of one proposition becomes the subject (or predicate) of the next is limited in one direction, can it be infinite in the other ? If not, the chain must be finite, and our original question is answered : there cannot be infinite interpolation, because if there could be an infinite number of middles between any two terms in our chain, the chain as a whole would be infinite ; which *ex hypothesi* it is not.

To ensure that his proof shall be comprehensive Aristotle shows that if a chain proving an affirmative conclusion must be limited at both ends, so must a chain proving a negative conclusion ; because the mediation of a negative premiss always involves (in any figure) the introduction of a new affirmative premiss, so that if the number of affirmative premisses in a chain is limited, so is the number of negative premisses. It remains to prove that an affirmative chain must be limited at both ends.

Aristotle first offers two dialectical proofs. (1) In strict predication as it is used by the sciences the subject is a substance, which (not being itself predicable) is the downward limit of predication. From this extend upward chains of predication (whether of essential attributes, properties or accidents) terminating in the categories, which are the upward

9

limit ; they are finite in number, and so are the attributes in any category ; therefore there can be no infinite chain.

(2) The conclusion of any chain of propositions can be known only if it is proved ; but if the chain is infinite it cannot be traversed and proof is impossible. Therefore, unless the claim of certainty made by science is to be abandoned, the chain cannot be infinite.

(3) The third proof is called analytical as being based upon arguments proper to demonstrative science. Essential attributes (with which alone science is concerned) either are elements in the definition of their subject or include their subject in their own definition. Catenary predication to infinity of either kind of attribute would entail definition containing an infinite number of elements, and this, as Aristotle has observed (84 a 7), is impossible (chs. xix-xxii).

Two corollaries follow : (1) that an attribute is not necessarily to be proved common to two subjects in virtue of something else common to them—this would result in an infinity of middle terms ; (2) to prove a connexion we must pack the interval by selecting middle terms that give a chain of immediate premisses, whether affirmative or negative (ch. xxiii).

Sundry comparisons and distinctions

Aristotle now discusses at some length the respective merits of universal and particular demonstration, and shows that on many grounds the former is superior. Similarly, affirmative is superior to negative demonstration, and ostensive proof to *reductio ad impossibile* (chs. xxiv-xxvi). Next he shows (1) on what grounds one science is to be preferred to another, and (2) how one science may be distinguished from another (chs. xxvii-xxviii).

The rest of the book (except ch. xxxii, which consists of arguments to show that syllogisms cannot all have the same premisses) touches upon various deviations from or approximations to scientific knowledge. First we are shown that there may be more than one proof (but not scientific proof) of the same conclusion ; then that there is demonstration (in some sense) of connexions which are not invariable. Finally, knowledge is contrasted with sense-perception and opinion, and " quickness of wit " is mentioned as a special flair for apprehending causes (chs. xxix-xxxiv).

Demonstration and Definition

In the second book Aristotle turns to definition. Difficulties begin as soon as he enunciates the " four kinds of question " which science tries to answer : τὸ ὅτι, τὸ διότι, εἰ ἔστι, τί ἐστιν. " The fact, the reason, whether it is, what it is " ; it seems clear from Aristotle's first examples that his questions are (1) Is X Y ? (2) Why is X Y ? (3) Does X exist ? (4) What is X ?—X being a substance (centaur, god, man). But when he goes on to say that in every case we are looking for a middle term or cause, doubts arise ; because it is not obviously true that when we ask whether a substance exists, or what it is, we are inquiring for its cause. It is true that every substance has its place in the natural order, and that it is what it is for some natural purpose ; but to judge from the examples which follow in ch. ii, that is not the sort of cause that Aristotle has in mind ; he has already turned his attention to attributes and events, with

11

which the rest of his discussion is chiefly concerned. It seems, then, that the opening formula, designed to be comprehensive, is misleading, and the questions resolve themselves into two : Is X Y ? and Why is X Y ? The implication is that definition should be causal ; we shall see later how Aristotle develops this view (chs. i-ii).

There follows an aporematic survey of problems connected with demonstration and definition. Among the conclusions tentatively drawn are (1) that the two operations are quite distinct, (2) that a definition cannot be proved (*a*) by syllogism or (*b*) by division or (*c*) hypothetically, (3) that definition proves nothing, and (4) that neither demonstration nor definition enables us to know the essence of a thing (chs. iii-vii).

Aristotle now begins to inquire how definition really is related to demonstration. Bare knowledge that a given event, *e.g.*, eclipse, exists leads to nothing ; but if we once grasp by induction what sort of thing it is, *i.e.* to what genus it belongs, we can then look for the cause that explains why that generic attribute belongs to the subject. Any middle term that establishes an actual connexion between attribute and subject will prove that the event takes place or exists ; thus we can prove that privation of light (the genus of eclipse) applies to the moon ; and this by re-arrangement gives (1) the crude verbal definition that eclipse is privation of light of the moon. But if we can prove the attribute of the subject by immediate premisses through one or more middle terms we can, by a re-arrangement of the whole demonstration, reach (2) a causal definition, *viz.*, that eclipse is a privation of the light of the moon by such-and-such a cause or causes. Thus, although definition cannot be demonstrated, we can reach it by the help of demonstration (ch. viii).

These are the two methods by which the definitions of attributes and events can be exhibited. There is a third kind of definition—that of substances and the primary subjects of the sciences—which can only be directly apprehended or assumed (chs. ix-x).

Inference and Causation

From considering the place of cause in definition Aristotle now turns to discuss certain problems of causation in their bearing upon demonstration. First he tries to show how each type of cause can stand as middle term. The types are not the usual four ; the place of the material cause (which is clearly inappropriate) is taken by the necessitating condition or eternal ground, which operates as a cause in mathematical reasoning. It cannot be said that Aristotle's arguments are always convincing ; in fact, it is sometimes hard to be sure what he is trying to prove. But his general contention can be justified in so far as all the other three can be regarded as aspects of the formal cause and therefore part of the essence (ch. xi).

Turning next to deal with the causation of events, Aristotle begins by considering events (such as eclipse or the formation of ice) in which cause and effect are complementary aspects of the same process, and rightly says that here cause and effect are simultaneous. But causes frequently appear to precede their effects in time. Assuming that in such a case the cause and effect are single events separated by an interval of time, Aristotle argues that although

13

the earlier can be inferred from the later, the later cannot be inferred from the earlier event ; because during the interval it will not be true to say that the later event has happened, or even that it will happen ; therefore the earlier does not directly imply the later. What then is the bond of connexion between a completed event and another subsequent event ? Aristotle approaches the problem along the lines of his discussions of time and continuity in *Physics* IV and VI, and arrives at no satisfactory conclusion. This is hardly surprising ; for he appears to confuse a past or completed event with the completion of a process, which is an indivisible limit, and therefore cannot be contiguous either with another completion or with a process. From this he seems to infer (though he has not proved that two processes cannot be contiguous) that no two events can be contiguous. This naturally makes it doubtful whether in reasoning from effect to cause we can ever reach immediate premisses (ch. xii).

(But the whole of Aristotle's reasoning rests upon a false assumption. Events are not discrete units ; they are merely such portions of the continuous world-process as we choose to isolate in thought because, for a particular purpose, it suits us to consider them as units. There is no *actual* completion— or beginning—of any such " event " ; only the limit set to it in our minds. When we relate two such " events " as cause and effect we are really isolating a minute section of the world-process and trying to trace the connexions that traverse it in so far as they link a particular aspect of the " event " regarded as cause to the " event " regarded as effect. But (1) we beg the whole question if we assume as the *whole* cause what is only one factor or stage in the process ; the *whole* cause is the sum of all the connexions viewed from one direction, and the *whole* effect is the same viewed from the opposite direction : in fact, the question of an interval does not arise ; (2) unless the section that we are examining is infinitesimally small the connexions will be so complex that some at least will escape our knowledge or attention, and so give the impression of an interval.

I hope that I make my general meaning plain ; my excuse for the disquisition is Ross's remark on p. 80 of his introduction : "Aristotle is clearly conscious of the difficulty which everyone must feel if he asks the question why a cause precedes its effect ; for it is hard to see how a mere lapse of time can be necessary for the occurrence of an event when the other conditions are already present ; this is a mystery which has never been explained." Unless I misunderstand him utterly, the mystery (if such it is) is explicable along the lines which I have indicated : there is no " mere lapse of time " ; as soon as *all* " the other conditions are already present " the so-called effect follows as part of the same continuous process.)

Definition, Division and Systematization

After noting the possibility of cyclic sequence and of reasoning about that which happens usually but not invariably, Aristotle returns to complete his account of definition. He has shown in ch. viii how to reach definitions of attributes ; now he explains how to do the same for the primary subjects of a given science. We take one of the *infimae species* and look for all the attributes within the genus that apply to the whole of that species and to others as well ;

15

collectively these attributes will be commensurate
with the species and will give its definition. When we
have defined all the *infimae species* we proceed to infer
the properties of the more complex species, and so
by degrees systematize the genus. In so doing we
ensure accuracy and completeness by the use of
dichotomic division. In defining we must move upwards from narrower to wider terms, because this is
both the easier way and the only way in which to
avoid ambiguity. On the other hand, when we come
to study the problems of a given science we should
work downwards from genus to species. In so doing
we must be careful to distinguish species correctly,
even if there are no ready-made names to fit them.
Several problems may have a common explanation,
and the solution of one problem may lead to the
solution of another (chs. xiii-xv).

This suggests the question whether there can be
more than one cause of the same effect. Cause and
effect certainly imply one another, but they are not
reciprocal causes ; the cause explains the effect, but
the effect does not explain the cause. In general, if
an attribute belongs to the whole of a subject, it
must do so through a cause that is commensurate
with that attribute. But can the same attribute
belong to different subjects through different middle
terms ? Aristotle first points out that the attribute
may be the same only by equivocation, and then the
causes are different ; or both attribute and subject
may be the same by analogy, and then so is the middle
term. But it is also possible, within the same genus,
for different species to have the same attribute.
When this is so, the attribute is connected to each
subject by two middle terms ; the first, which is

16

nearer to the attribute and definitory of it, is the same for each; the other, which connects the common middle to the separate subjects, is different for each. Thus in so far as there is a different middle term for each species, there is more than one cause (chs. xvi-xviii).

There remains the question for whose answer Aristotle has repeatedly—by a dramatic instinct—whetted our appetite : How do we apprehend the first principles themselves, which are not susceptible of demonstration ? Is it by scientific knowledge—the same kind of knowledge by which we cognize demonstrable facts—or by a different faculty ? If it is by a different faculty, how is this acquired ? Still dramatic, Aristotle postpones his climax by taking the second point first. The faculty of sense-perception is common to all animals ; but whereas in some the act of perception leaves no lasting impression, in others the impression persists and gives rise to memory ; and (in rational beings) repeated memories produce experience, that is the establishment in the mind of a " universal " or general notion, which is the first step in the development of a coherent art or science. When we have once learned to generalize we can advance higher and higher until we reach the most universal concepts of all ; and by the same inductive process we can advance from simple propositions to immediate truths and the axioms themselves. As for the faculty by which we know these, since it cannot be either science or inferior to science, it must be the only other intellectual faculty that is infallible, *viz.*, νοῦς or intuition, which supervenes upon our logical processes as a direct vision of the truth (ch. xix).

There are obvious defects in this treatise. One could wish that Aristotle had edited it a little more ; that he had made his meaning a little plainer, and had been more consistent in his use of technical terms. There are hasty statements and misapprehensions as well as deficiencies of knowledge ; and on the positive side it is easy to see (in spite of frequent repudiations) how much is owed to Plato's teaching at the Academy. Nevertheless, the *Posterior Analytics* is the work of a remarkably acute and discriminating mind ; and it is the first systematic attempt to apply logic to the ordering of scientific knowledge. If Aristotle had left us nothing else we should still be greatly in his debt.

III. Manuscripts and other Sources

The five oldest manuscripts of the *Posterior Analytics* are :

A	Urbinas 35	saec. ix-x ineunt.
B	Marcianus 201	an. 955
C	Coislinianus 330 (ad 82 a 2)	saec. xi
d	Laurentianus 72.5	,, ,,
n	Ambrosianus 490 (L 93)	,, ix

These are the five chosen by Ross to establish his text, and there can be little doubt that they are the most important. Ross has shown that ABCd belong to one family and n to another ; and that, while B is the best representative of its group and in general the most accurate manuscript, n is very often alone in preserving the right reading.

I have occasionally recorded the readings (when

they seemed to have any evidential value) of six other manuscripts, *viz.* :

D	Parisinus 1843	saec. xiii
M	Marcianus App. iv. 51	?
c	Vaticanus 1024	saec. x-xi
f	Marcianus App. iv. 5	saec. xiv
p	Ambrosianus 535 (M 89)	,,
u	Basileensis 54 (F ii. 21)	saec. xii

The commentaries of Philoponus (6th cent.) and Themistius (4th cent.) on both books, and those of Eustratius (about 1100) and an anonymous scholar (of uncertain date) on Book II, sometimes throw some light on the text. A reading implied by any one of these commentators is attributed to him by name, but where they seem to be unanimous I have referred to them collectively as " comm.".

In the critical apparatus I have only recorded departures from the wording of Bekker's text. I worked from this in the first place, modifying the punctuation as seemed necessary, and referring frequently to the edition of Waitz, which was then without a rival. In this way I established a provisional text incorporating a good many of Waitz's readings and some suggestions of my own. When Ross's edition of the *Analytics* was published in 1949 I found myself in rather an awkward position. I had completed a first draft of my translation, but there were still many points about which I felt extremely doubtful ; and in trying to clear these up I could neither ignore the conclusions of a leading authority nor seem to appropriate them, while if I disagreed with them I must be prepared to defend my conduct. Moreover, the interruption caused by the war, and

19

an infinity of unavoidable distractions, had already delayed my work to an exasperating degree. However, it seemed necessary to be realistic, so I carefully read through Ross's text and commentary. In doing so I found, with some natural regret, that he had anticipated most of the suggestions that I had intended to make. In such cases I hope that I have always yielded him full credit for the improvement. Where his reading or interpretation was different from mine, it was generally better ; and I adopted it with proper acknowledgement. There remain a few places in which I still prefer my own view. But I am conscious that I (like all amateur Aristotelians) owe an immense debt to Sir David's profound scholarship and penetrating criticism, which have opened my eyes to many things that I should otherwise have missed. I must also pay tribute to the Oxford Translation by G. R. G. Mure, which I have often consulted and always found helpful and stimulating. Finally, I am greatly obliged to the late Professor J. Tate for clarifying my mind on some difficult points, and to my colleague Miss N. P. Miller for saving me from many inaccuracies. In spite of these aids I cannot claim to have carried out this task even to my own satisfaction. I should have liked to continue the effort ; but it has taken far too long already.

THE TRADITIONAL MOOD-NAMES

In my notes I have frequently had occasion to use the Latin (or quasi-Latin) names invented by medieval logicians to designate the various moods of syllogism. They are as follows :

First figure : Barbara, Celarent, Darii, Ferio.

Second figure : Cesare, Camestres, Festino, Baroco.
Third figure : Darapti, Felapton, Disamis, Datisi,
Bocardo, Ferison.

For present purposes this list is sufficient ; a fuller
one with more detailed information will be found in
the introduction to the *Prior Analytics*. Here it is
only necessary to understand that in each name the
vowels indicate the quantity and quality of the
premisses and conclusion : thus A stands for the
universal affirmative (All X is Y), E for the universal
negative (No X is Y), I for the particular affirmative
(Some X is Y), and O for the particular negative
(Some X is not Y).

SELECT BIBLIOGRAPHY

I append a short list of the principal editions, translations, works of reference and articles that are likely to be helpful in a study of the *Posterior Analytics*.

TEXTS AND EDITIONS

Aristotelis Opera, ed. I. Bekker (Berlin, 1831 ; Oxford, 1837).

Organum, ed. I. Pacius (Frankfurt, 1592).

Organon, ed. T. Waitz (Leipzig, 1844–1846).

Prior and Posterior Analytics, ed. W. D. Ross (Oxford, 1949).

TRANSLATIONS

Posterior Analytics in English by E. Poste (Oxford, 1850), E. S. Bouchier (Oxford, 1901) and G. R. G. Mure (Oxford, 1906) ; in French by J. B.-Saint-Hilaire (Paris, 1837) and J. Tricot (Paris, 1938) ; in German by J. H. von Kirchmann (Heidelberg, 1877) and E. Rolfes (Leipzig, 1922).

WORKS OF REFERENCE

Commentaria in Aristotelem Graeca :

Themistii in *An. Post.* II Paraphrasis, ed. M. Wallies (Berlin, 1899).

Eustratius in *An. Post.* II, ed. M. Hayduck (Berlin, 1907).

POSTERIOR ANALYTICS

Ioannes Philoponus in *An. Post.* et Anonymus in *An. Post.* II, ed. M. Wallies (Berlin, 1909).

Cherniss, H. : *Aristotle's Criticism of Plato and the Academy* (Baltimore, 1944).

Gohlke, P. : *Die Entstehung der aristotelischen Logik* (Berlin, 1936).

Heath, Sir Thomas : *Mathematics in Aristotle* (Oxford, 1949).

Maier, H. : *Die Syllogistik des Aristoteles* (Tübingen, 1900).

Solmsen, F. : *Die Entwicklung der aristotelischen Logik und Rhetorik* (Berlin, 1929).

Zabarella, I. : *In duos Arist. libros Post. An. Commentaria* (Venice, 1582).

ARTICLES

Einarson, B. : " On certain Mathematical Terms in Aristotle's Logic " (*A.J.P.* (1936), pp. 33-54, 151-172).

Lee, H. D. P. : " Geometrical Method and Aristotle's Account of First Principles " (*C.Q.* (1925), pp. 113-129).

Stocks, J. L. : " The Composition of Aristotle's Logical Works " (*C.Q.* (1933), pp. 115-124).

ΑΡΙΣΤΟΤΕΛΟΥΣ
ΑΝΑΛΥΤΙΚΩΝ ΥΣΤΕΡΩΝ

Α

71 a 1 I. Πᾶσα διδασκαλία καὶ πᾶσα μάθησις διανο-
ητικὴ ἐκ προϋπαρχούσης γίγνεται γνώσεως. φανερὸν δὲ τοῦτο θεωροῦσιν ἐπὶ πασῶν· αἵ τε γὰρ
μαθηματικαὶ τῶν ἐπιστημῶν διὰ τούτου τοῦ τρόπου
παραγίγνονται καὶ τῶν ἄλλων ἑκάστη τεχνῶν.[a]
5 ὁμοίως δὲ καὶ περὶ τοὺς λόγους οἵ τε διὰ συλλογισμῶν καὶ οἱ δι᾽ ἐπαγωγῆς· ἀμφότεροι γὰρ διὰ
προγιγνωσκομένων ποιοῦνται τὴν διδασκαλίαν, οἱ
μὲν λαμβάνοντες ὡς παρὰ ξυνιέντων, οἱ δὲ δεικνύντες τὸ καθόλου διὰ τοῦ δῆλον εἶναι τὸ καθ᾽
ἕκαστον. ὡς δ᾽ αὕτως καὶ οἱ ῥητορικοὶ συμπείθου-
10 σιν· ἢ γὰρ διὰ παραδειγμάτων, ὅ ἐστιν ἐπαγωγή,
ἢ δι᾽ ἐνθυμημάτων, ὅπερ ἐστὶ συλλογισμός.[b]

Διχῶς δ᾽ ἀναγκαῖον προγιγνώσκειν· τὰ μὲν γὰρ

---

[a] τέχνη is used here, as often, to cover the sense of productive (as opposed to theoretical) science ; cf. 100 a 9.

[b] Clearly Aristotle is thinking of " dialectic," as a means
of instruction distinct from science (which seeks only to
discover and demonstrate the truth) and rhetoric (which aims
at persuasion by means of probabilities). For Aristotle dia-

24

ARISTOTLE'S
POSTERIOR ANALYTICS

BOOK I

I. ALL teaching and learning that involves the use of reason proceeds from pre-existent knowledge. This is evident if we consider all the different branches of learning, because both the mathematical sciences and every other art *a* are acquired in this way. Similarly too with logical arguments,*b* whether syllogistic or inductive ; both effect instruction by means of facts already recognized, the former making assumptions as though granted by an intelligent audience, and the latter proving the universal from the self-evident nature of the particular. The means by which rhetorical arguments carry conviction are just the same ; for they use either examples,*c* which are a kind of induction, or enthymemes,*d* which are a kind of syllogism.

There are two senses in which previous knowledge

lectic is the application of logical methods to argument with a real or imaginary opponent; it is by no means infallible, since neither its premises nor its conclusions are necessarily true, but (properly used) it can be a useful auxiliary to science.

c Cf. *An. Pr.* II. xxiv.
d *Ibid.* 70 a 10-24.

71 a

ὅτι ἔστι προϋπολαμβάνειν ἀναγκαῖον, τὰ δὲ τί τὸ
λεγόμενόν ἐστι ξυνιέναι δεῖ, τὰ δ᾿ ἄμφω, οἷον ὅτι
μὲν ἅπαν ἢ φῆσαι ἢ ἀποφῆσαι ἀληθές, ὅτι ἔστι, τὸ
15 δὲ τρίγωνον, ὅτι τοδὶ σημαίνει, τὴν δὲ μονάδα
ἄμφω, καὶ τί σημαίνει καὶ ὅτι ἔστιν· οὐ γὰρ ὁμοίως
τούτων ἕκαστον δῆλον ἡμῖν. ἔστι δὲ γνωρίζειν τὰ
μὲν πρότερον γνωρίσαντα,[1] τῶν δὲ καὶ ἅμα λαμ-
βάνοντα τὴν γνῶσιν, οἷον ὅσα τυγχάνει ὄντα ὑπὸ
τὸ καθόλου οὗ[2] ἔχει τὴν γνῶσιν· ὅτι μὲν γὰρ πᾶν
20 τρίγωνον ἔχει δυσὶν ὀρθαῖς ἴσας προῄδει, ὅτι δὲ
τόδε τὸ ἐν τῷ ἡμικυκλίῳ τρίγωνόν ἐστιν ἅμα ἐπ-
αγόμενος ἐγνώρισεν (ἐνίων γὰρ τοῦτον τὸν τρόπον
ἡ μάθησίς ἐστι, καὶ οὐ διὰ τοῦ μέσου τὸ ἔσχατον
γνωρίζεται, ὅσα ἤδη τῶν καθ᾿ ἕκαστα τυγχάνει
ὄντα καὶ μὴ καθ᾿ ὑποκειμένου τινός). πρὶν δ᾿
25 ἐπαχθῆναι ἢ λαβεῖν συλλογισμὸν τρόπον μέν τινα
ἴσως φατέον ἐπίστασθαι, τρόπον δ᾿ ἄλλον οὔ. ὃ
γὰρ μὴ ᾔδει εἰ ἔστιν ἁπλῶς, τοῦτο πῶς ᾔδει ὅτι
δύο ὀρθὰς ἔχει ἁπλῶς; ἀλλὰ δῆλον ὡς ὡδὶ μὲν
ἐπίσταται, ὅτι καθόλου ἐπίσταται, ἁπλῶς δὲ οὐκ
ἐπίσταται.

Εἰ δὲ μή, τὸ ἐν τῷ Μένωνι ἀπόρημα συμβήσεται·
30 ἢ γὰρ οὐδὲν μαθήσεται ἢ ἃ οἶδεν. οὐ γὰρ δὴ ὥς γέ

---

[1] Ross : γνωρίζοντα codd.   [2] Ross : ὧν codd.

---

[a] Probably we should suppose that the figure is not drawn
as a triangle ; cf. Heath, *Mathematics in Aristotle*, p. 38.
[b] The attributes of an individual are inferred from a
knowledge of the attributes of the species, but the individual
itself is directly apprehended as such.
[c] Plato, *Meno* 80 D-E.

is necessary. Sometimes it is necessary to assume the *fact* beforehand, and sometimes one must understand the *meaning* of the term ; sometimes both are necessary. *E.g.*, we must assume as a fact that either the assertion or the negation of every statement is true ; and we must know what the term " triangle " means ; and as regards the unit, we must both know what it means and assume that it exists. This is because these truths are not all equally apparent to us. Recognition of a fact may sometimes entail both previous knowledge and knowledge acquired in the act of recognition ; *viz.*, knowledge of the particulars which actually fall under the universal, which is known to us. We knew already that every triangle has the sum of its interior angles equal to two right angles ; but that *this* figure [a] inscribed in the semi-circle is a triangle we recognize only as we are led to relate the particular to the universal (for some things, *viz.*, such as are ultimate particulars not predicable of anything else as subject, are only learnt in this way, *i.e.*, the minor is not recognized by means of the middle term [b]). Before the process of relation is completed or the conclusion drawn, we should presumably say that in one sense the fact is understood and in another it is not. For how could we know in the full sense that the figure contains angles equal to the sum of two right angles if we did not know in the full sense whether it exists ? Clearly we apprehend the fact not absolutely but in the qualified sense that we apprehend a general principle.

Unless we make this distinction, we shall be faced with the dilemma reached in the *Meno* [c] : either one can learn nothing, or one can only learn what is already known. We certainly must not offer the

be know-ledge of fact or of meaning.

Previous knowledge distin-guished from actualiza-tion of po-tential knowledge.

This is the escape from the di-lemma of the *Meno*.

71 a

τινες ἐγχειροῦσι λύειν λεκτέον· ἆρ' οἶδας ἅπασαν
δυάδα ὅτι ἀρτία ἢ οὔ; φήσαντος δὲ προήνεγκάν
τινα δυάδα ἣν οὐκ ᾤετ' εἶναι, ὥστ' οὐδ' ἀρτίαν.
λύουσι γὰρ οὐ φάσκοντες εἰδέναι πᾶσαν δυάδα ἀρ-
71 b τίαν οὖσαν, ἀλλ' ἣν ἴσασιν ὅτι δυάς. καίτοι ἴσασι
μὲν οὗπερ τὴν ἀπόδειξιν ἔχουσι καὶ οὗ ἔλαβον, ἔλαβον δ' οὐχὶ παντὸς οὗ ἂν εἰδῶσιν ὅτι τρίγωνον ἢ ὅτι
ἀριθμός, ἀλλ' ἁπλῶς κατὰ παντὸς ἀριθμοῦ καὶ τρι-
γώνου· οὐδεμία γὰρ πρότασις λαμβάνεται τοιαύτη,
5 ὅτι ὃν σὺ οἶδας ἀριθμὸν ἢ ὃ σὺ οἶδας εὐθύγραμμον,
ἀλλὰ κατὰ παντός. ἀλλ' οὐδὲν (οἶμαι) κωλύει ὃ
μανθάνει ἔστιν ὡς ἐπίστασθαι, ἔστι δ' ὡς ἀγνοεῖν·
ἄτοπον γὰρ οὐκ εἰ οἶδέ πως ὃ μανθάνει, ἀλλ' εἰ ὡδί,
οἷον ᾗ μανθάνει καὶ ὥς.

II. Ἐπίστασθαι δὲ οἰόμεθ' ἕκαστον ἁπλῶς, ἀλλὰ
10 μὴ τὸν σοφιστικὸν τρόπον τὸν κατὰ συμβεβηκός,
ὅταν τήν τ' αἰτίαν οἰώμεθα γιγνώσκειν δι' ἣν τὸ
πρᾶγμά ἐστιν, ὅτι ἐκείνου αἰτία ἐστί, καὶ μὴ ἐνδέχεσθαι τοῦτ' ἄλλως ἔχειν. δῆλον τοίνυν ὅτι
τοιοῦτόν τι τὸ ἐπίστασθαί ἐστι· καὶ γὰρ οἱ μὴ
ἐπιστάμενοι καὶ οἱ ἐπιστάμενοι οἱ μὲν οἴονται αὐτοὶ
15 οὕτως ἔχειν, οἱ δ' ἐπιστάμενοι καὶ ἔχουσιν· ὥστε

---

^a The reference is unknown.

^b The sophist's knowledge is called " accidental " because,
not knowing the species as such, but only as qualified by
accidental attributes, he has no conception of what is essential to it.

explanation by which certain thinkers [a] attempt to solve the difficulty. Supposing that a man is asked "Do you or do you not know that every pair is even?" When he says "Yes," his opponents produce some pair which he did not know to exist, and therefore did not know to be even. These thinkers solve the difficulty by saying that they do not know that every pair is even, but only that such things as they know to be pairs are even. But what they know to be even is that which they have proved to be such, *i.e.*, that which they have taken as the subject of their premiss : and that is not everything which they know to be a triangle or a number, but every number and every triangle, without qualification. No premiss is ever assumed with such a term as "what you know to be a number" or "what you know to be a rectilinear figure "; the predication applies to every instance of the subject. But I presume that there is no reason why a man should not in one sense know, and in another not know, that which he is learning. The absurdity consists not in his knowing in some qualified sense that which he learns, but in his knowing it in a certain particular sense, *viz.*, in the exact way and manner in which he learns it.

II. We consider that we have unqualified knowledge of anything (as contrasted with the accidental knowledge of the sophist) [b] when we believe that we know (i) that the cause from which the fact results is the cause of that fact, and (ii) that the fact cannot be otherwise. Clearly knowledge is something of this sort ; for both those who do not know and those who do know agree on the subject ; but whereas the former merely think that they are in the condition described above, the latter are actually in it. Hence

Absolute knowledge

71 b

οὗ ἁπλῶς ἔστιν ἐπιστήμη, τοῦτ᾽ ἀδύνατον ἄλλως ἔχειν.

Εἰ μὲν οὖν καὶ ἕτερος ἔστι τοῦ ἐπίστασθαι τρόπος ὕστερον ἐροῦμεν, φαμὲν δὲ καὶ δι᾽ ἀποδείξεως εἰδέναι. ἀπόδειξιν δὲ λέγω συλλογισμὸν ἐπιστημονικόν· ἐπιστημονικὸν δὲ λέγω καθ᾽ ὃν τῷ ἔχειν αὐτὸν ἐπιστάμεθα.

20 Εἰ τοίνυν ἐστὶ τὸ ἐπίστασθαι οἷον ἔθεμεν, ἀνάγκη καὶ τὴν ἀποδεικτικὴν ἐπιστήμην ἐξ ἀληθῶν τ᾽ εἶναι καὶ πρώτων καὶ ἀμέσων καὶ γνωριμωτέρων καὶ προτέρων καὶ αἰτίων τοῦ συμπεράσματος· οὕτω γὰρ ἔσονται καὶ αἱ ἀρχαὶ οἰκεῖαι τοῦ δεικνυμένου. συλλογισμὸς μὲν γὰρ ἔσται καὶ ἄνευ τούτων, ἀπό-
25 δειξις δ᾽ οὐκ ἔσται· οὐ γὰρ ποιήσει ἐπιστήμην.

Ἀληθῆ μὲν οὖν δεῖ εἶναι, ὅτι οὐκ ἔστι τὸ μὴ ὂν ἐπίστασθαι, οἷον ὅτι ἡ διάμετρος σύμμετρος. ἐκ πρώτων δ᾽ ἀναποδείκτων, ὅτι οὐκ ἐπιστήσεται μὴ ἔχων ἀπόδειξιν αὐτῶν· τὸ γὰρ ἐπίστασθαι ὧν ἀπόδειξις ἔστι μὴ κατὰ συμβεβηκὸς τὸ ἔχειν ἀπόδειξίν
30 ἐστιν. αἴτιά τε καὶ γνωριμώτερα δεῖ εἶναι καὶ πρότερα, αἴτια μὲν ὅτι τότε ἐπιστάμεθα ὅταν τὴν αἰτίαν εἰδῶμεν, καὶ πρότερα, εἴπερ αἴτια, καὶ προγιγνωσκόμενα οὐ μόνον τὸν ἕτερον τρόπον τῷ ξυνιέναι, ἀλλὰ καὶ τῷ εἰδέναι ὅτι ἔστιν.

Πρότερα δ᾽ ἐστὶ καὶ γνωριμώτερα διχῶς· οὐ γὰρ ταὐτὸν πρότερον τῇ φύσει καὶ πρὸς ἡμᾶς πρότερον,

---

[a] In ch. iii and Book II, ch. xix.   [b] Cf. 71 a 11 ff.

if any fact is the object of unqualified knowledge, that fact cannot be otherwise than it is.

Whether there is any other method of knowing will *is acquired* be discussed later.[a] Our contention now is that we *(in one way)* do at any rate obtain knowledge by demonstration. *stration.* By demonstration I mean a syllogism which produces scientific knowledge, in other words one which enables us to know by the mere fact that we grasp it.

Now if knowledge is such as we have assumed, *The pre-* demonstrative knowledge must proceed from pre- *misses of* misses which are true, primary, immediate, better *tion.* known than, prior to, and causative of the conclusion. On these conditions only will the first principles be properly applicable to the fact which is to be proved. Syllogism indeed will be possible without these conditions, but not demonstration; for the result will not be knowledge.

The premisses, then, must be true statements; because it is impossible to know that which is contrary to fact, *e.g.*, that the diagonal of a square is commensurable with the sides. They must be primary and indemonstrable, because otherwise we shall not know them unless we have proof of them; for to know (otherwise than accidentally) that which is capable of proof implies that one has proof of it. They must be causative, better known and prior: causative, because we only have knowledge of a thing when we know its cause; prior, inasmuch as they are causative; and already known, not merely in the one[b] sense that their meaning is understood, but also in the sense that they are known as facts.

There are two senses in which things are prior and *Sundry dis-* more knowable. That which is prior in nature is not *tinctions* the same as that which is prior in relation to us, and *tions.*

31

72 a οὐδὲ γνωριμώτερον καὶ ἡμῖν γνωριμώτερον. λέγω
δὲ πρὸς ἡμᾶς μὲν πρότερα καὶ γνωριμώτερα τὰ
ἐγγύτερον τῆς αἰσθήσεως, ἁπλῶς δὲ πρότερα καὶ
γνωριμώτερα τὰ πορρώτερον. ἔστι δὲ πορρωτάτω
5 μὲν τὰ καθόλου μάλιστα, ἐγγυτάτω δὲ τὰ καθ' ἕ-
καστα· καὶ ἀντίκειται ταῦτ' ἀλλήλοις.

Ἐκ πρώτων δ' ἐστὶ τὸ ἐξ ἀρχῶν οἰκείων· ταὐτὸ
γὰρ λέγω πρῶτον καὶ ἀρχήν. ἀρχὴ δ' ἐστὶν ἀποδείξεως πρότασις ἄμεσος, ἄμεσος δὲ ἧς μὴ ἔστιν
ἄλλη προτέρα. πρότασις δ' ἐστὶν ἀποφάνσεως τὸ
ἕτερον μόριον, ἓν καθ' ἑνός, διαλεκτικὴ μὲν ἡ
10 ὁμοίως λαμβάνουσα ὁποτερονοῦν, ἀποδεικτικὴ δὲ ἡ
ὡρισμένως θάτερον, ὅτι ἀληθές. ἀπόφανσις δὲ ἀντιφάσεως ὁποτερονοῦν μόριον. ἀντίφασις δὲ ἀντίθεσις ἧς οὐκ ἔστι μεταξὺ καθ' αὑτήν. μόριον δ'
ἀντιφάσεως τὸ μὲν τὶ κατὰ τινός κατάφασις, τὸ
15 δὲ τὶ ἀπὸ τινός ἀπόφασις. ἀμέσου δ' ἀρχῆς συλ-
λογιστικῆς θέσιν μὲν λέγω ἣν μὴ ἔστι δεῖξαι μηδ'
ἀνάγκη ἔχειν τὸν μαθησόμενόν τι· ἣν δ' ἀνάγκη
ἔχειν τὸν ὁτιοῦν μαθησόμενον, ἀξίωμα· ἔστι γὰρ
ἔνια τοιαῦτα· τοῦτο γὰρ μάλιστ' ἐπὶ τοῖς τοιούτοις
εἰώθαμεν ὄνομα λέγειν. θέσεως δ' ἡ μὲν ὁποτε-
20 ρονοῦν τῶν μορίων τῆς ἀποφάνσεως[1] λαμβάνουσα,
οἷον λέγω τὸ εἶναί τι ἢ μὴ εἶναί τι, ὑπόθεσις, ἡ δ'

---

[1] ἀντιφάσεως n, Ross.

---

[a] Cf. Met. 1029 b 3 ff.
[b] Or simply " starting-point."
[c] i.e., it is either affirmative or negative.
[d] The dialectician is equally prepared to accept " A is B "
or " A is not B " as the object of his attack.

32

that which is ⟨naturally⟩ more knowable is not the same as that which is more knowable by us. By "prior" or "more knowable" in relation to us I mean that which is nearer to our perception, and by "prior" or "more knowable" in the absolute sense I mean that which is further from it. The most universal concepts are furthest from our perception, and particulars are nearest to it[a]; and these are opposite to one another.

To argue from primary premisses is to argue from appropriate first principles; for by "primary premiss" and "first principle" I mean the same thing. The first principle[b] of a demonstration is an immediate premiss; and an immediate premiss is one which has no other premiss prior to it. A premiss is one or the other part of a proposition,[c] and consists of one term predicated of another. If dialectical, it assumes either part indifferently[d]; if demonstrative, it definitely assumes that one part is true. A proposition is either part of a contradiction. A contradiction is an opposition which of its very nature excludes any middle. That part of a contradiction which affirms something of something else is an affirmation; that which denies something of something else is a negation. I apply the term *thesis* to an immediate indemonstrable first principle of syllogism the grasp of which is not necessary for the acquisition of certain kinds of knowledge; but that which must be grasped if any knowledge is to be acquired, I call an *axiom*; for there are certain things of this nature and we are accustomed to apply this name especially to them. A thesis which assumes one or the other part of a proposition, *i.e.*, that something does, or does not exist, is a *hypothesis*; a thesis which does

ἄνευ τούτου ὁρισμός. ὁ γὰρ ὁρισμὸς θέσις μέν
ἐστι· τίθεται γὰρ ὁ ἀριθμητικὸς μονάδα τὸ ἀδιαίρετον εἶναι κατὰ τὸ ποσόν· ὑπόθεσις δ' οὐκ ἔστι· τὸ
25 γὰρ τί ἐστι μονὰς καὶ τὸ εἶναι μονάδα οὐ ταὐτόν.

Ἐπεὶ δὲ δεῖ πιστεύειν τε καὶ εἰδέναι τὸ πρᾶγμα
τῷ τοιοῦτον ἔχειν συλλογισμὸν ὃν καλοῦμεν ἀπόδειξιν, ἔστι δ' οὗτος τῷ ταδὶ[1] εἶναι ἐξ ὧν ὁ συλλογισμός, ἀνάγκη μὴ μόνον προγιγνώσκειν τὰ
πρῶτα, ἢ πάντα ἢ ἔνια, ἀλλὰ καὶ μᾶλλον· ἀεὶ γὰρ
30 δι' ὃ ὑπάρχει ἕκαστον, ἐκείνῳ[2] μᾶλλον ὑπάρχει,
οἷον δι' ὃ φιλοῦμεν, ἐκεῖνο φίλον μᾶλλον· ὥστ'
εἴπερ ἴσμεν διὰ τὰ πρῶτα καὶ πιστεύομεν, κἀκεῖνα
ἴσμεν τε καὶ πιστεύομεν μᾶλλον, ὅτι δι' ἐκεῖνα καὶ
τὰ ὕστερον. οὐχ οἷόν τε δὲ πιστεύειν μᾶλλον ὧν
οἶδεν ἃ μὴ τυγχάνει μήτε εἰδὼς μήτε βέλτιον δια-
35 κείμενος ἢ εἰ ἐτύγχανεν εἰδώς. συμβήσεται δὲ
τοῦτο εἰ μή τις προγνώσεται τῶν δι' ἀπόδειξιν
πιστευόντων· μᾶλλον γὰρ ἀνάγκη πιστεύειν ταῖς
ἀρχαῖς ἢ πάσαις ἢ τισὶ τοῦ συμπεράσματος. τὸν
δὲ μέλλοντα ἕξειν τὴν ἐπιστήμην τὴν δι' ἀποδείξεως
οὐ μόνον δεῖ τὰς ἀρχὰς μᾶλλον γνωρίζειν καὶ μᾶλ-

---

[1] ταδὶ n, Ross : τάδ'.
[2] ἐκείνῳ Ross, habent comm. : ἐκεῖνο codd.

---

[a] The latter part of this attempt to systematize terminology seems rather abortive. Elsewhere (e.g. 76 b 23 ff.) a
ὑπόθεσις is not necessarily indemonstrable, and θέσις does not
seem to be used technically at all. It is even difficult to be
sure what Aristotle includes under ἀξιώματα. From a comparison of 76 b 11-22, 77 a 26-34, 88 a 31-b 29 it would seem
that the term is convertible with κοιναὶ ἀρχαί or τὰ κοινά, and
covers not only principles like the Law of Contradiction,
which are really " common," but also others, like the mathe-

not do this is a definition. A definition is a kind of thesis (or laying-down), because the arithmetician lays it down that to be a unit is to be quantitatively indivisible ; but it is not a hypothesis, because to define the nature of a unit is not the same as to assert its existence.[a]

Now since the required condition of our knowledge or conviction of a fact consists in grasping a syllogism of the kind which we call demonstration, and since the syllogism depends upon the truth of its premisses, it is necessary not merely to know the primary premisses—either all or some of them—beforehand, but to know them better than the conclusion. For that which causes an attribute to apply to a subject always possesses that attribute in a still greater degree ; e.g., that which causes us to love something is itself still dearer to us. Hence if the primary premisses are the cause of our knowledge and conviction, we know and are convinced of them also in a higher degree, since they cause our knowledge of all that follows from them. But to believe in anything more than in the things which we know, if we neither actually know it nor are in a better situation than if we actually knew it, is impossible ; yet this is what will happen if anyone whose conviction rests upon demonstration is to have no prior knowledge ; because we must believe in the first principles (some if not all of them) more than in the conclusion. And if a man is to possess the knowledge which is effected by demonstration, not only must he recognize and

The primary premisses must be known before and better than the conclusion.

matical axioms about equals, which are at once common and special to a particular group of sciences. For a discussion of the use of such terms in logic and mathematics see H. D. P. Lee in *C.Q.* xxix, pp. 113-124, and Heath, *Mathematics in Aristotle*, pp. 53-57.

72 b λον αὐταῖς πιστεύειν ἢ τῷ δεικνυμένῳ, ἀλλὰ μηδ'
ἄλλο αὐτῷ πιστότερον εἶναι μηδὲ γνωριμώτερον
τῶν ἀντικειμένων ταῖς ἀρχαῖς ἐξ ὧν ἔσται συλλογισμὸς ὁ τῆς ἐναντίας ἀπάτης, εἴπερ δεῖ τὸν ἐπιστάμενον ἁπλῶς ἀμετάπειστον εἶναι.

5 III. Ἐνίοις μὲν οὖν διὰ τὸ δεῖν τὰ πρῶτα ἐπίστασθαι οὐ δοκεῖ ἐπιστήμη εἶναι, τοῖς δ' εἶναι μέν,
πάντων μέντοι ἀποδείξεις¹ εἶναι· ὧν οὐδέτερον οὔτ'
ἀληθὲς οὔτ' ἀναγκαῖον. οἱ μὲν γὰρ ὑποθέμενοι μὴ
εἶναι ὅλως ἐπίστασθαι, οὗτοι εἰς ἄπειρον ἀξιοῦσιν
ἀνάγεσθαι ὡς οὐκ ἂν ἐπισταμένους τὰ ὕστερα διὰ
10 τὰ πρότερα, ὧν μή ἐστι πρῶτα, ὀρθῶς λέγοντες·
ἀδύνατον γὰρ τὰ ἄπειρα διελθεῖν. εἴ τε ἵσταται
καὶ εἰσὶν ἀρχαί, ταύτας ἀγνώστους εἶναι ἀποδείξεώς
γε μὴ οὔσης αὐτῶν, ὅπερ φασὶν εἶναι τὸ ἐπίστασθαι
μόνον· εἰ δὲ μὴ ἔστι τὰ πρῶτα εἰδέναι, οὐδὲ τὰ ἐκ
15 τούτων εἶναι ἐπίστασθαι ἁπλῶς οὐδὲ κυρίως, ἀλλ'
ἐξ ὑποθέσεως, εἰ ἐκεῖνα ἔστιν. οἱ δὲ περὶ μὲν τοῦ
ἐπίστασθαι ὁμολογοῦσι· δι' ἀποδείξεως γὰρ εἶναι
μόνον· ἀλλὰ πάντων εἶναι ἀπόδειξιν οὐδὲν κωλύειν·
ἐνδέχεσθαι γὰρ κύκλῳ γίγνεσθαι τὴν ἀπόδειξιν καὶ
ἐξ ἀλλήλων.

Ἡμεῖς δέ φαμεν οὔτε πᾶσαν ἐπιστήμην ἀπο-
20 δεικτικὴν εἶναι, ἀλλὰ τὴν τῶν ἀμέσων ἀναπόδεικτον
(καὶ τοῦθ' ὅτι ἀναγκαῖον, φανερόν· εἰ γὰρ ἀνάγκη

¹ ἀπόδειξις d.

ᵃ Probably Antisthenes ; see Maier, *Syllogistik* II. ii. 15,
n. 2.
ᵇ Possibly " certain followers of Xenocrates " ; Cherniss,
Aristotle's Criticism of Plato and the Academy, I. 68.

believe in the first principles more than in that which is being proved, but nothing which is opposed to the first principles and from which will result a syllogism of the contrary error, must be more credible or better known to him than those principles ; since one who has absolute knowledge should be unshakable in his belief.

III. The necessity of knowing the primary truths has led some persons [a] to think that there is no knowledge, and others,[b] admitting the possibility of knowledge, to think that all facts are demonstrable. Neither of these views is true or logically unavoidable. The former school, who assume that there is no knowledge at all, claim that there is an infinite regress, on the ground that we cannot know posterior by prior truths unless the latter themselves depend upon primary truths (in which they are right ; for it is impossible to traverse an infinite series) ; while if the series comes to an end, and there are first principles, they are unknowable, since they do not admit of demonstration, which these thinkers hold to be the sole condition of knowledge ; and if it is not possible to know the primary truths, neither is it possible to know in the strict and absolute sense that the inferences drawn from them are true ; we can only know them hypothetically, by assuming that the former are true. The other school agrees with this one as regards the conditions of knowledge, for they hold that it can only be secured by demonstration ; but they maintain that there is no reason why there should not be demonstration of everything, since the demonstration may be circular or reciprocal.

We, however, hold that not all knowledge is demonstrative ; the knowledge of immediate premisses is not by demonstration. It is evident that this must

Two false views : (1) that scientific knowledge is impossible, (2) that all truths are demonstrable by circular proof.

Answer to (1). There is no infinite regress,

μὲν ἐπίστασθαι τὰ πρότερα καὶ ἐξ ὧν ἡ ἀπόδειξις,
ἵσταται δέ ποτε τὰ ἄμεσα, ταῦτ' ἀναπόδεικτα
ἀνάγκῃ εἶναι)—ταῦτά τ' οὖν οὕτω λέγομεν, καὶ οὐ
μόνον ἐπιστήμην ἀλλὰ καὶ ἀρχὴν ἐπιστήμης εἶναί
25 τινά φαμεν ᾗ τοὺς ὅρους γνωρίζομεν.

Κύκλῳ δ' ὅτι ἀδύνατον ἀποδείκνυσθαι ἁπλῶς,
δῆλον, εἴπερ ἐκ προτέρων δεῖ τὴν ἀπόδειξιν εἶναι
καὶ γνωριμωτέρων· ἀδύνατον γάρ ἐστι τὰ αὐτὰ τῶν
αὐτῶν ἅμα πρότερα καὶ ὕστερα εἶναι, εἰ μὴ τὸν
ἕτερον τρόπον, οἷον τὰ μὲν πρὸς ἡμᾶς τὰ δ' ἁπλῶς,
30 ὅνπερ τρόπον ἡ ἐπαγωγὴ ποιεῖ γνώριμον. εἰ δ'
οὕτως, οὐκ ἂν εἴη τὸ ἁπλῶς εἰδέναι καλῶς ὡρισμένον, ἀλλὰ διττόν· ἢ οὐχ ἁπλῶς ἡ ἑτέρα ἀπόδειξις
γιγνομένη ἐκ τῶν ἡμῖν γνωριμωτέρων.

Συμβαίνει δὲ τοῖς λέγουσι κύκλῳ τὴν ἀπόδειξιν
εἶναι οὐ μόνον τὸ νῦν εἰρημένον, ἀλλ' οὐδὲν ἄλλο
λέγειν ἢ ὅτι τοῦτ' ἔστιν εἰ τοῦτ' ἔστιν· οὕτω δὲ
35 πάντα ῥάδιον δεῖξαι. δῆλον δ' ὅτι τοῦτο συμβαίνει
τριῶν ὅρων τεθέντων· τὸ μὲν γὰρ διὰ πολλῶν ἢ
δι' ὀλίγων ἀνακάμπτειν φάναι οὐδὲν διαφέρει, δι'

---

[a] Viz. νοῦς or intuition ; see Book II, ch. xix.

[b] For this sense of ὅρος (=ἀρχή) cf. Eth. Nic. 1142 a 26,
1143 a 36, b 2.

[c] Which proceeds from that which is " prior to us " to
that which is " prior in nature."

[d] As based on " prior " premisses (71 b 22).

[e] Although the " terms " doubtless represent propositions,
I suspect that (pace Ross ad loc.) Aristotle here really means
" terms " by ὅροι, because he is primarily concerned with the
form of the argument. He says that circular proof claims to
establish by the propositions " if A is true, B is true " and " if
B is true, A is true " (using two terms only) the absolute
truth of A ; the fallacy can be easily seen if the argument is
cast in the form of a normal syllogism (using three terms),
in which the propositions " if A is true, B is true " and " if B

be so ; for if it is necessary to know the prior pre- ^{because not} misses from which the demonstration proceeds, and ^{all knowledge is} if the regress ends with the immediate premisses, the ^{demonstrative.} latter must be indemonstrable. Such is our contention on this point. Indeed we hold not only that scientific knowledge is possible, but that there is a definite first principle of knowledge [a] by which we recognize ultimate truths.[b]

Demonstration in the absolute sense is obviously ^{Answer to} impossible by the circular method ; that is, if demon- ^{(2). Circular proof} stration must proceed from premisses which are ^{(a) is not} prior and better known ; for the same things cannot ^{scientific,} be at once prior and posterior to the same things, except in different senses,—I mean the distinction between " prior to us " and " absolutely prior "—with which we become familiar through induction.[c] In this case our definition of absolute knowledge [d] will be unsatisfactory, because it will have a double meaning. But presumably the other mode of demonstration, proceeding from that which is better known to us, is not demonstration in the absolute sense.

Those who profess that demonstration is circular ^{(b) proves} are faced not only by the consequence just described, ^{nothing} but also by the following : their theory simply ^{new,} amounts to this, that a thing is so if it is so ; and it is easy to prove anything by this method. That this is all that follows will be clearly seen if we take three terms ; for it makes no difference whether we say that a circular proof is effected through many or few terms, provided that there are not fewer than two.[e]

is true, C is true " give the conclusion " *if A is true*, C is true " : because similarly the conclusion of " if A is true, B is true " and " if B is true, A is true " is " *if A is true*, A is true," which proves nothing.

72 b

ὀλίγων δ' ἢ δυοῖν. ὅταν γὰρ τοῦ Α ὄντος ἐξ ἀνάγκης ᾖ τὸ Β, τούτου δὲ τὸ Γ, τοῦ Α ὄντος ἔσται τὸ
Γ. εἰ δὴ τοῦ Α ὄντος ἀνάγκη τὸ Β εἶναι, τούτου
73 a δ' ὄντος τὸ Α (τοῦτο γὰρ ἦν τὸ κύκλῳ), κείσθω τὸ
Α ἐφ' οὗ τὸ Γ. τὸ οὖν τοῦ Β ὄντος τὸ Α εἶναι
λέγειν ἐστὶ τὸ Γ εἶναι λέγειν, τοῦτο δ' ὅτι τοῦ Α
ὄντος τὸ Γ ἐστί· τὸ δὲ Γ τῷ Α τὸ αὐτό. ὥστε
5 συμβαίνει λέγειν τοὺς κύκλῳ φάσκοντας εἶναι τὴν
ἀπόδειξιν οὐδὲν ἕτερον πλὴν ὅτι τοῦ Α ὄντος τὸ Α
ἐστίν. οὕτω δὲ πάντα δεῖξαι ῥᾴδιον.

Οὐ μὴν ἀλλ' οὐδὲ τοῦτο δυνατὸν πλὴν ἐπὶ τούτων
ὅσα ἀλλήλοις ἕπεται, ὥσπερ τὰ ἴδια. ἑνὸς μὲν οὖν
κειμένου δέδεικται ὅτι οὐδέποτ' ἀνάγκη τι εἶναι
ἕτερον (λέγω δ' ἑνός, ὅτι οὔτε ὅρου ἑνὸς οὔτε
10 θέσεως μιᾶς τεθείσης), ἐκ δύο δὲ θέσεων πρώτων
καὶ ἐλαχίστων ἐνδέχεται, εἴπερ καὶ συλλογίσασθαι.
ἐὰν μὲν οὖν τό τε Α τῷ Β καὶ τῷ Γ ἕπηται, καὶ
ταῦτ' ἀλλήλοις καὶ τῷ Α, οὕτω μὲν ἐνδέχεται ἐξ
ἀλλήλων δεικνύναι πάντα τὰ αἰτηθέντα ἐν τῷ πρώτῳ σχήματι, ὡς δέδεικται ἐν τοῖς περὶ συλλογισμοῦ.
15 δέδεικται δὲ καὶ ὅτι ἐν τοῖς ἄλλοις σχήμασιν ἢ οὐ
γίγνεται συλλογισμὸς ἢ οὐ περὶ τῶν ληφθέντων.
τὰ δὲ μὴ ἀντικατηγορούμενα οὐδαμῶς ἔστι δεῖξαι
κύκλῳ· ὥστ' ἐπειδὴ ὀλίγα τοιαῦτα ἐν ταῖς ἀποδείξεσι, φανερὸν ὅτι κενόν τε καὶ ἀδύνατον τὸ

---

[a] Sc. in conjunction with the major premiss " when A is,
B is."

For when if A is, B must be, and if B is, C must be, then if A is, C must be. Then if when A is, B must be, and when B is, A must be (this is what is meant by circular proof), let A represent C in the first proof. Then to say that when B is, A is, is equivalent to saying that when B is, C is ; and this [a] is equivalent to saying that when A is, C is. But C is the same as A. Thus it follows that those who assert that demonstration is circular are merely maintaining that when A is, A is ; by which method it is easy to prove anything.

Moreover, even this mode of proof is impossible except in the case of attributes which are reciprocal consequents, e.g., properties.[b] It has been shown [c] that from the positing of one thing—by which I mean either one term or one proposition—nothing else ever necessarily follows ; two is the first and least number of propositions from which a necessary consequence is possible, since this is the minimum requirement for any logical conclusion. Thus if A is a consequent of B and of C, and the latter are consequents both of one another and of A, it is possible to prove reciprocally in the first figure all the assumptions which we have made. This has been shown in our discussion of syllogism.[d] But it has also been shown [e] that in the other figures either no syllogism results or none which confirms our assumptions. Propositions whose terms are not reciprocally predicable cannot be proved at all by circular demonstration. Hence, since such terms rarely occur in demonstrations, it is evidently futile

[b] Cf. Top. 102 a 18. Definition and differentia are also predicable convertibly.
[c] An. Pr. I. xxv.
[d] Ibid. II. v.
[e] Ibid. vi, vii.

73 a

λέγειν ἐξ ἀλλήλων εἶναι τὴν ἀπόδειξιν καὶ διὰ
20 τοῦτο πάντων ἐνδέχεσθαι εἶναι ἀπόδειξιν.

IV. Ἐπεὶ δ' ἀδύνατον ἄλλως ἔχειν οὗ ἐστιν ἐπιστήμη ἁπλῶς, ἀναγκαῖον ἂν εἴη τὸ ἐπιστητὸν τὸ
κατὰ τὴν ἀποδεικτικὴν ἐπιστήμην. ἀποδεικτικὴ δ'
ἐστὶν ἣν ἔχομεν τῷ ἔχειν ἀπόδειξιν· ἐξ ἀναγκαίων
25 ἄρα συλλογισμός ἐστιν ἡ ἀπόδειξις. ληπτέον ἄρα
ἐκ τίνων καὶ ποίων αἱ ἀποδείξεις εἰσίν. πρῶτον δὲ
διορίσωμεν τί λέγομεν τὸ κατὰ παντὸς καὶ τί τὸ
καθ' αὑτὸ καὶ τί τὸ καθόλου.

Κατὰ παντὸς μὲν οὖν τοῦτο λέγω ὃ ἂν ᾖ μὴ ἐπὶ
τινὸς μὲν τινὸς δὲ μή, μηδὲ ποτὲ μὲν ποτὲ δὲ μή·
30 οἷον εἰ κατὰ παντὸς ἀνθρώπου ζῷον, εἰ ἀληθὲς τόνδ'
εἰπεῖν ἄνθρωπον, ἀληθὲς καὶ ζῷον, καὶ εἰ νῦν
θάτερον, καὶ θάτερον, καὶ εἰ ἐν πάσῃ γραμμῇ
στιγμή, ὡσαύτως. σημεῖον δέ· καὶ γὰρ τὰς ἐνστάσεις οὕτω φέρομεν ὡς κατὰ παντὸς ἐρωτώμενοι, ἢ
εἰ ἐπί τινι μή, ἢ εἴ ποτε μή.

35 Καθ' αὑτὰ δ' ὅσα ὑπάρχει τε ἐν τῷ τί ἐστιν,
οἷον τριγώνῳ γραμμὴ καὶ γραμμῇ στιγμή (ἡ γὰρ
οὐσία αὐτῶν ἐκ τούτων ἐστί, καὶ ἐν τῷ λόγῳ τῷ
λέγοντι τί ἐστιν ἐνυπάρχει)· καὶ ὅσοις τῶν ὑπαρχόντων[1] αὐτοῖς αὐτὰ ἐν τῷ λόγῳ ἐνυπάρχουσι τῷ τί

---

[1] Bonitz: ἐνυπαρχόντων.

---

[a] Here καθόλου is used in a special sense : see 73 b 25 ff.
[b] i.e., this will be true of any line at any time.
[c] Although Aristotle's examples are of essential constituents, he obviously intends to include essential attributes.

and impossible to maintain that demonstration is reciprocal and that therefore everything can be demonstrated.

IV. Since the object of scientific knowledge in the absolute sense cannot be otherwise than it is, the notion reached by demonstrative knowledge will be necessarily true. Now knowledge is demonstrative when we possess it in virtue of having a demonstration ; therefore the premisses from which demonstration is inferred are necessarily true. Therefore we must comprehend the nature and character of the premisses from which demonstrations proceed. Let us first define what we mean by the terms " predicated of all " and " *per se* " and " universal " [a] ⟨as applied to attributes⟩.

Before discussing the premisses we must define certain terms.

I apply the term " predicated of all " to whatever is *not* predicated of one instance but not of another, or predicated at one time but not at another. *E.g.*, if " animal " is predicated of all " man," if it is true to call X a man, it is also true to call him an animal ; and if the former statement is true now, so is the latter. Similarly too if every line contains a point.[b] There is evidence to corroborate this definition ; for the objection which we adduce against a proposition which involves " predication of all " implies either an example to which or a time at which the predicate does not apply.

" Predicated of all."

I describe one thing as " belonging *per se* " to another (i) if it is an element in the essential nature of the other,[c] as, *e.g.*, a line belongs to a triangle and a point to a line (for the line or point is a constituent of the being of the triangle or line, and is an element in the formula which describes its essence) ; (ii) if it is an attribute the formula of whose essence includes

" Per se " as applied to attributes,

43

73 a

ἐστι δηλοῦντι, οἷον τὸ εὐθὺ ὑπάρχει γραμμῇ καὶ
40 τὸ περιφερές, καὶ τὸ περιττὸν καὶ ἄρτιον ἀριθμῷ,
73 b καὶ τὸ πρῶτον καὶ σύνθετον καὶ ἰσόπλευρον καὶ
ἑτερόμηκες· καὶ πᾶσι τούτοις ἐνυπάρχουσιν ἐν τῷ
λόγῳ τῷ τί ἐστι λέγοντι ἔνθα μὲν γραμμὴ ἔνθα δ'
ἀριθμός. ὁμοίως δὲ καὶ ἐπὶ τῶν ἄλλων τὰ τοιαῦθ'
ἑκάστοις καθ' αὑτὰ λέγω, ὅσα δὲ μηδετέρως ὑπάρ-
5 χει συμβεβηκότα, οἷον τὸ μουσικὸν ἢ λευκὸν τῷ
ζῴῳ. ἔτι ὃ μὴ καθ' ὑποκειμένου λέγεται ἄλλου
τινός, οἷον τὸ βαδίζον ἕτερόν τι ὂν βαδίζον ἐστί, καὶ
τὸ¹ λευκόν, ἡ δ' οὐσία καὶ ὅσα τόδε τι σημαίνει οὐχ
ἕτερόν τι ὄντα ἐστὶν ὅπερ ἐστί. τὰ μὲν δὴ μὴ καθ'
ὑποκειμένου καθ' αὑτὰ λέγω, τὰ δὲ καθ' ὑποκει-
10 μένου συμβεβηκότα. ἔτι δ' ἄλλον τρόπον τὸ μὲν
δι' αὑτὸ ὑπάρχον ἑκάστῳ καθ' αὑτό, τὸ δὲ μὴ δι'
αὑτὸ συμβεβηκός, οἷον εἰ βαδίζοντος ἤστραψε, συμ-
βεβηκός· οὐ γὰρ διὰ τὸ βαδίζειν ἤστραψεν, ἀλλὰ
συνέβη, φαμέν, τοῦτο. εἰ δὲ δι' αὑτό, καθ' αὑτό,
15 οἷον εἴ τι σφαττόμενον ἀπέθανε καὶ κατὰ τὴν
σφαγήν, ὅτι διὰ τὸ σφάττεσθαι, ἀλλ' οὐ συνέβη
σφαττόμενον ἀποθανεῖν. τὰ ἄρα λεγόμενα ἐπὶ τῶν
ἁπλῶς ἐπιστητῶν καθ' αὑτὰ οὕτως ὡς ἐνυπάρχειν

¹ τὸ om. ABCd.

---

^a An oblong number is a compound number that is not a
square. Both names refer to the geometrical patterns in
which pebbles or other objects representing the units can be
arranged.

^b Although in Greek a participle or adjective can be used
as an apparent substantive, it is still an attribute predicated
of an unexpressed subject apart from which it has no separate
existence.

^c We should call them attributes.

^d (iii) and (iv) are irrelevant for Aristotle's present pur-

the subject to which the attribute itself belongs. *E.g.*, " straight " and " curved " belong to " line," " odd " and " even," " prime " and " compound," " square " and " oblong " [a] belong to number ; and the formula of the essence of each one of these includes line or number respectively. Similarly in all other cases I describe all terms of either of the kinds just described as belonging *per se* to their several subjects ; whereas such as belong in neither of these senses—as *e.g.*, " cultured " or " white " belongs to " animal "—I call accidents. (iii) I also describe as ⟨existing⟩ *per se* whatever is not stated of something else as subject. I mean, *e.g.*, that " the walking " is something else which walks, and similarly " the white " [b] ; whereas substance, or whatever denotes an individual, is not anything other than just itself. Thus I call *per se* those terms which are not predicated of a subject ; those which are so predicated I call accidents.[c] (iv) Again in another sense that which happens to something else in virtue of the latter's own nature is said to happen to it *per se* ; while that which does not so happen is called an accident. *E.g.*, if it lightens while a man is walking, it is an accident ; for it was not because he was walking that it lightened ; it was, as we say, an accident. But an event which happens in virtue of a thing's own nature happens to it *per se*, *e.g.*, if something dies while being slaughtered and in accordance with the act of slaughtering, since it died because it was slaughtered, it was not an accident that it died while being slaughtered. Thus [d] in the sphere of what is knowable in the absolute sense, attributes which are called *per se*

individual substances,

and events.

pose ; they may even have been added by another hand ; at any rate Aristotle treats them as parenthetical.

45

73 b

τοῖς κατηγορουμένοις ἢ ἐνυπάρχεσθαι δι' αὐτά τέ
ἐστι καὶ ἐξ ἀνάγκης. οὐ γὰρ ἐνδέχεται μὴ ὑπάρχειν
20 ἢ ἁπλῶς ἢ τὰ ἀντικείμενα, οἷον γραμμῇ τὸ εὐθὺ ἢ
τὸ καμπύλον καὶ ἀριθμῷ τὸ περιττὸν ἢ τὸ ἄρτιον.
ἔστι γὰρ τὸ ἐναντίον ἢ στέρησις·ἢ ἀντίφασις ἐν τῷ
αὐτῷ γένει, οἷον ἄρτιον τὸ μὴ περιττὸν ἐν ἀριθμοῖς
ᾗ ἕπεται. ὥστ' εἰ ἀνάγκη φάναι ἢ ἀποφάναι, ἀνάγκη καὶ τὰ καθ' αὑτὰ ὑπάρχειν.

25   Τὸ μὲν οὖν κατὰ παντὸς καὶ καθ' αὑτὸ διωρίσθω
τὸν τρόπον τοῦτον· καθόλου δὲ λέγω ὃ ἂν κατὰ
παντός τε ὑπάρχῃ καὶ καθ' αὑτὸ καὶ ᾗ αὐτό.
φανερὸν ἄρα ὅτι ὅσα καθόλου ἐξ ἀνάγκης ὑπάρχει
τοῖς πράγμασιν. τὸ καθ' αὑτὸ δὲ καὶ ᾗ αὐτὸ ταὐ-
30 τόν, οἷον καθ' αὑτὴν τῇ γραμμῇ ὑπάρχει στιγμὴ καὶ
τὸ εὐθύ· καὶ γὰρ ᾗ γραμμή· καὶ τῷ τριγώνῳ ᾗ
τρίγωνον δύο ὀρθαί· καὶ γὰρ καθ' αὑτὸ τὸ τρίγωνον
δύο ὀρθαῖς ἴσον. τὸ καθόλου δὲ ὑπάρχει τότε, ὅταν
ἐπὶ τοῦ τυχόντος καὶ πρώτου δεικνύηται. οἷον τὸ
35 δύο ὀρθὰς ἔχειν οὔτε τῷ σχήματί ἐστι καθόλου
(καίτοι ἔστι δεῖξαι κατὰ σχήματος ὅτι δύο ὀρθὰς

---

[a] Type (i).
[b] Type (ii).
[c] A colour is either white or not-white in the sense that it
is either pure white or a colour containing little or no white
(privation) ; number is either odd or not-odd in the sense
that if it is not odd it must be even (contradictory).
[d] By the Law of Excluded Middle.
[e] This limitation of the meaning of καθ' αὐτό by equating
it with ᾗ αὐτό comes in oddly here. The point is that strictly
an attribute only belongs *per se* to the highest class to which
it is essential. The same idea is expressed in a different way
by πρῶτον below.

as implying or implied by their subjects belong to those subjects in virtue of their own nature and of necessity. It is impossible that they should not belong to their subjects—either absolutely [a] or in the way that opposite attributes belong,[b] e.g., either straight or curved to a line and either odd or even to a number ; because the contrary of an attribute is either the privation or the contradictory of that attribute in the same genus ; e.g., in number the not-odd is even, inasmuch as evenness is a consequent of non-oddness.[c] Thus since an attribute must be either asserted or denied of a subject,[d] per se attributes must belong to their subjects of necessity.

So much for the definition of what is meant by "predication of all" and "per se." By a "universal" attribute I mean one which belongs as "predicated of all" to its subject, and belongs to that subject per se and qua itself. Thus it is evident that all universal attributes belong to their subjects of necessity. A per se attribute is identical with that which belongs to its subject qua itself [e] ; e.g., "point" and "straight" belong per se to "line," for they also belong to it qua line ; and "having the sum of its interior angles equal to two right angles" belongs to triangle qua triangle ; for a triangle per se has the sum of its interior angles equal to two right angles. An attribute only belongs to a subject universally when it can be shown to belong to any chance instance of that subject, and to belong to that subject primarily.[f] (i) E.g., "having the sum of its interior angles equal to two right angles" is not universally applicable to "figure." It is indeed possible to prove of a figure that the sum of its interior angles is equal to

" Universal " attributes.

[f] See previous note.

73 b

ἔχει, ἀλλ' οὐ τοῦ τυχόντος σχήματος, οὐδὲ χρῆται
τῷ τυχόντι σχήματι δεικνύς[1]· τὸ γὰρ τετράγωνον
σχῆμα μέν, οὐκ ἔχει δὲ δύο ὀρθαῖς ἴσας). τὸ δ'
ἰσοσκελὲς ἔχει μὲν τὸ τυχὸν δύο ὀρθαῖς ἴσας, ἀλλ'
οὐ πρῶτον, ἀλλὰ τὸ τρίγωνον πρότερον. ὃ τοίνυν τὸ
40 τυχὸν πρῶτον δείκνυται δύο ὀρθὰς ἔχον ἢ ὁτιοῦν
74 a ἄλλο, τούτῳ πρώτῳ ὑπάρχει καθόλου, καὶ ἡ ἀπόδειξις καθ' αὑτὸ τούτου καθόλου ἐστί, τῶν δ' ἄλλων
τρόπον τινὰ οὐ καθ' αὑτό· οὐδὲ τοῦ ἰσοσκελοῦς οὐκ
ἔστι καθόλου ἀλλ' ἐπὶ πλέον.

V. Δεῖ δὲ μὴ λανθάνειν ὅτι πολλάκις συμβαίνει
5 διαμαρτάνειν καὶ μὴ ὑπάρχειν τὸ δεικνύμενον πρῶτον καθόλου, ᾗ δοκεῖ δείκνυσθαι καθόλου πρῶτον.
ἀπατώμεθα δὲ ταύτην τὴν ἀπάτην ὅταν ἢ μηδὲν ᾖ
λαβεῖν ἀνώτερον παρὰ τὸ καθ' ἕκαστον ἢ τὰ καθ'
ἕκαστα,[2] ἢ ᾗ μέν, ἀλλ' ἀνώνυμον ᾗ ἐπὶ διαφόροις
10 εἴδει πράγμασιν, ἢ τυγχάνῃ ὂν ὡς ἐν μέρει ὅλον ἐφ'
ᾧ δείκνυται· τοῖς γὰρ ἐν μέρει ὑπάρξει μὲν ἡ ἀπόδειξις, καὶ ἔσται κατὰ παντός, ἀλλ' ὅμως οὐκ ἔσται
τούτου πρώτου καθόλου ἡ ἀπόδειξις. λέγω δὲ

---

[1] δεικνύς] ὁ δεικνύς Bekker.
[2] ἢ τὰ καθ' ἕκαστα secl. Ross.

---

[a] Unless Aristotle is writing very carelessly ἢ τὰ καθ'
ἕκαστα is a mistaken gloss, which Ross rightly brackets. καθ'

48

two right angles, but this cannot be proved of any chance figure ; nor does one use any chance figure for the proof, for a square is a figure, but it does not contain angles equal to the sum of two right angles. Again, any chance isosceles triangle has angles equal to the sum of two right angles, but it is not the first figure to fulfil this requirement ; the triangle is prior to it. Thus that which can be shown in any chance instance primarily to fulfil the condition of containing the sum of two right angles, or any other requirement, is the subject to which that universal attribute primarily belongs ; and the demonstration that this predicate is true universally of its subject establishes a *per se* relation between them, whereas the relation established for other predicates is in a sense not *per se.* (ii) Nor again is " containing angles equal to the sum of two right angles " a universal attribute of " isosceles " ; it has a wider extension.

V. We must not overlook the fact that a mistake often occurs, and the attribute which we are trying to prove does not apply primarily and universally in the sense in which we think that it is being proved. We fall into this error either (i) when we cannot find any higher term apart from the individual [or individuals] [a] ; or (ii) when there is such a term, but it has no name as applied to objects which differ in species ; or (iii) when the subject of the demonstration happens to be a whole which is a part of some other ; for although the demonstration will hold good of the particulars contained in it and will be predicated of all of it, still the demonstration will not apply to it primarily and universally. When I say

Error may vitiate the proof of universal attributes. Three causes for this error.

ἕκαστον seems here to mean not an individual but a single species the genus of which is unrecognizable.

ARISTOTLE

74 a

τούτου πρώτου, ᾗ τοῦτο, ἀπόδειξιν ὅταν ᾖ πρώτου καθόλου.

Εἰ οὖν τις δείξειεν ὅτι αἱ ὀρθαὶ οὐ συμπίπτουσι, 15 δόξειεν ἂν τούτου εἶναι ἡ ἀπόδειξις διὰ τὸ ἐπὶ πασῶν εἶναι τῶν ὀρθῶν· οὐκ ἔστι δέ, εἴπερ μὴ ὅτι ὡδὶ ἴσαι γίγνεται τοῦτο, ἀλλ᾽ ᾗ ὁπωσοῦν ἴσαι.

Καὶ εἰ τρίγωνον μὴ ἦν ἄλλο ἢ ἰσοσκελές, ᾗ ἰσοσκελὲς ἂν ἐδόκει ὑπάρχειν.

Καὶ τὸ ἀνάλογον ὅτι ἐναλλάξ, ᾗ ἀριθμοὶ καὶ ᾗ γραμμαὶ καὶ ᾗ στερεὰ καὶ ᾗ χρόνοι, ὥσπερ 20 ἐδείκνυτό ποτε χωρίς, ἐνδεχόμενόν γε κατὰ πάντων μιᾷ ἀποδείξει δειχθῆναι· ἀλλὰ διὰ τὸ μὴ εἶναι ὠνομασμένον τι πάντα ταῦτα ἕν, ἀριθμοὶ μήκη χρόνος στερεά, καὶ εἴδει διαφέρειν ἀλλήλων, χωρὶς ἐλαμβάνετο· νῦν δὲ καθόλου δείκνυται· οὐ γὰρ ᾗ γραμμαὶ ἢ ᾗ ἀριθμοὶ ὑπῆρχεν ἀλλ᾽ ᾗ τοδί, ὃ 25 καθόλου ὑποτίθενται ὑπάρχειν. διὰ τοῦτο οὐδ᾽ ἂν τις δείξῃ καθ᾽ ἕκαστον τὸ τρίγωνον ἀποδείξει ἢ μιᾷ ἢ ἑτέρᾳ ὅτι δύο ὀρθὰς ἔχει ἕκαστον, τὸ ἰσόπλευρον χωρὶς καὶ τὸ σκαληνὲς καὶ τὸ ἰσοσκελές, οὔπω οἶδε τὸ τρίγωνον ὅτι δύο ὀρθαῖς εἰ μὴ τὸν

---

[a] An example of (iii). The fact is true of the lines primarily *qua* parallel, only secondarily *qua* perpendicular.

[b] An example of (i).

[c] *i.e.*, that if A : B = C : D, A : C = B : D. The illustration which follows is an example of (ii); but *cf.* Heath, *Mathematics in Aristotle*, pp. 41-44.

[d] *i.e.*, with the unco-ordinated unscientific knowledge of the sophist.

that demonstration applies to a subject primarily and universally, I mean that it applies to that subject primarily as such.

Thus if one were to prove that perpendiculars ⟨to the same straight line⟩ never meet, it might be supposed that this quality of perpendiculars was the proper subject of the demonstration, since it holds good of all perpendiculars. But it is not ; inasmuch as the result follows, not because the ⟨alternate⟩ angles are equal in this particular way, but if they are equal at all.[a]

Again, if there were no triangle except the isosceles, the proof that it contains angles equal to the sum of two right angles would be supposed to apply to it *qua* isosceles.[b]

Again, the law that *proportionals alternate* [c] might be supposed to apply to numbers *qua* numbers, and similarly to lines, solids and periods of time ; as indeed it used to be demonstrated of these subjects separately. It could, of course, have been proved of them all by a single demonstration, but since there was no single term to denote the common quality of numbers, lengths, time and solids, and they differ in species from one another, they were treated separately ; but now the law is proved universally ; for the property did not belong to them *qua* lines or *qua* numbers, but *qua* possessing this special quality which they are assumed to possess universally. Hence, even if a man proves separately—whether by the same demonstration or not—of each kind of triangle, equilateral, scalene and isosceles, that it contains angles equal to the sum of two right angles, he still does not know, except in the sophistical sense,[d] that a triangle has its angles equal to the sum of two right angles, or

51

σοφιστικὸν τρόπον, οὐδὲ καθόλου τρίγωνον, οὐδ' εἰ
30 μηδέν ἐστι παρὰ ταῦτα τρίγωνον ἕτερον· οὐ γὰρ ᾗ
τρίγωνον οἶδεν, οὐδὲ πᾶν τρίγωνον ἀλλ' ἢ κατ'
ἀριθμόν· κατ' εἶδος δ' οὐ πᾶν, καὶ εἰ μηδὲν ἔστιν ὃ
οὐκ οἶδεν.

Πότ' οὖν οὐκ οἶδε καθόλου, καὶ πότ' οἶδεν ἁπλῶς; δῆλον δὴ ὅτι εἰ ταὐτὸν ἦν τριγώνῳ εἶναι καὶ
ἰσοπλεύρῳ ἢ ἑκάστῳ ἢ πᾶσιν· εἰ δὲ μὴ ταὐτὸν ἀλλ'
35 ἕτερον, ὑπάρχει δ' ᾗ τρίγωνον, οὐκ οἶδεν. πότερον
δ' ᾗ τρίγωνον ἢ ᾗ ἰσοσκελὲς ὑπάρχει; καὶ πότε
κατὰ τοῦθ' ὑπάρχει πρῶτον; καὶ καθόλου τίνος
ἡ ἀπόδειξις; δῆλον ὅτι ὅταν ἀφαιρουμένων ὑπάρξῃ
πρώτῳ. οἷον τῷ ἰσοσκελεῖ χαλκῷ τριγώνῳ ὑπ-
74b άρξουσι δύο ὀρθαί, ἀλλὰ καὶ τοῦ χαλκοῦν εἶναι
ἀφαιρεθέντος καὶ τοῦ ἰσοσκελές. ἀλλ' οὐ τοῦ σχήματος ἢ πέρατος. ἀλλ' οὐ πρώτων. τίνος οὖν
πρώτου; εἰ δὴ τριγώνου, κατὰ τοῦτο ὑπάρχει
καὶ τοῖς ἄλλοις, καὶ τούτου καθόλου ἐστὶν ἡ ἀπόδειξις.

5 VI. Εἰ οὖν ἐστιν ἡ ἀποδεικτικὴ ἐπιστήμη ἐξ
ἀναγκαίων ἀρχῶν (ὃ γὰρ ἐπίσταται οὐ δυνατὸν
ἄλλως ἔχειν), τὰ δὲ καθ' αὑτὰ ὑπάρχοντα ἀναγκαῖα

---

that this is a universal property of triangles, even if there is no other kind of triangle besides these; for he does not know that this property belongs to a triangle *qua* triangle, nor that it belongs to every triangle, except numerically[a]; for he does not know that it belongs to every triangle specifically, even if there is no triangle which he does not know to possess it.

When, then, do we not know universally, and when do we know absolutely? Clearly, if " triangle " were essentially the same as " equilateral " in each or every instance, we should have absolute knowledge; but if it is not the same but different, and the property belongs to the equilateral *qua* triangle, our knowledge is not universal. We must ask " Does the property belong to its subject *qua* triangle or *qua* isosceles? When does it apply to its subject primarily? What is the subject of which it can be demonstrated universally? " Clearly the first subject to which it applies as the differentiae are removed. *E.g.*, the property of having angles equal to the sum of two right angles will apply to " bronze isosceles triangle "; and it will still apply when " bronze " and " isosceles " are removed. " But not if you remove ' figure ' or ' limit.' " No, but these are not the first differentiae whose removal makes the attribute inapplicable. " Then what is the first? " If it is " triangle," then it is with respect to triangularity that the attribute applies to all the rest of the subjects, and it is of " triangle " that the attribute can be universally demonstrated.

VI. If, then, demonstrative knowledge proceeds from necessary first principles (because that which we know cannot possibly be otherwise), and essential

74 b

τοῖς πράγμασιν (τὰ μὲν γὰρ ἐν τῷ τί ἐστιν ὑπάρχει·
τοῖς δ' αὐτὰ ἐν τῷ τί ἐστιν ὑπάρχει κατηγορουμένοις
αὐτῶν, ὧν θάτερον τῶν ἀντικειμένων ἀνάγκη
10 ὑπάρχειν), φανερὸν ὅτι ἐκ τοιούτων τινῶν ἂν εἴη ὁ
ἀποδεικτικὸς συλλογισμός· ἅπαν γὰρ ἢ οὕτως ὑπάρχει ἢ κατὰ συμβεβηκός, τὰ δὲ συμβεβηκότα οὐκ
ἀναγκαῖα.

Ἢ δὴ οὕτω λεκτέον, ἢ ἀρχὴν θεμένοις ὅτι ἡ ἀπόδειξις ἀναγκαῖόν[1] ἐστι, καὶ εἰ ἀποδέδεικται, οὐχ
15 οἷόν τ' ἄλλως ἔχειν· ἐξ ἀναγκαίων ἄρα δεῖ εἶναι τὸν
συλλογισμόν. ἐξ ἀληθῶν μὲν γὰρ ἔστι καὶ μὴ ἀποδεικνύντα συλλογίσασθαι, ἐξ ἀναγκαίων δ' οὐκ
ἔστιν ἀλλ' ἢ ἀποδεικνύντα· τοῦτο γὰρ ἤδη ἀποδείξεώς ἐστι.

Σημεῖον δ' ὅτι ἡ ἀπόδειξις ἐξ ἀναγκαίων ὅτι καὶ
τὰς ἐνστάσεις οὕτω φέρομεν πρὸς τοὺς οἰομένους
20 ἀποδεικνύναι, ὅτι οὐκ ἀνάγκη, ἂν οἰώμεθα ἢ ὅλως
ἐνδέχεσθαι ἄλλως ἢ ἕνεκά γε τοῦ λόγου.

Δῆλον δ' ἐκ τούτων καὶ ὅτι εὐήθεις οἱ λαμβάνειν
οἰόμενοι καλῶς τὰς ἀρχὰς ἐὰν ἔνδοξος ᾖ ἡ πρότασις
καὶ ἀληθής, οἷον οἱ σοφισταὶ ὅτι τὸ ἐπίστασθαι τὸ
ἐπιστήμην ἔχειν. οὐ γὰρ τὸ ἔνδοξον ἢ μή[2] ἀρχή

---

[1] ἀναγκαίων Philoponus (?), Ross : ἀναγκαίου Mure.
[2] ἢ μή] ἡμῖν n[1], Ross.

---

[a] e.g., ' nose ' is part of the definition of ' snubness '
(*Met.* 1064 a 25), and every nose is either snub or not snub.
[b] i.e., necessary.
[c] This sense can, I think, be extracted from the vulgate
without having recourse to emendation.

attributes are necessary to their subjects (for some *demonstra-*
of them inhere in the essence of their subjects, while *tion are*
necessary.
others have the subjects of which they are predicated
inherent in their own essence, and in this latter class
one member of the pair of opposite attributes must
apply),[a] it is evident that the premisses from which
demonstrative syllogisms are drawn will be of this
nature[b]; for every attribute applies either in this or
in the accidental sense, and accidental attributes are
not necessary.

We may either argue in this way, or lay down the
principle that demonstration implies necessity,[c] *i.e.*,
that if a thing has been proved, it cannot be otherwise.
Then it follows that the premisses of the ⟨demonstra-
tive⟩ syllogism must be necessary; for whereas it is
possible to draw a conclusion from true premisses
without demonstrating anything, it is impossible to
draw one from necessary premisses without doing so;
for necessity directly implies demonstration.

Evidence that the premisses from which demonstration proceeds are necessary may be found in the
fact that the way in which we raise objections against
those who imagine that they are demonstrating is
by saying " it is not *necessary*," that is if we think that
it is possible, either without qualification or for the
purposes of the argument, that the fact should be
otherwise.

⟨It is also clear from these arguments that it is
foolish to think that one is choosing the right starting-
point if the premiss is ⟨merely⟩ generally accepted
and true; as the sophists assume that to know is to
have knowledge.[d] The starting-point is not that
which is generally accepted or the reverse, but that

[d] *Cf.* Plato, *Euthydemus* 277 B.

74 b

25 ἐστιν, ἀλλὰ τὸ πρῶτον τοῦ γένους περὶ ὃ δείκνυται·
καὶ τἀληθὲς οὐ πᾶν οἰκεῖον.

Ὅτι δ' ἐξ ἀναγκαίων εἶναι δεῖ τὸν συλλογισμὸν
φανερὸν καὶ ἐκ τῶνδε. εἰ γὰρ ὁ μὴ ἔχων λόγον τοῦ
διὰ τί οὔσης ἀποδείξεως οὐκ ἐπιστήμων, εἴη δ' ἂν
ὥστε τὸ Α κατὰ τοῦ Γ ἐξ ἀνάγκης ὑπάρχειν, τὸ δὲ
30 Β τὸ μέσον δι' οὗ ἀπεδείχθη μὴ ἐξ ἀνάγκης, οὐκ
οἶδε διότι. οὐ γάρ ἐστι τοῦτο διὰ τὸ μέσον· τὸ μὲν
γὰρ ἐνδέχεται μὴ εἶναι, τὸ δὲ συμπέρασμα ἀναγκαῖον.

Ἔτι εἴ τις μὴ οἶδε νῦν ἔχων τὸν λόγον καὶ σῳζό-
μενος, σῳζομένου τοῦ πράγματος, μὴ ἐπιλελησ-
μένος, οὐδὲ πρότερον ᾔδει. φθαρείη δ' ἂν τὸ μέσον
35 εἰ μὴ ἀναγκαῖον, ὥστε ἕξει μὲν τὸν λόγον σῳζό-
μενος σῳζομένου τοῦ πράγματος, οὐκ οἶδε δέ· οὐδ'
ἄρα πρότερον ᾔδει. εἰ δὲ μὴ ἔφθαρται, ἐνδέχεται
δὲ φθαρῆναι, τὸ συμβαῖνον ἂν εἴη δυνατὸν καὶ
ἐνδεχόμενον. ἀλλ' ἔστιν ἀδύνατον οὕτως ἔχοντα
εἰδέναι.

75 a Ὅταν μὲν οὖν τὸ συμπέρασμα ἐξ ἀνάγκης ᾖ,
οὐδὲν κωλύει τὸ μέσον μὴ ἀναγκαῖον εἶναι δι' οὗ
ἐδείχθη· ἔστι γὰρ τὸ ἀναγκαῖον καὶ μὴ ἐξ ἀναγκαίων[1] συλλογίσασθαι, ὥσπερ καὶ ἀληθὲς μὴ ἐξ
5 ἀληθῶν· ὅταν δὲ τὸ μέσον ἐξ ἀνάγκης, καὶ τὸ

---

[1] ἀναγκαίων n, Philoponus : ἀναγκαίου.

---

[a] But in neither case is the conclusion proved. This paragraph is a parenthetical comment on the main argument.

which is primarily true of the genus with which the demonstration deals ; and not every true fact is peculiar to a given genus.)

That our syllogism must be based upon necessary premisses is evident also from the following argument. Since the man who cannot give an account of the reason for a fact, although there is a proof available, is not possessed of scientific knowledge, if we assume a syllogism such that while A necessarily applies as predicate to C, B, the middle term by which the conclusion was proved, is not in a necessary relation to the other terms, then he does not know the reason. For the conclusion does not depend upon the middle term, since the latter may not be true, whereas the conclusion is necessary.

Again, if a man does not know a fact now, although he can give an account of it and both he himself and the fact are unchanged, and he has not forgotten it, then he was also ignorant of it before. But if the middle term is not necessary, it may cease to operate. In that case, although the man himself and the fact are unchanged, and he will still have his account of it, he does not know the fact. Therefore he was also ignorant of it before. Even if the middle term has not actually ceased, if it *may* cease, the conclusion will be problematic and contingent ; and under such conditions knowledge is impossible.

(When the conclusion is necessary, it is not essential that the middle term by which it was proved should be necessary, for it is possible to reach a necessary conclusion even from premisses which are not necessary, just as it is possible to reach a true conclusion from premisses which are not true.[a] But when the middle term is necessarily true, the con-

Parenthesis: Non-necessary premisses may give, but necessary premisses must give, a necessary conclusion.

συμπέρασμα ἐξ ἀνάγκης, ὥσπερ καὶ ἐξ ἀληθῶν
ἀληθὲς ἀεί· ἔστω γὰρ τὸ Α κατὰ τοῦ Β ἐξ ἀνάγκης,
καὶ τοῦτο κατὰ τοῦ Γ· ἀναγκαῖον τοίνυν καὶ τὸ Α
τῷ Γ ὑπάρχειν· ὅταν δὲ μὴ ἀναγκαῖον ᾖ τὸ συμπέρασμα, οὐδὲ τὸ μέσον ἀναγκαῖον οἷόν τ᾽ εἶναι·
ἔστω γὰρ τὸ Α τῷ Γ μὴ ἐξ ἀνάγκης ὑπάρχειν, τῷ
10 δὲ Β, καὶ τοῦτο τῷ Γ ἐξ ἀνάγκης· καὶ τὸ Α ἄρα
τῷ Γ ἐξ ἀνάγκης ὑπάρξει· ἀλλ᾽ οὐχ ὑπέκειτο.

Ἐπεὶ τοίνυν εἰ ἐπίσταται ἀποδεικτικῶς, δεῖ ἐξ
ἀνάγκης ὑπάρχειν, δῆλον ὅτι καὶ διὰ μέσου ἀναγκαίου δεῖ ἔχειν τὴν ἀπόδειξιν· ἢ οὐκ ἐπιστήσεται
15 οὔτε διότι οὔτε ὅτι ἀνάγκη ἐκεῖνο εἶναι, ἀλλ᾽ ἢ οἰήσεται οὐκ εἰδώς, ἐὰν ὑπολάβῃ ὡς ἀναγκαῖον τὸ μὴ
ἀναγκαῖον, ἢ οὐδ᾽ οἰήσεται, ὁμοίως ἐάν τε τὸ ὅτι
εἰδῇ διὰ μέσων ἐάν τε τὸ διότι καὶ δι᾽ ἀμέσων.

Τῶν δὲ συμβεβηκότων μὴ καθ᾽ αὑτά, ὃν τρόπον διωρίσθη τὰ καθ᾽ αὑτά, οὐκ ἔστιν ἐπιστήμη
20 ἀποδεικτική. οὐ γὰρ ἔστιν ἐξ ἀνάγκης δεῖξαι τὸ
συμπέρασμα· τὸ συμβεβηκὸς γὰρ ἐνδέχεται μὴ ὑπ-
άρχειν· περὶ τοῦ[1] τοιούτου γὰρ λέγω συμβεβηκότος.
καίτοι ἀπορήσειεν ἄν τις ἴσως τίνος ἕνεκα ταῦτα
δεῖ ἐρωτᾶν περὶ τούτων, εἰ μὴ ἀνάγκη τὸ συμπέρασμα εἶναι· οὐδὲν γὰρ διαφέρει εἴ τις ἐρόμενος τὰ
25 τυχόντα εἶτα εἴπειεν τὸ συμπέρασμα. δεῖ δ᾽ ἐρωτᾶν οὐχ ὡς ἀναγκαῖον εἶναι διὰ τὰ ἠρωτημένα, ἀλλ᾽

[1] om. Ad.

---

[a] 73 a 37 ff., 74 b 8 ff.

clusion is also necessary ; just as the conclusion from true premises is always true. For let A be necessarily predicated of B, and B of C ; then the conclusion that A applies to C is also necessary. But when the conclusion is not necessary, neither can the middle term be necessary. For suppose that A applies necessarily to B but not to C, and that B necessarily applies to C. Then A will also apply necessarily to C. But this was not the original assumption.)

Therefore since, if we have demonstrative knowledge of a proposition, the predicate must apply necessarily to the subject, it is obvious that the middle term upon which the proof depends must also be necessary. Otherwise we shall recognize neither the fact of the conclusion not the reason for it as necessary ; we shall either think that we know, although we do not—that is if we assume as necessary that which is not necessary—or we shall not even think that we know, alike whether we know the fact by intermediate terms or whether we know the reason immediately.

Thus in demonstration the middle term must be necessary.

Attributes which are not essential in the sense which we have defined [a] do not admit of demonstrative knowledge, since it is not possible to give a necessary proof of the conclusion ; for an accidental attribute may not apply to its subject, and it is of this kind of attribute that I am speaking. At the same time it might be questioned why ⟨in dialectic⟩, if the conclusion is not necessarily true, we should ask for the concession of such premises for such a conclusion ; one might as well suggest any premises at random, and then state the conclusion. The answer is that we should put definite questions, not because the answers affect the necessity of the conclusion, but

No demonstrative knowledge of non-essential attributes.

75 a

ὅτι λέγειν ἀνάγκη τῷ ἐκεῖνα λέγοντι, καὶ ἀληθῶς λέγειν, ἐὰν ἀληθῶς ᾖ ὑπάρχοντα.

Ἐπεὶ δ' ἐξ ἀνάγκης ὑπάρχει περὶ ἕκαστον γένος ὅσα καθ' αὐτὰ ὑπάρχει, καὶ ᾗ ἕκαστον, φανερὸν ὅτι
30 περὶ τῶν καθ' αὑτὰ ὑπαρχόντων αἱ ἐπιστημονικαὶ ἀποδείξεις καὶ ἐκ τῶν τοιούτων εἰσίν. τὰ μὲν γὰρ συμβεβηκότα οὐκ ἀναγκαῖα, ὥστ' οὐκ ἀνάγκη τὸ συμπέρασμα εἰδέναι διότι ὑπάρχει, οὐδ' εἰ ἀεὶ εἴη, μὴ καθ' αὑτὸ δέ, οἷον οἱ διὰ σημείων συλλογισμοί. τὸ γὰρ καθ' αὑτὸ οὐ καθ' αὑτὸ ἐπιστήσεται, οὐδὲ
35 διότι. τὸ δὲ διότι ἐπίστασθαί ἐστι τὸ διὰ τοῦ αἰτίου ἐπίστασθαι. δι' αὐτὸ ἄρα δεῖ καὶ τὸ μέσον τῷ τρίτῳ καὶ τὸ πρῶτον τῷ μέσῳ ὑπάρχειν.

VII. Οὐκ ἄρα ἔστιν ἐξ ἄλλου γένους μεταβάντα δεῖξαι, οἷον τὸ γεωμετρικὸν ἀριθμητικῇ. τρία γάρ
40 ἐστι τὰ ἐν ταῖς ἀποδείξεσιν, ἓν μὲν τὸ ἀποδεικνύ- μενον τὸ συμπέρασμα (τοῦτο δ' ἐστὶ τὸ ὑπάρχον γένει τινὶ καθ' αὑτό), ἓν δὲ τὰ ἀξιώματα (ἀξιώματα
75 b δ' ἐστὶν ἐξ ὧν), τρίτον τὸ γένος τὸ ὑποκείμενον, οὗ τὰ πάθη καὶ τὰ καθ' αὑτὰ συμβεβηκότα δηλοῖ ἡ ἀπόδειξις. ἐξ ὧν μὲν οὖν ἡ ἀπόδειξις, ἐνδέχεται τὰ αὐτὰ εἶναι· ὧν δὲ τὸ γένος ἕτερον, ὥσπερ ἀριθμη- τικῆς καὶ γεωμετρίας, οὐκ ἔστι τὴν ἀριθμητικὴν
5 ἀπόδειξιν ἐφαρμόσαι ἐπὶ τὰ τοῖς μεγέθεσι συμβε- βηκότα, εἰ μὴ τὰ μεγέθη ἀριθμοί εἰσι· τοῦτο δ' ὡς

---

[a] Even the syllogisms of dialectic should be formally valid.

[b] Where the connexion is neither causal nor necessary ; cf. *An. Pr.* 70 a 7 ff.

[c] To describe the common axioms as ἐξ ὧν suggests that they serve as premisses ; but this is true only of such as are

because in stating them our opponent must state the conclusion, and state it truly if the attributes apply truly.[a]

Since in each genus it is the attributes that belong essentially to that particular genus that belong to it of necessity, it is evident that scientific demonstrations are concerned with essential attributes and proceed from them. For accidental attributes are not necessary, and therefore we do not necessarily know why the conclusion is true ; not even if the attributes belong always, but not *per se*, as in syllogisms through signs.[b] For we shall not have knowledge of the essential *fact* as essential, nor shall we know its reason. To know the reason of a thing is to know it through its cause. Therefore the middle term must apply *per se* to the third, and also the first *per se* to the middle.

Hence our premisses must state per se connexions.

VII. Hence it is not possible to prove a fact by passing from one genus to another—*e.g.*, to prove a geometrical proposition by arithmetic. There are three factors in a demonstration : (1) The conclusion which is required to be proved, *i.e.*, the application of an essential attribute to some genus ; (2) the axioms, on which the proof is based [c] ; (3) the underlying genus, whose modifications or essential attributes are disclosed by the demonstration. Now where different genera, *e.g.*, arithmetic and geometry, are involved, although the basis of proof may be the same, it is not possible to apply the arithmetical demonstration to the attributes of extended magnitudes, unless extended magnitudes are numbers.[d] How transference is possible in some cases

They must state them of attributes belonging to the same genus as the proposition to be proved.

quantitative. Normally the axioms are δι' ὧν (*cf.* 76 b 10, 88 a 36 ff.).   [d] For Aristotle they are not ; *cf. Cat.* 4 b 22 ff.

ἐνδέχεται ἐπί τινων, ὕστερον λεχθήσεται. ἡ δ᾿
ἀριθμητικὴ ἀπόδειξις ἀεὶ ἔχει τὸ γένος περὶ ὃ ἡ
ἀπόδειξις, καὶ αἱ ἄλλαι ὁμοίως· ὥστ᾿ ἢ ἁπλῶς
ἀνάγκη τὸ αὐτὸ εἶναι γένος ἢ πῇ, εἰ μέλλει ἡ ἀπό-
10 δειξις μεταβαίνειν· ἄλλως δ᾿ ὅτι ἀδύνατον δῆλον·
ἐκ γὰρ τοῦ αὐτοῦ γένους ἀνάγκη τὰ ἄκρα καὶ τὰ
μέσα εἶναι. εἰ γὰρ μὴ καθ᾿ αὑτά, συμβεβηκότα
ἔσται. διὰ τοῦτο τῇ γεωμετρίᾳ οὐκ ἔστι δεῖξαι ὅτι
τῶν ἐναντίων μία ἐπιστήμη, ἀλλ᾿ οὐδ᾿ ὅτι οἱ δύο
κύβοι κύβος· οὐδ᾿ ἄλλῃ ἐπιστήμῃ τὸ ἑτέρας, ἀλλ᾿ ἢ
15 ὅσα οὕτως ἔχει πρὸς ἄλληλα ὥστ᾿ εἶναι θάτερον ὑπὸ
θάτερον, οἷον τὰ ὀπτικὰ πρὸς γεωμετρίαν καὶ τὰ
ἁρμονικὰ πρὸς ἀριθμητικήν. οὐδ᾿ εἴ τι ὑπάρχει
ταῖς γραμμαῖς μὴ ᾗ γραμμαὶ καὶ ᾗ ἐκ τῶν ἀρχῶν
τῶν ἰδίων, οἷον εἰ καλλίστη τῶν γραμμῶν ἡ εὐθεῖα
20 ἢ εἰ ἐναντίως ἔχει τῇ περιφερείᾳ· οὐ γὰρ ᾗ τὸ ἴδιον
γένος αὐτῶν ὑπάρχει, ἀλλ᾿ ᾗ κοινόν τι.

VIII. Φανερὸν δὲ καὶ ἐὰν ὦσιν αἱ προτάσεις
καθόλου ἐξ ὧν ὁ συλλογισμός, ὅτι ἀνάγκη καὶ τὸ
συμπέρασμα ἀΐδιον εἶναι τῆς τοιαύτης ἀποδείξεως
καὶ τῆς ἁπλῶς εἰπεῖν ἀποδείξεως. οὐκ ἔστιν ἄρα
25 ἀπόδειξις τῶν φθαρτῶν οὐδ᾿ ἐπιστήμη ἁπλῶς, ἀλλ᾿
οὕτως ὥσπερ κατὰ συμβεβηκός, ὅτι οὐ καθόλου
αὐτοῦ ἐστιν ἀλλὰ ποτὲ καὶ πώς. ὅταν δ᾿ ᾖ, ἀνάγκη
τὴν ἑτέραν μὴ καθόλου εἶναι πρότασιν καὶ φθαρτήν,

---

[a] 76 a 9 ff., 78 b 34 ff.
[b] In the case of subaltern sciences.
[c] The reference is to cube numbers ; cf. Euclid, *Elementa*
ix. 4.

62

will be explained later.[a] Arithmetical demonstration always keeps to the genus which is the subject of the demonstration, and similarly with all other sciences. Thus the genus must be the same, either absolutely or in some respect,[b] if the demonstration is to be *transferable*. Clearly this is impossible in any other way; the extreme and middle terms must belong to the same genus; if the connexion is not essential it must be accidental. This is why we cannot prove by geometry that contraries are studied by the same science, nor even that the product of two cubes is a cube.[c] Nor can a proposition of one science be proved by another science, except when the relation is such that the propositions of the one are subordinate to those of the other, as the propositions of optics are subordinate to geometry and those of harmonics to arithmetic. Nor can geometry decide whether a given attribute applies to lines otherwise than *qua* lines and derived from their own peculiar principles, *e.g.*, whether the straight line is the most beautiful of lines, or whether it is the contrary of the curved; for these attributes apply to lines not in virtue of their peculiar genus, but in virtue of a characteristic common to other genera.

VIII. It is also evident that if the premisses of the syllogism are universal, the conclusion of a demonstration of this kind—demonstration in the strict sense—must be eternal. Hence of connexions that are not eternal, there is no demonstration or knowledge in the strict sense, but only in the accidental sense that the attribute belongs to the subject not universally but at a given time or under given conditions. When this is so, the minor premiss must be non-eternal and non-universal : non-eternal because *Only eternal connexions can be demonstrated.*

63

75 b

φθαρτὴν μὲν ὅτι καὶ[1] τὸ συμπέρασμα οὔσης, μὴ
καθόλου δὲ ὅτι τῷ[2] μὲν ἔσται τῷ δὲ οὐκ ἔσται ἐφ'
30 ὧν, ὥστε οὐκ ἔστι συλλογίσασθαι καθόλου, ἀλλ'
ὅτι νῦν. ὁμοίως δ' ἔχει καὶ περὶ ὁρισμούς, ἐπείπερ
ἐστὶν ὁ ὁρισμὸς ἢ ἀρχὴ ἀποδείξεως ἢ ἀπόδειξις
θέσει διαφέρουσα ἢ συμπέρασμά τι ἀποδείξεως. αἱ
δὲ τῶν πολλάκις γιγνομένων ἀποδείξεις καὶ ἐπι-
35 στῆμαι, οἷον σελήνης ἐκλείψεως, δῆλον ὅτι ᾗ μὲν
τοιοῦδ'[3] εἰσίν, ἀεί εἰσιν, ᾗ δ' οὐκ ἀεί, κατὰ μέρος
εἰσίν. ὥσπερ δ' ἡ ἔκλειψις, ὡσαύτως τοῖς ἄλλοις.

IX. Ἐπεὶ δὲ φανερὸν ὅτι ἕκαστον ἀποδεῖξαι οὐκ
ἔστιν ἀλλ' ἢ ἐκ τῶν ἑκάστου ἀρχῶν, ἂν τὸ δεικνύμενον ὑπάρχῃ ᾗ ἐκεῖνο, οὐκ ἔστι τὸ ἐπίστασθαι
40 τοῦτο, ἂν ἐξ ἀληθῶν καὶ ἀναποδείκτων δειχθῇ καὶ
ἀμέσων. ἔστι γὰρ οὕτω δεῖξαι, ὥσπερ Βρύσων τὸν
τετραγωνισμόν. κατὰ κοινόν τε γὰρ δεικνύουσιν
οἱ τοιοῦτοι λόγοι, ὃ καὶ ἑτέρῳ ὑπάρξει· διὸ καὶ
76 a ἐπ' ἄλλων ἐφαρμόττουσιν οἱ λόγοι οὐ συγγενῶν.
οὐκοῦν οὐχ ᾗ ἐκεῖνο ἐπίσταται, ἀλλὰ κατὰ συμβε-
βηκός· οὐ γὰρ ἂν ἐφήρμοττεν ἡ ἀπόδειξις καὶ ἐπ'
ἄλλο γένος.

---

[1] καὶ] ἔσται καὶ n, Ross.
[2] τῷ . . . τῷ C[1]: τὸ . . . τὸ C[2] n: ᾧ . . . ᾧ ABd.
[3] τοιοῦδ' B, Philoponus : (μέν)τοι οὐδ' A : τοιαῖδ' C : alii alia.

---

[a] If the minor premiss stated an eternal connexion the
conclusion would also be eternal.
[b] Cf. Book II, ch. x.
[c] What Bryson actually tried to prove is not clear (though
the attempt is also described—guardedly—as ' squaring the
circle ' in Soph. Elench. 171 b 16, 172 a 3) ; but he seems to
have used the comparative areas of inscribed and circum-
scribed figures, whether squares or polygons. The objection,
however, is to his ' sophistical ' method of starting from a

only so will the conclusion also be non-eternal,[a] and non-universal because the conclusion will be true in some cases but not in others, and so cannot be proved to be true universally, but only at a given time. Similarly too with respect to definitions, inasmuch as a definition is either a starting-point of demonstration, or a demonstration in a different form, or a conclusion of a demonstration.[b] It is clear that demonstration and knowledge of intermittent events, such as an eclipse of the moon, are eternal in so far as they refer to events of a specific kind ; but in so far as they are not eternal, they are particular. Attributes may apply intermittently to other subjects just as an eclipse does to the moon.

IX. Since it is evidently impossible to demonstrate the application of a particular attribute as such to its subject except from the first principles proper to its genus, scientific knowledge does not consist in proof from principles which are merely true, indemonstrable and immediate. I say this because one can conduct a proof in this way, just as Bryson, for example, proved his theory of squaring the circle [c] ; for such arguments prove the conclusion by using a common middle term which will refer equally to a different subject ; hence they are also applicable to subjects of other genera. Thus they enable us to know the attribute as applying to its subject not *qua* itself but only accidentally ; otherwise the demonstration would not be applicable to another genus also.

The premisses of demonstration must be peculiar to their own science,

general postulate of the form ' Things which are both greater than the same ⟨set of⟩ things and less than the same ⟨set of⟩ things are equal to one another ' (obviously invalid, by the way, unless the two sets taken together exhaust all the possibilities) instead of a geometrical axiom. See Heath, *Greek Mathematics*, I. 223-225 ; *Mathematics in Aristotle*, 48-50.

Ἕκαστον δ' ἐπιστάμεθα μὴ κατὰ συμβεβηκός,
5 ὅταν κατ' ἐκεῖνο γιγνώσκωμεν καθ' ὃ ὑπάρχει, ἐκ
τῶν ἀρχῶν τῶν ἐκείνου. ᾗ ἐκεῖνο, οἷον τὸ δυσὶν
ὀρθαῖς ἴσας ἔχειν, ᾧ ὑπάρχει καθ' αὑτὸ τὸ εἰρημένον, ἐκ τῶν ἀρχῶν τῶν τούτου. ὥστ' εἰ καθ'
αὑτὸ κἀκεῖνο ὑπάρχει ᾧ ὑπάρχει, ἀνάγκη τὸ μέσον
10 ἐν τῇ αὐτῇ συγγενείᾳ εἶναι. εἰ δὲ μή, ἀλλ' ὡς τὰ
ἁρμονικὰ δι' ἀριθμητικῆς. τὰ δὲ τοιαῦτα δείκνυται
μὲν ὡσαύτως, διαφέρει δέ· τὸ μὲν γὰρ ὅτι ἑτέρας
ἐπιστήμης (τὸ γὰρ ὑποκείμενον γένος ἕτερον), τὸ
δὲ διότι τῆς ἄνω, ἧς καθ' αὑτὰ τὰ πάθη ἐστίν.
15 ὥστε καὶ ἐκ τούτων φανερὸν ὅτι οὐκ ἔστιν ἀποδεῖξαι ἕκαστον ἁπλῶς, ἀλλ' ἢ ἐκ τῶν ἑκάστου ἀρχῶν.
ἀλλὰ τούτων αἱ ἀρχαὶ ἔχουσι τὸ κοινόν.

Εἰ δὲ φανερὸν τοῦτο, φανερὸν καὶ ὅτι οὐκ ἔστι
τὰς ἑκάστου ἰδίας ἀρχὰς ἀποδεῖξαι· ἔσονται γὰρ
ἐκεῖναι ἁπάντων ἀρχαί, καὶ ἐπιστήμη ἡ ἐκείνων
κυρία πάντων. καὶ γὰρ ἐπίσταται μᾶλλον ὁ ἐκ τῶν
20 ἀνωτέρων[1] αἰτίων εἰδώς· ἐκ τῶν προτέρων γὰρ
οἶδεν ὅταν ἐκ μὴ αἰτιατῶν εἰδῇ αἰτίων. ὥστ' εἰ
μᾶλλον οἶδε καὶ μάλιστα, κἂν ἐπιστήμη ἐκείνη εἴη
καὶ μᾶλλον καὶ μάλιστα. ἡ δ' ἀπόδειξις οὐκ ἐφαρμόττει ἐπ' ἄλλο γένος, ἀλλ' ἢ ὡς εἴρηται αἱ γεω-

---

[1] ἀνωτέρων A²d : ἀνωτέρω B².

---

[a] The middle term, subject of the major, predicate of the minor premiss.
[b] e.g., Plato's dialectic, which Aristotle repudiates.
[c] 75 b 14 ff., 76 a 9 ff.

Our knowledge of any given attribute is only non-accidental when we recognize it in respect of the subject in virtue of which it is an attribute, and from the principles proper to that subject as such ; *e.g.*, the attribute of " having the sum of its angles equal to two right angles " as belonging to the subject to which it applies *per se*, and from the principles proper to this subject. Therefore if this latter term [a] applies *per se* to its own subject, the middle must belong to the same genus as the extreme terms. The only exceptions are such as the propositions of harmonics which are proved by arithmetic. Such propositions are proved in the same way, but with this difference ; that while the fact proved belongs to a different science (for the subject genus is different), the grounds of the fact belong to the superior science, to which the attributes belong *per se*. Thus it is evident from these considerations also that absolute demonstration of any attribute is impossible except from its own principles. In the examples just given, however, the principles have a common element. except in the case of subaltern sciences.

If this is evident, it is evident also that the special principles of each genus cannot be demonstrated ; for the principles from which they would be demonstrable would be principles of all existing things, and the science of those principles would be supreme over all.[b] For a man knows a fact in a truer sense if he knows it from more ultimate causes, since he knows it from prior premisses when he knows it from causes which are themselves uncaused. Thus if he knows in a truer or the truest sense, his knowledge will be science in a truer or the truest sense. However, demonstration is not applicable to a different genus, except as we have explained [c] that geometrical proofs Hence the special principles of the sciences are indemonstrable.

67

76 a

μετρικαὶ ἐπὶ τὰς μηχανικὰς ἢ ὀπτικὰς καὶ αἱ
25 ἀριθμητικαὶ ἐπὶ τὰς ἁρμονικάς.

Χαλεπὸν δ' ἐστὶ τὸ γνῶναι εἰ οἶδεν ἢ μή. χαλεπὸν γὰρ τὸ γνῶναι εἰ ἐκ τῶν ἑκάστου ἀρχῶν ἴσμεν
ἢ μή· ὅπερ ἐστὶ τὸ εἰδέναι. οἰόμεθα δ', ἂν ἔχωμεν
ἐξ ἀληθινῶν τινῶν συλλογισμὸν καὶ πρώτων, ἐπί-
30 στασθαι. τὸ δ' οὐκ ἔστιν, ἀλλὰ συγγενῆ δεῖ εἶναι
τοῖς πρώτοις.

Χ. Λέγω δ' ἀρχὰς ἐν ἑκάστῳ γένει ταύτας ἃς
ὅτι ἔστι μὴ ἐνδέχεται δεῖξαι. τί μὲν οὖν σημαίνει
καὶ τὰ πρῶτα καὶ τὰ ἐκ τούτων, λαμβάνεται, ὅτι
δ' ἔστι, τὰς μὲν ἀρχὰς ἀνάγκη λαμβάνειν, τὰ δ'
35 ἄλλα δεικνύναι, οἷον τί μονὰς ἢ τί τὸ εὐθὺ καὶ τρί-
γωνον· εἶναι δὲ τὴν μὲν μονάδα λαβεῖν καὶ μέγεθος,
τὰ δ' ἕτερα δεικνύναι.

Ἔστι δ' ὧν χρῶνται ἐν ταῖς ἀποδεικτικαῖς ἐπιστήμαις τὰ μὲν ἴδια ἑκάστης ἐπιστήμης τὰ δὲ κοινά,
κοινὰ δὲ κατ' ἀναλογίαν, ἐπεὶ χρήσιμόν γε ὅσον ἐν
40 τῷ ὑπὸ τὴν ἐπιστήμην γένει. ἴδια μὲν οἷον γραμμὴν
εἶναι τοιανδί, καὶ τὸ εὐθύ, κοινὰ δὲ οἷον τὸ ἴσα ἀπὸ
ἴσων ἂν ἀφέλῃ ὅτι ἴσα τὰ λοιπά. ἱκανὸν δ' ἕκαστον
76 b τούτων ὅσον ἐν τῷ γένει· ταὐτὸ γὰρ ποιήσει, κἂν
μὴ κατὰ πάντων λάβῃ ἀλλ' ἐπὶ μεγεθῶν μόνον, τῷ

68

apply to the propositions of mechanics or optics, and arithmetical proofs to those of harmonics.

It is difficult to be certain whether one knows or not ; for it is difficult to be certain whether our knowledge is based upon the principles appropriate to each case—it is this that constitutes true knowledge —or not. We suppose that we have scientific knowledge if we draw an inference from any true and primary premisses, but it is not so ; the inference must be homogeneous with the primary truths of the science.

X. I call " first principles " in each genus those facts which cannot be proved. Thus the meaning both of the primary truths and of the attributes demonstrated from them is assumed ; as for their existence, that of the principles must be assumed, but that of the attributes must be proved. *E.g.*, we assume the meaning of " unit," " straight " and " triangular " ; but while we assume the existence of the unit and geometrical magnitude, that of the rest must be proved. *Every science assumes certain principles,*

Of the first principles used in the demonstrative sciences some are special to particular sciences, and some are common ; but only in the analogical sense, since each is only to be employed in so far as it is contained in the genus which falls under the science concerned. Special principles are such as that a line, or straightness, is of such-and-such a nature ; common principles are such as that when equals are taken from equals the remainders are equal. Each of these latter truths need only be assumed for the given genus. The effect will be the same for the geometrician if he assumes the truth not universally but only of magnitudes, and for the arithmetician if he assumes *which are either special to it, or special aspects of a common principle.*

69

76 b

δ' ἀριθμητικῷ ἐπ' ἀριθμῶν. ἔστι δ' ἴδια μὲν καὶ
ἃ λαμβάνεται εἶναι, περὶ ἃ ἡ ἐπιστήμη θεωρεῖ τὰ
5 ὑπάρχοντα καθ' αὑτά, οἷον μονάδας ἡ ἀριθμητική, ἡ
δὲ γεωμετρία σημεῖα καὶ γραμμάς. ταῦτα γὰρ
λαμβάνουσι τὸ εἶναι καὶ τοδὶ εἶναι. τὰ δὲ τούτων
πάθη καθ' αὑτά, τί μὲν σημαίνει ἕκαστον, λαμβάνουσιν, οἷον ἡ μὲν ἀριθμητικὴ τί περιττὸν ἢ ἄρτιον
ἢ τετράγωνον ἢ κύβος, ἡ δὲ γεωμετρία τί τὸ ἄλογον
10 ἢ τὸ κεκλάσθαι ἢ νεύειν, ὅτι δ' ἔστι δεικνύουσι διά
τε τῶν κοινῶν καὶ ἐκ τῶν ἀποδεδειγμένων. καὶ ἡ
ἀστρολογία ὡσαύτως.

Πᾶσα γὰρ ἀποδεικτικὴ ἐπιστήμη περὶ τρία ἐστίν,
ὅσα τε εἶναι τίθεται (ταῦτα δ' ἐστὶ τὸ γένος, οὗ τῶν
καθ' αὑτὰ παθημάτων ἐστὶ θεωρητική), καὶ τὰ
κοινὰ λεγόμενα ἀξιώματα, ἐξ ὧν πρώτων ἀποδείκ-
15 νυσι, καὶ τρίτον τὰ πάθη, ὧν τί σημαίνει ἕκαστον
λαμβάνει. ἐνίας μέντοι ἐπιστήμας οὐδὲν κωλύει
ἔνια τούτων παρορᾶν, οἷον τὸ γένος μὴ ὑποτίθεσθαι
εἶναι ἂν ᾖ φανερὸν ὅτι ἔστιν (οὐ γὰρ ὁμοίως δῆλον
ὅτι ἀριθμὸς ἔστι καὶ ὅτι ψυχρὸν καὶ θερμόν), καὶ
20 τὰ πάθη μὴ λαμβάνειν τί σημαίνει ἂν ᾖ δῆλα·
ὥσπερ οὐδὲ τὰ κοινὰ οὐ λαμβάνει τί σημαίνει τὸ
ἴσα ἀπὸ ἴσων ἀφελεῖν, ὅτι γνώριμον. ἀλλ' οὐδὲν
ἧττον τῇ γε φύσει τρία ταῦτά ἐστι, περὶ ὅ τε δείκνυσι καὶ ἃ δείκνυσι καὶ ἐξ ὧν.

Οὐκ ἔστι δ' ὑπόθεσις οὐδ' αἴτημα ὃ ἀνάγκη
εἶναι δι' αὑτὸ καὶ δοκεῖν ἀνάγκη. οὐ γὰρ πρὸς τὸν

---

[a] νεύειν is used technically of a straight line's tending,
when produced, to pass through a given point. The term is
unimportant and scarcely appropriate here; I suggest a
more general sense.

[b] They are common only by analogy; cf. 75 a 38. Ross
compares Met. 1005 a 20 τὰ ἐν τοῖς μαθήμασι καλούμενα ἀξιώ-

it only of numbers. Also special to each science are those subjects whose existence it assumes, and whose essential attributes it studies, as arithmetic studies units and geometry points and lines. Of these subjects both the existence and the meaning are assumed; but of their essential attributes only the meaning is assumed. *E.g.*, arithmetic assumes the meaning of odd or even or square or cube, and geometry that of incommensurable or of deflection or inclination[a]; but their existence is proved by means of the common principles and from conclusions already demonstrated. The same is true of astronomy.

Every demonstrative science is concerned with three things : the subjects which it posits (*i.e.*, the genus whose essential attributes it studies), the so-called[b] common axioms upon which the demonstration is ultimately based, and thirdly the attributes whose several meanings it assumes. There is no reason, however, why certain sciences should not disregard some of these three things ; *e.g.*, omit to posit the existence of the genus if its existence is evident (for the existence of number is not so obvious as that of hot and cold), or to assume the meaning of the attributes if it is quite clear ; just as in the case of the common principles the meaning of " when equals are subtracted from equals the remainders are equal " is not assumed, because it is well known. Nevertheless there holds good this natural threefold division into the subject, the object, and the basis of demonstration. *Thus there are three kinds of primary premiss, though not all need be explicitly assumed.*

That which is in itself necessarily true and must be thought to be so is not a hypothesis nor a postulate ; *Axioms, hypotheses and postulates.*

μᾱτᾱ. If the term was generally accepted by mathematicians in Aristotle's time, it was abandoned by Euclid.

76 b

25 ἔξω λόγον ἡ ἀπόδειξις, ἀλλὰ πρὸς τὸν ἐν τῇ ψυχῇ,
ἐπεὶ οὐδὲ συλλογισμός. ἀεὶ γὰρ ἔστιν ἐνστῆναι
πρὸς τὸν ἔξω λόγον, ἀλλὰ πρὸς τὸν ἔσω λόγον οὐκ
ἀεί. ὅσα μὲν οὖν δεικτὰ ὄντα λαμβάνει αὐτὸς μὴ
δείξας, ταῦτ᾽, ἐὰν μὲν δοκοῦντα λαμβάνῃ τῷ μανθάνοντι, ὑποτίθεται, καὶ ἔστιν οὐχ ἁπλῶς ὑπόθεσις
30 ἀλλὰ πρὸς ἐκεῖνον μόνον, ἂν δὲ ἢ μηδεμιᾶς ἐνούσης
δόξης ἢ καὶ ἐναντίας ἐνούσης λαμβάνῃ τὸ αὐτό,
αἰτεῖται. καὶ τούτῳ διαφέρει ὑπόθεσις καὶ αἴτημα·
ἔστι γὰρ αἴτημα τὸ ὑπεναντίον τοῦ μανθάνοντος τῇ
δόξῃ, ἢ ὃ ἄν τις ἀποδεικτὸν ὂν λαμβάνῃ καὶ χρῆται
μὴ δείξας.

35 Οἱ μὲν οὖν ὅροι οὐκ εἰσὶν ὑποθέσεις (οὐδὲν[1] γὰρ
εἶναι ἢ μὴ εἶναι λέγεται[2]), ἀλλ᾽ ἐν ταῖς προτάσεσιν
αἱ ὑποθέσεις. τοὺς δ᾽ ὅρους μόνον ξυνίεσθαι δεῖ·
τοῦτο δ᾽ οὐχ ὑπόθεσις, εἰ μὴ καὶ τὸ ἀκούειν ὑπό-
θεσίν τις φήσειεν εἶναι, ἀλλ᾽ ὅσων ὄντων τῷ ἐκεῖνα
εἶναι γίγνεται τὸ συμπέρασμα. οὐδ᾽ ὁ γεωμέτρης
40 ψευδῆ ὑποτίθεται, ὥσπερ τινὲς ἔφασαν, λέγοντες ὡς
οὐ δεῖ τῷ ψεύδει χρῆσθαι, τὸν δὲ γεωμέτρην ψεύδεσθαι λέγοντα ποδιαίαν τὴν οὐ ποδιαίαν ἢ εὐθεῖαν
77 a τὴν γεγραμμένην οὐκ εὐθεῖαν οὖσαν. ὁ δὲ γεωμέτρης οὐδὲν συμπεραίνεται τῷ τήνδε εἶναι γραμμὴν
ἣν αὐτὸς ἔφθεγκται, ἀλλὰ τὰ διὰ τούτων δηλούμενα.

---

[1] οὐδὲν ABdn, Philoponus : οὐδὲ B²C.   [2] Ross : λέγονται.

---

[a] The axioms used in demonstration appeal directly to the
inner reason and are accepted by it, but the assumptions of
spoken argument or instruction are always open to verbal
objection.
[b] There is perhaps a reference to the narrower sense of
hypothesis given in 72 a 18 ff.
[c] I doubt whether " two definitions of αἴτημα are offered "

72

for demonstration, like syllogism, is concerned not with external but with internal discourse ; and it is always possible to object to the former, but not always possible to do so to the latter.[a] Thus any provable proposition that a teacher assumes without proving it, if the student accepts it, is a hypothesis— a hypothesis not absolutely but relatively to the student[b]; but the same assumption, if it is made when the student has no opinion or a contrary opinion about it, is a postulate. This is the difference between a hypothesis and a postulate ; the latter is the contrary of the student's opinion, or any provable proposition that is assumed and used without being proved.[c]

Definitions are not hypotheses, because they make no assertion of existence or non-existence. Hypotheses have their place among propositions, whereas definitions only need to be understood ; and this does not constitute a hypothesis, unless it is claimed that listening is a kind of hypothesis.[d] Hypotheses consist of assumptions from which the conclusion follows in virtue of their being what they are. Thus the geometrician's hypotheses are not false, as some have maintained, saying that one should not make use of falsehood, and that the geometrician is guilty of falsehood in asserting that the line which he has drawn is a foot long, or straight, when it is not ; the geometrician does not infer anything from the existence of the particular line which he himself has mentioned, but only from the facts which his diagrams

Definition distin- guished from hypo- thesis.

here, as Ross concludes. What Aristotle appears to say is that any provable but unproved assumption is a postulate unless it is accepted by the respondent, when it becomes (relatively to him) a hypothesis.

[d] If the qualification is not entirely sarcastic it may hint that listening implies some degree of acceptance.

ἔτι τὸ αἴτημα καὶ ὑπόθεσις πᾶσα ἢ ὡς ὅλον ἢ ὡς
ἐν μέρει, οἱ δ' ὅροι οὐδέτερον τούτων.

5 XI. Εἴδη μὲν οὖν εἶναι ἢ ἕν τι παρὰ τὰ πολλὰ
οὐκ ἀνάγκη, εἰ ἀπόδειξις ἔσται, εἶναι μέντοι ἓν
κατὰ πολλῶν ἀληθὲς εἰπεῖν ἀνάγκη· οὐ γὰρ ἔσται
τὸ καθόλου ἂν μὴ τοῦτο ᾖ· ἐὰν δὲ τὸ καθόλου μὴ
ᾖ, τὸ μέσον οὐκ ἔσται, ὥστ' οὐδ' ἀπόδειξις. δεῖ
ἄρα τι ἓν καὶ τὸ αὐτὸ ἐπὶ πλειόνων εἶναι μὴ ὁμώνυμον.[1]

10 Τὸ δὲ μὴ ἐνδέχεσθαι ἅμα φάναι καὶ ἀποφάναι
οὐδεμία λαμβάνει ἀπόδειξις ἀλλ' ἢ ἐὰν δέῃ δεῖξαι
καὶ τὸ συμπέρασμα οὕτως. δείκνυται δὲ λαβοῦσι
τὸ πρῶτον κατὰ τοῦ μέσου ὅτι ἀληθές, ἀποφάναι δ'
οὐκ ἀληθές. τὸ δὲ μέσον οὐδὲν διαφέρει εἶναι καὶ
15 μὴ εἶναι λαβεῖν, ὡς δ' αὕτως καὶ τὸ τρίτον. εἰ γὰρ
ἐδόθη καθ' οὗ ἄνθρωπον ἀληθὲς εἰπεῖν—εἰ καὶ μὴ
ἄνθρωπον ἀληθές, ἀλλ' εἰ μόνον ἄνθρωπον—ζῷον
εἶναι, μὴ ζῷον δὲ μή, ἔσται [γὰρ][2] ἀληθὲς εἰπεῖν
Καλλίαν, εἰ καὶ μὴ Καλλίαν, ὅμως ζῷον, μὴ ζῷον
20 δ' οὔ. αἴτιον δ' ὅτι τὸ πρῶτον οὐ μόνον κατὰ τοῦ
μέσου λέγεται ἀλλὰ καὶ κατ' ἄλλου διὰ τὸ εἶναι ἐπὶ
πλειόνων, ὥστ' οὐδ' εἰ τὸ μέσον καὶ αὐτό ἐστι καὶ
μὴ αὐτό, πρὸς τὸ συμπέρασμα οὐδὲν διαφέρει.

---

[1] εἴδη μὲν οὖν . . . ὁμώνυμον ad 83 a 35 transponenda ci.
Ross.
[2] seclusit Ross.

---

[a] Cf. An. Pr. 49 b 35, Met. 1078 a 20.
[b] Aristotle's objection to the Platonic Forms is that they
exist independently of particulars, whereas his own universals are abstractions. The paragraph seems to be displaced.
Ross would transfer it to 83 a 35.
[c] Because the middle must be distributed in at least one
premiss.

illustrate.[a] Further, all postulates and hypotheses are either universal or particular, whereas definitions are neither.

XI. It is not necessary, in order to make demonstration possible, that there should be Forms or some One apart from the Many [b]; but it is necessary that it should be true to state a single predicate of a plurality of subjects. Otherwise there will be no universal term; and if there is no universal there will be no middle term,[c] and hence no demonstration. Therefore there must be something which is one and the same above the several particulars, and does not merely share a common name with them.[d] *Demonstration needs universals, but not Forms.*

No demonstration makes use of the principle that simultaneous assertion and negation are impossible, unless it is required to prove the conclusion also in this form.[e] The proof is effected by assuming that it is true to assert and not true to deny the first term of the middle. It makes no difference to add the negation of the contradictory to the middle or to the third term. For if it is granted that whatever is truly called " man " is truly called an animal—even if " not-man " is also truly called an animal, provided only that it is true that man is an animal, and not true that he is not an animal—it will be true to call Callias an animal even if it is true to call not-Callias an animal, and it will not be true to call him not-animal. The reason for this is that the first term is stated not only of the middle but also of another term or terms, because it has a wider extension; so that even if the middle term is both itself and its contradictory the conclusion is unaffected. *How demonstration uses the Law of Contradiction*

---

[d] *Sc.*, without sharing their common character.
[e] In the form " C is A and not not-A."

Τὸ δ' ἅπαν φάναι ἢ ἀποφάναι ἡ εἰς τὸ ἀδύνατον
ἀπόδειξις λαμβάνει, καὶ ταῦτα οὐδ' ἀεὶ καθόλου,
ἀλλ' ὅσον ἱκανόν, ἱκανὸν δ' ἐπὶ τοῦ γένους. λέγω
25 δ' ἐπὶ τοῦ γένους οἷον περὶ ὃ γένος τὰς ἀποδείξεις
φέρει, ὥσπερ εἴρηται καὶ πρότερον.

Ἐπικοινωνοῦσι δὲ πᾶσαι αἱ ἐπιστῆμαι ἀλλήλαις
κατὰ τὰ κοινά (κοινὰ δὲ λέγω οἷς χρῶνται ὡς ἐκ
τούτων ἀποδεικνύντες, ἀλλ' οὐ περὶ ὧν δεικνύουσιν
οὐδ' ὃ δεικνύουσι), καὶ ἡ διαλεκτικὴ πάσαις, καὶ εἴ
30 τις καθόλου πειρῷτο δεικνύναι τὰ κοινά, οἷον ὅτι
ἅπαν φάναι ἢ ἀποφάναι, ἢ ὅτι ἴσα ἀπὸ ἴσων, ἢ τῶν
τοιούτων ἄττα. ἡ δὲ διαλεκτικὴ οὐκ ἔστιν οὕτως
ὡρισμένων τινῶν, οὐδὲ γένους τινὸς ἑνός. οὐ γὰρ
ἂν ἠρώτα· ἀποδεικνύντα γὰρ οὐκ ἔστιν ἐρωτᾶν διὰ
τὸ τῶν ἀντικειμένων ὄντων μὴ δείκνυσθαι τὸ αὐτό.
35 δέδεικται δὲ τοῦτο ἐν τοῖς περὶ συλλογισμοῦ.

XII. Εἰ δὲ τὸ αὐτό ἐστιν ἐρώτημα συλλογιστικὸν
καὶ πρότασις ἀντιφάσεως, προτάσεις δὲ καθ' ἑκάσ-

---

[b] The reference is probably to *An. Pr.* 57 b 4 ff. Dialectic
proceeds by interrogation, giving the opponent an open
choice between opposite answers, either of which is prepared to attack. Science is concerned with the proof of
facts ; and since the same conclusion cannot be correctly
inferred from opposite data, the " questions " of science offer
no real choice, because only the right answer will furnish a
true premiss for the required proof.
[c] By " syllogistic question " Aristotle means the interro-
gative form of an affirmative or negative premiss from which
it is proposed to draw a scientific conclusion. Since (as we

The law that either the assertion or the negation and the Law
of every predicate must be true is used in demonstra- of Excluded
tion by *reductio ad impossibile*. It is not always Middle.
applied universally, but only so far as is sufficient,
i.e., in reference to the genus. By " in reference to
the genus " I mean, *e.g.*, as regards the genus which
is the subject of the demonstrations in question, as
we have observed above.[a]

All the sciences share with one another in the use All the
of the common principles. By " common principles " sciences,
I mean what they use for the purpose of demonstra- lectic too,
tion, not the subjects about which they conduct their common
proofs, nor the connexions which they prove. Dia- axioms.
lectic shares the principles of all the other sciences ;
and so too would any science which might attempt to
prove universally the common principles, *e.g.*, that
either the assertion or the negation of every predicate is true, or that equals subtracted from equals
leave equal remainders, or any other axioms of this
kind. But dialectic has no sphere thus defined, nor
is it concerned with any one class of objects. If it
were, it would not proceed by interrogation ; for
interrogation is impossible in demonstration, since
the opposite facts do not allow proof of the same
result. This has been explained in my treatise on
the syllogism.[b]

XII. If a syllogistic question is the same as a Every
proposition stating one half of a contradiction,[c] and science has
every science has its own premisses from which are questions.

have seen) only the right answer will serve, Ross regards
ἐρώτημα as meaning " assumption " in this chapter. But
Aristotle seems (to judge from the context and the examples
quoted below) to be thinking of discussion rather than formal
demonstration, so that the normal sense should perhaps be
preferred.

77 a

την ἐπιστήμην ἐξ ὧν ὁ συλλογισμὸς ὁ καθ᾽ ἑκάστην,
εἴη ἄν τι ἐρώτημα ἐπιστημονικόν, ἐξ ὧν ὁ καθ᾽
40 ἑκάστην οἰκεῖος γίγνεται συλλογισμός. δῆλον ἄρα
ὅτι οὐ πᾶν ἐρώτημα γεωμετρικὸν ἂν εἴη οὐδ᾽ ἰατρι-
77 b κόν, ὁμοίως δὲ καὶ ἐπὶ τῶν ἄλλων· ἀλλ᾽ ἐξ ὧν[1]
δείκνυταί τι περὶ ὧν ἡ γεωμετρία ἐστίν, ἢ ἃ[2] ἐκ
τῶν αὐτῶν δείκνυται τῇ γεωμετρίᾳ, ὥσπερ τὰ ὀπ-
τικά. ὁμοίως δὲ καὶ ἐπὶ τῶν ἄλλων. καὶ περὶ
μὲν τούτων καὶ λόγον ὑφεκτέον ἐκ τῶν γεωμετρικῶν
5 ἀρχῶν καὶ συμπερασμάτων, περὶ δὲ τῶν ἀρχῶν
λόγον οὐχ ὑφεκτέον τῷ γεωμέτρῃ ᾗ γεωμέτρης·
ὁμοίως δὲ καὶ ἐπὶ τῶν ἄλλων ἐπιστημῶν.

Οὔτε πᾶν ἄρα ἕκαστον ἐπιστήμονα ἐρώτημα ἐρω-
τητέον, οὔθ᾽ ἅπαν τὸ ἐρωτώμενον ἀποκριτέον περὶ
ἑκάστου, ἀλλὰ τὰ κατὰ τὴν ἐπιστήμην διορισθέντα.
10 εἰ δὲ διαλέξεται γεωμέτρῃ ᾗ γεωμέτρης οὕτως,
φανερὸν ὅτι καὶ καλῶς, ἐὰν ἐκ τούτων τι δεικνύῃ·
εἰ δὲ μή, οὐ καλῶς. δῆλον δ᾽ ὅτι οὐδ᾽ ἐλέγχει
γεωμέτρην ἀλλ᾽ ἢ κατὰ συμβεβηκός· ὥστ᾽ οὐκ ἂν
εἴη ἐν ἀγεωμετρήτοις περὶ γεωμετρίας διαλεκτέον·
λήσει γὰρ ὁ φαύλως διαλεγόμενος. ὁμοίως δὲ καὶ
15 ἐπὶ τῶν ἄλλων ἔχει ἐπιστημῶν.

Ἐπεὶ δ᾽ ἔστι γεωμετρικὰ ἐρωτήματα, ἆρ᾽ ἔστι
καὶ ἀγεωμέτρητα; καὶ παρ᾽ ἑκάστην ἐπιστήμην
τὰ κατὰ τὴν ἄγνοιαν τὴν ποίαν[3] γεωμετρικά

---

[1] ὧν ἢ ABCd.   [2] om. ABC²d.
[3] ποίαν A², Philoponus : ποιὰν.

---

[a] Because the principles of a science are assumed, not
proved, by that science.

drawn the conclusions proper to that science, then there must be a scientific question corresponding to the premises from which the conclusions proper to science are drawn. Hence it is clear that not every question will be geometrical (or medical, and similarly with the other sciences), but only those which correspond to the grounds for the proof of geometrical theorems, or the theorems of any science, such as optics, which uses for its proofs the same axioms as geometry (and similarly with the other sciences). Of these questions the geometrician must give an account, based upon the principles and conclusions of geometry; but he need not, as a geometrician, account for the principles [a] (and similarly with the other sciences).

Hence we must not ask every question of each individual expert, nor is the expert bound to answer everything that is asked him about each given subject, but only such questions as fall within the scope of his own science. If in arguing with a geometrician *qua* geometrician one argues by proving any given point from geometrical principles, evidently he will be arguing properly; otherwise he will not. It is clear also that in the latter case one cannot refute a geometrician, except accidentally.[b] Therefore one should not discuss geometry among people who are not geometricians, because they will not recognize an unsound argument. The same applies to all other sciences.

Since there are geometrical questions, are there also ungeometrical questions? In any given science ⟨*e.g.* geometry⟩, what sort of ignorance is it that

Sources of Error in scientific reasoning.

---

[b] Because *qua* geometrician he can only be refuted by a geometrical argument.

77 b

ἐστιν;[1] καὶ πότερον ὁ κατὰ τὴν ἄγνοιαν συλλογισ-
20 μὸς ὁ ἐκ τῶν ἀντικειμένων συλλογισμός, ἢ ὁ[2] παραλογισμός, κατὰ γεωμετρίαν δέ; ἢ ἐξ ἄλλης τέχνης,
οἷον τὸ μουσικόν ἐστιν ἐρώτημα ἀγεωμέτρητον
περὶ γεωμετρίας, τὸ δὲ τὰς παραλλήλους συμπί-
πτειν οἴεσθαι γεωμετρικόν πως καὶ ἀγεωμέτρητον
ἄλλον τρόπον; διττὸν γὰρ τοῦτο, ὥσπερ τὸ ἄρρυθ-
25 μον, καὶ τὸ μὲν ἕτερον ἀγεωμέτρητον τῷ μὴ ἔχειν
[ὥσπερ τὸ ἄρρυθμον],[3] τὸ δ᾽ ἕτερον τῷ φαύλως
ἔχειν· καὶ ἡ ἄγνοια αὕτη καὶ[4] ἡ ἐκ τῶν τοιούτων
ἀρχῶν ἐναντία. ἐν δὲ τοῖς μαθήμασιν οὐκ ἔστιν
ὁμοίως ὁ παραλογισμός, ὅτι τὸ μέσον ἐστὶν ἀεὶ τὸ[5]
διττόν· κατά τε γὰρ τούτου παντός, καὶ τοῦτο πάλιν
30 κατ᾽ ἄλλου λέγεται παντός· τὸ δὲ κατηγορούμενον
οὐ λέγεται πᾶν. ταῦτα δ᾽ ἐστὶν οἷον ὁρᾶν τῇ νοήσει,
ἐν δὲ τοῖς λόγοις λανθάνει. ἆρα πᾶς κύκλος σχῆμα;
ἂν δὲ γράψῃ, δῆλον. τί δέ; τὰ ἔπη κύκλος; φανερὸν ὅτι οὐκ ἔστιν.

Οὐ δεῖ δ᾽ ἔνστασιν εἰς αὐτὸ φέρειν ἐν ᾗ[6] ἡ πρό-

---

[1] ἐστιν καὶ ἀγεωμέτρητα f : ἐστιν ἢ ἀγεωμέτρητα Bekker.
[2] ὁ om. Cn.   [3] secl. Mure.
[4] καὶ om. Aldina, Bekker.   [5] om. C²d.
[6] ἐν ᾗ ci. Ross, leg. fort. comm. : ἂν ᾖ.

---

[a] *i.e.* relevant although mistaken. A " question " may
be (a) proper to a given science, but " ignorant " because
based (1) on false premises or (2) false inference from true
premises, or (b) proper to a quite different science.
[b] *Cf. Met.* 1022 b 35.

makes questions still geometrical ? [a] Is an ignorant conclusion one which is drawn from premises opposite to the true ones, or an inference which though invalid is nevertheless geometrical ? Or is it an inference drawn from a different science, as, e.g., a musical question is ungeometrical with reference to geometry, while to think that parallel lines meet is in a sense geometrical, although in another sense ungeometrical ? (For " ungeometrical," like " unrhythmical," has two senses ; in one sense a thing is ungeometrical because it lacks the quality altogether, and in another sense because it possesses the quality but slightly.[b]) It is ignorance in this latter sense, i.e., ignorance which proceeds from premises of this kind,[c] which is contrary to scientific knowledge. In mathematics formal invalidity is not so common, because it is always the middle term that provides the ambiguity (for one term is predicated of all the middle, and this in turn is predicated of all another, but the predicate is not distributed[d]) ; and in mathematics middle terms are clearly visualized whereas ambiguities pass unnoticed in dialectical argument. " Is every circle a figure ? " If one draws a circle the answer is obvious. " Well, are the epic poems [e] a circle ? " Evidently they are not.

One should not meet an argument with an objec- Objections

[c] Exhibiting defective knowledge of the right science.
[d] Aristotle is thinking of a syllogism in Barbara, the only figure useful for demonstration.
[e] The Epic Cycle was the name given to a sequence of early epic poems which, supplementing the *Iliad* and *Odyssey*, narrated the whole story of the Trojan War (and perhaps also the legends connected with Thebes). To call this " cycle " a " circle " would be an absurd quibble, although the words are the same in Greek.

ARISTOTLE

35 τασις ἐπακτική. ὥσπερ γὰρ οὐδὲ πρότασίς ἐστιν
ἢ μή ἐστιν ἐπὶ πλειόνων (οὐ γὰρ ἔσται ἐπὶ πάντων,
ἐκ τῶν καθόλου δ' ὁ συλλογισμός), δῆλον ὅτι οὐδ'
ἔνστασις. αἱ αὐταὶ γὰρ προτάσεις καὶ ἐνστάσεις·
ἣν γὰρ φέρει ἔνστασιν, αὕτη γένοιτ' ἂν πρότασις ἢ
ἀποδεικτικὴ ἢ διαλεκτική.

40 Συμβαίνει δ' ἐνίους ἀσυλλογίστως λέγειν διὰ τὸ
λαμβάνειν ἀμφοτέροις τὰ ἑπόμενα, οἷον καὶ ὁ
78 a Καινεὺς ποιεῖ, ὅτι τὸ πῦρ ἐν τῇ πολλαπλασίᾳ ἀνα-
λογίᾳ· καὶ γὰρ τὸ πῦρ ταχὺ γεννᾶται, ὥς φησι, καὶ
αὕτη ἡ ἀναλογία. οὕτω δ' οὐκ ἔστι συλλογισμός·
ἀλλ' εἰ τῇ ταχίστῃ ἀναλογίᾳ ἕπεται ἡ πολλαπλά-
5 σιος καὶ τῷ πυρὶ ἡ ταχίστη ἐν τῇ κινήσει ἀναλογία.
ἐνίοτε μὲν οὖν οὐκ ἐνδέχεται συλλογίσασθαι ἐκ τῶν
εἰλημμένων, ὅτε δ' ἐνδέχεται, ἀλλ' οὐχ ὁρᾶται.

Εἰ δ' ἦν ἀδύνατον ἐκ ψεύδους ἀληθὲς δεῖξαι,
ῥᾴδιον ἂν ἦν τὸ ἀναλύειν· ἀντέστρεφε γὰρ ἂν ἐξ
ἀνάγκης. ἔστω γὰρ τὸ Α ὄν· τούτου δ' ὄντος ταδὶ
10 ἔστιν, ἃ οἶδα ὅτι ἔστιν, οἷον τὸ Β. ἐκ τούτων ἄρα
δείξω ὅτι ἔστιν ἐκεῖνο. ἀντιστρέφει δὲ μᾶλλον τὰ

---

[a] For "objections" see *An. Pr.* 69 a 37 ff. There particular objections are admitted as logically possible ; here
they are excluded because we are dealing with scientific
demonstration, in which any objection must be capable of
serving as premiss in a fresh proof. The reading adopted
here seems to be that of the commentators and gives a better
sense than the vulgate.

[b] *Sc.* " as middles in the second figure," and undistributed
middles at that. It is in fact a common type of paralogism.
Aristotle goes on to show how the terms must be related to
give a valid conclusion in the first figure. Caeneus *may* be
the Lapith in Antiphanes' play of that name, but he may

tion in which the ⟨minor⟩ premiss is inductive.[a] Just must not be inductive.
as a premiss which does not hold good of more than
one case is no true premiss (because it will not hold
good of all cases, and syllogism proceeds from universal judgements), so an objection of this nature
is no true objection. Premisses and objections are
the same, in that any objection which is brought
may become a premiss, either demonstrative or dialectical.

We find that some persons argue fallaciously Paralogism in the second figure.
through taking consequents of both terms [b]; as
Caeneus does in maintaining that fire spreads in
geometrical progression, on the ground that both fire
and this kind of progression increase rapidly. But
with these conditions there is no syllogism ; only if
the most rapid rate of increase implies geometrical
proportion, and fire in its motion implies the most
rapid rate of increase. Sometimes it is not possible
to draw an inference from the assumptions ; sometimes it is possible,[c] but the method of procedure is
overlooked.

If it were impossible to prove a true conclusion Error in the analysis of problems.
from false premisses,[d] analysis would be easy ; be-
cause conclusion and premisses would necessarily
reciprocate. Let A be a real fact, whose reality
implies that of certain other facts, e.g., B, which I
know to be real ; then from the latter I will prove
the existence of A. Reciprocation is more usual in

equally well have been a real person, though unknown to
us.
    [c] If the major premiss is convertible.
    [d] But it is not : *An. Pr.* II. ii-iv. The analysis in question
is the analysis of a problem, *i.e.* the discovery of the premisses necessary to prove a given conclusion. *Cf. Eth. Nic.*
1112 b 20 ff.

ἐν τοῖς μαθήμασιν, ὅτι οὐδὲν συμβεβηκὸς λαμβάνουσιν (ἀλλὰ καὶ τούτῳ διαφέρουσι τῶν ἐν τοῖς δια-
λόγοις) ἀλλ' ὁρισμούς.

Αὔξεται δ' οὐ διὰ τῶν μέσων, ἀλλὰ τῷ προσλαμ-
15 βάνειν, οἷον τὸ Α τοῦ Β, τοῦτο δὲ τοῦ Γ, πάλιν
τοῦτο τοῦ Δ, καὶ τοῦτ' εἰς ἄπειρον· καὶ εἰς τὸ
πλάγιον, οἷον τὸ Α καὶ κατὰ τοῦ Γ καὶ κατὰ τοῦ·
Ε, οἷον ἔστιν ἀριθμὸς ποσὸς ἢ καὶ ἄπειρος τοῦτο
ἐφ' ᾧ Α, ὁ περιττὸς ἀριθμὸς ποσὸς ἐφ' οὗ Β,
ἀριθμὸς περιττὸς ἐφ' οὗ Γ· ἔστιν ἄρα τὸ Α κατὰ
20 τοῦ Γ. καὶ ἔστιν ὁ ἄρτιος ποσὸς ἀριθμὸς ἐφ' οὗ
Δ, ὁ ἄρτιος ἀριθμὸς ἐφ' οὗ Ε· ἔστιν ἄρα τὸ Α
κατὰ τοῦ Ε.

XIII. Τὸ δ' ὅτι διαφέρει καὶ τὸ διότι ἐπίστασθαι,
πρῶτον μὲν ἐν τῇ αὐτῇ ἐπιστήμῃ, καὶ ἐν ταύτῃ
διχῶς, ἕνα μὲν τρόπον ἐὰν μὴ δι' ἀμέσων γίγνηται
25 ὁ συλλογισμός (οὐ γὰρ λαμβάνεται τὸ πρῶτον αἴτιον,
ἡ δὲ τοῦ διότι ἐπιστήμη κατὰ τὸ πρῶτον αἴτιον),
ἄλλον δὲ εἰ δι' ἀμέσων μέν, ἀλλὰ μὴ διὰ τοῦ αἰτίου
ἀλλὰ τῶν ἀντιστρεφόντων διὰ τοῦ γνωριμωτέρου.
κωλύει γὰρ οὐδὲν τῶν ἀντικατηγορουμένων γνωριμώτερον εἶναι ἐνίοτε τὸ μὴ αἴτιον, ὥστ' ἔσται διὰ
30 τούτου ἡ ἀπόδειξις, οἷον ὅτι ἐγγὺς οἱ πλάνητες διὰ
τοῦ μὴ στίλβειν. ἔστω ἐφ' ᾧ Γ πλάνητες, ἐφ' ᾧ Β
τὸ μὴ στίλβειν, ἐφ' ᾧ Α τὸ ἐγγὺς εἶναι. ἀληθὲς δὴ
τὸ Β κατὰ τοῦ Γ εἰπεῖν· οἱ γὰρ πλάνητες οὐ στίλβουσιν. ἀλλὰ καὶ τὸ Α κατὰ τοῦ Β· τὸ γὰρ μὴ

---

[a] *Cf.* 77 b 27.
[b] *Sc.* lower than any which have hitherto been used. In
this way the system can be extended downwards. The
middle terms of the main system are already established ;
otherwise it would not be scientific. But it is also possible

mathematical problems, because mathematics never assumes an accident but only definitions. This is another [a] respect in which mathematical differs from dialectical reasoning.

A science expands not by the interpolation of middle terms but by the addition of extreme terms [b]; *e.g.*, A is predicated of B, and the latter of C, and this again of D, and so *ad infinitum*. It may also be extended laterally ; *e.g.*, A may be predicated of both C and E. For example, A is number (determinate or indeterminate), B is determinate odd number, C is a particular odd number ; then A is predicable of C. Again, D is determinate even number, and E a particular even number ; then A is predicable of E.

XIII. Knowledge of a fact and knowledge of the reason for it differ when both fall under the same science, under several conditions : (1) if the conclusion is not drawn from immediate premises (for then the proximate cause is not contained in them, and knowledge of the reason depends upon the proximate cause) ; (2) if the premises are immediate, but the conclusion is drawn not from the cause but from the more familiar of two convertible terms ; for it may well be that of two reciprocally predicable terms that which is not the cause is sometimes the more familiar, so that the demonstration will proceed by it ; *e.g.*, the proof that the planets are near because they do not twinkle. Let C stand for " planets," B for " not twinkling," and A for " being near." Then it is true to state B of C ; because the planets do not twinkle. But it is also true to state A of B ; because that which

Expansion of a science.

Knowledge of a fact and knowledge of its reason may differ although both fall under one science.

to extend the system laterally at any stage, as in the example, by linking a fresh minor (E) to a given major (A) by a fresh middle (D).

35 στίλβον ἐγγύς ἐστι· τοῦτο δ᾽ εἰλήφθω δι᾽ ἐπαγωγῆς
ἢ δι᾽ αἰσθήσεως. ἀνάγκη οὖν τὸ Α τῷ Γ ὑπάρχειν,
ὥστ᾽ ἀποδέδεικται ὅτι οἱ πλάνητες ἐγγύς εἰσιν.
οὗτος οὖν ὁ συλλογισμὸς οὐ τοῦ διότι ἀλλὰ τοῦ ὅτι
ἐστίν· οὐ γὰρ διὰ τὸ μὴ στίλβειν ἐγγύς εἰσιν, ἀλλὰ
διὰ τὸ ἐγγὺς εἶναι οὐ στίλβουσιν. ἐγχωρεῖ δὲ καὶ
40 διὰ θατέρου θάτερον δειχθῆναι, καὶ ἔσται τοῦ διότι
78 b ἡ ἀπόδειξις, οἷον ἔστω τὸ Γ πλάνητες, ἐφ᾽ ᾧ Β τὸ
ἐγγὺς εἶναι, τὸ Α τὸ μὴ στίλβειν· ὑπάρχει δὴ καὶ
τὸ Β τῷ Γ καὶ τὸ Α τῷ Β [τὸ μὴ στίλβειν],[1] ὥστε
καὶ τῷ Γ τὸ Α. καὶ ἔστι τοῦ διότι ὁ συλλογισμός·
εἴληπται γὰρ τὸ πρῶτον αἴτιον. πάλιν ὡς τὴν
5 σελήνην δεικνύουσιν ὅτι σφαιροειδής, διὰ τῶν αὐ-
ξήσεων· εἰ γὰρ τὸ αὐξανόμενον οὕτω σφαιροειδές,
αὐξάνει δ᾽ ἡ σελήνη, φανερὸν ὅτι σφαιροειδής· οὕτω
μὲν οὖν τοῦ ὅτι γέγονεν ὁ συλλογισμός, ἀνάπαλιν
δὲ τεθέντος τοῦ μέσου τοῦ διότι· οὐ γὰρ διὰ τὰς
αὐξήσεις σφαιροειδής ἐστιν, ἀλλὰ διὰ τὸ σφαι-
10 ροειδὴς εἶναι λαμβάνει τὰς αὐξήσεις τοιαύτας.
σελήνη ἐφ᾽ ᾧ Γ, σφαιροειδὴς ἐφ᾽ ᾧ Β, αὔξησις ἐφ᾽
ᾧ Α.

Ἐφ᾽ ὧν δὲ τὰ μέσα μὴ ἀντιστρέφει καὶ ἔστι
γνωριμώτερον τὸ ἀναίτιον, τὸ ὅτι μὲν δείκνυται, τὸ
διότι δ᾽ οὔ. ἔτι ἐφ᾽ ὧν τὸ μέσον ἔξω τίθεται· καὶ
γὰρ ἐν τούτοις τοῦ ὅτι καὶ οὐ τοῦ διότι ἡ ἀπόδειξις·
15 οὐ γὰρ λέγεται τὸ αἴτιον. οἷον διὰ τί οὐκ ἀναπνεῖ

[1] secl. Ross.

---

[a] Sc. as middle.
[b] Sc. with the majors. This is a corollary to the foregoing
case, the difference being that it is no longer possible to establish the reason by converting the major premiss.

does not twinkle is near (this may have been assumed either by induction or through sense-perception). Then A must apply to C; and so it has been proved that the planets are near. Thus this syllogism proves not the reason but the fact; for it is not because the planets do not twinkle that they are near, but because they are near that they do not twinkle. (It is possible, however, to prove the middle by means of the major term, and then the demonstration will establish the reason. *E.g.*, let C stand for " planets," B for " being near " and A for " not twinkling." Then B applies to C, and A—[" not twinkling "]—to B, and so A also applies to C; and the syllogism establishes the reason, because the proximate cause has been assumed.[a]) Or again as the moon is proved to be spherical from its phases; for if that which exhibits phases of this kind is spherical, and the moon exhibits phases, it is evident that the moon is spherical. In this form the syllogism proves the fact, but when the middle term is interchanged with the major, we can establish the reason; for it is not on account of its phases that the moon is spherical, but because it is spherical that it exhibits phases of this kind. C stands for " moon," B for " spherical " and A for " phase."

(3) Where the middle terms are not convertible [b] and that which is not the cause is better known than the cause, the fact can be proved but the reason cannot. (4) This is true also of syllogisms whose middle term falls outside [c]; in these too the demonstration establishes the fact and not the reason, since the cause is not stated. *E.g.*, why does the wall not

---

[c] In the second figure; the third, giving no universal conclusion, is useless for demonstration.

78 b

ὁ τοῖχος; ὅτι οὐ ζῷον. εἰ γὰρ τοῦτο τοῦ μὴ
ἀναπνεῖν αἴτιον, ἔδει τὸ ζῷον εἶναι αἴτιον τοῦ ἀναπνεῖν, οἷον εἰ ἡ ἀπόφασις αἰτία τοῦ μὴ ὑπάρχειν, ἡ
20 κατάφασις τοῦ ὑπάρχειν, ὥσπερ εἰ τὸ ἀσύμμετρα
εἶναι τὰ θερμὰ καὶ ψυχρὰ τοῦ μὴ ὑγιαίνειν, τὸ σύμ-
μετρα εἶναι τοῦ ὑγιαίνειν· ὁμοίως δὲ καὶ εἰ ἡ κατάφασις τοῦ ὑπάρχειν, ἡ ἀπόφασις τοῦ μὴ ὑπάρχειν.
ἐπὶ δὲ τῶν οὕτως ἀποδεδομένων οὐ συμβαίνει τὸ
λεχθέν· οὐ γὰρ ἅπαν ἀναπνεῖ ζῷον. ὁ δὲ συλλογισμὸς γίγνεται τῆς τοιαύτης αἰτίας ἐν τῷ μέσῳ σχή-
25 ματι. οἷον ἔστω τὸ Α ζῷον, ἐφ᾽ οὗ τὸ Β τὸ
ἀναπνεῖν, ἐφ᾽ ᾧ Γ τοῖχος. τῷ μὲν οὖν Β παντὶ
ὑπάρχει τὸ Α (πᾶν γὰρ τὸ ἀναπνέον ζῷον), τῷ δὲ
Γ οὐθενί, ὥστε οὐδὲ τὸ Β τῷ Γ οὐθενί· οὐκ ἄρα
ἀναπνεῖ ὁ τοῖχος. ἐοίκασι δ᾽ αἱ τοιαῦται τῶν
αἰτιῶν τοῖς καθ᾽ ὑπερβολὴν εἰρημένοις· τοῦτο δ᾽
30 ἔστι τὸ πλέον ἀποστήσαντα τὸ μέσον εἰπεῖν, οἷον
τὸ τοῦ Ἀναχάρσιος, ὅτι ἐν Σκύθαις οὐκ εἰσὶν αὐλητρίδες,[1] οὐδὲ γὰρ ἄμπελοι.

Κατὰ μὲν δὴ τὴν αὐτὴν ἐπιστήμην καὶ κατὰ τὴν
τῶν μέσων θέσιν αὗται διαφοραί εἰσιν τοῦ ὅτι πρὸς
τὸν τοῦ διότι συλλογισμόν· ἄλλον δὲ τρόπον διαφέρει
35 τὸ διότι τοῦ ὅτι τῷ[2] δι᾽ ἄλλης ἐπιστήμης ἑκάτερον
θεωρεῖν. τοιαῦτα δ᾽ ἐστὶν ὅσα οὕτως ἔχει πρὸς

---

[1] αὐλητρίδες np, Philoponus, Themistius : αὐληταί ABCd.
[2] τῷ np : τό.

---

[a] But it is not; see below.
[b] According to Aristotle only warm-blooded animals
breathe (cf. De Resp. 478 a 28 ff.), so in the example "animal"
is too wide a middle term.

breathe ? Because it is not an animal. If this were the reason for its not breathing, " being an animal " ought to be the reason for breathing [a]; on the principle that if a negative statement gives the reason for an attribute's not applying, the corresponding affirmative statement will give the reason for its applying ; e.g., if the disproportion of the hot and cold elements in us is the cause of our not being healthy, their due proportion is the cause of our being healthy. Similarly too if the affirmative statement gives the reason for an attribute's applying, the negative statement will give the reason for its not applying. But in the given instance the conclusion does not follow ; for not every animal breathes.[b] A syllogism which proves this sort of cause occurs in the middle figure. E.g., let A stand for " animal," B for " respiration " and C for " wall." Then A applies to all B (for everything that breathes is an animal), but to no C, and so neither does B apply to any C. Hence the wall does not breathe. Such causes as these are like far-fetched explanations ; I mean stating the middle term in too remote a form, e.g., the dictum of Anacharsis that there are no flute-players among the Scythians because there are no vines.[c]

These, then, are the differences between the syllogism which proves the fact and that which proves the reason, within the same science and according to the position of the middle terms. But there is another way in which the fact and the reason differ, viz., in each being studied by a different science. This is true of all subjects which are so related that one is

A fact and its reason may belong to different sciences.

[c] The full chain of implication is something like " flute-playing—thirsty work—heavy drinking—wine—grapes—vines." Anacharsis was a Scythian ethnologist of the sixth century B.C. (Herodotus iv. 76).

78 b

ἄλληλα ὥστ᾽ εἶναι θάτερον ὑπὸ θάτερον, οἷον τὰ
ὀπτικὰ πρὸς γεωμετρίαν καὶ τὰ μηχανικὰ πρὸς
στερεομετρίαν καὶ τὰ ἁρμονικὰ πρὸς ἀριθμητικὴν
καὶ τὰ φαινόμενα πρὸς ἀστρολογικήν. σχεδὸν δὲ
40 συνώνυμοί εἰσιν ἔνιαι τούτων τῶν ἐπιστημῶν, οἷον
79 a ἀστρολογία ἥ τε μαθηματικὴ καὶ ἡ ναυτική, καὶ
ἁρμονικὴ ἥ τε μαθηματικὴ καὶ ἡ κατὰ τὴν ἀκοήν.
ἐνταῦθα γὰρ τὸ μὲν ὅτι τῶν αἰσθητικῶν εἰδέναι, τὸ
δὲ διότι τῶν μαθηματικῶν· οὗτοι γὰρ ἔχουσι τῶν
αἰτίων τὰς ἀποδείξεις, καὶ πολλάκις οὐκ ἴσασι τὸ
5 ὅτι, καθάπερ οἱ τὸ καθόλου θεωροῦντες πολλάκις
ἔνια τῶν καθ᾽ ἕκαστον οὐκ ἴσασι δι᾽ ἀνεπισκεψίαν.
ἔστι δὲ ταῦτα ὅσα ἕτερόν τι ὄντα τὴν οὐσίαν κέχρηται τοῖς εἴδεσιν. τὰ γὰρ μαθήματα περὶ εἴδη ἐστίν·
οὐ γὰρ καθ᾽ ὑποκειμένου τινός· εἰ γὰρ καὶ καθ᾽
ὑποκειμένου τινὸς τὰ γεωμετρικά ἐστιν, ἀλλ᾽ οὐχ
10 ᾗ γε καθ᾽ ὑποκειμένου. ἔχει δὲ καὶ πρὸς τὴν
ὀπτικήν, ὡς αὕτη πρὸς τὴν γεωμετρίαν, ἄλλη πρὸς
ταύτην, οἷον τὸ περὶ τῆς ἴριδος· τὸ μὲν γὰρ ὅτι
φυσικοῦ εἰδέναι, τὸ δὲ διότι ὀπτικοῦ, ἢ ἁπλῶς ἢ
τοῦ κατὰ τὸ μάθημα. πολλαὶ δὲ καὶ τῶν μὴ ὑπ᾽
ἀλλήλας ἐπιστημῶν ἔχουσιν οὕτως, οἷον ἰατρικὴ
15 πρὸς γεωμετρίαν· ὅτι μὲν γὰρ τὰ ἕλκη τὰ περιφερῆ
βραδύτερον ὑγιάζεται τοῦ ἰατροῦ εἰδέναι, διότι δὲ
τοῦ γεωμέτρου.

---

^a i.e., studied by more than one science.

^b Up to this point it might be supposed that Aristotle
recognizes two " levels " of science, concerned respectively
with form and with informed matter. It now appears that
there are three " levels," the highest studying universals, the
lowest particulars, and the other mediating between them.

^c Philoponus offers two explanations : (1) because such

subordinate to the other, as is the relation of optical problems to plane and of mechanical problems to solid geometry and of harmonical problems to arithmetic and of the study of phenomena to astronomy. Some of these sciences have practically the same name ; *e.g.*, both mathematical and nautical astronomy are called astronomy, and both mathematical and acoustic harmonics are called harmonics. In these cases it is for the collectors of data to know the fact, and for the mathematicians to establish the reason. The latter can demonstrate the causes, whereas they are often ignorant of the fact ; just as those who are studying the universal are often ignorant of some of the particular instances, through lack of thorough investigation. Of this kind [a] are all objects which, while having a separate substantial existence, yet exhibit certain specific forms. For the mathematical sciences are concerned with forms ; they do not confine their demonstrations to a particular substrate. Even if geometrical problems refer to a particular substrate, they do so only incidentally. As optics is related to geometry, so is another science to optics, namely, the study of the rainbow.[b] To know the fact of the rainbow's existence is for the natural scientist ; to know the reason is for the optician, either simply as such or as a mathematical optician. Many of the sciences which are not strictly subordinate stand in this relation ; *e.g.*, medicine to geometry. It is for the doctor to know the fact that circular wounds heal more slowly, but it is for the geometrician to know the reason for the fact.[c]

wounds have the greatest area in relation to their perimeter, (2) because the healing surfaces are farther apart and nature has difficulty in joining them.

XIV. Τῶν δὲ σχημάτων ἐπιστημονικὸν μάλιστα τὸ πρῶτόν ἐστιν. αἵ τε γὰρ μαθηματικαὶ τῶν ἐπιστημῶν διὰ τούτου φέρουσι τὰς ἀποδείξεις, οἷον
20 ἀριθμητικὴ καὶ γεωμετρία καὶ ὀπτική, καὶ σχεδὸν ὡς εἰπεῖν ὅσαι τοῦ διότι ποιοῦνται τὴν σκέψιν· ἢ γὰρ ὅλως ἢ ὡς ἐπὶ τὸ πολὺ καὶ ἐν τοῖς πλείστοις διὰ τούτου τοῦ σχήματος ὁ τοῦ διότι συλλογισμός. ὥστε κἂν διὰ τοῦτ᾽ εἴη μάλιστα ἐπιστημονικόν· κυριώτατον γὰρ τοῦ εἰδέναι τὸ διότι θεωρεῖν. εἶτα
25 τὴν τοῦ τί ἐστιν ἐπιστήμην διὰ μόνου τούτου θη-
ρεῦσαι δυνατόν. ἐν μὲν γὰρ τῷ μέσῳ σχήματι οὐ γίγνεται κατηγορικὸς συλλογισμός, ἡ δὲ τοῦ τί ἐστιν ἐπιστήμη καταφάσεως· ἐν δὲ τῷ ἐσχάτῳ γίγνεται μὲν ἀλλ᾽ οὐ καθόλου, τὸ δὲ τί ἐστι τῶν καθόλου ἐστίν· οὐ γὰρ πῇ ἐστι ζῷον δίπουν ὁ ἄν-
30 θρωπος. ἔτι τοῦτο μὲν ἐκείνων οὐδὲν προσδεῖται, ἐκεῖνα δὲ διὰ τούτου καταπυκνοῦται καὶ αὔξεται, ἕως ἂν εἰς τὰ ἄμεσα ἔλθῃ. φανερὸν οὖν ὅτι κυριώ-
τατον τοῦ ἐπίστασθαι τὸ πρῶτον σχῆμα.

XV. Ὥσπερ δὲ ὑπάρχειν τὸ Α τῷ Β ἐνεδέχετο ἀτόμως, οὕτω καὶ μὴ ὑπάρχειν ἐγχωρεῖ. λέγω δὲ
35 τὸ ἀτόμως ὑπάρχειν ἢ μὴ ὑπάρχειν τὸ μὴ εἶναι αὐτῶν μέσον· οὕτω γὰρ οὐκέτι ἔσται κατ᾽ ἄλλο τὸ ὑπάρχειν ἢ μὴ ὑπάρχειν. ὅταν μὲν οὖν ἢ τὸ Α ἢ τὸ Β ἐν ὅλῳ τινὶ ᾖ, ἢ καὶ ἄμφω, οὐκ ἐνδέχεται τὸ

---

[a] *An. Pr.* I. v. [b] *Ibid.* vi.
[c] *Cf. An. Pr.* 29 a 30 ff.
[d] 72 b 18-25.
[e] *i.e.*, immediately.
[f] Aristotle means when (*a*) A belongs to a genus which excludes B, or (*b*) B belongs to a genus which excludes A, or (*c*) A and B belong to different genera. It is not clear whether he intends the fourth case—when A and B belong to the same

XIV. The most scientific of the figures is the first. Not only do the mathematical sciences, such as arithmetic, geometry and optics, advance their demonstrations by means of this figure, but so, broadly speaking, do practically all sciences which investigate reasons ; for it is by this figure, if not universally, at least as a general rule and in most cases, that the syllogism establishing the reason is effected. Hence on this account too the first figure may be regarded as the most scientific ; for the most essential part of knowledge is the study of reasons. Further, by this figure alone is it possible to pursue knowledge of the essence ; for in the middle figure we get no affirmative conclusion,[a] and the knowledge of a thing's essence must be affirmative ; while in the last figure we get an affirmative conclusion, but it is not universal,[b] whereas the essence belongs to the category of universals ; it is not in any particular sense that man is a two-footed animal. Finally the first figure is independent of the others, whereas they are supplemented and augmented by it until immediate premisses are obtained.[c] Thus it is evident that the first figure is most essential to knowledge.

XV. Just as A may (as we saw[d]) apply atomically[e] to B, so also it may not-apply atomically. By applying or not-applying atomically I mean that there is no middle term between them ; for in this case the applying or not-applying will no longer depend upon some other term. (1) When either A or B or both are contained in some whole,[f] it is impossible that A

The first figure is supreme for purposes of science.

Immediate negative propositions, impossible if either term is, or both terms are, contained in a genus,

genus—to be included in his formula, or whether he dismisses it as self-evident. He is probably thinking of A and B as species ; and if they are different species of the same proximate genus their disconnexion can be proved through one or other of their differentiae.

93

79 a

Α τῷ Β πρώτως μὴ ὑπάρχειν. ἔστω γὰρ τὸ Α ἐν
ὅλῳ τῷ Γ. οὐκοῦν εἰ τὸ Β μή ἐστιν ἐν ὅλῳ τῷ Γ
40 (ἐγχωρεῖ γὰρ τὸ μὲν Α εἶναι ἔν τινι ὅλῳ, τὸ δὲ Β
μὴ εἶναι ἐν τούτῳ), συλλογισμὸς ἔσται τοῦ μὴ ὑπάρ-
79 b χειν τὸ Α τῷ Β· εἰ γὰρ τῷ μὲν Α παντὶ τὸ Γ τῷ
δὲ Β μηδενί, οὐδενὶ τῷ Β τὸ Α. ὁμοίως δὲ καὶ εἰ
τὸ μὲν Β ἐν ὅλῳ τινί ἐστιν, οἷον ἐν τῷ Δ· τὸ μὲν
γὰρ Δ παντὶ τῷ Β ὑπάρχει, τὸ δὲ Α οὐδενὶ τῷ¹ Δ,
ὥστε τὸ Α οὐδενὶ τῷ Β ὑπάρξει διὰ συλλογισμοῦ.
5 τὸν αὐτὸν δὲ τρόπον δειχθήσεται καὶ εἰ ἄμφω ἐν
ὅλῳ τινί ἐστιν.

Ὅτι δ' ἐνδέχεται τὸ Β μὴ εἶναι ἐν ᾧ ὅλῳ ἐστὶ
τὸ Α, ἢ πάλιν τὸ Α ἐν ᾧ τὸ Β, φανερὸν ἐκ τῶν
συστοιχιῶν, ὅσαι μὴ ἐπαλλάττουσιν ἀλλήλαις. εἰ
γὰρ μηδὲν τῶν ἐν τῇ ΑΓΔ συστοιχίᾳ κατὰ μη-
10 δενὸς κατηγορεῖται τῶν ἐν τῇ ΒΕΖ, τὸ δ' Α ἐν
ὅλῳ ἐστὶ τῷ Θ συστοίχῳ ὄντι, φανερὸν ὅτι τὸ Β
οὐκ ἔσται ἐν τῷ Θ· ἐπαλλάξουσι γὰρ αἱ συστοιχίαι.
ὁμοίως δὲ καὶ εἰ τὸ Β ἐν ὅλῳ τινί ἐστιν.

Ἐὰν δὲ μηδέτερον ᾖ ἐν ὅλῳ μηδενί, μὴ ὑπάρχῃ
δὲ τὸ Α τῷ Β, ἀνάγκη ἀτόμως μὴ ὑπάρχειν. εἰ
15 γὰρ ἔσται τι μέσον, ἀνάγκη θάτερον αὐτῶν ἐν ὅλῳ
τινὶ εἶναι· ἢ γὰρ ἐν τῷ πρώτῳ σχήματι ἢ ἐν τῷ
μέσῳ ἔσται ὁ συλλογισμός. εἰ μὲν οὖν ἐν τῷ
πρώτῳ, τὸ Β ἔσται ἐν ὅλῳ τινί (καταφατικὴν γὰρ
δεῖ τὴν πρὸς τοῦτο γίγνεσθαι πρότασιν), εἰ δ' ἐν
τῷ μέσῳ, ὁπότερον ἔτυχεν· πρὸς ἀμφοτέροις γὰρ

¹ τῶν n, Bekker.

ᵃ This again means " immediately."

94

should not-apply in the primary sense ^{a} to B. For let A be contained in the whole of C. Then if B is not contained in the whole of C (for it is possible for A to be contained in a whole although B is not also contained in it), there will be a syllogism proving that A does not apply to B.^{b} For if C applies to all A but to no B, A will apply to no B. Similarly too if B is contained in some whole, e.g., D; for D applies to all B, and A to no D,^{c} so that by syllogism A will apply to no B. The proof will take the same form also if both terms are contained in some whole.

That B may not be contained in the whole which contains A, and *vice versa*, will be evident from the consideration of series ^{d} of mutually exclusive predicates. For if none of the terms in the series ACD is predicable of any of the terms in the series BEF, and A is wholly contained in H, a term in the former series, obviously B will not be contained in H; for then the series would not be mutually exclusive. Similarly too if B is wholly contained in some other term.

On the other hand if neither is wholly contained in any term, and A does not apply to B, it must not-apply atomically. For if there is to be a middle term, one of the terms A and B must be wholly contained in some genus. The syllogism will occur either in the first or in the middle figure. If it occurs in the first, it will be B that is wholly contained in some genus (for the premiss relating to B must be affirmative); if in the middle figure, it will be either A or B indifferently, since we get a syllogism when the negative statement

[margin: are possible if neither term is so contained.]

---

^{b} So the relation of A to B is not atomic.
^{c} By conversion.
^{d} Consisting of genera with their species and sub-species.

95

20 ληφθέντος τοῦ στερητικοῦ γίγνεται συλλογισμός·
ἀμφοτέρων δ' ἀποφατικῶν οὐσῶν οὐκ ἔσται.

Φανερὸν οὖν ὅτι ἐνδέχεταί τε ἄλλο[1] ἄλλῳ μὴ
ὑπάρχειν ἀτόμως, καὶ πότ' ἐνδέχεται καὶ πῶς
εἰρήκαμεν.

XVI. Ἄγνοια δ' ἡ μὴ κατ' ἀπόφασιν ἀλλὰ κατὰ
διάθεσιν λεγομένη ἔστι μὲν ἡ διὰ συλλογισμοῦ γιγ-
25 νομένη ἀπάτη, αὕτη δ' ἐν μὲν τοῖς πρώτως ὑπάρχουσιν ἢ μὴ ὑπάρχουσι συμβαίνει διχῶς· ἢ γὰρ
ὅταν ἁπλῶς ὑπολάβῃ ὑπάρχειν ἢ μὴ ὑπάρχειν, ἢ
ὅταν διὰ συλλογισμοῦ λάβῃ τὴν ὑπόληψιν. τῆς μὲν
οὖν ἁπλῆς ὑπολήψεως ἁπλῆ ἡ ἀπάτη, τῆς δὲ διὰ
συλλογισμοῦ πλείους. μὴ ὑπαρχέτω γὰρ τὸ Α μη-
30 δενὶ τῷ[2] Β ἀτόμως· οὐκοῦν ἐὰν συλλογίζηται ὑπάρχειν τὸ Α τῷ Β, μέσον λαβὼν τὸ Γ, ἠπατημένος
ἔσται διὰ συλλογισμοῦ. ἐνδέχεται μὲν οὖν ἀμφοτέρας τὰς προτάσεις εἶναι ψευδεῖς, ἐνδέχεται δὲ τὴν
ἑτέραν μόνον. εἰ γὰρ μήτε τὸ Α μηδενὶ τῶν Γ
35 ὑπάρχει μήτε τὸ Γ μηδενὶ τῶν Β, εἴληπται δ'
ἑκατέρα ἀνάπαλιν, ἄμφω ψευδεῖς ἔσονται. ἐγχωρεῖ
δ' οὕτως ἔχειν τὸ Γ πρὸς τὸ Α καὶ Β ὥστε μήτε
ὑπὸ τὸ Α εἶναι μήτε καθόλου τῷ Β. τὸ μὲν γὰρ Β
ἀδύνατον εἶναι ἐν ὅλῳ τινί (πρώτως γὰρ ἐλέγετο
αὐτῷ τὸ Α μὴ ὑπάρχειν), τὸ δὲ Α οὐκ ἀνάγκη πᾶσι
40 τοῖς οὖσιν εἶναι καθόλου, ὥστ' ἀμφότεραι ψευδεῖς.
ἀλλὰ καὶ τὴν ἑτέραν ἐνδέχεται ἀληθῆ λαμβάνειν, οὐ
80 a μέντοι ὁποτέραν ἔτυχεν, ἀλλὰ τὴν ΑΓ· ἡ γὰρ ΓΒ
πρότασις ἀεὶ ψευδὴς ἔσται διὰ τὸ ἐν μηδενὶ εἶναι
τὸ Β, τὴν δὲ ΑΓ ἐγχωρεῖ, οἷον εἰ τὸ Α καὶ τῷ Γ

---

[1] om. Bekker.   [2] τῶν ABCd, Bekker.

is assumed in connexion with either of them, but when both are negative there will be no syllogism.

Thus it is evident that one term may not-apply atomically to another; and we have explained when and how this is possible.

XVI. Ignorance, considered not in a negative sense but as a positive disposition of mind, is error reached through inference.[a] In propositions stating an immediate positive or negative relation it arises in two ways: (a) when we directly suppose[b] that one term applies or does not apply to another, and (b) when we reach this supposition by inference. The error arising from direct supposition is simple, but that which is based on inference takes more than one form. Let A apply atomically to no B. Then if we infer, taking C as the middle, that A applies to B, our error will be based on inference. It is possible either for both premisses or for one only to be false. (i) For if A applies to no C and C to no B, and we have assumed the contrary in each case, both premisses will be false (it is possible for C to be so related to A and B that it neither falls under A nor applies universally to B. For B cannot be wholly contained in a genus, since we stated above[c] that A is directly inapplicable to it; and A need not necessarily apply universally to everything: hence both premisses are false.) (ii) It is also possible to assume one true premiss: not either premiss indifferently, but AC (the premiss CB will always be false, because B is contained in no genus; but AC may be true); e.g., if A applies

Error in respect of terms immediately related.

(1) Negative relation.

(i) Both premisses false.

(ii) Major true, minor false.

<hr />

[a] This is a hasty statement, and Aristotle proceeds at once to correct it; but since the direct misapprehension described under (a) does not admit logical analysis he says no more about it and confines his attention to (b).

[b] Sc. wrongly. [c] b 29.

80 a

καὶ τῷ Β ὑπάρχει ἀτόμως. ὅταν γὰρ πρώτως κατηγορῆται ταὐτὸ πλειόνων οὐδέτερον ἐν[1] οὐδε- 5 τέρῳ ἔσται. διαφέρει δ᾽ οὐδέν, οὐδ᾽ εἰ μὴ ἀτόμως ὑπάρχει.

Ἡ μὲν οὖν τοῦ ὑπάρχειν ἀπάτη διὰ τούτων τε καὶ οὕτω γίγνεται μόνως (οὐ γὰρ ἦν ἐν ἄλλῳ σχή- ματι τοῦ ὑπάρχειν συλλογισμός), ἡ δὲ τοῦ μὴ ὑπάρ- χειν ἔν τε τῷ πρώτῳ καὶ ἐν τῷ μέσῳ σχήματι. 10 πρῶτον οὖν εἴπωμεν ποσαχῶς ἐν τῷ πρώτῳ γίγ- νεται, καὶ πῶς ἐχουσῶν τῶν προτάσεων.

Ἐνδέχεται μὲν οὖν ἀμφοτέρων ψευδῶν οὐσῶν, οἷον εἰ τὸ Α καὶ τῷ Γ καὶ τῷ Β ὑπάρχει ἀτόμως· ἐὰν γὰρ ληφθῇ τὸ μὲν Α τῷ Γ μηδενί, τὸ δὲ Γ παντὶ τῷ Β, ψευδεῖς αἱ προτάσεις. ἐνδέχεται δὲ 15 καὶ τῆς ἑτέρας ψευδοῦς οὔσης, καὶ ταύτης ὁποτέρας ἔτυχεν. ἐγχωρεῖ γὰρ τὴν μὲν ΑΓ ἀληθῆ εἶναι, τὴν δὲ ΓΒ ψευδῆ, τὴν μὲν ΑΓ ἀληθῆ, ὅτι οὐ πᾶσι τοῖς οὖσιν ὑπάρχει τὸ Α, τὴν δὲ ΓΒ ψευδῆ ὅτι ἀδύνατον ὑπάρχειν[2] τῷ Β τὸ Γ, ᾧ μηδενὶ ὑπάρχει τὸ Α· οὐ γὰρ ἔτι ἀληθὴς ἔσται ἡ ΑΓ πρότασις· 20 ἅμα δέ, εἰ καί εἰσιν ἀμφότεραι ἀληθεῖς, καὶ τὸ συμ- πέρασμα ἔσται ἀληθές. ἀλλὰ καὶ τὴν ΓΒ ἐνδέ- χεται ἀληθῆ εἶναι τῆς ἑτέρας οὔσης ψευδοῦς, οἷον εἰ τὸ Β καὶ ἐν τῷ Γ καὶ ἐν τῷ Α ἐστίν· ἀνάγκη γὰρ θάτερον ὑπὸ θάτερον εἶναι, ὥστ᾽ ἂν λάβῃ τὸ Α μηδενὶ τῷ Γ ὑπάρχειν, ψευδὴς ἔσται ἡ πρότασις. 25 φανερὸν οὖν ὅτι καὶ τῆς ἑτέρας ψευδοῦς οὔσης καὶ ἀμφοῖν ἔσται ψευδὴς ὁ συλλογισμός.

---

[1] ἐν om. ABCd, Bekker.
[2] ὑπάρχει Bekker.

atomically both to C and to B ; for when the same term is immediately predicated of more than one subject, neither of these latter terms will apply to the other. It makes no difference to the result if the relation ⟨of A to C⟩ is not atomic.

Thus erroneous affirmative attribution arises only from these causes and in these conditions (for we have seen [a] that a syllogism proving the ⟨universal⟩ affirmative relation occurs in no other figure) ; but erroneous negative attribution occurs in the second figure as well as in the first. Let us first state in how many forms it occurs in the first figure and how the premisses are related. (2) Affirmative relation.

A. Syllogism in first figure.

Error is possible (i) when both premisses are false, e.g., if A applies immediately to both C and B ; for if A is assumed to apply to no C, and C to all B, the premisses will be false. (ii) It is possible when either premiss indifferently is false. For AC may be true and CB false : AC true because A does not apply to all things, and CB false because C cannot apply to B when A applies to no C ; for the premiss AC will no longer be true, and moreover, if both premisses are true, the conclusion will also be true. Again, CB may be true, the other premiss being false ; e.g., if B is contained in both C and A. For one of these terms must be subordinate to the other [b] ; so that if we assume that A applies to no C, the premiss will be false. Thus it is evident that the syllogism will be false whether only one of the premisses is false or both are false. (i) Both premisses false.

(ii) One premiss false.

[a] *An. Pr.* I. v-vi.
[b] A to C ; in the other case A would apply to all C, and therefore by inference to B, whereas it applies immediately to B. In fact, as Ross points out, A and C might be co-ordinate and overlapping.

Ἐν δὲ τῷ μέσῳ σχήματί ὅλας μὲν εἶναι τὰς προτάσεις ἀμφοτέρας ψευδεῖς οὐκ ἐνδέχεται (ὅταν γὰρ
τὸ Α παντὶ τῷ Β ὑπάρχῃ, οὐδὲν ἔσται λαβεῖν ὃ τῷ
30 μὲν ἑτέρῳ παντὶ θατέρῳ δ' οὐδενὶ ὑπάρξει, δεῖ δ'
οὕτω λαμβάνειν τὰς προτάσεις ὥστε τῷ μὲν ὑπάρχειν τῷ δὲ μὴ ὑπάρχειν, εἴπερ ἔσται συλλογισμός·
εἰ οὖν οὕτω λαμβανόμεναι ψευδεῖς, δῆλον ὡς ἐναντίως ἀνάπαλιν ἕξουσι· τοῦτο δ' ἀδύνατον), ἐπί τι δ'
ἑκατέραν οὐδὲν κωλύει ψευδῆ εἶναι, οἷον εἰ τὸ Γ
35 καὶ τῷ Α καὶ τῷ Β τινὶ ὑπάρχοι· ἂν γὰρ τῷ μὲν Α
παντὶ ληφθῇ ὑπάρχον τῷ δὲ Β μηδενί, ψευδεῖς μὲν
ἀμφότεραι αἱ προτάσεις, οὐ μέντοι ὅλαι ἀλλ' ἐπί τι.
καὶ ἀνάπαλιν δὲ τεθέντος τοῦ στερητικοῦ ὡσαύτως.
τὴν δ' ἑτέραν εἶναι ψευδῆ καὶ ὁποτερανοῦν ἐν-
40 δέχεται. ὃ γὰρ ὑπάρχει τῷ Α παντί, καὶ τῷ Β
80 b ὑπάρξει· ἐὰν οὖν ληφθῇ τῷ μὲν Α ὅλῳ ὑπάρχειν τὸ
Γ τῷ δὲ Β ὅλῳ μὴ ὑπάρχειν, ἡ μὲν ΓΑ ἀληθὴς
ἔσται, ἡ δὲ ΓΒ ψευδής. πάλιν ὃ τῷ Β μηδενὶ
ὑπάρχει οὐδὲ τῷ Α παντὶ ὑπάρξει· εἰ γὰρ τῷ Α,
καὶ τῷ Β· ἀλλ' οὐχ ὑπῆρχεν. ἐὰν οὖν ληφθῇ τὸ Γ
5 τῷ μὲν Α ὅλῳ ὑπάρχειν τῷ δὲ Β μηδενί, ἡ μὲν ΓΒ
πρότασις ἀληθής, ἡ δ' ἑτέρα ψευδής. ὁμοίως δὲ
καὶ μετατεθέντος τοῦ στερητικοῦ. ὃ γὰρ μηδενὶ
ὑπάρχει τῷ Α, οὐδὲ τῷ Β οὐδενὶ ὑπάρξει· ἐὰν οὖν
ληφθῇ τὸ Γ τῷ μὲν Α ὅλῳ μὴ ὑπάρχειν τῷ δὲ Β
ὅλῳ ὑπάρχειν, ἡ μὲν ΑΓ πρότασις ἀληθὴς ἔσται,
10 ἡ ἑτέρα δὲ ψευδής. καὶ πάλιν, ὃ παντὶ τῷ Β
ὑπάρχει, μηδενὶ λαβεῖν τῷ Α ὑπάρχον ψεῦδος. ἀνάγκη γάρ, εἰ τῷ Β παντί, καὶ τῷ Α τινὶ ὑπάρχειν·

---

a For a valid syllogism the premisses must be either AaC,

100

In the middle figure (i) it is impossible for both premisses to be wholly false; for when A applies to all B we shall not be able to find any term which will apply to all of the one and to none of the other, yet we must assume the premisses in such a way that the middle applies to one but not the other extreme term, if there is to be a syllogism. If, then, the premisses so assumed are false, clearly if their contraries are assumed the converse result should follow; but this is impossible.[a] But (ii) there is no reason why both premisses should not be partly false; *e.g.*, supposing that C should apply to some of both A and B; for if it is assumed to apply to all A and to no B, both premisses will be false: not wholly, however, but partly. So too if the negative is posited in the other premiss. (iii) Either premiss singly may be ⟨wholly⟩ false. For that which applies to all A will also apply to B; then if C is assumed to apply to the whole of A but to be inapplicable to the whole of B, CA will be true, and CB false. Again, that which applies to no B will not apply to all A; for if it applies to A it will apply to B, which *ex hypothesi* it does not. Then if C is assumed to apply to the whole of A but to none of B, the premiss CB will be true, and the other will be false. Similarly too when the negative premiss is transposed; for that which applies to no A will not apply to any B. Thus if C is assumed to be inapplicable to the whole of A, but to apply to the whole of B, the premiss AC will be true, and the other false. Again, it is false to assume that that which applies to all B applies to no A; for if it applies to all B it must also apply to some

Marginal notes: B. Syllogism in second figure. (i) Both premisses cannot be wholly false, (ii) but may be partly false, (iii) and one may be wholly false.

BeC or Aec, BaC; and if both premisses are wholly false, either BeC, BaC or AaC, BeC must be true; but neither pair is compatible with BaA.

101

80 b

ἐὰν οὖν ληφθῇ τῷ μὲν Β παντὶ ὑπάρχειν τὸ Γ τῷ
δὲ Α μηδενί, ἡ μὲν ΓΒ ἀληθὴς ἔσται, ἡ δὲ ΓΑ
ψευδής.

15 Φανερὸν οὖν ὅτι καὶ ἀμφοτέρων οὐσῶν ψευδῶν
καὶ τῆς ἑτέρας μόνον ἔσται συλλογισμὸς ἀπατη-
τικὸς ἐν τοῖς ἀτόμοις.

XVII. Ἐν δὲ τοῖς μὴ ἀτόμως ὑπάρχουσιν ἢ μὴ
ὑπάρχουσιν,[1] ὅταν μὲν διὰ τοῦ οἰκείου μέσου γίγνηται τοῦ ψεύδους ὁ συλλογισμός, οὐχ οἷόν τε ἀμφο-
20 τέρας ψευδεῖς εἶναι τὰς προτάσεις, ἀλλὰ μόνον τὴν
πρὸς τῷ μείζονι ἄκρῳ. (λέγω δ' οἰκεῖον μέσον δι'
οὗ γίγνεται τῆς ἀντιφάσεως ὁ συλλογισμός.) ὑπαρχέτω γὰρ τὸ Α τῷ Β διὰ μέσου τοῦ Γ. ἐπεὶ οὖν
ἀνάγκη τὴν ΓΒ καταφατικὴν λαμβάνεσθαι συλλογισμοῦ γιγνομένου, δῆλον ὅτι ἀεὶ αὕτη ἔσται ἀλη-
25 θής· οὐ γὰρ ἀντιστρέφεται. ἡ δὲ ΑΓ ψευδής·
ταύτης γὰρ ἀντιστρεφομένης ἐναντίος γίγνεται ὁ
συλλογισμός. ὁμοίως δὲ καὶ εἰ ἐξ ἄλλης συστοιχίας
ληφθείη τὸ μέσον, οἷον τὸ Δ εἰ καὶ ἐν τῷ Α ὅλῳ
ἐστὶ καὶ κατὰ τοῦ Β κατηγορεῖται παντός· ἀνάγκη
30 γὰρ τὴν μὲν ΔΒ πρότασιν μένειν, τὴν δ' ἑτέραν
ἀντιστρέφεσθαι, ὥσθ' ἡ μὲν ἀεὶ ἀληθής, ἡ δ' ἀεὶ
ψευδής. καὶ σχεδὸν ἥ γε τοιαύτη ἀπάτη ἡ αὐτή
ἐστι τῇ διὰ τοῦ οἰκείου μέσου. ἐὰν δὲ μὴ διὰ τοῦ
οἰκείου μέσου γίγνηται ὁ συλλογισμός, ὅταν μὲν ὑπὸ
τὸ Α ᾖ τὸ μέσον τῷ δὲ Β μηδενὶ ὑπάρχῃ, ἀνάγκη
35 ψευδεῖς εἶναι ἀμφοτέρας. ληπτέαι γὰρ ἐναντίως ἢ
ὡς ἔχουσιν αἱ προτάσεις, εἰ μέλλει συλλογισμὸς
ἔσεσθαι· οὕτω δὲ λαμβανομένων ἀμφότεραι γίγ-

[1] ἢ μὴ ὑπάρχουσιν om. ABn.

102

A. Thus if C is assumed to apply to all B but to no A, CB will be true and CA false.

Thus it is evident that in atomic propositions erroneous inference will be possible when both premisses are false and when only one is false.

XVII. In non-atomic attribution, whether affirmative or negative,[a] when the false conclusion is reached by means of the proper middle term, it is not possible for both premisses to be false, but only for the major premiss. (By " proper " middle I mean that by which the contradictory [b] conclusion is reached.) Let A apply to B through C as middle term. Then since the premiss BC must be assumed as affirmative to produce a syllogism, clearly it must always be true ; for it is not converted.[c] But AC is false ; for it is upon the conversion of this that the contrary conclusion results. Similarly too supposing that the middle term should be taken from another series of predicates [d] ; e.g., if D is both wholly contained in A and also predicated of all B ; for the premiss DB must remain unchanged while the other is converted, so that the former is always true and the latter always false. Error of this kind is practically the same as that which is inferred by the proper middle. If, however, the syllogism is not effected by means of the proper middle, when the middle is subordinate to A but applies to no B, both premisses must be false ; for the premisses must be assumed in the contrary sense if there is to be a syllogism, and when they are

Marginal notes: Error in respect of terms mediately related. (1) Affirmative relation. A. First figure. (i) Inference by the proper middle. (ii) Inference by a middle not proper but valid. (iii) Inference by an improper middle.

---

[a] The latter is first considered at 81 a 15.

[b] i.e. the true conclusion.

[c] i.e. changed in quality. Throughout this section ἀντιστρέφεσθαι refers to qualitative change, not interchange of subject and predicate. Cf. An. Pr. 45 b 6, and II. viii-x.

[d] Non-essential attributes.

80 b

νονται ψευδεῖς. οἷον εἰ τὸ μὲν Α ὅλῳ τῷ Δ ὑπάρχει τὸ δὲ Δ μηδενὶ τῶν Β· ἀντιστραφέντων γὰρ τούτων συλλογισμός τ᾽ ἔσται καὶ αἱ προτάσεις ἀμ-
40 φότεραι ψευδεῖς. ὅταν δὲ μὴ ᾖ ὑπὸ τὸ Α τὸ μέσον,
81 a οἷον τὸ Δ, ἡ μὲν ΑΔ ἀληθὴς ἔσται, ἡ δὲ ΔΒ ψευδής. ἡ μὲν γὰρ ΑΔ ἀληθής, ὅτι οὐκ ἦν ἐν τῷ Α τὸ Δ, ἡ δὲ ΔΒ ψευδής, ὅτι εἰ ἦν ἀληθής, κἂν τὸ συμπέρασμα ἦν ἀληθές· ἀλλ᾽ ἦν ψεῦδος.
5 Διὰ δὲ τοῦ μέσου σχήματος γιγνομένης τῆς ἀπάτης, ἀμφοτέρας μὲν οὐκ ἐνδέχεται ψευδεῖς εἶναι τὰς προτάσεις ὅλας (ὅταν γὰρ ᾖ τὸ Β ὑπὸ τὸ Α, οὐδὲν ἐνδέχεται τῷ μὲν παντὶ τῷ δὲ μηδενὶ ὑπάρχειν, καθάπερ ἐλέχθη καὶ πρότερον), τὴν ἑτέραν δ᾽
10 ἐγχωρεῖ, καὶ ὁποτέραν ἔτυχεν. εἰ γὰρ τὸ Γ καὶ τῷ Α καὶ τῷ Β ὑπάρχει, ἐὰν ληφθῇ τῷ μὲν Α ὑπάρχειν τῷ δὲ Β μὴ ὑπάρχειν, ἡ μὲν ΓΑ¹ ἀληθὴς ἔσται, ἡ δ᾽ ἑτέρα ψευδής. πάλιν δ᾽ εἰ τῷ μὲν Β ληφθείη τὸ Γ ὑπάρχον τῷ δὲ Α μηδενί, ἡ μὲν ΓΒ ἀληθὴς ἔσται, ἡ δ᾽ ἑτέρα ψευδής.
15 Ἐὰν μὲν οὖν στερητικὸς ᾖ τῆς ἀπάτης ὁ συλλογισμός, εἴρηται πότε καὶ διὰ τίνων ἔσται ἡ ἀπάτη· ἐὰν δὲ καταφατικός, ὅταν μὲν διὰ τοῦ οἰκείου μέσου, ἀδύνατον ἀμφοτέρας εἶναι ψευδεῖς· ἀνάγκη γὰρ τὴν ΓΒ μένειν, εἴπερ ἔσται συλλογισμός,
20 καθάπερ ἐλέχθη καὶ πρότερον· ὥστε ἡ ΑΓ² ἀεὶ ἔσται ψευδής, αὕτη γάρ ἐστιν ἡ ἀντιστρεφομένη. ὁμοίως δὲ καὶ εἰ ἐξ ἄλλης συστοιχίας λαμβάνοιτο τὸ μέσον, ὥσπερ ἐλέχθη καὶ ἐπὶ τῆς στερητικῆς ἀπάτης· ἀνάγκη γὰρ τὴν μὲν ΔΒ μένειν τὴν δ᾽

¹ ΓΑ Mure, Ross :. ΑΓ. ² ΑΓ Mure, Ross : ΓΑ.

104

so assumed, both become false : *e.g.*, if A applies to the whole of D, and D applies to no B ; for when these propositions are converted, there will be a syllogism and both premisses will be false. But when the middle term, *e.g.* D, is not subordinate to A, the premiss AD will be true and DB false. AD will be true because D was not contained in A ; DB will be false because if it had been true, the conclusion would have been true too ; whereas it is *ex hypothesi* false.

When the error arises in the middle figure, it is impossible that both premisses should be wholly false (for when B is subordinate to A, nothing can apply to all of the one and to none of the other, as we observed above [a]), but one premiss, and that either one indifferently, may be false. For when C applies to both A and B, if it is assumed to apply to A but not to B, the premiss CA will be true, but the other will be false. Again, supposing that C is assumed as applying to B, but to no A, CB will be true but the other will be false. B. Second figure. Either premiss may be false, but both cannot be wholly false.

Thus we have stated when and from what sort of premisses the error will arise if the erroneous conclusion is negative. If it is affirmative, when (i) it is reached through the proper middle term, it is impossible that both premisses should be false ; for the premiss CB must remain unchanged, if there is to be a syllogism, as we observed above.[b] Hence AC will always be false ; for this is the premiss whose quality is converted. Similarly too (ii) supposing that the middle term is taken from another predicate-series, as we observed with reference to negative error [c] ; for DB must remain unchanged, and AD must be (2) Negative relation. (First figure.) (i) Inference by the proper middle. (ii) Inference by a middle not proper but valid.

<hr>

[a] 80 a 29.   [b] 80 b 23.   [c] 80 b 26.

81 a

ΑΔ ἀντιστρέφεσθαι, καὶ ἡ ἀπάτη ἡ αὐτὴ τῇ πρό-
25 τερον. ὅταν δὲ μὴ διὰ τοῦ οἰκείου, ἐὰν μὲν ᾖ τὸ
Δ ὑπὸ τὸ Α, αὕτη μὲν ἔσται ἀληθής, ἡ ἑτέρα δὲ
ψευδής· ἐγχωρεῖ γὰρ τὸ Α πλείοσιν ὑπάρχειν ἃ
οὐκ ἔστιν ὑπ' ἄλληλα. ἐὰν δὲ μὴ ᾖ τὸ Δ ὑπὸ τὸ Α,
αὕτη μὲν ἀεὶ δῆλον ὅτι ἔσται ψευδής (καταφατικὴ
γὰρ λαμβάνεται), τὴν δὲ ΔΒ¹ ἐνδέχεται καὶ ἀληθῆ
30 εἶναι καὶ ψευδῆ· οὐδὲν γὰρ κωλύει τὸ μὲν Α τῷ Δ
μηδενὶ ὑπάρχειν τὸ δὲ Δ τῷ Β παντί, οἷον ζῷον
ἐπιστήμη, ἐπιστήμη δὲ μουσικῇ. οὐδ' αὖ μήτε τὸ
Α μηδενὶ τῶν Δ μήτε τὸ Δ μηδενὶ τῶν² Β. [φανε-
ρὸν οὖν ὅτι μὴ ὄντος τοῦ μέσου ὑπὸ τὸ Α καὶ
ἀμφοτέρας ἐγχωρεῖ ψευδεῖς εἶναι καὶ ὁποτέραν
ἔτυχεν.]³
35 Ποσαχῶς μὲν οὖν καὶ διὰ τίνων ἐγχωρεῖ γίγνεσθαι τὰς κατὰ συλλογισμὸν ἀπάτας ἔν τε τοῖς
ἀμέσοις καὶ ἐν τοῖς δι' ἀποδείξεως, φανερόν.

XVIII. Φανερὸν δὲ καὶ ὅτι, εἴ τις αἴσθησις ἐκ-
λέλοιπεν, ἀνάγκη καὶ ἐπιστήμην τινὰ ἐκλελοιπέναι,
40 ἣν ἀδύνατον λαβεῖν, εἴπερ μανθάνομεν ἢ ἐπαγωγῇ
81 b ἢ ἀποδείξει, ἔστι δ' ἡ μὲν ἀπόδειξις ἐκ τῶν καθόλου
ἡ δ' ἐπαγωγὴ ἐκ τῶν κατὰ μέρος, ἀδύνατον δὲ τὰ
καθόλου θεωρῆσαι μὴ δι' ἐπαγωγῆς (ἐπεὶ καὶ τὰ ἐξ
ἀφαιρέσεως λεγόμενα ἔσται δι' ἐπαγωγῆς γνώριμα
ποιεῖν, ὅτι ὑπάρχει ἑκάστῳ γένει ἔνια, καὶ εἰ μὴ

---

¹ ΒΔ Bekker.
² τῷ ΑΒ, Bekker.
³ φανερὸν . . . ἔτυχεν secl. Ross.

ᵃ Ross points out that this case (in which if the false premiss is corrected a valid though unscientific syllogism is
obtained) does not belong under (iii) but is identical with
that already mentioned under (ii).

converted in quality, and the error is the same as before. But when (iii) the conclusion is not reached through the proper middle term, if D is subordinate to A, this premiss will be true, and the other false, since A may apply to two or more terms which are not subordinate to one another; but if D is not subordinate to A, clearly this premiss will always be false (since it is assumed as affirmative), whereas DB may be true [a] or false ; for there is no reason why A should not apply to no D, and D to all B (as *e.g.*, " animal " applies to no " science," but " science " to all " music "), nor why A should not apply to no D and D to no B. [Thus it is evident that when the middle term is not subordinate to A not only both premisses but either indifferently may be false.] [b]

(iii) Inference by an improper middle.

Thus it is evident in how many ways and by what sort of premisses syllogistic error may occur both in immediate attribution and in demonstrative attribution.

XVIII. It is evident also that if any sense-faculty has been lost, some knowledge must be irrevocably lost with it ; since we learn either by induction or by demonstration. Now demonstration proceeds from universals and induction from particulars ; but it is impossible to gain a view of universals except through induction (since even what we call abstractions [c] can only be grasped by induction, because, although they cannot exist in separation, some of them inhere in each class of objects, in so far as each class has

Lack of a sense-faculty as a cause of ignorance.

---

[b] This sentence is unlikely to be Aristotelian (since if D is not subordinate to A the major premiss must be false) and Philoponus ignores it. It is probably a rash observation by an early " editor."

[c] τὰ ἐξ ἀφαιρέσεως generally means " mathematical abstractions," *e.g.*, continuity or dimension (*cf. Met.* 1061 a 28); possibly here the sense is wider.

5 χωριστά ἐστιν, ᾗ τοιονδὶ ἕκαστον), ἐπαχθῆναι δὲ μὴ
ἔχοντας αἴσθησιν ἀδύνατον. τῶν γὰρ καθ' ἕκαστον ἡ αἴσθησις· οὐ γὰρ ἐνδέχεται λαβεῖν αὐτῶν
τὴν ἐπιστήμην· οὔτε γὰρ ἐκ τῶν καθόλου ἄνευ ἐπαγωγῆς, οὔτε δι' ἐπαγωγῆς ἄνευ τῆς αἰσθήσεως.

10 XIX. Ἔστι δὲ πᾶς συλλογισμὸς διὰ τριῶν ὅρων,
καὶ ὁ μὲν δεικνύναι δυνάμενος ὅτι ὑπάρχει τὸ Α τῷ
Γ διὰ τὸ ὑπάρχειν τῷ Β καὶ τοῦτο τῷ Γ, ὁ δὲ στερη-
τικός, τὴν μὲν ἑτέραν πρότασιν ἔχων ὅτι ὑπάρχει τι
ἄλλο ἄλλῳ, τὴν δ' ἑτέραν ὅτι οὐχ ὑπάρχει. φανερὸν
15 οὖν ὅτι αἱ μὲν ἀρχαὶ καὶ αἱ λεγόμεναι ὑποθέσεις
αὐταί εἰσι· λαβόντα γὰρ ταῦτα οὕτως ἀνάγκη δεικνύναι, οἷον ὅτι τὸ Α τῷ Γ ὑπάρχει διὰ τοῦ Β, πάλιν
δ' ὅτι τὸ Α τῷ Β δι' ἄλλου μέσου, καὶ ὅτι τὸ Β τῷ
Γ ὡσαύτως. κατὰ μὲν οὖν δόξαν συλλογιζομένοις
καὶ μόνον διαλεκτικῶς δῆλον ὅτι τοῦτο μόνον σκε-
20 πτέον, εἰ ἐξ ὧν ἐνδέχεται ἐνδοξοτάτων γίγνεται ὁ
συλλογισμός, ὥστ' εἰ καὶ μὴ ἔστι τι τῇ ἀληθείᾳ τῶν
ΑΒ μέσον, δοκεῖ δὲ εἶναι, ὁ διὰ τούτου συλλογιζόμενος συλλελόγισται διαλεκτικῶς· πρὸς δ' ἀλήθειαν ἐκ τῶν ὑπαρχόντων δεῖ σκοπεῖν. ἔχει δ' οὕτως·
ἐπειδὴ ἔστιν ὃ αὐτὸ μὲν κατ' ἄλλου κατηγορεῖται
25 μὴ κατὰ συμβεβηκός—λέγω δὲ τὸ κατὰ συμβεβηκὸς οἷον τὸ λευκόν ποτ' ἐκεῖνό φαμεν εἶναι ἄνθρωπον, οὐχ ὁμοίως λέγοντες καὶ τὸν ἄνθρωπον λευκόν·
ὁ μὲν γὰρ οὐχ ἕτερόν τι ὢν λευκόν ἐστι, τὸ δὲ
λευκὸν ὅτι συμβέβηκε τῷ ἀνθρώπῳ εἶναι λευκῷ—

a determinate nature); and we cannot employ induction if we lack sense-perception, because it is sense-perception that apprehends particulars. It is impossible to gain scientific knowledge of them, since they can neither be apprehended from universals without induction, nor through induction apart from sense-perception.

XIX. Every syllogism is effected by means of three terms. One kind has the effect of proving that A applies to C because A applies to B and B to C; the other is negative, and has for one premiss the affirmative and for the other the negative attribution of one term to another. It is evident, then, that these are the starting-points and so-called hypotheses (of syllogism); for it is by assuming them in this way that one must effect one's proof, *e.g.*, that A applies by means of B to C, and again that A applies to B through some other term as middle, and similarly that B applies to C. Now if we are arguing with a view to plausibility, *i.e.*, only dialectically, clearly we need only consider whether the conclusion proceeds from premisses which are as widely as possible accepted; so that although a given term is not really the middle between A and B, provided that it is accepted as such, if we draw our inference through it the inference is dialectically sound. But if our object is truth, we must base our investigation on the actual facts. Now the position is this. There are terms which are predicable of something else not accidentally—by "accidentally" I mean as we sometimes say "that white ⟨thing⟩ is a man," which is not the same as saying "the man is white," since a man is not a white thing because he is something else, but the white ⟨thing⟩ is a man because it is an accident of the man to be

81 b

ἔστιν οὖν ἔνια τοιαῦτα ὥστε καθ' αὑτὰ κατηγορεῖ-
30 σθαι. ἔστω δὴ τὸ Γ τοιοῦτον ὃ αὐτὸ μὲν μηκέτι
ὑπάρχει ἄλλῳ, τούτῳ δὲ τὸ Β πρώτῳ, καὶ οὐκ
ἔστιν ἄλλο μεταξύ· καὶ πάλιν τὸ Ε τῷ Ζ ὡσαύτως,
καὶ τοῦτο τῷ Β. ἆρ' οὖν τοῦτο ἀνάγκη στῆναι, ἢ
ἐνδέχεται εἰς ἄπειρον ἰέναι; καὶ πάλιν εἰ τοῦ μὲν
Α μηδὲν κατηγορεῖται καθ' αὑτὸ τὸ δὲ Α τῷ Θ
35 ὑπάρχει πρώτῳ, μεταξὺ δε μηδενὶ προτέρῳ, καὶ τὸ
Θ τῷ Η, καὶ τοῦτο τῷ Β, ἆρα καὶ τοῦτο ἵστασθαι
ἀνάγκη, ἢ καὶ τοῦτ' ἐνδέξεται εἰς ἄπειρον ἰέναι;
· διαφέρει δὲ τοῦτο τοῦ πρότερον τοσοῦτον, ὅτι τὸ
μέν ἐστιν, ἆρα ἐνδέχεται ἀρξαμένῳ ἀπὸ τοιούτου ὃ
40 μηδενὶ ὑπάρχει ἑτέρῳ ἀλλ' ἄλλο ἐκείνῳ, ἐπὶ τὸ
ἄνω εἰς ἄπειρον ἰέναι, θάτερον δὲ ἀρξάμενον ἀπὸ
82 a τοιούτου ὃ αὐτὸ μὲν ἄλλου ἐκείνου δὲ μηδὲν κατηγορεῖται, ἐπὶ τὸ κάτω σκοπεῖν εἰ ἐνδέχεται εἰς
ἄπειρον ἰέναι. ἔτι τὰ μεταξὺ ἆρ' ἐνδέχεται ἄπειρα
εἶναι ὡρισμένων τῶν ἄκρων; λέγω δ' οἷον εἰ τὸ Α
5 τῷ Γ ὑπάρχει, μέσον δ' αὐτῶν τὸ Β, τοῦ δὲ Β καὶ
τοῦ Α ἕτερα, τούτων δ' ἄλλα, ἆρα καὶ ταῦτα εἰς
ἄπειρον ἐνδέχεται ἰέναι, ἢ ἀδύνατον; ἔστι δὲ τοῦτο
σκοπεῖν ταὐτὸ καὶ εἰ αἱ ἀποδείξεις εἰς ἄπειρον
ἔρχονται, καὶ εἰ ἔστιν ἀπόδειξις ἅπαντος, ἢ πρὸς
ἄλληλα περαίνεται. ὁμοίως δὲ λέγω καὶ ἐπὶ τῶν
10 στερητικῶν συλλογισμῶν καὶ προτάσεων, οἷον εἰ τὸ
Α μὴ ὑπάρχει τῷ Β μηδενί, ἤτοι πρώτῳ, ἢ ἔσται
τι μεταξὺ ᾧ προτέρῳ οὐχ ὑπάρχει (οἷον εἰ τῷ[1] Η,

[1] τῷ A²n : τὸ ABd.

---

[a] The distinction which Aristotle is drawing between
natural subjects and natural attributes is partly obscured in
Greek by the substantival use of the neuter adjective. What
he seems to mean here is that " white " is not really the sub-

white [a]—, some things, then, are such that they are of their own nature predicable. Let C be such that it does not further apply to any other term, but B applies directly to C, and there is no other term mediating between them. Again, let E apply in the same way to F, and F to B. Is there then any necessary limit to this series, or may it proceed to infinity? Again, if nothing is of itself predicable of A, but A applies directly to H and to no intermediate term first, and H applies to G and G to B, must this series too come to an end, or may it too proceed to infinity? The latter question differs from the former in that the first asks " Is it possible, if we start from a term such that it applies to nothing else, but something else applies to it, to proceed to infinity in the upward direction? " and the latter asks whether, if we start from a term such that it is itself predicable of something else, but nothing is predicable of it, we can proceed to infinity in the downward direction. Further, can the intermediate terms be infinite in number when the extremes are definite? I mean, e.g., if A applies to C, and B is their middle term, and other terms are predicable of B and A, and again other terms are predicable of these, can these too proceed to infinity, or is this impossible? To inquire into this is the same as to inquire whether demonstrations form an infinite series, i.e., whether there is a demonstration of everything, or the extremes are limited in relation one to the other. Similarly too in the case of negative syllogisms and premisses ; e.g., if A applies to no B, either it does so directly, or there will be some intermediate term, e.g., G, to which it first does not apply,

Can predication form an infinite chain (1) of attributes from a fixed subject, (2) of subjects from a fixed attribute,

(3) by interpolation between fixed extremes?

ject of which " man " is predicated, but an accidental attribute of that subject.

ὃ τῷ Β ὑπάρχει παντί) καὶ πάλιν τούτου ἔτι ἄλλῳ
προτέρῳ, οἷον εἰ τῷ[1] Θ, ὃ τῷ Η παντὶ ὑπάρχει. καὶ
γὰρ ἐπὶ τούτων ἢ ἄπειρα οἷς ὑπάρχει προτέροις ἢ
ἵσταται.

15 Ἐπὶ δὲ τῶν ἀντιστρεφόντων οὐχ ὁμοίως ἔχει. οὐ
γὰρ ἔστιν ἐν τοῖς ἀντικατηγορουμένοις[2] οὗ πρώτου
κατηγορεῖται ἢ τελευταίου· πάντα γὰρ πρὸς πάντα
ταύτῃ γε ὁμοίως ἔχει, εἴτ' ἐστὶν ἄπειρα τὰ κατ'
αὐτοῦ κατηγορούμενα εἴτ' ἀμφότερά ἐστι τὰ ἀπορη-
θέντα ἄπειρα· πλὴν εἰ μὴ ὁμοίως ἐνδέχεται ἀντι-
20 στρέφειν, ἀλλὰ τὸ μὲν ὡς συμβεβηκὸς τὸ δ' ὡς
κατηγορίαν.

XX. Ὅτι μὲν οὖν τὰ μεταξὺ οὐκ ἐνδέχεται ἄπειρα εἶναι, εἰ ἐπὶ τὸ κάτω καὶ τὸ ἄνω ἵστανται αἱ
κατηγορίαι, δῆλον (λέγω δ' ἄνω μὲν τὴν ἐπὶ τὸ
καθόλου μᾶλλον, κάτω δὲ τὴν ἐπὶ τὸ κατὰ μέρος).
25 εἰ γὰρ τοῦ Α κατηγορουμένου κατὰ τοῦ Ζ ἄπειρα
τὰ μεταξύ, ἐφ' ὧν Β, δῆλον ὅτι ἐνδέχοιτ' ἂν ὥστε
καὶ ἀπὸ τοῦ Α ἐπὶ τὸ κάτω ἕτερον ἑτέρου κατηγορεῖσθαι εἰς ἄπειρον (πρὶν γὰρ ἐπὶ τὸ Ζ ἐλθεῖν
ἄπειρα τὰ μεταξύ) καὶ ἀπὸ τοῦ Ζ ἐπὶ τὸ ἄνω
ἄπειρα πρὶν ἐπὶ τὸ Α ἐλθεῖν· ὥστ' εἰ ταῦτα ἀδύνατα,
30 καὶ τοῦ Α καὶ Ζ ἀδύνατον ἄπειρα εἶναι μεταξύ.

---

[1] τῷ A[2]n : τὸ ABd.
[2] κατηγορουμένοις A[1]Bd.

---

[a] In the sense that predicate and subject are strictly interchangeable.
[b] i.e., additional attributes or additional subjects. In this
case, however, the distinction is meaningless, because (the

but which applies to all B; and again some other term prior to G, *e.g.*, H, to which A does not apply, but which applies to all G. In this case too either the intermediate terms to which A is more directly related in attribution are infinite in number, or the series has a limit.

If the premises are convertible,[a] however, the conditions are not the same. Where the terms are reciprocally predicable there is none of which another is primarily or ultimately predicated, since in this respect all are similarly related, whether the terms predicated of the subject are infinite in number or both classes [b] about which we expressed uncertainty are infinite in number. The only exception is if the terms are not convertible in the same way, but one only accidentally and the other as a true predicate.[c]

XX. It is obvious that the intermediate terms cannot be infinite in number if there is an upward and a downward limit to predication (by " upward " I mean in the direction of the universal, and by " downward " in that of the particular). For if when A is predicated of F the intermediate terms—B—are infinite in number, clearly it would be possible both starting from A to predicate one term of another in the downward direction to infinity (since the intermediate terms before one reaches F are infinite in number), and starting from F to predicate to infinity in the upward direction before one reaches A. Thus if these results are impossible, it is also impossible that there should be infinitely many intermediate terms between A and

terms being mutually predicable of one another) none is either subject or attribute more than another. Such terms (*e.g.*, properties of a species) form a circle, not a series, of predication.

  [c] *Cf.* 81 b 25-29.

If subject and predicate are interchangeable there is no series.

Between fixed extremes there is no infinite chain in affirmative predication.

82 a

οὐδὲ γὰρ εἴ τις λέγοι ὅτι τὰ μέν ἐστι τῶν ΑΒΖ¹
ἐχόμενα ἀλλήλων ὥστε μὴ εἶναι μεταξύ, τὰ δ' οὐκ
ἔστι λαβεῖν, οὐδὲν διαφέρει. ὃ γὰρ ἂν λάβω τῶν
Β, ἔσται πρὸς τὸ Α ἢ πρὸς τὸ Ζ ἢ ἄπειρα τὰ
μεταξὺ ἢ οὔ. ἀφ' οὗ δὴ πρῶτον ἄπειρα, εἴτ' εὐθὺς
35 εἴτε μὴ εὐθύς, οὐδὲν διαφέρει· τὰ γὰρ μετὰ ταῦτα
ἄπειρά ἐστιν.

XXI. Φανερὸν δὲ καὶ ἐπὶ τῆς στερητικῆς ἀποδείξεως ὅτι στήσεται, εἴπερ ἐπὶ τῆς κατηγορικῆς
ἵσταται ἐπ' ἀμφότερα. ἔστω γὰρ μὴ ἐνδεχόμενον
μήτε ἐπὶ τὸ ἄνω ἀπὸ τοῦ ὑστάτου εἰς ἄπειρον ἰέναι
82 b (λέγω δ' ὕστατον ὃ αὐτὸ μὲν ἄλλῳ μηδενὶ ὑπάρχει,
ἐκείνῳ δὲ ἄλλο, οἷον τὸ Ζ) μήτε ἀπὸ τοῦ πρώτου
ἐπὶ τὸ ὕστατον (λέγω δὲ πρῶτον ὃ αὐτὸ μὲν κατ'
ἄλλου, κατ' ἐκείνου δὲ μηδὲν ἄλλο). εἰ δὴ ταῦτ'
ἔστι, καὶ ἐπὶ τῆς ἀποφάσεως στήσεται. τριχῶς γὰρ
5 δείκνυται μὴ ὑπάρχον. ἢ γὰρ ᾧ μὲν τὸ Γ, τὸ Β
ὑπάρχει παντί, ᾧ δὲ τὸ Β, οὐδενὶ τὸ Α. τοῦ μὲν
τοίνυν ΒΓ, καὶ ἀεὶ τοῦ ἑτέρου διαστήματος, ἀνάγκη βαδίζειν εἰς ἄμεσα· κατηγορικὸν γὰρ τοῦτο τὸ
διάστημα. τὸ δ' ἕτερον δῆλον ὅτι εἰ ἄλλῳ οὐχ
ὑπάρχει προτέρῳ, οἷον τῷ Δ, τοῦτο δεήσει τῷ Β
10 παντὶ ὑπάρχειν· καὶ εἰ πάλιν ἄλλῳ τοῦ Δ προτέρῳ
οὐχ ὑπάρχει, ἐκεῖνο δεήσει τῷ Δ παντὶ ὑπάρχειν·

¹ ΑΒΖ Waitz : ΑΒΓ ABdn : ΑΒ Μ, Bekker.

ᵃ Sc., from A or F.
ᵇ The argument is : A negative conclusion can be proved
in each of the three figures. In any example (Aristotle gives
one in each figure, viz. Celarent, Camestres and Bocardo) (1)
we cannot assume an infinitive number of middles between

114

F. Nor does it affect the case supposing that it be said that some of the terms in the series AB . . . F are contiguous, so that there can be no intermediates between them, and that others cannot be grasped at all ; for whatever B we take, the intermediates in the direction of either A or F will either be infinite in number or not. It makes no difference where the infinite series first starts, whether immediately[a] or not ; the rest of the terms are infinite in number.

XXI. If there is a limit to the series in both directions in affirmative demonstration, evidently there will be a limit in negative demonstrations also. Let it be impossible to continue to infinity either upwards from the last term (by " last term " I mean that which applies to no other term, whereas some other term, *e.g.*, F, applies to it) or from the first term towards the last (by " first term " I mean that which is predicable of another but has no other term predicated of it). If these conditions obtain, there will be a limit in negation too. There are three ways in which one term can be proved not to apply to another.[b] (1) B applies to all that to which C applies, but A to none of that to which B applies. Now in the premiss BC, and generally in the minor premiss, we must reach immediate propositions, because this premiss is affirmative. As for the other term,[c] clearly if it is inapplicable to another prior term, *e.g.*, D, this term will have to apply to all B. Again, if it is inapplicable to another term prior to D, that term will have to

If affirmative predication must have limits, so must negative.

Proof in the first figure.

the terms of an affirmative premiss ; (2) mediation of a negative premiss always gives two new premisses, one affirmative and one negative ; since the former are limited in number, the latter must be too.

[c] *Viz.* A. BeA is proved by DeA and BaD ; and similarly with DeA.

ὥστ' ἐπεὶ ἡ ἐπὶ τὸ ἄνω[1] ἵσταται ὁδός, καὶ ἡ ἐπὶ τὸ
Α[2] στήσεται, καὶ ἔσται τι πρῶτον ᾧ οὐχ ὑπάρχει.

Πάλιν εἰ τὸ μὲν Β παντὶ τῷ Α τῷ δὲ Γ μηδενί,
τὸ Α τῶν[3] Γ οὐδενὶ ὑπάρχει. πάλιν τοῦτο εἰ δεῖ δεῖ-
15 ξαι, δῆλον ὅτι ἢ διὰ τοῦ ἄνω τρόπου δειχθήσεται
ἢ διὰ τούτου ἢ διὰ τοῦ τρίτου. ὁ μὲν οὖν πρῶτος
εἴρηται, ὁ δὲ δεύτερος δειχθήσεται. οὕτω δ' ἂν
δεικνύοι, οἷον ὅτι τὸ Δ τῷ μὲν Β παντὶ ὑπάρχει τῷ
δὲ Γ οὐδενί, εἰ ἀνάγκη ὑπάρχειν τι τῷ Β. καὶ
πάλιν εἰ τοῦτο τῷ Γ μὴ ὑπάρξει, ἄλλο τῷ Δ
20 ὑπάρχει, ὃ τῷ Γ οὐχ ὑπάρχει. οὐκοῦν ἐπεὶ τὸ
ὑπάρχειν ἀεὶ τῷ ἀνωτέρω ἵσταται, στήσεται καὶ τὸ
μὴ ὑπάρχειν.

Ὁ δὲ τρίτος τρόπος ἦν· εἰ τὸ μὲν Α τῷ Β παντὶ
ὑπάρχει, τὸ δὲ Γ μὴ ὑπάρχει, οὐ παντὶ ὑπάρχει τὸ
Γ ᾧ τὸ Α. πάλιν δὲ τοῦτο ἢ διὰ τῶν ἄνω εἰ-
25 ρημένων ἢ ὁμοίως δειχθήσεται. ἐκείνως μὲν δὴ
ἵσταται· εἰ δ' οὕτω, πάλιν λήψεται τὸ Β τῷ Ε
ὑπάρχειν, ᾧ τὸ Γ μὴ παντὶ ὑπάρχει. καὶ τοῦτο
πάλιν ὁμοίως. ἐπεὶ δ' ὑπόκειται ἵστασθαι καὶ ἐπὶ
τὸ κάτω, δῆλον ὅτι στήσεται καὶ τὸ Γ οὐχ ὑπάρχον.

Φανερὸν δ' ὅτι καὶ ἐὰν μὴ μιᾷ ὁδῷ δεικνύηται
30 ἀλλὰ πάσαις, ὁτὲ μὲν ἐκ τοῦ πρώτου σχήματος ὁτὲ

---

[1] κάτω fecit n, Bekker.
[2] Α n[1], Ross: Δ ABd: ἄνω n[2].   [3] τῷ D.

---

[a] The required sense is fairly clear, and Ross's readings,
which I have adopted, are at least compatible with it; but
the text is barely convincing.
[b] Not the conclusion, but the negative premiss CeB.
[c] i.e., by the first, second or third figure.
[d] As before, not only a negative but an affirmative premiss

apply to all D. Thus since the upward ⟨affirmative⟩ process is limited, the ⟨negative⟩ process towards A will be limited too,[a] and there will be some first term to which A does not apply.

(2) If B applies to all A but to no C, A applies to no C. If it is now required to prove this,[b] clearly the proof will either be by the method described above, or by the present method, or by the third.[c] The first has been stated already ; the second will be proved now. The proof will be as follows : D applies to all B, but to no C (since some predicate must apply to B).[d] Again, since D is not to apply to C, some other term which does not apply to C applies to D. Thus since the affirmative series of attribution is limited in the upward direction, the negative series will also be limited. *Proof in the second figure.*

(3) The third case is, as we have seen [e] ; if A applies and C does not apply to all B, C does not apply to all that to which A applies. This [f] again can be proved either by the foregoing methods or by a similar one. In the former case the series is clearly limited ; in the latter we shall assume this time that B applies to E, to not all of which C applies ; and this again will be proved similarly. Since we have assumed that there is a downward limit also,[g] clearly there will be a limit to the non-attribution of C. *Proof in the third figure.*

It is evident that even if the proof is not effected by one method but by all three—now by the first *If all three figures are used, the result is the same.*

must be interpolated. Ross's interpretation " if in fact there is any particular term D that necessarily belongs to B " seems improbable.

[e] If this is the meaning here of the " philosophical imperfect," the reference is presumably to the discussion of the third figure in *An. Pr.* I. vi.

[f] The negative premiss BoC.   [g] 82 a 37.

82 b

δὲ ἐκ τοῦ δευτέρου ἢ τρίτου, ὅτι καὶ οὕτω στήσεται· πεπερασμέναι γάρ εἰσιν αἱ ὁδοί, τὰ δὲ πεπερασμένα πεπερασμενάκις ἀνάγκη πεπεράνθαι πάντα.

35 Ὅτι μὲν οὖν ἐπὶ τῆς στερήσεως, εἴπερ καὶ ἐπὶ τοῦ ὑπάρχειν, ἵσταται, δῆλον· ὅτι δ᾽ ἐπ᾽ ἐκείνων, λογικῶς μὲν θεωροῦσιν ὧδε φανερόν.

XXII. Ἐπὶ μὲν οὖν τῶν ἐν τῷ τί ἐστι κατηγορουμένων δῆλον· εἰ γὰρ ἔστιν ὁρίσασθαι ἢ εἰ γνωστὸν τὸ τί ἦν εἶναι, τὰ δ᾽ ἄπειρα μὴ ἔστι δι-

83 a ελθεῖν, ἀνάγκη πεπεράνθαι τὰ ἐν τῷ τί ἐστι κατηγορούμενα. καθόλου δὲ ὧδε λέγωμεν. ἔστι γὰρ εἰπεῖν ἀληθῶς τὸ λευκὸν βαδίζειν καὶ τὸ μέγα ἐκεῖνο ξύλον εἶναι, καὶ πάλιν τὸ ξύλον μέγα εἶναι καὶ τὸν ἄνθρωπον βαδίζειν. ἕτερον δή ἐστι τὸ

5 οὕτως εἰπεῖν καὶ τὸ ἐκείνως. ὅταν μὲν γὰρ τὸ λευκὸν εἶναι φῶ ξύλον, τότε λέγω ὅτι ᾧ συμβέβηκε λευκῷ εἶναι ξύλον ἐστίν, ἀλλ᾽ οὐχ ὡς τὸ ὑποκείμενον τῷ ξύλῳ τὸ λευκόν ἐστι· καὶ γὰρ οὔτε λευκὸν ὂν οὔθ᾽ ὅπερ λευκόν τι ἐγένετο ξύλον, ὥστ᾽ οὐκ ἔστιν ἀλλ᾽ ἢ κατὰ συμβεβηκός. ὅταν δὲ τὸ ξύλον

10 λευκὸν εἶναι φῶ, οὐχ ὅτι ἕτερόν τί ἐστι λευκόν, ἐκείνῳ δὲ συμβέβηκε ξύλῳ εἶναι, οἷον ὅταν τὸν μουσικὸν λευκὸν εἶναι φῶ (τότε γὰρ ὅτι ὁ ἄνθρωπος λευκός ἐστιν, ᾧ συμβέβηκεν εἶναι μουσικῷ, λέγω), ἀλλὰ τὸ ξύλον ἐστὶ τὸ ὑποκείμενον, ὅπερ καὶ ἐγένετο, οὐχ ἕτερόν τι ὂν ἢ ὅπερ ξύλον ἢ ξύλον τί. εἰ

---

a Cf. 81 b 25-29.

figure, now by the second or third—even so the series will be limited ; for the methods are finite in number, and the product of a finite number of things taken in a finite number of ways must always be finite.

Thus it is clear that there is a limit to the series of negative attribution, if there is a limit in affirmative attribution also. That there is one in the latter case will be apparent in the light of the following dialectical argument.

Now to prove that predication has a limit.

XXII. In the case of predicates which form part of the essence, it is obvious ⟨that there is a limit⟩ ; since if definition is possible, *i.e.*, if the essential nature is knowable, and things infinite in number cannot be exhausted, the predicates which form part of the essence must be limited in number. But we can treat the question generally as follows. It is possible to state truly " the white ⟨object⟩ walks " and " that large thing is wood " and again " the ⟨piece of⟩ wood is large " and " the man walks." [a] The two latter statements are quite different from the two former. When I say " the white thing is wood " I mean that the subject of which whiteness is an accident is wood, not that whiteness is the substrate in which the wood inheres ; for it was not *qua* white or *qua* a particular kind of white that the white thing became wood, and so it is wood only accidentally. But when I say " the wood is white," I do not mean that something else is white, and that it is an accident of that something else to be wood, as when I say " the cultured ⟨person⟩ is white " ; for then I mean that the man, of whom it is an accident to be cultured, is white ; but the wood is the substrate, which actually became white, not *qua* anything else, but *qua* wood in general or a par-

Predication. Essential attributes must be limited.

Predication proper distinguished from accidental predication.

119

83 a

15 δὴ δεῖ νομοθετῆσαι, ἔστω τὸ οὕτω λέγειν κατηγορεῖν, τὸ δ' ἐκείνως ἤτοι μηδαμῶς κατηγορεῖν, ἢ
κατηγορεῖν μὲν μὴ ἁπλῶς, κατὰ συμβεβηκὸς δὲ
κατηγορεῖν. ἔστι δ' ὡς μὲν τὸ λευκὸν τὸ κατηγορούμενον, ὡς δὲ τὸ ξύλον τὸ οὗ κατηγορεῖται.
20 ὑποκείσθω δὴ τὸ κατηγορούμενον κατηγορεῖσθαι
ἀεί, οὗ κατηγορεῖται, ἁπλῶς, ἀλλὰ μὴ κατὰ συμ-
βεβηκός· οὕτω γὰρ αἱ ἀποδείξεις ἀποδεικνύουσιν.
ὥστε ἢ ἐν τῷ τί ἐστιν ἢ ὅτι ποιὸν ἢ ποσὸν ἢ πρός
τι ἢ ποιοῦν ἢ πάσχον ἢ ποὺ ἢ ποτέ, ὅταν ἓν καθ'
ἑνὸς κατηγορηθῇ.

Ἔτι τὰ μὲν οὐσίαν σημαίνοντα ὅπερ ἐκεῖνο ἢ
25 ὅπερ ἐκεῖνό τι σημαίνει καθ' οὗ κατηγορεῖται· ὅσα
δὲ μὴ οὐσίαν σημαίνει, ἀλλὰ κατ' ἄλλου ὑποκειμένου λέγεται ὃ μή ἐστι μήτε ὅπερ ἐκεῖνο μήτε
ὅπερ ἐκεῖνό τι, συμβεβηκότα, οἷον κατὰ τοῦ ἀνθρώπου τὸ λευκόν. οὐ γάρ ἐστιν ὁ ἄνθρωπος οὔτε
30 ὅπερ λευκὸν οὔτε ὅπερ λευκόν τι, ἀλλὰ ζῷον ἴσως·
ὅπερ γὰρ ζῷόν ἐστιν ὁ ἄνθρωπος. ὅσα δὲ μὴ
οὐσίαν σημαίνει, δεῖ κατά τινος ὑποκειμένου κατηγορεῖσθαι, καὶ μὴ εἶναί τι λευκὸν ὃ οὐχ ἕτερόν τι
ὂν λευκόν ἐστιν. τὰ γὰρ εἴδη χαιρέτω· τερετίσ-
ματά τε γάρ ἐστι, καὶ εἰ ἔστιν, οὐδὲν πρὸς τὸν
35 λόγον ἐστίν· αἱ γὰρ ἀποδείξεις περὶ τῶν τοιούτων
εἰσίν.

_____

ᵃ Here, as often, the categories of " position " and " state "
are omitted (for the full list see *Cat.* 1 b 25). In any case
completeness is unnecessary since the distinction is between
essential and non-essential attributes.

ᵇ In the sense of non-essential attributes.

ticular piece of wood. Thus if we are to lay down a general rule, let us call the latter kind of assertion predication, and the former kind either not predication at all, or predication not in an unqualified but in an accidental sense. The predicate corresponds to " white " in the example, and the subject to " wood." Let us assume, then, that the predicate is predicated of the subject, not accidentally but always without qualification, for that is how demonstrations conduct their proofs. Then, when one term is predicated of another, that which is stated is either part of the essence, or quality, quantity, relation, activity, passivity, place or time.[a]

Further, predicates which denote essence indicate that the subject is identical with the predicate or with some part of the predicate ; but those which do not denote essence, but are stated of some other subject, which is identical neither with the predicate nor with some part of the predicate, indicate accidents,[b] as e.g., " white " is predicated of " man " ; man is identical neither with " white " nor with some particular form of " white " ; but he is presumably an animal ; for man is identical with a particular kind of animal. Predicates which do not denote essence must be predicated of some subject ; a thing cannot be white unless it is something else first. The Forms may be dismissed—they are mere prattle[c] ; and even if they exist, they are irrelevant, because demonstrations are concerned only with such predicates as we have described.

Non-essential predicates require a subject of their own.

[c] In view of Aristotle's debt to the Platonic Forms, it is ungenerous of him to describe the theory by a word which in Greek suggests the twittering of birds or a person's aimless humming. No doubt his indignation is roused by the thought of Forms as self-subsistent attributes.

ARISTOTLE

Ἔτι εἰ μή ἐστι τόδε τοῦδε[1] ποιότης κἀκεῖνο
τούτου, μηδὲ ποιότητος ποιότης, ἀδύνατον ἀντι-
κατηγορεῖσθαι ἀλλήλων οὕτως, ἀλλ' ἀληθὲς μὲν
ἐνδέχεται εἰπεῖν, ἀντικατηγορῆσαι δ' ἀληθῶς οὐκ
ἐνδέχεται. ἢ γάρ τοι ὡς οὐσία κατηγορηθήσεται,
οἷον ἢ γένος ὂν ἢ διαφορὰ τοῦ κατηγορουμένου.
ταῦτα δὲ δέδεικται ὅτι οὐκ ἔσται ἄπειρα, οὔτ' ἐπὶ
τὸ κάτω· οὔτ' ἐπὶ τὸ ἄνω (οἷον ἄνθρωπος δίπουν,
τοῦτο ζῷον, τοῦτο δ' ἕτερον· οὐδὲ τὸ ζῷον κατ'
5 ἀνθρώπου, τοῦτο δὲ κατὰ Καλλίου, τοῦτο δὲ κατ'
ἄλλου ἐν τῷ τί ἐστιν), τὴν μὲν γὰρ οὐσίαν ἅπασαν
ἔστιν ὁρίσασθαι τὴν τοιαύτην, τὰ δ' ἄπειρα οὐκ
ἔστι διεξελθεῖν νοοῦντα. ὥστ' οὔτ' ἐπὶ τὸ ἄνω οὔτ'
ἐπὶ τὸ κάτω ἄπειρα· ἐκείνην γὰρ οὐκ ἔστιν ὁρίσασθαι, ἧς τὰ ἄπειρα κατηγορεῖται. ὡς μὲν δὴ γένη
10 ἀλλήλων οὐκ ἀντικατηγορηθήσεται· ἔσται γὰρ αὐτὸ
ὅπερ αὐτό τι. οὐδὲ μὴν τοῦ ποιοῦ ἢ τῶν ἄλλων
οὐδέν, ἂν μὴ κατὰ συμβεβηκὸς κατηγορηθῇ· πάντα
γὰρ ταῦτα συμβέβηκε καὶ κατὰ τῶν οὐσιῶν κατηγορεῖται. ἀλλὰ δὴ ὅτι οὐδ' εἰς τὸ ἄνω ἄπειρα
ἔσται· ἑκάστου γὰρ κατηγορεῖται ὃ ἂν σημαίνῃ ἢ
15 ποιόν τι ἢ ποσόν τι ἤ τι τῶν τοιούτων ἢ τὰ ἐν τῇ
οὐσίᾳ· ταῦτα δὲ πεπέρανται, καὶ τὰ γένη τῶν κατηγοριῶν πεπέρανται· ἢ γὰρ ποιὸν ἢ ποσὸν ἢ πρός τι
ἢ ποιοῦν ἢ πάσχον ἢ ποὺ ἢ ποτέ.

---

[1] τόδε τοῦδε n, Philoponus : τοῦτο τουδὶ ABd.

---

[a] *Sc.*, " and the downward limit is the individual."
[b] If X = part of Y, and Y = part of X, each will be identical
with part of (part of) itself.
[c] 82 b 37.

Further, if it is not possible both for X to be a quality of Y and *vice versa*, *i.e.*, if there cannot be a quality of a quality, X and Y cannot be predicated reciprocally in the way in which we have laid down. It may be true to state one of the other, but the reciprocating statement cannot be true. For (1) the predicate may be stated as substance, *i.e.*, the genus or differentia of the subject. (It has been shown that predication of this kind cannot proceed to infinity either upwards or downwards—*e.g.*, man is biped, biped is animal, animal is something else ; or animal is predicated of man, man of Callias, and Callias of something else which is part of the essence—for every substance of this sort can be defined, but it is impossible to exhaust in thought an infinite series. Hence the series cannot be infinite either upwards or downwards, for we cannot define a substance of which an infinite number of terms is predicated.[a]) Then they cannot be predicated as genera of each other, for then a thing will be identical with a particular part of itself.[b] (2) Nor can anything be predicated reciprocally of quality or any of the other categories, except accidentally ; for all these are attributes and are predicable only of substances. As for the proof that the series will not be infinite in the upper direction, at every step the predicate denotes either quality or quantity or one of the other categories, or else the elements in the essence. But the latter are limited in number,[c] and so are the kinds of categories, *viz.*, quality, quantity, relation, activity, passivity, place and time.[d]

Predication proper is non-recipro-cating.

[d] *Cf.* 83 a 21. That even the full list of ten categories is exhaustive is nowhere proved, nor indeed is it capable of proof.

Ὑπόκειται δὲ ἓν καθ' ἑνὸς κατηγορεῖσθαι, αὐτὰ
δὲ αὑτῶν, ὅσα μὴ τί ἐστι, μὴ κατηγορεῖσθαι. συμ-
20 βεβηκότα γάρ ἐστι πάντα, ἀλλὰ τὰ μὲν καθ' αὑτά,
τὰ δὲ καθ' ἕτερον τρόπον· ταῦτα δὲ πάντα καθ'
ὑποκειμένου τινὸς κατηγορεῖσθαί φαμεν, τὸ δὲ συμβεβηκὸς οὐκ εἶναι ὑποκείμενόν τι· οὐδὲν γὰρ τῶν
τοιούτων τίθεμεν εἶναι ὃ οὐχ ἕτερόν τι ὂν λέγεται
ὃ λέγεται, ἀλλ' αὐτὸ ἄλλου καὶ ἄλλ' ἄττα καθ'
25 ἑτέρου. οὔτ' εἰς τὸ ἄνω ἄρα ἓν καθ' ἑνὸς οὔτ' εἰς
τὸ κάτω ὑπάρχειν λεχθήσεται. καθ' ὧν μὲν γὰρ
λέγεται τὰ συμβεβηκότα, ὅσα ἐν τῇ οὐσίᾳ ἑκάστου·
ταῦτα δὲ οὐκ ἄπειρα· ἄνω δὲ ταῦτά τε καὶ τὰ συμβεβηκότα, ἀμφότερα οὐκ ἄπειρα. ἀνάγκη ἄρα
εἶναί τι οὗ πρῶτόν τι κατηγορεῖται καὶ τούτου
30 ἄλλο, καὶ τοῦτο ἵστασθαι καὶ εἶναί τι ὃ οὐκέτι οὔτε
κατ' ἄλλου προτέρου οὔτε κατ' ἐκείνου ἄλλο πρότερον κατηγορεῖται.

Εἷς μὲν οὖν τρόπος λέγεται ἀποδείξεως οὗτος,
ἔτι δ' ἄλλος, εἰ ὧν πρότερα ἄττα κατηγορεῖται,
ἔστι τούτων ἀπόδειξις, ὧν δ' ἔστιν ἀπόδειξις, οὔτε
35 βέλτιον ἔχειν ἐγχωρεῖ πρὸς αὐτὰ τοῦ εἰδέναι, οὔτ'
εἰδέναι ἄνευ ἀποδείξεως, εἰ δὲ τόδε διὰ τῶνδε γνώ-

---

[a] Definitory predicates are (in a sense at least) convertible with their subjects.

[b] i.e., as a subject. Mure and Ross seem to be mistaken in taking τοιούτων as referring to συμβεβηκότα.

[c] Cf. 82 b 37, 83 b 15.

[d] Cf. 83 b 13.

[e] Predication is limited at one end by the individual substance, at the other by the highest genus or category.

[f] i.e., premises which depend upon other premises.

We have now established that in predication one Recapitula-
tion, lead-
ing to predicate is asserted of one subject, and that predicates (except those which denote essence [a]) are not predicated of one another. They are all attributes, some *per se* and others in a different sense ; but we hold that they are all predicated of some subject, whereas an attribute is not a kind of subject ; because we do not regard as such [b] anything which is not something else distinct from the statement which is made about it, but is merely stated of some other term, while other attributes are predicated of a different subject. It follows that the assertion of a first dia-
lectical
proof. single predicate of a single subject cannot form an infinite series either upwards or downwards ; for the subjects of which the attributes are stated are no more than those which are implied in the essence of the individual, and these are not infinite in number [c]; while in the upward direction we have these subjects and their attributes, both of which are limited in number.[d] Hence there must be some subject of which something is first predicated, and something else must be predicated of this, and the series must be finite ; *i.e.*, there must be a term which is not predicated of any other term prior to it, and of which no other prior term is predicated.[e]

This is a statement of one manner of proof, but Second dia-
lectical
proof. there is another also ; predicates of whose subjects other prior predicates can be predicated [f] are demonstrable ; and it is not possible to stand in a better relation [g] than that of knowledge to anything which is demonstrable, nor to know it apart from demonstration. Moreover, if one thing is knowable through

[g] Aristotle refers to intuition, by which we apprehend the indemonstrable ; *cf.* Book II, ch. xix.

ριμον, τάδε δὲ μὴ ἴσμεν μηδὲ βέλτιον ἔχομεν πρὸς
αὐτὰ τοῦ εἰδέναι, οὐδὲ τὸ διὰ τούτων γνώριμον ἐπι-
στησόμεθα. εἰ οὖν ἔστι τι εἰδέναι δι᾽ ἀποδείξεως
ἁπλῶς καὶ μὴ ἐκ τινῶν μηδ᾽ ἐξ ὑποθέσεως, ἀνάγκη
84 a ἵστασθαι τὰς κατηγορίας τὰς μεταξύ. εἰ γὰρ μὴ
ἵστανται, ἀλλ᾽ ἔστιν ἀεὶ τοῦ ληφθέντος ἐπάνω,
ἁπάντων ἔσται ἀπόδειξις· ὥστ᾽ εἰ τὰ ἄπειρα μὴ ἐγχωρεῖ διελθεῖν, ὧν ἔστιν ἀπόδειξις, ταῦτ᾽ οὐκ εἰσό-
μεθα δι᾽ ἀποδείξεως. εἰ οὖν μηδὲ βέλτιον ἔχομεν
5 πρὸς αὐτὰ τοῦ εἰδέναι, οὐκ ἔσται οὐδὲν ἐπίστασθαι
δι᾽ ἀποδείξεως ἁπλῶς, ἀλλ᾽ ἐξ ὑποθέσεως.

Λογικῶς μὲν οὖν ἐκ τούτων ἄν τις πιστεύσειε
περὶ τοῦ λεχθέντος, ἀναλυτικῶς δὲ διὰ τῶνδε φανερὸν συντομώτερον, ὅτι οὔτ᾽ ἐπὶ τὸ ἄνω οὔτ᾽ ἐπὶ τὸ
10 κάτω ἄπειρα τὰ κατηγορούμενα ἐνδέχεται εἶναι ἐν
ταῖς ἀποδεικτικαῖς ἐπιστήμαις, περὶ ὧν ἡ σκέψις
ἐστίν.

Ἡ μὲν γὰρ ἀπόδειξίς ἐστι τῶν ὅσα ὑπάρχει καθ᾽
αὐτὰ τοῖς πράγμασιν. καθ᾽ αὐτὰ δὲ διττῶς· ὅσα τε
γὰρ ἐν[1] ἐκείνοις ἐνυπάρχει ἐν τῷ τί ἐστι, καὶ οἷς
αὐτὰ ἐν τῷ τί ἐστιν ὑπάρχουσιν αὐτοῖς· οἷον τῷ
15 ἀριθμῷ τὸ περιττόν, ὃ ὑπάρχει μὲν ἀριθμῷ, ἐνυπάρχει δ᾽ αὐτὸς ὁ ἀριθμὸς ἐν τῷ λόγῳ αὐτοῦ, καὶ
πάλιν πλῆθος ἢ τὸ διαιρετὸν ἐν τῷ λόγῳ τοῦ
ἀριθμοῦ ἐνυπάρχει. τούτων δ᾽ οὐδέτερα ἐνδέχεται

[1] ἐν secl. Jaeger.

---

[a] The proof is called analytical because it is based upon
a principle of the relevant science, viz., demonstration.
[b] See a 18 infra.

certain others, and we do not know the latter or stand in a better relation to them than that of knowledge, we shall have no scientific knowledge of that which is knowable through them. If, then, it is possible to know a thing absolutely through demonstration, and not as a qualified or hypothetical consequence, the series of intermediate predications must have a limit. If there is no limit, and there is always something higher than the term last taken, everything will be demonstrable. Therefore, since it is impossible to traverse the numerically infinite, we shall not know by means of demonstration those predicates which are demonstrable. Hence if at the same time we do not stand in a better relation to them than that of knowledge, it will not be possible to have scientific knowledge of anything absolutely through demonstration, but only hypothetically.

One might be convinced dialectically of the truth of our contention from the foregoing discussion; but by analytical [a] method it can be apprehended more readily from the following arguments that there cannot be either in the upward or in the downward direction an infinite series of predicates in the demonstrative sciences, which are the subject of our investigation.

Demonstration is concerned with the essential *Analytical* attributes of things. There are two senses in which *proof.* attributes may be essential; (*a*) because they inhere in the essence of their subjects, or (*b*) because their subjects inhere in their essence. An example of (*b*) is the relation of " odd " [b] to number; " odd " is an attribute of number, and number itself is inherent in the definition of " odd." On the other hand, (*a*) plurality or divisibility is inherent in the definition of number. Neither of these processes of attribution

127

ἄπειρα εἶναι, οὔθ' ὡς τὸ περιττὸν τοῦ ἀριθμοῦ
(πάλιν γὰρ ἂν ἐν τῷ περιττῷ ἄλλο εἴη ᾧ ἐνυπῆρχεν
20 ὑπάρχοντι· τοῦτο δ' εἰ ἔστι, πρῶτον ὁ ἀριθμὸς
ἐνυπάρξει ὑπάρχουσιν αὐτῷ· εἰ οὖν μὴ ἐνδέχεται
ἄπειρα τοιαῦτα ὑπάρχειν ἐν τῷ ἑνί, οὐδ' ἐπὶ τὸ
ἄνω ἔσται ἄπειρα· ἀλλὰ μὴν ἀνάγκη γε πάντα
ὑπάρχειν τῷ πρώτῳ, οἷον τῷ ἀριθμῷ, κἀκείνοις
τὸν ἀριθμόν, ὥστ' ἀντιστρέφοντα ἔσται, ἀλλ' οὐχ
25 ὑπερτείνοντα)· οὐδὲ μὴν ὅσα ἐν τῷ τί ἐστιν ἐνυπάρχει, οὐδὲ ταῦτα ἄπειρα· οὐδὲ γὰρ ἂν εἴη ὁρίσασθαι. ὥστ' εἰ τὰ μὲν κατηγορούμενα καθ' αὑτὰ
πάντα λέγεται, ταῦτα δὲ μὴ ἄπειρα, ἵσταιτο ἂν τὰ
ἐπὶ τὸ ἄνω, ὥστε καὶ ἐπὶ τὸ κάτω.

Εἰ δ' οὕτω, καὶ τὰ ἐν τῷ μεταξὺ δύο ὅρων ἀεὶ
30 πεπερασμένα. εἰ δὲ τοῦτο, δῆλον ἤδη καὶ τῶν
ἀποδείξεων ὅτι ἀνάγκη ἀρχάς τε εἶναι, καὶ μὴ πάντων εἶναι ἀπόδειξιν, ὅπερ ἔφαμέν τινας λέγειν κατ'
ἀρχάς. εἰ γὰρ εἰσὶν ἀρχαί, οὔτε πάντ' ἀποδεικτὰ
οὔτ' εἰς ἄπειρον οἷόν τε βαδίζειν· τὸ γὰρ εἶναι
τούτων ὁποτερονοῦν οὐδὲν ἄλλο ἐστὶν ἢ τὸ εἶναι
35 μηδὲν διάστημα ἄμεσον καὶ ἀδιαίρετον, ἀλλὰ πάντα
διαιρετά. τῷ γὰρ ἐντὸς ἐμβάλλεσθαι ὅρον, ἀλλ'
οὐ τῷ προσλαμβάνεσθαι, ἀποδείκνυται τὸ ἀποδεικ-
νύμενον, ὥστ' εἰ τοῦτ' εἰς ἄπειρον ἐνδέχεται ἰέναι,
ἐνδέχοιτ' ἂν δύο ὅρων ἄπειρα μεταξὺ εἶναι μέσα.

---

[a] Number is assumed to be the downward limit; if there
is no upward limit there will be terms with infinitely many
elements in their essence.

[b] Thus they form not a vertical series but a kind of circle.
Since they are convertible, " odd " must stand for " odd or
even."

[c] Cf. 82 b 38.

[d] Proved in ch. xx.

[e] 72 b 6.

can proceed to infinity. (*b*) The series cannot be infinite when the relation is that of " odd " to number ; for then in its turn " odd " would have another attribute in which " odd " was inherent ; and if so, number must be ultimately inherent in the several " odds " which are its attributes. Thus since an infinite number of such attributes cannot apply to a single subject, the series will not be infinite in the upward direction either.[a] Actually all such attributes must so inhere in the ultimate subject—the attributes of number in number and number in them— that they will be commensurate with it and not extend beyond it.[b] Nor again are the attributes which inhere in the essence of their subject infinite in number ; if they were, definition would be impossible.[c] Thus if all the attributes are predicated as essential, and as such cannot be infinite in number, the upward series must have a limit, and therefore so must the downward.

If this is so, the intermediates between any two terms must always be finite in number[d] ; and if this is so, it is obvious at once that there must be first principles of demonstration, and that the view that everything is demonstrable (which we mentioned at the beginning[e] as held by some) is false. For if there are first principles, (1) not everything is demonstrable, and (2) demonstration cannot form an infinite series ; because the rejection of either consequence immediately implies that no premiss is immediate and indivisible, but all are divisible. For it is by adding a term internally, and not externally, that a proposition is demonstrated. Thus if the process of demonstration can continue to infinity, it would be possible for there to be an infinite number of middles

84 b ἀλλὰ τοῦτ' ἀδύνατον, εἰ ἵστανται αἱ κατηγορίαι ἐπὶ
τὸ ἄνω καὶ τὸ κάτω. ὅτι δὲ ἵστανται, δέδεικται
λογικῶς μὲν πρότερον, ἀναλυτικῶς δὲ νῦν.

XXIII. Δεδειγμένων δὲ τούτων φανερὸν ὅτι, ἐάν
τι τὸ αὐτὸ δυσὶν ὑπάρχῃ, οἷον τὸ Α τῷ τε Γ καὶ
5 τῷ Δ, μὴ κατηγορουμένου θατέρου κατὰ θατέρου,
ἢ μηδαμῶς ἢ μὴ κατὰ παντός, ὅτι οὐκ ἀεὶ κατὰ
κοινόν τι ὑπάρξει. οἷον τῷ ἰσοσκελεῖ καὶ τῷ
σκαληνῷ τὸ δυσὶν ὀρθαῖς ἴσας ἔχειν κατὰ κοινόν τι
ὑπάρχει (ᾗ γὰρ σχῆμά τι ὑπάρχει, καὶ οὐχ ᾗ
ἕτερον), τοῦτο δ' οὐκ ἀεὶ οὕτως ἔχει. ἔστω γὰρ τὸ
10 Β καθ' ὃ τὸ Α τῷ ΓΔ ὑπάρχει. δῆλον τοίνυν ὅτι
καὶ τὸ Β τῷ Γ καὶ[1] Δ κατ' ἄλλο κοινόν, κἀκεῖνο
καθ' ἕτερον, ὥστε δύο ὅρων μεταξὺ ἄπειροι ἂν
ἐμπίπτοιεν ὅροι. ἀλλ' ἀδύνατον. κατὰ μὲν τοίνυν
κοινόν τι ὑπάρχειν οὐκ ἀνάγκη ἀεὶ τὸ αὐτὸ πλείοσιν,
15 εἴπερ[2] ἔσται ἄμεσα διαστήματα. ἐν μέντοι τῷ
αὐτῷ γένει καὶ ἐκ τῶν αὐτῶν ἀτόμων ἀνάγκη τοὺς
ὅρους εἶναι, εἴπερ τῶν καθ' αὑτὰ ὑπαρχόντων ἔσται
τὸ κοινόν· οὐ γὰρ ἦν ἐξ ἄλλου γένους εἰς ἄλλο δια-
βῆναι τὰ δεικνύμενα.

Φανερὸν δὲ καὶ ὅτι, ὅταν τὸ Α τῷ Β ὑπάρχῃ, εἰ
20 μὲν ἔστι τι μέσον, ἔστι δεῖξαι ὅτι τὸ Α τῷ Β
ὑπάρχει· καὶ στοιχεῖα τούτου ἐστὶ ταὐτὰ[3] καὶ το-

---

[1] καὶ] καὶ τῷ D.
[2] εἴπερ ci. Jaeger : ἐπείπερ.
[3] ταὐτὰ Ross : ταῦτα.

---

[a] 84 a 39.   [b] Ch. vii.

between two terms. This, however, is impossible, if the series of predications has an upward and a downward limit. That it has these limits was proved above by dialectical, and has now been proved by analytical method.

XXIII. Now that this fact has been established, it is evident that if the same attribute applies to two subjects, e.g., if A applies both to C and to D, which are not reciprocally predicable of each other, at least not universally, the predicate will not always apply in virtue of a common characteristic. E.g., " having the sum of its angles equal to two right angles " applies in virtue of a common characteristic to the isosceles and to the scalene triangle : it belongs to each of them *qua* a particular kind of figure, and not *qua* different. But this is not always so. Let B stand for the characteristic in virtue of which A applies to C and D. Then clearly B also applies to C and D in virtue of some other characteristic, and this in virtue of another ; so that an infinite number of terms will be interpolated between the original two. But this is impossible.[a] Thus if there are to be immediate premisses it will not necessarily be in virtue of some common characteristic that the same predicate applies to more than one subject. If, however, it is an essential attribute that is to be proved common, the ⟨middle⟩ terms must belong to the same genus and ⟨the premisses⟩ be derived from the same immediate premisses ; for we saw [b] that in proving propositions we cannot pass from one genus to another.

It is evident also that when A applies to B, if there is a middle term, it is possible to prove that A applies to B ; and the elements of this proof are identical with the middle terms, or rather the same in number ;

Corollaries : (1) Common attributes need not be identically mediated.

(2) Connexions are provable by middle terms.

131

84 b

σαῦθ' ὅσα μέσα ἐστίν· αἱ γὰρ ἄμεσοι προτάσεις
στοιχεῖα, ἢ πᾶσαι ἢ αἱ καθόλου. εἰ δὲ μὴ ἔστιν,
οὐκέτι ἔστιν ἀπόδειξις, ἀλλ' ἡ ἐπὶ τὰς ἀρχὰς ὁδὸς
αὕτη ἐστίν. ὁμοίως δὲ καὶ εἰ τὸ Α τῷ Β μὴ ὑπάρ-
25 χει, εἰ μὲν ἔστιν ἢ μέσον ἢ πρότερον ᾧ οὐχ ὑπάρχει,
ἔστιν ἀπόδειξις, εἰ δὲ μή, οὐκ ἔστιν, ἀλλ' ἀρχή· καὶ
στοιχεῖα τοσαῦτ' ἐστὶν ὅσοι ὅροι· αἱ γὰρ τούτων
προτάσεις ἀρχαὶ τῆς ἀποδείξεώς εἰσιν. καὶ ὥσπερ
ἔνιαι ἀρχαί εἰσιν ἀναπόδεικτοι, ὅτι ἔστι τόδε τοδὶ
30 καὶ ὑπάρχει τόδε τῳδί, οὕτω καὶ ὅτι οὐκ ἔστι τόδε
τοδὶ οὐδ' ὑπάρχει τόδε τῳδί· ὥσθ' αἱ μὲν εἶναί τι,
αἱ δὲ μὴ εἶναί τι ἔσονται ἀρχαί.

Ὅταν δὲ δέῃ δεῖξαι, ληπτέον ὃ τοῦ Β πρῶτον
κατηγορεῖται. ἔστω τὸ Γ, καὶ τούτου ὁμοίως τὸ
Δ.[1] καὶ οὕτως ἀεὶ βαδίζοντι οὐδέποτ' ἐξωτέρω
πρότασις οὐδ' ὑπάρχον λαμβάνεται τοῦ Α ἐν τῷ
35 δεικνύναι, ἀλλ' ἀεὶ τὸ μέσον πυκνοῦται ἕως ἀδιαίρετα γένηται καὶ ἕν. ἔστι δ' ἓν ὅταν ἄμεσον γένηται, καὶ μία πρότασις ἁπλῶς ἡ ἄμεσος. καὶ ὥσπερ
ἐν τοῖς ἄλλοις ἡ ἀρχὴ ἁπλοῦν, τοῦτο δ' οὐ ταὐτὸ
πανταχοῦ, ἀλλ' ἐν βάρει μὲν μνᾶ, ἐν δὲ μέλει δίεσις,
85 a ἄλλο δ' ἐν ἄλλῳ, οὕτως ἐν συλλογισμῷ τὸ ἓν πρότασις ἄμεσος, ἐν δ' ἀποδείξει καὶ ἐπιστήμῃ ὁ νοῦς.

Ἐν μὲν οὖν τοῖς δεικτικοῖς συλλογισμοῖς τοῦ

[1] Δ n, Ross : Α.

[a] Assuming that there are several middles, forming with
A and B a chain of immediate premisses, all of which, except
the last, are " universal," *i.e.* majors.

for it is the immediate premisses—either all or those which are universal—that are elements.[a] If there is no middle term, demonstration is impossible ; we are approaching first principles. Similarly too if A does not apply to B, if there is either a middle or a prior term to which A does not apply, demonstration is possible (otherwise it is not possible ; we are dealing with a first principle) ; and there will be as many elements as there are ⟨middle⟩ terms ; for it is the premisses containing these that are the principles of the demonstration. Just as there are some indemonstrable premisses to the effect that X is Y or X applies to Y, so there are others to the effect that X is not Y or does not apply to Y ; so that some will be principles making an affirmative and others making a negative statement.

When, however, proof is required, we must assume ⟨as middle⟩ the immediate predicate of B. Let this be C, and let D similarly be predicated of C. If we continue this process we never assume in our proof a premiss or an attribute which falls outside A, but we go on packing the space between until the intervals are indivisible or unitary : and we have one unit when the premiss is immediate. It is only the immediate premiss that is *one* in the unqualified sense. Just as in all other genera the basic measure is something simple, and this is not the same in all cases, but in weight is the mina,[b] in music the quarter-tone, and so on in each genus, so in syllogism the unit is the immediate premiss, while in demonstration and understanding the unit is an act of intuition.[c]

In affirmative syllogisms, then, nothing falls outside

How to select these in (a) affirmative proof,

(b) negative proof.

---

[b] About 1 lb. avoirdupois.
[c] Which cognizes the immediate premiss.

ὑπάρχοντος οὐδὲν ἔξω πίπτει, ἐν δὲ τοῖς στερη-
τικοῖς, ἔνθα μὲν ὃ δεῖ ὑπάρχειν, οὐδὲν τούτου ἔξω
5 πίπτει, οἷον εἰ τὸ Α τῷ Β διὰ τοῦ Γ μή (εἰ γὰρ τῷ
μὲν Β παντὶ τὸ Γ, τῷ δὲ Γ μηδενὶ τὸ Α)· πάλιν ἂν
δέῃ ὅτι τῷ Γ τὸ Α οὐδενὶ ὑπάρχει, μέσον ληπτέον
τοῦ Α καὶ Γ, καὶ οὕτως ἀεὶ πορεύσεται. ἐὰν δὲ
δέῃ δεῖξαι ὅτι τὸ Δ τῷ Ε οὐχ ὑπάρχει τῷ τὸ Γ τῷ
μὲν Δ παντὶ ὑπάρχειν τῷ δὲ Ε μηδενὶ [ἢ μὴ παντί],[1]
10 τοῦ Ε οὐδέποτ᾽ ἔξω πεσεῖται· τοῦτο δ᾽ ἐστὶν ᾧ [οὗ][2]
δεῖ ὑπάρχειν. ἐπὶ δὲ τοῦ τρίτου τρόπου οὔτε ἀφ᾽
οὗ δεῖ οὔτε ὃ δεῖ στερῆσαι οὐδέποτ᾽ ἔξω βαδιεῖται.

XXIV. Οὔσης δ᾽ ἀποδείξεως τῆς μὲν καθόλου
τῆς δὲ κατὰ μέρος, καὶ τῆς μὲν κατηγορικῆς τῆς
15 δὲ στερητικῆς, ἀμφισβητεῖται ποτέρα βελτίων· ὡς
δ᾽ αὕτως καὶ περὶ τῆς ἀποδεικνύναι λεγομένης καὶ
τῆς εἰς τὸ ἀδύνατον ἀγούσης ἀποδείξεως. πρῶτον
μὲν οὖν ἐπισκεψώμεθα περὶ τῆς καθόλου καὶ τῆς
κατὰ μέρος· δηλώσαντες δὲ τοῦτο, καὶ περὶ τῆς
δεικνύναι λεγομένης καὶ τῆς εἰς τὸ ἀδύνατον
εἴπωμεν.

---

[1] ἢ μὴ παντί secl. Ross.
[2] οὗ om. Dn[1], Ross.

---

[a] *i.e.*, no middle term is assumed that is wider than the predicate.

[b] Celarent in the first figure.

[c] Strictly non-attribution ; Aristotle again means the predicate or major term.

[d] Ross is doubtless right in bracketing ἢ μὴ παντί and so confining the reference to Camestres, because Aristotle seems to have only universal conclusions in view.

[e] Since the major and minor terms are regarded as extremes, " outside " here means " below " ; no middle will be narrower than the subject. It may, however (though Aristotle does not actually say so), be wider than the predicate.

the attribute.[a] In negative syllogisms (1) in one mood [b] nothing falls outside the term whose attribution [c] is required to be proved ; *e.g.*, supposing that it is required to be proved by means of C that A does not apply to B (the premisses being C applies to all B, and A to no C) ; if in turn it is required to prove that A applies to no C, a middle term must be assumed between A and C, and the process will continue in this way. (2) If, however, it is required to prove that D does not apply to E because C applies to all D but to none [or not to all] [d] of E, the additional terms will never fall outside [e] E, *i.e.*, the subject to which the predicate is required ⟨not⟩[f] to apply. (3) In the third mood [g] the additional terms will never proceed beyond the subject or the predicate of the required negative conclusion.

XXIV. Since demonstration may be either universal or particular,[h] and either affirmative or negative, it may be debated which is the better. So too with regard to so-called ostensive proof and *reductio ad impossibile*. First, then, let us consider universal and particular demonstration. When we have cleared up this question let us discuss direct proof and *reductio ad impossibile*.[i]

Is universal superior to particular demonstration ?

---

[f] The negative, required in English, is dispensable in Aristotle's formula (*cf.* ὃ δεῖ ὑπάρχειν in a 3 above). It was probably inserted in the text by a zealous corrector.

[g] Clearly not the third figure (which, as Ross points out, does not satisfy the conditions) but Cesare in the second—the only other mood which gives a universal negative conclusion.

[h] Not in the ordinary sense of the terms, because demonstration proper is not concerned with particular or singular propositions (the argument adduced and rejected below is unscientific) ; the distinction is between degrees of universality. [i] See ch. xxvi.

20 Δόξειε μὲν οὖν τάχ' ἂν τισιν ὡδὶ σκοποῦσιν ἡ
κατὰ μέρος εἶναι βελτίων. εἰ γὰρ καθ' ἣν μᾶλλον
ἐπιστάμεθα ἀπόδειξιν βελτίων ἀπόδειξις (αὕτη γὰρ
ἀρετὴ ἀποδείξεως), μᾶλλον δ' ἐπιστάμεθα ἕκαστον
ὅταν αὐτὸ εἰδῶμεν καθ' αὑτὸ ἢ ὅταν κατ' ἄλλο (οἷον
25 τὸν μουσικὸν Κορίσκον ὅταν ὅτι ὁ Κορίσκος μουσικὸς ἢ ὅταν ὅτι ἄνθρωπος[1] μουσικός· ὁμοίως δὲ
καὶ ἐπὶ τῶν ἄλλων), ἡ δὲ καθόλου ὅτι ἄλλο, οὐχ
ὅτι αὐτὸ τετύχηκεν ἐπιδείκνυσιν (οἷον ὅτι τὸ ἰσοσκελὲς οὐχ ὅτι ἰσοσκελὲς ἀλλ' ὅτι τρίγωνον), ἡ δὲ
κατὰ μέρος ὅτι αὐτό· εἰ δὴ βελτίων μὲν ἡ καθ' αὑτό,
30 τοιαύτη δ' ἡ κατὰ μέρος τῆς καθόλου μᾶλλον, καὶ
βελτίων ἂν ἡ κατὰ μέρος ἀπόδειξις εἴη. ἔτι εἰ τὸ
μὲν καθόλου μή ἐστί τι παρὰ τὰ καθ' ἕκαστα, ἡ δ'
ἀπόδειξις δόξαν ἐμποιεῖ εἶναί τι τοῦτο καθ' ὃ ἀποδείκνυσι, καί τινα φύσιν ὑπάρχειν ἐν τοῖς οὖσι ταύτην, οἷον τριγώνου παρὰ τὰ τινὰ καὶ σχήματος παρὰ
35 τὰ τινὰ καὶ ἀριθμοῦ παρὰ τοὺς τινὰς ἀριθμούς,
βελτίων δ' ἡ περὶ ὄντος ἢ μὴ ὄντος καὶ δι' ἣν μὴ
ἀπατηθήσεται ἢ δι' ἥν, ἔστι δ' ἡ μὲν καθόλου τοιαύτη (προϊόντες γὰρ δεικνύουσιν, ὥσπερ περὶ τοῦ ἀνὰ

---

[1] ἄνθρωπος Ross.

---

[a] Of Scepsis in Mysia; a friend whose name Aristotle
often uses in illustrative examples. The epithet μουσικός is
probably used with its wider meaning.
[b] Probably either Academic mathematicians or actual
disciples of Eudoxus, who discovered the general theory of
proportion.

Some people, looking at the question in the following way, might suppose that particular demonstration is superior. (1) If the superior method of demonstration is that by which we gain more knowledge (since this is the distinctive merit of demonstration), and we have more knowledge of an individual thing when we recognize it in virtue of itself than when we do so in virtue of something else (as, *e.g.*, we have more knowledge of " cultured Coriscus " [a] when we know that Coriscus is cultured than when we only know that man is cultured ; and similarly in all other cases) ; and whereas universal demonstration informs us that something else, not that the particular thing, has a given attribute—*e.g.*, does not tell us that an isosceles triangle has a given attribute because it is isosceles but because it is a triangle—, particular demonstration informs us that the particular thing has it ;—if, then, the better demonstration is that which informs us of something in virtue of itself, and particular is more of this nature than universal demonstration, then particular will also be superior to universal demonstration. (2) Further, if the universal does not exist apart from particulars, and demonstration produces in us a belief that there is something of this nature in virtue of which the demonstration proceeds, and that this inheres as a definite characteristic in things (*e.g.*, the characteristics triangle, figure and number apart from particular triangles, figures and numbers) ; and if the demonstration which treats of the existent and is infallible is superior to that which treats of the non-existent and is fallible ; and if universal demonstration is of the latter kind (since it is by proceeding in this way that they [b] attempt proofs like that which

λόγον, οἷον ὅτι ὃ ἂν ᾖ τι τοιοῦτον ἔσται ἀνὰ λόγον,
ὃ οὔτε γραμμὴ οὔτ' ἀριθμὸς οὔτε στερεὸν οὔτ' ἐπί-
85 b πεδον, ἀλλὰ παρὰ ταῦτά τι)—εἰ οὖν καθόλου μὲν
μᾶλλον αὕτη, περὶ ὄντος δ' ἧττον τῆς κατὰ μέρος
καὶ ἐμποιεῖ δόξαν ψευδῆ, χείρων ἂν εἴη ἡ καθόλου
τῆς κατὰ μέρος.

Ἢ πρῶτον μὲν οὐδὲν μᾶλλον ἐπὶ τοῦ καθόλου ἢ
5 τοῦ κατὰ μέρος ἅτερος λόγος ἐστίν; εἰ γὰρ τὸ δυσὶν
ὀρθαῖς ὑπάρχει μὴ ᾗ ἰσοσκελὲς ἀλλ' ᾗ τρίγωνον, ὁ
εἰδὼς ὅτι ἰσοσκελὲς ἧττον οἶδεν ᾗ αὐτὸ ἢ ὁ εἰδὼς
ὅτι τρίγωνον. ὅλως τε, εἰ μὲν μὴ ὄντος ᾗ τρίγωνον
εἶτα δείκνυσιν, οὐκ ἂν εἴη ἀπόδειξις, εἰ δὲ ὄντος, ὁ
εἰδὼς ἕκαστον ᾗ ἕκαστον ὑπάρχει μᾶλλον οἶδεν. εἰ
10 δὴ τὸ τρίγωνον ἐπὶ πλέον ἐστί, καὶ ὁ αὐτὸς λόγος,
καὶ μὴ καθ' ὁμωνυμίαν τὸ τρίγωνον, καὶ ὑπάρχει
παντὶ τριγώνῳ τὸ δύο, οὐκ ἂν τὸ τρίγωνον ᾗ ἰσοσκελές, ἀλλὰ τὸ ἰσοσκελὲς ᾗ τρίγωνον, ἔχοι τοιαύτας
τὰς γωνίας. ὥστε ὁ καθόλου εἰδὼς μᾶλλον οἶδεν ᾗ
15 ὑπάρχει ἢ ὁ κατὰ μέρος. βελτίων ἄρα ἡ καθόλου
τῆς κατὰ μέρος. ἔτι εἰ μὲν εἴη τις λόγος εἷς καὶ μὴ
ὁμωνυμία τὸ καθόλου, εἴη τ'[1] ἂν οὐδὲν ἧττον ἐνίων

[1] τ' om. n.

asserts that a proportional is anything which has a certain definite characteristic, and that it is neither a line nor a number nor a solid nor a plane, but something distinct from these)—, if, then, this kind of proof is closer to universal demonstration, and treats less of the existent than particular demonstration, and produces a false opinion, universal will be inferior to particular demonstration.

In point of fact, however, (1) the first argument applies no more to universal than to particular demonstration. If the attribute of having the sum of its interior angles equal to two right angles belongs to a figure not *qua* isosceles but *qua* triangle, the man who knows that the figure possesses this attribute because it is isosceles knows less of the essential reason for the fact than he who knows that it is so because the figure is a triangle. And in general if, when an attribute does not belong to a given subject *qua* triangle, the attribute is proved of that subject, the proof cannot amount to demonstration; but if it does apply to the subject (*qua* triangle), then he has the greater knowledge who knows that a given attribute belongs to a given subject as such. Thus if " triangle " is the wider term, and has an invariable meaning, the term " triangle " not being equivocal; and if the attribute of having the sum of its interior angles equal to two right angles applies to every triangle, then it is the isosceles *qua* triangle, and not the triangle *qua* isosceles, that will possess such angles. Thus the man who knows the universal has more knowledge than he who knows the particular. Therefore universal is superior to particular demonstration. (2) If the meaning is invariable and the universal term is not merely equivocal, it will be not

139

85 b

τῶν κατὰ μέρος, ἀλλὰ καὶ μᾶλλον; ὅσῳ τὰ ἄφθαρτα
ἐν ἐκείνοις ἐστί, τὰ δὲ κατὰ μέρος φθαρτὰ μᾶλλον,
ἔτι τε οὐδεμία ἀνάγκη ὑπολαμβάνειν τι εἶναι τοῦτο
20 παρὰ ταῦτα ὅτι ἓν δηλοῖ, οὐδὲν μᾶλλον ἢ ἐπὶ τῶν
ἄλλων ὅσα μὴ τὶ σημαίνει ἀλλ' ἢ ποιὸν ἢ πρός τι
ἢ ποιεῖν. εἰ δὲ ἄρα, οὐχ ἡ ἀπόδειξις αἰτία ἀλλ' ὁ
ἀκούων.

Ἔτι εἰ ἡ ἀπόδειξις μέν ἐστι συλλογισμὸς δεικτι-
κὸς αἰτίας καὶ τοῦ διὰ τί, τὸ καθόλου δ' αἰτιώτερον
25 (ᾧ γὰρ καθ' αὑτὸ ὑπάρχει τι, τοῦτο αὐτὸ αὑτῷ
αἴτιον· τὸ δὲ καθόλου πρῶτον· αἴτιον ἄρα τὸ καθόλου)· ὥστε καὶ ἡ ἀπόδειξις βελτίων· μᾶλλον γὰρ τοῦ
αἰτίου καὶ τοῦ διὰ τί ἐστιν.

Ἔτι μέχρι τούτου ζητοῦμεν τὸ διὰ τί, καὶ τότε
οἰόμεθα εἰδέναι ὅταν μὴ ᾖ ὅτι τι ἄλλο τοῦτο ἢ
30 γιγνόμενον ἢ ὄν· τέλος γὰρ καὶ πέρας τὸ ἔσχατον
ἤδη οὕτως ἐστίν. οἷον τίνος ἕνεκα ἦλθεν; ὅπως
λάβῃ τἀργύριον, τοῦτο δ' ὅπως ἀποδῷ ὃ ὤφειλε,
τοῦτο δ' ὅπως μὴ ἀδικήσῃ· καὶ οὕτως ἰόντες, ὅταν
μηκέτι δι' ἄλλο μηδ' ἄλλου ἕνεκα, διὰ τοῦτο ὡς τέλος φαμὲν ἐλθεῖν καὶ εἶναι καὶ γίγνεσθαι, καὶ τότε
35 εἰδέναι μάλιστα διὰ τί ἦλθεν. εἰ δὴ ὁμοίως ἔχει ἐπὶ
πασῶν τῶν αἰτιῶν καὶ τῶν διὰ τί, ἐπὶ δὲ τῶν ὅσα

---

[a] Genera and species being (for Aristotle at least) permanent types.

[b] In the sense that the subject of a (commensurately) universal attribute is the first subject to which it can be shown
to apply : 73 b 32.

less but more really existent than some of the particulars, inasmuch as universals include imperishable things,[a] whereas particulars tend rather to be perishable. Further, there is no need to assume that the universal is some one entity apart from the particulars simply because it has a single denotation; no more than in the case of the other categories which denote not substance but quality or relation or activity. If this assumption is made, the fault lies not in the demonstration but in the hearer.

(3) There is also the argument that demonstration is a syllogism proving the cause or reasoned fact, and the universal is more of the nature of a cause (for a subject which possesses an attribute *per se* is itself the cause of its own possession of that attribute; and the universal is primary [b]; therefore the universal is the cause). Therefore universal demonstration is superior, because it more properly proves the cause or reasoned fact. *Further positive arguments.*

(4) Again, we cease our inquiry for the reason and assume that we know it when we reach a fact whose existence or coming into existence does not depend upon any other fact; for the last stage of an inquiry by this method is *ipso facto* the end and limit. *E.g.*, why did X come? To get the money; and this was in order to repay what he owed, and this again in order not to do wrong. When, as we proceed in this way, we reach a cause which neither depends upon anything else nor has anything else as its object, we say that this is the end for which the man came, or exists, or comes into being; it is then that we say that we understand most completely *why* the man came. If, then, the same principle applies to all causes and reasoned facts, and if our knowledge of

αἴτια οὕτως ὡς οὗ ἕνεκα οὕτως ἴσμεν μάλιστα, καὶ
ἐπὶ τῶν ἄλλων ἄρα τότε μάλιστα ἴσμεν ὅταν μηκέτι
ὑπάρχῃ τοῦτο ὅτι ἄλλο. ὅταν μὲν οὖν γιγνώσκωμεν ὅτι τέτταρσιν αἱ ἔξω ἴσαι, ὅτι ἰσοσκελές, ἔτι
λείπεται διὰ τί τὸ ἰσοσκελές, ὅτι τρίγωνον, καὶ
τοῦτο, ὅτι σχῆμα εὐθύγραμμον. εἰ δὲ τοῦτο μηκέτι
διότι ἄλλο, τότε μάλιστα ἴσμεν. καὶ καθόλου δὲ
τότε· ἡ καθόλου ἄρα βελτίων.

Ἔτι ὅσῳ ἂν μᾶλλον κατὰ μέρος ᾖ, εἰς τὰ ἄπειρα
ἐμπίπτει, ἡ δὲ καθόλου εἰς τὸ ἁπλοῦν καὶ τὸ πέρας.
ἔστι δ᾽, ᾗ μὲν ἄπειρά, οὐκ ἐπιστητά, ᾗ δὲ πεπέρανται, ἐπιστητά. ᾗ ἄρα καθόλου, μᾶλλον ἐπι-
στητὰ ἢ ᾗ κατὰ μέρος. ἀποδεικτὰ ἄρα μᾶλλον τὰ
καθόλου. τῶν δὲ ἀποδεικτῶν μᾶλλον μᾶλλον ἀπό-
δειξις· ἅμα γὰρ μᾶλλον τὰ πρός τι. βελτίων ἄρα ἡ
καθόλου, ἐπείπερ καὶ μᾶλλον ἀπόδειξις.

Ἔτι εἰ[1] αἱρετωτέρα καθ᾽ ἣν τοῦτο καὶ ἄλλο ἢ καθ᾽
ἣν τοῦτο μόνον οἶδεν· ὁ δὲ τὴν καθόλου ἔχων οἶδε
καὶ τὸ κατὰ μέρος, οὗτος δὲ τὸ καθόλου οὐκ οἶδεν·
ὥστε κἂν οὕτως αἱρετωτέρα εἴη.

Ἔτι δὲ ὧδε. τὸ γὰρ καθόλου μᾶλλον δεικνύναι

[1] εἰ om. DM.

all final causes is most complete under the conditions which we have just described, then in all other cases too our knowledge is most complete when we reach a fact which does not depend further upon any other fact. So when we recognize that the sum of the exterior angles of a figure is equal to four right angles, because the figure is isosceles, there still remains the reason why the figure is isosceles, *viz.*, that it is a triangle, and this because it is a right-lined figure. If this reason depends upon nothing else, our knowledge is now complete. Moreover our knowledge is now universal ; and therefore universal knowledge is superior.

(5) Again, the more particular causes are, the more they tend to form an infinite regress, whereas universal demonstration tends towards the simple and finite ; and causes *qua* infinite are not knowable, whereas *qua* finite they are knowable. Hence causes are more knowable *qua* universal than *qua* particular; and therefore universal causes are more demonstrable. But the demonstration of things which are more demonstrable is more truly demonstration ; for correlatives vary simultaneously in degree. Hence universal demonstration is superior, inasmuch as it is more truly demonstration.

(6) Again, that kind of demonstration by which one knows a given fact *and* another fact as well is preferable to that by which one knows only the given fact. But he who has universal knowledge knows the particular cause as well, whereas the man who has only particular knowledge does not know the universal cause. Hence on this ground also universal demonstration will be preferable.

(7) Again, there is the following argument. Proof

143

15 ἐστὶ τὸ διὰ μέσου δεικνύναι ἐγγυτέρω ὄντος τῆς
ἀρχῆς. ἐγγυτάτω δὲ τὸ ἄμεσον· τοῦτο δ' ἀρχή.
εἰ οὖν ἡ ἐξ ἀρχῆς τῆς μὴ ἐξ ἀρχῆς, ἡ μᾶλλον ἐξ
ἀρχῆς τῆς ἧττον ἀκριβεστέρα ἀπόδειξις. ἔστι δὲ
τοιαύτη ἡ καθόλου μᾶλλον· κρείττων ἄρ' ἂν εἴη ἡ
καθόλου. οἷον εἰ ἔδει ἀποδεῖξαι τὸ Α κατὰ τοῦ Δ·
20 μέσα τὰ ἐφ' ὧν ΒΓ· ἀνωτέρω δὴ τὸ Β, ὥστε ἡ
διὰ τούτου καθόλου μᾶλλον.

Ἀλλὰ τῶν μὲν εἰρημένων ἔνια λογικά ἐστι· μάλιστα δὲ δῆλον ὅτι ἡ καθόλου κυριωτέρα ὅτι τῶν
προτάσεων τὴν μὲν προτέραν ἔχοντες ἴσμεν πως
25 καὶ τὴν ὑστέραν καὶ ἔχομεν δυνάμει, οἷον εἴ τις
οἶδεν ὅτι πᾶν τρίγωνον δυσὶν ὀρθαῖς, οἶδέ πως καὶ
τὸ ἰσοσκελὲς ὅτι δύο ὀρθαῖς, δυνάμει, καὶ εἰ μὴ οἶδε
τὸ ἰσοσκελὲς ὅτι τρίγωνον· ὁ δὲ ταύτην ἔχων τὴν
πρότασιν τὸ καθόλου οὐδαμῶς οἶδεν, οὔτε δυνάμει
οὔτ' ἐνεργείᾳ. καὶ ἡ μὲν καθόλου νοητή, ἡ δὲ
30 κατὰ μέρος εἰς αἴσθησιν τελευτᾷ.

XXV. Ὅτι μὲν οὖν ἡ καθόλου βελτίων τῆς κατὰ
μέρος, τοσαῦθ' ἡμῖν εἰρήσθω· ὅτι δ' ἡ δεικτικὴ τῆς

---

a The implication is that (6), which Aristotle now proceeds
to expand, is (or can be made) truly scientific.

b Not a major and a minor, but the two premisses mentioned in the following lines.

c When it reaches individuals, which are perceptible
rather than intelligible.

of the more universal fact consists in proving by a middle which is nearer to the first principle. Now that which is nearest to the first principle is the immediate premiss, *i.e.*, the first principle itself. If, then, demonstration from the first principle is more accurate than demonstration which is not from the first principle, that demonstration which is more nearly from the first principle is more accurate than that which is less nearly from it. Now it is universal demonstration which is more truly of this nature ; and therefore universal demonstration is superior. *E.g.*, suppose that it is required to demonstrate A of D, the middle terms being B and C. B is the *higher* term, and so the demonstration by means of B is the more universal.

Some of the foregoing arguments, however, are merely dialectical.[a] The clearest indication that universal demonstration is more authoritative is that when we comprehend the former of the two premisses[b] we have knowledge in a sense of the latter as well, and comprehend it potentially. *E.g.*, if anyone knows that every triangle has the sum of its interior angles equal to two right angles, he knows in a sense also (*viz.*, potentially) that the sum of the interior angles of an isosceles triangle is equal to two right angles, even if he does not know that the isosceles is a triangle. But the man who comprehends the latter premiss does not in any sense know the universal fact, neither potentially nor actually. Moreover universal demonstration is intelligible, whereas particular demonstration terminates in sense perception.[c]

Final proofs that universal demonstration is superior.

XXV. The foregoing account may suffice to show that universal is superior to particular demonstration.

Affirmative is superior to negative

145

ARISTOTLE

ἀπόδειξις βελτίων τῶν ἄλλων τῶν αὐτῶν ὑπαρ-
35 χόντων, ἡ ἐξ ἐλαττόνων αἰτημάτων ἢ ὑποθέσεων ἢ
προτάσεων. εἰ γὰρ γνώριμοι ὁμοίως, τὸ θᾶττον
γνῶναι διὰ τούτων ὑπάρξει· τοῦτο δ' αἱρετώτερον.
λόγος δὲ τῆς προτάσεως, ὅτι βελτίων ἡ ἐξ ἐλαττόνων, καθόλου ὅδε[1]· εἰ γὰρ ὁμοίως εἴη τὸ γνώριμα
εἶναι τὰ μέσα, τὰ δὲ πρότερα γνωριμώτερα, ἔστω
86 b ἡ μὲν διὰ μέσων ἀπόδειξις τῶν ΒΓΔ ὅτι τὸ Α τῷ
Ε ὑπάρχει, ἡ δὲ διὰ τῶν ΖΗ ὅτι τὸ Α τῷ Ε.
ὁμοίως δὴ[2] ἔχει τὸ ὅτι τὸ Α τῷ Δ ὑπάρχει καὶ τὸ Α
τῷ Ε. τὸ δ' ὅτι τὸ Α τῷ Δ πρότερον καὶ γνωριμώτερον ἢ ὅτι τὸ Α τῷ Ε· διὰ γὰρ τούτου ἐκεῖνο ἀπο-
5 δείκνυται, πιστότερον δὲ τὸ δι' οὗ. καὶ ἡ διὰ τῶν
ἐλαττόνων ἄρα ἀπόδειξις βελτίων τῶν ἄλλων τῶν
αὐτῶν ὑπαρχόντων. ἀμφότεραι μὲν οὖν διά τε
ὅρων τριῶν καὶ προτάσεων δύο δείκνυνται, ἀλλ' ἡ
μὲν εἶναί τι λαμβάνει, ἡ δὲ καὶ εἶναι καὶ μὴ εἶναί
τι· διὰ πλειόνων ἄρα, ὥστε χείρων.

10 Ἔτι ἐπειδὴ δέδεικται ὅτι ἀδύνατον ἀμφοτέρων
οὐσῶν στερητικῶν τῶν προτάσεων γενέσθαι συλλογισμόν, ἀλλὰ τὴν μὲν δεῖ τοιαύτην εἶναι, τὴν δ'

---

[1] ὅδε Dnp : ὥδε Waitz : δέ codd. plerique.
[2] δὴ np : δέ.

---

[a] i.e., more universal.
[b] Presumably because it is proved by the same number of
middle terms.
[c] The argument is blatantly dialectical, since it turns
upon an equivocation. The premises of a negative syllogism are the same in *number* as those of an affirmative one;
they are " more " only in *kind*.
[d] *An. Pr.* I. vii.

146

That affirmative is superior to negative demonstra- demonstration will be clear from the following argument. (1) It First argu-
may be assumed that, given the same conditions, ment.
that form of demonstration is superior to the rest
which depends upon fewer postulates or hypotheses
or premisses ; for supposing that they are equally
well known, when there are fewer of them knowledge
will be more quickly attained, and this result is to be
preferred. The argument that demonstration from
fewer premisses is superior may be stated universally
as follows. Supposing that in both cases alike the
middle terms are known, and that middle terms are
better known in proportion as they are prior,[a] let us
assume demonstration that A applies to E in one case
by means of the middle terms B, C and D, and in
another by means of F and G. Then the proposition
that A applies to D is equally evident [b] with the proposition (in the second case) that A applies to E.
But the proposition that A applies to D is prior and
more knowable than the proposition (in the first
case) that A applies to E ; for the latter is proved by
the former, and the means of proof is more certain
than the thing proved. Therefore the demonstration
which proceeds from fewer premisses is superior to
any other conducted under the same conditions. Now
both affirmative and negative demonstration are
proved by three terms and two premisses, but whereas
the former assumes that something is so, the latter
assumes both that something is and that something
is not so. Hence it proceeds from more [c] premisses,
and is therefore inferior.

(2) It has already been proved [d] that there can be Second
no syllogism when both premisses are negative ; if argument.
one is of this kind, the other must make an affirmative

147

ὅτι ὑπάρχει, ἔτι πρὸς τούτῳ δεῖ τόδε λαβεῖν. τὰς
μὲν γὰρ κατηγορικὰς αὐξανομένης τῆς ἀποδείξεως
ἀναγκαῖον γίγνεσθαι πλείους, τὰς δὲ στερητικὰς
15 ἀδύνατον πλείους εἶναι μιᾶς ἐν ἅπαντι συλλογισμῷ.
ἔστω γὰρ μηδενὶ ὑπάρχον τὸ Α ἐφ' ὅσων τὸ Β,
τῷ δὲ Γ ὑπάρχον παντὶ τὸ Β. ἂν δὴ δέῃ πάλιν
αὔξειν ἀμφοτέρας τὰς προτάσεις, μέσον ἐμβλητέον.
τοῦ μὲν ΑΒ ἔστω τὸ Δ, τοῦ δὲ ΒΓ τὸ Ε. τὸ μὲν
20 δὴ Ε φανερὸν ὅτι κατηγορικόν, τὸ δὲ Δ τοῦ μὲν
Β κατηγορικόν, πρὸς δὲ τὸ Α ὡς στερητικὸν κεῖται.
τὸ μὲν γὰρ Δ παντὸς τοῦ Β, τὸ δὲ Α οὐδενὶ δεῖ τῶν
Δ ὑπάρχειν. γίγνεται οὖν μία στερητικὴ πρότασις
ἡ τὸ ΑΔ. ὁ δ' αὐτὸς τρόπος καὶ ἐπὶ τῶν ἑτέρων
συλλογισμῶν. ἀεὶ γὰρ τὸ μέσον τῶν κατηγορικῶν
25 ὅρων κατηγορικὸν ἐπ' ἀμφότερα· τοῦ δὲ στερητικοῦ
ἐπὶ θάτερα στερητικὸν ἀναγκαῖον εἶναι, ὥστε αὕτη
μία τοιαύτη γίγνεται πρότασις, αἱ δ' ἄλλαι κατη-
γορικαί. εἰ δὴ γνωριμώτερον δι' οὗ δείκνυται καὶ
πιστότερον, δείκνυται δ' ἡ μὲν στερητικὴ διὰ τῆς
κατηγορικῆς, αὕτη δὲ δι' ἐκείνης οὐ δείκνυται,
30 προτέρα καὶ γνωριμωτέρα οὖσα καὶ πιστοτέρα βελτίων ἂν εἴη.

Ἔτι εἰ ἀρχὴ συλλογισμοῦ ἡ καθόλου πρότασις
ἄμεσος, ἔστι δ' ἐν μὲν τῇ δεικτικῇ καταφατικὴ ἐν
δὲ τῇ στερητικῇ ἀποφατικὴ ἡ καθόλου πρότασις, ἡ
δὲ καταφατικὴ τῆς ἀποφατικῆς προτέρα καὶ γνωριμωτέρα (διὰ γὰρ τὴν κατάφασιν ἡ ἀπόφασις
35 γνώριμος, καὶ προτέρα ἡ κατάφασις, ὥσπερ καὶ τὸ
εἶναι τοῦ μὴ εἶναι)· ὥστε βελτίων ἡ ἀρχὴ τῆς

statement. Now in addition to this we must grasp
the following fact. As the demonstration is expanded,[a] the affirmative premisses must increase in
number, but there cannot be more than one negative
premiss in any syllogism. Let us suppose that A
applies to no instances of B, and that B applies to all
C. Then if it is further required to expand both these
premisses, a middle term must be interpolated in
them. Let D be the middle of AB, and E of BC.
Then obviously E is affirmative, but D, though related
affirmatively to B, is related negatively to A ; for D
must be predicated of all B, but A must apply to no D.
Thus we get one negative premiss, *viz.*, AD. The same
holds good of all other syllogisms. Where the terms
are affirmative, the middle is always related affirmatively to both the others ; but in a negative syllogism
the middle term must be related negatively to one
of the others, and therefore this is the only premiss of this kind that we obtain ; the rest are affirmative. Now if the means of proof is more knowable
and more certain than the thing proved, and negative
is proved by affirmative demonstration, but not affirmative by negative, the affirmative, being prior and
more knowable and more certain, must be superior.

(3) Again, if the starting-point of a syllogism is the Third
universal immediate premiss and if in affirmative argument.
proof the universal premiss is affirmative and in
negative proof negative, and if the affirmative is prior
to and more knowable than the negative premiss (for
it is through the affirmation that the negation becomes known, and the affirmation is prior to the negation, just as being is prior to not-being),—then the
starting-point of the affirmative is superior to that of

[a] By the interpolation of middle terms.

149

86 b

δεικτικῆς ἢ τῆς στερητικῆς· ἡ δὲ βελτίοσιν ἀρχαῖς χρωμένη βελτίων.

Ἔτι ἀρχοειδεστέρα· ἄνευ γὰρ τῆς δεικνυούσης οὐκ ἔστιν ἡ στερητική.

87 a XXVI. Ἐπεὶ δ' ἡ κατηγορικὴ τῆς στερητικῆς βελτίων, δῆλον ὅτι καὶ τῆς εἰς τὸ ἀδύνατον ἀγούσης. δεῖ δ' εἰδέναι τίς ἡ διαφορὰ αὐτῶν. ἔστω δὴ τὸ Α μηδενὶ ὑπάρχον τῷ Β, τῷ δὲ Γ τὸ Β παντί· ἀνάγκη 5 δὴ τῷ Γ μηδενὶ ὑπάρχειν τὸ Α. οὕτω μὲν οὖν ληφθέντων δεικτικὴ ἡ στερητικὴ ἂν εἴη ἀπόδειξις ὅτι τὸ Α τῷ Γ οὐχ ὑπάρχει. ἡ δ' εἰς τὸ ἀδύνατον ὧδ' ἔχει. εἰ δέοι δεῖξαι ὅτι τὸ Α τῷ Β οὐχ ὑπάρχει, ληπτέον ὑπάρχειν, καὶ τὸ Β τῷ Γ, ὥστε συμβαίνει τὸ Α τῷ Γ ὑπάρχειν. τοῦτο δ' ἔστω γνώριμον καὶ 10 ὁμολογούμενον ὅτι ἀδύνατον. οὐκ ἄρα οἷόν τε τὸ Α τῷ Β ὑπάρχειν. εἰ οὖν τὸ Β τῷ Γ ὁμολογεῖται ὑπάρχειν, τὸ Α τῷ Β ἀδύνατον ὑπάρχειν. οἱ μὲν οὖν ὅροι ὁμοίως τάττονται, διαφέρει δὲ τὸ ὁπο- τέρα ἂν ᾖ γνωριμωτέρα ἡ πρότασις ἡ στερητική, πότερον ὅτι τὸ Α τῷ Β οὐχ ὑπάρχει ἢ ὅτι τὸ Α τῷ 15 Γ. ὅταν μὲν οὖν ᾖ τὸ συμπέρασμα γνωριμώτερον ὅτι οὐκ ἔστιν, ἡ εἰς τὸ ἀδύνατον γίγνεται ἀπόδειξις, ὅταν δ' ἡ ἐν τῷ συλλογισμῷ, ἡ ἀποδεικτική. φύσει

---

[a] Here again there seems to be an equivocation, though Aristotle may not have been conscious of it. In the previous sentence ἀρχή has been translated " starting-point " because that is all that it seems to be intended to mean ; but here it seems rather to mean " logical principle." The argument which follows tends to confirm this view.

[b] i.e., an affirmative premiss.

the negative demonstration. But the demonstration which uses superior first principles [a] is itself superior.

(4) Again, affirmative demonstration is more of the nature of a first principle ; for negative demonstration is impossible without another ⟨affirmative⟩ demonstration [b] to prove it. Fourth argument.

XXVI. Since affirmative demonstration is superior to negative, clearly it is also superior to *reductio ad impossibile*. We must, however, understand what is the difference between them.[c] Let us suppose that A applies to no B, but that B applies to all C ; then A must apply to no C. When the terms are taken in this way the negative demonstration that A does not apply to C will be ostensive. But *reductio ad impossibile* takes the following form. Supposing that it is required to prove that A does not apply [d] to B, we must assume that it does apply, and that B applies to C, so that it follows that A applies to C. Let it be known and admitted that this is impossible. Then A cannot apply to B. Thus if B is admitted to apply to C, A cannot apply to B.[e] The terms, then, are arranged in the same way ; the difference depends upon this : in which form the negative premiss is better known, whether as the statement " A does not apply to B " or " A does not apply to C." Thus when it is the negative statement in the conclusion that is better known, we get demonstration by *reductio ad impossibile* ; when it is one of the premisses of the syllogism, we get ostensive demonstration. Ostensive demonstration is superior to *reductio ad impossibile*.

[c] *Sc.*, negative ostensive proof and *reductio ad impossibile*.
[d] In this example Aristotle ignores quantity as being complicative and unnecessary for his argument.
[e] Because the conjunction of two true premisses cannot give a false conclusion : *An. Pr.* II. 53 b 12-25.

δὲ προτέρα ἢ ὅτι τὸ Α τῷ Β ἢ ὅτι τὸ Α τῷ Γ.
πρότερα γάρ ἐστι τοῦ συμπεράσματος ἐξ ὧν τὸ
συμπέρασμα· ἔστι δὲ τὸ μὲν Α τῷ Γ μὴ ὑπάρχειν
20 συμπέρασμα, τὸ δὲ Α τῷ Β ἐξ οὗ τὸ συμπέρασμα.
οὐ γὰρ εἰ συμβαίνει ἀναιρεῖσθαί τι, τοῦτο συμπέρασμά ἐστιν, ἐκεῖνα δὲ ἐξ ὧν, ἀλλὰ τὸ μὲν ἐξ οὗ
συλλογισμός ἐστιν ὃ ἂν οὕτως ἔχῃ ὥστε ἢ ὅλον
πρὸς μέρος ἢ μέρος πρὸς ὅλον ἔχειν, αἱ δὲ τὸ ΑΓ
25 καὶ ΒΓ¹ προτάσεις οὐκ ἔχουσιν οὕτω πρὸς ἀλλήλας.
εἰ οὖν ἡ ἐκ γνωριμωτέρων καὶ προτέρων κρείττων,
εἰσὶ δ' ἀμφότεραι ἐκ τοῦ μὴ εἶναί τι πισταί, ἀλλ' ἡ
μὲν ἐκ προτέρου ἡ δ' ἐξ ὑστέρου, βελτίων ἁπλῶς
ἂν εἴη τῆς εἰς τὸ ἀδύνατον ἡ στερητικὴ ἀπόδειξις,
ὥστε καὶ ἡ ταύτης βελτίων ἡ κατηγορικὴ δῆλον
30 ὅτι καὶ τῆς εἰς τὸ ἀδύνατόν ἐστι βελτίων.

XXVII. Ἀκριβεστέρα δ' ἐπιστήμη ἐπιστήμης καὶ
προτέρα ἥ τε τοῦ ὅτι καὶ διότι ἡ αὐτή, ἀλλὰ μὴ
χωρὶς τοῦ ὅτι τῆς τοῦ διότι, καὶ ἡ μὴ καθ' ὑποκειμένου τῆς καθ' ὑποκειμένου, οἷον ἀριθμητικὴ ἁρ-
35 μονικῆς, καὶ ἡ ἐξ ἐλαττόνων τῆς ἐκ προσθέσεως,
οἷον γεωμετρίας ἀριθμητική. λέγω δ' ἐκ προσθέ-

But the statement " A does not apply to B " is prior in nature to " A does not apply to C " ; for the premisses from which the conclusion is drawn are prior to the conclusion, and the statement " A does not apply to C " is the conclusion, while " A does not apply to B " is one of the premisses from which the conclusion is drawn. For if we obtain a destructive result,[a] this result is not a conclusion, nor are the statements from which it is drawn premisses, in the strict sense. The statements from which a syllogism follows are premisses related to one another as whole to part or part to whole ; and the premisses AC and BC are not so related to one another. Therefore if that demonstration is superior which proceeds from better known and prior premisses, and both these kinds of demonstration depend upon negative statements, of which one is prior and the other posterior, then negative demonstration will be absolutely superior to *reductio ad impossibile* ; and therefore affirmative demonstration, being superior to negative, will *a fortiori* also be superior to demonstration by *reductio ad impossibile*.

XXVII. Knowledge at the same time of the fact and of the reasoned fact, as contrasted with knowledge of the former without the latter, is more accurate and prior. So again is knowledge of objects which do not inhere in a substrate as contrasted with that of objects which do so inhere (*e.g.*, arithmetic and harmonics) and that which depends upon fewer factors as contrasted with that which uses additional factors (*e.g.*, arithmetic and geometry). What I mean by

Ranking of sciences according to their aims and subject-matter.

---

[a] Involving the disproof of a hypothesis.

---

[1] BΓ C², Ross : AB.

ARISTOTLE

σεως οἷον μονὰς οὐσία ἄθετος, στιγμὴ δὲ οὐσία
θετός· ταύτην ἐκ προσθέσεως.

XXVIII. Μία δ' ἐπιστήμη ἐστὶν ἡ ἑνὸς γένους,
ὅσα ἐκ τῶν πρώτων σύγκειται καὶ μέρη ἐστὶν ἢ
40 πάθη τούτων καθ' αὐτά. ἑτέρα δ' ἐπιστήμη ἐστὶν
87 b ἑτέρας, ὅσων αἱ ἀρχαὶ μήτ' ἐκ τῶν αὐτῶν μήθ'
ἅτεραι[1] ἐκ τῶν ἑτέρων. τούτου δὲ σημεῖον ὅταν
εἰς τὰ ἀναπόδεικτα ἔλθῃ· δεῖ γὰρ αὐτὰ ἐν τῷ αὐτῷ
γένει εἶναι τοῖς ἀποδεδειγμένοις. σημεῖον δὲ καὶ
τούτου ὅταν τὰ δεικνύμενα δι' αὐτῶν ἐν τῷ αὐτῷ
γένει ὦσι καὶ συγγενῆ.

5 XXIX. Πλείους δ' ἀποδείξεις εἶναι τοῦ αὐτοῦ
ἐγχωρεῖ οὐ μόνον ἐκ τῆς αὐτῆς συστοιχίας λαμβάνοντι μὴ τὸ συνεχὲς μέσον, οἷον τῶν ΑΒ τὸ Γ
καὶ Δ καὶ Ζ, ἀλλὰ καὶ ἐξ ἑτέρας. οἷον ἔστω τὸ Α
μεταβάλλειν, τὸ δ' ἐφ' ᾧ Δ κινεῖσθαι, τὸ δὲ Β
ἥδεσθαι, καὶ πάλιν τὸ Η ἠρεμίζεσθαι. ἀληθὲς οὖν
10 καὶ τὸ Δ τοῦ Β καὶ τὸ Α τοῦ Δ κατηγορεῖν· ὁ γὰρ
ἡδόμενος κινεῖται καὶ τὸ κινούμενον μεταβάλλει.
πάλιν τὸ Α τοῦ Η καὶ τὸ Η τοῦ Β ἀληθὲς κατη-
γορεῖν· πᾶς γὰρ ὁ ἡδόμενος ἠρεμίζεται καὶ ὁ ἠρεμι-
ζόμενος μεταβάλλει. ὥστε δι' ἑτέρων μέσων καὶ
οὐκ ἐκ τῆς αὐτῆς συστοιχίας ὁ συλλογισμός. οὐ μὴν
15 ὥστε μηδέτερον κατὰ μηδετέρου λέγεσθαι τῶν
μέσων· ἀνάγκη γὰρ τῷ αὐτῷ τινι ἄμφω ὑπάρχειν.

1 ἅτεραι Philoponus (?), ci. Mure : ἕτεραι Bn : ἕτερα Ad.

a Not in the strict sense : cf. Met. XIII (M) ii.
b The species and their essential attributes.
c If one set of principles is derived from the other, they
belong respectively to a lower and a higher branch of the
same science.   d The ultimate truths or postulates.
e Sc., with either or both of the extreme terms.

additional factors is this : a unit is a substance [a]
without position, but a point is a substance with
position : I regard the latter as containing an additional factor.

XXVIII. A science is one if it is concerned with a
single genus or class of objects which are composed
of the primary elements of that genus and are parts
of it or essential modifications of those parts.[b] One
science is different from another if their principles
do not belong to the same genus, or if the principles
of the one are not derived from the principles of the
other.[c] This is verified when one reaches the in-
demonstrables,[d] because these must be in the same
genus as the things demonstrated. This again is
verified when the conclusions proved by their means
are in the same genus and cognate.

XXIX. It is possible to have more than one demonstration of the same conclusion, not only by selecting
a middle term, not directly connected,[e] from the
same series, e.g., by choosing C or D or F as the
middle term for AB, but also by choosing one from
another series.[f] For example, A is change, D being
moved, B pleasure and G relaxation. Then it is true
both to predicate D of B and A of D ; because if a
man is pleased he is moved, and that which is moved
changes. Again it is true to predicate A of G and
G of B ; because everyone who is pleased relaxes,
and one who relaxes changes. Thus the conclusion
can be drawn by means of different middle terms
which do not belong to the same series. Of course
the two middles must not exclude one another ; both
must apply to some of the same subject. We must

What makes a science one.

There may be more than one proof of the same con-clusion.

[f] *i.e.,* another chain of reasoning. There can, however,
be only one *scientific* demonstration of any given fact.

ἐπισκέψασθαι δὲ καὶ διὰ τῶν ἄλλων σχημάτων
ὁσαχῶς ἐνδέχεται τοῦ αὐτοῦ γενέσθαι συλλογισμόν.

XXX. Τοῦ δ' ἀπὸ τύχης οὐκ ἔστιν ἐπιστήμη δι'
20 ἀποδείξεως. οὔτε γὰρ ὡς ἀναγκαῖον οὔθ' ὡς ἐπὶ
τὸ πολὺ τὸ ἀπὸ τύχης ἐστίν, ἀλλὰ τὸ παρὰ ταῦτα
γιγνόμενον· ἡ δ' ἀπόδειξις θατέρου τούτων. πᾶς
γὰρ συλλογισμὸς ἢ δι' ἀναγκαίων ἢ διὰ τῶν ὡς ἐπὶ
τὸ πολὺ προτάσεων· καὶ εἰ μὲν αἱ προτάσεις ἀναγ-
25 καῖαι, καὶ τὸ συμπέρασμα ἀναγκαῖον, εἰ δ' ὡς ἐπὶ
τὸ πολύ, καὶ τὸ συμπέρασμα τοιοῦτον. ὥστ' εἰ τὸ
ἀπὸ τύχης μήθ' ὡς ἐπὶ τὸ πολὺ μήτ' ἀναγκαῖον,
οὐκ ἂν εἴη αὐτοῦ ἀπόδειξις.

XXXI. Οὐδὲ δι' αἰσθήσεως ἔστιν ἐπίστασθαι. εἰ
γὰρ καὶ ἔστιν ἡ αἴσθησις τοῦ τοιοῦδε καὶ μὴ τοῦδέ
30 τινος, ἀλλ' αἰσθάνεσθαί γε ἀναγκαῖον τόδε τι καὶ
πού καὶ νῦν. τὸ δὲ καθόλου καὶ ἐπὶ πᾶσιν ἀδύνατον
αἰσθάνεσθαι· οὐ γὰρ τόδε οὐδὲ νῦν· οὐ γὰρ ἂν ἦν
καθόλου· τὸ γὰρ ἀεὶ καὶ πανταχοῦ καθόλου φαμὲν
εἶναι. ἐπεὶ οὖν αἱ μὲν ἀποδείξεις καθόλου, ταῦτα
δ' οὐκ ἔστιν αἰσθάνεσθαι, φανερὸν ὅτι οὐδ' ἐπίστα-
35 σθαι δι' αἰσθήσεως ἔστιν, ἀλλὰ δῆλον ὅτι καὶ εἰ
ἦν αἰσθάνεσθαι τὸ τρίγωνον ὅτι δυσὶν ὀρθαῖς ἴσας
ἔχει τὰς γωνίας, ἐζητοῦμεν ἂν ἀπόδειξιν καὶ οὐχ

---

^a It is tempting to regard this observation as a sort of
" marginal jotting " in Aristotle's lecture notes. The project
is not carried out.

^b For chance see *Physics* II. iv-vi, and *cf. Met.* 1064 b
32 ff.

^c When we perceive a sensible object, what we perceive is,
in one sense, a complex of sensible qualities (colour, shape,
size, etc.) which constitute a recognizable type. But the

examine this point in the other figures to see in how many ways it is possible to draw the same inference.[a]

XXX. There can be no demonstrative knowledge of the fortuitous.[b] What happens by chance is neither a necessary nor a usual event, but something which happens in a different way from either; whereas demonstration is concerned with one or the other of them. Every syllogism proceeds through premisses which are either necessary or usual ; if the premisses are necessary, the conclusion is necessary too ; and if the premisses are usual, so is the conclusion. Hence if the fortuitous is neither usual nor necessary, there can be no demonstration of it.

There is no science of the fortuitous.

XXXI. Scientific knowledge cannot be acquired by sense-perception. Even granting that perception is of the object as qualified, and not of a mere particular,[c] still what we perceive must be a particular thing at a particular place and time. On the other hand a universal term of general application cannot be perceived by the senses, because it is not a particular thing or at a given time ; if it were, it would not be universal ; for we describe as universal only that which obtains always and everywhere. Therefore since demonstrations are universal, and universals cannot be perceived by the senses, obviously knowledge cannot be acquired by sense-perception. Again it is obvious that even if it were possible to perceive by the senses that the sum of the angles of a triangle is equal to two right angles, we should still require a proof of this ; we should not (as some [d]

Sense-perception cannot give scientific knowledge,

fact remains that the object perceived is only one particular instance of the type.

[d] *e.g.*, Protagoras—if Plato represents his meaning fairly (which is questionable) in *Theaetetus* 151 E. *Cf.* Diogenes Laertius ix. 51.

87 b

ὥσπερ φασί τινες ἠπιστάμεθα· αἰσθάνεσθαι μὲν γὰρ
ἀνάγκη καθ᾽ ἕκαστον, ἡ δ᾽ ἐπιστήμη τῷ[1] τὸ καθόλου
γνωρίζειν ἐστίν. διὸ καὶ εἰ ἐπὶ τῆς σελήνης ὄντες
40 ἑωρῶμεν ἀντιφράττουσαν τὴν γῆν, οὐκ ἂν ᾔδειμεν

88 a τὴν αἰτίαν τῆς ἐκλείψεως. ᾐσθανόμεθα γὰρ ἂν ὅτι
νῦν ἐκλείπει, καὶ οὐ διότι ὅλως· οὐ γὰρ ἦν τοῦ
καθόλου αἴσθησις. οὐ μὴν ἀλλ᾽ ἐκ τοῦ θεωρεῖν
τοῦτο πολλάκις συμβαῖνον τὸ καθόλου ἂν θηρεύ-
σαντες ἀπόδειξιν εἴχομεν· ἐκ γὰρ τῶν καθ᾽ ἕκαστα
5 πλειόνων τὸ καθόλου δῆλον. τὸ δὲ καθόλου τίμιον,
ὅτι δηλοῖ τὸ αἴτιον· ὥστε περὶ τῶν τοιούτων ἡ
καθόλου τιμιωτέρα τῶν αἰσθήσεων καὶ τῆς νοή-
σεως, ὅσων ἕτερον τὸ αἴτιον· περὶ δὲ τῶν πρώτων
ἄλλος λόγος.

Φανερὸν οὖν ὅτι ἀδύνατον τῷ αἰσθάνεσθαι ἐπί-
10 στασθαί τι τῶν ἀποδεικτῶν,[2] εἰ μή τις τὸ αἰσθάνεσθαι τοῦτο λέγει, τὸ ἐπιστήμην ἔχειν δι᾽ ἀποδείξεως. ἔστι μέντοι ἔνια ἀναγόμενα εἰς αἰσθήσεως
ἔκλειψιν ἐν τοῖς προβλήμασιν. ἔνια γὰρ εἰ ἑωρῶμεν
οὐκ ἂν ἐζητοῦμεν, οὐχ ὡς εἰδότες τῷ ὁρᾶν, ἀλλ᾽
ὡς ἔχοντες τὸ καθόλου ἐκ τοῦ ὁρᾶν. οἷον εἰ τὴν
15 ὕαλον τετρυπημένην ἑωρῶμεν καὶ τὸ φῶς διόν,

---

[1] τῷ] τὸ B, Philoponus (?), Ross.
[2] ἀποδεικτικῶν ABd.

---

[a] Particular facts (given by sense-perception) have their
causes in ultimate laws or truths (apprehended by intuition).

maintain) *know* that it is so. Sense-perception must be concerned with particulars, whereas knowledge depends upon recognition of the universal. Hence if we were on the moon and saw the earth intercepting the light of the sun, we should not know the cause of the eclipse. We should only perceive that an eclipse was taking place at that moment ; we should have no perception at all of the reason for it, because (as we have seen) sense-perception does not tell us anything about universals. If, however, by observing repeated instances we had succeeded in grasping the universal, we should have our proof ; because it is from the repetition of particular experiences that we obtain our view of the universal. The value of the universal is that it exhibits the cause. Thus in considering facts of this kind which have a cause other than themselves, knowledge of the universal is more valuable than perception by the senses or intuition.[a] Primary truths call for separate consideration.[b]

Clearly then it is impossible to acquire knowledge although its of any demonstrable fact by sense-perception, unless limitations by sense-perception one means the acquisition of may impede knowledge by demonstration. There are some pro- hension. blems, however, which are referable to a failure of sense-perception ; *e.g.*, there are phenomena whose explanation would cause no difficulty if we could see what happens ; not because we know a thing by seeing it, but because seeing it enables us to grasp the universal. For example, if we could see the channels in the burning-glass and the light passing

Logic shows their connexion by proving the specific truth which covers all relevant particulars.
[b] *Cf.* 100 b 12.

88 a

δῆλον ἂν ἦν καὶ διὰ τί καίει, τῷ ὁρᾶν μὲν χωρὶς
ἐφ᾽ ἑκάστης, νοῆσαι δ᾽ ἅμα ὅτι ἐπὶ πασῶν οὕτως.

XXXII. Τὰς δ᾽ αὐτὰς ἀρχὰς ἁπάντων εἶναι τῶν
συλλογισμῶν ἀδύνατον, πρῶτον μὲν λογικῶς θεω-
20 ροῦσιν. οἱ μὲν γὰρ ἀληθεῖς εἰσι τῶν συλλογισμῶν, οἱ δὲ ψευδεῖς. καὶ γὰρ εἰ¹ ἔστιν ἀληθὲς ἐκ
ψευδῶν συλλογίσασθαι, ἀλλ᾽ ἅπαξ τοῦτο γίγνεται,
οἷον εἰ τὸ Α κατὰ τοῦ Γ ἀληθές, τὸ δὲ μέσον τὸ Β
ψεῦδος· οὔτε γὰρ τὸ Α τῷ Β ὑπάρχει οὔτε τὸ Β
25 τῷ Γ. ἀλλ᾽ ἐὰν τούτων μέσα λαμβάνηται τῶν
προτάσεων, ψευδεῖς ἔσονται διὰ τὸ πᾶν συμπέρασμα ψεῦδος ἐκ ψευδῶν εἶναι, τὰ δ᾽ ἀληθῆ ἐξ
ἀληθῶν, ἕτερα δὲ τὰ ψευδῆ καὶ τἀληθῆ. εἶτα οὐδὲ
τὰ ψευδῆ ἐκ τῶν αὐτῶν ἑαυτοῖς· ἔστι γὰρ ψευδῆ
ἀλλήλοις καὶ ἐναντία καὶ ἀδύνατα ἅμα εἶναι, οἷον
30 τὸ τὴν δικαιοσύνην εἶναι ἀδικίαν ἢ δειλίαν, καὶ τὸν
ἄνθρωπον ἵππον ἢ βοῦν, ἢ τὸ ἴσον μεῖζον ἢ ἔλαττον.

Ἐκ δὲ τῶν κειμένων ὧδε· οὐδὲ γὰρ τῶν ἀληθῶν
αἱ αὐταὶ ἀρχαὶ πάντων. ἕτεραι γὰρ πολλῶν τῷ
γένει αἱ ἀρχαί, καὶ οὐδ᾽ ἐφαρμόττουσαι, οἷον αἱ
μονάδες ταῖς στιγμαῖς οὐκ ἐφαρμόττουσιν· αἱ μὲν
γὰρ οὐκ ἔχουσι θέσιν, αἱ δὲ ἔχουσιν. ἀνάγκη δέ
35 γε ἢ εἰς μέσα ἁρμόττειν ἢ ἄνωθεν ἢ κάτωθεν, ἢ

¹ εἰ om. ABd.

ᵃ According to Gorgias, fr. 5 (Diels) = Theophrastus, *de Igne* 73.

ᵇ Cf. *An. Pr.* II. ii-iv.

ᶜ This is inaccurate. A false conclusion can have one true premiss, and a true conclusion can have one or both premisses false. Thus there is no guarantee that the irregularity " only happens once." However, the general distinction between true and false syllogisms is fair enough.

ᵈ As being peculiar to different sciences.

through,[a] it would also be obvious why it burns; because we should see the effect severally in each particular instance, and appreciate at the same time that this is what happens in every case.

XXXII. Syllogisms cannot all have the same first principles. (1) This can be shown, in the first place, by dialectical arguments. (a) Some syllogisms are true, others are false. It is, of course, possible to draw a true conclusion from false premisses,[b] but this only happens once ⟨in a chain of inference⟩; e.g., if it is true to assert A of C, but false to assert the middle term B, because A does not apply to B nor B to C; now if we take middle terms in these premisses, the ⟨new⟩ premisses will be false, because every false conclusion is based upon false premisses, whereas true conclusions are drawn from true premisses,[c] and what is false is different from what is true. (b) Even false conclusions do not always have identical first principles; because a false judgement may either involve a contradiction, e.g., that justice is injustice or that the equal is greater or smaller; or incompatibility, e.g., that justice is cowardice, or that a man is a horse or an ox.

(2) The impossibility can be shown from what we have established already, as follows. (a) Not even all true syllogisms have the same principles. Many have first principles which are generically different,[d] and cannot be interchanged; as for example units cannot be interchanged with points, since the latter have position and the former have not. In any case the terms [e] must be introduced either as middles, or as majors or minors, to the original terms; or partly as

Syllogisms cannot all have the same first principles. First dialectical proof.

Second dialectical proof.

Five logical arguments.

---

[e] Sc., belonging to the principle of the second science, by which it is hoped to prove the facts of the first.

τοὺς μὲν εἴσω ἔχειν τοὺς δ' ἔξω τῶν ὅρων. ἀλλ'
οὐδὲ τῶν κοινῶν ἀρχῶν οἷόν τ' εἶναί τινας ἐξ ὧν
88 b ἅπαντα δειχθήσεται (λέγω δὲ κοινὰς οἷον τὸ πᾶν
φάναι ἢ ἀποφάναι)· τὰ γὰρ γένη τῶν ὄντων ἕτερα,
καὶ τὰ μὲν τοῖς ποσοῖς τὰ δὲ τοῖς ποιοῖς ὑπάρχει
μόνοις, μεθ' ὧν δείκνυται διὰ τῶν κοινῶν. ἔτι αἱ
5 ἀρχαὶ οὐ πολλῷ ἐλάττους τῶν συμπερασμάτων·
ἀρχαὶ μὲν γὰρ αἱ προτάσεις, αἱ δὲ προτάσεις ἢ προσ-
λαμβανομένου ὅρου ἢ ἐμβαλλομένου εἰσίν. ἔτι τὰ
συμπεράσματα ἄπειρα, οἱ δ' ὅροι πεπερασμένοι.
ἔτι αἱ ἀρχαὶ αἱ μὲν ἐξ ἀνάγκης, αἱ δ' ἐνδεχόμεναι.

Οὕτω μὲν οὖν σκοπουμένοις ἀδύνατον τὰς αὐτὰς
10 εἶναι πεπερασμένας, ἀπείρων ὄντων τῶν συμπερασμάτων. εἰ δ' ἄλλως πως λέγοι τις, οἷον ὅτι αἱδὶ

---

[a] Sc., so that terms from different genera will be predicated of one another ; which is impossible (75 b 10).

[b] It would be truer to say that the common principles
provide the general conditions of the proof which is drawn
from the special principles.

[c] This argument smacks of equivocation. In the hypothesis that all syllogisms have the same ἀρχαί the word ἀρχαί
seems to bear the sense of " ultimate principles," which
might well be expected to be few in comparison with the
many conclusions drawn from them. On the other hand
premisses are surely ἀρχαί only as " starting-points " relatively to the conclusion. If there is no equivocation, the
hypothesis is equivalent to " All syllogisms have the same
premisses," which scarcely needs refutation.

The effects of adding terms to a syllogism have been considered in *An. Pr.* 42 b 16 ff., where Aristotle decides that
" there will be many more conclusions than either terms or
premisses." Noting the inconsistency, Ross suspects that
the present passage expresses an earlier and superficial view.
But the rule stated in the other passage (quoted by Ross in

the former and partly as the latter.[a] (b) It is impossible that any of the common principles (e.g., the law of the excluded middle) should serve as premisses for all proofs ; because subjects belong to different genera, some of which are predicated only of quantities and others only of qualities. It is with the help of these that proofs are effected by means of the common first principles.[b] (c) The principles are not much fewer in number than the conclusions ; because the premisses are principles, and premisses are formed by adding another term either externally or internally.[c] (d) The conclusions are infinite in number whereas the terms are finite.[d] (e) Some principles are apodeictic, others problematic.[e]

If we regard the question in this way the principles cannot be the same for all or finite in number when the conclusions are infinite. (3) Supposing that " the Answers to the form " n premisses give $\frac{n(n-1)}{2}$ conclusions ") is valid only if we deny the name " premiss " to those conclusions from which as premisses the remaining conclusions are proved. E.g., to take one of Ross's examples : " from four premisses 'A is B,' ' B is C,' ' C is D,' ' D is E ' we get six conclusions ' A is C,' ' A is D,' ' A is E,' ' B is D,' ' B is E,' ' C is E ' " ; here only the first, fourth and sixth are proved directly from the original four premisses ; the remainder are proved by the help of three further premisses supplied from the conclusions. By this more accurate reckoning the premisses will always be one more than the conclusions, so Aristotle's statement in the present passage (if treated as a meiosis) is not far from the truth.

[d] The conclusions are infinitely many because we know of no limit that can be set to them ; but the principles, if " the same for all," must be limited, and so must the premisses and terms, if the premisses are principles. Yet we have just seen that the principles are " not much fewer " than the conclusions.

[e] And the conclusions drawn from them differ accordingly.

163

88 b

μὲν γεωμετρίας αἱδὶ δὲ λογισμῶν αἱδὶ δὲ ἰατρικῆς,
τί ἂν εἴη τὸ λεγόμενον ἄλλο πλὴν ὅτι εἰσὶν ἀρχαὶ
τῶν ἐπιστημῶν; τὸ δὲ τὰς αὐτὰς φάναι γελοῖον,
15 ὅτι αὐταὶ αὐταῖς αἱ αὐταί· πάντα γὰρ οὕτω γίγνεται
ταὐτά. ἀλλὰ μὴν οὐδὲ τὸ ἐξ ἁπάντων δείκνυσθαι
ὁτιοῦν, τοῦτ᾽ ἐστὶ τὸ ζητεῖν ἁπάντων εἶναι τὰς
αὐτὰς ἀρχάς· λίαν γὰρ εὔηθες. οὔτε γὰρ ἐν τοῖς
φανεροῖς μαθήμασι τοῦτο γίγνεται, οὔτ᾽ ἐν τῇ
ἀναλύσει δυνατόν· αἱ γὰρ ἄμεσοι προτάσεις ἀρχαί,
20 ἕτερον δὲ συμπέρασμα προσληφθείσης γίγνεται προτάσεως ἀμέσου. εἰ δὲ λέγοι τις τὰς πρώτας ἀμέσους προτάσεις ταύτας εἶναι ἀρχάς, μία ἐν ἑκάστῳ
γένει ἐστίν. εἰ δὲ μήτ᾽ ἐξ ἁπασῶν ὡς δέον δείκνυσθαι ὁτιοῦν μήθ᾽ οὕτως ἑτέρας ὥσθ᾽ ἑκάστης
25 ἐπιστήμης εἶναι ἑτέρας, λείπεται εἰ συγγενεῖς αἱ
ἀρχαὶ πάντων, ἀλλ᾽ ἐκ τωνδὶ μὲν ταδί, ἐκ δὲ τωνδὶ
ταδί. φανερὸν δὲ καὶ τοῦθ᾽ ὅτι οὐκ ἐνδέχεται·
δέδεικται γὰρ ὅτι ἄλλαι ἀρχαὶ τῷ γένει εἰσὶν αἱ
τῶν διαφόρων τῷ γένει. αἱ γὰρ ἀρχαὶ διτταί, ἐξ
ὧν τε καὶ περὶ ὅ· αἱ μὲν οὖν ἐξ ὧν κοιναί, αἱ δὲ
περὶ ὃ ἴδιαι, οἷον ἀριθμός, μέγεθος.

---

^a Viz., the definition of the subject-matter.
^b In ch. vii.
^c Cf. 75 b 2.

same " is used with another meaning, as if one should say " these are the very principles of geometry and these of arithmetic and these of medicine," this would simply mean no more than that there are principles of the sciences. It is absurd to say that they are the same *as themselves* ; because on this basis anything can be called the same. (4) Nor again does the attempt to maintain that all syllogisms have the same principles mean that any given proposition can be proved from the totality of first principles. This would be too absurd. It is not the case in the mathematical sciences whose methods are obvious ; and it is not possible in analysis, because here it is the immediate premisses that are the first principles, and each new conclusion is formed by the addition of a new immediate premiss. (5) If it be suggested that it is the primary immediate premisses that are the first principles, there is one [a] in each genus. (6) If, however, while it is not claimed that any conclusion must be provable from the totality of the first principles, it is still denied that the latter differ to the extent of being generically different for each science, it remains to consider whether the first principles of all propositions are cognate, but some are proper to the proofs of one and some to those of another particular science. It is obvious however that even this is impossible, because we have shown [b] that the first principles of things which differ in genus are themselves generically different. The fact is that first principles are of two kinds : the premisses from which demonstration proceeds, and the genus with which the demonstration is concerned.[c] The former are common, while the latter (*e.g.*, number and magnitude) are peculiar.

possible objections or evasions.

165

XXXIII. Τὸ δ' ἐπιστητὸν καὶ ἐπιστήμη διαφέρει
τοῦ δοξαστοῦ καὶ δόξης, ὅτι ἡ μὲν ἐπιστήμη καθόλου καὶ δι' ἀναγκαίων, τὸ δ' ἀναγκαῖον οὐκ ἐνδέχεται ἄλλως ἔχειν. ἔστι δέ τινα ἀληθῆ μὲν καὶ
ὄντα, ἐνδεχόμενα δὲ καὶ ἄλλως ἔχειν. δῆλον οὖν
ὅτι περὶ μὲν ταῦτα ἐπιστήμη οὐκ ἔστιν· εἴη γὰρ
35 ἂν ἀδύνατα ἄλλως ἔχειν τὰ δυνατὰ ἄλλως ἔχειν.
ἀλλὰ μὴν οὐδὲ νοῦς (λέγω γὰρ νοῦν ἀρχὴν ἐπιστήμης) οὐδ' ἐπιστήμη ἀναπόδεικτος (τοῦτο δ' ἐστὶν
89 a ὑπόληψις τῆς ἀμέσου προτάσεως). ἀληθὴς δ' ἐστὶ
νοῦς καὶ ἐπιστήμη καὶ δόξα καὶ τὸ διὰ τούτων
λεγόμενον· ὥστε λείπεται δόξαν εἶναι περὶ τὸ ἀληθὲς μὲν ἢ ψεῦδος, ἐνδεχόμενον δὲ καὶ ἄλλως ἔχειν.
τοῦτο δ' ἐστὶν ὑπόληψις τῆς ἀμέσου προτάσεως
5 καὶ μὴ ἀναγκαίας. καὶ ὁμολογούμενον δ' οὕτω
τοῖς φαινομένοις· ἥ τε γὰρ δόξα ἀβέβαιον, καὶ ἡ
φύσις ἡ τοιαύτη. πρὸς δὲ τούτοις οὐδεὶς οἴεται
δοξάζειν ὅταν οἴηται ἀδύνατον ἄλλως ἔχειν, ἀλλ'
ἐπίστασθαι· ἀλλ' ὅταν εἶναι μὲν οὕτως, οὐ μὴν
ἀλλὰ καὶ ἄλλως οὐδὲν κωλύειν, τότε δοξάζειν, ὡς
10 τοῦ μὲν τοιούτου δόξαν οὖσαν, τοῦ δ' ἀναγκαίου
ἐπιστήμην.

Πῶς οὖν ἔστι τὸ αὐτὸ δοξάσαι καὶ ἐπίστασθαι,
καὶ διὰ τί οὐκ ἔσται[1] ἡ δόξα ἐπιστήμη, εἴ τις θήσει
ἅπαν ὃ οἶδεν ἐνδέχεσθαι δοξάζειν; ἀκολουθήσει

---

[1] ἔστιν Dc.

---

[a] It does not seem that Aristotle intends any distinction
between intuition and indemonstrable knowledge.

[b] i.e., mental states or activities.

XXXIII. Knowledge and its object differ from opinion and its object in that knowledge is of the universal and proceeds by necessary propositions ; and that which is necessary cannot be otherwise ; but there are some propositions which, though true and real, are also capable of being otherwise. Obviously it is not knowledge that is concerned with these ; if it were, that which is capable of being otherwise would be incapable of being otherwise. Nor is it intuition—by which I mean the starting-point of knowledge—or indemonstrable knowledge,[a] which is the apprehension of an immediate premiss. But the only things [b] that are true are intuition, knowledge and opinion, and the discourse resulting from these. Therefore we are left with the conclusion that it is opinion that is concerned with that which is true or false and which may be otherwise. In other words opinion is the assumption of a premiss which is neither mediated nor necessary. This description agrees with observed usage ; for opinion, like events of the character which we have just described, is uncertain. Besides, no one thinks that he is " opining " when he thinks that a thing cannot be otherwise ; he thinks that he has knowledge. It is when he thinks that a thing is so, but nevertheless there is no reason why it should not be otherwise, that he thinks that he is opining ; which implies that opinion is concerned with this sort of proposition, while knowledge is concerned with that which must be so.

How, then, is it possible for the same thing to be an object of both opinion and knowledge ? and if someone maintains that he can opine everything that he knows, what reason can we give to show why opinion is not knowledge ? Both the man who knows

Knowledge contrasted with opinion.

Opinion is of the contingent.

How can knowledge and opinion have the same object ?

89 a

γὰρ ὁ μὲν εἰδὼς ὁ δὲ δοξάζων διὰ τῶν μέσων ἕως
15 εἰς τὰ ἄμεσα ἔλθῃ, ὥστ' εἴπερ ἐκεῖνος οἶδε, καὶ ὁ
δοξάζων οἶδεν. ὥσπερ γὰρ καὶ τὸ ὅτι δοξάζειν
ἔστι, καὶ τὸ διότι· τοῦτο δὲ τὸ μέσον. ἢ εἰ μὲν
οὕτως ὑπολήψεται τὰ μὴ ἐνδεχόμενα ἄλλως ἔχειν
ὥσπερ [ἔχει]¹ τοὺς ὁρισμοὺς δι' ὧν αἱ ἀποδείξεις,
20 οὐ δοξάσει ἀλλ' ἐπιστήσεται· εἰ δ' ἀληθῆ μὲν εἶναι,
οὐ μέντοι ταῦτά γε αὐτοῖς ὑπάρχειν κατ' οὐσίαν
καὶ κατὰ τὸ εἶδος, δοξάσει καὶ οὐκ ἐπιστήσεται
ἀληθῶς, καὶ τὸ ὅτι καὶ τὸ διότι, ἐὰν μὲν διὰ τῶν
ἀμέσων δοξάσῃ· ἐὰν δὲ μὴ διὰ τῶν ἀμέσων, τὸ ὅτι
μόνον δοξάσει; τοῦ δ' αὐτοῦ δόξα καὶ ἐπιστήμη
οὐ πάντως ἐστίν, ἀλλ' ὥσπερ καὶ ψευδὴς καὶ ἀλη-
25 θὴς τοῦ αὐτοῦ τρόπον τινά, οὕτω καὶ ἐπιστήμη καὶ
δόξα τοῦ αὐτοῦ. καὶ γὰρ δόξαν ἀληθῆ καὶ ψευδῆ
ὡς μέν τινες λέγουσι τοῦ αὐτοῦ εἶναι, ἄτοπα συμβαίνει αἱρεῖσθαι ἄλλα τε καὶ μὴ δοξάζειν ὃ δοξάζει
ψευδῶς· ἐπεὶ δὲ τὸ αὐτὸ πλεοναχῶς λέγεται, ἔστι
30 μὲν ὡς ἐνδέχεται, ἔστι δ' ὡς οὔ. τὸ μὲν γὰρ σύμ-
μετρον εἶναι τὴν διάμετρον ἀληθῶς δοξάζειν ἄτοπον·
ἀλλ' ὅτι ἡ διάμετρος, περὶ ἣν αἱ δόξαι, τὸ αὐτό,
οὕτω τοῦ αὐτοῦ, τὸ δὲ τί ἦν εἶναι ἑκατέρῳ κατὰ
τὸν λόγον οὐ τὸ αὐτό. ὁμοίως δὲ καὶ ἐπιστήμη καὶ
δόξα τοῦ αὐτοῦ. ἡ μὲν γὰρ οὕτως τοῦ ζῴου ὥστε
35 μὴ ἐνδέχεσθαι μὴ εἶναι ζῷον, ἡ δ' ὥστ' ἐνδέχεσθαι,

¹ secl. Ross : ἔχειν M, Bekker, Waitz.

---

[a] *Cf.* the discussion of the Law of Contradiction in *Met.*
IV (Γ) iv-viii.
[b] The true opinion—that the diagonal is incommensurable
—recognizes a property of the diagonal which follows from
its essence as expressed in definition ; the contrary false
opinion does not.

and the man who opines will proceed by means of the middle terms until they reach the immediate premisses; so that if the former knows, so does the latter; because it is equally possible to opine the fact and the reason for it; *i.e.*, the middle term. The solution is probably this. If you apprehend Because they regard it differently, propositions which cannot be otherwise in the same way as you apprehend the definitions through which demonstrations are effected, you will have not opinion but knowledge; but if you only apprehend that the attributes are true and not that they apply in virtue of the essence and specific nature of their subject, you will have not true knowledge but an opinion, of both the fact and the reason for it,—that is, if you have reached your opinion through the immediate premisses; otherwise you will have an opinion only of the fact. It is not in every sense that opinion and just as true and false opinion do, knowledge have the same object, but only in the sense that true and false opinion have, in a manner, the same object. (The sense in which some authorities [a] hold true and false opinion to apply to the same object involves, amongst other absurdities, the view that false opinion is not opinion at all.) Since " the same " is an equivocal expression, there is a sense in which this is possible, and another in which it is not. It would be absurd to have a true opinion that the diagonal of a square is commensurable with the sides; but since the diagonal, with which the opinions are concerned, is the same, in this sense the true and the false opinion have the same object; but the essence (in accordance with the definition) of the two objects is not the same.[b] It is in this sense that knowledge and opinion can have the same object. Knowledge knowledge seeing an essential apprehends the term " animal " as a necessary,

169

89 a

οἷον εἰ ἡ μὲν ὅπερ ἀνθρώπου ἐστίν, ἡ δ' ἀνθρώπου
μέν, μὴ ὅπερ δ' ἀνθρώπου. τὸ αὐτὸ γὰρ ὅτι ἄνθρωπος, τὸ δ' ὡς οὐ τὸ αὐτό.

Φανερὸν δ' ἐκ τούτων ὅτι οὐδὲ δοξάζειν ἅμα τὸ
αὐτὸ καὶ ἐπίστασθαι ἐνδέχεται. ἅμα γὰρ ἂν ἔχοι
89 b ὑπόληψιν τοῦ ἄλλως ἔχειν καὶ μὴ ἄλλως τὸ αὐτό·
ὅπερ οὐκ ἐνδέχεται. ἐν ἄλλῳ μὲν γὰρ ἑκάτερον
εἶναι ἐνδέχεται τοῦ αὐτοῦ ὡς εἴρηται, ἐν δὲ τῷ
αὐτῷ οὐδ' οὕτως οἷόν τε· ἕξει γὰρ ὑπόληψιν ἅμα,
5 οἷον ὅτι ὁ ἄνθρωπος ὅπερ ζῷον (τοῦτο γὰρ ἦν τὸ
μὴ ἐνδέχεσθαι εἶναι μὴ ζῷον) καὶ μὴ ὅπερ ζῷον·
τοῦτο γὰρ ἔστω[1] τὸ ἐνδέχεσθαι.

Τὰ δὲ λοιπὰ πῶς δεῖ διανεῖμαι ἐπί τε διανοίας
καὶ νοῦ καὶ ἐπιστήμης καὶ τέχνης καὶ φρονήσεως
καὶ σοφίας, τὰ μὲν φυσικῆς τὰ δὲ ἠθικῆς θεωρίας
μᾶλλόν ἐστιν.

10 XXXIV. Ἡ δ' ἀγχίνοιά ἐστιν εὐστοχία τις ἐν
ἀσκέπτῳ χρόνῳ τοῦ μέσου, οἷον εἴ τις ἰδὼν ὅτι ἡ
σελήνη τὸ λαμπρὸν ἀεὶ ἔχει πρὸς τὸν ἥλιον, ταχὺ
ἐνενόησε διὰ τί τοῦτο, ὅτι διὰ τὸ λάμπειν ἀπὸ τοῦ
ἡλίου· ἢ διαλεγόμενον πλουσίῳ ἔγνω διότι δανεί-
15 ζεται· ἢ διότι φίλοι, ὅτι ἐχθροὶ τοῦ αὐτοῦ. πάντα
γὰρ τὰ αἴτια τὰ μέσα [ὁ][2] ἰδὼν τὰ ἄκρα ἐγνώρισεν.

---

[1] ἔσται A[2].   [2] secl. Ross: om. Philoponus (?).

---

[a] Cf. 73 b 16 ff.

[b] Exact equivalents are hard to find in English. διάνοια
is a comprehensive term for coherent thinking; νοῦς is direct
apprehension of the indemonstrable (cf. De Anima III. iv-
vii); ἐπιστήμη is the logical exploration of scientific facts;
τέχνη the application of thought to production; φρόνησις the
appreciation of moral values; σοφία the study of reality at
the highest level. The last five are discussed in Eth. Nic. VI.
iii-vii.

opinion as a contingent attribute ; *e.g.*, knowledge apprehends it as essentially predicable of " man " ; opinion as predicable of " man " but not essentially. The subject " man " is the same in both cases, but the mode of predication is not the same. connexion where opinion does not.

These considerations make it clear that it is impossible to have opinion and knowledge at the same time about the same object ; otherwise one would apprehend that the same thing both could and could not be otherwise, which is impossible. Knowledge and opinion of the same object may exist separately in different minds in the sense which we have explained ; but they cannot so exist in the same mind. This would imply the apprehension at one and the same time (*e.g.*) that man is essentially an animal (we have seen [a] that this is what it means to say that it is impossible for man not to be an animal) and is not essentially an animal (which we may take to be the meaning of the contrary assertion). Hence one cannot have both at once about the same object.

How the other modes of thought should be distributed between cogitation, intuition, science, art, practical intelligence and wisdom will be better considered partly by natural science and partly by ethics.[b] Other modes of thought to be discussed elsewhere.

XXXIV. Quickness of wit is a sort of flair for hitting upon the middle term without a moment's hesitation. A man sees that the moon always has its bright side facing the sun, and immediately realizes the reason : that it is because the moon derives its brightness from the sun ; or he sees someone talking to a rich man, and decides that it is because he is trying to borrow money ; or he understands why people are friends, because they have a common enemy. In all these cases, perception of the extreme terms enables him to recognize the cause or middle term. Quickness of wit.

171

τὸ λαμπρὸν εἶναι τὸ πρὸς τὸν ἥλιον ἐφ' οὗ Α, τὸ
λάμπειν ἀπὸ τοῦ ἡλίου Β, σελήνη τὸ Γ. ὑπάρχει
δὴ τῇ μὲν σελήνῃ τῷ Γ τὸ Β, τὸ λάμπειν ἀπὸ τοῦ
ἡλίου· τῷ δὲ Β τὸ Α, τὸ πρὸς τοῦτ' εἶναι τὸ
20 λαμπρὸν ἀφ' οὗ λάμπει· ὥστε καὶ τῷ Γ τὸ Α διὰ
τοῦ Β.

A stands for " bright side facing the sun," B for " deriving brightness from the sun," and C for " moon." Then B, " deriving brightness from the sun," applies to C, " moon," and A, " having its bright side facing the source of its brightness," applies to B. Thus A applies to C through B.

B

I. Τὰ ζητούμενά ἐστιν ἴσα τὸν ἀριθμὸν ὅσαπερ
ἐπιστάμεθα. ζητοῦμεν δὲ τέτταρα, τὸ ὅτι, τὸ
25 διότι, εἰ ἔστι, τί ἐστιν. ὅταν μὲν γὰρ πότερον τόδε
ἢ τόδε ζητῶμεν, εἰς ἀριθμὸν θέντες, οἷον πότερον
ἐκλείπει ὁ ἥλιος ἢ οὔ, τὸ ὅτι ζητοῦμεν. σημεῖον δὲ
τούτου· εὑρόντες γὰρ ὅτι ἐκλείπει πεπαύμεθα· καὶ
ἐὰν ἐξ ἀρχῆς εἰδῶμεν ὅτι ἐκλείπει, οὐ ζητοῦμεν
πότερον. ὅταν δὲ εἰδῶμεν τὸ ὅτι, τὸ διότι ζητοῦ-
30 μεν, οἷον εἰδότες ὅτι ἐκλείπει καὶ ὅτι κινεῖται ἡ γῆ,
τὸ διότι ἐκλείπει ἢ διότι κινεῖται ζητοῦμεν. ταῦτα
μὲν οὖν οὕτως, ἔνια δ' ἄλλον τρόπον ζητοῦμεν, οἷον
εἰ ἔστιν ἢ μὴ ἔστι κένταυρος ἢ θεός (τὸ δ' εἰ ἔστιν ἢ
μὴ ἁπλῶς λέγω, ἀλλ' οὐκ εἰ λευκὸς ἢ μή)· γνόντες
δὲ ὅτι ἔστι, τί ἐστι ζητοῦμεν, οἷον τί οὖν ἐστι θεός,
35 ἢ τί ἐστιν ἄνθρωπος;

II. Ἃ μὲν οὖν ζητοῦμεν καὶ ἃ εὑρόντες ἴσμεν,
ταῦτα καὶ τοσαῦτά ἐστι. ζητοῦμεν δέ, ὅταν μὲν
ζητῶμεν τὸ ὅτι ἢ τὸ εἰ ἔστιν ἁπλῶς, ἆρ' ἔστι μέσον

---

[a] *i.e.*, a predicate as well as a subject.

[b] The four questions intended seem clearly to be (1) Is
S P ? (2) Why is S P ? (3) Does S exist ? (4) What is (the
174

BOOK II

I. THERE are four kinds of question that we ask, and they correspond to the kinds of things that we know. They are : the question of fact, the question of reason or cause, the question of existence, and the question of essence. (1) When we ask whether this or that is so, introducing a plurality of terms [a] (*e.g.*, whether the sun suffers eclipse or not), we are asking the question of fact. The proof is that when we have discovered that it does suffer eclipse our inquiry is finished ; and if we know at the outset that it does so, we do not ask whether it does. It is when we know the fact that we ask (2) the reason ; *e.g.*, if we know that the sun suffers eclipse and that the earth moves, we ask the reasons for these facts. That is how we ask these questions ; but there are others which take a different form : *e.g.* (3) whether a centaur or a god exists. The question of existence refers to simple existence, and not to whether the subject is (say) white or not. When we know that the subject exists, we ask (4) what it is ; *e.g.*, " what, then, is a god ? " or " a man ? " [b]

II. These are the four kinds of question which we ask and the four kinds of knowledge which we have when we have discovered the answers. When we ask the question of fact or of simple existence, we

definition of) S ?—*i.e.*, it is implied that each is asked about a subject term or substance. But *cf.* Introd. p. 12.

175

αὐτοῦ ἢ οὐκ ἔστιν· ὅταν δὲ γνόντες ἢ τὸ ὅτι ἢ εἰ
90 a ἔστιν, ἢ τὸ ἐπὶ μέρους ἢ τὸ ἁπλῶς, πάλιν τὸ διὰ τί
ζητῶμεν ἢ τὸ τί ἐστι, τότε ζητοῦμεν τί τὸ μέσον.
λέγω δὲ τὸ ὅτι ἢ εἰ ἔστιν ἐπὶ μέρους καὶ ἁπλῶς,
ἐπὶ μέρους μέν, ἆρ' ἐκλείπει ἡ σελήνη ἢ αὔξεται;
εἰ γάρ ἐστι τὶ ἢ μή ἐστι τὶ ἐν τοῖς τοιούτοις ζητοῦ-
5 μεν· ἁπλῶς δ', εἰ ἔστιν ἢ μὴ σελήνη ἢ νύξ.

Συμβαίνει ἄρα ἐν ἁπάσαις ταῖς ζητήσεσι ζητεῖν
ἢ εἰ ἔστι μέσον ἢ τί ἐστι τὸ μέσον. τὸ μὲν γὰρ
αἴτιον τὸ μέσον, ἐν ἅπασι δὲ τοῦτο ζητεῖται. ἆρ'
ἐκλείπει; ἆρ' ἔστι τι αἴτιον ἢ οὔ; μετὰ ταῦτα
γνόντες ὅτι ἔστι τι, τί οὖν τοῦτ' ἔστι ζητοῦμεν. τὸ
10 γὰρ αἴτιον τοῦ εἶναι μὴ τοδὶ ἢ τοδὶ ἀλλ' ἁπλῶς τὴν
οὐσίαν, ἢ τοῦ[1] μὴ ἁπλῶς ἀλλά τι τῶν καθ' αὑτὸ ἢ
κατὰ συμβεβηκός, τὸ μέσον ἐστίν. λέγω δὲ τὸ μὲν
ἁπλῶς τὸ ὑποκείμενον, οἷον σελήνην ἢ γῆν ἢ ἥλιον ἢ
τρίγωνον, τὸ δὲ τὶ ἔκλειψιν ἰσότητα ἀνισότητα, εἰ

---

[1] τοῦ Bonitz : τὸ codd.

---

[a] The "thing" for which the middle term is sought must
properly be an attribute or a connexion. It is only in so far
as middle term = cause that the formula can be applied to
substance. In a strictly teleological system to ask whether a
substance exists is to ask whether it has a cause, and to
ask what a substance is amounts to demanding a causal
definition. (Ross well compares *Met.* 1041 a 26, b 4, 1043 a
14-21, remarking truly that Aristotle seldom observes this
principle of definition.) But, as the examples show, Aristotle
is already thinking less of substances than of phenomena
and attributes. His analysis is indeed over-simplified.

are asking whether the thing [a] has a middle term or
not; but when, after ascertaining that the proposition is a fact or that the subject exists (in other words,
that the subject *is* in a particular sense, or simply *is*),
we then proceed to ask the reason for the fact, or
what the subject is, we are asking what the middle
term is. In describing the " fact " and " existence "
as particular and simple modes of being I mean this :
an example of particular being is " Does the moon
suffer eclipse ? " or " Does the moon wax ? " because
in such questions we are asking whether an attribute
is predicable of the subject ; an example of simple
being is " Does the moon exist ? " or " Does night [b]
exist ? "

It follows, then, that in all these questions we are
asking either " Is there a middle term ? " or " What
is the middle term ? " because the middle term is because we
the cause, and that is what we are trying to find out are always
in every case. " Does it suffer eclipse ? " means " Is cause.
there or is there not a cause ⟨for its being eclipsed⟩ ? " ;
and then, when we have ascertained that there is
a cause, we ask " then what is the cause ? " The
cause for a substance's being—not being this or that,
but simply existing—and the cause, not for its simply
existing, but for its being coupled with some essential
or accidental [c] attribute—is in both cases the middle
term. By that which simply exists I mean the subject—moon, earth, sun or triangle—; by that which
the subject is in a particular sense I mean the predicate : being eclipsed, equality, inequality, inter-

[b] Night is not a substance, like the moon, but either an
event or a privative attribute. If Aristotle intends to vary
his choice of subject, he should do so explicitly.

[c] Or rather " non-essential." A purely accidental attribute would be outside the scope of science.

90 a

ἐν μέσῳ ἢ μή. ἐν ἅπασι γὰρ τούτοις φανερόν ἐστιν
15 ὅτι τὸ αὐτό ἐστι τὸ τί ἐστι καὶ διὰ τί ἔστιν. τί
ἔστιν ἔκλειψις; στέρησις φωτὸς ἀπὸ σελήνης ὑπὸ
γῆς ἀντιφράξεως. διὰ τί ἔστιν ἔκλειψις, ἢ διὰ τί
ἐκλείπει ἡ σελήνη; διὰ τὸ ἀπολείπειν τὸ φῶς ἀντι-
φραττούσης τῆς γῆς. τί ἐστι συμφωνία; λόγος
20 ἀριθμῶν ἐν ὀξεῖ καὶ¹ βαρεῖ. διὰ τί συμφωνεῖ τὸ
ὀξὺ τῷ βαρεῖ; διὰ τὸ λόγον ἔχειν ἀριθμῶν τὸ ὀξὺ
καὶ τὸ βαρύ. ἆρ' ἔστι συμφωνεῖν τὸ ὀξὺ καὶ τὸ
βαρύ; ἆρ' ἐστὶν ἐν ἀριθμοῖς ὁ λόγος αὐτῶν;
λαβόντες δ' ὅτι ἔστι, τίς οὖν ἐστιν ὁ λόγος;

Ὅτι δ' ἐστὶ τοῦ μέσου ἡ ζήτησις, δηλοῖ ὅσων τὸ
25 μέσον αἰσθητόν. ζητοῦμεν γὰρ μὴ ᾐσθημένοι, οἷον
τῆς ἐκλείψεως, εἰ ἔστιν ἢ μή. εἰ δ' ἦμεν ἐπὶ τῆς
σελήνης, οὐκ ἂν ἐζητοῦμεν οὔτ' εἰ γίγνεται οὔτε διὰ
τί, ἀλλ' ἅμα δῆλον ἂν ἦν. ἐκ γὰρ τοῦ αἰσθέσθαι
καὶ τὸ καθόλου ἐγένετο ἂν ἡμῖν εἰδέναι. ἡ μὲν γὰρ
30 αἴσθησις ὅτι νῦν ἀντιφράττει (καὶ γὰρ δῆλον ὅτι
νῦν ἐκλείπει)· ἐκ δὲ τούτου τὸ καθόλου ἂν ἐγένετο.

Ὥσπερ οὖν λέγομεν, τὸ τί ἐστιν εἰδέναι ταυτό
ἐστι καὶ διὰ τί ἔστιν· τοῦτο δ' ἢ ἁπλῶς καὶ μὴ τῶν

---

¹ καὶ n, Philoponus : ἢ.

ᵃ Of the earth, in an eclipse of the moon. That this is the
sense of ἐν μέσῳ here seems clear from 95 a 14, 15, 98 b 18 ;
I do not see why Ross takes it to mean " centrality in the
universe."

ᵇ Viz., 1 : 2 (octave), 2 : 3 (fifth), 3 : 4 (fourth) ; their discovery is attributed to Pythagoras.

178.

position or non-interposition.[a] In all these cases it is obvious that the question of essence and the question of cause are identical. Q. " What is an eclipse?" A. " The moon's deprivation of light through obstruction by the earth," is the same as Q. " What is the cause of an eclipse ? " or " Why does the moon suffer eclipse ? " A. " Because the (sun's) light fails owing to the obstruction of the earth." Again, Q. " What is a concord ? " A. " A numerical ratio [b] of high and low pitch," is the same as Q. " Why is the high note concordant with the low one ? " A. " Because they exhibit a numerical ratio " ; and Q. " Are the high and low notes concordant ? " is the same as Q. " Is their ratio *numerical* ? " And when we have grasped that it is, the question follows " Then what is their ratio ? "

That the object of our inquiry is the middle term can be clearly seen in cases where the middle term is perceptible by the senses. We ask our question when we have not yet perceived whether there is a middle term or not ; e.g., in the case of an eclipse. If we were on the moon, we should ask neither whether nor why it was taking place ; the answers to both questions would be simultaneously obvious, because from the act of perception we should be able to apprehend the universal.[c] The fact that the eclipse was now taking place would be obvious, and since sense-perception would tell us that the earth was now obstructing the light, from this the universal would follow.

As we said, then, to know the essence of a thing is the same as to know the cause of it. This is so whether the subject simply *is*, apart from *being* any of its

This is obvious when the middle term is perceptible to sense.

To know the essence is to know the cause.

90 a
ὑπαρχόντων τι, ἢ τῶν ὑπαρχόντων οἷον ὅτι δύο
ὀρθαί, ἢ ὅτι μεῖζον ἢ ἔλαττον.

III. Ὅτι μὲν οὖν πάντα τὰ ζητούμενα μέσου
35 ζήτησίς ἐστι, δῆλον· πῶς δὲ τὸ τί ἐστι δείκνυται,
καὶ τίς ὁ τρόπος τῆς ἀναγωγῆς, καὶ τί ἐστιν ὁρισμὸς καὶ τίνων, εἴπωμεν, διαπορήσαντες πρῶτον
90 b περὶ αὐτῶν. ἀρχὴ δ' ἔστω τῶν μελλόντων ἥπερ
ἐστὶν οἰκειοτάτη τῶν ἐχομένων λόγων.

Ἀπορήσειε γὰρ ἄν τις, ἆρ' ἔστι τὸ αὐτὸ καὶ κατὰ
τὸ αὐτὸ ὁρισμῷ εἰδέναι καὶ ἀποδείξει, ἢ ἀδύνατον;
ὁ μὲν γὰρ ὁρισμὸς τοῦ τί ἐστιν εἶναι δοκεῖ, τὸ δὲ
5 τί ἐστιν ἅπαν καθόλου καὶ κατηγορικόν· συλλογισμοὶ δ' εἰσὶν οἱ μὲν στερητικοί, οἱ δ' οὐ καθόλου,
οἷον οἱ μὲν ἐν τῷ δευτέρῳ σχήματι στερητικοὶ
πάντες, οἱ δ' ἐν τῷ τρίτῳ οὐ καθόλου. εἶτα οὐδὲ
τῶν ἐν τῷ πρώτῳ σχήματι κατηγορικῶν ἁπάντων
10 ἔστιν ὁρισμός, οἷον ὅτι πᾶν τρίγωνον δυσὶν ὀρθαῖς
ἴσας ἔχει. τούτου δὲ λόγος ὅτι τὸ ἐπίστασθαί ἐστιν
τὸ ἀποδεικτὸν[1] τὸ ἀπόδειξιν ἔχειν, ὥστ' εἰ ἐπὶ τῶν
τοιούτων ἀπόδειξίς ἐστι, δῆλον ὅτι οὐκ ἂν εἴη
αὐτῶν καὶ ὁρισμός. ἐπίσταιτο γὰρ ἄν τις καὶ
κατὰ τὸν ὁρισμόν, οὐκ ἔχων τὴν ἀπόδειξιν· οὐδὲν
γὰρ κωλύει μὴ ἅμα ἔχειν. ἱκανὴ δὲ πίστις καὶ ἐκ
15 τῆς ἐπαγωγῆς· οὐδὲν γὰρ πώποτε ὁρισάμενοι ἔγνω-

[1] ἀποδεικτὸν c², Philoponus: ἀποδεικτικόν Ad: ἀποδεικτικῶς BDMnu.

attributes; or whether it *is* one of its attributes, *e.g.*, having the sum of its angles equal to two right angles, or greater or smaller.

III. It is clear, then, that in all our inquiries we are trying to find a middle term. We must now explain how the essence is brought to light, and in what way it is referable to demonstration, and what definition is, and what things are definable; first examining the difficulties involved in these questions.[a] Let us begin this next section with a discussion which is most pertinent to the ensuing inquiry.

It might be asked whether it is possible to know the same thing in the same respect both by definition and by demonstration. (1) Definition is generally held to be of the essence, and essence is always universal and affirmative, but some conclusions are negative and some are not universal. *E.g.*, all those in the second figure are negative, and those in the third are not universal. (2) Again, even the affirmative conclusions in the first figure are not all appropriate to definition (*e.g.*, " every triangle has the sum of its angles equal to two right angles "). The reason for this is that to have scientific knowledge of what is demonstrable is the same as to have a demonstration of it, and so if demonstration is possible in the case of the aforesaid conclusions, clearly they cannot be definable as well; otherwise one could know the conclusion in virtue of the definition without possessing the demonstration, since there is no reason why he should not have one without the other. (3) Induction too affords sufficient grounds for holding that definition and demonstration are not the same, be-

Programme of the inquiry.

First we must discuss some difficulties.

Can we gain knowledge the same by demonstration and by definition? Not everything demonstrable is definable,

(beginning in ch. viii) by an aporematic survey (chs. iii–vii) of possible theories and arguments.

ARISTOTLE

μεν, οὔτε τῶν καθ' αὑτὸ ὑπαρχόντων οὔτε τῶν
συμβεβηκότων. ἔτι εἰ ὁ ὁρισμὸς οὐσίας τινὸς γνω-
ρισμός, τά γε τοιαῦτα φανερὸν ὅτι οὐκ οὐσίαι.

Ὅτι μὲν οὖν οὐκ ἔστιν ὁρισμὸς ἅπαντος οὗπερ
καὶ ἀπόδειξις, δῆλον. τί δαί;[1] οὗ ὁρισμός, ἆρα
20 παντὸς ἀπόδειξις ἔστιν ἢ οὔ; εἷς μὲν δὴ λόγος καὶ
περὶ τούτου ὁ αὐτός. τοῦ γὰρ ἑνός, ᾗ ἕν, μία
ἐπιστήμη. ὥστ' εἴπερ τὸ ἐπίστασθαι τὸ ἀποδεικ-
τόν ἐστι τὸ τὴν ἀπόδειξιν ἔχειν, συμβήσεταί τι
ἀδύνατον· ὁ γὰρ τὸν ὁρισμὸν ἔχων ἄνευ τῆς ἀποδείξεως ἐπιστήσεται. ἔτι αἱ ἀρχαὶ τῶν ἀποδείξεων
25 ὁρισμοί, ὧν ὅτι οὐκ ἔσονται ἀποδείξεις δέδεικται
πρότερον· ἢ ἔσονται αἱ ἀρχαὶ ἀποδεικταὶ καὶ τῶν
ἀρχῶν ἀρχαί, καὶ τοῦτ' εἰς ἄπειρον βαδιεῖται, ἢ τὰ
πρῶτα ὁρισμοὶ ἔσονται ἀναπόδεικτοι.

Ἀλλ' ἆρα, εἰ μὴ παντὸς τοῦ αὐτοῦ, ἀλλὰ τινὸς
τοῦ αὐτοῦ ἔστιν ὁρισμὸς καὶ ἀπόδειξις; ἢ ἀδύνα-
30 τον; οὐ γὰρ ἔστιν ἀπόδειξις οὗ ὁρισμός. ὁρισμὸς
μὲν γὰρ τοῦ τί ἐστι καὶ οὐσίας· αἱ δ' ἀποδείξεις
φαίνονται πᾶσαι ὑποτιθέμεναι καὶ λαμβάνουσαι τὸ
τί ἐστιν, οἷον αἱ μαθηματικαὶ τί μονὰς καὶ τί τὸ
περιττόν, καὶ αἱ ἄλλαι ὁμοίως. ἔτι πᾶσα ἀπόδειξις
τὶ κατὰ τινὸς δείκνυσιν, οἷον ὅτι ἔστιν ἢ οὐκ ἔστιν·
35 ἐν δὲ τῷ ὁρισμῷ οὐδὲν ἕτερον ἑτέρου κατηγορεῖται,
οἷον οὔτε τὸ ζῷον κατὰ τοῦ δίποδος οὔτε τοῦτο
κατὰ τοῦ ζῴου, οὐδὲ δὴ κατὰ τοῦ ἐπιπέδου τὸ

[1] δαί B: δ'.

cause we never get to know any attribute, whether essential or accidental,[a] by defining it. Also, (4) if definition is the method of getting to know the essence, obviously such attributes are not essences.

Clearly then not everything that is demonstrable is also definable. Very well ; is everything that is definable demonstrable, or not ?   (1) One of the *nor is every-thing defin-able demon-strable ;* arguments given above also applies here. Of one fact, *qua* one, there is only one knowledge ; therefore if to know the demonstrable is to possess the demonstration, an impossible result will follow : the possessor of the definition will have knowledge without possessing the demonstration. (2) The starting-points of demonstrations are definitions, and it has been shown above [b] that of these there can be no demonstration : either the starting-points will be demonstrable, and will have starting-points that are demonstrable, and there will be an infinite regress ; or the primary truths will be indemonstrable definitions.

But perhaps some things, if not all, are both defin- *in fact, nothing is both de-monstrable and definable.* able and demonstrable. Surely this is impossible ; because (1) there is no demonstration of the definable. Definition is of the essence or essential nature, and it is obvious that all demonstrations assume the essence as a received fact ; *e.g.*, mathematics assumes the nature of unity and oddness, and similarly in the other sciences. (2) Every demonstration proves some predicate of some subject, either affirmatively or negatively ; but in a definition nothing is predicated of anything else ; " animal " is not predicated of " two-footed " nor *vice versa,* nor is " figure " pre-

[a] *Cf.* 90 a 11.
[b] 72 b 18-25, 84 a 29-b 2.

90 b

σχῆμα· οὐ γάρ ἐστι τὸ ἐπίπεδον σχῆμα, οὐδὲ τὸ
σχῆμα ἐπίπεδον. ἔτι ἕτερον τὸ τί ἐστι καὶ ὅτι ἔστι

91 a δεῖξαι. ὁ μὲν οὖν ὁρισμὸς τί ἐστι δηλοῖ, ἡ δὲ ἀπόδειξις ὅτι[1] ἐστὶ τόδε κατὰ τοῦδε ἢ οὐκ ἔστιν.
ἑτέρου δὲ ἑτέρα ἀπόδειξις, ἐὰν μὴ ὡς μέρος ᾖ τι τῆς
ὅλης. τοῦτο δὲ λέγω, ὅτι δέδεικται τὸ ἰσοσκελὲς
5 δύο ὀρθαῖς, εἰ πᾶν τρίγωνον δέδεικται· μέρος γάρ,
τὸ δ' ὅλον. ταῦτα δὲ πρὸς ἄλληλα οὐκ ἔχει οὕτως,
τὸ ὅτι ἔστι καὶ τί ἐστιν· οὐ γάρ ἐστι θατέρου
θάτερον μέρος.

Φανερὸν ἄρα ὅτι οὔτε οὗ ὁρισμός, τούτου παντὸς
ἀπόδειξις, οὔτε οὗ ἀπόδειξις, τούτου παντὸς ὁρισμός, οὔτε[2] ὅλως τοῦ αὐτοῦ οὐδενὸς ἐνδέχεται ἄμφω
10 ἔχειν· ὥστε δῆλον ὡς οὐδὲ ὁρισμὸς καὶ ἀπόδειξις
οὔτε τὸ αὐτὸ ἂν εἴη οὔτε θάτερον ἐν θατέρῳ· καὶ
γὰρ ἂν τὰ ὑποκείμενα ὁμοίως εἶχεν.

IV. Ταῦτα μὲν οὖν μέχρι τούτου διηπορήσθω.
τοῦ δὲ τί ἐστι πότερον ἔστι συλλογισμὸς καὶ ἀπόδειξις ἢ οὐκ ἔστι, καθάπερ νῦν ὁ λόγος ὑπέθετο;
15 ὁ μὲν γὰρ συλλογισμὸς τὶ κατὰ τινὸς δείκνυσι διὰ
τοῦ μέσου· τὸ δὲ τί ἐστιν ἴδιόν τε καὶ ἐν τῷ τί ἐστι
κατηγορεῖται. ταῦτα δ' ἀνάγκη ἀντιστρέφειν. εἰ
γὰρ τὸ Α τοῦ Γ ἴδιον, δῆλον ὅτι καὶ τοῦ Β καὶ
τοῦτο τοῦ Γ, ὥστε πάντα ἀλλήλων. ἀλλὰ μὴν

---

[1] ὅτι ἢ n. [2] Pacius : ὥστε.

---

[a] By " definition " Aristotle means the complex of genus
and differentia (e.g. " two-footed animal " or " plane figure
bounded by three straight lines ") which is itself predicated
of the definiendum.

[b] Aristotle is tiresomely vague in his use of the phrase τί
ἐστι, which approximates sometimes to τί ἦν εἶναι, sometimes
to ὁρισμός. Here it seems to mean first one and then the
other. [c] Cf. note on 73 a 7.

dicated of " plane " ; a plane is not a figure, nor a figure a plane.[a] (3) To reveal the essence of a thing is not the same as to prove a proposition about it ; now definition exhibits the essence, but demonstration proves that an attribute is, or is not, predicated of a subject. Also different things have different demonstrations, unless they are related as part to whole (by this qualification I mean, *e.g.*, that if it is proved that every triangle has the sum of its angles equal to two right angles, this is also proved of the isosceles triangle, " isosceles " being the part and " triangle " the whole). But the proposition and the essence are not so related, because one is not a part of the other.

It is evident, then, that not everything that is definable is demonstrable, and not everything that is demonstrable is definable ; and that in no case is it possible to have both definition and demonstration of the same thing. Thus it is clear also that definition and demonstration cannot be the same, and that neither can be included in the other ; otherwise their objects would be similarly related. *It follows that demonstration and definition are quite distinct.*

IV. The foregoing difficulties may now be regarded as sufficiently stated. But is syllogism or demonstration of the essence possible, or is it impossible, as our discussion assumed just now ? Syllogism proves an attribute of a subject through the middle term ; but the definition [b] is both (1) peculiar [c] to its subject and (2) predicated as belonging to its essence. Now (1) terms so related must be convertible ; for if A is peculiar to C, clearly it is also peculiar to B, and B to C, so that all are peculiar to one another.[d] Further, *Can a definition be proved syllogistically ?*

[a] Since A and C are co-extensive, B, the middle term, must be co-extensive with them both.

καὶ εἰ τὸ Α ἐν τῷ τί ἐστιν ὑπάρχει παντὶ τῷ Β,
20 καὶ καθόλου τὸ Β παντὸς τοῦ Γ ἐν τῷ τί ἐστι λέγεται, ἀνάγκη καὶ τὸ Α ἐν τῷ τί ἐστι τοῦ Γ λέγεσθαι.
εἰ δὲ μὴ οὕτω τις λήψεται διπλώσας, οὐκ ἀνάγκη
ἔσται τὸ Α τοῦ Γ κατηγορεῖσθαι ἐν τῷ τί ἐστιν, εἰ
τὸ μὲν Α τοῦ Β ἐν τῷ τί ἐστι, μὴ καθ᾿ ὅσων δὲ τὸ
Β ἐν τῷ τί ἐστιν. τὸ δὴ τί ἐστιν ἄμφω ταῦτα ἕξει·
25 ἔσται ἄρα καὶ τὸ Β κατὰ τοῦ Γ τὸ τί ἐστιν. εἰ δὴ
τὸ τί ἐστι καὶ τὸ τί ἦν εἶναι ἄμφω ἔχει, ἐπὶ τοῦ
μέσου ἔσται πρότερον τὸ τί ἦν εἶναι. ὅλως τε, εἰ
ἔστι δεῖξαι τί ἐστιν ἄνθρωπος, ἔστω τὸ Γ ἄνθρωπος, τὸ δὲ Α τὸ τί ἐστιν, εἴτε ζῷον δίπουν εἴτ᾿
ἄλλο τι. εἰ τοίνυν συλλογιεῖται, ἀνάγκη κατὰ τοῦ
30 Γ[1] τὸ Α παντὸς κατηγορεῖσθαι. τούτου[2] δ᾿ ἔσται
ἄλλος λόγος μέσος, ὥστε καὶ τοῦτο ἔσται τί ἐστιν
ἄνθρωπος. λαμβάνει οὖν ὃ δεῖ δεῖξαι· καὶ γὰρ τὸ
Β ἔσται[3] τί ἐστιν ἄνθρωπος. δεῖ δ᾿ ἐν ταῖς δυσὶ
προτάσεσι καὶ τοῖς πρώτοις καὶ ἀμέσοις σκοπεῖν·
35 μάλιστα γὰρ φανερὸν τὸ λεγόμενον γίγνεται. οἱ
μὲν οὖν διὰ τοῦ ἀντιστρέφειν δεικνύντες τί ἐστι
ψυχή, ἢ τί ἐστιν ἄνθρωπος ἢ ἄλλο ὁτιοῦν τῶν
ὄντων, τὸ ἐξ ἀρχῆς αἰτοῦνται, οἷον εἴ τις ἀξιώσειε
ψυχὴν εἶναι τὸ αὐτὸ αὑτῷ αἴτιον τοῦ ζῆν, τοῦτο δ᾿
ἀριθμὸν αὐτὸν αὑτὸν κινοῦντα· ἀνάγκη γὰρ αἰτῆσαι

---

[1] Γ scripsi : Β.
[2] τούτου] τοῦτο ci. Bonitz, prob. Ross.
[3] ἔσται ci. Bonitz : ἐστι codd.

---

[a] Presumably Aristotle means that the minor premiss (in
which B is predicate) will supply the definition, so that we
are assuming what we arc trying to prove.

[b] It is hard to get a satisfactory sense from the vulgate,

(2) if A is an essential attribute of all B, and B is asserted universally and essentially of all C, A must be asserted essentially of C; but without this double assumption it will not necessarily follow that A is predicated essentially of C—I mean, if A is essentially predicated of B, but B is not essentially true of everything of which it is predicated. So both premisses must state the essence; therefore B too will be predicated as essence of C. Then since both premisses state the essence or essential nature, the essence will appear in the case of the middle term before it appears in the conclusion.[a] In general, if it is required to prove the essence of "man," let C be "man" and A the essence—"two-footed animal," or whatever else it may be. Then if we are to have a syllogism, A must be predicated of all C.[b] But this premiss will be mediated by another definition, so that this too will be the essence of "man." Thus we are assuming what we are required to prove, since B will also be the essence of "man." We should consider the case, however, in relation to the two premisses and to primary and immediate connexions; because this throws most light upon the point that we are discussing. Those who try to prove the essence of "soul" or "man" or anything else by conversion are guilty of *petitio principii*. *E.g.*, suppose that somebody asserts that soul is that which is the cause of its own life, and that this is a self-moving number [c]; he is necessarily postulating that soul is

Only by a petitio principii.

and Bonitz' τοῦτο, which Ross adopts, seems barely convincing. I have therefore ventured to write Γ for B, which I suppose to be a "correction" made by an editor or copyist who was puzzled by finding B first at l. 31.

[c] *Cf. De Anima* 404 b 29, 408 b 32. The view is ascribed to Xenocrates by Plutarch, *Moralia* 1012 d.

91 b τὴν ψυχὴν ὅπερ ἀριθμὸν εἶναι αὐτὸν αὐτὸν κινοῦντα,
οὕτως ὡς τὸ αὐτὸ ὄν. οὐ γὰρ εἰ ἀκολουθεῖ τὸ Α
τῷ Β καὶ τοῦτο τῷ Γ, ἔσται τῷ Γ τὸ Α τὸ τί ἦν
εἶναι, ἀλλ' ἀληθὲς¹ εἰπεῖν ἔσται μόνον· οὐδ' εἰ ἔστι
τὸ Α ὅπερ τι καὶ κατὰ τοῦ Β κατηγορεῖται παντός.
5 καὶ γὰρ τὸ ζῴῳ εἶναι κατηγορεῖται κατὰ τοῦ ἀνθρώπῳ εἶναι· ἀληθὲς γὰρ πᾶν τὸ ἀνθρώπῳ εἶναι
ζῴῳ εἶναι, ὥσπερ καὶ πάντα ἄνθρωπον ζῷον, ἀλλ'
οὐχ οὕτως ὥστε ἓν εἶναι. ἐὰν μὲν οὖν μὴ οὕτω
λάβῃ, οὐ συλλογιεῖται ὅτι τὸ Α ἐστὶ τῷ Γ τὸ τί ἦν
εἶναι καὶ ἡ οὐσία· ἐὰν δὲ οὕτω λάβῃ, πρότερον
10 ἔσται εἰληφὼς τῷ Γ τί ἐστι τὸ τί ἦν εἶναι [τὸ Β].²
ὥστ' οὐκ ἀποδέδεικται· τὸ γὰρ ἐν ἀρχῇ εἴληφεν.

V. Ἀλλὰ μὴν οὐδ' ἡ διὰ τῶν διαιρέσεων ὁδὸς
συλλογίζεται, καθάπερ ἐν τῇ ἀναλύσει τῇ περὶ τὰ
σχήματα εἴρηται. οὐδαμοῦ γὰρ ἀνάγκη γίγνεται
15 τὸ πρᾶγμα ἐκεῖνο εἶναι τωνδὶ ὄντων, ἀλλ' ὥσπερ οὐδ' ὁ ἐπάγων ἀποδείκνυσιν. οὐ γὰρ δεῖ τὸ
συμπέρασμα ἐρωτᾶν, οὐδὲ τῷ δοῦναι εἶναι, ἀλλ'
ἀνάγκη εἶναι ἐκείνων ὄντων, κἂν μὴ φῇ ὁ ἀποκρινόμενος. ἆρ' ὁ ἄνθρωπος ζῷον ἢ ἄψυχον; εἶτ'
ἔλαβε ζῷον, οὐ συλλελόγισται. πάλιν ἅπαν ζῷον
20 ἢ πεζὸν ἢ ἔνυδρον· ἔλαβε πεζόν. καὶ τὸ εἶναι τὸν
ἄνθρωπον τὸ ὅλον, ζῷον πεζόν, οὐκ ἀνάγκη ἐκ τῶν
εἰρημένων, ἀλλὰ λαμβάνει καὶ τοῦτο. διαφέρει δ'

---

¹ ἀληθὲς n, Eustratius (?) : ἀληθὲς ἦν.
² secl. Ross.

essentially a self-moving number in the sense of being identical with it. For if A is a consequent of B, and B of C, A will not be the essence of C—it will only be true to predicate it of C ; nor ⟨will A be the essence of C⟩ if A is predicated of all B as genus of species. Animality is predicated of all humanity, because it is true that all humanity is a species of animality, just as it is true that every man is an animal ; but not in the sense that they are identical. Thus unless the premisses are taken in the way that we have described, it cannot be inferred that A is the essence or real nature of C ; and if they are so taken, it will have been already assumed what the essence of C is. Therefore the conclusion is not proved, because there has been *petitio principii.*

V. Nor again does the method of division lead to a conclusion, as has been explained in my logical analysis of the figures.[a] At no stage do we find the logical necessity that, given certain conditions, the object must have the required definition ; the process is just as inconclusive as induction. The conclusion must not be a question, nor stand by concession only ; it must follow necessarily from the premisses, even if the respondent rejects it. ⟨The exponent of division asks⟩ " Is ' man ' animate or inanimate ? " and then assumes " animate " ; it is not the result of inference. Next " every animal is either terrestrial or aquatic," and he assumes " terrestrial." It does not follow necessarily from stated premisses that " man " is the whole expression, " terrestrial animal " ; he assumes this too. (It makes no differ-

A definition cannot be proved by division, for this proves nothing,

---

[a] *An. Pr.* I. xxxi. The Platonic method of division is illustrated in *Sophist* 219 A ff., *Politicus* 258 B ff. For Aristotle's view of the proper use of division see chs. xiii and xiv.

91 b

οὐδὲν ἐπὶ πολλῶν ἢ ὀλίγων οὕτω ποιεῖν· τὸ αὐτὸ
γάρ ἐστιν. ἀσυλλόγιστος μὲν οὖν καὶ ἡ χρῆσις
γίγνεται τοῖς οὕτω μετιοῦσι καὶ τῶν ἐνδεχομένων
25 συλλογισθῆναι. τί γὰρ κωλύει τοῦτο ἀληθὲς μὲν
τὸ πᾶν εἶναι κατὰ τοῦ ἀνθρώπου, μὴ μέντοι τὸ τί
ἐστι μηδὲ τὸ τί ἦν εἶναι δηλοῦν; ἔτι τί κωλύει
ἢ προσθεῖναί τι ἢ ἀφελεῖν ἢ ὑπερβεβηκέναι τῆς
 οὐσίας;

Ταῦτα μὲν οὖν παρίεται μέν, ἐνδέχεται δὲ λῦσαι
τῷ λαμβάνειν τὰ ἐν τῷ τί ἐστι πάντα, καὶ τὸ
30 ἐφεξῆς τῇ διαιρέσει ποιεῖν, αἰτούμενον τὸ πρῶτον,
καὶ μηδὲν παραλείπειν. τοῦτο δὲ ἀναγκαῖον, εἰ
ἅπαν εἰς τὴν διαίρεσιν ἐμπίπτει καὶ μηδὲν ἐλλείπει·
[τοῦτο δ' ἀναγκαῖον,][1] ἄτομον γὰρ ἤδη δεῖ εἶναι.

Ἀλλὰ συλλογισμὸς ὅμως οὐκ ἔνεστιν,[2] ἀλλ' εἴπερ,
ἄλλον τρόπον γνωρίζειν ποιεῖ. καὶ τοῦτο μὲν οὐδὲν
35 ἄτοπον· οὐδὲ γὰρ ὁ ἐπάγων ἴσως ἀποδείκνυσιν, ἀλλ'
ὅμως δηλοῖ τι. συλλογισμὸν δ' οὐ λέγει ὁ ἐκ
τῆς διαιρέσεως λέγων τὸν ὁρισμόν· ὥσπερ γὰρ ἐν
τοῖς συμπεράσμασι τοῖς ἄνευ τῶν μέσων, ἐάν τις
εἴπῃ ὅτι τούτων ὄντων ἀνάγκη τοδὶ εἶναι, ἐνδέχεται
ἐρωτῆσαι διὰ τί, οὕτως καὶ ἐν τοῖς διαιρετικοῖς
92 a ὅροις. τί ἐστιν ἄνθρωπος; ζῷον, θνητόν, ὑπόπουν,
δίπουν, ἄπτερον. διὰ τί; παρ' ἑκάστην πρόσθε-
σιν· ἐρεῖ γάρ, καὶ δείξει τῇ διαιρέσει, ὡς οἴεται, ὅτι

---

[1] secl. Waitz.   [2] ἔνεστιν] ἔστι n, Philoponus, Ross.

---

[a] i.e., including a non-essential or passing over an essential element in the definition.
[b] i.e., the next widest.

190

ence whether the process involves many steps or few ; the position is just the same.) Indeed the method, when used in this way, fails to draw even those inferences that are available. It is quite possible that the whole expression should be truly predicable of " man," and yet not exhibit the essence or essential nature of man. Besides, what is there to prevent the division from adding something, or omitting something,[a] or missing out a step in the definition of the real nature ?

These defects are usually ignored, but they can be dealt with by (a) taking at each stage only elements in the essence, (b) dividing consecutively, always postulating the first [b] ⟨differentia⟩, and (c) leaving out nothing. This result is bound to follow if the term to be defined is entirely covered by the division ⟨at each stage⟩, without any omission ; for the process must lead directly to a term that requires no further division. *though it can be used systematically.*

Even so, however, there is no inference in the process ; if it conveys any knowledge to us, it does so in a different way. There is nothing abnormal in this, since presumably induction too *proves* nothing, but nevertheless it gives us some information. But in selecting the definition by means of division one does not state a logical inference. As in the case of conclusions reached without the use of middle terms, if it is stated that, given certain conditions, suchand-such must follow, one is entitled to ask " Why ?", so too in definitions reached by division. What is man ? An animate being—mortal—footed—twofooted—wingless. At every added predicate one may ask " Why ? " ; because the divider can state, and prove (as he supposes) by his division, that everything *The results of division are not reached by inference.*

191

92 a

πᾶν ἢ θνητὸν ἢ ἀθάνατον. ὁ δὲ τοιοῦτος λόγος
ἅπας οὐκ ἔστιν ὁρισμός, ὥστ' εἰ καὶ ἀπεδείκνυτο
5 τῇ διαιρέσει, ἀλλ' ὅ γ' ὁρισμὸς οὐ συλλογισμὸς
γίγνεται.

VI. 'Αλλ' ἆρα ἔστι καὶ ἀποδεῖξαι τὸ τί ἐστι κατ'
οὐσίαν, ἐξ ὑποθέσεως δέ, λαβόντα τὸ μὲν τί ἦν εἶναι
τὸ ἐκ τῶν ἐν τῷ τί ἐστιν ἴδιον,[1] ταδὶ δὲ ἐν τῷ τί
ἐστι μόνα, καὶ ἴδιον τὸ πᾶν; τοῦτο γάρ ἐστι τὸ
10 εἶναι ἐκείνῳ. ἢ πάλιν εἴληφε τὸ τί ἦν εἶναι καὶ ἐν
τούτῳ; ἀνάγκη γὰρ διὰ τοῦ μέσου δεῖξαι. ἔτι
ὥσπερ οὐδ' ἐν συλλογισμῷ λαμβάνεται τί ἐστι τὸ
συλλελογίσθαι (ἀεὶ γὰρ ὅλη ἢ μέρος ἡ πρότασις, ἐξ
ὧν ὁ συλλογισμός), οὕτως οὐδὲ τὸ τί ἦν εἶναι δεῖ
ἐνεῖναι ἐν τῷ συλλογισμῷ, ἀλλὰ χωρὶς τοῦτο τῶν
15 κειμένων εἶναι, καὶ πρὸς τὸν ἀμφισβητοῦντα εἰ συλλελόγισται ἢ μή, τοῦτο ἀπαντᾶν ὅτι "τοῦτο γὰρ
ἦν συλλογισμός"· καὶ πρὸς τὸν ὅτι οὐ τὸ τί ἦν
εἶναι συλλελόγισται, ὅτι "ναί· τοῦτο γὰρ ἔκειτο
ἡμῖν τὸ τί ἦν εἶναι." ὥστε ἀνάγκη καὶ ἄνευ τοῦ
τί συλλογισμὸς ἢ τὸ[2] τί ἦν εἶναι συλλελογίσθαι τι.

20   Κἂν ἐξ ὑποθέσεως δὲ δεικνύῃ, οἷον εἰ τὸ[3] κακῷ

---

[1] ἴδιον Pacius, Ross : ἰδίων.
[2] τὸ] τοῦ Bn.   [3] τὸ] τῷ Adn[2].

---

[a] Which is here lacking, the minor premiss being a mere
petitio principii. The hypothetical proof rejected here is
used in *Top.* 153 a ff., but dialectically (*cf.* Cherniss, *Aristotle's Criticism of Plato and the Academy*, i. 34-6, note 28).
[b] Aristotle is thinking of the first figure (which alone is

is either mortal or immortal; but such a proposition, taken as a whole, is not a definition. Thus even if the proposition could be proved by division, the definition still does not amount to a logical inference.

VI. It may be suggested, however, that it is actually possible to demonstrate the essential definition of a subject hypothetically by assuming that the definition consists of the elements in the essence, and is peculiar to the subject; and that this and that are the only elements in the essence; and that the aggregate of them is peculiar to the subject, because this aggregate represents its essential nature. But (1) surely in this ⟨minor premiss⟩ the definition has once more been *assumed*; because proof must proceed through a middle term.[a] (2) Just as in a syllogism we do not assume ⟨as a premiss⟩ the definition of syllogism (since the premisses from which the conclusion is drawn are always related as whole and part [b]), so neither must the definition of definition appear in the syllogism [c]—it must be something apart from the premisses laid down; and when an opponent disputes whether there has been syllogistic proof or not, we should ⟨be able to⟩ answer " Yes, because we agreed that that is what syllogism is "; and if one objects that the syllogism has not proved the definition, " Yes, because that is what definition was assumed to be." Thus we must have already drawn some inference without ⟨using as a premiss⟩ the definition of syllogism or of definition.[d]

Equally invalid is proof from a hypothesis in the

One suggested method of proving a definition not only assumes the essence, but improperly assumes the definition of definition as a premiss.

Another

useful for establishing scientific facts) where the relation is normally genus : species or species : sub-species.

[c] *Sc.* by which we hope to prove a particular definition.

[d] *Sc.*, before appealing to the said definition, which is a pre-condition, not a part, of the argument.

92 a

ἐστὶ τὸ διαιρετῷ εἶναι, τὸ[1] δ᾿ ἐναντίῳ τὸ τῷ
ἐναντίῳ ⟨ἐναντίῳ⟩[2] εἶναι, ὅσοις ἔστι τι ἐναντίον·
τὸ δ᾿ ἀγαθὸν τῷ κακῷ ἐναντίον καὶ τὸ ἀδιαίρετον
τῷ διαιρετῷ· ἔστιν ἄρα τὸ ἀγαθῷ εἶναι τὸ ἀδιαι-
ρέτῳ εἶναι. καὶ γὰρ ἐνταῦθα λαβὼν τὸ τί ἦν εἶναι
25 δείκνυσι· λαμβάνει δ᾿ εἰς τὸ δεῖξαι τὸ τί ἦν εἶναι.
ἕτερον μέντοι· ἔστω· καὶ γὰρ ἐν ταῖς ἀποδείξεσιν,
ὅτι ἐστὶ τόδε κατὰ τοῦδε ἀλλὰ μὴ αὐτό, μηδὲ οὗ ὁ
αὐτὸς λόγος, καὶ ἀντιστρέφει.

Πρὸς ἀμφοτέρους δέ, τόν τε κατὰ διαίρεσιν δεικνύντα καὶ πρὸς τὸν οὕτω συλλογισμόν, τὸ αὐτὸ
30 ἀπόρημα· διὰ τί ἔσται ὁ ἄνθρωπος ζῷον [δίπουν][3]
πεζόν, ἀλλ᾿ οὐ ζῷον καὶ πεζόν; ἐκ γὰρ τῶν λαμβανομένων οὐδεμία ἀνάγκη ἐστὶν ἓν γίγνεσθαι τὸ
κατηγορούμενον, ἀλλ᾿ ὥσπερ ἂν ἄνθρωπος ὁ αὐτὸς
εἴη μουσικὸς καὶ γραμματικός.

VII. Πῶς οὖν δὴ ὁ ὁριζόμενος δείξει τὴν οὐσίαν
35 ἢ τὸ τί ἐστιν; οὔτε γὰρ ὡς ἀποδεικνὺς ἐξ ὁμολο-
γουμένων εἶναι δῆλον ποιήσει ὅτι ἀνάγκη ἐκείνων
ὄντων ἕτερόν τι εἶναι (ἀπόδειξις γὰρ τοῦτο), οὔθ᾿
ὡς ὁ ἐπάγων διὰ τῶν καθ᾿ ἕκαστα δήλων ὄντων,

---

[1] τὸ Bonitz : τῷ.
[2] ἐναντίῳ add. Bonitz.
[3] δίπουν seclusi : δίπουν πεζόν codd. : πεζὸν δίπουν comm.,
Ross, qui post καὶ πεζόν add. καὶ δίπουν.

---

[a] This method of proof, ἐκ τοῦ ἐναντίου, is illustrated and
discussed in *Topics* 153 a 26–b 24 and 147 a 29–b 25 (where
it is criticized as in the present passage). It was freely used
in the Academy ; *cf.* Cherniss, *op. cit.* i. 36-38.

[b] Speusippus' view ; for the evidence see Cherniss, *loc. cit.*

[c] *Viz.*, that of the subject's contrary.

[d] The major term.

[e] To secure consistency we must either bracket δίπουν
here or add καὶ δίπουν in l. 30. The former course seems

194

following way [a] : If evil is definable as divisibility,[b] and if any term that has a contrary is definable by the contrary of that contrary's definition, and if good is contrary to evil, and indivisibility to divisibility, then goodness is definable as indivisibility. Here too the proof first assumes the definition, and assumes it to prove the definition. " But it is a different definition." [c] Granted, ⟨but the objection still holds,⟩ because in demonstrations too we assume that one term is predicable of another, but it [d] must not be the very term ⟨that is to be proved⟩, nor one which has the same definition or rather is correlative with it.

assumes a term correlative with the essence.

Both the opponent who attempts proof by division and the one who offers syllogism in this form have to face the same difficulty : why should " man " be " terrestrial animal " [e] and not " terrestrial " *and* " animal " ? There is nothing in the assumptions to make it necessary that the predicate should be a unity, and not ⟨consist of non-essential attributes⟩, as the same man may be musical and literary.[f]

None of these proofs shows that the definition is a unity.

VII. How then can the person who is trying to define prove the essence or definition ? (1) He cannot exhibit deductively from admitted facts that, given these facts, a conclusion distinct from them must follow—that is demonstration ; nor can he show inductively by enumeration of manifest particular instances that every case is like this, because none

How can one prove the essence ? (1) If neither deductively nor inductively, how else ?

better. Only two attributes are required, and I believe δίπουν to be an intruder from the parallel passages in *Met.* 1037 b 11 ff., 1045 a 14 ff., where the attributes are ζῷον and δίπουν. The fact that the commentators have δίπουν after πεζόν may point the same way, since an added word is always liable to displacement.

[f] *Cf. Met. locc. citt.* Aristotle gives his own solution of the " difficulty " in the latter passage.

92 b ὅτι πᾶν οὕτως τῷ μηδὲν ἄλλως· οὐ γὰρ τί ἐστι
δείκνυσιν, ἀλλ' ὅτι ἢ ἔστιν ἢ οὐκ ἔστιν. τίς οὖν
ἄλλος τρόπος λοιπός; οὐ γὰρ δὴ δείξει γε τῇ
αἰσθήσει ἢ τῷ δακτύλῳ.

Ἔτι πῶς δείξει τὸ τί ἐστιν; ἀνάγκη γὰρ τὸν
5 εἰδότα τὸ τί ἐστιν ἄνθρωπος ἢ ἄλλο ὁτιοῦν, εἰδέναι
καὶ ὅτι ἔστιν· τὸ γὰρ μὴ ὂν οὐδεὶς οἶδεν ὅτι ἐστίν,
ἀλλὰ τί μὲν σημαίνει ὁ λόγος ἢ τὸ ὄνομα, ὅταν
εἴπω τραγέλαφος, τί δ' ἐστὶ τραγέλαφος ἀδύνατον
εἰδέναι. ἀλλὰ μὴν εἰ δείξει τί ἐστι καὶ ὅτι ἔστι,
πῶς τῷ αὐτῷ λόγῳ δείξει; ὅ τε γὰρ ὁρισμὸς ἕν
10 τι δηλοῖ καὶ ἡ ἀπόδειξις· τὸ δὲ τί ἐστιν ἄνθρωπος
καὶ τὸ εἶναι ἄνθρωπον ἄλλο.

Εἶτα καὶ δι' ἀποδείξεώς φαμεν ἀναγκαῖον εἶναι
δείκνυσθαι ἅπαν ὅτι ἔστιν, εἰ μὴ οὐσία εἴη. τὸ δ'
εἶναι οὐκ οὐσία οὐδενί· οὐ γὰρ γένος τὸ ὄν. ἀπό-
15 δειξις ἄρ' ἔσται ὅτι ἔστιν. ὅπερ καὶ νῦν ποιοῦσιν
αἱ ἐπιστῆμαι· τί μὲν γὰρ σημαίνει τὸ τρίγωνον,
ἔλαβεν ὁ γεωμέτρης, ὅτι δ' ἔστι, δείκνυσιν. τί
οὖν δείξει ὁ ὁριζόμενος τί ἔστιν; ἢ[1] τὸ τρίγωνον;
εἰδὼς ἄρα τις ὁρισμῷ τί ἐστιν, εἰ ἔστιν οὐκ εἴσεται.
ἀλλ' ἀδύνατον.

Φανερὸν δὲ καὶ κατὰ τοὺς νῦν τρόπους τῶν

---

[1] τί ἐστιν; ἢ] ἢ τί ἐστι Ross.

[a] Strictly " goat-deer," a type of fabulous animal ; cf.
An. Pr. 49 a 24.

[b] It is hard to accept Ross's ὅ τι ἐστιν. Aristotle could not,
like a modern editor, make his meaning plain by spacing
and accentuation ; and without these aids, in such a context,
the phrase would have been quite misleading. In b 6 above,
on the other hand, the sense is sufficiently obvious.

is otherwise; for this does not prove *what* the subject is, but the *fact* that it is, or is not. What other way then remains? because he cannot presumably prove ⟨the definition⟩ by reference to sense-perception, or point to it with his finger.

(2) How can one prove the essence? Anyone who knows *what* "man" or any other thing is must also know *that* it is; because no one knows *what* a non-existent thing is. (He may know the meaning of a phrase, or of a name if, *e.g.*, I speak of a unicorn [a]; but it is impossible to know *what* a unicorn is.) But (*a*) if it is proposed to prove *what* a thing is and *that* it is, how can they be proved by the same argument? Both definition and demonstration give us *one* piece of information; but *what* man is and *that* man is are two different things.

(*b*) Again, we hold that it is by demonstration that everything must be proved to exist,[b] except essence; and existence is not the essence of anything, because being is not a genus.[c] So there will be demonstration *that* a thing is. This is how the sciences actually proceed; the geometrician assumes what "triangle" means, but proves that the triangle exists.[d] Of what, then, will the definer exhibit *what* it is [e]? The triangle? Then one will know by definition *what* a thing is without knowing that it exists; but this is impossible.

(*c*) It is evident also from the methods of defining now in use that those who define do not prove the

Marginal notes: (2) Knowledge of essence implies knowledge of existence; but (*a*) both cannot be proved by the same argument, (*b*) if the proofs are distinct, we can have one without the other, (*c*) definition as practised

---

[c] *Cf. Met.* 998 b 22 ff.

[d] *i.e.*, proves it as an attribute; *cf.* 71 a 14, 76 a 35, 93 b 31.

[e] Understood in this way the vulgate gives quite a good sense; and although the commentators give some support to Ross's transposition, I question its necessity.

20 ὁρῶν ὡς οὐ δεικνύουσιν οἱ ὁριζόμενοι ὅτι ἔστιν.
εἰ γὰρ καὶ ἔστιν ἐκ τοῦ μέσου τι¹ ἴσον, ἀλλὰ διὰ τί
ἔστι τὸ ὁρισθέν; καὶ διὰ τί τοῦτ' ἔστι κύκλος;
εἴη γὰρ ἂν καὶ ὀρειχάλκου φάναι εἶναι αὐτόν. οὔτε
γὰρ ὅτι δυνατὸν εἶναι τὸ λεγόμενον προσδηλοῦσιν οἱ
ὅροι οὔτε ὅτι ἐκεῖνο οὗ φασὶν εἶναι ὁρισμοί, ἀλλ'
25 ἀεὶ ἔξεστι λέγειν τὸ διὰ τί.

Εἰ ἄρα ὁ ὁριζόμενος δείκνυσιν ἢ τί ἐστιν ἢ τί
σημαίνει τοὔνομα, εἰ μή ἐστι μηδαμῶς τοῦ τί ἐστιν,
εἴη ἂν ὁ ὁρισμὸς λόγος ὀνόματι τὸ αὐτὸ σημαίνων.
ἀλλ' ἄτοπον. πρῶτον μὲν γὰρ καὶ μὴ οὐσιῶν ἂν
30 εἴη καὶ τῶν μὴ ὄντων· σημαίνειν γὰρ ἔστι καὶ τὰ
μὴ ὄντα. ἔτι πάντες οἱ λόγοι ὁρισμοὶ ἂν εἶεν· εἴη
γὰρ ἂν ὄνομα θέσθαι ὁποιῳοῦν λόγῳ, ὥστε ὅρους
ἂν διαλεγοίμεθα πάντες καὶ ἡ Ἰλιὰς ὁρισμὸς ἂν εἴη.
ἔτι οὐδεμία ἀπόδειξις² ἀποδείξειεν³ ἂν ὅτι τοῦτο
τοὔνομα τουτὶ δηλοῖ· οὐδ' οἱ ὁρισμοὶ τοίνυν τοῦτο
προσδηλοῦσιν.

35 Ἐκ μὲν τοίνυν τούτων οὔτε ὁρισμὸς καὶ συλλογισμὸς φαίνεται ταὐτὸν ὄν, οὔτε ταὐτοῦ συλλογισμὸς καὶ ὁρισμός· πρὸς δὲ τούτοις, ὅτι οὔτε ὁ
ὁρισμὸς οὐδὲν οὔτε ἀποδείκνυσιν οὔτε δείκνυσιν,
οὔτε τὸ τί ἐστιν οὔθ' ὁρισμῷ οὔτ' ἀποδείξει ἔστι
γνῶναι.

93 a VIII. Πάλιν δὲ σκεπτέον τί τούτων λέγεται

¹ τι] τὸ B, Bekker.
² ἀπόδειξις d : om. AB : ἐπιστήμη B²n.
³ εἶεν d.

ᵃ *Viz.*, a line ; the reference is to a crude definition of a
circle.
ᵇ Or " non-essences." In an aporematic passage it is not
198

existence of the definiendum. Even supposing that proves neither existence nor its own validity. there is something *a* equidistant from the centre, why does the object so defined exist ? and why is it a circle ? One might equally well assert that it is the definition of mountain-copper. Definitions do not include evidence that it is possible for what they describe to exist, nor that it is identical with that which they claim to define. It is always possible to ask *why*.

Thus since in defining one exhibits either what the It is no solution to say that definition merely explains the name. object is or what its name means, if definition is in no sense of the essence, it must be an expression meaning the same as a name. But this is absurd. (1) In the first place, there would be definition not only of non-substances *b* but also of non-existents ; because even these can have a significant name. (2) All expressions would be definitions, because a name could be attached to any one of them ; so we should all converse in formulae, and the *Iliad* would be a definition.*c* (3) No demonstration can prove that a given name has a given meaning ; therefore neither do definitions ⟨in establishing the meaning of a term⟩ furnish evidence also that the name has a given meaning.

These considerations make it clear that definition Conclusions from the arguments of chs. iii-vii. is not the same as syllogism, and that they have not the same objects. It is also clear that definition neither demonstrates nor exhibits anything ; and that neither by definition nor by demonstration can we acquire knowledge of the essence.

VIII. We must now review what we have said above, and consider which of the arguments are valid

<hr/>

easy to be certain from what standpoint Aristotle is arguing.   *c* *Cf. Met.* 1030 a 7 ff.

ARISTOTLE

καλῶς καὶ τί οὐ καλῶς, καὶ τί ἐστιν ὁ ὁρισμός, καὶ
τοῦ τί ἐστιν· ἆρά πως ἔστιν ἀπόδειξις καὶ ὁρισμὸς
ἢ οὐδαμῶς.

Ἐπεὶ δ᾽ ἐστίν, ὡς ἔφαμεν, ταὐτὸν τὸ εἰδέναι τί
5 ἐστι καὶ τὸ εἰδέναι τὸ αἴτιον τοῦ εἰ[1] ἐστι (λόγος δὲ
τούτου ὅτι ἔστι τι τὸ αἴτιον· καὶ τοῦτο ἢ τὸ αὐτὸ ἢ
ἄλλο, κἂν ᾖ ἄλλο, ἢ ἀποδεικτὸν ἢ ἀναπόδεικτον)—
εἰ τοίνυν ἐστὶν ἄλλο καὶ ἐνδέχεται ἀποδεῖξαι, ἀνάγκη μέσον εἶναι τὸ αἴτιον καὶ ἐν τῷ σχήματι τῷ
πρώτῳ δείκνυσθαι· καθόλου τε γὰρ καὶ κατηγορικὸν τὸ δεικνύμενον.

10 Εἷς μὲν δὴ τρόπος ἂν εἴη ὁ νῦν ἐξητασμένος, τὸ
δι᾽ ἄλλου τὸ τί ἐστι δείκνυσθαι. τῶν τε γὰρ τί ἐστιν
ἀνάγκη τὸ μέσον εἶναι τί ἐστι, καὶ τῶν ἰδίων ἴδιον·
ὥστε τὸ μὲν δείξει, τὸ δ᾽ οὐ δείξει τῶν τί ἦν εἶναι
τῷ αὐτῷ πράγματι.

Οὗτος μὲν οὖν ὁ τρόπος ὅτι οὐκ ἂν εἴη ἀπόδειξις,
15 εἴρηται πρότερον· ἀλλ᾽ ἔστι λογικὸς συλλογισμὸς
τοῦ τί ἐστιν. ὃν δὲ τρόπον ἐνδέχεται λέγωμεν,
εἰπόντες πάλιν ἐξ ἀρχῆς. ὥσπερ γὰρ τὸ διότι ζητοῦμεν ἔχοντες τὸ ὅτι, ἐνίοτε δὲ καὶ ἅμα δῆλα
γίγνεται, ἀλλ᾽ οὔτι πρότερόν γε τὸ διότι δυνατὸν
γνωρίσαι τοῦ ὅτι, δῆλον ὅτι ὁμοίως καὶ τὸ τί ἦν
20 εἶναι οὐκ ἄνευ τοῦ ὅτι ἐστίν. ἀδύνατον γὰρ εἰδέναι
τί ἐστιν ἀγνοοῦντας εἰ ἔστιν. τὸ δ᾽ εἰ ἔστιν ὁτὲ μὲν

_____
[1] εἰ AB²d : τί Bn.

_____
[a] In ch. ii.
[b] Substance has no cause other than its own form ; that
which has an external cause is an attribute or event. It
is with these latter that the following chapters are chiefly
concerned.

and which are not; and what definition is; and whether the essence is in any sense demonstrable and definable, or not at all.

As we have said above,[a] to know what a thing is is the same as to know the cause of its existence; and the reason for this is that the thing has a definite cause, which is either identical with it or distinct from it,[b] and which, if distinct, is either demonstrable[c] or indemonstrable. Then if this cause is distinct and can be demonstrated, it must be a middle term, and be proved in the first figure; for ⟨only⟩ in this is the proved connexion universal and affirmative.

Now one way of employing such a proof will be the method which we criticized just now,[d] of proving one definition by another. For the middle term through which essences are inferred must itself be essence, and that through which peculiar attributes are inferred must be a peculiar attribute. Thus for the self-same subject one statement of its essential nature will be proved and one will not.

It has been observed above[e] that this method cannot have the force of a demonstration; it is only a dialectical inference of the essence. Let us now make a fresh start and explain in what way demonstration *is* possible. It is when we are sure of the *fact* that we look for the *reason*; sometimes we become aware of them simultaneously, but it is quite impossible to recognize the reason before the fact. Clearly in the same way the essential nature implies the fact; it is impossible to know *what* a thing is if we do not know *whether* it exists. Now we may be

To know what a thing is we must grasp clearly that it is.

[c] Not demonstrable itself, but serviceable for demonstration, *i.e.*, for explaining the attribute or event.

[d] 91 a 14–b 11.

[e] 91 b 10.

93 a

κατὰ συμβεβηκὸς ἔχομεν, ὁτὲ δ' ἔχοντές τι αὐτοῦ
τοῦ πράγματος, οἷον βροντήν, ὅτι ψόφος τις νεφῶν,
καὶ ἔκλειψιν, ὅτι στέρησίς τις φωτός, καὶ ἄνθρωπον, ὅτι ζῷόν τι, καὶ ψυχήν, ὅτι αὐτὸ αὑτὸ κινοῦν.
25 ὅσα μὲν οὖν κατὰ συμβεβηκὸς οἴδαμεν ὅτι ἔστιν,
ἀναγκαῖον μηδαμῶς ἔχειν πρὸς τὸ τί ἐστιν· οὐδὲ
γὰρ ὅτι ἔστιν ἴσμεν· τὸ δὲ ζητεῖν τί ἐστι μὴ ἔχοντας
ὅτι ἔστι, μηδὲν ζητεῖν ἐστιν. καθ' ὅσων δ' ἔχομέν
τι, ῥᾷον. ὥστε ὡς ἔχομεν ὅτι ἔστιν, οὕτως ἔχομεν
καὶ πρὸς τὸ τί ἐστιν.

Ὧν οὖν ἔχομέν τι τοῦ τί ἐστιν, ἔστω πρῶτον μὲν
30 ὧδε· ἔκλειψις ἐφ' οὗ τὸ Α, σελήνη ἐφ' οὗ Γ,
ἀντίφραξις γῆς ἐφ' οὗ Β. τὸ μὲν οὖν πότερον ἐκλείπει ἢ οὔ, τὸ Β ζητεῖν ἐστιν, ἆρ' ἔστιν ἢ οὔ.
τοῦτο δ' οὐδὲν διαφέρει ζητεῖν ἢ εἰ ἔστι λόγος αὐ-
τοῦ· καὶ ἐὰν ᾖ τοῦτο, κἀκεῖνό φαμεν εἶναι. ἢ
35 ποτέρας τῆς ἀντιφάσεώς ἐστιν ὁ λόγος, πότερον
τοῦ ἔχειν δύο ὀρθὰς ἢ τοῦ μὴ ἔχειν. ὅταν δ' εὕρω-
μεν, ἅμα τὸ ὅτι καὶ τὸ διότι ἴσμεν, ἂν δι' ἀμέσων[1]
ᾖ. εἰ δὲ μή, τὸ ὅτι, τὸ διότι δ' οὔ. σελήνη Γ,
ἔκλειψις Α, τὸ πανσελήνου σκιὰν μὴ δύνασθαι
ποιεῖν μηδενὸς ἡμῶν μεταξὺ ὄντος φανεροῦ, ἐφ' οὗ
Β. εἰ τοίνυν τῷ Γ ὑπάρχει τὸ Β τὸ μὴ δύνασθαι
93 b ποιεῖν σκιὰν μηδενὸς μεταξὺ ἡμῶν ὄντος, τούτῳ

---

[1] δι' ἀμέσων n : διὰ μέσων.

---

[a] i.e., on the ground of some non-essential connexion.
[b] Plato's view : cf. Phaedrus 245 c ff., Laws 895 E. If
Aristotle is here assuming Xenocrates' definition of soul
(91 a 37 supra), all four examples illustrate knowledge of the
genus without knowledge of the differentia.
[c] Here the " grasp " is so good that the true reason is

202

aware of a thing's existence either accidentally [a] or because we have some grasp of the thing itself, *e.g.*, that thunder is a noise in the clouds, that an eclipse is a privation of light, that man is a kind of animal, and that soul is self-moving.[b] When our knowledge of the thing's existence is only accidental we cannot be in any position to grasp what the thing is, because we do not even *know* that it exists; and to inquire what a thing is when we are not sure that it exists is no inquiry at all. But when we have some grasp of the thing itself, the task is easier. Thus our capacity for discovering what a thing is depends upon our awareness that it is.

Let us first take an example of something of whose essence we have some grasp, and let A stand for "eclipse," C for "moon," and B for "obstruction by the earth."[c] Then to inquire whether there is an eclipse or not is to inquire whether B exists or not; and this is equivalent to inquiring whether there is anything to account for it; if there is, we assert that B *is* too. Similarly we may ask which of a pair of contradictories is true (*e.g.*, having or not having the sum of the angles equal to two right angles); and when we have discovered the answer we know simultaneously both the fact and the reason for it—if the premisses are immediate; otherwise we know the fact but not the reason.[d] C is "moon," A "eclipse," B "the inability of the moon at its full to cast a shadow, there being nothing visible in the way." Then if B, "inability to cast a shadow although there is nothing in the way," applies to C, and A, "being directly assumed, so that fact and reason are discovered simultaneously.

We may then look for immediate premisses to explain the connexion,

[d] As in the following example, where the minor premiss is not immediate, and the real reason has to be sought.

δὲ τὸ Α τὸ ἐκλελοιπέναι, ὅτι μὲν ἐκλείπει δῆλον,
διότι δ' οὔπω, καὶ ὅτι μὲν ἔστιν ἔκλειψις[1] ἴσμεν, τί
δ' ἐστιν οὐκ ἴσμεν. δῆλου δ' ὄντος ὅτι τὸ Α τῷ Γ
5 ὑπάρχει, ἀλλὰ διὰ τί ὑπάρχει, τὸ ζητεῖν τὸ Β τί
ἐστι, πότερον ἀντίφραξις ἢ στροφὴ τῆς σελήνης ἢ
ἀπόσβεσις. τοῦτο δ' ἐστὶν ὁ λόγος τοῦ ἑτέρου ἄκρου,
οἷον ἐν τούτοις τοῦ Α· ἔστι γὰρ ἡ ἔκλειψις ἀντίφραξις ὑπὸ γῆς. τί ἐστι βροντή; πυρὸς ἀπόσβεσις
ἐν νέφει. διὰ τί βροντᾷ; διὰ τὸ ἀποσβέννυσθαι τὸ
10 πῦρ ἐν τῷ νέφει. νέφος Γ, βροντὴ Α, ἀπόσβεσις
πυρὸς τὸ Β. τῷ δὴ Γ τῷ νέφει ὑπάρχει τὸ Β, ἀποσβέννυται γὰρ ἐν αὐτῷ τὸ πῦρ· τούτῳ δὲ τὸ Α,
ψόφος· καὶ ἔστι γε λόγος τὸ Β τοῦ Α τοῦ πρώτου
ἄκρου. ἂν δὲ πάλιν τούτου ἄλλο μέσον ᾖ, ἐκ τῶν
παραλοίπων ἔσται λόγων.
15 Ὡς μὲν τοίνυν λαμβάνεται τὸ τί ἐστι καὶ γίγνεται
γνώριμον, εἴρηται, ὥστε συλλογισμὸς μὲν τοῦ τί
ἐστιν οὐ γίγνεται οὐδ' ἀπόδειξις, δῆλον μέντοι διὰ
συλλογισμοῦ καὶ δι' ἀποδείξεως· ὥστ' οὔτ' ἄνευ
ἀποδείξεως ἔστι γνῶναι τὸ τί ἐστιν, οὗ ἐστιν αἴτιον
20 ἄλλο, οὔτ' ἔστιν ἀπόδειξις αὐτοῦ, ὥσπερ καὶ ἐν τοῖς
διαπορήμασιν εἴπομεν.

IX. Ἔστι δὲ τῶν μὲν ἕτερόν τι αἴτιον, τῶν δ'
οὐκ ἔστιν. ὥστε δῆλον ὅτι καὶ τῶν τί ἐστι τὰ μὲν

---

[1] ἔστιν ἔκλειψις n : ἔκλειψίς ἐστιν ΑΒd.

---

[a] Or " explanation " ; see below.
[b] i.e., major.
[c] λόγος seems to have a wider meaning here than in b 6.
Aristotle means that B either is itself the definition or implies

eclipsed," to B, it is obvious that there is an eclipse, but it is not yet obvious *why* ; and we know that the eclipse is a fact, but we do not know *what* it is. When it is clear that A applies to C, to ask *why* it does so is equivalent to asking what B is : whether an obstruction or a rotation or an extinction of the moon ; and this is the definition [a] of the other extreme [b] term, *viz.* (in these examples) A ; because an eclipse is an obstruction by the earth of the moon's light. What is thunder ? An extinction of fire in a cloud. Why does it thunder ? Because the fire is being extinguished in the cloud. "Cloud" is C, "thunder" A, "extinction of fire" B. Then B applies to the cloud, C, because the fire is being extinguished in it ; and A, "noise," applies to B ; and B is undoubtedly the explanation of A, the major term. If B in its turn has another middle term for its cause, this will be one of the remaining explanations [c] of A. *and the middle term or terms will constitute the definition.*

We have now stated how the essence is apprehended, and becomes known to us, to the effect that although it does not admit of syllogism or demonstration, yet it is through syllogism and demonstration that it becomes clear to us.[d] It follows that the essence of a thing which has a cause other than itself cannot be known apart from demonstration, while at the same time it cannot be demonstrated ; as we said [e] in reviewing the difficulties of the subject. *Thus demonstration does not prove but reveals the essence.*

IX. Some things have a cause distinct from themselves, and others have not.[f] Thus it is clear that of *Immediate essences*

an additional cause, which, together with B, constitutes the definition.

[d] Although the essence or definition cannot be proved as the conclusion of a syllogism, yet syllogism enables us to see the facts in their true relation.

[e] In chs. ii and iii. [f] *Cf.* note on 93 a 5.

93 b

ἄμεσα καὶ ἀρχαί εἰσιν, ἃ καὶ εἶναι καὶ τί ἐστιν
ὑποθέσθαι δεῖ ἢ ἄλλον τρόπον φανερὰ ποιῆσαι (ὅπερ
25 ὁ ἀριθμητικὸς ποιεῖ· καὶ γὰρ τί ἐστι τὴν μονάδα
ὑποτίθεται, καὶ ὅτι ἔστιν)· τῶν δ᾿ ἐχόντων μέσον,
καὶ ὧν ἔστι τι ἕτερον αἴτιον τῆς οὐσίας, ἔστι δι᾿
ἀποδείξεως, ὥσπερ εἴπομεν, δηλῶσαι, μὴ τὸ τί
ἐστιν ἀποδεικνύντας.

X. Ὁρισμὸς δ᾿ ἐπειδὴ λέγεται εἶναι λόγος τοῦ
30 τί ἐστι, φανερὸν ὅτι ὁ μέν τις ἔσται λόγος τοῦ τί
σημαίνει τὸ ὄνομα ἢ λόγος ἕτερος ὀνοματώδης, οἷον
τὸ¹ τί σημαίνει [τί ἐστι]² τρίγωνον. ὅπερ ἔχοντες
ὅτι ἔστι, ζητοῦμεν διὰ τί ἔστιν· χαλεπὸν δ᾿ οὕτως
ἐστὶ λαβεῖν ἃ μὴ ἴσμεν ὅτι ἔστιν. ἡ δ᾿ αἰτία
35 εἴρηται πρότερον τῆς χαλεπότητος, ὅτι οὐδ᾿ εἰ
ἔστιν ἢ μὴ ἴσμεν, ἀλλ᾿ ἢ κατὰ συμβεβηκός. (λόγος
δ᾿ εἷς ἐστι διχῶς, ὁ μὲν συνδέσμῳ, ὥσπερ ἡ Ἰλιάς,
ὁ δὲ τῷ ἓν καθ᾿ ἑνὸς δηλοῦν μὴ κατὰ συμβεβηκός.)

Εἷς μὲν δὴ ὅρος ἐστὶν ὅρου ὁ εἰρημένος, ἄλλος δ᾿
ἐστὶν ὅρος λόγος ὁ δηλῶν διὰ τί ἔστιν· ὥστε ὁ μὲν
94 a πρότερος σημαίνει μέν, δείκνυσι δ᾿ οὔ, ὁ δ᾿ ὕστερος
φανερὸν ὅτι ἔσται οἷον ἀπόδειξις τοῦ τί ἐστι, τῇ
θέσει διαφέρων τῆς ἀποδείξεως. διαφέρει γὰρ
εἰπεῖν διὰ τί βροντᾷ καὶ τί ἐστι βροντή· ἐρεῖ γὰρ
οὕτω μὲν διότι ἀποσβέννυται τὸ πῦρ ἐν τοῖς νέφεσι·

---

¹ τὸ om. n¹.
² τί ἐστι secl. Ross : τί ἐστιν ᾗ Ad.

ᵃ In ch. viii.
ᵇ Considered (apparently) as an attribute, not as a subject
of geometry ; for then it would be a quasi-substance and its
definition would fall under type (3).
ᶜ 93 a 24 ff.
ᵈ Cf. Met. 1045 a 13, and supra 92 b 32.

essences too some are immediate ; *i.e.*, they are first must be
principles, and both their existence and their defini- assumed or
tion have to be assumed or exhibited in some other another
way. (This is what an arithmetician does : he as- method.
sumes both what a unit is, and that it exists.) As for
things which have a middle term, *i.e.*, something
distinct from themselves which is a cause of their
being, it is possible (as we have said [a]) to exhibit
their essence by demonstration, although we do not
actually demonstrate it.

X. Since definition means " an account of what a The three
thing is," obviously (1) one kind of definition will be kinds of
an explanation of the meaning of the name, or of an definition.
equivalent denomination ; *e.g.*, it will explain the
meaning of " triangularity." [b] If we are aware that
such a thing exists, we inquire why it exists ; but it
is difficult to apprehend in this way the definition
of things which we do not know to exist. We have
explained above [c] the cause of this difficulty, *viz.*,
that we do not really know, except in an accidental
sense, whether the thing exists or not. (An account
may be a unity in two ways : either by connexion,
like the *Iliad*,[d] or because it exhibits one term as
predicated of one other term in a non-accidental
relation.)

The above is one definition of definition ; but (2)
in another sense definition is a form of words which
explains *why* a thing exists. Thus type (1) conveys
a meaning but does not prove, whereas type (2) will
obviously be a quasi-demonstration of the essence,
differing from demonstration in the arrangement of
its terms. To explain why it thunders is not the same
as to explain what thunder is. In the former case we
shall say " because the fire is being extinguished in

94 a

5 τί δ' ἐστὶ βροντή; ψόφος ἀποσβεννυμένου πυρὸς
ἐν νέφεσιν· ὥστε ὁ αὐτὸς λόγος ἄλλον τρόπον λέγεται, καὶ ὡδὶ μὲν ἀπόδειξις συνεχής, ὡδὶ δὲ ὁρισμός. ἔτι ἐστὶν ὅρος βροντῆς ψόφος ἐν νέφεσι· τοῦτο
δ' ἐστὶ τῆς τοῦ τί ἐστιν ἀποδείξεως συμπέρασμα.
ὁ δὲ τῶν ἀμέσων ὁρισμὸς θέσις ἐστὶ τοῦ τί ἐστιν
10 ἀναπόδεικτος.

Ἔστιν ἄρα ὁρισμὸς εἷς μὲν λόγος τοῦ τί ἐστιν
ἀναπόδεικτος, εἷς δὲ συλλογισμὸς τοῦ τί ἐστι πτώ-
σει διαφέρων τῆς ἀποδείξεως, τρίτος δὲ τῆς τοῦ τί
ἐστιν ἀποδείξεως συμπέρασμα. φανερὸν οὖν ἐκ
15 τῶν εἰρημένων καὶ πῶς ἔστι τοῦ τί ἐστιν ἀπόδειξις
καὶ πῶς οὐκ ἔστι, καὶ τίνων ἔστι καὶ τίνων οὐκ
ἔστιν, ἔτι δ' ὁρισμὸς ποσαχῶς τε λέγεται καὶ πῶς
τὸ τί ἐστι δείκνυσι καὶ πῶς οὔ, καὶ τίνων ἔστι καὶ
τίνων οὔ, ἔτι δὲ πρὸς ἀπόδειξιν πῶς ἔχει, καὶ πῶς
ἐνδέχεται τοῦ αὐτοῦ εἶναι καὶ πῶς οὐκ ἐνδέχεται.

20 XI. Ἐπεὶ δὲ ἐπίστασθαι οἰόμεθα ὅταν εἰδῶμεν
τὴν αἰτίαν, αἰτίαι δὲ τέτταρες, μία μὲν τὸ τί ἦν
εἶναι, μία δὲ τὸ τίνων ὄντων ἀνάγκη τοῦτ' εἶναι,
ἑτέρα δὲ ἡ τί πρῶτον ἐκίνησε, τετάρτη δὲ τὸ τίνος
ἕνεκα, πᾶσαι αὗται διὰ τοῦ μέσου δείκνυνται. τό τε

---

^a Continuous " because its premisses are parts which are
conterminous (as linked by middle terms), and there is a
movement from premisses to conclusion. Definition resembles rather the indivisible simplicity of a point " (Mure).

^b See 93 b 21 ff.

^c The three types are recapitulated in reverse order.

^d i.e., in the arrangement of the terms (cf. 94 a 2).

^e Three of these causes belong to Aristotle's standard doc-
trine of causation as set out in Phys. II. iii ; but here the
place of the material cause, which is inappropriate for the
present logical purpose, is taken by the " necessitating con-

the clouds " ; but the answer to the question " What is thunder ? " is " Noise due to the extinguishing of fire in the clouds." Thus the same account is expressed in a different way ; in one form it is a continuous [a] demonstration, in the other a definition. Further, whereas thunder can be defined as a noise in the clouds, which is the conclusion of the syllogism that demonstrates the essence, (3) the definition of immediate terms [b] consists in an indemonstrable assumption of their essence.

Thus in one sense [c] definition is an indemonstrable account of the essence ; in another it is a logical inference of the essence, differing from demonstration in grammatical form [d] ; and in a third it is the conclusion of the syllogism which demonstrates the essence. The foregoing discussion shows clearly (a) in what sense essence is demonstrable, and in what sense it is not ; (b) of what things the essence is demonstrable, and of what it is not ; (c) the different aspects of definition ; (d) in what sense it does or does not exhibit the essence ; (e) what things are or are not definable ; (f) the relation of definition to demonstration ; (g) in what sense there can be definition and demonstration of the same thing. *Summary of this and the two preceding chapters.*

XI. We only think that we have knowledge of a thing when we know its cause. There are four kinds of cause : the essence, the necessitating conditions, the efficient cause which started the process, and the final cause.[e] All these are exhibited through the *The four kinds of logical cause are all exhibited through a middle term. (1) The ground,*

dition " or " ground." The formula (barely reproducible in English) by which Aristotle describes this recalls the definition of syllogism (*An. Pr.* 24 b 18 ff.), and in l. 24 it becomes plain that he has in mind the conjunction of two premisses as the ground of their conclusion. Although there is some analogy between this ground and the material cause, there

25 γὰρ οὗ ὄντος τοδὶ ἀνάγκη εἶναι μιᾶς μὲν προτάσεως

ληφθείσης οὐκ ἔστι, δυοῖν δὲ τοὐλάχιστον· τοῦτο δ᾽

ἐστὶν ὅταν ἓν μέσον ἔχωσι. τούτου οὖν ἑνὸς ληφ-

θέντος τὸ συμπέρασμα ἀνάγκη εἶναι. δῆλον δὲ καὶ

ὧδε. διὰ τί ὀρθὴ ἡ ἐν ἡμικυκλίῳ; τίνος[1] ὄντος

ὀρθή; ἔστω δὴ ὀρθὴ ἐφ᾽ ἧς Α, ἡμίσεια δυοῖν ὀρ-

30 θαῖν ἐφ᾽ ἧς Β, ἡ ἐν ἡμικυκλίῳ ἐφ᾽ ἧς Γ. τοῦ δὴ

τὸ Α τὴν ὀρθὴν ὑπάρχειν τῷ Γ τῇ ἐν τῷ ἡμικυκλίῳ

αἴτιον τὸ Β. αὕτη μὲν γὰρ τῇ Α ἴση· ἡ δὲ τὸ Γ

τῇ Β· δύο γὰρ ὀρθῶν ἡμίσεια. τοῦ Β οὖν ὄντος

ἡμίσεος δύο ὀρθῶν τὸ Α τῷ Γ ὑπάρχει· τοῦτο δ᾽

ἦν τὸ ἐν ἡμικυκλίῳ ὀρθὴν εἶναι. τοῦτο δὲ ταὐτόν

[1] τίνος] ἢ τίνος D.

---

is no reason to suppose that Aristotle means to identify them. The error of such a view is fully demonstrated by Ross *ad loc.* Here it is enough to point out that the material could never be equated with the formal cause (a 34 *infra*). Aristotle is simply trying (with qualified success) to offer an analysis of causation which will enable him to represent each type of cause as a kind of middle term.

[a] From the sequel it appears that this odd and perhaps deliberately vague phrase is intended to mean that each type can actually serve as middle term in a syllogism.

[b] *i.e.*, common.

[c] The choice of " the half of two right angles " as middle term clearly implies that Aristotle had in mind a proof in

middle term.[a] (1) There is no necessitating ground
if only one premiss is assumed; two at least are
necessary; and the condition is satisfied when the
premisses have one [b] middle term. Thus the assumption of this one term necessitates the conclusion.
This is clear from the following example. Why is the
angle in a semicircle a right angle? What is the
ground of its being a right angle? Let A be a right
angle, B the half of two right angles, C the angle in a
semicircle.[c] Then the cause for the attachment of
A, right angle, to C, the angle in a semicircle, is B;
for this is equal to A, and the angle C to B, since B
is the half of two right angles. Thus the fact that
B is the half of two right angles is the ground necessitating that A applies to C, *i.e.* (by our assumption),
that the angle in a semicircle is a right angle. Now

which this expression occurred (probably) at the penultimate
step; *e.g.*, not the proof of *Met.* 1051 a 27 (cited by Ross),
nor that of Euclid iii. 21, but the interpolated proof which
follows the latter, to this effect:

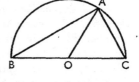

BAC is an ∠ in the semicircle
ABC, centre O. Since OB, OA,
OC are radii, ∠OBA = ∠OAB
and ∠OCA = ∠OAC. Then
∠AOC = 2∠BAO, and ∠AOB
= 2∠CAO.
∴ ∠BAC = ∠BAO + ∠CAO =
½(∠AOC + ∠AOB) = ½∠BOC
= ½(2 rt.∠s) = a rt∠.
(So Heath, *Mathematics in Aristotle*, p. 72.) It is tempting
to think that Aristotle might have directly perceived that
∠BAC = ½ the flat ∠BOC standing on the same arc; for
this would go far to justify " some such definition of the
rightness of the angle in a semicircle as its being right in
consequence of being the half of two right angles,'" for
which " little can be said " (Ross *ad loc.*). But although
Aristotle was an acute mathematician, it is hardly likely that
he was so far in advance of his times.

94 a

35 ἐστι τῷ τί ἦν εἶναι, τῷ τοῦτο σημαίνειν τὸν λόγον.
ἀλλὰ μὴν καὶ τὸ τί ἦν εἶναι αἴτιον δέδεικται τὸ
μέσον ὄν.[1] τὸ δὲ διὰ τί ὁ Μηδικὸς πόλεμος ἐγένετο
Ἀθηναίοις; τίς αἰτία τοῦ πολεμεῖσθαι Ἀθηναίους;
94 b ὅτι εἰς Σάρδεις μετ' Ἐρετριέων ἐνέβαλον· τοῦτο
γὰρ ἐκίνησε πρῶτον. πόλεμος ἐφ' οὗ Α, προ-
τέρους[2] εἰσβαλεῖν Β, Ἀθηναῖοι τὸ Γ. ὑπάρχει δὴ
τὸ Β τῷ Γ, τὸ προτέροις[3] ἐμβαλεῖν τοῖς Ἀθηναίοις·
5 τὸ δὲ Α τῷ Β· πολεμοῦσι γὰρ τοῖς πρότερον ἀδική-
σασιν. ὑπάρχει ἄρα τῷ μὲν Β τὸ Α, τὸ πολεμεῖσθαι τοῖς προτέροις[4] ἄρξασι· τοῦτο δὲ τὸ Β[5] τοῖς
Ἀθηναίοις· πρότεροι γὰρ ἦρξαν. μέσον ἄρα καὶ ἐνταῦθα τὸ αἴτιον τὸ πρῶτον κινῆσαν. ὅσων δὲ αἴτιον
τὸ ἕνεκά τινος, οἷον διὰ τί περιπατεῖ; ὅπως ὑγιαίνῃ·
10 διὰ τί οἰκία ἔστιν; ὅπως σῴζηται τὰ σκεύη· τὸ
μὲν ἕνεκα τοῦ ὑγιαίνειν, τὸ δὲ ἕνεκα τοῦ σῴζεσθαι.
διὰ τί δὲ ἀπὸ δείπνου δεῖ περιπατεῖν, καὶ ἕνεκα
τίνος δεῖ, οὐδὲν διαφέρει. περίπατος ἀπὸ δείπνου
Γ, τὸ μὴ ἐπιπολάζειν τὰ σιτία ἐφ' οὗ Β, τὸ ὑγιαίνειν ἐφ' οὗ Α. ἔστω δὴ τῷ ἀπὸ δείπνου περιπατεῖν
15 ὑπάρχον τὸ ποιεῖν μὴ ἐπιπολάζειν τὰ σιτία πρὸς
τῷ στόματι τῆς κοιλίας, καὶ τοῦτο ὑγιεινόν. δοκεῖ
γὰρ ὑπάρχειν τῷ περιπατεῖν τῷ Γ τὸ Β τὸ μὴ
ἐπιπολάζειν τὰ σιτία, τούτῳ δὲ τὸ Α τὸ ὑγιεινόν.
τί οὖν αἴτιον τῷ Γ τοῦ τὸ Α ὑπάρχειν τὸ οὗ ἕνεκα;[a]

---

[1] ὄν om. ABdn[1].   [2] πρότερον Bekker.
[3] πρότερον D, Bekker.
[4] προτέροις] πρότερον D.
[5] Β τῷ Γ D[2] f.

---

[a] i.e., the necessitating ground.

this [a] is the same as the essence, inasmuch as it is what the definition implies. (2) The cause in the sense of essence has also been proved to be the middle.[b] (3) Why did the Persian expedition [c] come against Athens ? or in other words, what was the cause of her becoming involved in war ? Because Athens had, in company with Eretria, raided Sardis [d]; this was what first started the war. A is " war," B " unprovoked aggression," C " Athens." Then B, unprovoked aggression, applies to C, Athens ; and A applies to B, because war is made upon those who commit an aggressive wrong. So A, becoming involved in war, applies to B, the side which began hostilities ; and B in its turn applies to C, Athens, because she began hostilities. Thus here too the cause—the efficient cause—is a middle. (4) Now take the case where the cause is final : e.g., Why does one take a walk ? In order to be healthy. What is the object of a house ? Preservation of the contents. The final causes are respectively health and preservation. It makes no difference whether we ask *why* or *for what purpose* one should take a walk after dinner. C stands for " walking after dinner," B for " normal digestion," [e] and A for " health." Let us assume that walking after dinner possesses the attribute of promoting normal digestion, and that the latter is conducive to health ; because it is generally accepted that B, normal digestion, applies to C, taking a walk, and that A, healthful, applies to B. Then what is the reason why A, the final cause, applies to C ? The

(marginal notes) (2) the essence, (3) the efficient cause, and (4) the final cause, can all stand as middle terms.

---

[b] In ch. viii ; *cf.* also 93 b 38 ff.
[c] Under Datis in 490 B.C.
[d] Under Aristagoras in 497 B.C.
[e] Literally " food not floating on the surface," with the added qualification in l. 15 " at the mouth of the stomach."

213

τὸ Β τὸ μὴ ἐπιπολάζειν. τοῦτο δ' ἐστὶν ὥσπερ
20 ἐκείνου λόγος· τὸ γὰρ Α οὕτως ἀποδοθήσεται. διὰ
τί δὲ¹ τὸ Β τῷ Γ ἐστίν; ὅτι τοῦτ' ἔστι τὸ ὑγιαίνειν, τὸ οὕτως ἔχειν. δεῖ δὲ μεταλαμβάνειν τοὺς
λόγους, καὶ οὕτως μᾶλλον ἕκαστα φανεῖται. αἱ δὲ
γενέσεις ἀνάπαλιν ἐνταῦθα καὶ ἐπὶ τῶν κατὰ κίνησιν αἰτίων· ἐκεῖ μὲν γὰρ τὸ μέσον δεῖ γενέσθαι
25 πρῶτον, ἐνταῦθα δὲ τὸ Γ τὸ ἔσχατον· τελευταῖον
δὲ τὸ οὗ ἕνεκα.

Ἐνδέχεται δὲ τὸ αὐτὸ καὶ ἕνεκά τινος εἶναι καὶ
ἐξ ἀνάγκης, οἷον διὰ τοῦ λαμπτῆρος τὸ φῶς· καὶ

---

¹ δὲ om. D.

ᵃ This passage is not clearly thought out, and interpretation can only be tentative. It seems that up to this point
Aristotle only professes to enunciate a syllogism of which the
major term is a final cause. In so doing he overlooks (or
disregards) the fact that a final cause can only function as
such in a " practical " syllogism, whereas the one which he
has in mind seems to be demonstrative, *viz.*,

What promotes digestion is healthful
Walking after dinner promotes digestion
∴ Walking after dinner is healthful.

This is valid, but it proves nothing about health *qua* final
cause. Aristotle would probably justify his reasoning on
teleological grounds by arguing that walking, etc., is healthful
because it is an activity subserving a natural end ; but this
is really another matter.

Ross, who interprets the passage quite differently, supposing
that Aristotle is already trying to exhibit the final cause as
middle term, shows that in this case the middle term must
be not " health " but " desirous of being healthy " (Those
who wish to be healthy walk after dinner, This man desires
to be healthy, Therefore this man walks after dinner), and
comments " Aristotle is in fact mistaken in his use of the

answer is " B, normal digestion." [a] This is a sort of definition of A, because A will be explained by this means.[b] Why does B apply to C? Because health is the condition represented by B. The expressions [c] should be transposed, and then the several facts will become clearer. In these examples the order of events is the reverse of what it is in the case of efficient causes. There it is the middle term that must come first[d]; but here it is the minor term C, and the end or purpose comes last.

The same effect may obtain both for a purpose and as a necessary consequence, as, *e.g.*, light shines

Possibility of double causation.

notion of final cause. It is never the so-called final cause that is operative, but the desire of an object ; and this desire operates as an efficient cause, being what corresponds, in the case of purposive action, to a mechanical or chemical cause in physical action." If my view is right, this criticism is scarcely justified. Moreover, it obscures the correlativity of the final and efficient causes : if it is the desire that " operates," that desire is still excited by the object of desire (the mouse wants the cheese, and the cheese attracts the mouse) ; the two are always complementary and often no more than different aspects of a single fact.

[b] Aristotle now tries to show that A, the final cause, can stand as middle between B and C. The steps seem to be : (1) B is " a sort of definition " of A ; *i.e.*, the final is expressible in terms of the efficient cause. (2) Similarly *vice versa*. (3) Therefore A and B are convertible, and B can be proved of C through A.

If this interpretation (which is virtually the same as Mure's) is correct, Aristotle can hardly be acquitted of juggling with terms, although the interdependence of efficient and final causes (noted above) and the tendency of both to merge in the formal cause (*Met.* 1044 b 1, 1070 b 26) provide some justification.

[c] Or perhaps " definitions," A being defined in terms of B, and *vice versa*. The vagueness of the language suggests that Aristotle is not quite satisfied with his demonstration.

[d] Not really first, but before the major.

94 b

γὰρ ἐξ ἀνάγκης διέρχεται τὸ μικρομερέστερον διὰ
30 τῶν μειζόνων πόρων, εἴπερ φῶς γίγνεται τῷ δι-
ιέναι, καὶ ἕνεκά τινος, ὅπως μὴ πταίωμεν.ᵃ ἆρ' οὖν
εἰ εἶναι ἐνδέχεται, καὶ γίγνεσθαι ἐνδέχεται, ὥσπερ εἰ
βροντᾷ ⟨ὅτι⟩¹ ἀποσβεννυμένου τε τοῦ πυρὸς ἀνάγκη
σίζειν καὶ ψοφεῖν, καὶ εἰ ὡς οἱ Πυθαγόρειοί φασιν,
ἀπειλῆς ἕνεκα τοῖς ἐν τῷ ταρτάρῳ, ὅπως φοβῶνται;
35 πλεῖστα δὲ τοιαῦτ' ἔστι, καὶ μάλιστα ἐν τοῖς κατὰ
φύσιν συνισταμένοις καὶ συνεστῶσιν· ἡ μὲν γὰρ
ἕνεκά του ποιεῖ φύσις, ἡ δ' ἐξ ἀνάγκης. ἡ δ' ἀνάγ-
95 a κη διττή· ἡ μὲν γὰρ κατὰ φύσιν καὶ τὴν ὁρμήν, ἡ
δὲ βίᾳ ἡ παρὰ τὴν ὁρμήν, ὥσπερ λίθος ἐξ ἀνάγκης
καὶ ἄνω καὶ κάτω φέρεται, ἀλλ' οὐ διὰ τὴν αὐτὴν
ἀνάγκην. ἐν δὲ τοῖς ἀπὸ διανοίας τὰ μὲν οὐδέποτε
ἀπὸ τοῦ αὐτομάτου ὑπάρχει, οἷον οἰκία ἢ ἀνδριάς,
5 οὐδ' ἐξ ἀνάγκης, ἀλλ' ἕνεκά του, τὰ δὲ καὶ ἀπὸ
τύχης, οἷον ὑγίεια καὶ σωτηρία. μάλιστα δὲ ἐν
ὅσοις ἐνδέχεται καὶ ὧδε καὶ ἄλλως, ὅταν μὴ ἀπὸ
τύχης ἡ γένεσις ᾖ ὥστε τὸ τέλος ἀγαθόν, ἕνεκά του

---

¹ ὅτι add. Ross, habent comm. (?).

ᵃ The lantern is probably of the type implied by A. in
Hist. An. 531 a 5, with a cylindrical parchment shield (τὸ
κύκλῳ δέρμα); and the light-particles pass through the pores
of the parchment. The theory goes back to Empedocles
(fr. 84, quoted in *De Sensu* 437 b 26 ff.), as no doubt does the
similar theory about the burning-glass (*supra* 88 a 14) attributed to Gorgias, who was his pupil.

ᵇ The purpose is surely artificial, not (as Ross thinks) an
instance of natural design ; for the translucence of (oiled ?)
parchment can hardly be tied to this particular use. If the
example is meant to be exactly parallel with that which
follows, it is ill-chosen.

through a lantern. Being composed of particles smaller than the pores ⟨in the shield⟩ of the lantern,[a] it cannot help passing through them (assuming that this is how the light is propagated); but it also shines for a purpose, so that we may not stumble.[b] If, then, an effect can obtain for two causes, can it also be brought about by two causes?—e.g., if it thunders both because there must be a hissing and roaring as the fire [c] is extinguished, and also (as the Pythagoreans hold) to threaten the souls in Tartarus and make them fear.[d] There are plenty of such examples, especially among the processes and products of nature; because nature in one aspect acts with a purpose and in another from necessity. Now necessity is of two kinds: one acts in accordance with the nature or natural tendency of an object, the other forcibly opposes it (thus both the upward and the downward movements of a stone are due to necessity, but not to the same necessity [e]). Among the products of rational thought some, such as a house or a statue, never owe their existence to spontaneity or necessity but always to some purpose; others, like health and security, may also be due to chance. It is especially in circumstances that admit of more than one result, when the process is not due to chance, so that the end is some good, that design

[c] Sc., of the lightning. The Greek seems to call for Ross's ὅτι, which has some support from the commentators; but I am by no means confident that Aristotle wrote it. It really looks as though the εἰ before βροντᾷ were intended to serve twice over.

[d] I know of no other authority for this doctrine.

[e] The downward movement is the stone's natural tendency to find its proper place in the universe (cf. De Caelo IV. iv); the upward is imparted by some external force.

217

95 a

γίγνεται, καὶ ἢ φύσει ἢ τέχνη. ἀπὸ τύχης δ᾽ οὐδὲν
ἕνεκά του γίγνεται.

10   XII. Τὸ δ᾽ αὐτὸ αἴτιόν ἐστι τοῖς γιγνομένοις καὶ
τοῖς γεγενημένοις καὶ τοῖς ἐσομένοις ὅπερ καὶ τοῖς
οὖσι (τὸ γὰρ μέσον αἴτιον), πλὴν τοῖς μὲν οὖσιν ὄν,
τοῖς δὲ γιγνομένοις γιγνόμενον, τοῖς δὲ γεγενημένοις γεγενημένον καὶ ἐσομένοις ἐσόμενον. οἷον
15 διὰ τί γέγονεν ἔκλειψις; διότι ἐν μέσῳ γέγονεν ἡ
γῆ· γίγνεται δὲ διότι γίγνεται, ἔσται δὲ διότι ἔσται
ἐν μέσῳ, καὶ ἔστι διότι¹ ἔστιν. τί ἐστι κρύσταλλος;
εἰλήφθω δὴ ὅτι ὕδωρ πεπηγός. ὕδωρ ἐφ᾽ οὗ Γ,
πεπηγὸς ἐφ᾽ οὗ Α, αἴτιον τὸ μέσον ἐφ᾽ οὗ Β, ἔκλειψις θερμοῦ παντελής. ὑπάρχει δὴ τῷ Γ τὸ Β,
20 τούτῳ δὲ τὸ πεπηγέναι τὸ ἐφ᾽ οὗ Α. γίγνεται δὲ
κρύσταλλος γιγνομένου τοῦ Β, γεγένηται δὲ γεγενημένου, ἔσται δ᾽ ἐσομένου.

Τὸ μὲν οὖν οὕτως αἴτιον καὶ οὗ αἴτιον ἅμα γίγνεται, ὅταν γίγνηται, καὶ ἔστιν, ὅταν ᾖ· καὶ ἐπὶ τοῦ
γεγονέναι καὶ ἔσεσθαι ὡσαύτως. ἐπὶ δὲ τῶν μὴ
25 ἅμα ἆρ᾽ ἔστιν ἐν τῷ συνεχεῖ χρόνῳ, ὥσπερ δοκεῖ
ἡμῖν, ἄλλα ἄλλων αἴτια εἶναι, τοῦ τόδε γενέσθαι
ἕτερον γενόμενον, καὶ τοῦ ἔσεσθαι ἕτερον ἐσόμενον,
καὶ τοῦ γίγνεσθαι δέ, εἴ τι ἔμπροσθεν ἐγένετο;
ἔστι δὴ ἀπὸ τοῦ ὕστερον γεγονότος ὁ συλλογισμός
(ἀρχὴ δὲ καὶ τούτων τὰ γεγονότα)· διὸ καὶ ἐπὶ τῶν

---

¹ διότι Dn : om. d : δὲ ὅτι AB.

ᵃ In the preceding examples the causes are both formal
and efficient. Aristotle does not say explicitly that causes
which are not simultaneous with their effects are not formal

occurs; it may be either natural or artificial. No designed result is due to chance.

XII. Present, past and future events are caused in just the same way as existing facts. The cause is always the middle term; but whereas the cause of a fact is a fact, the cause of a present event is a present event, and similarly with the past and the future. *E.g.*, why has an eclipse occurred? Because the earth has come in between; and an eclipse *is coming* about because the earth *is coming* in between, *will be* because the earth *will be* in between, and *is* because the earth *is* in between. What is ice? Assume that it is frozen water. Water is C, frozen A; the cause is the middle term B, complete failure of heat. Then B applies to C, and A, " frozen," applies to B. Ice forms when B comes about, has formed or will form when B has come or will come about.

Causes correspond in time with their effects.

Causes and effects which are related in this way [a] occur simultaneously when they occur at all, whether in the present, past or future; and co-exist when they exist. But the question suggests itself whether, as is commonly supposed, events which do *not* occur simultaneously in continuous time can be related as cause and effect—a past effect having a cause in the remoter past, a future effect a cause in the nearer future, and a present effect too a cause prior to it? On this view inference is possible from the posterior past event (although past events have their origin in previous events [b])—and therefore the same is true of

Can causes ever precede their effects?

If so, we can infer the cause from the effect, but not the effect from the cause.

but may be efficient or material; but he may intend to imply it.

[b] This qualification comes in oddly here. It seems to be merely a reminder that Aristotle does not dispute the causal connexion, although he does not accept it as a sufficient basis for inference.

30 γιγνομένων ὡσαύτως. ἀπὸ δὲ τοῦ προτέρου οὐκ
ἔστιν· οἷον ἐπεὶ τόδε γέγονεν, ὅτι τόδ᾿ ὕστερον
γέγονεν· καὶ ἐπὶ τοῦ ἔσεσθαι ὡσαύτως. οὔτε γὰρ
ἀορίστου οὔθ᾿ ὁρισθέντος ἔσται τοῦ χρόνου ὥστ᾿
ἐπεὶ τοῦτ᾿ ἀληθὲς εἰπεῖν γεγονέναι, τόδ᾿ ἀληθὲς
εἰπεῖν γεγονέναι τὸ ὕστερον· ἐν γὰρ τῷ μεταξὺ
35 ψεῦδος ἔσται τὸ εἰπεῖν τοῦτο, ἤδη θατέρου γεγονότος. ὁ δ᾿ αὐτὸς λόγος καὶ ἐπὶ τοῦ ἐσομένου, οὐδ᾿
ἐπεὶ τόδε γέγονε, τόδ᾿ ἔσται. τὸ γὰρ μέσον ὁμόγονον δεῖ εἶναι, τῶν γενομένων γενόμενον, τῶν ἐσο-
μένων ἐσόμενον, τῶν γιγνομένων γιγνόμενον, τῶν
ὄντων ὄν· τοῦ δὲ γέγονε καὶ τοῦ ἔσται οὐκ ἐνδέχεται
40 εἶναι ὁμόγονον. ἔτι οὔτε ἀόριστον ἐνδέχεται εἶναι
95 b τὸν χρόνον τὸν μεταξὺ οὔθ᾿ ὡρισμένον· ψεῦδος γὰρ
ἔσται τὸ εἰπεῖν ἐν τῷ μεταξύ. ἐπισκεπτέον δὲ τί
τὸ συνέχον ὥστε μετὰ τὸ γεγονέναι τὸ γίγνεσθαι
ὑπάρχειν ἐν τοῖς πράγμασιν. ἢ δῆλον ὅτι οὐκ ἔστιν

---

[a] But it might, of course, be true to say that Y *will*
happen; therefore Aristotle proceeds to deal with this
possibility.

[b] As Ross points out, " Aristotle says more than he means
here," for this principle would exclude inference from present
to past events, which he explicitly allows.

[c] If the effect does not follow immediately (as it does when
" simultaneous " with its cause) other factors may either
delay it so that it does not occur within a definite period of
time, or prevent it from happening at all. Thus while the
cause can be inferred as a necessary precondition of the
effect, the effect cannot be inferred to be a necessary consequence. On the whole question see Introd. pp. 15 f.

[d] The discussion is inconclusive; its superficiality is at
least partly due to an ambiguity in the terms used, and to
the lack of a Greek participle expressing continuous action

present events—but not from the prior; *e.g.*, we cannot argue that because X happened Y happened subsequently (and similarly in the case of future events); whether the interval be defined or not, it will not follow that because it is true to say that X has happened, it is also true to say that the posterior event Y has happened; because during the interval it will be false to say that Y has happened,[a] whereas X has happened already. The same argument applies to future events: it does not follow, because X has happened, that Y will happen. (1) The middle term must be homogeneous with the extremes: past when they are past, future when they are future, present when they are present, existent fact when they are existent facts[b]; and nothing can be homogeneous at once with what is past and what is future. (2) The interval between cause and effect can neither be indefinite nor definite; because during the interval it will be false to assert the effect.[c] We must investigate what is the bond of continuity that makes a present process follow the completion of a past event.[d] It is surely obvious that a present process is not con-

What is the causal link between events distinct in time?

in past time. Aristotle asks what is the connexion between a past event (γεγονός or γενόμενον, "a thing-having-happened) and a present one (γιγνόμενον, "a thing-happening"). But the former also means a completed process, or the completion of a process, and the latter a process still continuing. Since the completion of a process is momentary, it is indivisible and has no extremes (*Phys.* 235 b 30 ff.) and cannot be contiguous (*i.e.*, immediately successive: *Phys.* 227 a 6, *Met.* 1069 a 2) either to another completion or to a process; just as a point cannot be contiguous either to another point or to a line (which is not, of course, to be thought of as a finite aggregate of points). What Aristotle overlooks is that the completion of one process might coincide with the terminal point of a line: in other words, two processes may be actually continuous and separable only at an imaginary moment.

221

95 b

ἐχόμενον γεγονότος γιγνόμενον; οὐδὲ γὰρ γενό-
5 μενον γενομένου· πέρατα γὰρ καὶ ἄτομα· ὥσπερ
οὖν οὐδὲ στιγμαί εἰσιν ἀλλήλων ἐχόμεναι, οὐδὲ
γενόμενα· ἄμφω γὰρ ἀδιαίρετα. οὐδὲ δὴ γιγνόμενον γεγενημένου διὰ τὸ αὐτό· τὸ μὲν γὰρ γιγνόμενον διαιρετόν, τὸ δὲ γεγονὸς ἀδιαίρετον. ὥσπερ
οὖν γραμμὴ πρὸς στιγμὴν ἔχει, οὕτω τὸ γιγνό-
10 μενον πρὸς τὸ γεγονός· ἐνυπάρχει γὰρ ἄπειρα γεγονότα ἐν τῷ γιγνομένῳ. μᾶλλον δὲ φανερῶς ἐν τοῖς
καθόλου περὶ κινήσεως δεῖ λεχθῆναι περὶ τούτων.

Περὶ μὲν οὖν τοῦ πῶς ἂν ἐφεξῆς γιγνομένης τῆς
γενέσεως ἔχοι τὸ μέσον τὸ αἴτιον ἐπὶ τοσοῦτον
15 εἰλήφθω. ἀνάγκη γὰρ καὶ ἐν τούτοις τὸ μέσον
καὶ τὸ πρῶτον ἄμεσα εἶναι. οἷον τὸ Α γέγονεν
ἐπεὶ τὸ Γ γέγονεν (ὕστερον δὲ τὸ Γ γέγονεν, ἔμπροσθεν δὲ τὸ Α· ἀρχὴ δὲ τὸ Γ διὰ τὸ ἐγγύτερον
τοῦ νῦν εἶναι, ὅ ἐστιν ἀρχὴ τοῦ χρόνου). τὸ δὲ Γ
γέγονεν εἰ τὸ Δ γέγονε· τοῦ δὴ Δ γενομένου ἀνάγκη
20 τὸ Α γεγονέναι. αἴτιον δὲ τὸ Γ· τοῦ γὰρ Δ γενομένου τὸ Γ ἀνάγκη γεγονέναι, τοῦ δὲ Γ γεγονότος
ἀνάγκη πρότερον τὸ Α γεγονέναι. οὕτω δὲ λαμβάνοντι τὸ μέσον στήσεταί που εἰς ἄμεσον, ἢ ἀεὶ
παρεμπεσεῖται διὰ τὸ ἄπειρον; οὐ γάρ ἐστιν ἐχόμενον γεγονὸς γεγονότος, ὥσπερ ἐλέχθη. ἀλλ' ἄρξα-
25 σθαί γε ὅμως ἀνάγκη ἀπ' ἀμέσου[1] καὶ ἀπὸ τοῦ νῦν

---

[1] ἀπ' ἀμέσου n, Waitz : ἀπὸ μέσου ABd : ἀπὸ τοῦ μέσου
comm.

---

[a] See *Phys.* IV. x-xiv and VI, where Aristotle discusses
problems relating to time and continuity, and *cf.* Introd. p. 15.
[b] *i.e.*, the immediate cause (*causa cognoscendi*).

tiguous with a past completion; no more than one completed process is with another. Such completions are limits and indivisible. They are no more contiguous than are points in a line; both are equally indivisible. For the same reason a present process cannot be contiguous with the completion of a past event, because the former is divisible and the latter is not. Thus the relation of a present process to the completion of a past event is like that of a line to a point because in a process there is an infinite number of completions. We must treat this subject more explicitly, however, in our general discussion of Motion.[a]

We may take it that we have now shown how, in a sequence of events, the middle term can contain the cause. Here again the middle and major terms must be immediately connected. *E.g.*, A has happened because C has happened. C is the later, A the earlier event; but C is the starting-point, because it is nearer to the present, which is the starting-point in time. Now C has happened if D has happened. Then if D happens A must have happened. But the cause [b] is C, because if D happens C must have happened, and if C has happened A must have happened first. But if we take the middle term in this way, will the series terminate somewhere in an immediate premiss, or will it be infinite and always admit of the insertion of another term?—because one past event is not contiguous with another, as we have observed above.[c] In any case we must start from an immediate connexion and the present time.[d]

In reasoning from effect to cause we must proceed by immediate connexions;

but will the series ever terminate?

---

[c] 95 b 3-6.

[d] Or perhaps (as Ross, following the commentators, prefers), " we must start from a connexion that is immediate and is the first of the series, reckoning back from the present."

πρώτου. ὁμοίως δὲ καὶ ἐπὶ τοῦ ἔσται. εἰ γὰρ ἀληθὲς εἰπεῖν ὅτι ἔσται τὸ Δ, ἀνάγκη πρότερον ἀληθὲς
εἰπεῖν ὅτι τὸ Α ἔσται. τούτου δ' αἴτιον τὸ Γ· εἰ μὲν
γὰρ τὸ Δ ἔσται, πρότερον τὸ Γ ἔσται· εἰ δὲ τὸ Γ
30 ἔσται, πρότερον τὸ Α ἔσται. ὁμοίως δ' ἄπειρος ἡ
τομὴ καὶ ἐν τούτοις· οὐ γὰρ ἔστιν ἐσόμενα ἐχόμενα
ἀλλήλων. ἀρχὴ δὲ καὶ ἐν τούτοις ἄμεσος ληπτέα.
ἔχει δὲ οὕτως ἐπὶ τῶν ἔργων· εἰ γέγονεν οἰκία,
ἀνάγκη τετμῆσθαι λίθους καὶ γεγονέναι. τοῦτο διὰ
τί; ὅτι ἀνάγκη θεμέλιον γεγονέναι, εἴπερ καὶ οἰκία
35 γέγονεν.[1] εἰ δὲ θεμέλιον, πρότερον λίθους γεγονέναι ἀνάγκη. πάλιν εἰ ἔσται οἰκία, ὡσαύτως
πρότερον ἔσονται λίθοι. δείκνυται δὲ διὰ τοῦ μέσου
ὁμοίως· ἔσται γὰρ θεμέλιος[2] πρότερον.

Ἐπεὶ δ' ὁρῶμεν ἐν τοῖς γιγνομένοις κύκλῳ τινὰ
γένεσιν οὖσαν, ἐνδέχεται τοῦτο εἶναι εἴπερ ἔποιντο
40 ἀλλήλοις τὸ μέσον καὶ οἱ ἄκροι· ἐν γὰρ τούτοις τὸ
96 a ἀντιστρέφειν ἐστίν. δέδεικται δὲ τοῦτο ἐν τοῖς
πρώτοις, ὅτι ἀντιστρέφει τὰ συμπεράσματα· τὸ δὲ
κύκλῳ τοῦτό ἐστιν. ἐπὶ δὲ τῶν ἔργων φαίνεται
ὧδε· βεβρεγμένης τῆς γῆς ἀνάγκη ἀτμίδα γενέσθαι,[3]
τούτου δὲ γενομένου νέφος, τούτου δὲ γενομένου
5 ὕδωρ· τούτου δὲ γενομένου ἀνάγκη βεβρέχθαι
τὴν γῆν· τοῦτο δ' ἦν τὸ ἐξ ἀρχῆς, ὥστε κύκλῳ περι-
ελήλυθεν· ἑνὸς γὰρ αὐτῶν ὁτουοῦν ὄντος ἕτερον
ἔστι, κἀκείνου ἄλλο, καὶ τούτου τὸ πρῶτον.

Ἔστι δ' ἔνια μὲν γιγνόμενα καθόλου (ἀεί τε γὰρ

---

[1] οἰκία γέγονεν Ross, habet Eustratius : οἰκίαν γεγονέναι
codd.
[2] θεμέλιος n, Eustratius : θεμέλιον.
[3] γίνεσθαι Aldina, Bekker.

Similarly too in respect of the future. If it is true to say that D will be, it must be true at an earlier time to say that A will be. But C is the cause of A; because if D will be, C will be before it; and if C will be, A will be before C is. Here again the series will be infinitely divisible in the same way as before, because future events are not contiguous with one another. In this case too we must take as our starting-point an immediate connexion. The principle is exemplified in practical affairs. If a house has come into being, stones must have been cut and come into being. Why? Because the fact that a house has come into being implies that so has a foundation; and if so, stones must have come into being first. Again, if there is to be a house, similarly there will be stones first. The proof, as before, is by the middle term; there will be a foundation before there is a house. *Practical examples of such inference.*

It is a matter of observation that events sometimes occur in a cycle. This is possible when the middle and extreme terms are reciprocal consequents; because under these conditions the sequence is convertible. It has been shown in the first part of our treatise that conclusions are convertible,[a] and this is a form of cyclic sequence. The following is a practical example. When the earth is wet mist must form, and after mist comes cloud, and after cloud rain, and after rain the earth must be wet. This was the point from which we started, so events have moved in a cycle. Any one of them leads to another, and that to a third, and that back to the first. *How events can occur in a cycle.*

Some events occur universally (for a given state or *Inference of usual events.*

---

[a] *Sc.*, if both premisses are convertible. *Cf. An. Pr.* II. v, and *supra* 73 a 6 ff.

καὶ ἐπὶ παντὸς οὕτως ἢ ἔχει ἢ γίγνεται), τὰ δὲ ἀεὶ
10 μὲν οὔ, ὡς ἐπὶ τὸ πολὺ δέ, οἷον οὐ πᾶς ἄνθρωπος
ἄρρην τὸ γένειον τριχοῦται, ἀλλ' ὡς ἐπὶ τὸ πολύ.
τῶν δὴ τοιούτων ἀνάγκη καὶ τὸ μέσον ὡς ἐπὶ τὸ
πολὺ εἶναι. εἰ γὰρ τὸ Α κατὰ τοῦ Β καθόλου κατηγορεῖται, καὶ τοῦτο κατὰ τοῦ Γ καθόλου, ἀνάγκη
καὶ τὸ Α κατὰ τοῦ Γ ἀεὶ καὶ ἐπὶ παντὸς κατ-
15 ηγορεῖσθαι· τοῦτο γάρ ἐστι τὸ καθόλου, τὸ¹ ἐπὶ
παντὶ καὶ ἀεί. ἀλλ' ὑπέκειτο ὡς ἐπὶ τὸ πολύ· ἀνάγκη ἄρα καὶ τὸ μέσον ὡς ἐπὶ τὸ πολὺ εἶναι τὸ ἐφ'
οὗ τὸ Β. ἔσονται τοίνυν καὶ τῶν ὡς ἐπὶ τὸ πολὺ
ἀρχαὶ ἄμεσοι, ὅσα ὡς ἐπὶ τὸ πολὺ οὕτως ἔστιν ἢ
γίγνεται.

20 XIII. Πῶς μὲν οὖν τὸ τί ἐστιν εἰς τοὺς ὅρους
ἀποδίδοται, καὶ τίνα τρόπον ἀπόδειξις ἢ ὁρισμὸς
ἔστιν αὐτοῦ ἢ οὐκ ἔστιν, εἴρηται πρότερον· πῶς δὲ
δεῖ θηρεύειν τὰ ἐν τῷ τί ἐστι κατηγορούμενα, νῦν
λέγωμεν.

Τῶν δὴ ὑπαρχόντων ἀεὶ ἑκάστῳ ἔνια ἐπεκτείνει
25 ἐπὶ πλέον, οὐ μέντοι ἔξω τοῦ γένους. λέγω δὲ ἐπὶ
πλέον ὑπάρχειν ὅσα ὑπάρχει μὲν ἑκάστῳ καθόλου,
οὐ μὴν ἀλλὰ καὶ ἄλλῳ. οἷον ἔστι τι ὃ πάσῃ τριάδι
ὑπάρχει, ἀλλὰ καὶ μὴ τριάδι· ὥσπερ τὸ ὂν ὑπάρχει
τῇ τριάδι, ἀλλὰ καὶ μὴ ἀριθμῷ· ἀλλὰ καὶ τὸ περιτ-
30 τὸν ὑπάρχει τε πάσῃ τριάδι καὶ ἐπὶ πλέον ὑπάρχει

---

¹ τὸ n : καὶ ABd.

ᵃ For " usual " events as objects of science *cf. Met.* 1026
b 27 ff., 1064 b 32 ff.
ᵇ *Viz.*, that in a syllogism which leads to a causal defini-
226

process may be true always and of every case), while others occur not always but usually [a]; *e.g.*, not every male human being grows hair on the chin, but it happens usually. In such cases the middle term too must be a usual event. If A is predicated universally of B, and B universally of C, A must also be predicated of C, and of *all* C; because " universally " means always and in every case. But *ex hypothesi* A is predicated usually of C. Then the middle term B must also be " usual." Thus the immediate premisses of usual events must also describe states or processes which are usual.

XIII. We have explained above how the essence is distributed among the terms,[b] and in what sense it does or does not admit of demonstration or definition.[c] Let us now consider how we should hunt for the attributes which are predicated as elements in the definition.

Of the permanent [d] attributes of any given subject some [e] have a wider application—not, however, beyond the genus. By an attribute with a wider application I mean one which applies universally to a particular subject, and also to some other. *E.g.*, there are attributes which apply to every 3 and also to what is not 3, in the way that " being " applies to 3 and also to subjects which are not numbers.[f] On the other hand, oddness applies to every 3, and has a

How to find the elements in a definition,

by collecting attributes shared with other species but not with other genera.

tion of an attribute the attribute must be the major, the cause the middle, and the subject the minor term (93 a 14 ff.).

[c] In chs. viii-x. [d] *i.e.*, non-accidental.

[e] Others—*viz.*, properties and some differentiae—do not; but they are not in question here. Note that we are now concerned with the definition of substances.

[f] This type is mentioned only to be dismissed, because it extends beyond the genus, number.

96 a

(καὶ γὰρ τῇ πεντάδι ὑπάρχει), ἀλλ' οὐκ ἔξω τοῦ
γένους· ἡ μὲν γὰρ πεντὰς ἀριθμός, οὐδὲν δὲ ἔξω
ἀριθμοῦ περιττόν. τὰ δὴ τοιαῦτα ληπτέον μέχρι
τούτου, ἕως τοσαῦτα ληφθῇ πρῶτον ὧν ἕκαστον
μὲν ἐπὶ πλέον ὑπάρξει, ἅπαντα δὲ μὴ ἐπὶ πλέον·
35 ταύτην γὰρ ἀνάγκη οὐσίαν εἶναι τοῦ πράγματος.
οἷον τριάδι ὑπάρχει πάσῃ ἀριθμός, τὸ περιττόν, τὸ
πρῶτον ἀμφοτέρως, καὶ ὡς μὴ μετρεῖσθαι ἀριθμῷ
καὶ ὡς μὴ συγκεῖσθαι ἐξ ἀριθμῶν. τοῦτο τοίνυν
ἤδη ἐστὶν ἡ τριάς, ἀριθμὸς περιττὸς πρῶτος καὶ
ὡδὶ πρῶτος. τούτων γὰρ ἕκαστον τὰ μὲν καὶ
96 b τοῖς περιττοῖς πᾶσιν ὑπάρχει, τὸ δὲ τελευταῖον
καὶ τῇ δυάδι, πάντα δὲ οὐδενί. ἐπεὶ δὲ δεδήλωται
ἡμῖν ἐν τοῖς ἄνω ὅτι καθόλου[1] μέν ἐστι τὰ ἐν τῷ τί
ἐστι κατηγορούμενα, τὰ καθόλου δὲ ἀναγκαῖα, τῇ
δὲ τριάδι καὶ ἐφ' οὗ ἄλλου οὕτω λαμβάνεται ἐν τῷ
5 τί ἐστι τὰ λαμβανόμενα, οὕτως ἐξ ἀνάγκης μὲν
ἂν εἴη τριὰς ταῦτα. ὅτι δ' οὐσία, ἐκ τῶνδε δῆλον.
ἀνάγκη γάρ, εἰ μὴ τοῦτο ἦν τριάδι εἶναι, οἷον γένος
τί εἶναι τοῦτο, ἢ ὠνομασμένον ἢ ἀνώνυμον. ἔσται
τοίνυν ἐπὶ πλέον[2] ἢ τῇ τριάδι ὑπάρχον. ὑποκείσθω
γὰρ τοιοῦτον εἶναι τὸ γένος ὥστε ὑπάρχειν κατὰ
10 δύναμιν ἐπὶ πλέον.[3] εἰ τοίνυν μηδενὶ ὑπάρχει ἄλλῳ
ἢ ταῖς ἀτόμοις τριάσι, τοῦτ' ἂν εἴη τὸ τριάδι εἶναι·
ὑποκείσθω γὰρ καὶ τοῦτο, ἡ οὐσία ἡ ἑκάστου εἶναι

---

[1] καθόλου Ross : ἀναγκαῖα codd.
[2] πλεῖον AB.   [3] πλεῖον D, Bekker.

---

[a] i.e., this complex of attributes.
[b] i.e., as neither having factors nor being the sum of two
or more numbers. 3 = 2 + 1, but 1 was regarded not as a
number itself but as the " measure " or " starting-point " of
number (Met. 1088 a 4 ff.).

wider application, because it applies to 5 too ; but it does not extend beyond the genus, because 5 is a number, and nothing outside the genus number is odd. It is attributes of this kind that we must select, up to the point where, although singly they have a wider extension of meaning than the subject, collectively they have not ; for this [a] must be the essence of the thing. *E.g.*, 3 has the following universal attributes : it is a number, it is odd, it is prime in both senses, as being neither measurable by number nor composed of numbers.[b] We now have the essence of 3 : a number, odd, prime, and prime in this particular sense. The first two of these attributes apply to all odd numbers, and the last also applies to 2 ; but no other number has them all. Now since we have shown above [c] that attributes which are predicated as elements in the definition are universal,[d] and that universal attributes are necessary, and since the selected attributes are elements in the definition of 3 (or of any other subject in the case of which they are so selected), then " threeness " must consist in just these attributes. That they constitute its essence is clear from the following argument. If this combination of attributes were not the essence of 3, it must be a sort of genus, either with or without a name of its own. Then its application must extend beyond 3. Let us assume that the genus is such as to have the widest possible application. Then if it applies to nothing else but individual 3s, it must be " threeness " ; for we must further assume that the essence of any given thing is the

The complex of these will give the essence.

Proof that this is so.

[c] Book I, ch. iv.
[d] Ross's emendation, though supported by no evidence, seems to be required by the argument.

ἢ ἐπὶ τοῖς¹ ἀτόμοις ἔσχατος τοιαύτη κατηγορία·
ὥστε ὁμοίως καὶ ἄλλῳ ὁτῳοῦν τῶν οὕτω δειχθέν-
των τὸ αὐτῷ εἶναι ἔσται.

15 Χρὴ δέ, ὅταν ὅλον τι πραγματεύηταί τις, διελεῖν τὸ
γένος εἰς τὰ ἄτομα τῷ εἴδει τὰ πρῶτα, οἷον ἀριθμὸν
εἰς τριάδα καὶ δυάδα, εἶθ' οὕτως ἐκείνων ὁρισμοὺς πειρᾶσθαι λαμβάνειν, οἷον εὐθείας γραμμῆς
καὶ κύκλου καὶ ὀρθῆς γωνίας, μετὰ δὲ τοῦτο λαβόν-
20 τα τί τὸ γένος, οἷον πότερον τῶν ποσῶν ἢ τῶν
ποιῶν, τὰ ἴδια πάθη θεωρεῖν διὰ τῶν κοινῶν πρώτων. τοῖς γὰρ συντιθεμένοις ἐκ τῶν ἀτόμων τὰ
συμβαίνοντα ἐκ τῶν ὁρισμῶν ἔσται δῆλα, διὰ τὸ
ἀρχὴν εἶναι πάντων τὸν ὁρισμὸν καὶ τὸ ἁπλοῦν καὶ
τοῖς ἁπλοῖς καθ' αὑτὰ ὑπάρχειν τὰ συμβαίνοντα
25 μόνοις, τοῖς δ' ἄλλοις κατ' ἐκεῖνα. αἱ δὲ διαιρέσεις
αἱ κατὰ τὰς διαφορὰς χρήσιμοί εἰσιν εἰς τὸ οὕτω
μετιέναι· ὡς μέντοι δεικνύουσιν, εἴρηται ἐν τοῖς
πρότερον. χρήσιμοι δ' ἂν εἶεν ὧδε μόνον πρὸς τὸ
συλλογίζεσθαι τὸ τί ἐστιν. καίτοι δόξειέν γ' ἂν
οὐδέν, ἀλλ' εὐθὺς λαμβάνειν ἅπαντα, ὥσπερ ἂν εἰ
30 ἐξ ἀρχῆς ἐλάμβανέ τις ἄνευ τῆς διαιρέσεως. διαφέρει δέ τι τὸ πρῶτον καὶ ὕστερον τῶν κατηγορουμένων κατηγορεῖσθαι, οἷον εἰπεῖν ζῷον ἥμερον
δίπουν ἢ δίπουν ζῷον ἥμερον. εἰ γὰρ ἅπαν ἐκ

---

¹ τοῖς Ross : ταῖς.

ᵃ *i.e.*, those which exhibit the properties of the genus in
their simplest form. 3 and 2 are the first odd and even
numbers ; straight lines and circles are the simplest lines ;
the right angle is that by which other angles are measured

last predicate of this kind that applies to the individuals. Similarly any other combination of attributes thus exhibited will be the essence of the subject in question.

In making a systematic study of a whole class of objects, one should first divide the genus into the primary [a] *infimae species* (*e.g.*, number into 3 and 2), and then try to arrive at the definitions of these (*e.g.*, of straight line, circle and right angle) by the methods described above ; then, after ascertaining what the category of the genus is (*e.g.*, whether it is quantity or quality), examine its peculiar properties in the light of the primary common attributes. The attributes of subjects which are compounded of these *infimae species* will become clear from the definitions ⟨of the latter⟩, because in every case the starting-point is the definition and the simple subject and attributes belong *per se* only to simple subjects, and to others indirectly. For investigations of this kind division in accordance with the differentiae is useful ; how it exhibits the facts has been explained above.[b] But for inferring the essential nature of a subject its use is limited, as I shall explain. It might indeed seem that it has no use at all, but proceeds by direct assumption, just as if one took the facts for granted without employing division ; but it makes an appreciable difference whether the predicates are stated in the right order, *e.g.*, whether you say " animal, tame, two-footed," or " two-footed, animal, tame," because if every definiendum consists of

Division aids the systematic study of a genus.

In a search for the essence it enables us to take attributes in the right order,

and defined. When the essence of these has been grasped and formulated, we can compare their properties with those of the other *infimae species*, and so, working steadily upwards, systematize the whole genus.

[b] In ch. v ; *cf.* also *An. Pr.* I. xxxi.

96 b

δύο ἐστί, καὶ ἕν τι τὸ ζῷον ἥμερον, καὶ πάλιν ἐκ
τούτου καὶ τῆς διαφορᾶς ὁ ἄνθρωπός ἢ ὅτι δήποτ'
35 ἐστὶ τὸ ἓν γιγνόμενον, ἀναγκαῖον διελόμενον αἰτεῖσθαι. ἔτι πρὸς τὸ μηδὲν παραλιπεῖν ἐν τῷ τί ἐστιν
οὕτω μόνως ἐνδέχεται. ὅταν γὰρ τὸ πρῶτον ληφθῇ γένος, ἂν μὲν τῶν κάτωθέν τινα διαιρέσεων
λαμβάνῃ, οὐκ ἐμπεσεῖται ἅπαν εἰς τοῦτο, οἷον οὐ
πᾶν ζῷον ἢ ὁλόπτερον ἢ σχιζόπτερον, ἀλλὰ πτηνὸν
97 a ζῷον ἅπαν· τούτου γὰρ διαφορὰ αὕτη. πρώτη δὲ
διαφορά ἐστι ζῴου εἰς ἣν ἅπαν ζῷον ἐμπίπτει.
ὁμοίως δὲ καὶ τῶν ἄλλων ἑκάστου, καὶ τῶν ἔξω
γενῶν καὶ τῶν ὑπ' αὐτό, οἷον ὄρνιθος, εἰς ἣν ἅπας
ὄρνις, καὶ ἰχθύος, εἰς ἣν ἅπας ἰχθύς. οὕτω μὲν οὖν
5 βαδίζοντι ἔστιν εἰδέναι ὅτι οὐδὲν παραλέλειπται·
ἄλλως δὲ καὶ παραλιπεῖν ἀναγκαῖον καὶ μὴ εἰδέναι.

Οὐδὲν δὲ δεῖ τὸν ὁριζόμενον καὶ διαιρούμενον
ἅπαντα εἰδέναι τὰ ὄντα. καίτοι ἀδύνατόν φασί
τινες εἶναι τὰς διαφορὰς εἰδέναι τὰς πρὸς ἕκαστον
μὴ εἰδότα ἕκαστον· ἄνευ δὲ τῶν διαφορῶν οὐκ
10 εἶναι ἕκαστον εἰδέναι· οὗ γὰρ μὴ διαφέρει, ταὐτὸν
εἶναι τούτῳ, οὗ δὲ διαφέρει, ἕτερον τούτου. πρῶτον
μὲν οὖν τοῦτο ψεῦδος· οὐ γὰρ κατὰ πᾶσαν διαφορὰν
ἕτερον· πολλαὶ γὰρ διαφοραὶ ὑπάρχουσι τοῖς αὐτοῖς
τῷ εἴδει, ἀλλ' οὐ κατ' οὐσίαν οὐδὲ καθ' αὑτά. εἶτα

---

[a] Viz., genus and differentia. At every stage of division
the compound of these becomes the generic element in the
next stage below.

[b] All the commentators refer this argument to Speusippus.
For his, Plato's and Aristotle's attitudes towards division cf.

two elements,[a] and " animal, tame " is a unity, and
if " man " (or whatever single species we are trying
to define) consists in its turn of this genus *plus* its
differentia, we must use division in assuming the
elements. Besides, this is the only way to ensure and ensures
that no element in the definition is omitted. If, after that we
taking the highest genus, we next take one of the thing.
lower divisions, the class which we are dividing will
not all fall into this division, *e.g.*, not every animal is
either whole-winged or split-winged, although every
winged animal is one or the other, because this is the
class to which the differentia belongs. The primary
differentia of " animal " is that into which all " animal " falls. The same applies to every one of the
other genera, whether co-ordinate or subaltern; the
primary differentia of " bird " or " fish " is that into
which all " bird " or " fish " falls. If you proceed in
this way you can be sure that nothing has been left
out; otherwise omissions are bound to occur, without
any possibility of detection.

In defining by division there is no need to know all To define by
the facts. Some,[b] however, maintain that it is im- division one
possible to know the differentiae between each thing need not
and the rest without knowing each thing severally, know *all* the
and impossible to know each thing severally without facts.
knowing the differentiae; because if A does not
differ from B, they are identical, and if it does differ,
they are distinct species. Now in the first place this
is false, because not every differentia entails a specific
distinction; many differentiae are attributable (but
neither essentially nor *per se*) to things which are
specifically the same. Secondly, when one takes a

Cherniss, *Aristotle's Criticism of Plato and the Academy,* i.
59-63.

15 ὅταν λάβῃ τἀντικείμενα καὶ τὴν διαφορὰν καὶ ὅτι
πᾶν ἐμπίπτει ἐνταῦθα ἢ ἐνταῦθα, καὶ λάβῃ ἐν
θατέρῳ τὸ ζητούμενον εἶναι, καὶ τοῦτο γιγνώσκῃ,
οὐδὲν διαφέρει εἰδέναι ἢ μὴ εἰδέναι ἐφ' ὅσων κατηγοροῦνται ἄλλων αἱ διαφοραί. φανερὸν γὰρ ὅτι ἂν
οὕτω βαδίζων ἔλθῃ εἰς ταῦτα ὧν μηκέτι ἔστι δια-
20 φορά, ἕξει τὸν λόγον τῆς οὐσίας. τὸ δ' ἅπαν ἐμπί-
πτειν εἰς τὴν διαίρεσιν, ἂν ᾖ ἀντικείμενα ὧν μὴ ἔστι
μεταξύ, οὐκ αἴτημα· ἀνάγκη γὰρ ἅπαν ἐν θατέρῳ
αὐτῶν εἶναι, εἴπερ ἐκείνου διαφορά ἐστι.[1]

Εἰς δὲ τὸ κατασκευάζειν ὅρον διὰ τῶν διαιρέσεων τριῶν δεῖ στοχάζεσθαι, τοῦ λαβεῖν τὰ κατη-
25 γορούμενα ἐν τῷ τί ἐστι, καὶ ταῦτα τάξαι τί πρῶτον
ἢ δεύτερον, καὶ ὅτι ταῦτα πάντα. ἔστι δὲ τούτων
ἓν πρῶτον διὰ τοῦ δύνασθαι, ὥσπερ πρὸς συμβεβηκὸς συλλογίσασθαι ὅτι ὑπάρχει, καὶ διὰ τοῦ γένους
κατασκευάσαι. τὸ δὲ τάξαι ὡς δεῖ ἔσται ἐὰν τὸ
πρῶτον λάβῃ. τοῦτο δ' ἔσται ἐὰν ληφθῇ ὃ πᾶσιν
30 ἀκολουθεῖ, ἐκείνῳ δὲ μὴ πάντα· ἀνάγκη γὰρ εἶναί
τι τοιοῦτον. ληφθέντος δὲ τούτου ἤδη ἐπὶ τῶν
κάτω ὁ αὐτὸς τρόπος· δεύτερον γὰρ τὸ τῶν ἄλλων
πρῶτον ἔσται, καὶ τρίτον τὸ τῶν ἐχομένων·
ἀφαιρεθέντος γὰρ τοῦ ἄνωθεν τὸ ἐχόμενον τῶν

---

[1] ἔστι d, comm. (?), Ross : ἔσται.

---

[a] i.e., the definition.

[b] A topic (τόπος) is a commonplace of argument, or set of
rules for cogent reasoning, such as are to be found in Aristotle's *Topics*. They are not scientific but dialectical, since
they are based upon premisses which are not necessarily
true, but merely probable as being generally accepted. They
are valuable both as an equipment for serious debate and as
a supplement to scientific discussion, since they help (as in

pair of opposite attributes and the differentia which distinguishes them, and assumes that every individual falls under one or the other, and then assumes that the given term is contained in one of the two, and knows that class, it does not matter whether he knows or does not know all the other terms of which the differentiae are predicable ; because clearly, if he proceeds in this way until he reaches the point where there is no further differentia, he will have the formula of the essence.[a] It is not an " assumption " to assert that every member of the genus must fall under one or the other division, if the opposites are exhaustive ; because every member of a genus must be in one or the other of two species distinguished by a differentia of that genus.

In order to establish a definition by division, we must keep three things in mind : (1) to select attributes which describe the essence, (2) to arrange them in order of priority, and (3) to make sure that the selection is complete. (1) The first object can be achieved through the possibility of establishing the genus and differentia by the topic [b] of genus, just as we can infer the inherence of an attribute by the topic of accident. (2) We can arrange the attributes correctly if we take first the first in order, *i.e.*, that which is implied by, but does not imply, all the rest ; there must be *one* such term. When we have selected this, we can proceed at once in the same way with the lower terms ; the second will be the first of the remainder, and the third the first of those immediately following (because when the first of a series

Three rules to observe.

the present instance) to establish facts or judgements which do not admit of actual demonstration. Books II and III of the *Topics* deal with accidents and Book IV with genera.

ARISTOTLE

ARISTOTLE

97 a

ἄλλων πρῶτον ἔσται. ὁμοίως δὲ καὶ ἐπὶ τῶν ἄλλων.
35 ὅτι δ' ἅπαντα ταῦτα φανερὸν ἐκ τοῦ λαβεῖν τό τε
πρῶτον κατὰ διαίρεσιν, ὅτι ἅπαν ἢ τόδε ἢ τόδε
ζῷον, ὑπάρχει δὲ τόδε, καὶ πάλιν τούτου ὅλου τὴν
διαφοράν, τοῦ δὲ τελευταίου μηκέτι εἶναι διαφοράν,
ἢ καὶ εὐθὺς μετὰ τῆς τελευταίας διαφορᾶς τοῦ
97 b συνόλου μὴ διαφέρειν εἴδει ἔτι[1] τοῦτο. δῆλον γὰρ
ὅτι οὔτε πλεῖον πρόσκειται (πάντα γὰρ ἐν τῷ τί
ἐστιν εἴληπται τούτων) οὔτε ἀπολείπει οὐδέν· ἢ γὰρ
γένος ἢ διαφορὰ ἂν εἴη. γένος μὲν οὖν τό τε
πρῶτον, καὶ μετὰ τῶν διαφορῶν τοῦτο προσλαμ-
5 βανόμενον· αἱ διαφοραὶ δὲ πᾶσαι ἔχονται· οὐ γὰρ
ἔτι ἔστιν ὑστέρα· εἴδει γὰρ ἂν διεφέρε τὸ τελευταῖον,
τοῦτο δ' εἴρηται μὴ διαφέρειν.

Ζητεῖν δὲ δεῖ ἐπιβλέποντα ἐπὶ τὰ ὅμοια καὶ
ἀδιάφορα, πρῶτον τί ἅπαντα ταὐτὸν ἔχουσιν, εἶτα
πάλιν ἐφ' ἑτέροις, ἃ ἐν ταὐτῷ μὲν γένει ἐκείνοις,
10 εἰσὶ δὲ αὑτοῖς[2] μὲν ταὐτὰ τῷ εἴδει, ἐκείνων δ' ἕτερα.
ὅταν δ' ἐπὶ τούτων ληφθῇ τί πάντα ταὐτόν, καὶ ἐπὶ
τῶν ἄλλων ὁμοίως, ἐπὶ τῶν εἰλημμένων πάλιν
σκοπεῖν εἰ ταὐτόν, ἕως ἂν εἰς ἕνα ἔλθῃ λόγον· οὗτος
γὰρ ἔσται τοῦ πράγματος ὁρισμός.

---

[1] εἴδει ἔτι B[1] (?) : τῷ εἴδει ἔτι n : εἴ τι Ad : εἴδει B[2], comm.
[2] αὑτοῖς A[2], Eustratius : αὑτᾶς.

236

is removed, the next is the first of the remainder) ; and so on. (3) The completeness of our selection is evident from the fact that we first take the first class to be divided, and assume that every animal is either A or B, and then that one of these differentiae belongs to it ; and next take the differentia of the whole class thus obtained, until the class which we finally reach has no further differentia : *i.e.*, as soon as we have assumed the last differentia which characterizes the complex term ⟨to be defined⟩, the latter is not further divisible into species. Clearly nothing superfluous is included, because all the attributes have been assumed as forming part of the essence ; and nothing is left out—if it were, it would have to be either a genus or a differentia ; now the first term is a genus, and so is the combination of this term with its differentiae ; and the differentiae are all included, because we have reached a point at which there is no further differentiation. If there were, the last term would be divisible into species ; and we have laid down that it is not.

We must set about our search by looking out for a group of things which are alike in the sense of being specifically indifferent, and asking what they all have in common ; then we must do the same with another group in the same genus and belonging to the same species as one another but to a species different from that of the first group. When we have discovered in the case of this second group what its members have in common, and similarly in the case of all the other groups, we must consider again whether the common features which we have established have any feature which is common to them all, until we reach a single expression. This will be the required definition.

How to reach a general definition.

Ἐὰν δὲ μὴ βαδίζῃ εἰς ἕνα ἀλλ' εἰς δύο ἢ πλείους,[1]
15 δῆλον ὅτι οὐκ ἂν εἴη ἕν τι εἶναι τὸ ζητούμενον, ἀλλὰ
πλείω. οἷον λέγω, εἰ τί ἐστι μεγαλοψυχία ζητοῖ-
μεν, σκεπτέον ἐπί τινων μεγαλοψύχων οὓς ἴσμεν τί
ἔχουσιν ἐν πάντες ᾗ τοιοῦτοι. οἷον εἰ Ἀλκιβιάδης
μεγαλόψυχος ἢ ὁ Ἀχιλλεὺς καὶ ὁ Αἴας, τί ἓν
20 ἅπαντες; τὸ μὴ ἀνέχεσθαι ὑβριζόμενοι· ὁ μὲν γὰρ
ἐπολέμησεν, ὁ δ' ἐμήνισεν, ὁ δ' ἀπέκτεινεν ἑαυτόν.
πάλιν ἐφ' ἑτέρων, οἷον Λυσάνδρου ἢ Σωκράτους.
εἰ δὴ τὸ ἀδιάφοροι εἶναι εὐτυχοῦντες καὶ ἀτυχοῦν-
τες, ταῦτα δύο λαβὼν σκοπῶ τί τὸ αὐτὸ ἔχουσιν ἥ
25 τε ἀπάθεια ἡ περὶ τὰς τύχας καὶ ἡ μὴ ὑπομονὴ
ἀτιμαζομένων. εἰ δὲ μηδέν, δύο εἴδη ἂν εἴη τῆς
μεγαλοψυχίας. αἰεὶ δ' ἐστὶ πᾶς ὅρος καθόλου· οὐ
γάρ τινι ὀφθαλμῷ λέγει τὸ ὑγιεινὸν ὁ ἰατρός, ἀλλ'
ἢ παντὶ ἢ εἴδει ἀφορίσας.

Ῥᾷόν τε τὸ καθ' ἕκαστον ὁρίσασθαι ἢ τὸ καθόλου·
διὸ δεῖ ἀπὸ τῶν καθ' ἕκαστα ἐπὶ τὰ καθόλου μετα-
30 βαίνειν· καὶ γὰρ αἱ ὁμωνυμίαι λανθάνουσι μᾶλλον
ἐν τοῖς καθόλου ἢ ἐν τοῖς ἀδιαφόροις. ὥσπερ δὲ
ἐν ταῖς ἀποδείξεσι δεῖ τό γε συλλελογίσθαι[2] ὑπάρχειν, οὕτω καὶ ἐν τοῖς ὅροις τὸ σαφές. τοῦτο δ'
ἔσται ἐὰν διὰ τῶν καθ' ἕκαστον εἰλημμένων[3] ᾖ τὸ
ἐν ἑκάστῳ γένει ὁρίζεσθαι χωρίς, οἷον τὸ ὅμοιον

---

[1] πλείους comm. : πλείω codd.
[2] συλλογίσασθαι Ad.
[3] εἰλημμένων Eustratius (?), Mure : εἰρημένων codd., Philoponus.

---

[a] This seems to be the least unsatisfactory rendering of a
difficult word, which for most Greeks ranked as a virtue.
"Pride," advocated by Burnet and accepted by Ross,
scarcely conveys this effect. The quality is discussed in *Eth.
Nic.* 1123 a 34 ff.

If the series ends not in one expression but in two or more, clearly the definiendum cannot be one thing; it must be more than one. I mean, for example, supposing that we require a definition of high-mindedness,[a] we must consider individual high-minded persons whom we know, and see what one characteristic they all have *qua* high-minded. *E.g.*, if Alcibiades and Achilles and Ajax were high-minded, what was their common characteristic? Intolerance of dishonour; for this made the first go to war, roused the wrath of the second, and drove the third to commit suicide. Then we must apply the same process to another group, *e.g.*, Lysander and Socrates. Suppose that here the common characteristic is being unaffected by good and bad fortune. Now I take these two and consider what there is in common between indifference to fortune and intolerance of dishonour; and if there is nothing, there must be two kinds of high-mindedness.[b] But every definition is always universal. A doctor prescribes what is salutary not for some one eye but for all eyes, or for the eye in a specific condition.

The term to be defined may prove to be equivocal.

It is easier to define the particular [c] than the universal; and therefore we should proceed from particulars to universals. Ambiguities, too, are harder to detect in universals than in *infimae species*. Just as demonstration demands a completed inference, so definition demands clarity; and this will be achieved if we can, by means of the common features which we have established, define our concept separately in each class of objects (*e.g.*, define similarity not in

By working up from particulars we secure clarity and precision.

---

[b] *i.e.*, the term is equivocal, being used to describe two distinct species.

[c] Not, of course, the individual (which is indefinable), but the species as opposed to the genus.

97 b

35 μὴ πᾶν ἀλλὰ τὸ ἐν χρώμασι καὶ σχήμασι, καὶ
ὀξὺ τὸ ἐν φωνῇ, καὶ οὕτως ἐπὶ τὸ κοινὸν βαδίζειν,
εὐλαβούμενον μὴ ὁμωνυμίᾳ ἐντύχῃ. εἰ δὲ μὴ διαλέγεσθαι δεῖ μεταφοραῖς, δῆλον ὅτι οὐδ᾽ ὁρίζεσθαι
οὔτε μεταφοραῖς οὔτε ὅσα λέγεται μεταφοραῖς·
διαλέγεσθαι γὰρ ἀνάγκη ἔσται μεταφοραῖς.

98 a XIV. Πρὸς δὲ τὸ ἔχειν τὰ προβλήματα ἐκλέγειν
δεῖ τάς τε ἀνατομὰς καὶ τὰς διαιρέσεις, οὕτω δὲ
ἐκλέγειν, ὑποθέμενον τὸ γένος τὸ κοινὸν ἁπάντων,
οἷον εἰ ζῷα εἴη τὰ τεθεωρημένα, ποῖα παντὶ ζῴῳ
5 ὑπάρχει, ληφθέντων δὲ τούτων, πάλιν τῶν λοιπῶν
τῷ πρώτῳ ποῖα παντὶ ἕπεται, οἷον εἰ τοῦτο ὄρνις,
ποῖα παντὶ ἕπεται ὄρνιθι, καὶ οὕτως ἀεὶ τῷ ἐγγύ-
τατα· δῆλον γὰρ ὅτι ἕξομεν ἤδη λέγειν τὸ διὰ τί
ὑπάρχει τὰ ἑπόμενα τοῖς ὑπὸ τὸ κοινόν, οἷον διὰ τί
ἀνθρώπῳ ἢ ἵππῳ ὑπάρχει. ἔστω δὲ ζῷον ἐφ᾽ οὗ
10 Α, τὸ δὲ Β τὰ ἑπόμενα παντὶ ζῴῳ, ἐφ᾽ ὧν δὲ Γ Δ
Ε τὰ τινὰ ζῷα. δῆλον δὴ διὰ τί τὸ Β ὑπάρχει τῷ
Δ· διὰ γὰρ τὸ¹ Α. ὁμοίως δὲ καὶ τοῖς ἄλλοις· καὶ
ἀεὶ ἐπὶ τῶν κάτω² ὁ αὐτὸς λόγος.

Νῦν μὲν οὖν κατὰ τὰ παραδεδομένα κοινὰ ὀνόματα λέγομεν, δεῖ δὲ μὴ μόνον ἐπὶ τούτων σκοπεῖν,
15 ἀλλὰ καὶ ἂν ἄλλο τι ὀφθῇ ὑπάρχον κοινὸν ἐκλαμβά-
νοντα, εἶτα τίσι τοῦτ᾽ ἀκολουθεῖ καὶ ποῖα τούτῳ
ἕπεται, οἷον τοῖς κέρατα ἔχουσι τὸ ἔχειν ἐχῖνον, τὸ

¹ τὸ n, Eustratius : τοῦ.
² κάτω n : ἄλλων.

ᵃ i.e., the propositions or connexions which we are required to prove.

240

general but in respect of colours or shapes, and define sharpness in respect of sound), and so advance to the general definition, taking care not to become involved in equivocation. If we are to avoid arguing in metaphors, clearly we must also avoid defining in metaphors and defining metaphorical terms ; otherwise we are bound to argue in metaphors.

XIV. In order to formulate the problems [a] (of a given science) we must select the proper sections or divisions [b] ; and that in the following way. We must first posit the genus which is common to all the particulars ; e.g., if the subject of our study is animals, we must establish what attributes belong to every animal. When we have done this, we must next consider all the attributes belonging to the first of the remaining classes ; e.g., if this class is " bird," we must consider what attributes belong to every bird ; and so on, always taking the proximate sub-genus. In this way we shall obviously be able directly to show the reason why the attributes belong to each of the sub-genera, such as " man " or " horse." Let A stand for animal, B for the attributes belonging to every animal, and C, D, E for species of animal. Then it is obvious why B applies to D, viz., through A ; and similarly with C and E. The same principle holds for all the other sub-genera.

At the moment we are using the traditional class-names, but we must not confine ourselves to these in our inquiry ; we must pick out any other observed common characteristic, and then consider to what subjects it belongs, and what properties it entails : e.g., in the case of horned animals, the possession of

Division helps us to formulate problems correctly.

------

[b] Sc., of the subject-matter. The whole field must be mapped out by genera and species.

98 a

μὴ ἀμφώδοντ᾽ εἶναι· πάλιν τὸ κέρατ᾽ ἔχειν τίσιν
ἕπεται· δῆλον γὰρ διὰ τί ἐκείνοις ὑπάρξει τὸ εἰρη-
μένον· διὰ γὰρ τὸ κέρατ᾽ ἔχειν ὑπάρξει.

20 Ἔτι δ᾽ ἄλλος τρόπος ἐστὶ κατὰ τὸ ἀνάλογον ἐκλέγειν. ἐν γὰρ λαβεῖν οὐκ ἔστι τὸ αὐτὸ ὃ δεῖ
καλέσαι σήπιον[1] καὶ ἄκανθαν καὶ ὀστοῦν· ἔσται[2] δ᾽
ἐπόμενα καὶ τούτοις ὥσπερ μιᾶς τινος φύσεως τῆς
τοιαύτης οὔσης.

XV. Τὰ δ᾽ αὐτὰ προβλήματά ἐστι τὰ μὲν τῷ τὸ
25 αὐτὸ μέσον ἔχειν, οἷον ὅτι πάντα ἀντιπερίστασις.
τούτων δ᾽ ἔνια τῷ γένει ταὐτά, ὅσα ἔχει διαφορὰς
τῷ ἄλλων ἢ ἄλλως εἶναι, οἷον διὰ τί ἠχεῖ, ἢ διὰ τί
ἐμφαίνεται, καὶ διὰ τί ἶρις· ἅπαντα γὰρ ταῦτα τὸ
αὐτὸ πρόβλημά ἐστι γένει (πάντα γὰρ ἀνάκλασις),
ἀλλ᾽ εἴδει ἕτερα.

30 Τὰ δὲ τῷ τὸ μέσον ὑπὸ τὸ ἕτερον μέσον εἶναι
διαφέρει τῶν προβλημάτων, οἷον διὰ τί ὁ Νεῖλος
φθίνοντος τοῦ μηνὸς μᾶλλον ῥεῖ; διότι χειμεριώτερος φθίνων ὁ μείς.[3] διὰ τί δὲ χειμεριώτερος
φθίνων; διότι ἡ σελήνη ἀπολείπει. ταῦτα γὰρ
οὕτως ἔχει πρὸς ἄλληλα.

---

[1] σήπιον n, Eustratius : σήπειον vel σηπεῖον.
[2] ἔσται dn, Philoponus : ἔστι.
[3] μείς n : μήν volgo, sed ὁ . . . φθίνων om. ABd.

---

[a] i.e., front teeth in the lower jaw only.
[b] The extra material for the horns is secured at the cost of
the upper front teeth (Part. An. 663 b 31 ff.); and nature
compensates the deficiency of teeth by amplifying the
apparatus of digestion (ibid. 674 a 22 ff.).
[c] " Pounce " is the internal shell of a cuttle-fish, and
" spine " a fish-bone. They are analogues of animal bone,
and all three must fall under one genus.

a third stomach and a single row of teeth [a] ; and then ask " What animals have the property of possessing horns ? " It will be obvious why the specified characteristic belongs to these animals, *viz.*, because they have horns.[b]

There is another method of selection, *viz.*, by analogy. It is impossible to find a single name which should be applied to pounce, spine and bone [c] ; yet the fact that these too have ⟨common⟩ properties implies that there is a single natural substance of this kind.

XV. Some problems are identical in virtue of having the same middle term ; *e.g.*, they may all be explained by the principle of reciprocal replacement.[d] Of these middle terms some are ⟨only⟩ generically identical, *viz.*, such as differ in virtue of having different subjects, or operating in different ways : *e.g.*, the phenomena of echo, reflection and rainbow ; in all these the problem is generically the same (because they are all kinds of refraction) but specifically different.

Problems may have middle terms which are identical

Other problems differ ⟨only⟩ in the fact that the middle term of the one is subordinate [e] to the middle term of the other. *E.g.*, why does the Nile flow fuller in the latter part of the month ? Because the weather is more stormy then. And why is the weather more stormy then ? Because the moon is waning. The relation of the two middles is one of subordination.

or subordinate one to the other.

[d] The principle (since for Aristotle there is no void : *Phys.* IV. vii–ix, especially 214 a 28-32) that the space vacated by one body (A) in displacing another (B) must be occupied either by B or by another body displaced by B (Simplicius, *Phys.* 1350. 31). Ross *ad loc.* instances various phenomena susceptible of this explanation.

[e] As a cause.

35 XVI. Περὶ δ' αἰτίου καὶ οὗ αἴτιον ἀπορήσειε μὲν
ἄν τις, ἆρα ὅτε ὑπάρχει τὸ αἰτιατόν, καὶ τὸ αἴτιον
ὑπάρχει (ὥσπερ εἰ φυλλορροεῖ ἢ ἐκλείπει, καὶ τὸ
αἴτιον τοῦ ἐκλείπειν ἢ φυλλορροεῖν ἔσται· οἷον εἰ
98 b τοῦτ' ἔστι τὸ πλατέα ἔχειν τὰ φύλλα, τοῦ δ' ἐκλείπειν τὸ τὴν γῆν ἐν μέσῳ εἶναι· εἰ γὰρ μὴ ὑπάρχει,
ἄλλο τι ἔσται τὸ αἴτιον αὐτῶν)· εἴ τε¹ τὸ αἴτιον
ὑπάρχει, ἅμα καὶ τὸ αἰτιατόν, οἷον εἰ ἐν μέσῳ ἡ
γῆ, ἐκλείπει, ἢ εἰ πλατύφυλλον, φυλλορροεῖ. εἰ δ'
5 οὕτως, ἅμ' ἂν εἴη καὶ δεικνύοιτο δι' ἀλλήλων.
ἔστω γὰρ τὸ φυλλορροεῖν ἐφ' οὗ Α, τὸ δὲ πλατύφυλλον ἐφ' οὗ Β, ἄμπελος δὲ ἐφ' οὗ Γ. εἰ δὴ τῷ
Β ὑπάρχει τὸ Α (πᾶν γὰρ πλατύφυλλον φυλλορροεῖ),
τῷ δὲ Γ ὑπάρχει τὸ Β (πᾶσα γὰρ ἄμπελος πλατύ-
10 φυλλος), τῷ Γ ὑπάρχει τὸ Α, καὶ πᾶσα ἄμπελος
φυλλορροεῖ. αἴτιον δὲ τὸ Β τὸ μέσον. ἀλλὰ καὶ
ὅτι πλατύφυλλον ἡ ἄμπελος ἔστι διὰ τοῦ φυλλο-
ροεῖν ἀποδεῖξαι. ἔστω γὰρ τὸ μὲν Δ πλατύφυλλον,
τὸ δὲ Ε τὸ φυλλορροεῖν, ἄμπελος δὲ ἐφ' οὗ Ζ. τῷ
δὴ Ζ ὑπάρχει τὸ Ε (φυλλορροεῖ γὰρ πᾶσα ἄμπελος),
15 τῷ δὲ Ε τὸ Δ (ἅπαν γὰρ τὸ φυλλορροοῦν πλατύφυλλον)· πᾶσα ἄρα ἄμπελος πλατύφυλλον. αἴτιον
δὲ τὸ φυλλορροεῖν. εἰ δὲ μὴ ἐνδέχεται αἴτια εἶναι
ἀλλήλων (τὸ γὰρ αἴτιον πρότερον οὗ αἴτιον, καὶ
τοῦ μὲν ἐκλείπειν αἴτιον τὸ ἐν μέσῳ τὴν γῆν εἶναι,

¹ εἴ τε] εἴτε ΑΒ : εἴ γε n.

ᵃ This punctuation of the passage (i.e., treating ὥσπερ . . .

244

XVI. With regard to cause and effect the questions might be raised (1) whether the presence of the effect implies the presence of the cause (*e.g.*, whether, if a tree sheds its leaves or an eclipse occurs, the cause of the eclipse or of the leaf-shedding must also be present—*viz.*, in the latter case the fact that the tree is broad-leafed, and in the former the fact of the earth's interposition—because if the cause is not present there must be some other cause of these effects) [a]; and (2) whether, if the cause is present, the effect will be present too (*e.g.*, if the earth interposes there is an eclipse, or if the tree is broad-leafed it is deciduous). If so,[b] cause and effect will be compresent and reciprocally demonstrable. Let A stand for " deciduous," B for " broad-leafed " and C for " vine." Then if A applies to B (since all broad-leafed plants are deciduous) and B to C (since all vines are broad-leafed), A applies to C, *i.e.*, all vines are deciduous. The cause is the middle term B. But we can also prove that the vine is broad-leafed because it is deciduous. Let D be " broad-leafed," E " deciduous " and F " vine." Then E applies to F (since every vine is deciduous) and D to E (since every deciduous plant is broad-leafed) ; therefore all vines are broad-leafed. Here the cause is " shedding leaves." But since it is impossible for two things to be causes of each other (for the cause is prior [c] to its effect, and it is the interposition of the earth that is

αὐτῶν as a parenthesis) had suggested itself to me before I knew that Ross had adopted it. It certainly tidies up the sense, and I think it must be right.

[b] *i.e.*, if both answers are affirmative.

[c] Not necessarily in time, for the formal cause is simultaneous with its effect (95 a 14 ff.) ; but naturally and logically.

98 b

τοῦ δ' ἐν μέσῳ τὴν γῆν εἶναι οὐκ αἴτιον τὸ ἐκλεί-
20 πειν)—εἰ οὖν ἡ μὲν διὰ τοῦ αἰτίου ἀπόδειξις τοῦ
διὰ τί, ἡ δὲ μὴ διὰ τοῦ αἰτίου τοῦ ὅτι, ὅτι μὲν ἐν μέσῳ οἶδε, διότι δ' οὔ. ὅτι δ' οὐ τὸ ἐκλείπειν αἴτιον
τοῦ ἐν μέσῳ, ἀλλὰ τοῦτο τοῦ ἐκλείπειν, φανερόν·
ἐν γὰρ τῷ λόγῳ τῷ τοῦ ἐκλείπειν ἐνυπάρχει τὸ ἐν
μέσῳ, ὥστε δῆλον ὅτι διὰ τούτου ἐκεῖνο γνωρί-
ζεται· ἀλλ' οὐ τοῦτο δι' ἐκείνου.

25 Ἦ ἐνδέχεται ἑνὸς πλείω αἴτια εἶναι; καὶ γὰρ εἰ
ἔστι τὸ αὐτὸ πλειόνων πρώτων κατηγορεῖσθαι, ἔστω
τὸ Α τῷ Β πρώτῳ ὑπάρχον, καὶ τῷ Γ ἄλλῳ πρώτῳ,
καὶ ταῦτα τοῖς Δ Ε. ὑπάρξει ἄρα τὸ Α τοῖς Δ Ε,
αἴτιον δὲ τῷ μὲν Δ τὸ Β τῷ δὲ Ε τὸ Γ· ὥστε τοῦ
30 μὲν αἰτίου ὑπάρχοντος ἀνάγκη τὸ πρᾶγμα ὑπάρχειν, τοῦ δὲ πράγματος ὑπάρχοντος οὐκ ἀνάγκη
πᾶν ὃ ἂν ᾖ αἴτιον, ἀλλ' αἴτιον μέν, οὐ μέντοι
πᾶν.

Ἦ εἰ ἀεὶ καθόλου τὸ πρόβλημά ἐστι, καὶ τὸ
αἴτιον ὅλον τι καὶ οὗ αἴτιον καθόλου; οἷον τὸ
φυλλορροεῖν ὅλῳ τινὶ ἀφωρισμένον, κἂν εἴδη αὐτοῦ
35 ᾖ, καὶ τοισδὶ καθόλου, ἢ φυτοῖς ἢ τοιοισδὶ[1] φυτοῖς·
ὥστε καὶ τὸ μέσον ἴσον δεῖ εἶναι ἐπὶ τούτων καὶ
οὗ αἴτιον, καὶ ἀντιστρέφειν. οἷον διὰ τί τὰ δένδρα
φυλλορροεῖ; εἰ δὴ διὰ πῆξιν τοῦ ὑγροῦ, εἴτε φυλ-

---

[1] τοιοισδὶ] τοιοῖσδε ΑΒd.

[a] i.e., through the effect.

the cause of the eclipse, and not *vice versa*)—if demonstration by means of the cause proves the reasoned fact, while demonstration not through the cause [a] proves the mere fact, ⟨one who reasons in the latter way⟩ knows the fact of the earth's interposition, but not the reason for it. That the earth's interposition is the cause of the eclipse, and not *vice versa*, is obvious from the fact that the former is an element in the definition of the latter ; which clearly shows that we obtain our knowledge of the latter through the former, and not *vice versa*.

Or is it possible for one effect to have several causes ? If the same attribute can be predicated immediately of more than one subject, let A apply immediately to B and likewise to C, and let B and C apply immediately to D and E respectively. Then A will apply to D and E, the causes being B and C respectively. Thus the presence of the cause necessarily implies that of the effect, but the presence of the effect does not necessarily imply that of the whole range of possible causes ; it implies *some* cause, but not *every* cause. *Can there be several causes of one effect ?*

But surely if the " problem " is always universal,[b] the cause is a whole, and the effect is ⟨commensurately⟩ universal. *E.g.*, deciduousness is appropriated to a subject as a whole ; and if this consists of species, the attribute belongs to these also universally : either to plants or to particular species of plants ; hence in the case of these the middle term and the effect must be commensurate and convertible. *E.g.*, why are trees deciduous ? If it is because there is coagulation of the sap,[c] then if a tree is *No ; the cause is a whole and commensurate with the effect.*

---

[b] As it must be, since it is a scientific proposition.

[c] *Sc.*, at the junction of the leaf-stalk (99 a 29).

ARISTOTLE

άρχει, μὴ ὁτῳοῦν ἀλλὰ δένδρῳ, φυλλορροεῖν.

XVII. Πότερον δ᾿ ἐνδέχεται μὴ τὸ αὐτὸ αἴτιον
εἶναι τοῦ αὐτοῦ πᾶσιν ἀλλ᾿ ἕτερον, ἢ οὔ; ἢ εἰ
μὲν καθ᾿ αὑτὸ ἀποδέδεικται καὶ μὴ κατὰ σημεῖον ἢ
συμβεβηκός, οὐχ οἷόν τε; ὁ γὰρ λόγος τοῦ ἄκρου
5 τὸ μέσον ἐστίν· εἰ δὲ μὴ οὕτως, ἐνδέχεται. ἔστι δὲ
καὶ οὗ αἴτιον καὶ ᾧ σκοπεῖν κατὰ συμβεβηκός· οὐ
μὴν δοκεῖ προβλήματα εἶναι. εἰ δὲ μή, ὁμοίως
ἕξει τὸ μέσον· εἰ μὲν ὁμώνυμα, ὁμώνυμον τὸ μέσον·
εἰ δ᾿ ὡς ἐν γένει, ὁμοίως ἕξει. οἷον διὰ τί καὶ
ἐναλλὰξ ἀνάλογον; ἄλλο γὰρ αἴτιον ἐν γραμμαῖς
10 καὶ ἀριθμοῖς καὶ τὸ αὐτό γε, ᾗ μὲν γραμμή,[1] ἄλλο,
ᾗ δ᾿ ἔχον αὔξησιν τοιανδί, τὸ αὐτό. οὕτως ἐπὶ
πάντων. τοῦ δ᾿ ὅμοιον εἶναι χρῶμα χρώματι καὶ
σχῆμα σχήματι ἄλλο ἄλλῳ. ὁμώνυμον γὰρ τὸ
ὅμοιον ἐπὶ τούτων· ἔνθα μὲν γὰρ ἴσως τὸ ἀνάλογον
ἔχειν τὰς πλευρὰς καὶ ἴσας τὰς γωνίας, ἐπὶ δὲ

---

[1] γραμμή n : γραμμαί.

---

[a] This chapter appears to contain an alternative and presumably later treatment of the problem discussed in ch. xvi.

[b] An event has only one formal cause, which is present in
every instance ; but it may be inferred from any of the various
properties which are its " signs " (cf. An. Pr. II. xxvii) ; and
may have any number of accidental causes.

[c] Because a " problem " is a scientific proposition, and
accidents lie outside the sphere of scientific knowledge.

[d] Since the examples which follow do not illustrate accidental relations, εἰ δὲ μή must be taken (as Ross takes it) to
indicate their exclusion—in spite of the commentators, who
understand it to refer to οὗ δοκεῖ.

[e] Aristotle notes three different cases in which the same
effect has, in a sense, different causes. (a) The major may be
equivocal : as " similar " has different meanings in different

248

deciduous, there must be coagulation ; and if coagulation is present—not in any and every subject, but in a tree—the tree must be deciduous.

XVII. Can the same effect be produced not by the same cause in all cases but ⟨sometimes⟩ by a different cause ? [a] Surely this is (1) impossible if the effect has been demonstrated as essential (not proved from a " sign " or through an accidental connexion),[b] for then the middle is the definition of the major term ; (2) possible if it has not. It is possible to consider the effect and its subject in an accidental relation, but such connexions are not regarded as " problems." [c] Apart from the accidental relation,[d] the middle will correspond to the extreme [e] terms : (a) if they are equivocal, the middle will be equivocal, and (b) if they express a generic connexion, so will the middle. For example, (b) " why do proportionals alternate ? " [f] The cause is different for lines and for numbers, and yet it is the same ; different if the lines are considered as lines, and the same if they are considered as exhibiting a given increment. So with all proportionals. (a) The cause of similarity between colours is different from that of similarity between figures, because " similarity " in these two cases is equivocal ; in the latter it means, presumably, that the sides are proportional and the angles equal, while in colours it means that our perception

genera, so has the middle which is the cause of similarity. (b) The major may apply to a whole genus (e.g., quantity), of which different species may be taken as subjects : then the middle term will vary with the subject. (c) Analogical connexions (cf. 98 a 20 ff.) are in one sense the same and in another different : so are their causes.

[f] The reference is to the theory of proportion mentioned at 74 a 17, where see note.

99 a

15 χρωμάτων τὸ τὴν αἴσθησιν μίαν εἶναι ἤ τι ἄλλο
τοιοῦτον. τὰ δὲ κατ' ἀναλογίαν τὰ αὐτὰ καὶ τὸ
μέσον ἕξει κατὰ ἀναλογίαν.

Ἔχει δ' οὕτω τὸ παρακολουθεῖν τὸ αἴτιον ἀλλήλοις καὶ οὗ αἴτιον καὶ ᾧ αἴτιον· καθ' ἕκαστον μὲν
λαμβάνοντι τὸ οὗ αἴτιον ἐπὶ πλέον, οἷον τὸ τέτταρ-
20 σιν ἴσας τὰς ἔξω ἐπὶ πλέον ἢ τρίγωνον ἢ τετράγωνον,
ἅπασι δὲ ἐπ' ἴσον (ὅσα γὰρ τέτταρσιν ὀρθαῖς ἴσας
τὰς ἔξω)· καὶ τὸ μέσον ὁμοίως. ἔστι δὲ τὸ μέσον
λόγος τοῦ πρώτου ἄκρου, διὸ πᾶσαι αἱ ἐπιστῆμαι
δι' ὁρισμοῦ γίγνονται. οἷον τὸ φυλλορροεῖν ἅμα
ἀκολουθεῖ τῇ ἀμπέλῳ καὶ ὑπερέχει, καὶ συκῇ καὶ
25 ὑπερέχει· ἀλλ' οὐ πάντων, ἀλλ' ἴσον. εἰ δὴ λάβοις
τὸ πρῶτον μέσον, λόγος τοῦ φυλλορροεῖν ἐστιν.
ἔσται γὰρ πρῶτον μὲν ἐπὶ θάτερα μέσον, ὅτι τοιαδὶ
ἅπαντα· εἶτα τούτου μέσον, ὅτι ὀπὸς πήγνυται ἤ τι
ἄλλο τοιοῦτον. τί δ' ἐστὶ τὸ φυλλορροεῖν; τὸ
πήγνυσθαι τὸν ἐν τῇ συνάψει τοῦ σπέρματος ὀπόν.
30 Ἐπὶ δὲ τῶν σχημάτων ὧδε ἀποδώσει ζητοῦσι
τὴν παρακολούθησιν τοῦ αἰτίου καὶ οὗ αἴτιον. ἔστω

ª *E.g.*, in a proposition relating to bony structure the
middle term, though the same by analogy, is in fact different
for animal, fish and cuttle-fish (*cf.* 98 a 22).

ᵇ That is, with all rectilinear figures ; *cf.* 85 b 38 ff.

ᶜ *Cf.* ch. viii, and 94 a 20 ff.

ᵈ As necessary for the proof of their propositions.

ᵉ The two botanical syllogisms of ch. xvi are here combined
in a sorites, *viz.*,

All plants whose sap is coagulated are deciduous,
All broad-leafed plants are subject to coagulation of sap
(∴ All broad-leafed plants are deciduous),
All vines, figs, etc., are broad-leafed,
∴ All vines, figs, etc., are deciduous.

There are two middles, of which " the first," next to the major,

of them is one and the same, or something of that
sort. (c) Things which are the same by analogy will
have a middle term which is analogous.[a]

The proper view of the reciprocation of cause, _{How cause,}
effect and subject is as follows. If the species are _{subject are}
taken separately, the effect has a wider extension _{related.}
than the subject—e.g., " having the sum of the ex-
terior angles equal to four right angles " has a wider
extension than has triangularity or squareness—but
if they are taken all together, it is coextensive with
them, viz., with all figures that have the sum of their
exterior angles equal to four right angles [b]; and
similarly with the middle. The middle is the definition of the major term [c]; this is the reason why all
sciences are based upon definitions.[d] E.g., deciduousness is a universal attribute of the vine or fig,
and also has a wider extension than either ; but it
is not wider than, but equal to, the sum of all the
species. Thus if you take the first [e] middle term,
you have a definition of " deciduous." ⟨I say " the
first "⟩ because there is ⟨another⟩ middle term which
is first in the direction of the subjects, which it
describes as all having a certain characteristic ; and
this in turn has a middle " because the sap is coagulated," or something to that effect. What is
deciduousness ? Coagulation of the sap at the junction of the leaf-stalk.

If it is required to exhibit the correspondence _{The same}
of cause and effect schematically, it will run like <sub>expressed
schemati-
cally.</sub>

defines it ; the other, " first in the direction of the subject,"
is merely a sub-genus of deciduous species.

99 a

τὸ Α τῷ Β ὑπάρχειν παντί, τὸ δὲ Β ἑκάστῳ τῶν Δ,
ἐπὶ πλέον[1] δέ. τὸ μὲν δὴ Β καθόλου ἂν εἴη τοῖς Δ·
τοῦτο γὰρ λέγω καθόλου ᾧ[2] μὴ ἀντιστρέφει, πρῶ-
35 τον δὲ καθόλου ᾧ ἕκαστον μὲν μὴ ἀντιστρέφει,
ἅπαντα δὲ ἀντιστρέφει καὶ παρεκτείνει. τοῖς δὴ
Δ αἴτιον τοῦ Α τὸ Β. δεῖ ἄρα τὸ Α ἐπὶ πλέον τοῦ Β
ἐπεκτείνειν[3]· εἰ δὲ μή, τί μᾶλλον αἴτιον ἔσται τοῦτο
ἐκείνου; εἰ δὴ πᾶσιν ὑπάρχει τοῖς Ε τὸ Α, ἔσται
τι ἐκεῖνα ἓν ἅπαντα ἄλλο τοῦ Β. εἰ γὰρ μή, πῶς
99 b ἔσται εἰπεῖν ὅτι ᾧ τὸ Ε τὸ Α παντί, ᾧ δὲ τὸ Α οὐ
παντὶ τὸ Ε; διὰ τί γὰρ οὐκ ἔσται τι αἴτιον οἷον
[τὸ Α][4] ὑπάρχει πᾶσι τοῖς Δ; ἀλλ᾽ ἆρα καὶ τὰ Ε
ἔσται τι ἕν; ἐπισκέψασθαι δεῖ τοῦτο, καὶ ἔστω τὸ
Γ. ἐνδέχεται δὴ τοῦ αὐτοῦ πλείω αἴτια εἶναι, ἀλλ᾽
5 οὐ τοῖς αὐτοῖς τῷ εἴδει, οἷον τοῦ μακρόβια εἶναι τὰ
μὲν τετράποδα τὸ μὴ ἔχειν χολήν, τὰ δὲ πτηνὰ τὸ
ξηρὰ εἶναι ἢ ἕτερόν τι.

---

[1] πλεῖον ABd, comm.
[2] ᾧ B[1], Eustratius : ὅ.
[3] ἐπεκτείνειν Ross : παρεκτείνειν.
[4] τὸ Α secl. Ross : τοῦ τὸ Α ὑπάρχειν coni. Mure : τοῦ Α
ὑπάρχει vel τὸ Β ὑπάρχει coni. Hayduck.

---

[a] The exposition which follows is at best elliptical, and
the phrasing is unusual ; it seems likely to be a supplement
by another hand. If we try to fit the scheme to the preceding
example we get :

All broad-leafed plants (B) are deciduous (A),
All vines, figs . . . etc., (D) are broad-leafed (B).

The " first " or definitory middle, " subject to coagulation,"
is passed over. Probably it is taken for granted ; indeed the
remarkable inference " Therefore A must have a wider extension than B " implies that B is not definitory (for if it
were, B would be co-extensive with A) ; but the omission is

this.[a] Assume that A applies to all B, and B to each of the species of D, but with a wider extension. Then B will be a universal attribute of the Ds; for I call an attribute universal [b] even if the premiss is not convertible, although I call it universal in the primary sense only if, whereas each species separately is not convertible with it, the sum of the species is convertible and co-extensive with it. Thus B is the cause of A's applying to the Ds. Therefore A must have a wider extension than B; otherwise A might just as well be the cause of B.[c] If now A applies to all the species of E, they will constitute a single whole distinct from B; otherwise how can it be said that A applies to all that to which E applies, but not *vice versa*? Surely there must be some cause ⟨of A's applying to the Es⟩, just as there is for all the Ds. So it seems that the Es too will constitute a single whole. We must consider what this is; let it be represented by C. Thus it is possible for the same effect to have more than one cause, but not when the subjects are identical in species. *E.g.*, in quadrupeds the cause of longevity is not having a gall-bladder,[d] but in birds it is dryness of constitution, or some other distinct characteristic.

hard to condone. The point, however, of " inferring " that A is wider than B is to allow A to be true also of certain other species, E^1, E^2 . . . E^n, to which it is mediated through a different sub-genus, C. Then as B is the cause of the Ds' being A, so is C the cause of the Es' being A: *i.e.*, the same effect is produced by different causes in different subjects.

[b] *Cf.* 73 b 26 ff.

[c] See note on a 30. In any case the ambiguity is purely formal; in any concrete example the cause could easily be identified.

[d] A traditional view approved by Aristotle; *cf. Part. An.* 677 a 30.

ARISTOTLE

Εἰ δὲ εἰς τὸ ἄτομον μὴ εὐθὺς ἔρχονται, καὶ μὴ
μόνον ἓν τὸ μέσον ἀλλὰ πλείω, καὶ τὰ αἴτια πλείω.
XVIII. πότερον δ' αἴτιον τῶν μέσων τὸ πρὸς τὸ
10 καθόλου πρῶτον ἢ τὸ πρὸς τὸ καθ' ἕκαστον τοῖς
καθ' ἕκαστον; δῆλον δὴ ὅτι τὸ¹ ἐγγύτατα ἑκάστῳ
ᾧ αἴτιον. τοῦ γὰρ τὸ πρῶτον ὑπὸ τὸ καθόλου
ὑπάρχειν τοῦτο αἴτιον, οἷον τῷ Δ τὸ Γ τοῦ τὸ Β
ὑπάρχειν αἴτιον. τῷ μὲν οὖν Δ τὸ Γ αἴτιον τοῦ Α,
15 τῷ δὲ Γ τὸ Β, τούτῳ δὲ αὐτό.

XIX. Περὶ μὲν οὖν συλλογισμοῦ καὶ ἀποδείξεως,
τί τε ἑκάτερόν ἐστι καὶ πῶς γίγνεται, φανερόν,
ἅμα δὲ καὶ περὶ ἐπιστήμης ἀποδεικτικῆς· ταὐτὸν
γάρ ἐστιν. περὶ δὲ τῶν ἀρχῶν, πῶς τε γίγνονται
γνώριμοι καὶ τίς ἡ γνωρίζουσα ἕξις, ἐντεῦθεν ἔσται²
δῆλον προαπορήσασι πρῶτον.

20 Ὅτι μὲν οὖν οὐκ ἐνδέχεται ἐπίστασθαι δι' ἀποδείξεως μὴ γιγνώσκοντι τὰς πρώτας ἀρχὰς τὰς
ἀμέσους, εἴρηται πρότερον. τῶν δ' ἀμέσων τὴν
γνῶσιν, καὶ πότερον ἡ αὐτή ἐστιν ἢ οὐχ ἡ αὐτή,
διαπορήσειεν ἄν τις, καὶ πότερον ἐπιστήμη ἑκατέρου [ἢ οὔ],³ ἢ τοῦ μὲν ἐπιστήμη τοῦ δ' ἕτερόν τι

¹ τὸ A²n : τὰ Bd, comm. : om. A.
² ἔσται] ἐστι ABd.
³ ἢ οὔ secl. Ross.

ᵃ Assuming a series of four terms from D (minor) to A
(major), C and B being consecutive middles.
ᵇ i.e., the immediate premisses upon which all demonstration depends, described in 72 a 14 ff. These include both the
axioms or general principles of reasoning (whether common
to all categories or proper to a particular category) and the
special principles of single sciences, viz., definitions and
assumptions. (Cf. 76 a 31—77 a 4, and see Heath, Mathematics in Aristotle, pp. 50-55.) What Aristotle goes on to
describe is the formation of universal concepts rather than
254

If we do not come directly to immediate proposi- If there is tions, *i.e.*, if there is not merely one but more than more than one middle term, there will be also more than one one middle term, there cause. XVIII. Is the cause of the several species' will be more than possessing a given property the middle which is next one cause. to the universal, or the middle which is next to the species ? Clearly it is that which is nearest to the particular species which is its subject, because this middle is the cause of the proximate subject's falling under the universal. *E.g.*,[a] C is the cause of D's being B ; then C is the cause of D's being A, and B is the cause of being A for both C and itself.

XIX. We have now explained the nature of syllo- How do we gism and demonstration—and also of demonstrative apprehend science, which is the same as demonstration—and first principles ? how they are effected. We must next inquire how we obtain knowledge of first principles,[b] and what is the faculty [c] that secures this knowledge. The answer will be clear if we first examine some preliminary difficulties.

We have observed above [d] that it is impossible to reach scientific knowledge through demonstration unless one apprehends the immediate first principles. With regard to the apprehension of immediates the questions may be asked : (1) whether it is or is not Three the same ⟨as apprehension of mediated premisses⟩ ; questions (2) whether there is scientific knowledge of both, or to be faced. only of the latter, the former being cognized by a

the grasping of universal propositions, and it is not until 100 b 3 that he (rather casually) indicates that the processes are parallel.

[c] ἕξις is a developed faculty, as contrasted with a δύναμις, which is undeveloped ; but it has not seemed necessary always to mark the distinction in English.

[d] Book I, ch. i.

ARISTOTLE

99 b

25 γένος, καὶ πότερον οὐκ ἐνοῦσαι αἱ ἕξεις ἐγγίγνονται
ἢ ἐνοῦσαι λελήθασιν.

Εἰ μὲν δὴ ἔχομεν αὐτάς, ἄτοπον· συμβαίνει γὰρ
ἀκριβεστέρας ἔχοντας γνώσεις ἀποδείξεως λανθάνειν. εἰ δὲ λαμβάνομεν μὴ ἔχοντες πρότερον, πῶς
ἂν γνωρίζοιμεν καὶ μανθάνοιμεν ἐκ μὴ προϋπαρ-
30 χούσης γνώσεως; ἀδύνατον γάρ, ὥσπερ καὶ ἐπὶ
τῆς ἀποδείξεως ἐλέγομεν. φανερὸν τοίνυν ὅτι οὔτ᾽
ἔχειν οἷόν τε οὔτ᾽ ἀγνοοῦσι καὶ μηδεμίαν ἔχουσιν
ἕξιν ἐγγίγνεσθαι. ἀνάγκη ἄρα ἔχειν μέν τινα δύναμιν, μὴ τοιαύτην δ᾽ ἔχειν ἢ ἔσται τούτων τιμιωτέρα κατ᾽ ἀκρίβειαν. φαίνεται δὲ τοῦτό γε πᾶσιν
35 ὑπάρχον τοῖς ζῴοις. ἔχει γὰρ δύναμιν σύμφυτον
κριτικήν, ἣν καλοῦσιν αἴσθησιν· ἐνούσης δ᾽ αἰσθήσεως τοῖς μὲν τῶν ζῴων ἐγγίγνεται μονὴ τοῦ
αἰσθήματος, τοῖς δ᾽ οὐκ ἐγγίγνεται. ὅσοις μὲν οὖν
μὴ ἐγγίγνεται, ἢ ὅλως ἢ περὶ ἃ μὴ ἐγγίγνεται, οὐκ
ἔστι τούτοις γνῶσις ἔξω τοῦ αἰσθάνεσθαι· ἐν οἷς δ᾽
100 a ἔνεστιν αἰσθομένοις[1] ἔχειν ἔτι ἐν τῇ ψυχῇ. πολλῶν
δὲ τοιούτων γιγνομένων ἤδη διαφορά τις γίγνεται,
ὥστε τοῖς μὲν γίγνεσθαι λόγον ἐκ τῆς τῶν τοιούτων μονῆς, τοῖς δὲ μή.

Ἐκ μὲν οὖν αἰσθήσεως γίγνεται μνήμη, ὥσπερ
λέγομεν, ἐκ δὲ μνήμης πολλάκις τοῦ αὐτοῦ γιγνο-

---

[1] αἰσθομένοις ci. Ueberweg, scripsit Ross : αἰσθανομένοις codd.

[a] These two questions are answered at the end of the chapter, 100 b 5-17.　　[b] 71 a 1 ff.
[c] *i.e.*, demonstration and scientific knowledge.

different kind of knowledge [a]; and (3) whether we develop cognitive faculties which we did not possess before, or have always possessed these faculties without knowing it.

It seems paradoxical that we should have possessed them always, because then it follows that we possess, without knowing it, powers of apprehension which are more accurate than demonstration. If on the other hand we acquire them, not having possessed them before, how can we gain knowledge and learn without some pre-existent power of apprehension? It is an impossibility, just as we said [b] in the case of demonstration. Thus it is evident both that we cannot always have possessed them and that we cannot acquire them if we are completely ignorant and have no positive capacity. We must, then, have some faculty, but not such as to be superior in accuracy to those mentioned above.[c] Clearly this is a property of all animals. They have an innate faculty of discrimination, which we call sense-perception. All animals have it, but in some the perception persists, while in others it does not.[d] Where it does not, there is either no cognition at all outside the act of perception, or no cognition of those objects of which the perception does not persist. Where perception does persist, after the act of perception is over the percipients can still retain the perception in the soul. If this happens repeatedly, a distinction immediately arises between those animals which derive a coherent impression from the persistence and those which do not.

Thus sense-perception gives rise to memory, as we hold; and repeated memories of the same thing give

There must be a faculty which, starting as sense-perception,

in rational beings develops,

through memory

[d] *Cf. Met.* 980 b 21 ff.

100 a
5 μένης ἐμπειρία· αἱ γὰρ πολλαὶ μνῆμαι τῷ ἀριθμῷ
ἐμπειρία μία ἐστίν. ἐκ δ᾽ ἐμπειρίας ἢ ἐκ παντὸς
ἠρεμήσαντος τοῦ καθόλου ἐν τῇ ψυχῇ, τοῦ ἑνὸς
παρὰ τὰ πολλά, ὃ ἂν ἐν ἅπασιν ἓν ἐνῇ ἐκείνοις τὸ
αὐτό, τέχνης ἀρχὴ καὶ ἐπιστήμης, ἐὰν μὲν περὶ
γένεσιν, τέχνης, ἐὰν δὲ περὶ τὸ ὄν, ἐπιστήμης.
10 οὔτε δὴ ἐνυπάρχουσιν ἀφωρισμέναι αἱ ἕξεις, οὔτ᾽
ἀπ᾽ ἄλλων ἕξεων γίγνονται γνωστικωτέρων, ἀλλ᾽
ἀπὸ αἰσθήσεως, οἷον ἐν μάχῃ τροπῆς γενομένης
ἑνὸς στάντος ἕτερος ἔστη, εἶθ᾽ ἕτερος, ἕως ἐπὶ
ἀρχὴν ἦλθεν. ἡ δὲ ψυχὴ ὑπάρχει τοιαύτη οὖσα οἷα
15 δύνασθαι πάσχειν τοῦτο. ὃ δ᾽ ἐλέχθη μὲν πάλαι,
οὐ σαφῶς δὲ ἐλέχθη, πάλιν εἴπωμεν. στάντος γὰρ
τῶν ἀδιαφόρων ἑνός, πρῶτον μὲν ἐν τῇ ψυχῇ καθόλου (καὶ γὰρ αἰσθάνεται μὲν τὸ καθ᾽ ἕκαστον, ἡ δ᾽
100 b αἴσθησις τοῦ καθόλου ἐστίν, οἷον ἀνθρώπου, ἀλλ᾽
οὐ Καλλίου ἀνθρώπου)· πάλιν ἐν τούτοις ἵσταται,
ἕως ἂν τὰ ἀμερῆ στῇ καὶ τὰ καθόλου, οἷον τοιονδὶ

---

a Or, more exactly, "come to rest." (Ross rightly detects
a reminiscence of Plato, *Phaedo* 96 B ; note especially ἐκ δὲ
μνήμης καὶ δόξης λαβούσης τὸ ἠρεμεῖν, κατὰ ταῦτα γίγνεσθαι ἐπιστήμην. Whatever the truth about ἐπίσταμαι and ἐφίσταμαι,
Plato and Aristotle clearly connected the two ; *cf. Physics* 247
b 11 τῷ γὰρ ἠρεμῆσαι καὶ στῆναι τὴν διάνοιαν ἐπίστασθαι . . .
λέγομεθα.) The stream of transient particular sensations is
contrasted with the fixed general impression which they produce in a suitable subject.

b The point of the comparison is to suggest how a succession of unitary sensations can combine to form a permanent
whole. There is also an implication of order emerging from
disorder ; but this is to be found in the general sense, not in
the phrase ἕως ἐπὶ ἀρχὴν ἦλθεν, which simply means "until
it reaches the starting-point," *i.e.* until the rally has extended
to the man who first gave way. Perhaps a kind of pun is
intended, since Aristotle is considering the approach to the
πρῶται ἀρχαί.

rise to experience ; because the memories, though **and experi-** numerically many, constitute a single experience. **ence, the power of** And experience, that is the universal when estab- **generaliz-** lished [a] as a whole in the soul—the One that corre- **ing.** sponds to the Many, the unity that is identically present in them all—provides the starting-point of art and science : art in the world of process and science in the world of facts. Thus these faculties are neither innate as determinate and fully developed, nor derived from other developed faculties on a higher plane of knowledge ; they arise from sense-perception, just as, when a retreat has occurred in battle, if one man halts so does another, and then another, until the original position is restored.[b] The soul is so constituted that it is capable of the same sort of process. Let us re-state what we said just now [c] with insufficient precision. As soon as one individual [d] percept has " come to a halt " in the soul, this is the first beginning of the presence there of a universal (because although it is the particular that we perceive, the act of perception involves the universal, *e.g.*, " man," not " a man, Callias "). Then other " halts " occur among these ⟨proximate⟩ universals, until the indivisible genera [e] or ⟨ultimate⟩ universals are established. *E.g.*, a particular species

---

[c] 100 a 3-9.

[d] I do not see· how τὰ ἀδιάφορα can mean *infimae species* here. If Aristotle's illustration means anything, it is that the process begins with the perception of individuals, although the species is perceived in the individual. Since Aristotle appears to equate τὰ καθ' ἕκαστα with τὰ ἀδιάφορα in 97 b 29-31, it seems just possible that he is doing the converse here. Otherwise he would seem to be skipping an important stage in his description.

[e] The categories, which do not admit of analysis into genus and differentia. *Cf. Met.* 1014 b 6 ff.

ζῷον, ἕως ζῷον· καὶ ἐν τούτῳ ὡσαύτως. δῆλον δὴ
ὅτι ἡμῖν τὰ πρῶτα ἐπαγωγῇ γνωρίζειν ἀναγκαῖον·
καὶ γὰρ ἡ¹ αἴσθησις οὕτω τὸ καθόλου ἐμποιεῖ.

5 Ἐπεὶ δὲ τῶν περὶ τὴν διάνοιαν ἕξεων αἷς ἀλη-
θεύομεν αἱ μὲν ἀεὶ ἀληθεῖς εἰσιν, αἱ δὲ ἐπιδέχονται
τὸ ψεῦδος, οἷον δόξα καὶ λογισμός, ἀληθῆ δ' ἀεὶ
ἐπιστήμη καὶ νοῦς, καὶ οὐδὲν ἐπιστήμης ἀκριβέστερον ἄλλο γένος ἢ νοῦς, αἱ δ' ἀρχαὶ τῶν ἀποδείξεων
10 γνωριμώτεραι, ἐπιστήμη δ' ἅπασα μετὰ λόγου ἐστί,
τῶν ἀρχῶν ἐπιστήμη μὲν οὐκ ἂν εἴη, ἐπεὶ δ' οὐδὲν
ἀληθέστερον ἐνδέχεται εἶναι ἐπιστήμης ἢ νοῦν, νοῦς
ἂν εἴη τῶν ἀρχῶν, ἔκ τε τούτων σκοποῦσι καὶ ὅτι
ἀποδείξεως ἀρχὴ οὐκ ἀπόδειξις, ὥστ' οὐδ' ἐπιστήμης ἐπιστήμη. εἰ οὖν μηδὲν ἄλλο παρὰ ἐπιστήμην
15 γένος ἔχομεν ἀληθές, νοῦς ἂν εἴη ἐπιστήμης ἀρχή.
καὶ ἡ μὲν ἀρχὴ τῆς ἀρχῆς εἴη ἄν, ἡ δὲ πᾶσα ὁμοίως
ἔχει πρὸς τὸ πᾶν² πρᾶγμα.

¹ ἡ n, Eustratius : καὶ ABd.
² πᾶν n : ἅπαν AB : om. d.

of animal leads to the genus " animal," and so on. Clearly then it must be by induction that we acquire knowledge of the primary premisses, because this is also the way in which general concepts are conveyed to us by sense-perception.

Now of the intellectual faculties that we use in the pursuit of truth some (*e.g.*, scientific knowledge and intuition) are always true, whereas others (*e.g.*, opinion and calculation) admit falsity ; and no other kind of knowledge except intuition is more accurate than scientific knowledge. Also first principles are more knowable than demonstrations, and all scientific knowledge involves reason. It follows that there can be no scientific knowledge of the first principles ; and since nothing can be more infallible than scientific knowledge except intuition, it must be intuition that apprehends the first principles. This is evident not only from the foregoing considerations but also because the starting-point of demonstration is not itself demonstration, and so the starting-point of scientific knowledge is not itself scientific knowledge. Therefore, since we possess no other infallible faculty besides scientific knowledge, the source from which such knowledge starts must be intuition. Thus it will be the primary source of scientific knowledge that apprehends the first principles, while scientific knowledge as a whole is similarly related to the whole world of facts.

TOPICA

INTRODUCTION

I. THE PLACE OF THE *TOPICA* IN THE *ORGANON*

BOTH the *Topica* and the *de Sophisticis Elenchis* have always been regarded as genuine works of Aristotle. The two treatises are closely connected; the *de Sophisticis Elenchis* is an appendix to the *Topica* and its final section forms an epilogue to both treatises; indeed Aristotle himself seems sometimes to regard the two as forming a single work, since he twice quotes the *de Sophisticis Elenchis* under the title of the *Topica*.

It is generally admitted that what we call logic and Aristotle himself calls analytic was an early preoccupation of the philosopher and a direct outcome of discussions on scientific method held in the Platonic Academy. Plato himself, however, never attempted a formal treatment of the subject and the theories put forward, for example, in the *Theaetetus*, *Sophist*, *Parmenides* and *Politicus* were never developed into a regular system. But while Aristotle's systematic treatment of the process of inference and, above all, his discovery of the syllogism owe little to Plato, it has been generally recognized that the Platonic dialogues contain some of the germs from which the Aristotelian system was afterwards developed; for

265

example, in the *Theaetetus* the doctrine of the categories is already implicit in the recognition of the abstract notions of substance, quality, quantity, relation, activity and passivity.

Of the logical treatises of Aristotle, which since about A.D. 200 have passed under the title of the *Organon* or 'instrument' of science, the most important are (1) the *Prior Analytics*, in which he sets forth the doctrine of the syllogism in its formal aspect without reference to the subject-matter with which it deals, (2) the *Posterior Analytics*, in which he discusses the characteristics which reasoning must necessarily possess in order to be truly scientific, (3) the *Topica*, in which he treats of the modes of reasoning, which, while syllogistically correct, fall short of the conditions of scientific accuracy. The *Categories* and the *de Interpretatione* are subsidiary treatises dealing, in the main, with the term and the proposition.

A great deal of time and ingenuity has been expended, particularly by German scholars, in an attempt to fix the exact order in which the various treatises which constitute the *Organon* were composed. The problem is complicated by the fact that the treatises, in the form in which they have come down to us, seem to consist of rough notes, which were evidently subjected to a certain amount of revision due to the modification and development of his original doctrines. This process has naturally given rise to minor inconsistencies such as would naturally occur if corrections were made or additions inserted which were not completely adapted to the context in which they were placed.

It has been generally recognized that the whole

of the *Topica* does not belong to the same date. H. Maier [a] holds that the oldest portion consists of Books II-VII. 2 and that it was written under the direct influence of the Academy and belongs to the same period as the Aristotelian *Dialogues*, which have survived only in fragments ; in particular, he points out that the term συλλογισμός is not used in the technical sense which it afterwards acquired (or, if it is used in that sense, *e.g.*, in 130 a 7, it is a late insertion), whereas in the second half of Book VII the term is used in its well-known Aristotelian sense, and that, consequently, Books II-VII. 2 were composed before the philosopher made his greatest contribution to logic. He holds that Books I and VIII belong to the same period as Book VII. 4-5, and form an introduction and conclusion to the treatise written after the discovery of the syllogism, and that the *de Sophisticis Elenchis* was a subsequent addition to the *Topica*. On the other hand, F. Solmsen [a] and P. Gohlke [a] hold that Books I-VII form the earlier portion of the work and that Book VIII and the *de Sophisticis Elenchis* were added subsequently.

As regards the relation of the *Topica* to the rest of the *Organon*, Maier considers the *Topica* as a whole to be earlier than the *Analytics* ; Solmsen suggests that the order was (1) *Topica* I-VII, (2) *Posterior Analytics* I, (3) *Topica* VIII and *de Sophisticis Elenchis*, (4) *Posterior Analytics* II, (5) *Prior Analytics* ; Gohlke holds that the traditional order of the two *Analytics* is correct, and that the *Topica* and *de Sophisticis Elenchis* presuppose the *Analytics*.

In short, there is general agreement that the bulk of the *Topica* embodies Aristotle's earliest contribu-

[a] See Bibliography.

tion to the systematic study of logic and that it was
written in part before his discovery of the syllogism.

II. The Content of the *Topica*

The purpose of the *Topica* is, in the words of its
author (100 a 18 ff.), " to discover a method by which
we shall be able to reason from generally accepted
opinions about any problem set before us and shall
ourselves, when sustaining an argument, avoid saying
anything self-contradictory "; that is to say, it aims at
enabling the two participants, the ' questioner ' and
the ' answerer,' to sustain their parts in a dialectical
discussion. The subject, then, of the treatise may
be described as the dialectical syllogism based on
premises which are merely probable as contrasted
with the demonstrative, or scientific, syllogism, which
is the subject of the *Posterior Analytics* and is based
on premises which are true and immediate. The
probable premises which make up the dialectical
syllogism are described (100 b 21 f.) as " those which
commend themselves to all or to the majority or to
the wise." The uses of dialectic are, we are told,
three in number, (1) for mental training, (2) for
general conversation, and (3) for application to the
sciences, because (*a*) if we can argue a question *pro*
and *con*, we shall be in a better position to recognize
truth and falsehood, and (*b*) since the first principles
of the sciences cannot be scientifically demonstrated,
the approach to them must be through the study of
the opinions generally held about them.

After the general introduction in Book I, Aristotle,
in Books II-VII. 3, gives a collection of the τόποι which
give their name to the treatise. The term τόποι is
268

somewhat difficult to define. They may be described as ' commonplaces ' of argument or as general principles of probability which stand in the same relation to the dialectical syllogism as axioms stand to the demonstrative syllogism ; in other words, they are " the pigeon-holes from which dialectical reasoning is to draw its arguments." [a]

Books II and III deal with the problems of accident; Books IV and V with those of genus and property ; Books VI and VII. 1-3 with those of definition. Books VII. 4-5, and Book VIII, after giving some additional notes, conclude the treatise by describing the practice of dialectical reasoning.

III. The Manuscripts

The chief manuscripts for the *Topica* are :

A	Urbinas 35	saec. ix-x ineunt.
B	Marcianus 201	an. 955
C	Coislinianus 330	saec. xi
D	Parisinus 1843	saec. xiii
u	Basileensis 54 (F ii. 21)	saec. xii
c	Vaticanus 1024	saec. x-xi
P	Vaticanus 207	saec. xiii
f	Marcianus App. iv. 5	saec. xiv
q	Ambrosianus M. 71	saec. xv
N	Laurentianus 72. 18	saec. xv
i	Laurentianus 72. 15	saec. xiv
T	Laurentianus 72. 12	saec. xiii
O	Marcianus 204	saec. xiv

Of these A and B are in a class by themselves. Bekker preferred A, Waitz B ; the Teubner Editors

[a] W. D. Ross, *Aristotle*, p. 59.

give a slight preference to B, the readings of which are sometimes supported by papyrus fragments.   C sometimes preserves the true reading.

IV. Select Bibliography

EDITIONS

J. T. Buhle, Text, Latin Translation and Notes, Biponti, 1792.
I. Bekker, Text, Berlin, 1831, Oxford, 1837.
T. Waitz, Text and Notes, Leipzig, 1844–1846.
Y. Strache and M. Wallies, Teubner Text, Leipzig, 1923.
[The Oxford Classical Text, by W. D. Ross, Oxford, 1958, was not available to Professor Forster.]

TRANSLATIONS

T. Taylor, London, 1812.
O. F. Owen (Bohn's Classical Library), London, 1902.
W. A. Pickard-Cambridge (Oxford Translation), Oxford, 1928.
   In French :
J. B.-Saint-Hilaire, Paris, 1837.
   In German :
J. H. von Kirchmann, Heidelberg, 1877.
E. Rolfes, Leipzig, 1922.

ARTICLES AND DISSERTATIONS

P. Gohlke, *Die Entstehung der aristotelischen Logik*, Berlin, 1936.

TOPICA

H. Maier, *Die Syllogistik des Aristoteles*, Tübingen, 1900.

F. Solmsen, *Die Entwicklung der aristotelischen Logik und Rhetorik*, Berlin, 1929.

J. L. Stocks, " The Composition of Aristotle's Logical Works," *Classical Quarterly*, 1933, pp. 115-124.

In translating the *Topica* I have used the text of Bekker in the Berlin Edition, and when I translate any other reading this is noted at the foot of the page. I have constantly referred to the Teubner text of Strache-Wallies, which does not, however, seem to me to mark any considerable advance on that of Bekker. I have found Waitz's edition of the *Organon* of great use, and the Latin version of Pacius is often helpful. I have frequently consulted the Oxford translation by W. A. Pickard-Cambridge.

I have to thank my friend and former colleague Professor W. S. Maguinness, of King's College, London, for reading through my version and giving me the benefit of his fine scholarship and accuracy. He has suggested several improvements in the text which I have been glad to adopt.

E. S. F.

[This Introduction is, with some modifications, Professor Forster's. After his death, his edition of the *Topica* was seen through the press by D. J. Furley, who also compiled the Index.]

ΤΟΠΙΚΩΝ

Α

100 a 18　I. Ἡ μὲν πρόθεσις τῆς πραγματείας μέθοδον
εὑρεῖν, ἀφ᾽ ἧς δυνησόμεθα συλλογίζεσθαι περὶ παν-
20 τὸς τοῦ προτεθέντος προβλήματος ἐξ ἐνδόξων, καὶ
αὐτοὶ λόγον ὑπέχοντες μηθὲν ἐροῦμεν ὑπεναντίον.
πρῶτον οὖν ῥητέον τί ἐστι συλλογισμὸς καὶ τίνες
αὐτοῦ διαφοραί, ὅπως ληφθῇ ὁ διαλεκτικὸς συλλογισμός.　τοῦτον γὰρ ζητοῦμεν κατὰ τὴν προκειμένην πραγματείαν.

25　Ἔστι δὴ συλλογισμὸς λόγος ἐν ᾧ τεθέντων τινῶν
ἕτερόν τι τῶν κειμένων ἐξ ἀνάγκης συμβαίνει διὰ
τῶν κειμένων.　ἀπόδειξις μὲν οὖν ἐστίν, ὅταν ἐξ
ἀληθῶν καὶ πρώτων ὁ συλλογισμὸς ᾖ, ἢ ἐκ τοιούτων ἃ διά τινων πρώτων καὶ ἀληθῶν τῆς περὶ αὐτὰ
30 γνώσεως τὴν ἀρχὴν εἴληφεν· διαλεκτικὸς δὲ συλ-
100 b 18 λογισμὸς ὁ ἐξ ἐνδόξων συλλογιζόμενος.　ἔστι δὲ
ἀληθῆ μὲν καὶ πρῶτα τὰ μὴ δι᾽ ἑτέρων ἀλλὰ δι᾽
αὐτῶν ἔχοντα τὴν πίστιν· οὐ δεῖ γὰρ ἐν ταῖς
20 ἐπιστημονικαῖς ἀρχαῖς ἐπιζητεῖσθαι τὸ διὰ τί,
ἀλλ᾽ ἑκάστην τῶν ἀρχῶν αὐτὴν καθ᾽ ἑαυτὴν εἶναι
πιστήν. ἔνδοξα δὲ τὰ δοκοῦντα πᾶσιν ἢ τοῖς πλεί-
272

TOPICA

BOOK I

I. The purpose of the present treatise is to discover a method by which we shall be able to reason from generally accepted opinions about any problem set before us and shall ourselves, when sustaining an argument, avoid saying anything self-contradictory. First, then, we must say what reasoning is and what different kinds of it there are, in order that dialectical reasoning may be apprehended; for it is the search for this that we are undertaking in the treatise which lies before us.

Reasoning is a discussion in which, certain things having been laid down, something other than these things necessarily results through them. Reasoning is *demonstration* when it proceeds from premises which are true and primary or of such a kind that we have derived our original knowledge of them through premises which are primary and true. Reasoning is *dialectical* which reasons from generally accepted opinions. Things are true and primary which command belief through themselves and not through anything else; for regarding the first principles of science it is unnecessary to ask any further question as to 'why,' but each principle should of itself command belief. Generally accepted opinions, on the other hand, are those which commend themselves

100 b

στοις ἢ τοῖς σοφοῖς, καὶ τούτοις ἢ πᾶσιν ἢ τοῖς
πλείστοις ἢ τοῖς μάλιστα γνωρίμοις καὶ ἐνδόξοις.
ἐριστικὸς δ' ἐστὶ συλλογισμὸς ὁ ἐκ φαινομένων
25 ἐνδόξων, μὴ ὄντων δέ, καὶ ὁ ἐξ ἐνδόξων ἢ φαινομένων ἐνδόξων φαινόμενος. οὐ γὰρ πᾶν τὸ
φαινόμενον ἔνδοξον καὶ ἔστιν ἔνδοξον. οὐθὲν γὰρ
τῶν λεγομένων ἐνδόξων ἐπιπόλαιον ἔχει παντελῶς
τὴν φαντασίαν, καθὰ περὶ τὰς τῶν ἐριστικῶν λόγων
ἀρχὰς συμβέβηκεν ἔχειν· παραχρῆμα γὰρ καὶ ὡς
30 ἐπὶ τὸ πολὺ τοῖς καὶ μικρὰ συνορᾶν δυναμένοις
101 a κατάδηλος ἐν αὐτοῖς ἡ τοῦ ψεύδους ἐστὶ φύσις. ὁ
μὲν οὖν πρότερος τῶν ῥηθέντων ἐριστικῶν συλλογισμῶν καὶ συλλογισμὸς λεγέσθω, ὁ δὲ λοιπὸς
ἐριστικὸς μὲν συλλογισμός, συλλογισμὸς δ' οὔ,
ἐπειδὴ φαίνεται μὲν συλλογίζεσθαι, συλλογίζεται
δ' οὔ.

5   Ἔτι δὲ παρὰ τοὺς εἰρημένους ἅπαντας συλλογισμοὺς οἱ ἐκ τῶν περί τινας ἐπιστήμας οἰκείων γινό-
μενοι παραλογισμοί, καθάπερ ἐπὶ τῆς γεωμετρίας
καὶ τῶν ταύτῃ συγγενῶν συμβέβηκεν ἔχειν. ἔοικε
γὰρ ὁ τρόπος οὗτος διαφέρειν τῶν εἰρημένων συλ-
10 λογισμῶν· οὔτε γὰρ ἐξ ἀληθῶν καὶ πρώτων συλλογίζεται ὁ ψευδογραφῶν, οὔτ' ἐξ ἐνδόξων. εἰς γὰρ
τὸν ὅρον οὐκ ἐμπίπτει· οὔτε γὰρ τὰ πᾶσι δοκοῦντα
λαμβάνει οὔτε τὰ τοῖς πλείστοις οὔτε τὰ τοῖς σοφοῖς, καὶ τούτοις οὔτε τὰ πᾶσιν οὔτε τοῖς πλείστοις
οὔτε τοῖς ἐνδοξοτάτοις, ἀλλ' ἐκ τῶν οἰκείων μὲν τῇ
15 ἐπιστήμῃ λημμάτων, οὐκ ἀληθῶν δὲ τὸν συλλογισμὸν ποιεῖται. τῷ γὰρ ἢ τὰ ἡμικύκλια περιγρά-

274

to all or to the majority or to the wise—that is, to all
of the wise or to the majority or to the most famous
and distinguished of them. Reasoning is *contentious* (c) Conten-
if it is based on opinions which appear to be gener- tious.
ally accepted but are not really so, or if it merely
appears to be based on opinions which are, or appear
to be, generally accepted. For not every opinion
which appears to be generally accepted is actually
so accepted. For in none of the so-called generally
accepted opinions is the illusory appearance entirely
manifest, as happens in the case of the principles of
contentious arguments ; for usually the nature of un-
truth in these is immediately obvious to those who
have even a small power of comprehension. Therefore, of the above-mentioned contentious reasonings
the former should actually be called reasoning, but
the other should be called, not reasoning, but contentious reasoning, because it appears to reason but
does not really do so.

Furthermore, besides all the above-mentioned False
reasonings, there are false reasonings based on pre- reasonings.
mises peculiar to certain sciences, as happens in
geometry and the sciences kindred to it. For this
kind seems to differ from the reasonings already
mentioned ; for the man who constructs a false figure
reasons neither from true and primary premises nor
from generally accepted opinions ; for he does not
fall within the definition, since he does not take as
his premises either universally accepted opinions or
those which commend themselves to the majority or
to the wise—that is to all of the wise or to the majority
or to the most distinguished of them,—but his process of reasoning is based on assumptions which are
peculiar to the science but not true ; for he reasons

101 a

φειν μὴ ὡς δεῖ, ἢ γραμμάς τινας ἄγειν μὴ ὡς ἂν
ἀχθείησαν, τὸν παραλογισμὸν ποιεῖται.

Εἴδη μὲν οὖν τῶν συλλογισμῶν, ὡς τύπῳ περιλαβεῖν, ἔστω τὰ εἰρημένα. καθόλου δ' εἰπεῖν
20 περὶ πάντων τῶν εἰρημένων καὶ τῶν μετὰ ταῦτα
ῥηθησομένων, ἐπὶ τοσοῦτον ἡμῖν διωρίσθω, διότι
περὶ οὐδενὸς αὐτῶν τὸν ἀκριβῆ λόγον ἀποδοῦναι προαιρούμεθα, ἀλλ' ὅσον τύπῳ περὶ αὐτῶν
βουλόμεθα διελθεῖν, παντελῶς ἱκανὸν ἡγούμενοι
κατὰ τὴν προκειμένην μέθοδον τὸ δύνασθαι γνωρίζειν ὁπωσοῦν ἕκαστον αὐτῶν.

25 II. Ἑπόμενον δ' ἂν εἴη τοῖς εἰρημένοις εἰπεῖν
πρὸς πόσα τε καὶ τίνα χρήσιμος ἡ πραγματεία.
ἔστι δὴ πρὸς τρία, πρὸς γυμνασίαν, πρὸς τὰς
ἐντεύξεις, πρὸς τὰς κατὰ φιλοσοφίαν ἐπιστήμας.
ὅτι μὲν οὖν πρὸς γυμνασίαν χρήσιμος, ἐξ αὐτῶν
30 καταφανές ἐστι· μέθοδον γὰρ ἔχοντες ῥᾷον περὶ τοῦ
προτεθέντος ἐπιχειρεῖν δυνησόμεθα. πρὸς δὲ τὰς
ἐντεύξεις, διότι τὰς τῶν πολλῶν κατηριθμημένοι
δόξας οὐκ ἐκ τῶν ἀλλοτρίων ἀλλ' ἐκ τῶν οἰκείων
δογμάτων ὁμιλήσομεν πρὸς αὐτούς, μεταβιβά-
ζοντες ὅ τι ἂν μὴ καλῶς φαίνωνται λέγειν ἡμῖν.
35 πρὸς δὲ τὰς κατὰ φιλοσοφίαν ἐπιστήμας, ὅτι δυνάμενοι πρὸς ἀμφότερα διαπορῆσαι ῥᾷον ἐν ἑκάστοις
κατοψόμεθα τἀληθές τε καὶ τὸ ψεῦδος. ἔτι δὲ πρὸς
τὰ πρῶτα τῶν περὶ ἑκάστην ἐπιστήμην [ἀρχῶν][1]·
ἐκ μὲν γὰρ τῶν οἰκείων τῶν κατὰ τὴν προτεθεῖσαν
ἐπιστήμην ἀρχῶν ἀδύνατον εἰπεῖν τι περὶ αὐτῶν,
101 b ἐπειδὴ πρῶται αἱ ἀρχαὶ ἁπάντων εἰσί, διὰ δὲ τῶν
περὶ ἕκαστα ἐνδόξων ἀνάγκη περὶ αὐτῶν διελθεῖν.
τοῦτο δ' ἴδιον ἢ μάλιστα οἰκεῖον τῆς διαλεκτικῆς

[1] Omitting ἀρχῶν with B corr. and C.

falsely either by describing the semicircles improperly
or by drawing lines as they should not be drawn.

Let the above then be a description in outline
of the different kinds of reasoning. In general, as
regards all those already mentioned and to be mentioned hereafter, let this much distinction suffice for
us, since we do not propose to give the exact definition of any of them but merely wish to describe them
in outline, considering it quite enough, in accordance
with the method which we have set before us, to be
able to recognize each of them in some way or other.

II. After the above remarks the next point is to
explain for how many and for what purposes this
treatise is useful. They are three in number, mental
training, conversations and the philosophic sciences.
That it is useful for mental training is obvious on the
face of it ; for, if we have a method, we shall be able
more easily to argue about the subject proposed. It
is useful for conversations, because, having enumerated the opinions of the majority, we shall be dealing
with people on the basis of their own opinions, not of
those of others, changing the course of any argument
which they appear to us to be using wrongly. For the
philosophic sciences it is useful, because, if we are
able to raise difficulties on both sides, we shall more
easily discern both truth and falsehood on every
point. Further, it is useful in connexion with the
ultimate bases of each science; for it is impossible to
discuss them at all on the basis of the principles
peculiar to the science in question, since the principles
are primary in relation to everything else, and it is
necessary to deal with them through the generally
accepted opinions on each point. This process belongs peculiarly, or most appropriately to dialectic ;

The uses of the treatise.

101 b

ἐστίν· ἐξεταστικὴ γὰρ οὖσα πρὸς τὰς ἁπασῶν τῶν
μεθόδων ἀρχὰς ὁδὸν ἔχει.

5   III. Ἕξομεν δὲ τελέως τὴν μέθοδον, ὅταν ὁμοίως
ἔχωμεν ὥσπερ ἐπὶ ῥητορικῆς καὶ ἰατρικῆς καὶ τῶν
τοιούτων δυνάμεων. τοῦτο δ᾽ ἐστὶ τὸ ἐκ τῶν ἐνδεχομένων ποιεῖν ἃ προαιρούμεθα. οὔτε γὰρ ὁ
ῥητορικὸς ἐκ παντὸς τρόπου πείσει, οὔθ᾽ ὁ ἰατρικὸς
ὑγιάσει· ἀλλ᾽ ἐὰν τῶν ἐνδεχομένων μηδὲν παρα-
10 λείπῃ, ἱκανῶς αὐτὸν ἔχειν τὴν ἐπιστήμην φήσομεν.

IV. Πρῶτον οὖν θεωρητέον ἐκ τίνων ἡ μέθοδος.
εἰ δὴ λάβοιμεν πρὸς πόσα καὶ ποῖα καὶ ἐκ τίνων
οἱ λόγοι, καὶ πῶς τούτων εὐπορήσομεν, ἔχοιμεν
ἂν ἱκανῶς τὸ προκείμενον. ἔστι δ᾽ ἀριθμῷ ἴσα καὶ
15 ταὐτά, ἐξ ὧν τε οἱ λόγοι καὶ περὶ ὧν οἱ συλλογισμοί. γίνονται μὲν γὰρ οἱ λόγοι ἐκ τῶν προτάσεων·
περὶ ὧν δὲ οἱ συλλογισμοί, τὰ προβλήματά ἐστι.
πᾶσα δὲ πρότασις καὶ πᾶν πρόβλημα ἢ γένος ἢ
ἴδιον ἢ συμβεβηκὸς δηλοῖ· καὶ γὰρ τὴν διαφορὰν
ὡς οὖσαν γενικὴν ὁμοῦ τῷ γένει τακτέον. ἐπεὶ δὲ
20 τοῦ ἰδίου τὸ μὲν τὸ τί ἦν εἶναι σημαίνει, τὸ δ᾽ οὐ
σημαίνει, διῃρήσθω τὸ ἴδιον εἰς ἄμφω τὰ προειρημένα μέρη, καὶ καλείσθω τὸ μὲν τὸ τί ἦν εἶναι
σημαῖνον ὅρος, τὸ δὲ λοιπὸν κατὰ τὴν κοινὴν
περὶ αὐτῶν ἀποδοθεῖσαν ὀνομασίαν προσαγορευέ-
σθω ἴδιον. δῆλον οὖν ἐκ τῶν εἰρημένων ὅτι κατὰ τὴν
25 νῦν διαίρεσιν τέτταρα τὰ πάντα συμβαίνει γίνεσθαι,

for, being of the nature of an investigation, it lies along the path to the principles of all methods of inquiry.

III. We shall possess the method completely when we are in a position similar to that in which we are with regard to rhetoric and medicine and other such faculties ; that is to say, when we carry out our purpose with every available means. For neither will the rhetorician seek to persuade nor the physician to heal by every expedient ; but if he omits none of the available means, we shall say that he possesses the science in an adequate degree. *The limitations of the method proposed*

IV. We must, then, first consider on what bases our method rests ; for if we could grasp to how many and to what kind of objects our arguments are directed and on what bases they rest, and how we are to be well provided with these, we should sufficiently attain the end which is set before us. Now the bases of arguments are equal in number and identical with the subjects of reasonings. For arguments arise from ' propositions,' while the subjects of reasonings are ' problems.' Now every proposition and every problem indicates either a genus or a peculiarity or an accident ; for the differentia also, being generic in character, should be ranged with the genus. But since part of the peculiarity indicates the essence and part does not do so, let the peculiarity be divided into the two above-mentioned parts and let that which indicates the essence be called a ' definition,' and let the remaining part be termed a ' property ' in accordance with the nomenclature usually assigned in these cases. It is clear therefore, from what has been said, that, as a result of the division just made, there are four alternatives in all, either property or *SUBJECTS AND MATERIALS OF DISCUSSION (I. 4-12).* *Propositions and Problems.*

279

ARISTOTLE

101 b

ἢ ἴδιον ἢ ὅρον ἢ γένος ἢ συμβεβηκός. μηδεὶς δ᾽
ἡμᾶς ὑπολάβῃ λέγειν ὡς ἕκαστον τούτων καθ᾽ αὑτὸ
λεγόμενον πρότασις ἢ πρόβλημά ἐστιν, ἀλλ᾽ ὅτι
ἀπὸ τούτων καὶ τὰ προβλήματα καὶ αἱ προτάσεις
γίνονται. διαφέρει δὲ τὸ πρόβλημα καὶ ἡ πρότασις
30 τῷ τρόπῳ. οὕτω μὲν γὰρ ῥηθέντος, ἆρά γε τὸ
ζῷον πεζὸν δίπουν ὁρισμός ἐστιν ἀνθρώπου; καὶ
ἆρά γε τὸ ζῷον γένος ἐστὶ τοῦ ἀνθρώπου;, πρότασις γίνεται. ἐὰν δέ, πότερον τὸ ζῷον πεζὸν
δίπουν ὁρισμός ἐστιν ἀνθρώπου ἢ οὔ; [καὶ πότερον
τὸ ζῷον γένος ἐστίν;],[1] πρόβλημα γίνεται. ὁμοίως
δὲ καὶ ἐπὶ τῶν ἄλλων. ὥστ᾽ εἰκότως ἴσα τῷ
35 ἀριθμῷ τὰ προβλήματα καὶ αἱ προτάσεις εἰσίν.
ἀπὸ πάσης γὰρ προτάσεως πρόβλημα ποιήσεις
μεταβάλλων τῷ τρόπῳ.

V. Λεκτέον δὲ τί ὅρος, τί ἴδιον, τί γένος, τί συμβεβηκός. ἔστι δ᾽ ὅρος μὲν λόγος ὁ τὸ τί ἦν εἶναι
102 a σημαίνων. ἀποδίδοται δὲ ἢ λόγος ἀντ᾽ ὀνόματος ἢ
λόγος ἀντὶ λόγου· δυνατὸν γὰρ καὶ τῶν ὑπὸ λόγου
τινὰ σημαινομένων ὁρίσασθαι. ὅσοι δ᾽ ὁπωσοῦν
ὀνόματι τὴν ἀπόδοσιν ποιοῦνται, δῆλον ὡς οὐκ
5 ἀποδιδόασιν οὗτοι τὸν τοῦ πράγματος ὁρισμόν,
ἐπειδὴ πᾶς ὁρισμὸς λόγος τίς ἐστιν. ὁρικὸν μέντοι
καὶ τὸ τοιοῦτον θετέον, οἷον ὅτι καλόν ἐστι τὸ
πρέπον. ὁμοίως δὲ καὶ τὸ πότερον ταὐτὸν αἴσθησις
καὶ ἐπιστήμη ἢ ἕτερον· καὶ γὰρ περὶ τοὺς ὁρισμούς,
πότερον ταὐτὸν ἢ ἕτερον, ἡ πλείστη γίνεται δια-
τριβή. ἁπλῶς δὲ ὁρικὰ πάντα λεγέσθω τὰ ὑπὸ τὴν
10 αὐτὴν ὄντα μέθοδον τοῖς ὁρισμοῖς. ὅτι δὲ πάντα

---

[1] Omitting καὶ πότερον . . . ἐστίν; with A B.

definition or genus or accident. But let no one suppose that we mean that each of these stated by itself is a proposition or a problem, but only that problems and propositions are made up of these. The problem and the proposition differ in the way in which they are stated. If we say, " Is not ' pedestrian biped animal ' a definition of man ? " or " Is not ' animal ' the genus of man ? " a proposition is formed. But if we say, " Is ' pedestrian biped animal ' a definition of man, or not ? " a problem is formed. Similarly too with the other cases. It naturally follows, therefore, that the problems and the propositions are equal in number ; for you will be able to make a problem out of any proposition by altering the way in which it is stated.

V. We must next say what definition, property, genus and accident are. A *definition* is a phrase indicating the essence of something. The definition is asserted either as a phrase used in place of a term, or as a phrase used in place of a phrase ; for it is possible to define some things also which are indicated by a phrase. But it is obvious that everyone who makes an assertion by means of a term in any way whatever, does not assert the definition of the thing, because every definition is a phrase of a certain kind. However, such a statement as " That which is seemly is beautiful " must also be put down as being ' definitory,' and likewise the question " Are sensation and knowledge the same thing or different ? " For when we are dealing with definitions, we spend most of our time discussing whether things are the same or different. In a word, let us call ' definitory ' everything which comes under the same kind of inquiry as do definitions; and it is self-evident that all the above-

The four predicables : (a) Definition.

τὰ νῦν ῥηθέντα τοιαῦτ' ἐστί, δῆλον ἐξ αὐτῶν.
δυνάμενοι γὰρ ὅτι ταὐτὸν καὶ ὅτι ἕτερον διαλέγεσθαι, τῷ αὐτῷ τρόπῳ καὶ πρὸς τοὺς ὁρισμοὺς ἐπιχειρεῖν εὐπορήσομεν· δείξαντες γὰρ ὅτι οὐ ταὐτόν
ἐστιν ἀνῃρηκότες ἐσόμεθα τὸν ὁρισμόν. οὐ μὴν
15 ἀντιστρέφει γε τὸ νῦν ῥηθέν· οὐ γὰρ ἱκανὸν πρὸς
τὸ κατασκευάσαι τὸν ὁρισμὸν τὸ δεῖξαι ταὐτὸν ὄν.
πρὸς μέντοι τὸ ἀνασκευάσαι αὔταρκες τὸ δεῖξαι
ὅτι οὐ ταὐτόν.

    Ἴδιον δ' ἐστὶν ὃ μὴ δηλοῖ μὲν τὸ τί ἦν εἶναι, μόνῳ
δ' ὑπάρχει καὶ ἀντικατηγορεῖται τοῦ πράγματος,
20 οἷον ἴδιον ἀνθρώπου τὸ γραμματικῆς εἶναι δεκτικόν·
εἰ γὰρ ἄνθρωπός ἐστι, γραμματικῆς δεκτικός ἐστι,
καὶ εἰ γραμματικῆς δεκτικός ἐστιν, ἄνθρωπός ἐστιν.
οὐθεὶς γὰρ ἴδιον λέγει τὸ ἐνδεχόμενον ἄλλῳ ὑπάρχειν, οἷον τὸ καθεύδειν ἀνθρώπῳ, οὐδ' ἂν τύχῃ
25 κατά τινα χρόνον μόνῳ ὑπάρχον. εἰ δ' ἄρα τι καὶ
λέγοιτο τῶν τοιούτων ἴδιον, οὐχ ἁπλῶς ἀλλὰ ποτὲ
ἢ πρός τι ἴδιον ῥηθήσεται· τὸ μὲν γὰρ ἐκ δεξιῶν
εἶναι ποτὲ ἴδιόν ἐστι, τὸ δὲ δίπουν πρός τι ἴδιον
τυγχάνει λεγόμενον, οἷον τῷ ἀνθρώπῳ πρὸς ἵππον
καὶ κύνα. ὅτι δὲ τῶν ἐνδεχομένων ἄλλῳ ὑπάρχειν
30 οὐθὲν ἀντικατηγορεῖται, δῆλον· οὐ γὰρ ἀναγκαῖον,
εἴ τι καθεύδει, ἄνθρωπον εἶναι.

    Γένος δ' ἐστὶ τὸ κατὰ πλειόνων καὶ διαφερόντων

mentioned instances are of this kind. For when we can argue that things are the same or that they are different, we shall by the same method have an abundance of arguments for dealing with definitions also; for when we have shown that a thing is not the same as another we shall have destroyed the definition. The converse of what we have just said does not, however, hold good; for it is not enough for the construction of a definition to show that one thing is the same as another; but, in order to destroy a definition, it is enough to show that it is not the same.

A *property* is something which does not show the essence of a thing but belongs to it alone and is predicated convertibly of it. For example, it is a property of man to be capable of learning grammar; for if a certain being is a man, he is capable of learning grammar, and if he is capable of learning grammar, he is a man. For no one calls anything a property which can possibly belong to something else; for example, he does not say that sleep is a property of man, even though at one moment it might happen to belong to him only. If, therefore, any such thing were to be called a property, it will be so called not absolutely but as at a certain time or in a certain relation; for ' to be on the right-hand side ' is a property at a certain time, and ' biped ' is actually assigned as a property in a certain relation, for example, as a property of man in relation to a horse or a dog. That nothing which can possibly belong to something other than a certain thing is a convertible predicate of that thing is obvious; for it does not necessarily follow that if anything is sleeping it is a man. *(b)* Property.

A *genus* is that which is predicated in the category *(c)* Genus.

ARISTOTLE

102 a
τῷ εἴδει ἐν τῷ τί ἐστι κατηγορούμενον. ἐν τῷ τί
ἐστι δὲ κατηγορεῖσθαι τὰ τοιαῦτα λεγέσθω, ὅσα
ἁρμόττει ἀποδοῦναι ἐρωτηθέντα τί ἐστι τὸ προκεί-
35 μενον, καθάπερ ἐπὶ τοῦ ἀνθρώπου ἁρμόττει, ἐρωτηθέντα τί ἐστι τὸ προκείμενον, εἰπεῖν ὅτι ζῷον.
γενικὸν δὲ καὶ τὸ πότερον ἐν τῷ αὐτῷ γένει ἄλλο
ἄλλῳ ἢ ἐν ἑτέρῳ. καὶ γὰρ τὸ τοιοῦτον ὑπὸ τὴν
αὐτὴν μέθοδον πίπτει τῷ γένει· διαλεχθέντες γὰρ ὅτι
τὸ ζῷον γένος τοῦ ἀνθρώπου, ὁμοίως δὲ καὶ τοῦ
βοός, διειλεγμένοι ἐσόμεθα ὅτι ἐν τῷ αὐτῷ γένει.
102 b ἐὰν δὲ τοῦ μὲν ἑτέρου δείξωμεν ὅτι γένος ἐστί, τοῦ
δὲ ἑτέρου ὅτι οὐκ ἔστι, διειλεγμένοι ἐσόμεθα ὅτι
οὐκ ἐν τῷ αὐτῷ γένει ταῦτ' ἐστίν.

Συμβεβηκὸς δέ ἐστιν ὃ μηδὲν μὲν τούτων ἐστί,
5 μήτε ὅρος μήτε ἴδιον μήτε γένος, ὑπάρχει δὲ τῷ
πράγματι, καὶ ὃ ἐνδέχεται ὑπάρχειν ὁτῳοῦν ἑνὶ καὶ
τῷ αὐτῷ καὶ μὴ ὑπάρχειν, οἷον τὸ καθῆσθαι ἐνδέχεται ὑπάρχειν τινὶ τῷ αὐτῷ καὶ μὴ ὑπάρχειν.
ὁμοίως δὲ καὶ τὸ λευκόν· τὸ γὰρ αὐτὸ οὐθὲν κωλύει
10 ὁτὲ μὲν λευκὸν ὁτὲ δὲ μὴ λευκὸν εἶναι. ἔστι δὲ
τῶν τοῦ συμβεβηκότος ὁρισμῶν ὁ δεύτερος βελ-
τίων· τοῦ μὲν γὰρ πρώτου ῥηθέντος ἀναγκαῖον, εἰ
μέλλει τις συνήσειν, προειδέναι τί ἐστιν ὅρος καὶ
γένος καὶ ἴδιον, ὁ δὲ δεύτερος αὐτοτελής ἐστι πρὸς
τὸ γνωρίζειν τί ποτ' ἐστὶ τὸ λεγόμενον καθ' αὑτό.
15 προσκείσθωσαν δὲ τῷ συμβεβηκότι καὶ αἱ πρὸς
ἄλληλα συγκρίσεις, ὁπωσοῦν ἀπὸ τοῦ συμβεβηκότος
λεγόμεναι, οἷον πότερον τὸ καλὸν ἢ τὸ συμφέρον
284

of essence of several things which differ in kind. Predicates in the category of essence may be described as such things as are fittingly contained in the reply of one who has been asked " What is the object before you ? " For example, in the case of man, if someone is asked what the object before him is, it is fitting for him to say " An animal." The question whether one thing is in the same genus as another thing or in a different one, is also a ' generic ' question ; for such a question also falls under the same kind of inquiry as the genus. For having argued that ' animal ' is the genus of man and likewise also of ox, we shall have argued that they are in the same genus ; but if we show that it is the genus of the one but not of the other, we shall have argued that they are not in the same genus.

An *accident* is that which is none of these things— (d) Accident. neither definition, nor property, nor genus—but still belongs to the thing. Also it is something which can belong and not belong to any one particular thing ; for example, ' a sitting position ' can belong or not belong to some one particular thing. This is likewise true of ' whiteness ' ; for there is nothing to prevent the same thing being at one time white and at another not white. The second of these definitions of accident is the better ; for when the first is enunciated, it is necessary, if one is to understand it, to know beforehand what is meant by ' definition ' and ' genus ' and ' property,' whereas the second suffices of itself to enable us to know what is meant without anything more. We may place also in the category of accident comparisons of things with one another, when they are described in terms derived in any way from accident ; for example, the questions " Is the honour-

αἱρετώτερον, καὶ πότερον ὁ κατ᾽ ἀρετὴν ἢ ὁ κατ᾽
ἀπόλαυσιν ἡδίων βίος, καὶ εἴ τι ἄλλο παραπλησίως
τυγχάνει τούτοις λεγόμενον· ἐπὶ πάντων γὰρ τῶν
20 τοιούτων, ποτέρῳ μᾶλλον τὸ κατηγορούμενον συμβέβηκεν, ἡ ζήτησις γίνεται. δῆλον δ᾽ ἐξ αὐτῶν
ὅτι τὸ συμβεβηκὸς οὐθὲν κωλύει ποτὲ καὶ πρός τι
ἴδιον γίνεσθαι, οἷον τὸ καθῆσθαι συμβεβηκὸς ὄν,
ὅταν τις μόνος κάθηται, τότε ἴδιον ἔσται, μὴ μόνου
25 δὲ καθημένου πρὸς τοὺς μὴ καθημένους ἴδιον.
ὥστε καὶ πρός τι καὶ ποτὲ οὐθὲν κωλύει τὸ συμβεβηκὸς ἴδιον γίνεσθαι. ἁπλῶς δ᾽ ἴδιον οὐκ ἔσται.

VI. Μὴ λανθανέτω δ᾽ ἡμᾶς ὅτι τὰ πρὸς τὸ ἴδιον
καὶ τὸ γένος καὶ τὸ συμβεβηκὸς πάντα καὶ πρὸς
30 τοὺς ὁρισμοὺς ἁρμόσει λέγεσθαι. δείξαντες γὰρ
ὅτι οὐ μόνῳ ὑπάρχει τῷ ὑπὸ τὸν ὁρισμόν, ὥσπερ
καὶ ἐπὶ τοῦ ἰδίου, ἢ ὅτι οὐ γένος τὸ ἀποδοθὲν
ἐν τῷ ὁρισμῷ, ἢ ὅτι οὐχ ὑπάρχει τι τῶν ἐν τῷ
λόγῳ ῥηθέντων, ὅπερ καὶ ἐπὶ τοῦ συμβεβηκότος
ἂν ῥηθείη, ἀνῃρηκότες ἐσόμεθα τὸν ὁρισμόν· ὥστε
35 κατὰ τὸν ἔμπροσθεν ἀποδοθέντα λόγον ἅπαντ᾽ ἂν
εἴη τρόπον τινὰ ὁρικὰ τὰ κατηριθμημένα. ἀλλ᾽ οὐ
διὰ τοῦτο μίαν ἐπὶ πάντων καθόλου μέθοδον ζητη-
τέον· οὔτε γὰρ ῥᾴδιον εὑρεῖν τοῦτ᾽ ἐστίν, εἴ θ᾽
εὑρεθείη, παντελῶς ἀσαφὴς καὶ δύσχρηστος ἂν εἴη
πρὸς τὴν προκειμένην πραγματείαν. ἰδίας δὲ καθ᾽

able or the expedient preferable ? " and " Is the life
of virtue or the life of enjoyment more pleasant ? "
and any other question which happens to be expressed
in a similar kind of way ; for in all such cases the
question is to which of the two does the predicate
more properly belong as an accident. It is self-
evident that nothing prevents the accident from being
temporarily or relatively a property ; for example,
the position of sitting, though it is an accident, will
at the time be a property, when a man is the only
person seated, while, if he is not the only person
seated, it will be a property in relation to any persons
who are not seated. Thus nothing prevents the
accident from becoming both a relative and a temporary property, but it will never be a property
absolutely.

VI. We must not, however, omit to notice that How far can
everything which is applicable to property, genus and the pre-
accident can be fittingly applied to definitions also. treated
For when we have shown that some attribute does separately ?
not belong to the subject of the definition only (as we
do also in the case of a property), or that what is
assigned in the definition is not the true genus of the
subject, or that something mentioned in the statement does not belong (as would also be asserted in
the case of an accident), we shall have destroyed the
definition ; and so, in accordance with the statement
made above, all the cases which have been enumerated would be in a sense ' definitory.' But we must
not for this reason seek for a single method of inquiry
which is generally applicable to all of them ; for it is
not easy to discover, and if it were to be discovered,
it would be wholly obscure and difficult to apply to
our present treatise. If, however, a special method

287

ARISTOTLE

ἕκαστον τῶν διορισθέντων γενῶν ἀποδοθείσης μεθ-
όδου ῥᾷον ἐκ τῶν περὶ ἕκαστον οἰκείων ἡ διέξ-
οδος τοῦ προκειμένου γένοιτ' ἄν. ὥστε τύπῳ
μὲν, καθάπερ εἴρηται πρότερον, διαιρετέον, τῶν δὲ
λοιπῶν τὰ μάλισθ' ἑκάστοις οἰκεῖα προσαπτέον,
ὁρικά τε καὶ γενικὰ προσαγορεύοντας αὐτά. σχε-
5 δὸν δὲ προσῆπται τὰ ῥηθέντα πρὸς ἑκάστοις.

VII. Πρῶτον δὲ πάντων περὶ ταὐτοῦ διοριστέον,
ποσαχῶς λέγεται. δόξειε δ' ἂν τὸ ταὐτὸν ὡς τύπῳ
λαβεῖν τριχῇ διαιρεῖσθαι. ἀριθμῷ γὰρ ἢ εἴδει ἢ
γένει τὸ ταὐτὸν εἰώθαμεν προσαγορεύειν, ἀριθμῷ
10 μὲν ὧν ὀνόματα πλείω τὸ δὲ πρᾶγμα ἕν, οἷον
λώπιον καὶ ἱμάτιον, εἴδει δὲ ὅσα πλείω ὄντα ἀδιάφορα κατὰ τὸ εἶδός ἐστι, καθάπερ ἄνθρωπος ἀνθρώπῳ καὶ ἵππος ἵππῳ· τὰ γὰρ τοιαῦτα τῷ εἴδει
λέγεται ταὐτά, ὅσα ὑπὸ ταὐτὸ εἶδος. ὁμοίως δὲ
καὶ γένει ταὐτά, ὅσα ὑπὸ ταὐτὸ γένος ἐστίν, οἷον
15 ἵππος ἀνθρώπῳ. δόξειε δ' ἂν τὸ ἀπὸ τῆς αὐτῆς
κρήνης ὕδωρ ταὐτὸν λεγόμενον ἔχειν τινὰ διαφορὰν
παρὰ τοὺς εἰρημένους τρόπους· οὐ μὴν ἀλλὰ καὶ
τὸ τοιοῦτόν γε ἐν τῷ αὐτῷ τετάχθω τοῖς καθ' ἓν
εἶδος ὁπωσοῦν λεγομένοις. ἅπαντα γὰρ τὰ τοιαῦτα
συγγενῆ καὶ παραπλήσια ἀλλήλοις ἔοικεν εἶναι.
20 πᾶν μὲν γὰρ ὕδωρ παντὶ ταὐτὸν τῷ εἴδει λέγεται
διὰ τὸ ἔχειν τινὰ ὁμοιότητα, τὸ δ' ἀπὸ τῆς αὐτῆς
κρήνης ὕδωρ οὐδενὶ ἄλλῳ διαφέρει ἀλλ' ἢ τῷ
σφοδροτέραν εἶναι τὴν ὁμοιότητα· διὸ οὐ χωρίζομεν
288

of inquiry is provided for each of the different classes which we have distinguished, the exposition of the subject before us would be more easily performed on the basis of what is appropriate to each class. And so, as has already been said, we must make broad divisions and fit into them those of the other questions which are most appropriate to each, calling them ' definitory ' and ' generic.' The questions to which I referred have now been, for all intents and purposes, assigned to their several classes.

VII. First of all we must distinguish the various meanings of ' the same.' In general, ' sameness ' would seem to fall into three divisions ; for we usually speak of numerical, specific and generic sameness. There is *numerical* sameness when there is more than one name for the same thing, *e.g.*, ' mantle ' and ' cloak.' There is *specific* sameness when there are several things but they do not differ in species, *e.g.*, one man and another man, one horse and another horse ; for such things as fall under the same species are said to be specifically the same. Similarly things are *generically* the same when they fall under the same genus, *e.g.*, horse and man. Water from the same fountain described as ' the same water ' might seem to have a sameness differing somewhat from the above-mentioned kinds ; however, a case of this kind ought also to be placed in the same class as those which are called in any sense the same as belonging to one species. For all such things seem to be akin and similar to one another ; for any water is said to be specifically the same as any other water because it has a certain similarity to it, and water from the same fountain differs in no other respect than in its more striking degree of similarity ; and so we do not

The various uses of the term ' *sameness* ' :

(a) Numerical.

(b) Specific.

(c) Generic.

103 a

αὐτὸ τῶν καθ' ἓν εἶδος ὁπωσοῦν λεγομένων. μάλιστα δ' ὁμολογουμένως τὸ ἓν ἀριθμῷ ταὐτὸν παρὰ
25 πᾶσι δοκεῖ λέγεσθαι. εἴωθε δὲ καὶ τοῦτο ἀποδίδοσθαι πλεοναχῶς, κυριώτατα μὲν καὶ πρώτως
ὅταν ὀνόματι ἢ ὅρῳ τὸ ταὐτὸν ἀποδοθῇ, καθάπερ
ἱμάτιον λωπίῳ καὶ ζῷον πεζὸν δίπουν ἀνθρώπῳ,
δεύτερον δ' ὅταν τῷ ἰδίῳ, καθάπερ τὸ ἐπιστήμης
δεκτικὸν ἀνθρώπῳ καὶ τὸ τῇ φύσει ἄνω φερόμενον
30 πυρί, τρίτον δ' ὅταν ἀπὸ τοῦ συμβεβηκότος, οἷον
τὸ καθήμενον ἢ τὸ μουσικὸν Σωκράτει. πάντα γὰρ
ταῦτα τὸ ἓν ἀριθμῷ βούλεται σημαίνειν. ὅτι δ'
ἀληθὲς τὸ νῦν ῥηθέν ἐστιν, ἐκ τῶν μεταβαλλόντων
τὰς προσηγορίας μάλιστ' ἄν τις καταμάθοι. πολλάκις γὰρ ἐπιτάσσοντες ὀνόματι καλέσαι τινὰ τῶν
35 καθημένων μεταβάλλομεν, ὅταν τύχῃ μὴ συνιεὶς
ᾧ τὴν πρόσταξιν ποιούμεθα, ὡς ἀπὸ τοῦ συμβεβηκότος αὐτοῦ μᾶλλον συνήσοντος, καὶ κελεύομεν
τὸν καθήμενον ἢ διαλεγόμενον καλέσαι πρὸς ἡμᾶς,
δῆλον ὡς ταὐτὸν ὑπολαμβάνοντες κατά τε τοὔνομα
καὶ κατὰ τὸ συμβεβηκὸς σημαίνειν.

103 b   VIII. Τὸ μὲν οὖν ταὐτόν, καθάπερ εἴρηται, τριχῇ
διῃρήσθω. ὅτι δ' ἐκ τῶν πρότερον εἰρημένων οἱ
λόγοι καὶ διὰ τούτων καὶ πρὸς ταῦτα, μία μὲν

---

[a] But not saying he was seated.

distinguish it from the things called in any sense the same as belonging to one species. The term ' the same ' seems to be applied with the most general acceptance of everyone to that which is numerically one. But even this is usually employed in several senses. Its principal and primary sense occurs when sameness is applied to a name or a definition, *e.g.*, when a ' cloak ' is said to be the same as a ' mantle,' or when ' a biped pedestrian animal ' is said to be the same as a ' man.' A second sense occurs when sameness is applied to a property, *e.g.*, when ' capable of receiving knowledge ' is said to be the same as ' man,' and ' that which is naturally carried upwards ' is said to be the same as ' fire.' A third sense occurs when the sameness is based on an accident, *e.g.*, when ' that which is seated ' or ' that which is musical ' is said to be the same as ' Socrates.' All these uses aim at indicating numerical oneness. That what we have just said is true can best be understood by a change of the manner of description ; for often when we order someone to summon one of several seated persons, giving his name,[a] we change the description when the person to whom we are giving the order does not happen to understand, since he will understand better from some accidental feature ; we, therefore, tell him to summon ' the man who is seated ' or ' the man who is talking,' obviously conceiving that we are indicating the same thing both when we name it and when we state an accident of it.

VIII. Of ' sameness,' then, as has been said, three senses can be distinguished. Now that arguments start from the above-mentioned elements and proceed through them and lead up to them is proved, in the

Twofold proof of the division of predicables.

291

ARISTOTLE

πίστις ἡ διὰ τῆς ἐπαγωγῆς· εἰ γάρ τις ἐπισκοποίη
ἑκάστην τῶν προτάσεων καὶ τῶν προβλημάτων,
5 φαίνοιτ᾽ ἂν ἢ ἀπὸ τοῦ ὅρου ἢ ἀπὸ τοῦ ἰδίου ἢ ἀπὸ
τοῦ γένους ἢ ἀπὸ τοῦ συμβεβηκότος γεγενημένη.
ἄλλη δὲ πίστις ἡ διὰ συλλογισμοῦ. ἀνάγκη γὰρ
πᾶν τὸ περί τινος κατηγορούμενον ἤτοι ἀντικατ-
ηγορεῖσθαι τοῦ πράγματος ἢ μή. καὶ εἰ μὲν ἀντι-
10 κατηγορεῖται, ὅρος ἢ ἴδιον ἂν εἴη· εἰ μὲν γὰρ
σημαίνει τὸ τί ἦν εἶναι, ὅρος, εἰ δὲ μὴ σημαίνει,
ἴδιον· τοῦτο γὰρ ἦν ἴδιον, τὸ ἀντικατηγορούμενον
μέν, μὴ σημαῖνον δὲ τὸ τί ἦν εἶναι. εἰ δὲ μὴ
ἀντικατηγορεῖται τοῦ πράγματος, ἤτοι τῶν ἐν τῷ
ὁρισμῷ τοῦ ὑποκειμένου λεγομένων ἐστὶν ἢ οὔ.
15 καὶ εἰ μὲν τῶν ἐν τῷ ὁρισμῷ λεγομένων, γένος
ἢ διαφορὰ ἂν εἴη, ἐπειδὴ ὁ ὁρισμὸς ἐκ γένους καὶ
διαφορῶν ἐστίν· εἰ δὲ μὴ τῶν ἐν τῷ ὁρισμῷ
λεγομένων ἐστί, δῆλον ὅτι συμβεβηκὸς ἂν εἴη· τὸ
γὰρ συμβεβηκὸς ἐλέγετο ὃ μήτε ὅρος μήτε γένος
μήτε ἴδιόν ἐστιν, ὑπάρχει δὲ τῷ πράγματι.
20 IX. Μετὰ τοίνυν ταῦτα δεῖ διορίσασθαι τὰ γένη
τῶν κατηγοριῶν, ἐν οἷς ὑπάρχουσιν αἱ ῥηθεῖσαι
τέτταρες. ἔστι δὲ ταῦτα τὸν ἀριθμὸν δέκα, τί
ἐστι, ποσόν, ποιόν, πρός τι, ποῦ, ποτέ, κεῖσθαι,
ἔχειν, ποιεῖν, πάσχειν. ἀεὶ γὰρ τὸ συμβεβηκὸς
25 καὶ τὸ γένος καὶ τὸ ἴδιον καὶ ὁ ὁρισμὸς ἐν μιᾷ
τούτων τῶν κατηγοριῶν ἔσται· πᾶσαι γὰρ αἱ διὰ
τούτων προτάσεις ἢ τί ἐστιν ἢ ποιὸν ἢ ποσὸν ἢ
τῶν ἄλλων τινὰ κατηγοριῶν σημαίνουσιν. δῆλον

first place, by *induction*. For if one were to examine each separate proposition and problem, it would be clear that it has come into being either from the definition of something or from its property or from its genus or from its accident. Another proof is through *reasoning*; for necessarily anything which is predicated about something must either be or not be convertible with its subject. If it is convertible, it would be a definition or a property; for if it indicates the essence, it is a definition, but, if it does not do so, it is a property; for we saw [a] that this was a property, namely, that which is predicated convertibly but does not indicate the essence. If, however, it is not predicated convertibly with the subject, it either is or is not one of the terms given in the definition of the subject; and if it is one of the terms in the definition, it must be either the genus or the differentia, since the definition is composed of genus and differentiae. If, however, it is not one of the terms given in the definition, obviously it must be an accident; for the accident was said [b] to be that which, while it belongs to the subject, is neither a definition nor a genus nor a property.

IX. Next we must define the kinds of categories in which the four above-mentioned predicates are found. They are ten in number: essence, quantity, quality, relation, place, time, position, state, activity, passivity. For the accident, the genus, the property and the definition will always be in one of these categories; for all propositions made by means of these indicate either essence or quality or quantity or one of the other categories. It is self-evident that he who

The ten Categories and their relation to the predicables.

---

[a] 102 a 18.
[b] 102 b 4.

103 b

δ' ἐξ αὐτῶν ὅτι ὁ τὸ τί ἐστι σημαίνων ὁτὲ μὲν
οὐσίαν σημαίνει, ὁτὲ δὲ ποιόν, ὁτὲ δὲ τῶν ἄλλων
τινὰ κατηγοριῶν. ὅταν μὲν γὰρ ἐκκειμένου ἀν-
30 θρώπου φῇ τὸ ἐκκείμενον ἄνθρωπον εἶναι ἢ ζῷον,
τί ἐστι λέγει καὶ οὐσίαν σημαίνει· ὅταν δὲ χρώματος λευκοῦ ἐκκειμένου φῇ τὸ ἐκκείμενον λευκὸν
εἶναι ἢ χρῶμα, τί ἐστι λέγει καὶ ποιὸν σημαίνει.
ὁμοίως δὲ καὶ ἐὰν πηχυαίου μεγέθους ἐκκειμένου
φῇ τὸ ἐκκείμενον πηχυαῖον εἶναι μέγεθος, τί ἐστιν
35 ἐρεῖ καὶ ποσὸν σημαίνει. ὁμοίως δὲ καὶ ἐπὶ τῶν
ἄλλων· ἕκαστον γὰρ τῶν τοιούτων, ἐάν τε αὐτὸ
περὶ αὑτοῦ λέγηται ἐάν τε τὸ γένος περὶ τούτου,
τί ἐστι σημαίνει. ὅταν δὲ περὶ ἑτέρου, οὐ τί ἐστι
σημαίνει, ἀλλὰ ποσὸν ἢ ποιὸν ἢ τινα τῶν ἄλλων
κατηγοριῶν. ὥστε περὶ ὧν μὲν οἱ λόγοι καὶ ἐξ
104 a ὧν, ταῦτα καὶ τοσαῦτά ἐστι· πῶς δὲ ληψόμεθα καὶ
δι' ὧν εὐπορήσομεν, μετὰ ταῦτα λεκτέον.

X. Πρῶτον τοίνυν διωρίσθω, τί ἐστι πρότασις
διαλεκτικὴ καὶ τί πρόβλημα διαλεκτικόν. οὐ γὰρ
πᾶσαν πρότασιν οὐδὲ πᾶν πρόβλημα διαλεκτικὸν
5 θετέον· οὐδεὶς γὰρ ἂν προτείνειε νοῦν ἔχων τὸ μηδενὶ δοκοῦν, οὐδὲ προβάλοι τὸ πᾶσι φανερὸν ἢ τοῖς
πλείστοις· τὰ μὲν γὰρ οὐκ ἔχει ἀπορίαν, τὰ δ'
οὐδεὶς ἂν θείη. ἔστι δὲ πρότασις διαλεκτικὴ ἐρώ-
τησις ἔνδοξος ἢ πᾶσιν ἢ τοῖς πλείστοις ἢ τοῖς
10 σοφοῖς, καὶ τούτοις ἢ πᾶσιν ἢ τοῖς πλείστοις ἢ τοῖς

294

indicates the essence of something, indicates sometimes a substance, sometimes a quality, and sometimes one of the other categories.   For when a man
is put before him and he says that what is put before
him is a man or an animal, he states an essence and
indicates a substance ; but when a white colour is put
before him and he says that what is put before him is
white or a colour, he states an essence and indicates
a quality.   Similarly, if a magnitude of a cubit is put
before him and he says that what is put before him is
a magnitude of a cubit, he will be stating an essence
and is indicating a quantity.   Similarly with the other
kinds of predicates ; for each of such things, both if
it be asserted about itself and if its genus be asserted
about it, indicates an essence ; but when it is asserted about something else, it does not indicate an
essence but a quality or quantity or one of the other
categories.   Such then is the nature and such is
the number of the subjects about which arguments
take place and the materials on which they are
based.   How we shall derive them and by what
means we shall obtain a supply of them, must next
be stated.

X. In the first place then let us define the nature Dialectical
of a dialectical proposition and a dialectical problem. Proposi-
tions.
For not every proposition and every problem can be
put down as dialectical ; for no man of sense would
put into a proposition that which is no one's opinion,
nor into a problem that which is manifest to everyone
or to most people ; for the latter raises no question,
while the former no one would accept.   Now a *dialectical proposition* is a question which accords with the
opinion held by everyone or by the majority or by the
wise—either all of the wise or the majority or the most

104 a

μάλιστα γνωρίμοις, μὴ παράδοξος· θείη γὰρ ἄν τις
τὸ δοκοῦν τοῖς σοφοῖς, ἐὰν μὴ ἐναντίον ταῖς τῶν
πολλῶν δόξαις ᾖ. εἰσὶ δὲ προτάσεις διαλεκτικαὶ
καὶ τὰ τοῖς ἐνδόξοις ὅμοια, καὶ τἀναντία κατ' ἀντίφασιν τοῖς δοκοῦσιν ἐνδόξοις εἶναι προτεινόμενα,
15 καὶ ὅσαι δόξαι κατὰ τέχνας εἰσὶ τὰς εὑρημένας. εἰ
γὰρ ἔνδοξον τὸ τὴν αὐτὴν εἶναι τῶν ἐναντίων ἐπιστήμην, καὶ τὸ αἴσθησιν τὴν αὐτὴν εἶναι τῶν ἐναντίων ἔνδοξον ἂν φανείη, καὶ εἰ μίαν ἀριθμῷ
γραμματικὴν εἶναι, καὶ αὐλητικὴν μίαν, εἰ δὲ πλείους γραμματικάς, καὶ αὐλητικὰς πλείους· πάντα
20 γὰρ ὅμοια καὶ συγγενῆ ταῦτ' ἔοικεν εἶναι. ὁμοίως
δὲ καὶ τὰ τοῖς ἐνδόξοις ἐναντία κατ' ἀντίφασιν προτεινόμενα ἔνδοξα φανεῖται· εἰ γὰρ ἔνδοξον ὅτι δεῖ
τοὺς φίλους εὖ ποιεῖν, καὶ ὅτι οὐ δεῖ κακῶς ποιεῖν
ἔνδοξον. ἔστι δ' ἐναντίον μὲν ὅτι δεῖ κακῶς ποιεῖν
25 τοὺς φίλους, κατ' ἀντίφασιν δὲ ὅτι οὐ δεῖ κακῶς
ποιεῖν. ὁμοίως δὲ καὶ εἰ δεῖ τοὺς φίλους εὖ ποιεῖν,
τοὺς ἐχθροὺς οὐ δεῖ. ἔστι δὲ καὶ τοῦτο κατ' ἀντίφασιν τῶν ἐναντίων· τὸ γὰρ ἐναντίον ἐστὶν ὅτι
δεῖ τοὺς ἐχθροὺς εὖ ποιεῖν. ὡσαύτως δὲ καὶ ἐπὶ
τῶν ἄλλων. ἔνδοξον δ' ἐν παραβολῇ φανεῖται καὶ
τὸ ἐναντίον περὶ τοῦ ἐναντίου, οἷον εἰ τοὺς φίλους
30 δεῖ εὖ ποιεῖν, καὶ τοὺς ἐχθροὺς δεῖ κακῶς. φανείη

famous of them—and which is not paradoxical; for one would accept the opinion of the wise, if it is not opposed to the views of the majority. Views which are similar to received opinions are also dialectical propositions, and so also are propositions made by way of contradicting the contrary of received opinions, and also views which accord with the arts which have been discovered. For if it is a received opinion that the knowledge of contraries is the same, it might seem to be a received opinion that the perception also of contraries is the same; and if it is a received opinion that there is a single art of grammar, it might seem to be a received opinion that there is also only one art of flute-playing, whereas if it is a received opinion that there is more than one art of grammar, it might seem to be a received opinion that there is also more than one art of flute-playing; for all these seem to be similar and akin. In like manner, also, propositions made by way of contradicting the contrary of received opinions will seem to be received opinions; for if it is a received opinion that one ought to do good to one's friends, it will also be a received opinion that one ought not to do them harm. Now that we ought to harm our friends is contrary to the received opinion, and this stated in a contradictory form is that we ought not to harm our friends. Likewise also, if we ought to do good to our friends, we ought not to do good to our enemies; this also takes the form of a contradiction of contraries, for the contrary is that we ought to do good to our enemies. The same is true of all the other cases. The contrary stated about the contrary in a comparison will also appear to be a received opinion; for example, if we ought to do good to our friends, we ought also to do harm to our

ARISTOTLE

104 a

δ' ἂν καὶ ἐναντίον τὸ τοὺς φίλους εὖ ποιεῖν τῷ τοὺς
ἐχθροὺς κακῶς· πότερον δὲ καὶ κατ' ἀλήθειαν
οὕτως ἔχει ἢ οὔ, ἐν τοῖς ὑπὲρ τῶν ἐναντίων
λεγομένοις ῥηθήσεται. δῆλον δ' ὅτι καὶ ὅσαι δόξαι
κατὰ τέχνας εἰσί, διαλεκτικαὶ προτάσεις εἰσί· θείη
35 γὰρ ἄν τις τὰ δοκοῦντα τοῖς ὑπὲρ τούτων ἐπεσκεμ-
μένοις, οἷον περὶ μὲν τῶν ἐν ἰατρικῇ ὡς ὁ ἰατρός,
περὶ δὲ τῶν ἐν γεωμετρίᾳ ὡς ὁ γεωμέτρης· ὁμοίως
δὲ καὶ ἐπὶ τῶν ἄλλων.

104 b

XI. Πρόβλημα δ' ἐστὶ διαλεκτικὸν θεώρημα τὸ
συντεῖνον ἢ πρὸς αἵρεσιν καὶ φυγὴν ἢ πρὸς ἀλήθειαν καὶ γνῶσιν, ἢ αὐτὸ ἢ ὡς συνεργὸν πρός τι
ἕτερον τῶν τοιούτων· περὶ οὗ ἢ οὐδετέρως δοξά-
ζουσιν ἢ ἐναντίως οἱ πολλοὶ τοῖς σοφοῖς ἢ οἱ
5 σοφοὶ τοῖς πολλοῖς ἢ ἑκάτεροι αὐτοὶ ἑαυτοῖς. ἔνια
μὲν γὰρ τῶν προβλημάτων χρήσιμον εἰδέναι πρὸς
τὸ ἑλέσθαι ἢ φυγεῖν, οἷον πότερον ἡ ἡδονὴ αἱρετὸν
ἢ οὔ, ἔνια δὲ πρὸς τὸ εἰδέναι μόνον, οἷον πότερον
ὁ κόσμος ἀΐδιος ἢ οὔ, ἔνια δὲ αὐτὰ μὲν καθ' αὑτὰ
10 πρὸς οὐδέτερον τούτων, συνεργὰ δέ ἐστι πρός τινα
τῶν τοιούτων· πολλὰ γὰρ αὐτὰ μὲν καθ' αὑτὰ οὐ
βουλόμεθα γνωρίζειν, ἑτέρων δ' ἕνεκα, ὅπως διὰ
τούτων ἄλλο τι γνωρίσωμεν. ἔστι δὲ προβλήματα καὶ ὧν ἐναντίοι εἰσὶ συλλογισμοί (ἀπορίαν
γὰρ ἔχει πότερον οὕτως ἔχει ἢ οὐχ οὕτως διὰ τὸ

enemies. To do good to one's friends might also appear to be the contrary of doing harm to one's enemies ; but whether this is really true or not will be dealt with in our discussions of contraries.[a] It is also obvious that all opinions which accord with the arts are dialectical propositions ; for one would accept the opinions of those who have examined the subjects in question. For example, on questions of medicine one would think as the doctor thinks and in matters of geometry as the geometrician thinks, and so too with the other arts.

XI. A *dialectical problem* is an investigation leading either to choice and avoidance or to truth and knowledge, either by itself or as an aid to the solution of some other such problem. Its subject is something about which either men have no opinion either way, or most people hold an opinion contrary to that of the wise, or the wise contrary to that of most people, or about which members of each of these classes disagree among themselves. The knowledge of some of these problems is useful for the purpose of choice or avoidance ; for example, whether pleasure is worthy of choice or not. The knowledge of some of these is useful purely for the sake of knowledge, for example, whether the universe is eternal or not. Others, again, are not useful in themselves for either of these purposes but as an aid to the solution of some similar problem ; for there are many things which we do not wish to know for themselves but for other purposes, in order that through them we may obtain knowledge of something else. Problems also occur where reasonings are in conflict (for they involve a doubt whether something is so or not, because there

Dialectical Problems.

[a] 112 b 27 ff.

περὶ ἀμφοτέρων εἶναι λόγους πιθανούς) καὶ περὶ
15 ὧν λόγον μὴ ἔχομεν ὄντων μεγάλων, χαλεπὸν οἰόμενοι εἶναι τὸ διὰ τί ἀποδοῦναι, οἷον πότερον ὁ
κόσμος ἀΐδιος ἢ οὔ· καὶ γὰρ τὰ τοιαῦτα ζητήσειεν
ἄν τις.

Τὰ μὲν οὖν προβλήματα καὶ αἱ προτάσεις, καθάπερ εἴρηται, διωρίσθω· θέσις δέ ἐστιν ὑπόληψις
20 παράδοξος τῶν γνωρίμων τινὸς κατὰ φιλοσοφίαν,
οἷον ὅτι οὐκ ἔστιν ἀντιλέγειν, καθάπερ ἔφη Ἀντι-
σθένης, ἢ ὅτι πάντα κινεῖται καθ' Ἡράκλειτον,
ἢ ὅτι ἓν τὸ ὄν, καθάπερ Μέλισσός φησιν· τὸ γὰρ
τοῦ τυχόντος ἐναντία ταῖς δόξαις ἀποφηναμένου
φροντίζειν εὔηθες. ἢ περὶ ὧν λόγον ἔχομεν ἐναν-
25 τίον ταῖς δόξαις, οἷον ὅτι οὐ πᾶν τὸ ὂν ἤτοι γενό-
μενόν ἐστιν ἢ ἀΐδιον, καθάπερ οἱ σοφισταί φασιν·
μουσικὸν γὰρ ὄντα γραμματικὸν εἶναι οὔτε γενόμενον οὔτε ἀΐδιον ὄντα. τοῦτο γάρ, εἰ καί τινι μὴ
δοκεῖ, δόξειεν ἂν διὰ τὸ λόγον ἔχειν.

Ἔστι μὲν οὖν καὶ ἡ θέσις πρόβλημα· οὐ πᾶν δὲ
30 πρόβλημα θέσις, ἐπειδὴ ἔνια τῶν προβλημάτων
τοιαῦτ' ἐστὶ περὶ ὧν οὐδετέρως δοξάζομεν. ὅτι δέ
ἐστι καὶ ἡ θέσις πρόβλημα, δῆλον· ἀνάγκη γὰρ ἐκ
τῶν εἰρημένων ἢ τοὺς πολλοὺς τοῖς σοφοῖς περὶ τὴν
θέσιν ἀμφισβητεῖν ἢ ὁποτερουσοῦν ἑαυτοῖς, ἐπειδὴ
35 ὑπόληψίς τις παράδοξος ἡ θέσις ἐστίν. σχεδὸν δὲ
νῦν πάντα τὰ διαλεκτικὰ προβλήματα θέσεις κα-
λοῦνται. διαφερέτω δὲ μηδὲν ὁπωσοῦν λεγόμενον·
οὐ γὰρ ὀνοματοποιῆσαι βουλόμενοι διείλομεν οὕτως

are strong arguments on both sides), and also where, because the questions are so vast, we have no argument to offer, thinking it difficult to assign a reason, for example, whether the universe is eternal or not ; for one might inquire into such questions also.

Let problems, then, and propositions be defined in the manner already stated. A thesis is the conception contrary to general opinion but propounded by someone famous as a philosopher ; for example, "Contradiction is impossible," as Antisthenes said, or the opinion of Heraclitus that " All things are in a state of motion " or " Being is one," as Melissus says ; for to pay any attention when an ordinary person sets forth views which are contrary to received opinions is foolish. Or a thesis may concern matters about which we hold a reasoned view contrary to received opinions ; for example, the view of the sophists that not everything which is has come into being or is eternal ; for a musical man, who is a grammarian, is a grammarian, though he has not come to be so and is not so eternally. This view, even if it is not acceptable to some people, might be accepted on the ground that it is reasonable.

A thesis is also a problem ; but not every problem is a thesis, since some problems are such that we hold no opinion about them either way. That a thesis is also a problem is obvious ; for it necessarily follows from what has been already said that either the many are at variance with the wise about a thesis or that one of these two classes is at variance within itself, since a thesis is a conception which is contrary to accepted opinion. Almost all dialectical problems are now called theses. But it need not matter which of the two names is used ; for we distinguished them

105 a αὐτά, ἀλλ᾿ ἵνα μὴ λανθάνωσιν ἡμᾶς τίνες αὐτῶν
τυγχάνουσιν οὖσαι διαφοραί.

Οὐ δεῖ δὲ πᾶν πρόβλημα οὐδὲ πᾶσαν θέσιν ἐπισκοπεῖν, ἀλλ᾿ ἣν ἀπορήσειεν ἄν τις τῶν λόγου
5 δεομένων καὶ μὴ κολάσεως ἢ αἰσθήσεως· οἱ μὲν
γὰρ ἀποροῦντες πότερον δεῖ τοὺς θεοὺς τιμᾶν καὶ
τοὺς γονέας ἀγαπᾶν ἢ οὒ κολάσεως δέονται, οἱ δὲ
πότερον ἡ χιὼν λευκὴ ἢ οὒ αἰσθήσεως. οὐδὲ δὴ
ὧν σύνεγγυς ἡ ἀπόδειξις, οὐδ᾿ ὧν λίαν πόρρω· τὰ
μὲν γὰρ οὐκ ἔχει ἀπορίαν, τὰ δὲ πλείω ἢ κατὰ
γυμναστικήν.

10 XII. Διωρισμένων δὲ τούτων χρὴ διελέσθαι πόσα
τῶν λόγων εἴδη τῶν διαλεκτικῶν. ἔστι δὲ τὸ μὲν
ἐπαγωγή, τὸ δὲ συλλογισμός. καὶ συλλογισμὸς
μὲν τί ἐστιν, εἴρηται πρότερον, ἐπαγωγὴ δὲ ἡ ἀπὸ
τῶν καθ᾿ ἕκαστον ἐπὶ τὰ καθόλου ἔφοδος, οἷον εἰ
15 ἔστι κυβερνήτης ὁ ἐπιστάμενος κράτιστος καὶ ἡνί-
οχος, καὶ ὅλως ἐστὶν ὁ ἐπιστάμενος περὶ ἕκαστον
ἄριστος. ἔστι δ᾿ ἡ μὲν ἐπαγωγὴ πιθανώτερον καὶ
σαφέστερον καὶ κατὰ τὴν αἴσθησιν γνωριμώτερον
καὶ τοῖς πολλοῖς κοινόν, ὁ δὲ συλλογισμὸς βιαστι-
κώτερον καὶ πρὸς τοὺς ἀντιλογικοὺς ἐνεργέστερον.

20 XIII. Τὰ μὲν οὖν γένη περὶ ὧν τε οἱ λόγοι καὶ
ἐξ ὧν, καθάπερ ἔμπροσθεν εἴρηται, διωρίσθω· τὰ
δ᾿ ὄργανα, δι᾿ ὧν εὐπορήσομεν τῶν συλλογισμῶν
[καὶ τῶν ἐπαγωγῶν,][1] ἐστὶ τέτταρα, ἓν μὲν τὸ
προτάσεις λαβεῖν, δεύτερον δὲ ποσαχῶς ἕκαστον

---

[1] Omitting καὶ τῶν ἐπαγωγῶν with AB.

thus not from a desire to invent new terms, but that it might not escape us what differences actually exist between them.

It is not necessary to examine every problem and every thesis but only one about which doubt might be felt by the kind of person who requires to be argued with and does not need castigation or lack perception. For those who feel doubt whether or not the gods ought to be honoured and parents loved, need castigation, while those who doubt whether snow is white or not, lack perception. We ought not to discuss subjects the demonstration of which is too ready to hand or too remote ; for the former raise no difficulty, while the latter involve difficulties which are outside the scope of dialectical training.

XII. These definitions having been drawn up, we must distinguish how many kinds of dialectical argument there are. Now there is, firstly, induction, and, secondly, reasoning. What reasoning is has been already stated.[a] Induction is the progress from particulars to universals ; for example, " If the skilled pilot is the best pilot and the skilled charioteer the best charioteer, then, in general, the skilled man is the best man in any particular sphere." Induction is more convincing and clear and more easily grasped by sense-perception and is shared by the majority of people, but reasoning is more cogent and more efficacious against argumentative opponents. Induction and Reasoning.

XIII. Let the above, then, be the distinctions which we make in the kinds of things with which arguments are concerned and of which they consist. The means by which we shall obtain an abundance of reasonings are four in number : (1) the provision of propositions, (2) the ability to distinguish in how THE PRO-VISION OF ARGU-MENTS (I. 13-VII. 5). Four sources of Arguments.

105 a

25 λέγεται δύνασθαι διελεῖν, τρίτον τὰς διαφορὰς εὑρεῖν, τέταρτον δὲ ἡ τοῦ ὁμοίου σκέψις. ἔστι δὲ
τρόπον τινὰ καὶ τὰ τρία τούτων προτάσεις· ἔστι
γὰρ καθ' ἕκαστον αὐτῶν ποιῆσαι πρότασιν, οἷον
ὅτι αἱρετόν ἐστι τὸ καλὸν ἢ τὸ ἡδὺ ἢ τὸ συμφέρον,
καὶ ὅτι διαφέρει αἴσθησις ἐπιστήμης τῷ τὴν μὲν
30 ἀποβαλόντι δυνατὸν εἶναι πάλιν λαβεῖν, τὴν δ'
ἀδύνατον, καὶ ὅτι ὁμοίως ἔχει τὸ ὑγιεινὸν πρὸς
ὑγίειαν καὶ τὸ εὐεκτικὸν πρὸς εὐεξίαν. ἔστι δ' ἡ
μὲν πρώτη πρότασις ἀπὸ τοῦ πολλαχῶς λεγομένου,
ἡ δὲ δευτέρα ἀπὸ τῶν διαφορῶν, ἡ δὲ τρίτη ἀπὸ
τῶν ὁμοίων.

XIV. Τὰς μὲν οὖν προτάσεις ἐκλεκτέον ὁσαχῶς
35 διωρίσθη περὶ προτάσεως, ἢ τὰς πάντων δόξας προ-
χειριζόμενον ἢ τὰς τῶν πλείστων ἢ τὰς τῶν σοφῶν,
καὶ τούτων ἢ πάντων ἢ τῶν πλείστων ἢ τῶν γνω-
105 b ριμωτάτων, ἢ τὰς ἐναντίας ταῖς φαινομέναις, καὶ
ὅσαι δόξαι κατὰ τέχνας εἰσίν. δεῖ δὲ προτείνειν
καὶ τὰς ἐναντίας ταῖς φαινομέναις ἐνδόξοις κατ'
ἀντίφασιν, καθάπερ εἴρηται πρότερον. χρήσιμον δὲ
καὶ τὸ ποιεῖν αὐτὰς ἐν τῷ ἐκλέγειν μὴ μόνον τὰς
5 οὔσας ἐνδόξους, ἀλλὰ καὶ τὰς ὁμοίας ταύταις, οἷον
ὅτι τῶν ἐναντίων ἡ αὐτὴ αἴσθησις (καὶ γὰρ ἡ ἐπιστήμη) καὶ ὅτι ὁρῶμεν εἰσδεχόμενοί τι, οὐκ ἐκ-
πέμποντες· καὶ γὰρ καὶ ἐπὶ τῶν ἄλλων αἰσθήσεων
οὕτως· ἀκούομέν τε γὰρ εἰσδεχόμενοί τι, οὐκ ἐκ-
πέμποντες, καὶ γευόμεθα ὡσαύτως. ὁμοίως δὲ

---

^a 104 a 21.

many senses a particular expression is used, (3) the discovery of differences and (4) the investigation of similarities. The last three of these are also in a sense propositions ; for it is possible to make a proposition in accordance with each of them. For example, we can say (a) " An object of choice is the honourable or the pleasant or the expedient," (b) " Sensation differs from knowledge, because it is possible to recover the latter when one has lost it but not the former," and (c) " The healthy stands in the same relation to health as the sound to soundness." The first proposition is derived from the use of a word in several senses, the second from differences, and the third from similarities.

XIV. The number of ways in which the proposi- ^{How to} tions must be selected is the same as the number of ^{secure pro-} distinctions which we have made regarding proposi-^{positions.} tions. One may choose either universal opinions, or those of the majority, or those of the wise—of all of them, or of the majority or of the most famous— or opinions contrary to those which appear to be generally held, and also opinions which are in accord with the arts. Propositions must also be formed from opinions contrary to those which appear to be generally accepted put into a contradictory form, as has been described before.[a] Another useful method of forming them is by choosing not only opinions actually received but also opinions which resemble these, for example, " The perception of contraries is the same " (for the knowledge of them is also the same), and " We see by admitting, not by emitting, something " (for this is also true in respect of the other senses) ; for we hear by admitting, not by emitting something, and we taste in the same

105 b
10 καὶ ἐπὶ τῶν ἄλλων. ἔτι ὅσα ἐπὶ πάντων ἢ τῶν
πλείστων φαίνεται, ληπτέον ὡς ἀρχὴν καὶ δοκοῦσαν
θέσιν· τιθέασι γὰρ οἱ μὴ συνορῶντες ἐπί τινος οὐχ
οὕτως ἔχειν.[1] ἐκλέγειν δὲ χρὴ καὶ ἐκ τῶν γεγραμ-
μένων λόγων, τὰς δὲ διαγραφὰς ποιεῖσθαι περὶ
ἑκάστου γένους ὑποτιθέντας χωρίς, οἷον περὶ ἀγα-
15 θοῦ ἢ περὶ ζῴου καὶ περὶ ἀγαθοῦ παντός, ἀρξάμενον ἀπὸ τοῦ τί ἐστιν. παρασημαίνεσθαι δὲ καὶ
τὰς ἑκάστων δόξας, οἷον ὅτι Ἐμπεδοκλῆς τέτταρα
ἔφησε τῶν σωμάτων στοιχεῖα εἶναι· θείη γὰρ ἄν τις
τὸ ὑπό τινος εἰρημένον ἐνδόξου.

Ἔστι δ' ὡς τύπῳ περιλαβεῖν τῶν προτάσεων καὶ
20 τῶν προβλημάτων μέρη τρία. αἱ μὲν γὰρ ἠθικαὶ
προτάσεις εἰσίν, αἱ δὲ φυσικαί, αἱ δὲ λογικαί.
ἠθικαὶ μὲν οὖν αἱ τοιαῦται, οἷον πότερον δεῖ τοῖς
γονεῦσι μᾶλλον ἢ τοῖς νόμοις πειθαρχεῖν, ἐὰν δια-
φωνῶσιν· λογικαὶ δὲ οἷον πότερον τῶν ἐναντίων ἡ
25 αὐτὴ ἐπιστήμη ἢ οὔ· φυσικαὶ δὲ οἷον πότερον ὁ
κόσμος ἀΐδιος ἢ οὔ· ὁμοίως δὲ καὶ τὰ προβλήματα.
ποῖαι δ' ἕκασται τῶν προειρημένων, ὁρισμῷ μὲν
οὐκ εὐπετὲς ἀποδοῦναι περὶ αὐτῶν, τῇ δὲ διὰ τῆς
ἐπαγωγῆς συνηθείᾳ πειρατέον γνωρίζειν ἑκάστην
αὐτῶν, κατὰ τὰ προειρημένα παραδείγματα ἐπι-
σκοποῦντα.

30 Πρὸς μὲν οὖν φιλοσοφίαν κατ' ἀλήθειαν περὶ
αὐτῶν πραγματευτέον, διαλεκτικῶς δὲ πρὸς δόξαν.
ληπτέον δ' ὅτι μάλιστα καθόλου πάσας τὰς προτάσεις, καὶ τὴν μίαν πολλὰς ποιητέον, οἷον ὅτι τῶν
ἀντικειμένων ἡ αὐτὴ ἐπιστήμη, εἶθ' ὅτι τῶν ἐναν-

---

[1] Reading οὕτως ἔχειν with C. ἔχειν is omitted by the other mss.

manner. And so with the other instances. Further, opinions which are apparently true in all or most cases must be taken as a starting-point and an accepted thesis; for they are admitted by such as do not notice that there is a case in which they are not true. We ought also to select from written disquisitions and make up descriptions of each class of subject, putting them in separate lists, for example, about 'the good' (or about 'animal life'), dealing with every kind of good, beginning with the essence. We ought also to note in passing the opinion of individuals, for example, that Empedocles said that the elements of bodies are four in number; for one may accept the statement of some thinker of repute.

To put the matter briefly, there are three classes of propositions and problems. Some are ethical, some physical and some logical propositions. *Ethical* propositions are such propositions as " Should one rather obey parents or the laws, if they are at variance ? " *Logical* propositions are such as the following : " Is knowledge of contraries the same or not ? " *Physical* problems are of the type of " Is the universe eternal or not ? " There are similar classes of problems. The nature of each of the above classes is not easily explained by definition, but we must try to obtain knowledge of each of them by the habitual practice of induction, examining them in the light of the above examples.

For philosophic purposes we must deal with propositions from the point of view of truth, but for purposes of dialectic, with a view to opinion. Propositions must always be taken in their most universal form, and the one should be made into many; for example, " The knowledge of opposites is the same,"

Ethical, logical and physical propositions and problems.

307

105 b

τίων καὶ ὅτι τῶν πρός τι. τὸν αὐτὸν δὲ τρόπον
35 καὶ ταύτας πάλιν διαιρετέον, ἕως ἂν ἐνδέχηται δι-
αιρεῖν, οἷον ὅτι ἀγαθοῦ καὶ κακοῦ, καὶ λευκοῦ καὶ
μέλανος, καὶ ψυχροῦ καὶ θερμοῦ. ὁμοίως δὲ καὶ
ἐπὶ τῶν ἄλλων.

106 a   XV. Περὶ μὲν οὖν προτάσεως ἱκανὰ τὰ προειρη-
μένα· τὸ δὲ ποσαχῶς, πραγματευτέον μὴ μόνον ὅσα
λέγεται καθ᾽ ἕτερον τρόπον, ἀλλὰ καὶ τοὺς λόγους
αὐτῶν πειρατέον ἀποδιδόναι, οἷον μὴ μόνον ὅτι
5 ἀγαθὸν καθ᾽ ἕτερον μὲν τρόπον λέγεται δικαιοσύνη
καὶ ἀνδρία, εὐεκτικὸν δὲ καὶ ὑγιεινὸν καθ᾽ ἕτερον,
ἀλλ᾽ ὅτι καὶ τὰ μὲν τῷ αὐτὰ ποιά τινα εἶναι, τὰ δὲ
τῷ ποιητικά τινος καὶ οὐ τῷ ποιὰ αὐτά τινα εἶναι.
ὡσαύτως δὲ καὶ ἐπὶ τῶν ἄλλων.

Πότερον δὲ πολλαχῶς ἢ μοναχῶς τῷ εἴδει λέ-
10 γεται, διὰ τῶνδε θεωρητέον. πρῶτον μὲν ἐπὶ τοῦ
ἐναντίου σκοπεῖν εἰ πολλαχῶς λέγεται, ἐάν τε τῷ
εἴδει ἐάν τε τῷ ὀνόματι διαφωνῇ. ἔνια γὰρ εὐθὺς
καὶ τοῖς ὀνόμασιν ἕτερά ἐστιν, οἷον τῷ ὀξεῖ ἐν φωνῇ
μὲν ἐναντίον τὸ βαρύ, ἐν ὄγκῳ δὲ τὸ ἀμβλύ. δῆλον
15 οὖν ὅτι τὸ ἐναντίον τῷ ὀξεῖ πολλαχῶς λέγεται. εἰ
δὲ τοῦτο, καὶ τὸ ὀξύ· καθ᾽ ἑκάτερον γὰρ ἐκείνων

308

then " The knowledge of contraries is the same," and finally, " The knowledge of relative terms is the same." In the same way, those too must be divided again, as long as division is possible, for example, " the knowledge of good and evil," " of black and white," and " of cold and hot is the same " ; and so with the other cases.

XV. On the making of propositions what has been said above must suffice. As regards the number of ways in which a term can be used, we must not only deal with those terms which are used in another way but also try to assign their definitions. For example, we must not only say that in one sense ' good ' is said to be ' justice ' and ' courage,' in another sense ' good ' is said to be ' conducive to soundness ' and ' conducive to health,' but we must also say that some things are called ' good ' because they possess certain qualities in themselves, while other things are good because they are productive of a certain result and not because they possess certain qualities in themselves. And so likewise in the other cases also. *How to detect ambiguity of meaning.*

Whether a term is used in one kind of sense only or in many, can be seen by the following method. First, examine the case of its contrary and see if it is used in several senses, whether the difference be one of kind or in the use of a word. For in some cases a difference is immediately apparent in the words used. For example, the contrary of ' sharp ' when used of a note is ' flat ' ($\beta\alpha\rho\acute{\nu}$), when it is used of a material substance, it is ' dull ' ($\dot{\alpha}\mu\beta\lambda\acute{\nu}$). The contrary of ' sharp,' therefore, obviously has several meanings, and, this being so, so also has ' sharp ' ; for the contrary will have different mean- *(a)* From contraries expressed in different words.

106 a

ἕτερον ἔσται τὸ ἐναντίον. οὐ γὰρ τὸ αὐτὸ ὀξὺ
ἔσται τῷ ἀμβλεῖ καὶ τῷ βαρεῖ ἐναντίον, ἑκατέρῳ
δὲ τὸ ὀξὺ ἐναντίον. πάλιν τῷ βαρεῖ ἐν φωνῇ μὲν
τὸ ὀξὺ ἐναντίον, ἐν ὄγκῳ δὲ τὸ κοῦφον, ὥστε πολ-
20 λαχῶς τὸ βαρὺ λέγεται, ἐπειδὴ καὶ τὸ ἐναντίον.
ὁμοίως δὲ καὶ τῷ καλῷ τῷ μὲν ἐπὶ τοῦ ζῴου τὸ
αἰσχρόν, τῷ δ' ἐπὶ τῆς οἰκίας τὸ μοχθηρόν, ὥστε
ὁμώνυμον τὸ καλόν.

Ἐπ' ἐνίων δὲ τοῖς μὲν ὀνόμασιν οὐδαμῶς διαφωνεῖ, τῷ δ' εἴδει κατάδηλος ἐν αὐτοῖς εὐθέως ἡ
25 διαφορά ἐστιν, οἷον ἐπὶ τοῦ λευκοῦ καὶ μέλανος.
φωνὴ γὰρ λευκὴ καὶ μέλαινα λέγεται, ὁμοίως δὲ
καὶ χρῶμα. τοῖς μὲν οὖν ὀνόμασιν οὐδὲν διαφωνεῖ,
τῷ δ' εἴδει κατάδηλος ἐν αὐτοῖς εὐθέως ἡ διαφορά·
οὐ γὰρ ὁμοίως τό τε χρῶμα λευκὸν λέγεται καὶ ἡ
φωνή. δῆλον δὲ τοῦτο καὶ διὰ τῆς αἰσθήσεως· τῶν
30 γὰρ αὐτῶν τῷ εἴδει ἡ αὐτὴ αἴσθησις, τὸ δὲ λευκὸν
τὸ ἐπὶ τῆς φωνῆς καὶ τοῦ χρώματος οὐ τῇ αὐτῇ
αἰσθήσει κρίνομεν, ἀλλὰ τὸ μὲν ὄψει, τὸ δ' ἀκοῇ.
ὁμοίως δὲ καὶ τὸ ὀξὺ καὶ τὸ ἀμβλὺ ἐν χυμοῖς καὶ
ἐν ὄγκοις· ἀλλὰ τὸ μὲν ἀφῇ, τὸ δὲ γεύσει. οὐδὲ
γὰρ ταῦτα διαφωνεῖ τοῖς ὀνόμασιν, οὔτ' ἐπ' αὐτῶν
35 οὔτ' ἐπὶ τῶν ἐναντίων· ἀμβλὺ γὰρ καὶ τὸ ἐναντίον
ἑκατέρῳ.

Ἔτι εἰ τῷ μέν ἐστί τι ἐναντίον τῷ δ' ἁπλῶς
μηδέν, οἷον τῇ μὲν ἀπὸ τοῦ πίνειν ἡδονῇ ἡ ἀπὸ τοῦ
διψῆν λύπη ἐναντίον, τῇ δ' ἀπὸ τοῦ θεωρεῖν ὅτι

---

^a Lit. ' white ' and ' black.'

ings, corresponding to each of those meanings. For 'sharp' will not be the same when it is the contrary of 'blunt' and when it is the contrary of 'flat,' though 'sharp' is the contrary in both cases. Again, the contrary of βαρύ ('flat,' 'heavy') applied to a note is 'sharp,' but applied to a material substance it is 'light'; so that βαρύ is used in many senses, since its contrary is also so used. Similarly also the contrary of 'beautiful' applied to a living creature is 'ugly,' but applied to a house, 'mean'; so that 'beautiful' is an equivocal term.

Sometimes there is no difference in the terms used but the variation in kind is immediately obvious in their use; for example, in the case of 'clear' and 'dim,'[a] for sound is said to be 'clear' and 'dim' and so is colour. Now there is no difference in the terms used, but the variation in kind is immediately obvious in their use; for 'clear' is not used in the same sense as applied to colour and as applied to sound. This is manifest also through sense-perception; for sense-perception of things which are of the same kind is the same, but we do not judge 'clearness' of sound and of colour by the same sense, but the latter by sight and the former by hearing. Similarly with regard to 'sharp' and 'dull' in flavours and in material substances; we judge the latter by touch, the former by taste. Here, too, there is no difference in the terms used—either in the terms themselves or in their contraries; for 'dull' is the contrary of 'sharp' in both its senses.

Furthermore, we must see whether there is a contrary of a term in one sense, but absolutely none in another sense. For example, the pleasure due to drinking has a contrary in the pain due to thirst,

(b) From contraries different in kind.

(c) From the presence or absence of contraries.

311

ARISTOTLE

106 b ἡ διάμετρος τῇ πλευρᾷ ἀσύμμετρος οὐδέν, ὥστε
πλεοναχῶς ἡ ἡδονὴ λέγεται. καὶ τῷ μὲν κατὰ τὴν
διάνοιαν φιλεῖν τὸ μισεῖν ἐναντίον, τῷ δὲ κατὰ τὴν
σωματικὴν ἐνέργειαν οὐδέν· δῆλον οὖν ὅτι τὸ φιλεῖν
ὁμώνυμον. ἔτι ἐπὶ τῶν ἀνὰ μέσον, εἰ τῶν μέν
5 ἐστί τι ἀνὰ μέσον, τῶν δὲ μηδέν, ἢ εἰ ἀμφοῖν μέν
ἐστι, μὴ ταὐτὸν δέ, οἷον λευκοῦ καὶ μέλανος ἐν
χρώμασι μὲν τὸ φαιόν, ἐν φωνῇ δ' οὐδέν, ἢ εἰ ἄρα,
τὸ σομφόν, καθάπερ τινές φασι σομφὴν φωνὴν ἀνὰ
μέσον εἶναι, ὥσθ' ὁμώνυμον τὸ λευκόν, ὁμοίως δὲ
10 καὶ τὸ μέλαν. ἔτι εἰ τῶν μὲν πλείω τὰ ἀνὰ μέσον,
τῶν δὲ ἕν, καθάπερ ἐπὶ τοῦ λευκοῦ καὶ μέλανος·
ἐπὶ μὲν γὰρ τῶν χρωμάτων πολλὰ τὰ ἀνὰ μέσον,
ἐπὶ δὲ τῆς φωνῆς ἓν τὸ σομφόν.

Πάλιν ἐπὶ τοῦ κατ' ἀντίφασιν ἀντικειμένου σκοπεῖν εἰ πλεοναχῶς λέγεται. εἰ γὰρ τοῦτο πλεονα-
15 χῶς λέγεται, καὶ τὸ τούτῳ ἀντικείμενον πλεοναχῶς
ῥηθήσεται, οἷον τὸ μὴ βλέπειν πλεοναχῶς λέγεται,
ἓν μὲν τὸ μὴ ἔχειν ὄψιν, ἓν δὲ τὸ μὴ ἐνεργεῖν τῇ
ὄψει. εἰ δὲ τοῦτο πλεοναχῶς, ἀναγκαῖον καὶ τὸ
βλέπειν πλεοναχῶς λέγεσθαι· ἑκατέρῳ γὰρ τῷ μὴ
βλέπειν ἀντικείσεταί τι, οἷον τῷ μὲν μὴ ἔχειν ὄψιν
20 τὸ ἔχειν, τῷ δὲ μὴ ἐνεργεῖν τῇ ὄψει τὸ ἐνεργεῖν.

312

but the pleasure due to the contemplation that the diagonal is incommensurate with the side has no contrary ; so that ' pleasure ' is used in more senses than one. Also ' loving,' used of the mental state, has a contrary in ' hating,' but, used of the physical act, it has no contrary ; therefore ' loving ' is obviously an equivocal term. Further, with regard to *(d)* From intermediates, you must see whether some meanings intermediates. of terms and their contraries have intermediates and others none, or whether both have an intermediate but not the same one. For example, in colours the intermediate between ' clear ' (white) and ' dim ' (black) is ' grey,' but when the terms are used of a note, they have no intermediate, unless it be ' muffled,' as some people say that a muffled note is intermediate. Therefore ' clear ' is an equivocal term, as also is ' dim.' You must see also whether some terms have several intermediates, others only one, as in the case of ' clear ' and ' dim ' ; for when they are used of colour they have many intermediates, but when they are used of a note only one, namely, ' muffled.'

Again, with regard to the opposite put in a con- *(e)* From tradictory form, you must see whether it is used in contradictory more senses than one. For if it is used in several opposites. senses, then its opposite also will be used in several senses. For example, ' not to see ' is used in more than one sense, firstly, ' not to possess sight,' and, secondly, ' not to exercise the faculty of sight ' ; and if this has more than one meaning, ' to see ' must necessarily also have more than one meaning ; for each meaning of ' not to see ' will have an opposite, the opposite of ' not to possess sight ' being ' to possess sight,' and the opposite of ' not to exercise the faculty of sight ' being ' to exercise the faculty of sight.'

106 b

Ἔτι ἐπὶ τῶν κατὰ στέρησιν καὶ ἕξιν λεγομένων
ἐπισκοπεῖν· εἰ γὰρ θάτερον πλεοναχῶς λέγεται, καὶ
τὸ λοιπόν, οἷον εἰ τὸ αἰσθάνεσθαι πλεοναχῶς λέγεται κατά τε τὴν ψυχὴν καὶ τὸ σῶμα, καὶ τὸ
25 ἀναίσθητον εἶναι πλεοναχῶς ῥηθήσεται κατά τε τὴν
ψυχὴν καὶ τὸ σῶμα. ὅτι δὲ κατὰ στέρησιν καὶ
ἕξιν ἀντίκειται τὰ νῦν λεγόμενα, δῆλον, ἐπειδὴ
πέφυκεν ἑκατέραν τῶν αἰσθήσεων ἔχειν τὰ ζῷα
καὶ κατὰ τὴν ψυχὴν καὶ κατὰ τὸ σῶμα.

Ἔτι δ' ἐπὶ τῶν πτώσεων ἐπισκεπτέον. εἰ γὰρ
30 τὸ δικαίως πλεοναχῶς λέγεται, καὶ τὸ δίκαιον
πλεοναχῶς ῥηθήσεται· καθ' ἑκάτερον γὰρ τῶν
δικαίως ἐστὶ δίκαιον, οἷον εἰ τὸ δικαίως λέγεται
τό τε κατὰ τὴν ἑαυτοῦ γνώμην κρῖναι καὶ τὸ ὡς
δεῖ, ὁμοίως καὶ τὸ δίκαιον. ὡσαύτως δὲ καὶ εἰ
τὸ ὑγιεινὸν πλεοναχῶς, καὶ τὸ ὑγιεινῶς πλεοναχῶς
35 ῥηθήσεται, οἷον εἰ ὑγιεινὸν τὸ μὲν ὑγιείας ποιητικὸν τὸ δὲ φυλακτικὸν τὸ δὲ σημαντικόν, καὶ
τὸ ὑγιεινῶς ἢ ποιητικῶς ἢ φυλακτικῶς ἢ σημαν-
τικῶς ῥηθήσεται. ὁμοίως δὲ καὶ ἐπὶ τῶν ἄλλων,
107 a ὅταν αὐτὸ πλεοναχῶς λέγηται, καὶ ἡ πτῶσις ἡ
ἀπ' αὐτοῦ πλεοναχῶς ῥηθήσεται, καὶ εἰ ἡ πτῶσις,
καὶ αὐτό.

Σκοπεῖν δὲ καὶ τὰ γένη τῶν κατὰ τοὔνομα
κατηγοριῶν, εἰ ταὐτά ἐστιν ἐπὶ πάντων. εἰ γὰρ
5 μὴ ταὐτά, δῆλον ὅτι ὁμώνυμον τὸ λεγόμενον, οἷον

---

a πτῶσις is used of any modification of a word, such as
cases and genders of nouns and adjectives, adjectives derived
from nouns, adverbs formed from adjectives (as in the examples which Aristotle gives here), and the tenses of verbs.

314

Further, you must examine cases where the privation and presence of some state is asserted; for if either of the terms used has several meanings, so also will the other. For example, if 'to have sensation' is used in several senses in connexion both with the soul and with the body, 'lacking sensation' also will be used in several senses in connexion both with the soul and with the body. That the terms under discussion are opposed in respect of the privation and presence of a certain state is obvious, since living creatures naturally possess each kind of sensation, that is to say, as connected both with the soul and with the body. *(f) From the privation or presence of states.*

Further, you must examine the inflected forms of words.[a] For if 'justly' can be used in several senses, 'just' will also be used in several senses; for there is a meaning of 'just' for each of the meanings of 'justly.' For example, if to judge 'justly' means to judge 'according to one's opinion,' and also to judge 'as one ought,' then 'just' will have the two similar meanings. Likewise if 'healthy' has several meanings, so also will 'healthily'; for example, if 'healthy' means 'producing health' and 'preserving health' and 'denoting health,' then 'healthily' will mean 'in a manner which produces health' or 'in a manner which preserves health' or 'in a manner which denotes health.' Similarly in every other case, when the word itself is used in several senses, the inflexion formed from it will also be used in several senses, and *vice versa*. *(g) From inflected forms of words.*

You must also examine the kinds of predicates denoted by the word used and see if they are the same in every case; for, if they are not, it is obvious that the word is equivocal. For example, 'good' as *(h) From the kinds of predicates denoted by a word.*

315

107 a

τὸ ἀγαθὸν ἐν ἐδέσματι μὲν τὸ ποιητικὸν ἡδονῆς,
ἐν ἰατρικῇ δὲ τὸ ποιητικὸν ὑγιείας, ἐπὶ δὲ ψυχῆς
τὸ ποιὰν εἶναι, οἷον σώφρονα ἢ ἀνδρείαν ἢ δικαίαν·
ὁμοίως δὲ καὶ ἐπὶ ἀνθρώπου. ἐνιαχοῦ δὲ τὸ ποτέ,
10 οἷον τὸ ἐν τῷ καιρῷ [ἀγαθόν]¹· ἀγαθὸν γὰρ λέγεται
τὸ ἐν τῷ καιρῷ. πολλάκις δὲ τὸ ποσόν, οἷον ἐπὶ
τοῦ μετρίου· λέγεται γὰρ καὶ τὸ μέτριον ἀγαθόν.
ὥστε ὁμώνυμον τὸ ἀγαθόν. ὡσαύτως δὲ καὶ τὸ
λευκὸν ἐπὶ σώματος μὲν χρῶμα, ἐπὶ δὲ φωνῆς
τὸ εὐήκοον. παραπλησίως δὲ καὶ τὸ ὀξύ· οὐ γὰρ
15 ὡσαύτως ἐπὶ πάντων τὸ αὐτὸ λέγεται· φωνὴ μὲν
γὰρ ὀξεῖα ἡ ταχεῖα, καθάπερ φασὶν οἱ κατὰ τοὺς
ἀριθμοὺς ἁρμονικοί, γωνία δ' ὀξεῖα ἡ ἐλάσσων
ὀρθῆς, μάχαιρα δὲ ἡ ὀξυγώνιος.

Σκοπεῖν δὲ καὶ τὰ γένη τῶν ὑπὸ τὸ αὐτὸ ὄνομα,
εἰ ἕτερα καὶ μὴ ὑπ' ἄλληλα, οἷον ὄνος τό τε ζῷον
20 καὶ τὸ σκεῦος. ἕτερος γὰρ ὁ κατὰ τοὔνομα λόγος
αὐτῶν· τὸ μὲν γὰρ ζῷον ποιόν τι ῥηθήσεται,
τὸ δὲ σκεῦος ποιόν τι. ἐὰν δὲ ὑπ' ἄλληλα τὰ
γένη ᾖ, οὐκ ἀναγκαῖον ἑτέρους τοὺς λόγους εἶναι.
οἷον τοῦ κόρακος τὸ ζῷον καὶ τὸ ὄρνεον γένος
ἐστίν. ὅταν οὖν λέγωμεν τὸν κόρακα ὄρνεον εἶναι,
25 καὶ ζῷον ποιόν τί φαμεν αὐτὸν εἶναι, ὥστ' ἀμφότερα τὰ γένη περὶ αὐτοῦ κατηγορεῖται. ὁμοίως
δὲ καὶ ὅταν ζῷον πτηνὸν δίπουν τὸν κόρακα λέγωμεν, ὄρνεόν φαμεν αὐτὸν εἶναι· καὶ οὕτως οὖν
ἀμφότερα τὰ γένη κατηγορεῖται κατὰ τοῦ κόρακος,

---

¹ Omitting the first ἀγαθόν with W. S. Maguinness.

ª i.e. the windlass (Herod. vii. 36; [Aristot.] *Mech.*
853 b 12).

applied to food means 'productive of pleasure,' as applied to medicine it means 'productive of health,' as applied to the soul it denotes a certain quality such as 'temperate' or 'brave' or 'just,' and similarly also as applied to man. Sometimes it means what happens at a certain time, for example at the right time; for what happens at the right time is called 'good.' Often too it is applied to quantity, being used, for example, of that which is 'moderate'; for that which is 'moderate,' too, is called 'good.' Thus 'good' is an equivocal term. Similarly too λευκόν ('white,' 'clear') as applied to a body denotes colour, as applied to a note it means 'easily heard.' The case of 'sharp' also is similar, for it does not always bear the same meaning. For a quick note is 'sharp,' as the theorists of rhythmic harmony tell us, and an angle which is less than a right angle is 'sharp' (acute), and a knife with a sharp angle (edge) is 'sharp.'

You must also examine the genera of the things which fall under the same term and see if they are different and not subaltern. For example, ὄνος ('donkey') is both the animal and the machine [a]; for the definition applied to the word is different in the two cases, since one will be described as a kind of animal, the other as a kind of machine. But if the genera are subaltern, the definitions are not necessarily different. For example, 'animal' is the genus of 'raven,' and so is 'bird.' When, therefore, we say that the raven is a bird, we also say that it is a kind of animal, so that both the genera are predicated of it. Likewise too, when we call the raven 'a flying biped animal,' we are stating that it is a bird, so that in this way too both the genera are

(i) From an examination of the genera falling under the same term.

317

107 a

καὶ ὁ λόγος αὐτῶν. ἐπὶ δὲ τῶν μὴ ὑπ' ἄλληλα
30 γενῶν οὐ συμβαίνει τοῦτο· οὔτε γὰρ ὅταν σκεῦος
λέγωμεν, ζῷον λέγομεν, οὔθ' ὅταν ζῷον, σκεῦος.

Σκοπεῖν δὲ μὴ μόνον εἰ τοῦ προκειμένου ἕτερα
τὰ γένη καὶ μὴ ὑπ' ἄλληλα, ἀλλὰ καὶ ἐπὶ τοῦ
ἐναντίου· εἰ γὰρ τὸ ἐναντίον πολλαχῶς λέγεται,
35 δῆλον ὅτι καὶ τὸ προκείμενον.

Χρήσιμον δὲ καὶ τὸ ἐπὶ τὸν ὁρισμὸν ἐπιβλέπειν
τὸν ἐκ τοῦ συντιθεμένου γινόμενον, οἷον λευκοῦ
σώματος καὶ λευκῆς φωνῆς· ἀφαιρουμένου γὰρ
τοῦ ἰδίου τὸν αὐτὸν λόγον δεῖ λείπεσθαι. τοῦτο
107 b δ' οὐ συμβαίνει ἐπὶ τῶν ὁμωνύμων, οἷον ἐπὶ τῶν
νῦν εἰρημένων. τὸ μὲν γὰρ ἔσται σῶμα τοιόνδε
χρῶμα ἔχον, τὸ δὲ φωνὴ εὐήκοος· ἀφαιρεθέντος
οὖν τοῦ σώματος καὶ τῆς φωνῆς οὐ ταὐτὸν ἐν
ἑκατέρῳ τὸ λειπόμενον. ἔδει δέ γε, εἴπερ συν-
5 ώνυμον ἦν τὸ λευκὸν τὸ ἐφ' ἑκατέρου λεγόμενον.

Πολλάκις δὲ καὶ ἐν αὐτοῖς τοῖς λόγοις λανθάνει
παρακολουθοῦν τὸ ὁμώνυμον· διὸ καὶ ἐπὶ τῶν
λόγων σκεπτέον. οἷον ἄν τις τὸ σημαντικὸν καὶ
τὸ[1] ποιητικὸν ὑγιείας τὸ συμμέτρως ἔχον πρὸς
10 ὑγίειαν φῇ εἶναι, οὐκ ἀποστατέον ἀλλ' ἐπισκεπτέον
τί τὸ συμμέτρως καθ' ἑκάτερον εἴρηκεν, οἷον εἰ
τὸ μὲν τὸ τοσοῦτον[2] εἶναι ὥστε ποιεῖν ὑγίειαν,
τὸ δὲ τὸ τοιοῦτον οἷον σημαίνειν ποία τις ἡ ἕξις.

---

[1] Inserting τὸ with C.
[2] Reading τοσοῦτον with all the best mss.

predicated of the raven, and also their definition.
This does not happen in the case of genera which
are not subaltern; for when we say a ' machine '
we do not mean an ' animal,' nor *vice versa*.

You must also examine not only whether the *(j)* From the
genera of the term in question are different without contrary of
being subaltern but also look into the case of its used in
contrary; for if its contrary is used in several senses,
obviously the term in question will also be so used. senses.

It is useful also to look at the definition which *(k)* From
results from the use of the term in a composite tion of a
phrase, for example, in λευκὸν σῶμα (' a white body ') term in a
and λευκὴ φωνή (' a clear note '). For when what is phrase.
peculiar is taken away, the same meaning ought to
be left. But this does not happen when equivocal
terms are used, as in the phrases just mentioned;
for the former will be ' a body having such and such
a colour ' the latter ' a note which is easily heard.'
If, therefore, ' a body ' and ' a note ' are taken away,
what remains in each phrase is not the same. But it
ought to have been the same if the term λευκός in
each case had been synonymous.

Often too in the actual definitions the equivocal *(l)* From
slips in unnoticed; therefore examination must be of defini-
made of the definitions also. For example, if some- tion.
one states that what denotes and what produces
health are ' commensurably related to health,' we
must not shrink from the task but examine what he
has meant by ' commensurably ' in each case, for
example, whether in the latter case it means that
it is ' of the requisite quantity to produce health,'
whereas in the former case it means that it is ' of
the requisite quality to denote of what kind the state
is which is present.'

Ἔτι εἰ μὴ συμβλητὰ κατὰ τὸ μᾶλλον ἢ ὁμοίως, οἷον λευκὴ φωνὴ καὶ λευκὸν ἱμάτιον καὶ ὀξὺς
15 χυμὸς καὶ ὀξεῖα φωνή· ταῦτα γὰρ οὔθ᾽ ὁμοίως λέγεται λευκὰ ἢ ὀξέα, οὔτε μᾶλλον θάτερον. ὥσθ᾽ ὁμώνυμον τὸ λευκὸν καὶ τὸ ὀξύ. τὸ γὰρ συνώνυμον πᾶν συμβλητόν· ἢ γὰρ ὁμοίως ῥηθήσεται, ἢ μᾶλλον θάτερον.

Ἐπεὶ δὲ τῶν ἑτέρων γενῶν καὶ μὴ ὑπ᾽ ἄλληλα
20 ἕτεραι τῷ εἴδει καὶ αἱ διαφοραί, οἷον ζῴου καὶ ἐπιστήμης (ἕτεραι γὰρ τούτων αἱ διαφοραί), σκοπεῖν εἰ τὰ ὑπὸ τὸ αὐτὸ ὄνομα ἑτέρων γενῶν καὶ μὴ ὑπ᾽ ἄλληλα διαφοραί εἰσιν, οἷον τὸ ὀξὺ φωνῆς καὶ ὄγκου· διαφέρει γὰρ φωνὴ φωνῆς τῷ ὀξεῖα εἶναι, ὁμοίως δὲ καὶ ὄγκος ὄγκου. ὥστε
25 ὁμώνυμον τὸ ὀξύ· ἑτέρων γὰρ γενῶν καὶ οὐχ ὑπ᾽ ἄλληλα διαφοραί εἰσιν.

Πάλιν εἰ αὐτῶν τῶν ὑπὸ τὸ αὐτὸ ὄνομα ἕτεραι αἱ διαφοραί, οἷον χρώματος τοῦ τε ἐπὶ τῶν σω-μάτων καὶ τοῦ ἐν τοῖς μέλεσιν· τοῦ μὲν γὰρ ἐπὶ
30 τῶν σωμάτων διακριτικὸν καὶ συγκριτικὸν ὄψεως, τοῦ δ᾽ ἐπὶ τῶν μελῶν οὐχ αἱ αὐταὶ διαφοραί. ὥστε ὁμώνυμον τὸ χρῶμα· τῶν γὰρ αὐτῶν αἱ αὐταὶ διαφοραί.

Ἔτι ἐπεὶ τὸ εἶδος οὐδενός ἐστι διαφορά, σκοπεῖν

Further, you must see whether the terms are not comparable in respect of greater or similar degree, for example, a ' clear ' (λευκός) note and a ' white ' (λευκός) garment, and a ' sharp ' flavour and a ' sharp ' note. For these things are not said to be λευκός (' white,' ' clear ') or ' sharp ' in a similar degree or one in a greater degree than the other ; and so the terms λευκός and ' sharp ' are equivocal. For every synonymous term is comparable ; for it will be used either of a similar degree or of a greater degree in one thing than another. *(m) From a comparison in respect of degree.*

Now since the differentiae of genera which are different but not subaltern are also different in kind, for example, those of ' animal ' and ' knowledge ' (for the differentiae of these are different), you must see whether the meanings which fall under the same term are differentiae of genera which are different without being subaltern, for example ' sharp ' as applied to a note and to a solid substance ; for voice differs from voice in ' sharpness ' and similarly too one solid substance from another. ' Sharp,' therefore, is an equivocal term ; for its meanings are differentiae of genera which are different without being subaltern. *(n) From an examination of the differentiae.*

Again, you must see whether the differentiae of the actual meanings which fall under the same term are different, for example, those of colour in bodies and colour in tunes ; for the differentiae of colour in bodies are ' penetrative of sight ' and ' compressive of sight,' [a] but the same differentiae do not hold good of colour in tunes. Therefore colour is an equivocal term ; for when things are the same they have the same differentiae.

Further, since the species is never the differentia

107 b

τῶν ὑπὸ τὸ αὐτὸ ὄνομα εἰ τὸ μὲν εἶδός ἐστι τὸ δὲ
35 διαφορά, οἷον τὸ λευκὸν τὸ μὲν ἐπὶ τοῦ σώματος
εἶδος χρώματος, τὸ δ' ἐπὶ τῆς φωνῆς διαφορά·
διαφέρει γὰρ φωνὴ φωνῆς τῷ λευκῇ εἶναι.

XVI. Περὶ μὲν οὖν τοῦ πολλαχῶς διὰ τούτων
καὶ τῶν τοιούτων σκεπτέον· τὰς δὲ διαφορὰς ἐν
108 a αὐτοῖς τε τοῖς γένεσι πρὸς ἄλληλα θεωρητέον, οἷον
τίνι διαφέρει δικαιοσύνη ἀνδρίας καὶ φρόνησις
σωφροσύνης (ταῦτα γὰρ ἅπαντα ἐκ τοῦ αὐτοῦ
γένους ἐστίν), καὶ ἐξ ἄλλου πρὸς ἄλλο τῶν μὴ
πολὺ λίαν διεστηκότων, οἷον τίνι αἴσθησις ἐπι-
5 στήμης· ἐπὶ μὲν γὰρ τῶν πολὺ διεστηκότων
κατάδηλοι παντελῶς αἱ διαφοραί.

XVII. Τὴν δὲ ὁμοιότητα σκεπτέον ἐπί τε τῶν
ἐν ἑτέροις γένεσιν, ὡς ἕτερον πρὸς ἕτερόν τι,
οὕτως ἄλλο πρὸς ἄλλο, οἷον ὡς ἐπιστήμη πρὸς
10 ἐπιστητόν, οὕτως αἴσθησις πρὸς αἰσθητόν· καὶ ὡς
ἕτερον ἐν ἑτέρῳ τινί, οὕτως ἄλλο ἐν ἄλλῳ, οἷον
ὡς ὄψις ἐν ὀφθαλμῷ, νοῦς ἐν ψυχῇ, καὶ ὡς γαλήνη
ἐν θαλάσσῃ, νηνεμία ἐν ἀέρι. μάλιστα δ' ἐν τοῖς
πολὺ διεστῶσι γυμνάζεσθαι δεῖ· ῥᾷον γὰρ ἐπὶ τῶν
λοιπῶν δυνησόμεθα τὰ ὅμοια συνορᾶν. σκεπτέον
15 δὲ καὶ τὰ ἐν τῷ αὐτῷ γένει ὄντα, εἴ τι ἅπασιν
ὑπάρχει ταὐτόν, οἷον ἀνθρώπῳ καὶ ἵππῳ καὶ κυνί·
ᾗ γὰρ ὑπάρχει τι αὐτοῖς ταὐτόν, ταύτῃ ὅμοιά
ἐστιν.

322

of anything, you must look whether one of the meanings which fall under the same term is a species and another a differentia, for example, λευκός ('white,' 'clear') when applied to a body is a species of colour, but when applied to a note it is a differentia, for one note differs from another in being clear.

XVI. The number of meanings, then, of a term must be examined by these and similar methods. The differences must be viewed in their relation with one another both in the genera themselves— for example, "In what does justice differ from courage and wisdom from temperance?" (for all these belong to the same genus)—and also from one genus to another, where they are not too widely separated—for example, "In what does sensation differ from knowledge?"—for where the genera are widely separated, the differences are quite obvious.

How to note differences.

XVII. Likeness must be examined in things belonging to different genera—as A is to B, so is C to D (for example, 'As knowledge is related to the object of knowledge, so is sensation related to the object of sensation'), and also, as A is in B, so is C in D (for example, 'As sight is in the eye, so is reason in the soul' and 'As is calm in the sea, so is absence of wind in the air'). In particular we must have practice in dealing with genera which are widely separated; for in the other cases we shall be able to detect the similarities more readily. We must examine also things which are in the same genus, to see if there is any attribute belonging to them all which is the same, for example, to a man, a horse and a dog; for they are alike in as far as any attribute which they possess is the same.

How to note resemblances.

108 a

XVIII. Χρήσιμον δὲ τὸ μὲν ποσαχῶς λέγεται
ἐπεσκέφθαι πρός τε τὸ σαφές (μᾶλλον γὰρ ἄν τις
20 εἰδείη τί τίθησιν, ἐμφανισθέντος ποσαχῶς λέγεται)
καὶ πρὸς τὸ γίνεσθαι κατ᾽ αὐτὸ τὸ πρᾶγμα καὶ
μὴ πρὸς τοὔνομα τοὺς συλλογισμούς. ἀδήλου γὰρ
ὄντος ποσαχῶς λέγεται, ἐνδέχεται μὴ ἐπὶ ταὐτὸν
τόν τε ἀποκρινόμενον καὶ τὸν ἐρωτῶντα φέρειν
τὴν διάνοιαν· ἐμφανισθέντος δὲ ποσαχῶς λέγεται
25 καὶ ἐπὶ τί φέρων τίθησι, γελοῖος ἂν φαίνοιτο ὁ
ἐρωτῶν, εἰ μὴ πρὸς τοῦτο τὸν λόγον ποιοῖτο.
χρήσιμον δὲ καὶ πρὸς τὸ μὴ παραλογισθῆναι καὶ
πρὸς τὸ παραλογίσασθαι. εἰδότες γὰρ ποσαχῶς
λέγεται οὐ μὴ παραλογισθῶμεν, ἀλλ᾽ εἰδήσομεν
ἐὰν μὴ πρὸς ταὐτὸ τὸν λόγον ποιῆται ὁ ἐρωτῶν·
30 αὐτοί τε ἐρωτῶντες δυνησόμεθα παραλογίσασθαι,
ἐὰν μὴ τυγχάνῃ εἰδὼς ὁ ἀποκρινόμενος ποσαχῶς
λέγεται. τοῦτο δ᾽ οὐκ ἐπὶ πάντων δυνατόν, ἀλλ᾽
ὅταν ᾖ τῶν πολλαχῶς λεγομένων τὰ μὲν ἀληθῆ
τὰ δὲ ψευδῆ. ἔστι δὲ οὐκ οἰκεῖος ὁ τρόπος οὗτος
τῆς διαλεκτικῆς· διὸ παντελῶς εὐλαβητέον τοῖς
35 διαλεκτικοῖς τὸ τοιοῦτον, τὸ πρὸς τοὔνομα διαλέγεσθαι, ἐὰν μή τις ἄλλως ἐξαδυνατῇ περὶ τοῦ
προκειμένου διαλέγεσθαι.

Τὸ δὲ τὰς διαφορὰς εὑρεῖν χρήσιμον πρός τε
τοὺς συλλογισμοὺς τοὺς περὶ ταὐτοῦ καὶ ἑτέρου
108 b καὶ πρὸς τὸ γνωρίζειν τί ἕκαστόν ἐστιν. ὅτι μὲν
οὖν πρὸς τοὺς συλλογισμοὺς τοὺς περὶ ταὐτοῦ καὶ

XVIII. It is useful to have examined the various meanings of a term both with a view to clarity (for a man would know better what he is stating if the various senses in which it can be used had been made clear), and also in order that his reasonings may be directed to the actual thing and not to the name by which it is called. For if the various ways in which a term can be used are not clear, it is possible that the answerer and the questioner are not applying their mind to the same thing ; whereas, if it has been made clear what are the various ways in which a term can be used and to which of them the answerer is referring in his statement, the questioner would look absurd if he did not direct his argument to this. It is also useful so that one may not be misled and that one may mislead others by false reasoning. For if we know the various senses in which a term can be used, we shall never be misled by false reasoning, but we shall be aware of it if the questioner fails to direct his argument to the same point, and we shall ourselves, when we are asking questions, be able to mislead the answerer, if he does not happen to know the various meanings of a term. This, however, is not always possible but only when some of the various meanings are true and others false. This kind of argument, however, is not a proper part of dialectic ; therefore, dialecticians must be very much on their guard against such verbal discussion, unless it is quite impossible to discuss the subject otherwise.

The discovery of differences is useful both for reasonings about sameness and difference, and also for the recognition of what some particular thing is. Its usefulness for reasonings about sameness and

ἑτέρου χρήσιμον, δῆλον· εὑρόντες γὰρ διαφορὰν
τῶν προκειμένων ὁποιανοῦν δεδειχότες ἐσόμεθα
ὅτι οὐ ταὐτόν· πρὸς δὲ τὸ γνωρίζειν τί ἐστι, διότι
5 τὸν ἴδιον τῆς οὐσίας ἑκάστου λόγον ταῖς περὶ
ἕκαστον οἰκείαις διαφοραῖς χωρίζειν εἰώθαμεν.

Ἡ δὲ τοῦ ὁμοίου θεωρία χρήσιμος πρός τε τοὺς
ἐπακτικοὺς λόγους καὶ πρὸς τοὺς ἐξ ὑποθέσεως
συλλογισμοὺς καὶ πρὸς τὴν ἀπόδοσιν τῶν ὁρισμῶν.
10 πρὸς μὲν οὖν τοὺς ἐπακτικοὺς λόγους, διότι τῇ
καθ' ἕκαστα ἐπὶ τῶν ὁμοίων ἐπαγωγῇ τὸ καθόλου
ἀξιοῦμεν ἐπάγειν· οὐ γὰρ ῥᾴδιόν ἐστιν ἐπάγειν
μὴ εἰδότας τὰ ὅμοια. πρὸς δὲ τοὺς ἐξ ὑποθέσεως
συλλογισμούς, διότι ἔνδοξόν ἐστιν, ὡς ποτε ἐφ'
ἑνὸς τῶν ὁμοίων ἔχει, οὕτως καὶ ἐπὶ τῶν λοιπῶν.
15 ὥστε πρὸς ὅ τι ἂν αὐτῶν εὐπορῶμεν διαλέγεσθαι,
προδιομολογησόμεθα, ὡς ποτε ἐπὶ τούτων ἔχει,
οὕτω καὶ ἐπὶ τοῦ προκειμένου ἔχειν. δείξαντες
δὲ ἐκεῖνο καὶ τὸ προκείμενον ἐξ ὑποθέσεως δεδειχότες ἐσόμεθα· ὑποθέμενοι γάρ, ὡς ποτε ἐπὶ τούτων ἔχει, οὕτω καὶ ἐπὶ τοῦ προκειμένου ἔχειν,
τὴν ἀπόδειξιν πεποιήμεθα. πρὸς δὲ τὴν τῶν
20 ὁρισμῶν ἀπόδοσιν, διότι δυνάμενοι συνορᾶν τί ἐν
ἑκάστῳ ταὐτόν, οὐκ ἀπορήσομεν εἰς τί δεῖ γένος
ὁριζομένους τὸ προκείμενον τιθέναι· τῶν γὰρ κοινῶν τὸ μάλιστα ἐν τῷ τί ἐστι κατηγορούμενον

difference is obvious ; for when we have discovered a difference of some kind or other between the subjects under discussion, we shall have shown that they are not the same. It is useful for recognizing what some particular thing is, because we usually isolate the appropriate description of the essence of a particular thing by means of the differentiae which are peculiar to it.

The consideration of similarity is useful both for inductive arguments and for hypothetical reasoning and also for the assignment of definitions. For inductive reasoning it is useful because we maintain that it is by induction of particulars on the basis of similarities that we infer the universal ; for it is not easy to employ inference if we do not know the points of similarity. It is useful for hypothetical reasoning, because it is an accepted opinion that whatever holds good of one of several similars, holds good also of the rest. Therefore, if we have the proper material for discussing any one of them, we shall secure beforehand an admission that what holds good of other similars also holds good of the subject under discussion, and, having demonstrated the former, we shall have also demonstrated, on the basis of the hypothesis, the subject under discussion ; for we shall have completed our demonstration by the hypothetical assumption that whatever holds good of other similars holds good also of the subject under discussion. It is useful for the assignment of definitions because, if we can see what is identical in each particular case, we shall have no doubt about the genus in which we must place the subject under discussion when we are defining it ; for, of the common predicates, that which falls most definitely

Utility of the discovery of similarities.

327

γένος ἂν εἴη. ὁμοίως δὲ καὶ ἐν τοῖς πολὺ διεστῶσι
χρήσιμος πρὸς τοὺς ὁρισμοὺς ἡ τοῦ ὁμοίου θεωρία,
25 οἷον ὅτι ταὐτὸν γαλήνη μὲν ἐν θαλάσσῃ, νηνεμία
δ' ἐν ἀέρι (ἑκάτερον γὰρ ἡσυχία), καὶ ὅτι στιγμὴ
ἐν γραμμῇ καὶ μονὰς ἐν ἀριθμῷ· ἑκάτερον γὰρ
ἀρχή. ὥστε τὸ κοινὸν ἐπὶ πάντων γένος ἀποδι-
δόντες δόξομεν οὐκ ἀλλοτρίως ὁρίζεσθαι. σχεδὸν
δὲ καὶ οἱ ὁριζόμενοι οὕτως εἰώθασιν ἀποδιδόναι·
30 τήν τε γὰρ μονάδα ἀρχὴν ἀριθμοῦ φασὶν εἶναι καὶ
τὴν στιγμὴν ἀρχὴν γραμμῆς. δῆλον οὖν ὅτι εἰς
τὸ κοινὸν ἀμφοτέρων γένος τιθέασιν.

Τὰ μὲν οὖν ὄργανα δι' ὧν οἱ συλλογισμοὶ ταῦτ'
ἐστίν· οἱ δὲ τόποι πρὸς οὓς χρήσιμα τὰ λεχθέντα
οἵδε εἰσίν.

in the category of essence must be the genus. Likewise also the consideration of similarity is useful for the forming of definitions in dealing with widely separated subjects, for example, the statements that " calm at sea and absence of wind in the air are the same thing " (for each is a state of quiet), and that " a point on a line and a unit in number are the same thing " (for each is a starting-point). Thus, if we assign as the genus that which is common to all the cases, our definition will not be regarded as unsuitable. Those who deal in definitions usually form them on this principle ; for they say that the unit is the starting-point of number and the point the starting-point of a line ; it is obvious, therefore, that they assign genus to that which is common to both.

Such, then, are the means by which reasonings are carried out. The commonplaces for the application of which the said means are useful are our next subject.

B

I. Ἔστι δὲ τῶν προβλημάτων τὰ μὲν καθόλου
35 τὰ δ' ἐπὶ μέρους. καθόλου μὲν οὖν οἷον ὅτι πᾶσα
ἡδονὴ ἀγαθὸν καὶ ὅτι οὐδεμία ἡδονὴ ἀγαθόν, ἐπὶ
109 a μέρους δὲ οἷον ὅτι ἔστι τις ἡδονὴ ἀγαθὸν καὶ ὅτι
ἔστι τις ἡδονὴ οὐκ ἀγαθόν. ἔστι δὲ πρὸς ἀμφότερα
τὰ γένη τῶν προβλημάτων κοινὰ τὰ καθόλου
κατασκευαστικὰ καὶ ἀνασκευαστικά· δείξαντες
γὰρ ὅτι παντὶ ὑπάρχει, καὶ ὅτι τινὶ ὑπάρχει δε-
5 δειχότες ἐσόμεθα. ὁμοίως δὲ κἂν ὅτι οὐδενὶ
ὑπάρχει δείξωμεν, καὶ ὅτι οὐ παντὶ ὑπάρχει δεδειχότες ἐσόμεθα. πρῶτον οὖν περὶ τῶν καθόλου
ἀνασκευαστικῶν ῥητέον διά τε τὸ κοινὰ εἶναι τὰ
τοιαῦτα πρὸς τὰ καθόλου καὶ τὰ ἐπὶ μέρους, καὶ
διὰ τὸ μᾶλλον τὰς θέσεις κομίζειν ἐν τῷ ὑπάρχειν
10 ἢ μή, τοὺς δὲ διαλεγομένους ἀνασκευάζειν. ἔστι
δὲ χαλεπώτατον τὸ ἀντιστρέφειν τὴν ἀπὸ τοῦ
συμβεβηκότος οἰκείαν ὀνομασίαν· τὸ γὰρ πῇ καὶ
μὴ καθόλου ἐπὶ μόνων ἐνδέχεται τῶν συμβεβηκότων. ἀπὸ μὲν γὰρ τοῦ ὅρου καὶ τοῦ ἰδίου καὶ
τοῦ γένους ἀναγκαῖον ἀντιστρέφειν, οἷον εἰ ὑπάρχει
15 τινὶ ζῴῳ πεζῷ δίποδι εἶναι, ἀντιστρέψαντι ἀληθὲς
ἔσται λέγειν ὅτι ζῷον πεζὸν δίπουν ἐστίν. ὁμοίως

BOOK II

COMMON-
PLACES
ABOUT
PREDICA-
TIONS. (A)
OF ACCI-
DENT.

Problems,
universal
and
particular.

Peculiar
difficulties
of problems
based on
accident.

I. Some problems are universal, others particular. Examples of universal problems are " Every pleasure is good," and " No pleasure is good "; examples of particular problems are " Some pleasure is good," and " Some pleasure is not good." Universally constructive and destructive methods are common to both kinds of problem ; for when we have shown that some predicate belongs in all instances, we shall also have shown that it belongs in some particular instance, and, similarly, if we show that it does not belong in any instance, we shall also have shown that it does not belong in every instance. First, then, we must speak of universally destructive methods, because such methods are common both to universal and to particular problems and because people bring forward theses asserting the presence of a predicate rather than its absence, while those who are arguing against them seek to demolish them. It is very difficult to convert an appropriate appellation which is derived from an ' accident '; for only in the case of accidents can something be predicated conditionally and not universally. For conversion must necessarily be based on the definition and the property and the genus. For example, if " to be a biped pedestrian animal is an attribute of A," it will be true to say by conversion that " A is a biped pedestrian animal."

331

δὲ καὶ ἀπὸ τοῦ γένους· εἰ γὰρ ζῴῳ ὑπάρχει τινὶ
εἶναι, ζῷόν ἐστιν. τὰ δ' αὐτὰ καὶ ἐπὶ τοῦ ἰδίου·
εἰ γὰρ ὑπάρχει τινὶ γραμματικῆς δεκτικῷ εἶναι,
γραμματικῆς δεκτικὸν ἔσται. οὐδὲν γὰρ τούτων
20 ἐνδέχεται κατά τι ὑπάρχειν ἢ μὴ ὑπάρχειν, ἀλλ'
ἁπλῶς ἢ ὑπάρχειν ἢ μὴ ὑπάρχειν. ἐπὶ δὲ τῶν
συμβεβηκότων οὐδὲν κωλύει κατά τι ὑπάρχειν,
οἷον λευκότητα ἢ δικαιοσύνην, ὥστε οὐκ ἀπόχρη
τὸ δεῖξαι ὅτι ὑπάρχει λευκότης ἢ δικαιοσύνη πρὸς
τὸ δεῖξαι ὅτι λευκὸς ἢ δίκαιός ἐστιν· ἔχει γὰρ
25 ἀμφισβήτησιν ὅτι κατά τι λευκὸς ἢ δίκαιός ἐστιν.
ὥστ' οὐκ ἀναγκαῖον ἐπὶ τῶν συμβεβηκότων τὸ
ἀντιστρέφειν.

Διορίσασθαι δὲ δεῖ καὶ τὰς ἁμαρτίας τὰς ἐν τοῖς
προβλήμασιν, ὅτι εἰσὶ διτταί, ἢ τῷ ψεύδεσθαι ἢ
τῷ παραβαίνειν τὴν κειμένην λέξιν. οἵ τε γὰρ
30 ψευδόμενοι καὶ τὸ μὴ ὑπάρχον ὑπάρχειν τινὶ λέγοντες ἁμαρτάνουσι· καὶ οἱ τοῖς ἀλλοτρίοις ὀνόμασι
τὰ πράγματα προσαγορεύοντες, οἷον τὴν πλάτανον
ἄνθρωπον, παραβαίνουσι τὴν κειμένην ὀνομασίαν.

II. Εἷς μὲν δὴ τόπος τὸ ἐπιβλέπειν εἰ τὸ κατ'
35 ἄλλον τινὰ τρόπον ὑπάρχον ὡς συμβεβηκὸς ἀποδέδωκεν. ἁμαρτάνεται δὲ μάλιστα τοῦτο περὶ τὰ
γένη, οἷον εἴ τις τῷ λευκῷ φαίη συμβεβηκέναι χρώματι εἶναι· οὐ γὰρ συμβέβηκε τῷ λευκῷ χρώματι εἶναι, ἀλλὰ γένος αὐτοῦ τὸ χρῶμά ἐστιν.
ἐνδέχεται μὲν οὖν καὶ κατὰ τὴν ὀνομασίαν διορίσαι
109 b τὸν τιθέμενον, οἷον ὅτι συμβέβηκε τῇ δικαιοσύνῃ

---

^a *i.e.* that colour is an accident of white.

So too if the appellation is derived from genus; for, if " to be an animal is an attribute of A," then " A is an animal." The same thing occurs in the case of a property; if " to be receptive of grammar is an attribute of B," then " B will be receptive of grammar." For it is impossible for any of these attributes to belong or not belong in part only; but they must belong or not belong absolutely. In the case of accidents, however, there is nothing to prevent an attribute belonging in part only (*e.g.*, whiteness or justice), and so it is not enough to show that whiteness or justice is an attribute of a man in order to show that he is white or just; for it is possible to argue that he is only partly white or just. In the case of accidents, therefore, conversion is not necessarily possible.

We must also define the errors which occur in problems, which are of two kinds, being due either to misrepresentation or to violation of the established use of language. Those who employ misrepresentation and assert that a thing has some attribute which it has not, commit error; while those who call things by names which do not belong to them (*e.g.*, calling a plane-tree a man) violate the established nomenclature. *Two common errors.*

II. One commonplace is to look whether your opponent has assigned as an accident something which belongs in some other way. This mistake is usually committed in respect of genera, for example, if someone should say that white happens to be a colour [a]; for white does not happen to be a colour, but colour is its genus. Possibly, it is true, the man who is making the statement may expressly define the attribute as an accident, saying, for example, *Various rules regarding problems of Accident. (a) Proof that what has been assigned as accident is not accident.*

ARISTOTLE

109 b

ἀρετῇ εἶναι· πολλάκις δὲ καὶ μὴ διορίσαντι κατάδηλον ὅτι τὸ γένος ὡς συμβεβηκὸς ἀποδέδωκεν,
οἷον εἴ τις τὴν λευκότητα κεχρῶσθαι φήσειεν ἢ
5 τὴν βάδισιν κινεῖσθαι. ἀπ' οὐδενὸς γὰρ γένους
παρωνύμως ἡ κατηγορία κατὰ τοῦ εἴδους λέγεται,
ἀλλὰ πάντα συνωνύμως τὰ γένη τῶν εἰδῶν κατη-
γορεῖται· καὶ γὰρ τοὔνομα καὶ τὸν λόγον ἐπιδέχεται
τῶν γενῶν τὰ εἴδη. ὁ οὖν κεχρωσμένον εἴπας τὸ
λευκὸν οὔτε ὡς γένος ἀποδέδωκεν, ἐπειδὴ παρω-
10 νύμως εἴρηκεν, οὔθ' ὡς ἴδιον ἢ ὡς ὁρισμόν· ὁ γὰρ
ὁρισμὸς καὶ τὸ ἴδιον οὐδενὶ ἄλλῳ ὑπάρχει, κέχρωσται δὲ πολλὰ καὶ τῶν ἄλλων, οἷον ξύλον λίθος
ἄνθρωπος ἵππος. δῆλον οὖν ὅτι ὡς συμβεβηκὸς
ἀποδίδωσιν.

Ἄλλος τὸ ἐπιβλέπειν οἷς ὑπάρχειν ἢ πᾶσιν ἢ
μηδενὶ εἴρηται, σκοπεῖν δὲ κατ' εἴδη καὶ μὴ ἐν
15 τοῖς ἀπείροις· ὁδῷ γὰρ μᾶλλον καὶ ἐν ἐλάττοσιν
ἡ σκέψις. δεῖ δὲ σκοπεῖν καὶ ἄρχεσθαι ἀπὸ τῶν
πρώτων, εἶτ' ἐφεξῆς ἕως τῶν ἀτόμων, οἷον εἰ τῶν
ἀντικειμένων τὴν αὐτὴν ἐπιστήμην ἔφησεν εἶναι,
σκεπτέον εἰ τῶν πρός τι καὶ τῶν ἐναντίων καὶ
τῶν κατὰ στέρησιν καὶ ἕξιν καὶ τῶν κατ' ἀντίφα-
20 σιν λεγομένων ἡ αὐτὴ ἐπιστήμη· κἂν ἐπὶ τούτων
μήπω φανερὸν ᾖ, πάλιν ταῦτα διαιρετέον μέχρι

ᵃ The meaning of παρωνύμως is explained in *Cat.* 1 a 12 ff. :
" Things are named ' derivatively ' which derive their name
from something else, being given a different word-form,
e.g., ' grammarian ' from ' grammar ' and ' courageous '
from ' courage.' " *Cf.* also Aesch. *Eum.* 8 τὸ Φοίβης δ' ὄνομ'
ἔχει (sc. Φοῖβος) παρώνυμον.

334

" Justice happens to be a virtue," but often, even if he does not so define it, it is obvious that he has assigned the genus as an accident, for example, if one were to say that " whiteness is coloured," or that " walking is motion." For a predicate taken from a genus is never applied to a species in a derived verbal form,[a] but all genera are predicated unequivocally of their species; for the species take the name and the description of their genera. A man, therefore, who speaks of white as ' coloured ' has not assigned ' colour ' as a genus, since he has described it by a derived form of the word, nor as a property, nor as a definition; for the definition and the property of a thing belong to nothing but that thing, whereas many other things are ' coloured,' for example, a piece of wood, a stone, a man or a horse. It is obvious, therefore, that he is assigning ' coloured ' as an accident.

Another commonplace rule is to examine instances *(b)* Examination of the subjects of predication. in which a predicate has been said to belong to all or none of a particular thing, and to look at them according to species and not in their infinite number; for then the examination will be more methodical and in fewer stages. The examination must be carried on and begin from the primary classes and then go on step by step until further division is impossible. For example, if your opponent has said that " the knowledge of opposites is the same," you must examine whether the knowledge is the same of relative opposites and contraries and predicates based on the privation and presence of certain conditions, and of contradictory predicates. If the matter is not yet clear in the light of these, the process of division must be continued until the

109 b

τῶν ἀτόμων, οἷον εἰ τῶν δικαίων καὶ ἀδίκων,
ἢ τοῦ διπλασίου καὶ ἡμίσεος, ἢ τυφλότητος καὶ
ὄψεως, ἢ τοῦ εἶναι καὶ μὴ εἶναι. ἐὰν γὰρ ἐπί
τινος δειχθῇ ὅτι οὐχ ἡ αὐτή, ἀνῃρηκότες ἐσόμεθα
25 τὸ πρόβλημα· ὁμοίως δὲ καὶ ἐὰν μηδενὶ ὑπάρχῃ.
οὗτος δ' ὁ τόπος ἀντιστρέφει πρὸς τὸ ἀνασκευάζειν
καὶ κατασκευάζειν. ἐὰν γὰρ ἐπὶ πάντων φαίνηται
διαίρεσιν προενέγκασιν ἢ ἐπὶ πολλῶν, ἀξιωτέον
καὶ καθόλου τιθέναι ἢ ἔνστασιν φέρειν ἐπὶ τίνος
οὐχ οὕτως· ἐὰν γὰρ μηδέτερον τούτων ποιῇ,
ἄτοπος φανεῖται μὴ τιθείς.

30 Ἄλλος τὸ λόγους ποιεῖν τοῦ τε συμβεβηκότος καὶ
ᾧ συμβέβηκεν, ἢ ἀμφοτέρων καθ' ἑκάτερον ἢ τοῦ
ἑτέρου, εἶτα σκοπεῖν εἴ τι μὴ ἀληθὲς ἐν τοῖς λόγοις
ὡς ἀληθὲς εἴληπται. οἷον εἰ ἔστι θεὸν ἀδικεῖν,
τί τὸ ἀδικεῖν; εἰ γὰρ τὸ βλάπτειν ἑκουσίως, δῆλον
ὡς οὐκ ἔστι θεὸν ἀδικεῖσθαι· οὐ γὰρ ἐνδέχεται
35 βλάπτεσθαι τὸν θεόν. καὶ εἰ φθονερὸς ὁ σπουδαῖος,
τίς ὁ φθονερὸς καὶ τίς ὁ φθόνος; εἰ γὰρ ὁ φθόνος
ἐστὶ λύπη ἐπὶ φαινομένῃ εὐπραγίᾳ τῶν ἐπιεικῶν
τινός, δῆλον ὅτι ὁ σπουδαῖος οὐ φθονερός· φαῦλος
γὰρ ἂν εἴη. καὶ εἰ ὁ νεμεσητικὸς φθονερός, τίς
110 a ἑκάτερος αὐτῶν; οὕτω γὰρ καταφανὲς ἔσται
πότερον ἀληθὲς ἢ ψεῦδος τὸ ῥηθέν, οἷον εἰ φθονερὸς
μὲν ὁ λυπούμενος ἐπὶ ταῖς τῶν ἀγαθῶν εὐπραγίαις,

336

indivisible is reached, for example, until you see if it is true of "just and unjust actions," "the double and the half," "blindness and sight," or "being and not-being." For if it is shown in any instance that the knowledge is not the same, we shall have demolished the problem. Similarly, too, if the predicate does not belong in any instance. This commonplace is convertible both for destructive and for constructive purposes ; for if, after a long process of division, the predicate appears to apply in all or in numerous cases, we must claim that our opponent should admit its universal application or else bring forward an objection and show in what case it does not apply. If he does neither of these things, he will look foolish if he refuses to make the admission.

Another commonplace is to make definitions both of the accident and of that to which it belongs, either of both separately or one of them, and then see if anything untrue has been assumed as true in the definitions. For example, to see if it is possible to wrong a god, you must ask, what does 'wrong' mean ? For if it means 'to harm wittingly,' it is obvious that it is impossible for a god to be wronged, for it is impossible for God to be harmed. Again, to see whether the good man is envious, you must ask, who is 'envious' and what is 'envy' ? For if 'envy' is pain at the apparent prosperity of an honest man, clearly the good man is not envious ; for then he would be a bad man. Again, to see whether the indignant man is envious, you must ask, what does each of these terms mean ? For thus it will be manifest whether the statement is true or false ; for example, if the man is 'envious' who is pained at the prosperity of the good, and the

(c) Definition of the accident and its subject.

337

110 a

νεμεσητικὸς δ' ὁ λυπούμενος ἐπὶ ταῖς τῶν κακῶν
εὐπραγίαις, δῆλον ὅτι οὐκ ἂν εἴη φθονερὸς ὁ
5 νεμεσητικός. λαμβάνειν δὲ καὶ ἀντὶ τῶν ἐν τοῖς
λόγοις ὀνομάτων λόγους, καὶ μὴ ἀφίστασθαι ἕως
ἂν εἰς γνώριμον ἔλθῃ· πολλάκις γὰρ ὅλου μὲν τοῦ
λόγου ἀποδοθέντος οὔπω δῆλον τὸ ζητούμενον,
ἀντὶ δέ τινος τῶν ἐν τῷ λόγῳ ὀνομάτων λόγου
ῥηθέντος κατάδηλον γίνεται.

10 Ἔτι τὸ πρόβλημα πρότασιν ἑαυτῷ ποιούμενον
ἐνίστασθαι· ἡ γὰρ ἔνστασις ἔσται ἐπιχείρημα πρὸς
τὴν θέσιν. ἔστι δ' ὁ τόπος οὗτος σχεδὸν ὁ αὐτὸς
τῷ ἐπιβλέπειν οἷς ὑπάρχειν ἢ πᾶσιν ἢ μηδενὶ
εἴρηται· διαφέρει δὲ τῷ τρόπῳ.

Ἔτι διορίζεσθαι ποῖα δεῖ καλεῖν ὡς οἱ πολλοὶ
15 καὶ ποῖα οὔ· χρήσιμον γὰρ καὶ πρὸς τὸ κατασκευάζειν καὶ πρὸς τὸ ἀνασκευάζειν· οἷον ὅτι
ταῖς μὲν ὀνομασίαις τὰ πράγματα προσαγορευτέον
καθάπερ οἱ πολλοί, ποῖα δὲ τῶν πραγμάτων ἐστὶ
τοιαῦτα ἢ οὐ τοιαῦτα, οὐκέτι προσεκτέον τοῖς
πολλοῖς. οἷον ὑγιεινὸν μὲν ῥητέον τὸ ποιητικὸν
20 ὑγιείας, ὡς οἱ πολλοὶ λέγουσιν· πότερον δὲ τὸ
προκείμενον ποιητικὸν ὑγιείας ἢ οὔ, οὐκέτι ὡς
οἱ πολλοὶ κλητέον ἀλλ' ὡς ὁ ἰατρός.

III. Ἔτι ἐὰν πολλαχῶς λέγηται, κείμενον δὲ
ᾖ ὡς ὑπάρχει ἢ ὡς οὐχ ὑπάρχει, θάτερον δεικνύναι

---

^a *i.e.* the objection will enable you to examine the assertion
dialectically.
^b *Cf.* 109 b 13.

338

indignant man is he who is pained at the prosperity of the wicked, it is obvious that the indignant man could not be envious. One ought also to substitute definitions for the terms used in the definitions and to go on doing this until some familiar term is reached. For often, though the whole definition has been given, the object of our search is not yet clear, but it becomes clear when a definition has been given in place of one of the terms in the definition.

Furthermore, one ought to turn the problem for oneself into a proposition and then raise an objection to it; for an objection will be an argument against a thesis.[a] This commonplace rule is almost the same as examining instances in which a predicate has been said to belong to all or none of a particular thing,[b] but it differs in method. *(d) Change of the problem into a proposition.*

Furthermore, you must define what kinds of things should be called as the majority call them, and what should not; for this is useful both for constructive and destructive purposes. For instance, you ought to lay it down that things ought to be described in the language used by the majority, but when it is asked what things are of certain kinds and what are not, you must no longer pay attention to the majority. For example, you must say, as do the majority, that ' healthy ' is that which is productive of health; but when it is asked whether the subject under discussion is productive of health or not, you must no longer use the language of the majority, but that of the doctor. *(e) Definition of what vulgar denominations should be admitted and what rejected.*

III. Furthermore, if a term is used with more than one meaning and it has been stated that it belongs to or does not belong to something, we ought to *Rules for dealing with ambiguity. (a) If the*

339

25 τῶν πλεοναχῶς λεγομένων, ἐὰν μὴ ἄμφω ἐνδέχηται. χρηστέον δ᾿ ἐπὶ τῶν λανθανόντων· ἐὰν
γὰρ μὴ λανθάνῃ πολλαχῶς λεγόμενον, ἐνστήσεται
ὅτι οὐ διείλεκται ὅπερ αὐτὸς ἠπόρει, ἀλλὰ θάτερον. οὗτος δ᾿ ὁ τόπος ἀντιστρέφει καὶ πρὸς
τὸ κατασκευάσαι καὶ ἀνασκευάσαι. κατασκευάζειν
30 μὲν γὰρ βουλόμενοι δείξομεν ὅτι θάτερον ὑπάρχει,
ἐὰν μὴ ἄμφω δυνώμεθα· ἀνασκευάζοντες δὲ ὅτι
οὐχ ὑπάρχει θάτερον δείξομεν, ἐὰν μὴ ἄμφω
δυνώμεθα. πλὴν ἀνασκευάζοντι μὲν οὐδὲν δεῖ ἐξ
ὁμολογίας διαλέγεσθαι, οὔτ᾿ εἰ παντὶ οὔτ᾿ εἰ
μηδενὶ ὑπάρχειν εἴρηται· ἐὰν γὰρ δείξωμεν ὅτι
35 οὐχ ὑπάρχει ὁτῳοῦν, ἀνῃρηκότες ἐσόμεθα τὸ παντὶ
ὑπάρχειν, ὁμοίως δὲ κἂν ἑνὶ δείξωμεν ὑπάρχον,
ἀναιρήσομεν τὸ μηδενὶ ὑπάρχειν. κατασκευάζουσι
δὲ προδιομολογητέον ὅτι εἰ ὁτῳοῦν ὑπάρχει παντὶ
110 b ὑπάρχει, ἂν πιθανὸν ᾖ τὸ ἀξίωμα. οὐ γὰρ ἀπόχρη
πρὸς τὸ δεῖξαι ὅτι παντὶ ὑπάρχει τὸ ἐφ᾿ ἑνὸς
διαλεχθῆναι, οἷον εἰ ἡ τοῦ ἀνθρώπου ψυχὴ ἀθάνατος, διότι ψυχὴ πᾶσα ἀθάνατος, ὥστε προομο-
λογητέον ὅτι εἰ ἡτισοῦν ψυχὴ ἀθάνατος, πᾶσα
5 ἀθάνατος. τοῦτο δ᾿ οὐκ ἀεὶ ποιητέον, ἀλλ᾿ ὅταν
μὴ εὐπορῶμεν κοινὸν ἐπὶ πάντων ἕνα λόγον

demonstrate one of the several meanings if it is impossible to demonstrate both. This method should be used when the variety of meaning is unnoticed ; for, if it is noticed, the opponent will object that the question which he himself raised has not been discussed, but the other meaning. This commonplace is convertible for both constructive and destructive purposes. If we wish to argue constructively, we shall show that the attribute belongs in one of its senses, if we cannot show it belongs in both. For destructive criticism, we shall show that one of its senses does not belong, if we cannot show that both do not do so. In destructive criticism, however, there is no need to argue on the basis of an admission, either if the attribute is stated to belong universally or if it is stated not to belong to anything ; for if we show that there is anything whatsoever to which it does not belong, we shall have destroyed the assertion that it belongs universally, and, similarly, if we can show that it does belong in a single case, we shall demolish the assertion that it does not belong to anything. If, however, we are arguing constructively, we ought to obtain a preliminary admission that, if the attribute belongs to any one thing, it belongs universally, provided the claim is plausible. For it is not enough to argue in a single case in order to show that an attribute belongs universally—to argue, for example, that if the soul of man is immortal, then every soul is immortal. We must, therefore, obtain beforehand an admission that if any soul whatever is immortal, then every soul is immortal. This method must not be employed always, but only when we are not in a position to state a single argument which applies to all cases

ambiguity of a term escapes the opponent, use the meaning best suited to your argument.

341

ARISTOTLE

110 b

εἰπεῖν, καθάπερ ὁ γεωμέτρης ὅτι τὸ τρίγωνον
δυσὶν ὀρθαῖς ἴσας ἔχει.

Ἐὰν δὲ μὴ λανθάνῃ πολλαχῶς λεγόμενον, διελόμενον ὁσαχῶς λέγεται, καὶ ἀναιρεῖν καὶ κατα-
10 σκευάζειν. οἷον εἰ τὸ δέον ἐστὶ τὸ συμφέρον
ἢ τὸ καλόν, πειρατέον ἄμφω κατασκευάζειν ἢ
ἀναιρεῖν περὶ τοῦ προκειμένου, οἷον ὅτι καλὸν
καὶ συμφέρον, ἢ ὅτι οὔτε καλὸν οὔτε συμφέρον.
ἐὰν δὲ μὴ ἐνδέχηται ἀμφότερα, θάτερον δεικτέον,
ἐπισημαινόμενον ὅτι τὸ μὲν τὸ δ᾽ οὔ. ὁ δ᾽ αὐτὸς
15 λόγος κἂν πλείω ᾖ εἰς ἃ διαιρεῖται.

Πάλιν ὅσα μὴ καθ᾽ ὁμωνυμίαν λέγεται πολλαχῶς, ἀλλὰ κατ᾽ ἄλλον τρόπον, οἷον ἐπιστήμη
μία πλειόνων ἢ ὡς τοῦ τέλους καὶ τοῦ πρὸς τὸ
τέλος, οἷον ἰατρικὴ τοῦ ὑγίειαν ποιῆσαι καὶ τοῦ
20 διαιτῆσαι, ἢ ὡς ἀμφοτέρων τελῶν, καθάπερ τῶν
ἐναντίων ἡ αὐτὴ λέγεται ἐπιστήμη (οὐδὲν γὰρ
μᾶλλον τέλος τὸ ἕτερον τοῦ ἑτέρου), ἢ ὡς τοῦ
καθ᾽ αὑτὸ καὶ τοῦ κατὰ συμβεβηκός, οἷον καθ᾽
αὑτὸ μὲν ὅτι τὸ τρίγωνον δυσὶν ὀρθαῖς ἴσας ἔχει,
κατὰ συμβεβηκὸς δὲ ὅτι τὸ ἰσόπλευρον· ὅτι γὰρ
συμβέβηκε τῷ [τριγώνῳ]¹ ἰσοπλεύρῳ τριγώνῳ
25 εἶναι, κατὰ τοῦτο γνωρίζομεν ὅτι δυσὶν ὀρθαῖς
ἴσας ἔχει. εἰ οὖν μηδαμῶς ἐνδέχεται τὴν αὐτὴν
εἶναι πλειόνων ἐπιστήμην, δῆλον ὅτι ὅλως οὐκ

¹ Omitting τριγώνῳ with Buhle.

342

alike, as for example, when a geometrician states that the angles of a triangle are equal to two right angles.

If there is no concealing the fact that a term has a variety of meanings, you must distinguish all of them and then proceed to demolish or confirm it. For example, if the 'right' is the 'expedient' or the 'honourable,' we must try to confirm or demolish both of these terms as applied to the subject under discussion, showing that it is honourable and expedient, or that it is neither honourable nor expedient. If it is impossible to show both, we must show one, indicating also that one is true and the other not true. The same argument also holds good when the meanings into which the term can be divided are more than two. (b) If the ambiguity is obvious, distinguish the meanings of the term which suit the argument.

Again, there is the case of terms which are used in several senses not because they are equivocal but in some other way. Take, for example, "The science of many things is one"; here the things in question may be the ends or the means to an end (*e.g.*, medicine is the science of producing health and of diet), or they may be both of them ends, as the science of contraries is said to be the same (for one contrary is not more an end than the other), or they may be an essential and an accidental attribute—an example of the former being that the angles of a triangle are equal to two right angles, of the latter that this is true of an equilateral triangle; for we know that it is because the equilateral triangle happens to be a triangle that its angles are equal to two right angles. If, therefore, there is no sense in which it is possible for the science of many things to be the same, it is obvious that it is completely impossible that this can

343

110 b

ἐνδέχεται εἶναι, ἢ εἴ πως ἐνδέχεται, δῆλον ὅτι
ἐνδέχεται. διαιρεῖσθαι δὲ ὁσαχῶς χρήσιμον. οἷον
ἐὰν βουλώμεθα κατασκευάσαι, τὰ τοιαῦτα προ-
30 οιστέον ὅσα ἐνδέχεται, καὶ διαιρετέον εἰς ταῦτα
μόνον ὅσα καὶ χρήσιμα πρὸς τὸ κατασκευάσαι·
ἂν δ' ἀνασκευάσαι, ὅσα μὴ ἐνδέχεται, τὰ δὲ λοιπὰ παραλειπτέον. ποιητέον δὲ ⟨τοῦτο⟩[1] καὶ ἐπὶ
τούτων, ὅταν λανθάνῃ ποσαχῶς λέγεται. καὶ εἶναι δὲ τόδε τοῦδε ἢ μὴ εἶναι ἐκ τῶν αὐτῶν τόπων
35 κατασκευαστέον, οἷον ἐπιστήμην τήνδε τοῦδε ἢ
ὡς τέλους ἢ ὡς τῶν πρὸς τὸ τέλος ἢ ὡς τῶν κατὰ
συμβεβηκός, ἢ πάλιν μὴ εἶναί [τι][2] κατὰ μηδένα
τῶν ῥηθέντων τρόπων. ὁ δ' αὐτὸς λόγος καὶ περὶ
ἐπιθυμίας, καὶ ὅσα ἄλλα λέγεται πλειόνων. ἔστι
111 a γὰρ ἡ ἐπιθυμία τούτου ἢ ὡς τέλους, οἷον ὑγιείας,
ἢ ὡς τῶν πρὸς τὸ τέλος, οἷον τοῦ φαρμακευθῆναι,
ἢ ὡς τοῦ κατὰ συμβεβηκός, καθάπερ ἐπὶ τοῦ
οἴνου ὁ φιλόγλυκυς οὐχ ὅτι οἶνος ἀλλ' ὅτι γλυκύς
ἐστιν. καθ' αὐτὸ μὲν γὰρ τοῦ γλυκέος ἐπιθυμεῖ,
5 τοῦ δ' οἴνου κατὰ συμβεβηκός· ἐὰν γὰρ αὐστηρὸς
ᾖ, οὐκέτι ἐπιθυμεῖ. κατὰ συμβεβηκὸς οὖν ἐπιθυμεῖ. χρήσιμος δ' ὁ τόπος οὗτος ἐν τοῖς πρός
τι· σχεδὸν γὰρ τὰ τοιαῦτα τῶν πρός τί ἐστιν.

IV. Ἔτι τὸ μεταλαμβάνειν εἰς τὸ γνωριμώτερον
ὄνομα, οἷον ἀντὶ τοῦ ἀκριβοῦς ἐν ὑπολήψει τὸ
10 σαφὲς καὶ ἀντὶ τῆς πολυπραγμοσύνης τὴν φιλο-
πραγμοσύνην· γνωριμωτέρου γὰρ γινομένου τοῦ

---

[1] Adding τοῦτο. Pacius renders, *in his quoque hoc facien-
dum est.*   [2] Omitting τι with C.

344

be so, or, if there is some sense in which it is possible, then it is obvious that it is possible. We must distinguish as many senses as will serve our purpose. For example, if we wish to argue constructively, we must bring forward such meanings as are admissible and divide them only into those which are useful for constructive argument; for destructive criticism, on the other hand, we must bring forward only such as are not admissible and omit the rest. This must also be done when the variety of meanings is unnoticed. The same commonplaces must also be used to confirm that one thing is, or is not, ' of ' another; for example, that a particular science is ' of ' a particular thing, either as an end, or as a means to an end, or as an accidental circumstance, or, on the other hand, that it is not ' of ' it in any of the above ways. The same holds good of desire and any other terms which are said to be ' of ' more than one thing. For the desire of a particular thing may be the desire of it as an end (*e.g.*, health), or as a means to an end (*e.g.*, taking medicine), or as an accidental circumstance, as in the case of wine the man who likes sweet things desires it not because it is wine but because it is sweet. For his essential desire is for what is sweet, and he only desires wine accidentally; for, if it is dry, he no longer desires it, and so his desire is accidental. This commonplace is also useful in connexion with relative terms; for cases of this kind generally have to do with relative terms.

IV. Moreover, there is the commonplace of substituting for a term one that is more familiar, for example, using ' clear ' instead of ' exact ' in speaking of a conception, and ' meddlesomeness ' instead of ' officiousness.' For when the term is rendered more

Various Rules : (*a*) Substitute more familiar for less familiar terms.

345

ῥηθέντος εὐεπιχειρητοτέρα ἡ θέσις. ἔστι δὲ καὶ
οὗτος ὁ τόπος πρὸς ἄμφω κοινός, καὶ πρὸς τὸ
κατασκευάζειν καὶ ἀνασκευάζειν.

Πρὸς δὲ τὸ δεῖξαι τἀναντία τῷ αὐτῷ ὑπάρχοντα
15 σκοπεῖν ἐπὶ τοῦ γένους, οἷον ἐὰν βουλώμεθα δεῖξαι
ὅτι ἔστι περὶ αἴσθησιν ὀρθότης καὶ ἁμαρτία, τὸ
δ' αἰσθάνεσθαι κρίνειν ἐστί, κρίνειν δ' ἔστιν ὀρθῶς
καὶ μὴ ὀρθῶς, καὶ περὶ αἴσθησιν ἂν εἴη ὀρθότης
καὶ ἁμαρτία. νῦν μὲν οὖν ἐκ τοῦ γένους περὶ τὸ
εἶδος ἡ ἀπόδειξις· τὸ γὰρ κρίνειν γένος τοῦ αἰσθά-
20 νεσθαι· ὁ γὰρ αἰσθανόμενος κρίνει πως. πάλιν δ'
ἐκ τοῦ εἴδους τῷ γένει· ὅσα γὰρ τῷ εἴδει ὑπάρχει,
καὶ τῷ γένει, οἷον εἰ ἔστιν ἐπιστήμη φαύλη καὶ
σπουδαία, καὶ διάθεσις φαύλη καὶ σπουδαία· ἡ
γὰρ διάθεσις τῆς ἐπιστήμης γένος. ὁ μὲν οὖν
πρότερος τόπος ψευδής ἐστι πρὸς τὸ κατασκευάσαι,
25 ὁ δὲ δεύτερος ἀληθής. οὐ γὰρ ἀναγκαῖον, ὅσα
τῷ γένει ὑπάρχει, καὶ τῷ εἴδει ὑπάρχειν· ζῷον
μὲν γάρ ἐστι πτηνὸν καὶ τετράπουν, ἄνθρωπος δ'
οὔ. ὅσα δὲ τῷ εἴδει ὑπάρχει, ἀναγκαῖον καὶ τῷ
γένει· εἰ γάρ ἐστιν ἄνθρωπος σπουδαῖος, καὶ ζῷόν
ἐστι σπουδαῖον. πρὸς δὲ τὸ ἀνασκευάζειν ὁ μὲν
30 πρότερος ἀληθής, ὁ δὲ ὕστερος ψευδής· ὅσα γὰρ
τῷ γένει οὐχ ὑπάρχει, οὐδὲ τῷ εἴδει· ὅσα δὲ τῷ
εἴδει μὴ ὑπάρχει, οὐκ ἀναγκαῖον τῷ γένει μὴ
ὑπάρχειν.

Ἐπεὶ δ' ἀναγκαῖον, ὧν τὸ γένος κατηγορεῖται,

familiar, the thesis is more easily dealt with. This commonplace is common to both processes, the constructive and the destructive.

In order to show that contrary attributes belong to the same thing, we must look at its genus. For example, if we wish to show that there is correctness and error in perception, and if to perceive is to distinguish and distinguishing can be correct or incorrect, then there can be correctness and error in perception also. Here, then, the proof starts from the genus and is concerned with the species, for 'distinguishing' is the genus of 'perceiving,' since he who perceives is distinguishing in a certain way. On the other hand, the proof may start from the species and be concerned with the genus, for all attributes which belong to the species belong also to the genus. For instance, if there is good and bad knowledge, then there also is good and bad disposition ; for disposition is the genus of knowledge. The former commonplace is fallacious for constructive argument, but the latter is true. For it is not necessary that all the attributes of the genus should also belong to the species ; for 'animal' is winged and quadruped, but 'man' is not. But all the attributes which belong to the species, necessarily belong also to the genus ; for if 'man' is good, then 'animal' also is good. On the other hand, for destructive criticism, the former of these arguments is true, the latter fallacious ; for all the attributes which do not belong to the genus do not belong to the species either, while all those which fail to belong to the species do not necessarily fail to belong to the genus.

Since of all those things of which the genus is predicated, one of its species must necessarily also

(b) To prove the presence of contraries, examine the genus.

A note on genus and species.

347

111 a

καὶ τῶν εἰδῶν τι κατηγορεῖσθαι, καὶ ὅσα ἔχει τὸ
35 γένος ἢ παρωνύμως ἀπὸ τοῦ γένους λέγεται, καὶ
τῶν εἰδῶν τι ἀναγκαῖον ἔχειν ἢ παρωνύμως ἀπό
τινος τῶν εἰδῶν λέγεσθαι (οἷον εἴ τινος ἐπιστήμη
κατηγορεῖται, καὶ γραμματικὴ ἢ μουσικὴ ἢ τῶν
ἄλλων τις ἐπιστημῶν κατηγορηθήσεται, καὶ εἴ τις
111 b ἔχει ἐπιστήμην ἢ παρωνύμως ἀπὸ τῆς ἐπιστήμης
λέγεται, καὶ γραμματικὴν ἕξει ἢ μουσικὴν ἢ τινα
τῶν ἄλλων ἐπιστημῶν ἢ παρωνύμως ἀπό τινος
αὐτῶν ῥηθήσεται, οἷον γραμματικὸς ἢ μουσικός),
5 ἐὰν οὖν τι τεθῇ λεγόμενον ἀπὸ τοῦ γένους ὁπωσοῦν,
οἷον τὴν ψυχὴν κινεῖσθαι, σκοπεῖν εἰ κατά τι τῶν
εἰδῶν τῶν τῆς κινήσεως ἐνδέχεται τὴν ψυχὴν
κινεῖσθαι, οἷον αὔξεσθαι ἢ φθείρεσθαι ἢ γίνεσθαι
ἢ ὅσα ἄλλα κινήσεως εἴδη· εἰ γὰρ κατὰ μηδέν,
δῆλον ὅτι οὐ κινεῖται. οὗτος δ' ὁ τόπος κοινὸς
πρὸς ἄμφω, πρός τε τὸ ἀνασκευάζειν καὶ κατασκευ-
10 άζειν· εἰ γὰρ κατά τι τῶν εἰδῶν κινεῖται, δῆλον
ὅτι κινεῖται, καὶ εἰ κατὰ μηδὲν τῶν εἰδῶν κινεῖται,
δῆλον ὅτι οὐ κινεῖται.

Μὴ εὐποροῦντι δὲ ἐπιχειρήματος πρὸς τὴν θέσιν,
σκοπεῖν ἐκ τῶν ὁρισμῶν ἢ τῶν ὄντων τοῦ προκειμένου πράγματος ἢ τῶν δοκούντων, καὶ εἰ[1]
15 μὴ ἀφ' ἑνὸς ἀλλ' ἀπὸ πλειόνων. ῥᾷον γὰρ ὁρισα-

---

[1] Reading, with B, καὶ εἰ: κἂν εἰ P: καὶ Bekker.

be predicated, and since all those things which
possess that genus, or derive their description from
that genus, must also possess one of its species or
derive their description from one of its species—for
example, if knowledge is predicated of someone, then
grammatical knowledge or musical knowledge or one
of the other kinds of knowledge will be predicated
of him, and if a man possesses knowledge or if
the description which he has is derived from his
knowledge, then he will also possess grammatical
knowledge or musical knowledge, or one of the other
kinds of knowledge, or will derive his description
from one of them, being called, for example, a
' grammarian ' or a ' musician '—then, if a statement is made which is derived in any way from
the genus (for example, that the soul is in motion),
you must examine whether it is possible for the
soul to be in motion according to any of the species
of motion, for example, whether it can increase
or decay or come into being or move in any of
the other species of motion ; for if it cannot move
in accordance with any of them, obviously it is not
in motion. This commonplace is common to both
processes, the destructive and the constructive ; for
if it moves according to one of the species of motion,
obviously it is in motion, and if it does not move in
accordance with any of them, obviously it is not in
motion.

If you have not a supply of material for arguing
against the thesis, you should look for arguments
taken from the real or generally accepted definitions
of the subject under discussion, and if you cannot
argue from one, you must argue from several. For
it is easier to attack the subject when you have

(c) Obtain
material by
examining
the defini-
tions of the
subject.

349

111 b

μένοις ἐπιχειρεῖν ἔσται· πρὸς γὰρ τοὺς ὁρισμοὺς
ῥᾷον ἡ ἐπιχείρησις.

Σκοπεῖν δὲ ἐπὶ τοῦ προκειμένου, τίνος ὄντος τὸ
προκείμενόν ἐστιν, ἢ τί ἔστιν ἐξ ἀνάγκης εἰ τὸ
προκείμενον ἔστι, κατασκευάζειν μὲν βουλομένῳ,
20 τίνος ὄντος τὸ προκείμενον ἔσται (ἐὰν γὰρ ἐκεῖνο
δειχθῇ ὑπάρχον, καὶ τὸ προκείμενον δεδειγμένον
ἔσται), ἀνασκευάζειν δὲ βουλομένῳ, τί ἔστιν εἰ
τὸ προκείμενον ἔστιν· ἐὰν γὰρ δείξωμεν τὸ ἀκόλουθον τῷ προκειμένῳ μὴ ὄν, ἀνῃρηκότες ἐσόμεθα
τὸ προκείμενον.

Ἔτι ἐπὶ τὸν χρόνον ἐπιβλέπειν, εἴ που διαφωνεῖ,
25 οἷον εἰ τὸ τρεφόμενον ἔφησεν ἐξ ἀνάγκης αὔξεσθαι·
τρέφεται μὲν γὰρ ἀεὶ τὰ ζῷα, αὔξεται δ' οὐκ ἀεί.
ὁμοίως δὲ καὶ εἰ τὸ ἐπίστασθαι ἔφησε μεμνῆσθαι·
τὸ μὲν γὰρ τοῦ παρεληλυθότος χρόνου ἐστί, τὸ
δὲ καὶ τοῦ παρόντος καὶ τοῦ μέλλοντος. ἐπίστασ-
30 θαι μὲν γὰρ λεγόμεθα τὰ παρόντα καὶ τὰ μέλλοντα,
οἷον ὅτι ἔσται ἔκλειψις, μνημονεύειν δ' οὐκ ἐνδέχεται ἀλλ' ἢ τὸ παρεληλυθός.

V. Ἔτι ὁ σοφιστικὸς τρόπος, τὸ ἄγειν εἰς τοιοῦτον πρὸς ὃ εὐπορήσομεν ἐπιχειρημάτων. τοῦτο
δ' ἔσται ὁτὲ μὲν ἀναγκαῖον, ὁτὲ δὲ φαινόμενον
35 ἀναγκαῖον, ὁτὲ δ' οὔτε φαινόμενον οὔτ' ἀναγκαῖον.
ἀναγκαῖον μὲν οὖν, ὅταν ἀρνησαμένου τοῦ ἀπο-
κριναμένου τῶν πρὸς τὴν θέσιν τι χρησίμων πρὸς
τοῦτο τοὺς λόγους ποιῆται, τυγχάνῃ δὲ τοῦτο τῶν

made definitions; for the attack is easier when it is aimed at definitions.

You must examine as regards the subject in hand what it is on the existence of which the existence of the subject depends, or what necessarily exists if the subject exists. For constructive purposes, you must examine what it is on the existence of which the existence of the subject will depend (for if the former has been shown to exist, the subject will have been shown to exist); for destructive purposes, we must examine what exists if the subject exists; for if we show that what is consequent upon the subject does not exist, then we shall have demolished the subject. *(d) Consider on what the existence of the subject depends.*

Furthermore, you must look into the question of time and see if any discrepancy occurs anywhere, for example, if your opponent has said that that which is nourished necessarily grows; for animals are always being nourished but are not always growing. Similarly too, if he has said that knowledge is recollection; for the latter is of the past, the former also of the present and the future. For we are said to know things present and things future (for example, that there will be an eclipse), but it is impossible to remember anything except the past. *(e) The factor of time must be considered.*

V. Furthermore, there is the sophistic method, by which we lead an opponent into the sort of assertion against which we shall have a supply of arguments. This expedient will be sometimes necessary, at others it will only appear necessary, at others it neither is nor appears necessary. It is necessary when, after the answerer has denied some point that is useful for employment against the thesis, the questioner directs his remarks to the support of this point and it happens to be one of the kind about which it is possible to *Rules for extending the argument: (a) The sophistic method can be used for leading on an opponent to make an assertion which can easily be refuted.*

351

111 b

τοιούτων ὂν πρὸς ὃ εὐπορεῖν ἔστιν ἐπιχειρημάτων.

112 a ὁμοίως δὲ καὶ ὅταν ἐπαγωγὴν πρός τι διὰ τοῦ
κειμένου ποιησάμενος ἀναιρεῖν ἐπιχειρῇ· τούτου
γὰρ ἀναιρεθέντος καὶ τὸ προκείμενον ἀναιρεῖται.
φαινόμενον δ' ἀναγκαῖον, ὅταν φαίνηται μὲν
χρήσιμον καὶ οἰκεῖον τῆς θέσεως, μὴ ᾖ δέ, πρὸς
5 ὃ γίγνονται οἱ λόγοι, εἴτε ἀρνησαμένου τοῦ τὸν
λόγον ὑπέχοντος, εἴτε ἐπαγωγῆς ἐνδόξου διὰ τῆς
θέσεως πρὸς αὐτὸ γενομένης[1] ἀναιρεῖν ἐπιχειροίη
αὐτό. τὸ δὲ λοιπόν, ὅταν μήτ' ἀναγκαῖον ᾖ μήτε
φαινόμενον πρὸς ὃ γίνονται οἱ λόγοι, ἄλλως δὲ
παρεξελέγχεσθαι συμβαίνῃ τῷ ἀποκρινομένῳ. δεῖ
10 δ' εὐλαβεῖσθαι τὸν ἔσχατον τῶν ῥηθέντων τρόπων·
παντελῶς γὰρ ἀπηρτημένος καὶ ἀλλότριος ἔοικεν
εἶναι τῆς διαλεκτικῆς. διὸ δεῖ καὶ τὸν ἀποκρινόμενον μὴ δυσκολαίνειν, ἀλλὰ τιθέναι τὰ μὴ χρήσιμα πρὸς τὴν θέσιν, ἐπισημαινόμενον ὅσα μὴ
δοκεῖ, τίθησι δέ. μᾶλλον γὰρ ἀπορεῖν ὡς ἐπὶ τὸ
15 πολὺ συμβαίνει τοῖς ἐρωτῶσι πάντων τιθεμένων
αὐτοῖς τῶν τοιούτων, ἐὰν μὴ περαίνωσιν.

Ἔτι πᾶς ὁ εἰρηκὼς ὁτιοῦν τρόπον τινὰ πολλὰ
εἴρηκεν, ἐπειδὴ πλείω ἑκάστῳ ἐξ ἀνάγκης ἀκό-
λουθά ἐστιν, οἷον ὁ εἰρηκὼς ἄνθρωπον εἶναι καὶ
ὅτι ζῷόν ἐστιν εἴρηκε καὶ ὅτι ἔμψυχον καὶ ὅτι
δίπουν καὶ ὅτι νοῦ καὶ ἐπιστήμης δεκτικόν, ὥστε
20 ὁποιουοῦν ἑνὸς τῶν ἀκολούθων ἀναιρεθέντος ἀν-

---

[1] Reading γενομένης with C: γινομένης Bekker.

have a supply of arguments. It is in like manner necessary also when the questioner, having reached a certain point through induction by means of the view which his opponent has set forth, then attempts to demolish that point; for, if this has been demolished, the view originally set forth is also demolished. It appears necessary, when the point towards which the discussion is tending, appears to be useful and germane to the thesis but is not really so, either when the man who is sustaining an argument has denied the point or if the questioner has reached the point by plausible induction based on the thesis, and then attempts to demolish it. The other case is when the point to which the discussion is tending neither is necessary nor appears to be necessary, and it is the answerer's fate to be defeated on some irrelevant point. We must be on our guard against the last of the above-mentioned methods; for it seems to be completely divorced from and alien to dialectic. Therefore, also, the answerer must not show bad temper but admit such points as cannot usefully be urged against the thesis, indicating anything which he admits though he does not approve of it. For questioners usually only become involved in greater difficulty, when all such admissions are made, if they cannot reach a conclusion.

Furthermore, a man who has made an assertion of any kind whatsoever, has in a way made a number of assertions, because each assertion necessarily involves a number of consequences. For example, he who has said that " X is a man," has also said that X is an animal and a biped and is animate and is receptive of reason and knowledge; so that, if any single one of these consequences is demolished,

(b) An assertion can be demolished, if a consequence of it can be subverted.

112 a

αἱρεῖται καὶ τὸ ἐν ἀρχῇ. εὐλαβεῖσθαι δὲ χρὴ καὶ
τὸ χαλεπωτέρου τὴν μετάληψιν ποιεῖσθαι· ἐνίοτε
μὲν γὰρ ῥᾷον τὸ ἀκόλουθον ἀνελεῖν, ἐνίοτε δ᾽
αὐτὸ τὸ προκείμενον.

VI. Ὅσοις δ᾽ ἀνάγκη θάτερον μόνον ὑπάρχειν,
25 οἷον τῷ ἀνθρώπῳ τὴν νόσον ἢ τὴν ὑγίειαν, ἐὰν
πρὸς θάτερον εὐπορῶμεν διαλέγεσθαι ὅτι ὑπάρχει
ἢ οὐχ ὑπάρχει, καὶ πρὸς τὸ λοιπὸν εὐπορήσομεν.
τοῦτο δ᾽ ἀντιστρέφει πρὸς ἄμφω· δείξαντες μὲν
γὰρ ὅτι ὑπάρχει θάτερον, ὅτι οὐχ ὑπάρχει τὸ
λοιπὸν δεδειχότες ἐσόμεθα· ἐὰν δ᾽ ὅτι οὐχ ὑπάρχει
30 δείξωμεν, τὸ λοιπὸν ὅτι ὑπάρχει δεδειχότες ἐσόμεθα. δῆλον οὖν ὅτι πρὸς ἄμφω χρήσιμος ὁ
τόπος.

Ἔτι τὸ ἐπιχειρεῖν μεταφέροντα τοὔνομα ἐπὶ τὸν
λόγον, ὡς μάλιστα προσῆκον ἐκλαμβάνειν ἢ ὡς
κεῖται τοὔνομα, οἷον εὔψυχον μὴ τὸν ἀνδρεῖον,
35 καθάπερ νῦν κεῖται, ἀλλὰ τὸν εὖ τὴν ψυχὴν ἔχοντα,
καθάπερ καὶ εὔελπιν τὸν ἀγαθὰ ἐλπίζοντα· ὁμοίως
δὲ καὶ εὐδαίμονα, οὗ ἂν ὁ δαίμων ᾖ σπουδαῖος,
καθάπερ Ξενοκράτης φησὶν εὐδαίμονα εἶναι τὸν
τὴν ψυχὴν ἔχοντα σπουδαίαν· ταύτην γὰρ ἑκάστου
εἶναι δαίμονα.

112 b Ἐπεὶ δὲ τῶν πραγμάτων τὰ μὲν ἐξ ἀνάγκης
ἐστί, τὰ δ᾽ ὡς ἐπὶ τὸ πολύ, τὰ δ᾽ ὁπότερ᾽ ἔτυχεν,
ἐὰν τὸ ἐξ ἀνάγκης ὡς ἐπὶ τὸ πολὺ τεθῇ ἢ τὸ ὡς
ἐπὶ τὸ πολὺ ἐξ ἀνάγκης, ἢ αὐτὸ ἢ τὸ ἐναντίον τῷ
5 ὡς ἐπὶ τὸ πολύ, ἀεὶ δίδωσι τόπον ἐπιχειρήματος.

---

^a As well as one who inspires hope, cf. the English ' young
hopeful.'
^b As well as in the meaning of ' possessed of a good
fortune ' in the sense of wealth.   ^c Frag. 81 (Heinze).

the original assertion is also demolished. But we must be on our guard against changing the assertion into something more difficult; for sometimes the consequential assertion, and sometimes the proposition itself, is the easier to demolish.

VI. Where of necessity only one of two predicates must be true (for example, a man must have either disease or health), if we have a supply of material for arguing with regard to one of them that it is present or not, we shall have a supply of material also regarding the other. This rule is convertible for both purposes; for if we have shown that one is present, we shall have shown that the other is not present; if we have shown that one is not present, we shall have shown that the other is present. It is obvious, therefore, that this commonplace is useful for both purposes. *Various observations: (a) Where only one of two predicates can be true, it is easy to argue about the other.*

Another method of attack is to refer back a term to its original meaning on the ground that it is more fitting to take it in this sense than in that now established. For example, 'stout-souled' can be used to mean not 'courageous,' which is its established meaning, but it can be applied to a man whose soul is in a good condition; as also the term 'hopeful' can mean a man who hopes for good things[a]; and similarly 'fortunate' can be used of one whose fortune is good,[b] as Xenocrates[c] says "Fortunate is he who has a noble soul"; for his soul is each man's fortune. *(b) It can be argued that the original meaning of a word should be preferred to its current meaning.*

Seeing that some things happen of necessity, others usually, others as chance dictates, the assertion that a necessary occurrence is a usual occurrence or that a usual occurrence (or the contrary of a usual occurrence) is a necessary occurrence, always gives *(c) The usual should not be represented as the necessary and vice versa.*

112 b

ἐὰν γὰρ τὸ ἐξ ἀνάγκης ὡς ἐπὶ τὸ πολὺ τεθῇ, δῆλον
ὅτι οὐ παντί φησιν ὑπάρχειν, ὑπάρχοντος παντί,
ὥστε ἡμάρτηκεν· εἴ τε τὸ ὡς ἐπὶ τὸ πολὺ λεγόμενον ἐξ ἀνάγκης ἔφησε· παντὶ γάρ φησιν ὑπάρχειν, οὐχ ὑπάρχοντος παντί. ὁμοίως δὲ καὶ εἰ
10 τὸ ἐναντίον τῷ ὡς ἐπὶ τὸ πολὺ ἐξ ἀνάγκης εἴρηκεν·
ἀεὶ γὰρ ἐπ' ἔλαττον λέγεται τὸ ἐναντίον τῷ ὡς
ἐπὶ τὸ πολύ, οἷον εἰ ὡς ἐπὶ τὸ πολὺ φαῦλοι οἱ
ἄνθρωποι, ἀγαθοὶ ἐπ' ἔλαττον, ὥστ' ἔτι μᾶλλον
ἡμάρτηκεν, εἰ ἀγαθοὺς ἐξ ἀνάγκης εἴρηκεν. ὡς-
αύτως δὲ καὶ εἰ τὸ ὁπότερ' ἔτυχεν ἐξ ἀνάγκης
15 ἔφησεν ἢ ὡς ἐπὶ τὸ πολύ· οὔτε γὰρ ἐξ ἀνάγκης
τὸ ὁπότερ' ἔτυχεν οὔθ' ὡς ἐπὶ τὸ πολύ. ἐνδέχεται δέ, κἂν μὴ διορίσας εἴπῃ πότερον ὡς ἐπὶ
τὸ πολὺ ἢ ἐξ ἀνάγκης εἴρηκεν, ᾗ δὲ τὸ πρᾶγμα
ὡς ἐπὶ τὸ πολύ, διαλέγεσθαι ὡς ἐξ ἀνάγκης εἰρη-
κότος αὐτοῦ, οἷον εἰ φαύλους τοὺς ἀποκλήρους
20 ἔφησεν εἶναι μὴ διορίσας, ὡς ἐξ ἀνάγκης εἰρηκό-
τος αὐτοῦ διαλέγεσθαι.

Ἔτι καὶ εἰ αὐτὸ αὑτῷ συμβεβηκὸς ἔθηκεν ὡς
ἕτερον διὰ τὸ ἕτερον εἶναι ὄνομα, καθάπερ Πρό-
δικος διῃρεῖτο τὰς ἡδονὰς εἰς χαρὰν καὶ τέρψιν
καὶ εὐφροσύνην· ταῦτα γὰρ πάντα τοῦ αὐτοῦ τῆς
25 ἡδονῆς ὀνόματά ἐστιν. εἰ οὖν τις τὸ χαίρειν τῷ
εὐφραίνεσθαι φήσει συμβεβηκέναι, αὐτὸ ἂν αὑτῷ
φαίη συμβεβηκέναι.

356

an occasion for attack. For if a necessary occurrence is asserted to be a usual occurrence, it is obvious that the man who makes the assertion is stating that a universal attribute is not universal, and therefore he is in error; and the same is true if he has stated that a usual attribute is necessary, for he has stated that it belongs universally when it does not do so. Similarly, if he has asserted that the contrary of what is usual is necessary; for the contrary of a usual attribute is always rather rarely predicated. For example, if men are usually bad, they are rather rarely good, so that he has committed an even greater error if he has said that they are necessarily good. In like manner also, if he has declared that a chance occurrence happens necessarily or usually; for a chance occurrence does not happen either necessarily or usually. Even if he has made his assertion without distinguishing whether it is a usual or a necessary occurrence, and as a matter of fact it is a usual occurrence, it is possible to argue as though he meant that it was a necessary occurrence. For instance, if he has said that disinherited persons are bad, without making any distinction, you can argue as though he has said that they were necessarily bad.

Furthermore, you must see whether your opponent has stated something as an accidental attribute of itself, taking it as something different because it bears a different name, just as Prodicus divided pleasure into joy, delight and merriment; for these are all names for the same thing, namely pleasure. If, therefore, anyone shall assert that joy is an accidental attribute of merriment, he would be saying that it is an accidental attribute of itself. *(d) Terms which are only nominally different should not be stated as accidents of one another.*

VII. Ἐπεὶ δὲ τὰ ἐναντία συμπλέκεται μὲν
ἀλλήλοις ἑξαχῶς, ἐναντίωσιν δὲ ποιεῖ τετραχῶς
συμπλεκόμενα, δεῖ λαμβάνειν τὰ ἐναντία, ὅπως
30 ἂν χρήσιμον ᾖ καὶ ἀναιροῦντι καὶ κατασκευάζοντι.
ὅτι μὲν οὖν ἑξαχῶς συμπλέκεται, δῆλον· ἢ γὰρ
ἑκάτερον τῶν ἐναντίων ἑκατέρῳ συμπλακήσεται·
τοῦτο δὲ διχῶς, οἷον τὸ τοὺς φίλους εὖ ποιεῖν καὶ
τὸ τοὺς ἐχθροὺς κακῶς, ἢ ἀνάπαλιν τὸ τοὺς φίλους
κακῶς καὶ τοὺς ἐχθροὺς εὖ. ἢ ὅταν ἄμφω περὶ τοῦ
35 ἑνός· διχῶς δὲ καὶ τοῦτο, οἷον τὸ τοὺς φίλους
εὖ καὶ τὸ τοὺς φίλους κακῶς, ἢ τὸ τοὺς ἐχθροὺς
εὖ καὶ τοὺς ἐχθροὺς κακῶς. ἢ τὸ ἓν περὶ ἀμφο-
τέρων· διχῶς δὲ καὶ τοῦτο, οἷον τὸ τοὺς φίλους
εὖ καὶ τὸ τοὺς ἐχθροὺς εὖ, ἢ τοὺς φίλους κακῶς
καὶ τοὺς ἐχθροὺς κακῶς.

Αἱ μὲν οὖν πρῶται δύο ῥηθεῖσαι συμπλοκαὶ οὐ
ποιοῦσιν ἐναντίωσιν· τὸ γὰρ τοὺς φίλους εὖ ποιεῖν
τῷ τοὺς ἐχθροὺς κακῶς οὐκ ἔστιν ἐναντίον· ἀμφότερα γὰρ αἱρετὰ καὶ τοῦ αὐτοῦ ἤθους. οὐδὲ τὸ
τοὺς φίλους κακῶς τῷ τοὺς ἐχθροὺς εὖ· καὶ γὰρ
5 ταῦτα ἀμφότερα φευκτὰ καὶ τοῦ αὐτοῦ ἤθους.
οὐ δοκεῖ δὲ φευκτὸν φευκτῷ ἐναντίον εἶναι, ἐὰν
μὴ τὸ μὲν καθ᾿ ὑπερβολὴν τὸ δὲ κατ᾿ ἔνδειαν
λεγόμενον ᾖ· ἥ τε γὰρ ὑπερβολὴ τῶν φευκτῶν
δοκεῖ εἶναι, ὁμοίως δὲ καὶ ἡ ἔνδεια. τὰ δὲ λοιπὰ
πάντα τέτταρα ποιεῖ ἐναντίωσιν. τὸ γὰρ τοὺς
10 φίλους εὖ ποιεῖν τῷ τοὺς φίλους κακῶς ἐναντίον·

VII. Seeing that contraries may be combined with one another in six ways, and four of these combinations make a contrariety, we must avail ourselves of contraries in whatever way may be useful both for destructive and for constructive purposes. That there are six kinds of combination is obvious; for either (*a*) each of the contrary verbs will be combined with each of the contrary objects, and this in two ways, for example, " to do good to friends and to do harm to enemies," or, conversely, " to do harm to friends and to do good to enemies "; or (*b*) both verbs may be used with one object, and this also in two ways, for example, " to do good to friends and to do harm to friends," or, " to do good to enemies and to do harm to enemies "; or (*c*) one verb may be used with both objects, and this also in two ways, for example, " to do good to friends and to do good to enemies," or, " to do harm to friends and to do harm to enemies."

Rules drawn from contraries: (a) Since one proposition may have several contraries, the most suitable must be selected.

The first two of the above combinations do not form a contrariety, for " to do good to friends " is not the contrary of " to do harm to enemies "; for both these actions are objects of choice and belong to the same character. Nor is " to do harm to friends " the contrary of " to do good to enemies "; for both these actions are objects of avoidance and belong to the same character, and one object of avoidance is not generally regarded as the contrary of another object of avoidance, unless the one is used to denote excess and the other defect; for excess is generally regarded as an object of avoidance, and so likewise also is defect. But all the other four combinations form a contrariety; for " to do good to friends " is the contrary of " to do harm

359

ἀπό τε γὰρ ἐναντίου ἤθους ἐστί, καὶ τὸ μὲν αἱρετὸν
τὸ δὲ φευκτόν. ὡσαύτως δὲ καὶ ἐπὶ τῶν ἄλλων·
καθ᾽ ἑκάστην γὰρ συζυγίαν τὸ μὲν αἱρετὸν τὸ δὲ
φευκτόν, καὶ τὸ μὲν ἐπιεικοῦς ἤθους τὸ δὲ φαύλου.
δῆλον οὖν ἐκ τῶν εἰρημένων ὅτι τῷ αὐτῷ πλείονα
15 ἐναντία συμβαίνει γίνεσθαι. τῷ γὰρ τοὺς φίλους
εὖ ποιεῖν καὶ τὸ τοὺς ἐχθροὺς εὖ ποιεῖν ἐναντίον
καὶ τὸ τοὺς φίλους κακῶς. ὁμοίως δὲ καὶ τῶν
ἄλλων ἑκάστῳ τὸν αὐτὸν τρόπον ἐπισκοποῦσι δύο
τὰ ἐναντία φανήσεται. λαμβάνειν οὖν τῶν ἐναντίων
ὁπότερον ἂν ᾖ πρὸς τὴν θέσιν χρήσιμον.

20 Ἔτι εἰ ἔστι τι ἐναντίον τῷ συμβεβηκότι, σκοπεῖν
εἰ ὑπάρχει ᾧπερ τὸ συμβεβηκὸς εἴρηται ὑπάρχειν·
εἰ γὰρ τοῦτο ὑπάρχει, ἐκεῖνο οὐκ ἂν ὑπάρχοι·
ἀδύνατον γὰρ τἀναντία ἅμα τῷ αὐτῷ ὑπάρχειν.

Ἢ εἴ τι τοιοῦτον εἴρηται κατά τινος, οὗ ὄντος
25 ἀνάγκη τὰ ἐναντία ὑπάρχειν. οἷον εἰ τὰς ἰδέας ἐν
ἡμῖν ἔφησεν εἶναι· κινεῖσθαί τε γὰρ καὶ ἠρεμεῖν
αὐτὰς συμβήσεται, ἔτι δὲ αἰσθητὰς καὶ νοητὰς
εἶναι. δοκοῦσι γὰρ αἱ ἰδέαι ἠρεμεῖν καὶ νοηταὶ
εἶναι τοῖς τιθεμένοις ἰδέας εἶναι, ἐν ἡμῖν δὲ οὔσας
ἀδύνατον ἀκινήτους εἶναι· κινουμένων γὰρ ἡμῶν
30 ἀναγκαῖον καὶ τὰ ἐν ἡμῖν πάντα συγκινεῖσθαι.
δῆλον δ᾽ ὅτι καὶ αἰσθηταί, εἴπερ ἐν ἡμῖν εἰσί· διὰ

---

^a ἰδέαι seem to be used here in the Platonic sense.

to friends," for they proceed from contrary characters, and one is an object of choice and the other of avoidance. Similarly, also, with the other combinations; for in each pair one is an object of choice, the other of avoidance; one always belongs to a good character, the other to a bad. It is obvious, therefore, from what has been said that the same thing has in fact more than one contrary. For " to do good to friends " has as its contrary both " to do good to enemies " and " to do harm to friends." In like manner, if we examine them in the same way, it will be apparent that the contraries of each of the others are two in number. We must, therefore, take whichever of the two contraries is useful for dealing with the thesis.

Furthermore, if the accident of anything has a contrary, you must examine whether it belongs to that to which the accident has been said to belong. For, if the former belongs, the latter cannot belong; for it is impossible for two contraries to belong to the same thing at the same time.

(b) The contrary of the accident of anything cannot be predicated of the same thing as is the accident.

Again, you should see if anything has been said regarding something, such that, if it exists, contrary predicates must of necessity belong to the thing, for example, if your opponent has said that "ideas [a] exist in us." For, if so, it will follow that they are both in motion and at rest, and, further, that they are objects both of sensation and of thought. For ideas are considered, by those who assert their existence, to be both at rest and objects of thought, but if they exist in us it is impossible for them to be unmoved; for, when we move, everything that is in us must of necessity also move with us. Obviously, also, they are objects of sensation, if indeed they

(c) Nothing which can be predicated of a thing must involve contrary predicates.

361

113 a

γὰρ τῆς περὶ τὴν ὄψιν αἰσθήσεως τὴν ἐν ἑκάστῳ
μορφὴν γνωρίζομεν.

Πάλιν εἰ κεῖται συμβεβηκὸς ᾧ ἐστί τι ἐναντίον,
σκοπεῖν εἰ καὶ τοῦ ἐναντίου δεκτικόν, ὅπερ καὶ
35 τοῦ συμβεβηκότος· τὸ γὰρ αὐτὸ τῶν ἐναντίων
δεκτικόν, οἷον εἰ τὸ μῖσος ἕπεσθαι ὀργῇ ἔφησεν,
113 b εἴη ἂν τὸ μῖσος ἐν τῷ θυμοειδεῖ· ἐκεῖ γὰρ ἡ ὀργή.
σκεπτέον οὖν εἰ καὶ τὸ ἐναντίον ἐν τῷ θυμοειδεῖ,
ἡ φιλία· εἰ γὰρ μή, ἀλλ' ἐν τῷ ἐπιθυμητικῷ ἐστιν
ἡ φιλία, οὐκ ἂν ἕποιτο μῖσος ὀργῇ. ὁμοίως δὲ
καὶ εἰ τὸ ἐπιθυμητικὸν ἀγνοεῖν ἔφησεν. εἴη γὰρ
5 ἂν καὶ ἐπιστήμης δεκτικόν, εἴπερ καὶ ἀγνοίας·
ὅπερ οὐ δοκεῖ, τὸ ἐπιθυμητικὸν δεκτικὸν εἶναι
ἐπιστήμης. ἀνασκευάζοντι μὲν οὖν, καθάπερ εἴρηται, χρηστέον· κατασκευάζοντι δέ, ὅτι μὲν ὑπάρχει
τὸ συμβεβηκός, οὐ χρήσιμος ὁ τόπος, ὅτι δ'
ἐνδέχεται ὑπάρχειν, χρήσιμος. δείξαντες μὲν γὰρ
10 ὅτι οὐ δεκτικὸν τοῦ ἐναντίου, δεδειχότες ἐσόμεθα
ὅτι οὔτε ὑπάρχει τὸ συμβεβηκὸς οὔτ' ἐνδέχεται
ὑπάρξαι· ἐὰν δὲ δείξωμεν ὅτι ὑπάρχει τὸ ἐναντίον
ἢ ὅτι δεκτικὸν τοῦ ἐναντίου ἐστίν, οὐδέπω δεδειχότες ἐσόμεθα ὅτι καὶ τὸ συμβεβηκὸς ὑπάρχει,
ἀλλ' ὅτι ἐνδέχεται ὑπάρχειν, ἐπὶ τοσοῦτον μόνον
δεδειγμένον ἔσται.

15 VIII. Ἐπεὶ δ' αἱ ἀντιθέσεις τέτταρες, σκοπεῖν
ἐκ μὲν τῶν ἀντιφάσεων ἀνάπαλιν ἐκ τῆς ἀκολου-
θήσεως καὶ ἀναιροῦντι καὶ κατασκευάζοντι, λαμ-

exist in us ; for it is through the sensation connected with sight that we recognize the form which is in each thing.

Again, if an accident which has a contrary is asserted, you must look whether what admits of the accident admits also of its contrary ; for the same thing admits of contraries. For example, if your opponent has said that hatred follows anger, then hatred would be in the spirited faculty ; for anger is in that faculty. You must, therefore, look whether its contrary, namely friendship, is also in the spirited faculty ; for if it is not there but in the appetitive faculty, then hatred cannot follow anger. Similarly, too, if he has declared that the appetitive faculty is ignorant ; for if it were capable of ignorance, it would also be capable of knowledge, and it is not a generally accepted opinion that the appetitive faculty is capable of knowledge. This method, as has been said, should be used in destructive criticism ; but for constructive purposes the commonplace is of no use for proving that an accident belongs, though it is useful for proving that it may possibly belong. For, when we have shown that something does not admit of the contrary, we shall have shown that the accident neither belongs nor can possibly do so ; but if we show that the contrary belongs or that the subject admits of the contrary, we shall not yet have shown that the accident actually belongs, but we shall only have gone as far as to show that it may possibly belong.

(d) That which admits of an accident admits also of its contrary.

VIII. Since there are four kinds of opposition, you must see whether arguments can be derived from the contradictories, taking them in reverse order, for both destructive and constructive purposes, and

Rules based on different kinds of opposition ; (a) Four kinds of

ARISTOTLE

βάνειν δ' ἐξ ἐπαγωγῆς, οἷον εἰ ὁ ἄνθρωπος ζῷον,
τὸ μὴ ζῷον οὐκ ἄνθρωπος. ὁμοίως δὲ καὶ ἐπὶ
τῶν ἄλλων. ἐνταῦθα γὰρ ἀνάπαλιν ἡ ἀκολούθησις·
20 τῷ μὲν γὰρ ἀνθρώπῳ τὸ ζῷον ἕπεται, τῷ δὲ μὴ
ἀνθρώπῳ τὸ μὴ ζῷον οὔ, ἀλλ' ἀνάπαλιν τῷ μὴ
ζῴῳ τὸ οὐκ ἄνθρωπος. ἐπὶ πάντων οὖν τὸ τοιοῦτον ἀξιωτέον, οἷον εἰ τὸ καλὸν ἡδύ, καὶ τὸ μὴ
ἡδὺ οὐ καλόν· εἰ δὲ μὴ τοῦτο, οὐδ' ἐκεῖνο. ὁμοίως
25 δὲ καὶ εἰ τὸ μὴ ἡδὺ οὐ καλόν, τὸ καλὸν ἡδύ. δῆλον οὖν ὅτι πρὸς ἄμφω ἀντιστρέφει ἡ κατὰ τὴν
ἀντίφασιν ἀκολούθησις ἀνάπαλιν γινομένη.

Ἐπὶ δὲ τῶν ἐναντίων σκοπεῖν εἰ τῷ ἐναντίῳ τὸ
ἐναντίον ἕπεται, ἢ ἐπὶ ταὐτὰ ἢ ἀνάπαλιν, καὶ
ἀναιροῦντι καὶ κατασκευάζοντι· λαμβάνειν δὲ καὶ
30 τὰ τοιαῦτα ἐξ ἐπαγωγῆς, ἐφ' ὅσον χρήσιμον. ἐπὶ
ταὐτὰ μὲν οὖν ἡ ἀκολούθησις, οἷον τῇ ἀνδρίᾳ καὶ
τῇ δειλίᾳ· τῇ μὲν γὰρ ἀρετὴ ἀκολουθεῖ, τῇ δὲ
κακία, καὶ τῇ μὲν ἀκολουθεῖ τὸ αἱρετόν, τῇ δὲ τὸ
φευκτόν. ἐπὶ ταὐτὰ οὖν καὶ ἡ τούτων ἀκολούθησις·
ἐναντίον γὰρ τὸ αἱρετὸν τῷ φευκτῷ. ὁμοίως δὲ
35 καὶ ἐπὶ τῶν ἄλλων. ἀνάπαλιν δὲ ἡ ἀκολούθησις,
οἷον εὐεξίᾳ μὲν ἡ ὑγίεια ἀκολουθεῖ, καχεξίᾳ δὲ
νόσος οὔ, ἀλλὰ νόσῳ καχεξία. δῆλον οὖν ὅτι
ἀνάπαλιν ἐπὶ τούτων ἡ ἀκολούθησις. σπάνιον δὲ
τὸ ἀνάπαλιν ἐπὶ τῶν ἐναντίων συμβαίνει, ἀλλὰ
τοῖς πλείστοις ἐπὶ ταὐτὰ ἡ ἀκολούθησις. εἰ οὖν
μήτ' ἐπὶ ταὐτὰ τῷ ἐναντίῳ τὸ ἐναντίον ἀκολουθεῖ

you should obtain them by induction, for example, opposition must be used to show that if A follows B, not-B also follows not-A. "If man is an animal, not-animal is not-man," and so with the other cases. For here the order is reversed; for 'animal' follows 'man,' but 'not-animal' does not follow 'not-man,' but, conversely, 'not-man' follows 'not-animal.' In all cases, an axiom must be laid down of the following type, "If the honourable is pleasant, what is not pleasant is not honourable, but, if the latter is not true, then the former is not true either." Similarly, "If what is not pleasant is not honourable, the pleasant is honourable." It is clear, therefore, that the reversed sequence of the terms used in contradiction is convertible for both purposes.

You must look with regard to contraries whether (b) It must be observed whether the contrary follows the contrary directly or reversely. contrary follows upon contrary, either directly or in reverse order, both in destructive criticism and in constructive argument, and you should obtain such arguments also by induction as far as may be useful. Now the sequence is direct in the case, for example, of courage and cowardice; for virtue follows the former, vice the latter; and object of choice follows the former, object of avoidance the latter. The sequence, therefore, in the latter case also is direct; for object of choice is contrary to object of avoidance; so too in the other cases also. On the other hand, the sequence is in reverse order in such a case as this: "Health follows upon good condition; but disease does not follow upon bad condition, but bad condition upon disease." It is clear, therefore, that here the sequence is reversed; but reversed sequence is rare in the case of contraries, where the sequence is generally direct. If, then, the contrary does not follow the contrary either directly or in reverse

365

μήτε ἀνάπαλιν, δῆλον ὅτι οὐδ' ἐπὶ τῶν ῥηθέντων
5 ἀκολουθεῖ τὸ ἕτερον τῷ ἑτέρῳ. εἰ δ' ἐπὶ τῶν
ἐναντίων, καὶ ἐπὶ τῶν ῥηθέντων ἀναγκαῖον τὸ
ἕτερον τῷ ἑτέρῳ ἀκολουθεῖν.

Ὁμοίως δὲ τοῖς ἐναντίοις καὶ ἐπὶ τῶν στερήσεων
καὶ ἕξεων σκεπτέον. πλὴν οὐκ ἔστιν ἐπὶ τῶν
στερήσεων τὸ ἀνάπαλιν, ἀλλ' ἐπὶ ταὐτὰ τὴν ἀκολούθησιν ἀναγκαῖον ἀεὶ γίνεσθαι, καθάπερ ὄψει
10 μὲν αἴσθησιν, τυφλότητι δ' ἀναισθησίαν. ἀντίκειται γὰρ ἡ αἴσθησις τῇ ἀναισθησίᾳ ὡς ἕξις καὶ
στέρησις· τὸ μὲν γὰρ ἕξις αὐτῶν, τὸ δὲ στέρησίς
ἐστιν.

Ὁμοίως δὲ τῇ ἕξει καὶ τῇ στερήσει καὶ ἐπὶ
τῶν πρός τι χρηστέον· ἐπὶ ταὐτὰ γὰρ καὶ τούτων
ἡ ἀκολούθησις. οἷον εἰ τὸ τριπλάσιον πολλα-
15 πλάσιον, καὶ τὸ τριτημόριον πολλοστημόριον· λέγεται γὰρ τὸ μὲν τριπλάσιον πρὸς τὸ τριτημόριον,
τὸ δὲ πολλαπλάσιον πρὸς τὸ πολλοστημόριον.
πάλιν εἰ ἡ ἐπιστήμη ὑπόληψις, καὶ τὸ ἐπιστητὸν
ὑποληπτόν· καὶ εἰ ἡ ὅρασις αἴσθησις, καὶ τὸ
20 ὁρατὸν αἰσθητόν. ἔνστασις ὅτι οὐκ ἀνάγκη ἐπὶ
τῶν πρός τι τὴν ἀκολούθησιν γίνεσθαι, καθάπερ
εἴρηται· τὸ γὰρ αἰσθητὸν ἐπιστητόν ἐστιν, ἡ δ'
αἴσθησις οὐκ ἐπιστήμη. οὐ μὴν ἀληθής γε ἡ
ἔνστασις δοκεῖ εἶναι· πολλοὶ γὰρ οὔ φασι τῶν
αἰσθητῶν ἐπιστήμην εἶναι. ἔτι πρὸς τοὐναντίον
25 οὐχ ἧττον χρήσιμον τὸ ῥηθέν, οἷον ὅτι τὸ αἰσθητὸν
οὐκ ἔστιν ἐπιστητόν· οὐδὲ γὰρ ἡ αἴσθησις ἐπιστήμη.

IX. Πάλιν ἐπὶ τῶν συστοίχων καὶ ἐπὶ τῶν πτώσεων, καὶ ἀναιροῦντα καὶ κατασκευάζοντα. λέγε-

---

ᵃ See note on 106 b 29.

order, it is clear that neither does one of the terms in the statement follow the other; but if one follows the other in the case of the contraries, one term in the statement must also necessarily follow the other.

Just as you examine contraries, so also you should examine cases of the privation or presence of states, except that in the case of privation the reverse sequence is impossible but the sequence must always of necessity be direct; for example, sensation must follow sight and absence of sensation must follow blindness. For sensation is opposed to absence of sensation; for they are a state and a privation, the former being a state, the latter a privation.

(c) Cases of the privation or presence of states must be examined.

You must also deal with relative terms in the same manner as with the privation or presence of states; for here too the sequence is direct. For example, if three times is a multiple, a third is a fraction; for three times is described as relative to a third, and a multiple as relative to a fraction. Again, if knowledge is a conceiving, then the knowable is conceivable; and if sight is a sensation, then the visible is sensible. It may be objected that in the case of relative terms the sequence does not necessarily take place in the manner just described; for the sensible is knowable, but sensation is not knowledge. The objection, however, is not generally regarded as holding good; for many people deny that there is a knowledge of sensible things. Further, the above principle is not less useful for proving the contrary, for example, that the sensible is not knowable; for neither is sensation knowledge.

(d) Relative terms must also be considered.

IX. Again, you must look at the case of the co-ordinates and inflected forms of words [a] both in destructive and constructive argument. By ' co-

Various Rules: (a) What is true of one co-ordinate

114 a

ται δὲ σύστοιχα μὲν τὰ τοιάδε οἷον τὰ δίκαια
καὶ ὁ δίκαιος τῇ δικαιοσύνῃ καὶ τὰ ἀνδρεῖα καὶ ὁ
ἀνδρεῖος τῇ ἀνδρίᾳ. ὁμοίως δὲ καὶ τὰ ποιητικὰ ἢ
30 φυλακτικὰ σύστοιχα ἐκείνου οὗ ἐστι ποιητικὰ ἢ
φυλακτικά, οἷον τὰ ὑγιεινὰ ὑγιείας καὶ τὰ εὐεκτικὰ
εὐεξίας. τὸν αὐτὸν δὲ τρόπον καὶ ἐπὶ τῶν ἄλλων.
σύστοιχα μὲν οὖν τὰ τοιαῦτα εἴωθε λέγεσθαι,
πτώσεις δὲ οἷον τὸ δικαίως καὶ ἀνδρείως καὶ
ὑγιεινῶς καὶ ὅσα τοῦτον τὸν τρόπον λέγεται.
35 δοκεῖ δὲ καὶ τὰ κατὰ τὰς πτώσεις σύστοιχα εἶναι,
οἷον τὸ μὲν δικαίως τῇ δικαιοσύνῃ, τὸ δὲ ἀνδρείως
τῇ ἀνδρίᾳ. σύστοιχα δὲ λέγεται τὰ κατὰ τὴν
αὐτὴν συστοιχίαν ἅπαντα, οἷον δικαιοσύνη, δίκαιος,
δίκαιον, δικαίως. δῆλον οὖν ὅτι ἑνὸς ὁποιουοῦν
δειχθέντος τῶν κατὰ τὴν αὐτὴν συστοιχίαν ἀγαθοῦ
114 b ἢ ἐπαινετοῦ καὶ τὰ λοιπὰ πάντα δεδειγμένα ἔσται,
οἷον εἰ ἡ δικαιοσύνη τῶν ἐπαινετῶν, καὶ ὁ δίκαιος
καὶ τὸ δίκαιον καὶ τὸ δικαίως τῶν ἐπαινετῶν.
ῥηθήσεται δὲ τὸ δικαίως καὶ ἐπαινετῶς κατὰ τὴν
5 αὐτὴν πτῶσιν ἀπὸ τοῦ ἐπαινετοῦ, καθάπερ τὸ
δικαίως ἀπὸ τῆς δικαιοσύνης.

Σκοπεῖν δὲ μὴ μόνον ἐπ' αὐτοῦ τοῦ εἰρημένου,
ἀλλὰ καὶ ἐπὶ τοῦ ἐναντίου τὸ ἐναντίον, οἷον ὅτι
τὸ ἀγαθὸν οὐκ ἐξ ἀνάγκης ἡδύ· οὐδὲ γὰρ τὸ κακὸν
λυπηρόν· ἢ εἰ τοῦτο, κἀκεῖνο. καὶ εἰ ἡ δικαιοσύνη
10 ἐπιστήμη, καὶ ἡ ἀδικία ἄγνοια· καὶ εἰ τὸ δικαίως

ordinates ' are meant such terms as ' just actions ' is true of and ' just man,' which are co-ordinate with ' justice,' another. and ' courageous acts ' and ' courageous man,' which are co-ordinate with ' courage.' Similarly also things which create or preserve something are co-ordinate with that of which they are creative or preservative, for example ' healthy things ' are co-ordinate with ' health,' and ' things which produce a good con- dition ' are co-ordinate with ' good condition,' and so with the other cases. Such things, then, are usu- ally described as ' co-ordinates '; ' inflected forms ' are such words as ' justly,' ' courageously ' and ' healthily ' and other words formed in this way. Inflected forms are usually regarded also as co- ordinates, for example, ' justly ' as a co-ordinate of ' justice ' and ' courageously ' of ' courage.' All words which are in the same co-ordinate series are called co-ordinates, for example, ' justice,' ' just man,' ' just action ' and ' justly.' It is obvious, therefore, that when any one member of the co-ordinate series has been shown to be good or praiseworthy, all the rest will have been shown to be so also. For example, if ' justice ' is something praiseworthy, then ' the just man ' and ' the just action ' and ' justly ' will be something praiseworthy. And ' justly ' will denote ' praiseworthily,' this being the same inflexion of ' praiseworthy ' as ' justly ' is of ' justice.'

You must look for the contrary not only in the (b) It must case of the subject itself which is under discussion, be observed but also in the case of its contrary. For instance, contrary is you can say that the good is not necessarily pleasant, also of the for neither is the evil necessarily painful ; or, if the contrary. latter part is true, so also is the former ; and, if justice is knowledge, injustice is ignorance, and, if

369

114 b

ἐπιστημονικῶς καὶ ἐμπείρως, τὸ ἀδίκως ἀγνοούν
τως καὶ ἀπείρως. εἰ δὲ ταῦτα μή, οὐδ᾽ ἐκεῖνα,
καθάπερ ἐπὶ τοῦ νῦν ῥηθέντος· μᾶλλον γὰρ ἂν
φανείη τὸ ἀδίκως ἐμπείρως ἢ ἀπείρως. οὗτος
δ᾽ ὁ τόπος εἴρηται πρότερον ἐν ταῖς τῶν ἐναντίων
ἀκολουθήσεσιν· οὐδὲν γὰρ ἄλλο νῦν ἀξιοῦμεν ἢ
15 τὸ ἐναντίον τῷ ἐναντίῳ ἀκολουθεῖν.

Ἔτι ἐπὶ τῶν γενέσεων καὶ φθορῶν καὶ ποιη
τικῶν καὶ φθαρτικῶν, καὶ ἀναιροῦντι καὶ κατα
σκευάζοντι. ὧν γὰρ αἱ γενέσεις τῶν ἀγαθῶν,
καὶ αὐτὰ ἀγαθά, καὶ εἰ αὐτὰ ἀγαθά, καὶ αἱ γενέσεις·
20 εἰ δὲ αἱ γενέσεις τῶν κακῶν, καὶ αὐτὰ τῶν κακῶν.
ἐπὶ δὲ τῶν φθορῶν ἀνάπαλιν· εἰ γὰρ αἱ φθοραὶ
τῶν ἀγαθῶν, αὐτὰ τῶν κακῶν, εἰ δ᾽ αἱ φθοραὶ τῶν
κακῶν, αὐτὰ τῶν ἀγαθῶν. ὁ δ᾽ αὐτὸς λόγος καὶ
ἐπὶ ποιητικῶν καὶ φθαρτικῶν· ὧν μὲν γὰρ τὰ
ποιητικὰ ἀγαθά, καὶ αὐτὰ τῶν ἀγαθῶν, ὧν δὲ
τὰ φθαρτικὰ ἀγαθά, αὐτὰ τῶν κακῶν.

25 X. Πάλιν ἐπὶ τῶν ὁμοίων, εἰ ὁμοίως ἔχει, οἷον
εἰ ἐπιστήμη μία πλειόνων, καὶ δόξα, καὶ εἰ τὸ ὄψιν
ἔχειν ὁρᾶν, καὶ τὸ ἀκοὴν ἔχειν ἀκούειν. ὁμοίως
δὲ καὶ ἐπὶ τῶν ἄλλων, καὶ ἐπὶ τῶν ὄντων καὶ τῶν
δοκούντων. χρήσιμος δ᾽ ὁ τόπος πρὸς ἄμφω·

' justly ' is ' knowingly ' and ' skilfully,' ' unjustly ' is ' ignorantly ' and ' unskilfully,' but if the latter part is untrue, so is also the former, as in the example above ; for ' unjustly ' would appear nearer to ' skilfully ' than ' unskilfully.' This commonplace has been mentioned above in dealing with the sequence of contraries [a] ; for at the moment we are not postulating anything more than that contrary follows contrary.

Further, you must examine the generations and corruptions of things and their creative and corruptive agencies, both for destructive and for constructive purposes. For things of which the generations are good things are themselves also good ; and if they are themselves good, so also are their generations. If, however, their generations are bad things, they themselves are also bad things. Conversely, in the case of corruptions, if their corruptions are good things, they are themselves bad things, but if their corruptions are bad things, then they themselves are good things. The same argument holds good also of creative and corruptive agencies ; for those things of which the creative agencies are good are themselves also good things, while those things of which the corruptive agencies are good are themselves bad things. *(c) The generation and corruption of a thing will show whether it is good or bad.*

X. Again, you must take the case of like things and see if the same is true of them ; for example, if one form of knowledge deals with several subjects, so also does one form of opinion, and if to have sight is to see, then also to have hearing is to hear, and so with the other examples both of things which are like and of things that are generally considered to be like. This commonplace is useful for both pur- *Rules based on the likeness of things and on variation of degree : (a) What is true of one of like things is also true of the others.*

εἰ μὲν γὰρ ἐπί τινος τῶν ὁμοίων οὕτως ἔχει, καὶ
30 ἐπὶ τῶν ἄλλων τῶν ὁμοίων, εἰ δὲ ἐπί τινος μή,
οὐδ' ἐπὶ τῶν ἄλλων. σκοπεῖν δὲ καὶ εἰ ἐφ' ἑνὸς
καὶ εἰ ἐπὶ πολλῶν ὁμοίως ἔχει· ἐνιαχοῦ γὰρ διαφωνεῖ. οἷον εἰ τὸ ἐπίστασθαι διανοεῖσθαι, καὶ
τὸ πολλὰ ἐπίστασθαι πολλὰ διανοεῖσθαι. τοῦτο
δ' οὐκ ἀληθές· ἐπίστασθαι μὲν γὰρ ἐνδέχεται
35 πολλά, διανοεῖσθαι δ' οὔ. εἰ οὖν τοῦτο μή, οὐδ'
ἐκεῖνο τὸ ἐφ' ἑνός, ὅτι τὸ ἐπίστασθαι διανοεῖσθαί
ἐστιν.

Ἔτι ἐκ τοῦ μᾶλλον καὶ ἧττον. εἰσὶ δὲ τοῦ
μᾶλλον καὶ ἧττον τόποι τέσσαρες, εἷς μὲν εἰ
ἀκολουθεῖ τὸ μᾶλλον τῷ μᾶλλον, οἷον εἰ ἡδονὴ
115 a ἀγαθόν, καὶ ἡ μᾶλλον ἡδονὴ μᾶλλον ἀγαθόν, καὶ
εἰ τὸ ἀδικεῖν κακόν, καὶ τὸ μᾶλλον ἀδικεῖν μᾶλλον
κακόν. χρήσιμος δ' οὖν πρὸς ἄμφω ὁ τόπος·
εἰ μὲν γὰρ ἀκολουθεῖ τῇ τοῦ ὑποκειμένου ἐπιδόσει
ἡ τοῦ συμβεβηκότος ἐπίδοσις, καθάπερ εἴρηται,
5 δῆλον ὅτι συμβέβηκεν, εἰ δὲ μὴ ἀκολουθεῖ, οὐ
συμβέβηκεν. τοῦτο δ' ἐπαγωγῇ ληπτέον. ἄλλος·
ἑνὸς περὶ δύο λεγομένου, εἰ ᾧ μᾶλλον εἰκὸς ὑπάρχειν μὴ ὑπάρχει, οὐδ' ᾧ ἧττον, καὶ εἰ ᾧ ἧττον
εἰκὸς ὑπάρχειν ὑπάρχει, καὶ ᾧ μᾶλλον. πάλιν,

poses ; for if something is true of one of the like
things, it is also true of the others, but if it is not
true of one of them, it is not true of the others
either. You must also see whether conditions are
alike in the case of a single thing and a number of
things ; for there is sometimes a discrepancy. For
example, if to ' know ' a thing is to ' think of ' a thing,
then to ' know many things ' is to ' think of many
things.' But this is not so ; for it is possible to know
many things and not to be thinking of them. If, therefore, the second statement is not true, then the first,
which dealt with a single thing, namely, ' to know
a thing ' is ' to think of a thing,' is not true either.

Moreover you must derive material from the (b) Four
greater and the less degrees. There are four arguments
commonplaces connected with the greater and the rived from
less degrees. One is to see whether the greater the greater
degree follows the greater degree ; for example, if degree.
pleasure is good, and greater pleasure is a greater
good, and if to commit injustice is an evil, whether
to commit a greater injustice is also a greater evil.
This commonplace is useful for both purposes ; for,
if the increase of the accident follows the increase
of the subject, as described above, it is obvious that
it is really an accident of the subject, but if it
does not follow it, it is not an accident of it. This
result must be obtained by induction. Here is
another commonplace ; when one predicate is applied
to two subjects, then, if it does not belong to the
one to which there is the greater likelihood of its
belonging, it does not belong either to the one to
which it is less likely to belong ; and if it belongs to
that to which it is less likely to belong, it belongs also
to that to which it is more likely to belong. Again,

δυοῖν περὶ ἑνὸς λεγομένων, εἰ τὸ μᾶλλον ὑπάρχειν

10 δοκοῦν μὴ ὑπάρχει, οὐδὲ τὸ ἧττον, ἢ εἰ τὸ ἧττον
δοκοῦν ὑπάρχειν ὑπάρχει, καὶ τὸ μᾶλλον. ἔτι
δυοῖν περὶ δύο λεγομένων εἰ τὸ θατέρῳ μᾶλλον
ὑπάρχειν δοκοῦν μὴ ὑπάρχει, οὐδὲ τὸ λοιπὸν τῷ
λοιπῷ, ἢ εἰ τὸ ἧττον δοκοῦν τῷ ἑτέρῳ ὑπάρχειν
ὑπάρχει, καὶ τὸ λοιπὸν τῷ λοιπῷ.

15 Ἔτι ἐκ τοῦ ὁμοίως ὑπάρχειν ἢ δοκεῖν ὑπάρχειν
τριχῶς, καθάπερ ἐπὶ τοῦ μᾶλλον ἐπὶ τῶν ὕστερον
ῥηθέντων τριῶν τόπων ἐλέγετο. εἴτε γὰρ ἕν τι
δυσὶν ὁμοίως ὑπάρχει ἢ δοκεῖ ὑπάρχειν, εἰ τῷ
ἑτέρῳ μὴ ὑπάρχει, οὐδὲ τῷ ἑτέρῳ, εἰ δὲ θατέρῳ

20 ὑπάρχει, καὶ τῷ λοιπῷ· εἴτε δύο τῷ αὐτῷ ὁμοίως,
εἰ τὸ ἕτερον μὴ ὑπάρχει, οὐδὲ τὸ λοιπόν, εἰ δὲ
θάτερον, καὶ τὸ λοιπόν. τὸν αὐτὸν δὲ τρόπον
καὶ εἰ δύο δυσὶν ὁμοίως ὑπάρχει· εἰ γὰρ τὸ ἕτερον
τῷ ἑτέρῳ μὴ ὑπάρχει, οὐδὲ τὸ λοιπὸν τῷ λοιπῷ,
εἰ δὲ ὑπάρχει τὸ ἕτερον τῷ ἑτέρῳ, καὶ τὸ λοιπὸν
τῷ λοιπῷ.

if two predicates are applied to one subject, then, if the one which is more generally regarded as belonging to the one subject does not belong, neither does that which is less generally so regarded; or, if the predicate which is less generally regarded as belonging does belong, then so also does that which is more generally so regarded. Further, when two predicates are applied to two subjects, if the predicate which is more generally regarded as belonging to one of the subjects does not belong, neither does the other predicate belong to the other subject; or, if the predicate which is less generally regarded as belonging to the one subject does belong, then the other predicate also belongs to the other subject.

Furthermore, you can derive material from the fact that a predicate belongs, or is generally regarded as belonging, in a like degree, in three ways, namely, those described in the last three commonplaces already mentioned in connexion with the greater degree. For, if one predicate belongs, or is generally regarded as belonging, to two subjects in a like degree, then, if it does not belong to the one, it does not belong to the other either, and, if it belongs to the one, it belongs to the other also. Or, if two predicates belong in a like degree to the same subject, if the one does not belong, neither does the other, whereas, if the one does belong, so also does the other. The same thing also happens if two predicates belong in a like degree to two subjects; for if the one predicate does not belong to the one subject, neither does the other predicate belong to the other subject, while, if the one predicate belongs to the one subject, then the other predicate also belongs to the other subject. *(c)* Three arguments can be derived from the like degree.

375

115 a

25   XI. Ἐκ μὲν οὖν τοῦ μᾶλλον καὶ ἧττον καὶ τοῦ
ὁμοίως τοσαυταχῶς ἐνδέχεται ἐπιχειρεῖν· ἔτι δ'
ἐκ τῆς προσθέσεως. ἐὰν ἕτερον πρὸς ἕτερον προστεθὲν ποιῇ ἀγαθὸν ἢ λευκόν, μὴ ὂν πρότερον
λευκὸν ἢ ἀγαθόν, τὸ προστεθὲν ἔσται λευκὸν ἢ
ἀγαθόν, οἷόν περ καὶ τὸ ὅλον ποιεῖ. ἔτι εἰ πρὸς τὸ
30   ὑπάρχον προστεθέν τι μᾶλλον ποιεῖ τοιοῦτον οἷον
ὑπῆρχε, καὶ αὐτὸ ἔσται τοιοῦτον. ὁμοίως δὲ καὶ
ἐπὶ τῶν ἄλλων. χρήσιμος δὲ οὐκ ἐν ἅπασιν ὁ
τόπος, ἀλλ' ἐν οἷς τὴν τοῦ μᾶλλον ὑπεροχὴν συμβαίνει γίνεσθαι. οὗτος δὲ ὁ τόπος οὐκ ἀντιστρέφει
πρὸς τὸ ἀνασκευάζειν. εἰ γὰρ μὴ ποιεῖ τὸ προσ-
35   τιθέμενον ἀγαθόν, οὐδέπω δῆλον εἰ αὐτὸ μὴ
115 b   ἀγαθόν· τὸ γὰρ ἀγαθὸν κακῷ προστιθέμενον οὐκ
ἐξ ἀνάγκης ἀγαθὸν τὸ ὅλον ποιεῖ, οὐδὲ λευκὸν
μέλανι.

Πάλιν εἴ τι μᾶλλον καὶ ἧττον λέγεται, καὶ
ἁπλῶς ὑπάρχει· τὸ γὰρ μὴ ὂν ἀγαθὸν ἢ λευκὸν
5   οὐδὲ μᾶλλον ἢ ἧττον ἀγαθὸν ἢ λευκὸν ῥηθήσεται·
τὸ γὰρ κακὸν οὐδενὸς μᾶλλον ἢ ἧττον ἀγαθόν,
ἀλλὰ μᾶλλον κακὸν ἢ ἧττον ῥηθήσεται. οὐκ ἀντιστρέφει δ' οὐδ' οὗτος ὁ τόπος πρὸς τὸ ἀνα-
σκευάσαι· πολλὰ γὰρ τῶν οὐ λεγομένων μᾶλλον
⟨καὶ ἧττον⟩[1] ἁπλῶς ὑπάρχει· ἄνθρωπος γὰρ οὐ
10   λέγεται μᾶλλον καὶ ἧττον, ἀλλ' οὐ διὰ τοῦτο οὐκ
ἔστιν ἄνθρωπος.

Τὸν αὐτὸν δὲ τρόπον σκεπτέον καὶ ἐπὶ τοῦ κατά

---

[1] καὶ ἧττον added by Wallies.

XI. Such then are the various ways in which you *Further* can argue from the greater and the less and the like *Rules*: *(a)* How to degrees. You can, moreover, obtain arguments from argue from the addition of one thing to another. If the addition adding two of one thing to another makes the latter good or things white, whereas it was not white or good before, then that which was added will be white or good, *i.e.*, it will have the quality which it also bestows on the whole. Further, if something added to the existing quality of a thing imparts a greater degree of the same existing quality, it will be itself also of that quality. So likewise in the other cases. But this commonplace is not always useful, but only where the result of the addition is that a greater intensification is produced. This commonplace is not convertible for purposes of destructive criticism. For, if that which is added does not make a thing good, it is not yet clear whether it is itself not good ; for good added to evil does not necessarily make the whole good, nor does white added to black necessarily make the whole white.

Again, if anything is predicated in a greater or *(b)* Any-less degree, it also belongs absolutely ; for what is thing which not good (or white) will never be said to be good (or cated in a white) in a greater or less degree ; for an evil thing greater or will never be described as possessing a greater or less less degree degree of goodness than something else, but only of solutely. evil. This commonplace also is not convertible for purposes of destructive criticism ; for many predicates to which we cannot ascribe a greater or a less degree belong absolutely ; for ' man ' cannot be predicated in a greater or less degree, but a man does not on this account cease to be a man.

In the same manner you must examine predicates *(c)* What is

ARISTOTLE

τι καὶ ποτὲ καὶ ποῦ· εἰ γὰρ κατά τι ἐνδέχεται,
καὶ ἁπλῶς ἐνδέχεται. ὁμοίως δὲ καὶ τὸ ποτὲ ἢ
ποῦ· τὸ γὰρ ἁπλῶς ἀδύνατον οὔτε κατά τι οὔτε
15 ποῦ οὔτε ποτὲ ἐνδέχεται. ἔνστασις ὅτι κατά τι
μέν εἰσι φύσει σπουδαῖοι, οἷον ἐλευθέριοι ἢ σω-
φρονικοί, ἁπλῶς δὲ οὐκ εἰσὶ φύσει σπουδαῖοι·
οὐδεὶς γὰρ φύσει φρόνιμος. ὁμοίως δὲ καὶ ποτὲ
μὲν ἐνδέχεται τῶν φθαρτῶν τι μὴ φθαρῆναι,
ἁπλῶς δ' οὐκ ἐνδέχεται μὴ φθαρῆναι. τὸν αὐτὸν
20 δὲ τρόπον καὶ ποῦ μὲν συμφέρει τοιαύτῃ διαίτῃ
χρῆσθαι, οἷον ἐν τοῖς νοσώδεσι τόποις, ἁπλῶς δ'
οὐ συμφέρει. ἔτι δὲ ποῦ μὲν ἕνα μόνον δυνατὸν
εἶναι, ἁπλῶς δὲ οὐ δυνατὸν ἕνα μόνον εἶναι. τὸν
αὐτὸν δὲ τρόπον καὶ ποῦ μὲν καλὸν τὸν πατέρα
θύειν, οἷον ἐν Τριβαλλοῖς, ἁπλῶς δ' οὐ καλόν. ἢ
25 τοῦτο μὲν οὐ ποῦ σημαίνει ἀλλὰ τισίν; οὐδὲν γὰρ
διαφέρει ὅπου ἂν ὦσιν· πανταχοῦ γὰρ αὐτοῖς ἔσται
καλὸν οὖσι Τριβαλλοῖς. πάλιν ποτὲ μὲν συμφέρει
φαρμακεύεσθαι, οἷον ὅταν νοσῇ, ἁπλῶς δ' οὔ. ἢ
οὐδὲ τοῦτο ποτὲ σημαίνει, ἀλλὰ τῷ διακειμένῳ
πως; οὐδὲν γὰρ διαφέρει ὁποτεοῦν, ἐὰν οὕτω
30 μόνον διακείμενος ᾖ. τὸ δ' ἁπλῶς ἐστιν ὃ μηδενὸς

378

which apply only in a certain respect or at a certain ^{predicated} time or in a certain place ; for, if a predicate is possible in a certain respect, it is also possible absolutely. The same is true of predicates which are qualified in respect of time and place ; for what is impossible absolutely is not possible in any respect or in any place or at any time. An objection may be raised that in a certain respect men are naturally good, for example, they may be generous or inclined to self-control, but absolutely they are not by nature good, for no one is naturally prudent. Similarly, too, it is possible at a certain time for something which is corruptible not to be corrupted, but it is impossible for it to avoid corruption absolutely. In the same way, too, it is expedient in certain places to adopt a certain diet, *e.g.*, in unhealthy localities, but absolutely it is not expedient. Further, in certain places it is possible for a man to exist alone, but absolutely it is not possible for him to exist alone. In the same way, also, it is honourable in some places to sacrifice one's father, for example amongst the Triballi,ᵃ but absolutely it is not honourable. (Or is a relativity to persons rather than places indicated here ? For it makes no difference where they may be ; for, wherever they are, it will be honourable in their eyes because they are Triballi.) Again, it is expedient at certain times to take drugs, for example, when one is ill ; but it is not expedient absolutely. (Or is a relativity to a certain condition rather than to a certain time indicated here ? For it makes no difference when a man takes the drug, if only he is in a condition which requires it.) Now the 'absolutely' honourable or its contrary, is that

predicated with a qualification can also be predicated absolutely.

ᵃ A Thracian tribe who dwelt near the Danube.

προστεθέντος ἐρεῖς ὅτι καλόν ἐστιν ἢ τὸ ἐναντίον. οἷον τὸ τὸν πατέρα θύειν οὐκ ἐρεῖς καλὸν εἶναι, ἀλλὰ τισὶ καλὸν εἶναι· οὐκ ἄρα ἁπλῶς καλόν. ἀλλὰ τὸ τοὺς θεοὺς τιμᾶν ἐρεῖς καλὸν οὐδὲν προστιθείς· ἁπλῶς γὰρ καλόν ἐστιν. ὥστε ὃ ἂν μηδενὸς προστιθεμένου δοκῇ εἶναι καλὸν ἢ αἰσχρὸν 35 ἢ ἄλλο τι τῶν τοιούτων, ἁπλῶς ῥηθήσεται.

which you will say is honourable or its contrary, without any additional qualification. For example, you will not say that to sacrifice one's father is honourable, but that ' in the eyes of some people ' it is honourable ; it is not, therefore, honourable absolutely. But you will say that to honour the gods is honourable without adding any qualification ; for it is honourable absolutely. So whatever is generally regarded as honourable or disgraceful, or anything else of the kind, without any additional qualification, will be called so in an absolute sense.

Γ

I. Πότερον δ' αἱρετώτερον ἢ βέλτιον δυεῖν ἢ πλειόνων, ἐκ τῶνδε σκεπτέον. πρῶτον δὲ διορί-
5 σθω ὅτι τὴν σκέψιν ποιούμεθα οὐχ ὑπὲρ τῶν πολὺ διεστώτων καὶ μεγάλην πρὸς ἄλληλα διαφορὰν ἐχόντων (οὐδεὶς γὰρ ἀπορεῖ πότερον ἡ εὐδαιμονία ἢ ὁ πλοῦτος αἱρετώτερον) ἀλλ' ὑπὲρ τῶν σύνεγγυς, καὶ περὶ ὧν ἀμφισβητοῦμεν ποτέρῳ δεῖ προσ-
θέσθαι μᾶλλον, διὰ τὸ μηδεμίαν ὁρᾶν τοῦ ἑτέρου
10 πρὸς τὸ ἕτερον ὑπεροχήν. δῆλον οὖν ἐπὶ τῶν τοιούτων ὅτι δειχθείσης ὑπεροχῆς ἢ μιᾶς ἢ πλειό-νων συγκαταθήσεται ἡ διάνοια ὅτι τοῦτ' ἐστὶν αἱρετώτερον, ὁπότερον τυγχάνει αὐτῶν ὑπερέχον.

Πρῶτον μὲν οὖν τὸ πολυχρονιώτερον ἢ βεβαιό-τερον αἱρετώτερον τοῦ ἧττον τοιούτου. καὶ ὃ μᾶλλον ἂν ἕλοιτο ὁ φρόνιμος ἢ ὁ ἀγαθὸς ἀνήρ, ἢ
15 ὁ νόμος ὁ ὀρθός, ἢ οἱ σπουδαῖοι περὶ ἕκαστα αἱρούμενοι ᾗ τοιοῦτοί εἰσιν, ἢ οἱ ἐν ἑκάστῳ γένει ἐπιστήμονες, ἢ ὅσα οἱ πλείους ἢ πάντες, οἷον ἐν ἰατρικῇ ἢ τεκτονικῇ ἃ οἱ πλείους τῶν ἰατρῶν ἢ πάντες, ἢ ὅσα ὅλως οἱ πλείους ἢ πάντες ἢ πάντα,

BOOK III

I. Which is more worthy of choice or better of two (or more) things, must be examined in the light of the following considerations. But first a limitation must be laid down that our inquiry does not concern things which are widely separated and show a considerable divergence from one another (for no one is at a loss to decide whether happiness or wealth is more worthy of choice), but it is concerned with things that are closely related and about which we discuss which we ought preferably to support, because we cannot detect any superiority of the one over the other. It is clear, therefore, that, as regards such things, if one or more points of superiority can be shown, the mind will agree that whichever of the two alternatives is actually superior is the more worthy of choice.

In the first place, then, that which is more permanent or constant is more worthy of choice than that which is less so, and also that which the prudent or good man would prefer, or the right law, or those who are excellent in any particular sphere when they make their choice as such, and those who are skilled in some particular subject, or what most of them, or all, would choose, for example, in medicine (or carpentry) what most, or all, doctors would choose, or generally those things which most people or every-

Rules for the comparative valuation of two or more predicates:

(a) The more durable and what commends itself to the wise and good is preferable.

383

20 οἷον τἀγαθόν· πάντα γὰρ τἀγαθοῦ ἐφίεται. δεῖ
δ' ἄγειν πρὸς ὅ τι ἂν ᾖ χρήσιμον τὸ ῥηθησόμενον.
ἔστι δ' ἁπλῶς μὲν βέλτιον καὶ αἱρετώτερον τὸ
κατὰ τὴν βελτίω ἐπιστήμην, τινὶ δὲ τὸ κατὰ τὴν
οἰκείαν.

Ἔπειτα δὲ τὸ ὅπερ τόδε τι τοῦ μὴ ἐν γένει,
οἷον ἡ δικαιοσύνη τοῦ δικαίου· τὸ μὲν γὰρ ἐν γένει
τῷ ἀγαθῷ, τὸ δ' οὔ, καὶ τὸ μὲν ὅπερ ἀγαθόν, τὸ
25 δ' οὔ· οὐδὲν γὰρ λέγεται ὅπερ τὸ γένος, ὃ μὴ
τυγχάνει ἐν τῷ γένει ὄν, οἷον ὁ λευκὸς ἄνθρωπος
οὐκ ἔστιν ὅπερ χρῶμα. ὁμοίως δὲ καὶ ἐπὶ τῶν
ἄλλων.

Καὶ τὸ δι' αὑτὸ αἱρετὸν τοῦ δι' ἕτερον αἱρετοῦ
30 αἱρετώτερον, οἷον τὸ ὑγιαίνειν τοῦ γυμνάζεσθαι·
τὸ μὲν γὰρ δι' αὑτὸ αἱρετόν, τὸ δὲ δι' ἕτερον.
καὶ τὸ καθ' αὑτὸ τοῦ κατὰ συμβεβηκός, οἷον τὸ
τοὺς φίλους δικαίους εἶναι τοῦ τοὺς ἐχθρούς. τὸ
μὲν γὰρ καθ' αὑτὸ αἱρετόν, τὸ δὲ κατὰ συμ-
βεβηκός· τὸ γὰρ τοὺς ἐχθροὺς δικαίους εἶναι κατὰ
35 συμβεβηκὸς αἱρούμεθα, ὅπως μηδὲν ἡμᾶς βλά-
πτωσιν. ἔστι δὲ τοῦτο ταὐτὸ τῷ πρὸ τούτου,
διαφέρει δὲ τῷ τρόπῳ· τὸ μὲν γὰρ τοὺς φίλους
δικαίους εἶναι δι' αὑτὸ αἱρούμεθα, καὶ εἰ μηδὲν

body or all things would choose, for example, the good; for everything aims at the good. You must direct the future course of the discussion in whatever direction may be advantageous; but the absolute criterion of what is better and more worthy of choice is the better knowledge, though for the individual it may be his own particular knowledge.

Next, that which is of a certain kind is more worthy of choice than that which is not in the genus of that thing, for example, justice is more worthy of choice than the just man; for the former is in the genus 'good,' but the latter is not, and the former is that which is called 'good,' but the latter is not. For nothing is called by the name of the genus which does not actually belong to the genus; for example, the 'white man' is not a 'colour' and so likewise in the other cases. *(b) The genus is preferable to the accident.*

Also, that which is worthy of choice for its own sake is more worthy of choice than that which is so for some other reason; for example, health is more worthy of choice than exercise, for the former is worthy of choice for its own sake, the latter for the sake of something else. Also, that which is in itself worthy of choice is more worthy of choice than that which is accidentally so; for example, that one's friends should be just is more worthy of choice than that one's enemies should be so, for the former is worthy of choice in itself, the latter accidentally; for we choose that our enemies should be just only accidentally, in order that they may not do us harm. This rule is the same as the one which preceded it, but differs in the way in which it is stated; for that our friends should be just is a thing which we choose for its own sake, even if it is not going to affect us *(c) What is desirable for its own sake is preferable.*

385

116 a

ἡμῖν μέλλει ἔσεσθαι, κἂν ἐν Ἰνδοῖς ὦσιν· τὸ δὲ
τοὺς ἐχθροὺς δι᾽ ἕτερον, ὅπως μηθὲν ἡμᾶς βλά-
πτωσιν.

116 b   Καὶ τὸ αἴτιον ἀγαθοῦ καθ᾽ αὑτὸ τοῦ κατὰ συμβεβηκὸς αἰτίου, καθάπερ ἡ ἀρετὴ τῆς τύχης (ἡ
μὲν γὰρ καθ᾽ αὑτὴν ἡ δὲ κατὰ συμβεβηκὸς αἰτία
τῶν ἀγαθῶν) καὶ εἴ τι ἄλλο τοιοῦτον. ὁμοίως δὲ
5 καὶ ἐπὶ τοῦ ἐναντίου· τὸ γὰρ καθ᾽ αὑτὸ κακοῦ
αἴτιον φευκτότερον τοῦ κατὰ συμβεβηκός, οἷον
ἡ κακία καὶ ἡ τύχη· τὸ μὲν γὰρ καθ᾽ αὑτὸ κακόν,
ἡ δὲ τύχη κατὰ συμβεβηκός.

Καὶ τὸ ἁπλῶς ἀγαθὸν τοῦ τινὶ αἱρετώτερον,
οἷον τὸ ὑγιάζεσθαι τοῦ τέμνεσθαι· τὸ μὲν γὰρ
10 ἁπλῶς ἀγαθόν, τὸ δὲ τινὶ τῷ δεομένῳ τομῆς.
καὶ τὸ φύσει τοῦ μὴ φύσει, οἷον ἡ δικαιοσύνη τοῦ
δικαίου· τὸ μὲν γὰρ φύσει, τὸ δ᾽ ἐπίκτητον. καὶ
τὸ τῷ βελτίονι καὶ τιμιωτέρῳ ὑπάρχον αἱρετώτερον, οἷον θεῷ ἢ ἀνθρώπῳ καὶ ψυχῇ ἢ σώματι.
καὶ τὸ τοῦ βελτίονος ἴδιον βέλτιον ἢ τὸ τοῦ χεί-
15 ρονος, οἷον τὸ τοῦ θεοῦ ἢ τὸ τοῦ ἀνθρώπου· κατὰ
μὲν γὰρ τὰ κοινὰ ἐν ἀμφοτέροις οὐδὲν διαφέρει
ἀλλήλων, τοῖς δ᾽ ἰδίοις τὸ ἕτερον τοῦ ἑτέρου
ὑπερέχει. καὶ τὸ ἐν βελτίοσιν ἢ προτέροις ἢ

at all, and even though they may be in India; but we choose that our enemies should be just for another reason, namely, that they may do us no harm.

Also that which is in itself the cause of good is more worthy of choice than that which is accidentally the cause of good; for example, virtue is more worthy of choice than luck (for the former is in itself the cause of good things but the latter only accidentally), and so with any other similar case. So also in the contrary case; for what is in itself the cause of evil is more to be avoided than that which is only accidentally the cause of evil, as in the case of baseness and chance; for the former is in itself an evil, while chance is only accidentally so. *(d)* What is *per se* the cause of good is preferable to what is accidentally so.

Also, that which is good absolutely is more worthy of choice than that which is good for an individual, *e.g.*, the enjoyment of health than a surgical operation; for the former is good absolutely, the latter is good only for an individual, namely, the man who requires an operation. Also, that which is naturally good is more worthy of choice than that which is not so by nature, *e.g.*, justice rather than the just man; for the former is naturally good, whereas the goodness of the latter is acquired. Also what belongs to that which is better and more highly honoured is more worthy of choice, for example, that which belongs to God than that which belongs to man, and that which belongs to the soul than that which belongs to the body. Also the property of the better is better than that of the worse, for example, the property of God than that of man; for in those things which are common to both there is no difference between them, but it is in their properties that the one is superior to the other. Also, that is better *(e)* The absolutely and the naturally good are preferable. *(f)* What belongs to the better is preferable.

τιμιωτέροις βέλτιον, οἷον ὑγίεια ἰσχύος καὶ κάλλους.

ἡ μὲν γὰρ ἐν ὑγροῖς καὶ ξηροῖς καὶ θερμοῖς καὶ
20 ψυχροῖς, ἁπλῶς δ' εἰπεῖν ἐξ ὧν πρώτων συν-
έστηκε τὸ ζῷον, τὰ δ' ἐν τοῖς ὑστέροις· ἡ μὲν γὰρ
ἰσχὺς ἐν τοῖς νεύροις καὶ ὀστοῖς, τὸ δὲ κάλλος τῶν
μελῶν τις συμμετρία δοκεῖ εἶναι. καὶ τὸ τέλος
τῶν πρὸς τὸ τέλος αἱρετώτερον δοκεῖ εἶναι, καὶ
δυοῖν τὸ ἔγγιον τοῦ τέλους. καὶ ὅλως τὸ πρὸς
25 τὸ τοῦ βίου τέλος αἱρετώτερον μᾶλλον ἢ τὸ πρὸς
ἄλλο τι, οἷον τὸ πρὸς εὐδαιμονίαν συντεῖνον ἢ τὸ
πρὸς φρόνησιν. καὶ τὸ δυνατὸν τοῦ ἀδυνάτου.
ἔτι δύο ποιητικῶν, οὗ τὸ τέλος βέλτιον. ποιητικοῦ δὲ καὶ τέλους ἐκ τοῦ ἀνάλογον, ὅταν πλείονι
ὑπερέχῃ τὸ τέλος τοῦ τέλους ἢ ἐκεῖνο τοῦ οἰκείου
ποιητικοῦ, οἷον εἰ ἡ εὐδαιμονία πλείονι ὑπερέχει
30 ὑγιείας ἢ ὑγίεια ὑγιεινοῦ, τὸ ποιητικὸν εὐδαιμονίας βέλτιον ὑγιείας. ὅσῳ γὰρ ἡ εὐδαιμονία
ὑγιείας ὑπερέχει, τοσούτῳ καὶ τὸ ποιητικὸν τὸ
τῆς εὐδαιμονίας τοῦ ὑγιεινοῦ ὑπερέχει. ἡ δὲ
ὑγίεια τοῦ ὑγιεινοῦ ἐλάττονι ὑπερεῖχεν, ὥστε
πλείονι ὑπερέχει τὸ ποιητικὸν εὐδαιμονίας τοῦ

---

^a It is difficult to see what is the syntax of the words ποιη-
τικοῦ δὲ τέλους ἐκ τοῦ ἀνάλογον, but the meaning is clear.

which is inherent in things which are better or prior or more highly honoured; for example, health is better than strength or beauty. For health is inherent in moisture and dryness and in heat and cold, in a word in all the primary elements of which the living creature consists, whereas the others are inherent in secondary constituents; for strength is generally considered to reside in the sinews and bones, and beauty to be in a certain symmetry of the limbs. Also, the end is usually regarded as more worthy of choice than the means to the end, and of two means that which is nearer to the end. And, to speak generally, the means which has life as its end is more worthy of choice than that which has some other end; for example, that which tends to happiness is more worthy of choice than that which tends to prudence. Also the practicable is more worthy of choice than the impracticable. Further, of two productive agencies, that of which the end is better is more worthy of choice. We can judge between a productive agency and an end by drawing up a proportion,[a] when the superiority of one end over the other is greater than that of the latter over its own productive agency. For example, if happiness has a greater superiority over health than health has over the health-giving, then that which produces happiness is superior to health. For that which produces happiness is superior to the health-giving in the same degree as happiness is superior to health. But health shows less superiority over the health-giving; therefore that which produces happiness shows greater superiority over the health-giving than

(g) The end is preferable to the means, and the practicable to the impracticable.

Pacius renders, *cum alterum sit effectivum, alterum finis, ex proportione iudicandum est.* Wallies reads ποιητικὸν.

389

35 ὑγιεινοῦ ἢ ἡ ὑγίεια τοῦ ὑγιεινοῦ. δῆλον ἄρα ὅτι
αἱρετώτερον τὸ ποιητικὸν εὐδαιμονίας τῆς ὑγιείας·
τοῦ γὰρ αὐτοῦ πλείονι ὑπερέχει.

Ἔτι τὸ κάλλιον καθ᾽ αὑτὸ καὶ τιμιώτερον καὶ
ἐπαινετώτερον, οἷον φιλία πλούτου καὶ δικαιοσύνη
ἰσχύος. τὰ μὲν γὰρ καθ᾽ αὑτὰ τῶν τιμίων καὶ
117 a ἐπαινετῶν, τὰ δ᾽ οὐ καθ᾽ αὑτὰ ἀλλὰ δι᾽ ἕτερον·
οὐδεὶς γὰρ τιμᾷ τὸν πλοῦτον δι᾽ ἑαυτὸν ἀλλὰ δι᾽
ἕτερον, τὴν δὲ φιλίαν καθ᾽ αὑτό, καὶ εἰ μηδὲν
μέλλει ἡμῖν ἕτερον ἀπ᾽ αὐτῆς ἔσεσθαι.

5 II. Ἔτι ὅταν δύο τινὰ ᾖ σφόδρα ἀλλήλοις παραπλήσια καὶ μὴ δυνώμεθα ὑπεροχὴν μηδεμίαν
συνιδεῖν τοῦ ἑτέρου πρὸς τὸ ἕτερον, ὁρᾶν ἀπὸ τῶν
παρεπομένων· ᾧ γὰρ ἕπεται μεῖζον ἀγαθόν, τοῦθ᾽
αἱρετώτερον. ἂν δ᾽ ᾖ τὰ ἑπόμενα κακά, ᾧ τὸ
ἔλαττον ἀκολουθεῖ κακόν, τοῦθ᾽ αἱρετώτερον.
10 ὄντων γὰρ ἀμφοτέρων αἱρετῶν οὐδὲν κωλύει
δυσχερές τι παρέπεσθαι. διχῶς δ᾽ ἀπὸ τοῦ
ἕπεσθαι ἡ σκέψις· καὶ γὰρ πρότερον καὶ ὕστερον
ἕπεται, οἷον τῷ μανθάνοντι τὸ μὲν ἀγνοεῖν πρότερον, τὸ δ᾽ ἐπίστασθαι ὕστερον. βέλτιον δ᾽ ὡς
ἐπὶ τὸ πολὺ τὸ ὕστερον ἑπόμενον. λαμβάνειν οὖν
15 τῶν ἑπομένων ὁπότερον ἂν ᾖ χρήσιμον.

Ἔτι τὰ πλείω ἀγαθὰ τῶν ἐλαττόνων, ἢ ἁπλῶς,
ἢ ὅταν τὰ ἕτερα ἐν τοῖς ἑτέροις ὑπάρχῃ, τὰ ἐλάττω
ἐν τοῖς πλείοσιν. ἔνστασις, εἴ που θάτερον θατέρου

health shows over the health-giving. It is clear, then, that what produces happiness is more worthy of choice than health ; for it shows a greater superiority over the same thing.

Further, that which is in itself more noble and more valued and more praiseworthy is more worthy of choice ; for example, friendship is more worthy of choice than wealth, and justice than strength. For the former in themselves are among things valued and praiseworthy, while the latter are valued and praiseworthy not in themselves but for some other reason ; for no one values wealth for its own sake but for some other reason, but we value friendship for its own sake, even if we are not likely to get anything else from it. *(h)* What is *per se* more noble, valued and praiseworthy is preferable.

II. Further, when two things are very similar to one another and we cannot detect any superiority in the one over the other, we must judge from their consequences ; for that of which the consequence is a greater good is more worthy of choice, and, if the consequences are evil, that is more worthy of choice which is followed by the lesser evil. For, if both are worthy of choice, there is nothing to prevent some unpleasant secondary consequence. The examination based on consequence takes two forms ; for a consequence can be prior or posterior in time ; for example, for the man who learns, ignorance is prior, knowledge posterior. The posterior consequence is usually better. You should, then, take whichever of the consequences is advantageous. *Rules of preference can be based on :* *(a)* Antecedents and consequences.

Further, a greater number of good things is preferable to a lesser number, either absolutely or when the one exists in the other, *i.e.*, the lesser number is included in the greater. An objection may be *(b)* Numbers.

391

χάριν· οὐδὲν γὰρ αἱρετώτερα τὰ ἄμφω τοῦ ἑνός,
20 οἷον τὸ ὑγιάζεσθαι καὶ ἡ ὑγίεια τῆς ὑγιείας,
ἐπειδὴ τὸ ὑγιάζεσθαι τῆς ὑγιείας ἕνεκεν αἱρούμεθα.
καὶ μὴ ἀγαθὰ δὲ· ἀγαθῶν οὐδὲν κωλύει εἶναι
αἱρετώτερα, οἷον εὐδαιμονίαν καὶ ἄλλο τι ὃ μή
ἐστιν ἀγαθὸν δικαιοσύνης καὶ ἀνδρίας. καὶ ταὐτὰ
μεθ᾽ ἡδονῆς μᾶλλον ἢ ἄνευ ἡδονῆς, καὶ ταὐτὰ
25 μετ᾽ ἀλυπίας μᾶλλον ἢ μετὰ λύπης.

Καὶ ἕκαστον ἐν ᾧ καιρῷ μεῖζον δύναται, ἐν
τούτῳ καὶ αἱρετώτερον, οἷον τὸ ἀλύπως ἐν τῷ
γήρᾳ μᾶλλον ἢ ἐν τῇ νεότητι· μεῖζον γὰρ ἐν τῷ
γήρᾳ δύναται. κατὰ ταῦτα δὲ καὶ ἡ φρόνησις ἐν
30 τῷ γήρᾳ αἱρετώτερον· οὐδεὶς γὰρ τοὺς νέους
αἱρεῖται ἡγεμόνας διὰ τὸ μὴ ἀξιοῦν φρονίμους
εἶναι. ἡ δ᾽ ἀνδρία ἀνάπαλιν· ἐν τῇ νεότητι γὰρ
ἀναγκαιοτέρα ἡ κατὰ τὴν ἀνδρίαν ἐνέργεια. ὁμοίως
δὲ καὶ ἡ σωφροσύνη· μᾶλλον γὰρ οἱ νέοι τῶν
πρεσβυτέρων ὑπὸ τῶν ἐπιθυμιῶν ἐνοχλοῦνται.

35 Καὶ ὃ ἐν παντὶ καιρῷ ἢ ἐν τοῖς πλείστοις χρή-
σιμώτερον, οἷον δικαιοσύνη καὶ σωφροσύνη ἀν-
δρίας· αἱ μὲν γὰρ ἀεὶ ἡ δὲ ποτὲ χρησίμη. καὶ
ὃ πάντων ἐχόντων μηδὲν θατέρου δεόμεθα, ἢ ὃ
ἐχόντων προσδεόμεθα τοῦ λοιποῦ, καθάπερ ἐπὶ
δικαιοσύνης καὶ ἀνδρίας· δικαίων μὲν γὰρ πάντων

---

made if a case occurs in which one thing is preferred
for the sake of another; for the two things taken
together are in no way preferable to the one. For
example, to become healthy *plus* health is not preferable to health alone, since we choose to become
healthy for the sake of health. Also, there is nothing
to prevent even things which are not good *a* from
being preferable to things which are good; for
example, happiness *plus* something else which is not
good may be preferable to justice *plus* courage.
Also, the same things are more worthy of choice
when pleasure is added than when it is absent, and
when accompanied by freedom from pain than when
attended by pain.

Also, everything is preferable at the time when *(c)* Times
it has greater importance; for example, freedom and
seasons.
from pain in old age is preferable to freedom from
pain in youth, for it is more important in old age.
And on this principle also prudence is preferable in
old age; for no one chooses young men as leaders,
because he does not expect them to be prudent.
The converse holds good of courage; for in youth
courageous activity is more necessary. So too with
self-control; for the young are more troubled by
their passions than the old.

Also, that is preferable which is more useful on
every occasion or on most occasions, for example,
justice and self-control are preferable to courage,
for the two first are always useful, but courage only
sometimes. Also, of two things, that one, the *(d)* Self-
sufficiency.
possession of which by all causes us to have no need
of the other, is preferable to the one the universal
possession of which leaves us still in need of the
other. Take, for example, justice and courage; if

117 b ὄντων οὐδὲν χρήσιμος ἡ ἀνδρία, ἀνδρείων δὲ πάντων ὄντων χρήσιμος ἡ δικαιοσύνη.

Ἔτι ἐκ τῶν φθορῶν καὶ τῶν ἀποβολῶν καὶ τῶν
γενέσεων καὶ τῶν λήψεων καὶ τῶν ἐναντίων· ὧν
5 γὰρ αἱ φθοραὶ φευκτότεραι, αὐτὰ αἱρετώτερα.
ὁμοίως δὲ καὶ ἐπὶ τῶν ἀποβολῶν καὶ τῶν ἐναντίων·
οὗ γὰρ ἡ ἀποβολὴ ἢ τὸ ἐναντίον φευκτότερον,
αὐτὸ αἱρετώτερον. ἐπὶ δὲ τῶν γενέσεων καὶ τῶν
λήψεων ἀνάπαλιν· ὧν γὰρ αἱ λήψεις καὶ αἱ γενέσεις
αἱρετώτεραι, καὶ αὐτὰ αἱρετώτερα.

10 Ἄλλος τόπος, τὸ ἐγγύτερον τἀγαθοῦ βέλτιον
καὶ αἱρετώτερον, καὶ τὸ ὁμοιότερον τἀγαθῷ, οἷον
ἡ δικαιοσύνη δικαίου. καὶ τὸ τῷ βελτίονι αὐτοῦ
ὁμοιότερον, καθάπερ τὸν Αἴαντα τοῦ Ὀδυσσέως
φασὶ βελτίω τινὲς εἶναι, διότι ὁμοιότερος τῷ
15 Ἀχιλλεῖ. ἔνστασις τούτου ὅτι οὐκ ἀληθές· οὐδὲν
γὰρ κωλύει, μὴ ᾗ βέλτιστος ὁ Ἀχιλλεύς, ταύτῃ
ὁμοιότερον εἶναι τὸν Αἴαντα, τοῦ ἑτέρου ὄντος
μὲν ἀγαθοῦ μὴ ὁμοίου δέ. σκοπεῖν δὲ καὶ εἰ ἐπὶ
τὸ γελοιότερον εἴη ὅμοιον, καθάπερ ὁ πίθηκος τῷ
ἀνθρώπῳ, τοῦ ἵππου μὴ ὄντος ὁμοίου· οὐ γὰρ
κάλλιον ὁ πίθηκος, ὁμοιότερον δὲ τῷ ἀνθρώπῳ.
20 πάλιν ἐπὶ δυοῖν εἰ τὸ μὲν τῷ βελτίονι τὸ δὲ τῷ
χείρονι ὁμοιότερον, εἴη ἂν βέλτιον τὸ τῷ βελτίονι
ὁμοιότερον. ἔχει δὲ καὶ τοῦτο ἔνστασιν· οὐδὲν
γὰρ κωλύει τὸ μὲν τῷ βελτίονι ἠρέμα ὅμοιον εἶναι,

all men were just, there would be no use for courage, but if all men were brave, justice would still be useful.

Further, arguments can be derived from the corruptions, losses, generations, acquisitions and contraries of things ; for things of which the corruption is more to be avoided are themselves preferable. Similarly, too, in the case of losses and contraries ; for that of which the loss or the contrary is more to be avoided is itself preferable. The converse is true of generation and acquisition ; for things of which the acquisition and generation is preferable are themselves preferable. *(e) Corruptions, losses, generations, acquisitions and contraries.*

Another commonplace is that what is nearer to the good is better and preferable, and also what is more like the good ; for example, justice is preferable to a just man. Also that is preferable which is more like something better than itself ; for example, some people say that Ajax was a better man than Odysseus, because he was more like Achilles. To this an objection may be raised that it is not true ; for nothing prevents Ajax from being more like Achilles, but not in respect of that in which Achilles was best, while Odysseus might be a good man though not resembling Achilles. We must also see whether the resemblance tends towards the ridiculous, for example, that of a monkey to a man, whereas the horse bears no resemblance ; for the monkey is not more handsome than the horse, although he is more like a man. Again, of two things, if the one is more like that which is better and the other more like that which is worse, then that which is like the better would itself be better. Here also an objection is possible ; for there is no reason why the one should not resemble the better in a slight degree only, *(f) Likeness to some ideal pattern.*

395

117 b

τὸ δὲ τῷ χείρονι σφόδρα, οἷον εἰ ὁ μὲν Αἴας τῷ
Ἀχιλλεῖ ἠρέμα, ὁ δ' Ὀδυσσεὺς τῷ Νέστορι
25 σφόδρα. καὶ εἰ τὸ μὲν τῷ βελτίονι ὅμοιον ἐπὶ τὰ
χείρω ὅμοιον εἴη, τὸ δὲ τῷ χείρονι ἐπὶ τὰ βελτίω,
καθάπερ ἵππος ὄνῳ καὶ πίθηκος ἀνθρώπῳ.

Ἄλλος, τὸ ἐπιφανέστερον τοῦ ἧττον τοιούτου, καὶ
τὸ χαλεπώτερον· μᾶλλον γὰρ ἀγαπῶμεν ἔχοντες
30 ἃ μὴ ἔστι ῥᾳδίως λαβεῖν. καὶ τὸ ἰδιαίτερον τοῦ
κοινοτέρου. καὶ τὸ τοῖς κακοῖς ἀκοινωνητότερον·
αἱρετώτερον γὰρ ᾧ μηδεμία δυσχέρεια ἀκολουθεῖ
ἢ ᾧ ἀκολουθεῖ.

Ἔτι εἰ ἁπλῶς τοῦτο τούτου βέλτιον, καὶ τὸ
βέλτιστον τῶν ἐν τούτῳ βέλτιον τοῦ ἐν τῷ ἑτέρῳ
35 βελτίστου, οἷον εἰ βέλτιον ἄνθρωπος ἵππου, καὶ
ὁ βέλτιστος ἄνθρωπος τοῦ βελτίστου ἵππου βελτίων. καὶ εἰ τὸ βέλτιστον τοῦ βελτίστου βέλτιον,
καὶ ἁπλῶς τοῦτο τούτου βέλτιον, οἷον εἰ ὁ βέλτιστος ἄνθρωπος τοῦ βελτίστου ἵππου βελτίων,
καὶ ἁπλῶς ἄνθρωπος ἵππου βελτίων.

118 a Ἔτι ὧν ἔστι τοὺς φίλους μετασχεῖν, αἱρετώτερα
ἢ ὧν μή. καὶ ἃ πρὸς τὸν φίλον πρᾶξαι μᾶλλον
βουλόμεθα ἢ ἃ πρὸς τὸν τυχόντα, ταῦτα αἱρετώτερα, οἷον τὸ δικαιοπραγεῖν καὶ εὖ ποιεῖν μᾶλλον
5 ἢ τὸ δοκεῖν· τοὺς γὰρ φίλους εὖ ποιεῖν βουλόμεθα
μᾶλλον ἢ δοκεῖν, τοὺς δὲ τυχόντας ἀνάπαλιν.

396

while the other strongly resembles the worse; for example, Ajax may slightly resemble Achilles, while Odysseus strongly resembles Nestor. Also, that which resembles the better may resemble it for the worse, while that which resembles the worse may resemble it for the better, as in the likeness of the horse to the donkey and that of a monkey to a man.

Another commonplace is that what is more conspicuous is preferable to what is less conspicuous, also that which is more difficult; for we value more highly the possession of such things as are not easy to obtain. Also, what is more peculiar to ourselves is preferable to what is more common. We also prefer that which has less communion with evil; for that which is not accompanied by vexation is preferable to that which is so accompanied. *(g) Various other desirable qualities and criteria.*

Further, if A be absolutely better than B, then also the best specimen of A is better than the best specimen of B; for example, if man is better than horse, then also the best man is better than the best horse. Also, if the best in one class (A) is better than the best in the other class (B), then also A is absolutely better than B; for example, if the best man is better than the best horse, then also man is better than horse absolutely.

Further, those things in which our friends can share are preferable to those in which they cannot share. Also, things are preferable which we would rather do to a friend than to any chance person. For example, to act justly and to do good are preferable to merely seeming to do so; for we would rather actually do good to our friends than only seem to do so, whereas the converse is true of our attitude to chance persons.

118 a

Καὶ τὰ ἐκ περιουσίας τῶν ἀναγκαίων βελτίω,
ἐνίοτε δὲ καὶ αἱρετώτερα· βέλτιον γὰρ τοῦ ζῆν
τὸ εὖ ζῆν, τὸ δὲ εὖ ζῆν ἐστιν ἐκ περιουσίας, αὐτὸ
δὲ τὸ ζῆν ἀναγκαῖον. ἐνίοτε δὲ τὰ βελτίω οὐχὶ
10 καὶ αἱρετώτερα· οὐ γὰρ εἰ βελτίω, ἀναγκαῖον καὶ
αἱρετώτερα· τὸ γοῦν φιλοσοφεῖν βέλτιον τοῦ
χρηματίζεσθαι, ἀλλ' οὐχ αἱρετώτερον τῷ ἐνδεεῖ
τῶν ἀναγκαίων. τὸ δ' ἐκ περιουσίας ἐστίν, ὅταν
ὑπαρχόντων τῶν ἀναγκαίων ἄλλα τινὰ προσκατα-
σκευάζηταί τις τῶν καλῶν. σχεδὸν δὲ ἴσως
αἱρετώτερον τὸ ἀναγκαῖόν ἐστι, βέλτιον δὲ τὸ ἐκ
15 περιουσίας.

Καὶ ὃ μὴ ἔστι παρ' ἄλλου πορίσασθαι ἢ ὃ ἔστι
καὶ παρ' ἄλλου, οἷον πέπονθεν ἡ δικαιοσύνη πρὸς
τὴν ἀνδρίαν. καὶ εἰ τόδε μὲν ἄνευ τοῦδε αἱρετόν,
τόδε δὲ ἄνευ τοῦδε μή, οἷον δύναμις ἄνευ φρονή-
20 σεως οὐχ αἱρετόν, φρόνησις δ' ἄνευ δυνάμεως
αἱρετόν. καὶ δυοῖν εἰ θάτερον ἀρνούμεθα, ἵνα τὸ
λοιπὸν δόξῃ ἡμῖν ὑπάρχειν, ἐκεῖνο αἱρετώτερον
ὃ βουλόμεθα δοκεῖν ὑπάρχειν, οἷον φιλοπονεῖν
ἀρνούμεθα, ἵν' εὐφυεῖς εἶναι δόξωμεν.

Ἔτι οὗ τῇ ἀπουσίᾳ ἧττον ἐπιτιμητέον δυσ-
25 φοροῦσι, τοῦτο αἱρετώτερον. καὶ οὗ τῇ ἀπουσίᾳ
μὴ δυσφοροῦντι μᾶλλον ἐπιτιμητέον, τοῦτο αἱρετώτερον.

III. Ἔτι τῶν ὑπὸ τὸ αὐτὸ εἶδος τὸ ἔχον τὴν

Also, superfluities are better than bare necessities, and sometimes also preferable. For living a good life is better than merely living; and a good life is a superfluity, while life itself is a necessity. Sometimes better things are not also preferable; for it does not follow that, if they are better, they are also preferable. For example, to be a philosopher is better than to make money, but it is not preferable for him who lacks the necessities of life. Superfluity exists, when, being already in possession of the necessities of life, a man tries to procure some noble accessories. We shall perhaps not be far wrong if we say that the necessary is preferable, while the superfluous is better.

Also, that which cannot be procured from another is preferable to that which can also be procured from another; this, for example, is true of justice as compared with courage. Also A is preferable to B, if A is an object of choice without B, while B is not an object of choice without A; for example, power is not an object of choice without prudence, but prudence is an object of choice without power. Also, if we deny the possession of one of two things in order that we may seem to possess the other, that one is preferable which we wish to seem to possess; for example, we deny that we work hard in order that we may be thought gifted.

Furthermore, that is preferable at the absence of which it is less reprehensible to be annoyed; also that is preferable at whose absence it is more reprehensible not to be annoyed.

III. Furthermore, of the things which fall under the same species, that which possesses the peculiar *Further rules for the comparative*

399

118 a

οἰκείαν ἀρετὴν τοῦ μὴ ἔχοντος. ἄμφω δ' ἐχόντων
τὸ μᾶλλον ἔχον.

Ἔτι εἰ τὸ μὲν ποιεῖ ἀγαθὸν ἐκεῖνο ᾧ ἂν παρῇ,
30 τὸ δὲ μὴ ποιεῖ, τὸ ποιοῦν αἱρετώτερον, καθάπερ
καὶ θερμότερον τὸ θερμαῖνον τοῦ μή. εἰ δ' ἄμφω
ποιεῖ, τὸ μᾶλλον ποιοῦν· ἢ εἰ τὸ βέλτιον καὶ
κυριώτερον ποιεῖ ἀγαθόν, οἷον εἰ τὸ μὲν τὴν
ψυχὴν τὸ δὲ τὸ σῶμα.

Ἔτι ἀπὸ τῶν πτώσεων καὶ τῶν χρήσεων καὶ
35 τῶν πράξεων καὶ τῶν ἔργων, καὶ ταῦτα δὲ ἀπ'
ἐκείνων· ἀκολουθεῖ γὰρ ἀλλήλοις, οἷον εἰ τὸ
δικαίως αἱρετώτερον τοῦ ἀνδρείως, καὶ ἡ δικαιοσύνη τῆς ἀνδρίας αἱρετώτερον· καὶ εἰ ἡ δικαιοσύνη
τῆς ἀνδρίας αἱρετώτερον, καὶ τὸ δικαίως τοῦ ἀνδρείως. παραπλησίως δὲ καὶ ἐπὶ τῶν ἄλλων.

118 b

Ἔτι εἴ τινος τοῦ αὐτοῦ τὸ μὲν μεῖζον ἀγαθόν
ἐστι τὸ δὲ ἔλαττον, αἱρετώτερον τὸ μεῖζον. ἢ
εἰ μείζονος μεῖζον θάτερον. ἀλλὰ καὶ εἰ δύο τινὰ
τινὸς εἴη αἱρετώτερα, τὸ μᾶλλον αἱρετώτερον τοῦ
5 ἧττον αἱρετωτέρου αἱρετώτερον. ἔτι οὗ ἡ ὑπερβολὴ τῆς ὑπερβολῆς αἱρετωτέρα, καὶ αὐτὸ αἱρετώτερον, οἷον φιλία χρημάτων· αἱρετωτέρα γὰρ
ἡ τῆς φιλίας ὑπερβολὴ τῆς τῶν χρημάτων. καὶ
οὗ μᾶλλον ἂν ἕλοιτο αὐτὸς αὑτῷ αἴτιος εἶναι ἢ
οὗ ἕτερον, οἷον τοὺς φίλους τῶν χρημάτων.

ᵃ That is, we must decide whether one thing (*e.g.*, justice)
is preferable to another (*e.g.*, courage) by considering how
other words containing these ideas are used. These may be
adverbs which are πτώσεις (*cf.* 106 b 29, note), or denote
action or actual deed ; χρήσεις seems to refer to the different
usages of a word.

400

virtue of the species is preferable to that which does *valuation of two predicates:* not possess it. If both possess it, then that which possesses it in a greater degree is preferable. *(a) Preference of predicate which (1) possesses the peculiar virtue of the species, or (2) produces the greater good.*

Furthermore, if one thing does good to anything in which it is present and another does not, then that which does good is preferable (just as that which warms is warmer than that which does not). If both do good, that which does greater good, or does good to what is better or more important, is preferable, for example, if one thing does good to the soul the other to the body.

Furthermore, we can judge things from their inflected forms, uses, actions and deeds,[a] and also *vice versa* ; for they follow one another. For example, if 'justly' is preferable to 'courageously,' then 'justice' also is preferable to 'courage'; and if 'justice' is preferable to 'courage,' then 'justly' too is preferable to 'courageously.' And similarly too in the other cases. *(b) Consideration of inflexions and uses of predicates.*

Furthermore, if one thing is a greater and the other a lesser good than the same thing, the greater good is preferable ; or if one of them is greater than a greater good. Moreover also, if two things were to be preferable to something, that which was preferable to a greater degree would be preferable to that which is preferable to a less degree. Further, if the excess of one thing is preferable to the excess of the other, it is itself also preferable. For example, friendship is preferable to money ; for excess of friendship is preferable to excess of money. Also, that of which a man would prefer to be the cause by his own act is preferable to that of which he would wish another to be the cause ; for example, friends are preferable to money. *(c) Comparison with some common standard.*

401

10 Ἔτι ἐκ τῆς προσθέσεως, εἰ τῷ αὐτῷ προσ-
τιθέμενόν τι τὸ ὅλον αἱρετώτερον ποιεῖ. εὐλαβεῖσθαι δὲ δεῖ προτείνειν ἐφ' ὧν τῷ μὲν ἑτέρῳ
τῶν προστιθεμένων χρῆται τὸ κοινὸν ἢ ἄλλως
πως συνεργόν ἐστι, τῷ δὲ λοιπῷ μὴ χρῆται μηδὲ
συνεργόν ἐστιν, οἷον πρίονα καὶ δρέπανον μετὰ
15 τεκτονικῆς· αἱρετώτερον γὰρ ὁ πρίων συνδυα-
ζόμενος, ἁπλῶς δὲ οὐχ αἱρετώτερον. πάλιν εἰ
ἐλάττονι προστεθέν τι τὸ ὅλον μεῖζον ποιεῖ. ὁμοίως
δὲ καὶ ἐκ τῆς ἀφαιρέσεως· οὗ γὰρ ἀφαιρεθέντος
ἀπὸ τοῦ αὐτοῦ τὸ λειπόμενον ἔλαττον, ἐκεῖνο
μεῖζον ἂν εἴη, ὁπότε ἀφαιρεθὲν τὸ λειπόμενον
ἔλαττον ποιεῖ.

20 Καὶ εἰ τὸ μὲν δι' αὐτὸ τὸ δὲ διὰ τὴν δόξαν
αἱρετόν, οἷον ὑγίεια κάλλους. ὅρος δὲ τοῦ πρὸς
δόξαν τὸ μηδενὸς συνειδότος μὴ ἂν σπουδάσαι
ὑπάρχειν. καὶ εἰ τὸ μὲν δι' αὐτὸ καὶ διὰ τὴν
δόξαν αἱρετόν, τὸ δὲ διὰ θάτερον μόνον. καὶ
ὁπότερον μᾶλλον δι' αὐτὸ τίμιον, τοῦτο καὶ βέλτιον
25 καὶ αἱρετώτερον. τιμιώτερον δ' ἂν εἴη καθ' αὐτό,
ὃ μηδενὸς ἄλλου μέλλοντος ὑπάρξειν δι' αὐτὸ
αἱρούμεθα μᾶλλον.

Ἔτι διελέσθαι ποσαχῶς τὸ αἱρετὸν λέγεται καὶ

Furthermore, you can argue by means of an addition, and see if the addition of one predicate to the same thing as that to which another is added makes the whole more worthy of choice. But you must beware of making a proposition in cases where the common term uses, or in some other way co-operates with, one of the things added, but does not use or co-operate with the other. For example, if you were to combine a saw or a sickle with the art of carpentry ; for the saw in conjunction is preferable, but not preferable absolutely. Again, the same is true if something added to a lesser good makes the whole a greater good. So likewise in the case of subtraction also ; for something, the subtraction of which from the same thing as that from which another is subtracted makes the remainder a lesser good, would be a greater good, when its subtraction makes the remainder a lesser good. *(d) Comparison of predicates by adding them to or subtracting them from a known value.*

Also, you must consider whether one thing is worthy of choice for its own sake and the other for the impression which it makes on others, for example, health as compared with beauty. That which is worthy of choice for the impression it makes may be defined as that which one would not be eager to possess if no one knew about it. You must also consider whether one thing is worthy of choice for its own sake and also for the impression it makes, and the other for only one of these reasons. Also whichever is more valuable for its own sake, is also better and more worthy of choice. More valuable for its own sake would mean that which we choose by preference for its own sake, when nothing else is likely to result from it. *(e) Comparison of the ground of preference.*

Further, you must distinguish the various meanings which ' worthy of choice ' may bear and what are the

403

118 b

τίνων χάριν, οἷον τοῦ συμφέροντος ἢ τοῦ καλοῦ
ἢ τοῦ ἡδέος· τὸ γὰρ πρὸς ἅπαντα ἢ πρὸς τὰ πλείω
30 χρήσιμον αἱρετώτερον ἂν ὑπάρχοι τοῦ μὴ ὁμοίως.
τῶν δ' αὐτῶν ἀμφοτέροις ὑπαρχόντων, ὁποτέρῳ
μᾶλλον ὑπάρχει σκεπτέον, πότερον ἥδιον ἢ κάλλιον ἢ συμφερώτερον. πάλιν τὸ τοῦ βελτίονος
ἕνεκεν αἱρετώτερον, οἷον τὸ ἀρετῆς ἕνεκεν ἢ
ἡδονῆς. ὁμοίως δὲ καὶ ἐπὶ τῶν φευκτῶν· φευκτό-
35 τερον γὰρ τὸ μᾶλλον ἐμποδιστικὸν τῶν αἱρετῶν,
οἷον νόσος αἴσχους· καὶ γὰρ ἡδονῆς καὶ τοῦ σπουδαῖον εἶναι κωλυτικώτερον ἡ νόσος.

Ἔτι ἐκ τοῦ ὁμοίως δεικνύναι φευκτὸν καὶ
αἱρετὸν τὸ προκείμενον· ἧττον γὰρ αἱρετὸν τὸ
τοιοῦτον, ὃ καὶ ἕλοιτ' ἄν τις ὁμοίως καὶ φύγοι,
τοῦ ἑτέρου ὄντος αἱρετοῦ μόνον.

119 a IV. Τὰς μὲν οὖν πρὸς ἄλληλα συγκρίσεις,
καθάπερ εἴρηται, ποιητέον. οἱ αὐτοὶ δὲ τόποι
χρήσιμοι καὶ πρὸς τὸ δεικνύναι ὁτιοῦν αἱρετὸν
ἢ φευκτόν· ἀφαιρεῖν γὰρ μόνον δεῖ τὴν πρὸς ἕτερον
ὑπεροχήν. εἰ γὰρ τὸ τιμιώτερον αἱρετώτερον, καὶ
5 τὸ τίμιον αἱρετόν, καὶ εἰ τὸ χρησιμώτερον αἱρετώτερον, καὶ τὸ χρήσιμον αἱρετόν. ὁμοίως δὲ
καὶ ἐπὶ τῶν ἄλλων, ὅσα τοιαύτην ἔχει τὴν σύγκρισιν. ἐπ' ἐνίων γὰρ εὐθέως κατὰ τὴν πρὸς

ends in view, such as expediency or honour or
pleasure ; for that which is useful for all these ends,
or for most of them, would be more worthy of choice
than which is not so useful. If the same qualities
belong to both of two things, you should examine to
which they belong in a greater degree, that is, which
is more pleasant or honourable or expedient. Again,
that which serves the better purpose is more worthy
of choice, for example, that which aims at virtue
than that which aims at pleasure. So too with the
things which are to be avoided. That is more to
be avoided which is more likely to stand in the way
of that which is worthy of choice ; for example,
disease is more to be avoided than ugliness, for disease is a greater preventive both of pleasure and
of goodness.

Further, you can argue by showing that the
subject under discussion is equally an object of
avoidance and of choice ; for the kind of thing
which one would equally choose and avoid is less
worthy of choice than an alternative which is worthy
of choice only.

IV. Comparisons, then, of things with one another *Adaptation
of the above*
should be made in the manner described. The same *rules to*
commonplaces are useful also for showing that some- *simple predication of*
thing is simply worthy of choice or avoidance ; for *value.*
we need only subtract the excess of one thing over
the other. For if that which is more valuable is
more worthy of choice, then also that which is valuable is worthy of choice, and, if that which is more
useful is more worthy of choice, then also that which
is useful is worthy of choice ; and so too in the other
cases where such comparison is possible. For sometimes, while we are actually comparing two things,

119 a

ἕτερον σύγκρισιν καὶ ὅτι αἱρετὸν ἑκάτερον ἢ τὸ
ἕτερον λέγομεν, οἷον ὅταν τὸ μὲν φύσει ἀγαθὸν
10 τὸ δὲ μὴ φύσει λέγωμεν· τὸ γὰρ φύσει ἀγαθὸν
δῆλον ὅτι αἱρετόν ἐστιν.

V. Ληπτέον δ' ὅτι μάλιστα καθόλου τοὺς
τόπους περὶ τοῦ μᾶλλον καὶ τοῦ μείζονος· ληφ-
θέντες γὰρ οὕτως πρὸς πλείω χρήσιμοι ἂν εἴησαν.
15 ἔστι δ' αὐτῶν τῶν εἰρημένων ἐνίους καθόλου
μᾶλλον ποιεῖν μικρὸν παραλλάσσοντα τῇ προσ-
ηγορίᾳ, οἷον τὸ φύσει τοιοῦτο τοῦ μὴ φύσει
τοιούτου μᾶλλον τοιοῦτο. καὶ εἰ τὸ μὲν ποιεῖ τὸ
δὲ μὴ ποιεῖ τὸ ἔχον τοιόνδε ἢ ᾧ ἂν ὑπάρχῃ, μᾶλλον
τοιοῦτο ὅ ποτε ποιεῖ ἢ ὃ μὴ ποιεῖ. εἰ δ' ἄμφω
ποιεῖ, τὸ μᾶλλον ποιοῦν τοιοῦτο.

20 Ἔτι εἰ τοῦ αὐτοῦ τινὸς τὸ μὲν μᾶλλον τὸ δὲ
ἧττον τοιοῦτο, καὶ εἰ τὸ μὲν τοιούτου μᾶλλον
τοιοῦτο, τὸ δὲ μὴ τοιούτου ⟨μᾶλλον⟩ τοιοῦτο,[1]
δῆλον ὅτι τὸ πρῶτον μᾶλλον τοιοῦτο. ἔτι ἐκ τῆς
προσθέσεως, εἰ τῷ αὐτῷ προστιθέμενον τὸ ὅλον
μᾶλλον ποιεῖ τοιοῦτο, ἢ εἰ τῷ ἧττον τοιούτῳ
προστιθέμενον τὸ ὅλον μᾶλλον ποιεῖ τοιοῦτο.
25 ὁμοίως δὲ καὶ ἐκ τῆς ἀφαιρέσεως· οὗ γὰρ ἀφαι-

---

[1] Reading τοιούτου ⟨μᾶλλον⟩ τοιοῦτο. Pacius renders, *si
alterum sit tali re magis tale, alterum non sit tali re tale,
manifestum est*, etc.

we immediately assert that each or one of them is worthy of choice, for example, when we say that one thing is naturally good and another not naturally good; for what is naturally good is obviously worthy of choice.

V. The commonplaces which deal with the more and the greater degree must be taken as generally as possible; for when they are so taken they would be useful in a larger number of cases. Of the actual instances given above some can be made of more general application by a slight change in the way in which they are worded. We can say, for example, that that which naturally has a certain quality has that quality in a greater degree than that which does not possess it naturally. Also, if one thing does, and another thing does not, create a certain quality in that which possesses it, or in which it is present, then whichever creates it has that quality in a greater degree than that which does not create it; and, if both create it, then that which creates it in a greater degree, possesses it in a greater degree. *Rules for the comparative predication of accidents in general.*

Further, if one thing is of a certain quality in a greater degree and the other in a less degree than the same thing, and also, if one thing possesses a certain quality in a greater degree than some other thing which possesses it, and the other does not, it is obvious that the former in each case possesses the quality in a greater degree. Further, you must see, as a result of addition, whether something added to the same thing makes the whole of a certain quality in a greater degree, or whether, being added to something which possesses the quality in a less degree, it gives the whole that quality in a greater degree. And, similarly, if subtraction is used; for

ρεθέντος τὸ λειπόμενον ἧττον τοιοῦτο, αὐτὸ μᾶλλον
τοιοῦτο. καὶ τὰ τοῖς ἐναντίοις ἀμιγέστερα μᾶλλον
τοιαῦτα, οἷον λευκότερον τὸ τῷ μέλανι ἀμιγέστερον.
ἔτι παρὰ τὰ εἰρημένα πρότερον, τὸ μᾶλλον ἐπιδε-
30 χόμενον τὸν οἰκεῖον τοῦ προκειμένου λόγον, οἷον
εἰ τοῦ λευκοῦ ἐστὶ λόγος χρῶμα διακριτικὸν
ὄψεως, λευκότερον ὅ ἐστι μᾶλλον χρῶμα διακριτικὸν ὄψεως.

VI. Ἂν δ' ἐπὶ μέρους· καὶ μὴ καθόλου τὸ πρόβλημα τεθῇ, πρῶτον μὲν οἱ εἰρημένοι καθόλου
κατασκευαστικοὶ ἢ ἀνασκευαστικοὶ τόποι πάντες
35 χρήσιμοι. καθόλου γὰρ ἀναιροῦντες ἢ κατασκευάζοντες καὶ ἐπὶ μέρους δείκνυμεν· εἰ γὰρ παντὶ
ὑπάρχει, καὶ τινί, καὶ εἰ μηδενί, οὐδὲ τινί. μάλιστα
δ' ἐπίκαιροι καὶ κοινοὶ τῶν τόπων οἵ τ' ἐκ τῶν
ἀντικειμένων καὶ τῶν συστοίχων καὶ τῶν πτώσεων·
ὁμοίως γὰρ ἔνδοξον τὸ ἀξιῶσαι, εἰ πᾶσα ἡδονὴ
ἀγαθόν, καὶ λύπην πᾶσαν εἶναι κακόν, τῷ εἴ τις
119 b ἡδονὴ ἀγαθόν, καὶ λύπην εἶναί τινα κακόν. ἔτι
εἴ τις αἴσθησις μή ἐστι δύναμις, καὶ ἀναισθησία
τις οὐκ ἔστιν ἀδυναμία. καὶ εἴ τι ὑποληπτὸν
ἐπιστητόν, καὶ ὑπόληψίς τις ἐπιστήμη. πάλιν εἴ
5 τι τῶν ἀδίκων ἀγαθόν, καὶ τῶν δικαίων τι κακόν·
καὶ εἴ τι τῶν δικαίως κακόν, καὶ τῶν ἀδίκως τι

that the subtraction of which makes the remainder less of a certain quality, itself possesses more of that quality. Also things possess qualities in a greater degree which have less admixture of the contraries of those qualities; for example, a thing is whiter which has less admixture of black. Further, besides what has already been said, a thing possesses a quality in a greater degree when it admits of the particular definition of the subject in question to a greater degree; for example, if the definition of 'white' is 'a colour which penetrates the vision,' that is whiter which is in a greater degree a colour which penetrates the vision.

VI. If the problem is put in a particular and not in a universal way, in the first place the general commonplaces mentioned above as applicable in constructive and destructive argument are all of them useful. For, when we destroy or construct something universally, we also display it in particular; for if something belongs to all, it also belongs to a particular one, and if it belongs to none, neither does it belong to a particular one. Those commonplaces are especially convenient and widely applicable which are based on opposites and co-ordinates and inflexions; for the claim that if all pleasure is good, then all pain is evil, meets with the same general acceptance as the claim that if some pleasure is good, then some pain is evil. Further, if some kind of perception is not a capacity, then some absence of perception is not an incapacity. Also, if something conceivable is knowable, then some conception is knowledge. Again, if something which is unjust is good, then something which is just is bad; and if something which can be done justly is bad, something

Particular predications:
(a) Adoption of the previous rules.

(1) Rules based on opposites, co-ordinates and inflexions.

119 b

ἀγαθόν. καὶ εἴ τι τῶν ἡδέων φευκτόν, ἡδονή τις φευκτόν. κατὰ ταὐτὰ δὲ καὶ εἴ τι τῶν ἡδέων ὠφέλιμον, ἡδονή τις ὠφέλιμον. καὶ ἐπὶ τῶν φθαρτικῶν δὲ καὶ τῶν γενέσεων καὶ φθορῶν ὡσαύτως. εἰ γάρ τι φθαρτικὸν ἡδονῆς ἢ ἐπιστήμης 10 ὂν ἀγαθόν ἐστιν, εἴη ἄν τις ἡδονὴ ἢ ἐπιστήμη τῶν κακῶν. ὁμοίως δὲ καὶ εἰ φθορά τις ἐπιστήμης τῶν ἀγαθῶν ἢ ἡ γένεσις τῶν κακῶν, ἔσται τις ἐπιστήμη τῶν κακῶν, οἷον εἰ τὸ ἐπιλανθάνεσθαι ἅ τις αἰσχρὰ ἔπραξε τῶν ἀγαθῶν ἢ τὸ ἀναμι-μνήσκεσθαι τῶν κακῶν, εἴη ἂν τὸ ἐπίστασθαι ἅ 15 τις αἰσχρὰ ἔπραξε τῶν κακῶν. ὡσαύτως δὲ καὶ ἐπὶ τῶν ἄλλων· ἐν ἅπασι γὰρ ὁμοίως τὸ ἔνδοξον.

Ἔτι ἐκ τοῦ μᾶλλον καὶ ἧττον καὶ ὁμοίως. εἰ γὰρ μᾶλλον μὲν τῶν ἐξ ἄλλου γένους τι τοιοῦτο ἐκείνων δὲ μηδέν ἐστιν, οὐδ᾽ ἂν τὸ εἰρημένον εἴη 20 τοιοῦτον, οἷον εἰ μᾶλλον μὲν ἐπιστήμη τις ἀγαθὸν ἢ ἡδονή, μηδεμία δ᾽ ἐπιστήμη ἀγαθόν, οὐδ᾽ ἂν ἡδονὴ εἴη. καὶ ἐκ τοῦ ὁμοίως δὲ καὶ ἧττον ὡσαύτως· ἔσται γὰρ καὶ ἀναιρεῖν καὶ κατασκευά-ζειν, πλὴν ἐκ μὲν τοῦ ὁμοίως ἀμφότερα, ἐκ δὲ τοῦ ἧττον κατασκευάζειν μόνον, ἀνασκευάζειν δὲ

410

which can be done unjustly is good. Also, if some pleasant thing is to be avoided, pleasure is sometimes to be avoided. On the same principle, too, if a pleasant thing is sometimes beneficial, pleasure is sometimes beneficial. Similarly with regard to destructive agencies and the processes of generation and destruction. For, if something which is destructive of pleasure or knowledge is good, pleasure or knowledge would sometimes be an evil thing. Similarly, too, if the destruction of knowledge is sometimes a good thing or the production of it an evil thing, knowledge will be sometimes an evil thing ; for example, if the forgetting of someone's disgraceful deeds is a good thing or the remembrance of them a bad thing, the knowledge of the disgraceful things which he has done would be an evil thing. Similarly, too, in the other cases ; for in all of them the generally accepted opinion is formed in the same manner.

Further, arguments can be derived from the greater and the less and the like degree. If something in another genus has some quality in a greater degree than the object under discussion and none of the members of that genus possesses that quality, then neither could the object under discussion possess it ; for example, if some kind of knowledge were good in a greater degree than pleasure, while no kind of knowledge is good, then neither would pleasure be good. We can argue in a similar way from the like and the less degrees ; for it will be possible to argue thus both destructively and constructively, except that both processes can be based on the like degree, but the less degree can be used for constructive purposes only and not for destructive

(2) Rules based on the greater, the less and the like degree.

411

οὔ. εἰ γὰρ ὁμοίως δύναμίς τις ἀγαθὸν καὶ ἐπι-
25 στήμη, ἔστι δέ τις δύναμις ἀγαθόν, καὶ ἐπιστήμη
ἐστίν. εἰ δὲ μηδεμία δύναμις, οὐδ' ἐπιστήμη. εἰ
δ' ἧττον δύναμίς τις ἀγαθὸν ἢ ἐπιστήμη, ἔστι δέ
τις δύναμις ἀγαθόν, καὶ ἐπιστήμη. εἰ δὲ μηδεμία
δύναμις ἀγαθόν, οὐκ ἀνάγκη καὶ ἐπιστήμην μηδεμίαν εἶναι ἀγαθόν. δῆλον οὖν ὅτι κατασκευάζειν
30 μόνον ἐκ τοῦ ἧττον ἔστιν.

Οὐ μόνον δ' ἐξ ἄλλου γένους ἔστιν ἀνασκευάζειν,
ἀλλὰ καὶ ἐκ τοῦ αὐτοῦ λαμβάνοντι τὸ μάλιστα
τοιοῦτον, οἷον εἰ κεῖται ἐπιστήμη τις ἀγαθόν,
δειχθείη δ' ὅτι φρόνησις οὐκ ἀγαθόν, οὐδ' ἄλλη
35 οὐδεμία ἔσται, ἐπεὶ οὐδ' ἡ μάλιστα δοκοῦσα. ἔτι
ἐξ ὑποθέσεως, ὁμοίως ἀξιώσαντα, εἰ ἑνί, καὶ
πᾶσιν ὑπάρχειν ἢ μὴ ὑπάρχειν, οἷον εἰ ἡ τοῦ
ἀνθρώπου ψυχὴ ἀθάνατος, καὶ τὰς ἄλλας, εἰ δ'
αὕτη μή, μηδὲ τὰς ἄλλας. εἰ μὲν οὖν ὑπάρχειν
τινὶ κεῖται, δεικτέον ὅτι οὐχ ὑπάρχει τινί· ἀκολουθήσει γὰρ διὰ τὴν ὑπόθεσιν τὸ μηδενὶ ὑπάρχειν.
120 a εἰ δέ τινι μὴ ὑπάρχον κεῖται, δεικτέον ὅτι ὑπάρχει
τινί· καὶ γὰρ οὕτως ἀκολουθήσει τὸ πᾶσιν ὑπάρχειν.
δῆλον δ' ἐστὶν ὅτι ὁ ὑποτιθέμενος ποιεῖ τὸ πρό-

purposes. For if a certain capacity is good in a like degree to knowledge, and a certain capacity is good, then knowledge is also good; but if no capacity is good, knowledge is not good either. On the other hand, if a certain capacity is good in a less degree than knowledge, and a certain capacity is good, then so also is knowledge; but if no capacity is good, it does not necessarily follow that no knowledge is good either. It is clear, therefore, that arguments from the less degree can only be used for constructive purposes.

It is possible to destroy an opinion not only by means of another genus but also by means of the same genus by taking an extreme case; for example, if it were to be laid down that a certain kind of knowledge is good, and it were to be shown that prudence is not good, then no other kind of knowledge will be good, since not even that kind of knowledge is good which is generally reputed to be so. Further, you can argue by means of a hypothesis, claiming that if some attribute belongs or does not belong to one member of the genus, it also belongs or does not belong in a like degree to all; for example, that, if the soul of man is immortal, all other souls are also immortal, but if it is not, then neither are the other souls. If, therefore, it is laid down that an attribute belongs to some member of the genus, you must show that there is some member to which it does not belong; for it will follow in accordance with the hypothesis that it belongs to no member of the genus. But, if it is laid down that it does not belong to any member, it must be shown that there is a member to which it belongs; for thus it will follow that it belongs to all the members of the genus. Now it is clear that he who makes the

(b) De-
structive
argument
can be
drawn not
only from
another
genus but
also from
the same
genus.

413

βλημα καθόλου ἐπὶ μέρους τεθέν· τὸν γὰρ ἐπὶ
μέρους ὁμολογοῦντα καθόλου ἀξιοῖ ὁμολογεῖν,
5 ἐπειδή, εἰ ἑνί, καὶ πᾶσιν ὁμοίως ἀξιοῖ ὑπάρχειν.

Ἀδιορίστου μὲν οὖν ὄντος τοῦ προβλήματος
μοναχῶς ἀνασκευάζειν ἐνδέχεται, οἷον εἰ ἔφησεν
ἡδονὴν ἀγαθὸν εἶναι ἢ μὴ ἀγαθόν, καὶ μηδὲν ἄλλο
προσδιώρισεν. εἰ μὲν γάρ τινα ἔφησεν ἡδονὴν
ἀγαθὸν εἶναι, δεικτέον καθόλου ὅτι οὐδεμία, εἰ
10 μέλλει ἀναιρεῖσθαι τὸ προκείμενον. ὁμοίως δὲ
καὶ εἴ τινα ἔφησεν ἡδονὴν μὴ εἶναι ἀγαθόν, δεικτέον καθόλου ὅτι πᾶσα· ἄλλως δ᾽ οὐκ ἐνδέχεται
ἀναιρεῖν. ἐὰν γὰρ δείξωμεν ὅτι ἐστί τις ἡδονὴ
οὐκ ἀγαθὸν ἢ ἀγαθόν, οὔπω ἀναιρεῖται τὸ προκείμενον. δῆλον οὖν ὅτι ἀναιρεῖν μὲν μοναχῶς ἐνδέ-
15 χεται, κατασκευάζειν δὲ διχῶς· ἄν τε γὰρ καθόλου
δείξωμεν ὅτι πᾶσα ἡδονὴ ἀγαθόν, ἄν τε ὅτι ἐστί
τις ἡδονὴ ἀγαθόν, δεδειγμένον ἔσται τὸ προκείμενον. ὁμοίως δὲ κἂν δέῃ διαλεχθῆναι ὅτι ἐστί
τις ἡδονὴ οὐκ ἀγαθόν, ἐὰν δείξωμεν ὅτι οὐδεμία
ἀγαθὸν ἢ ὅτι τις οὐκ ἀγαθόν, διειλεγμένοι ἐσόμεθα
20 ἀμφοτέρως, καὶ καθόλου καὶ ἐπὶ μέρους, ὅτι ἐστί
τις ἡδονὴ οὐκ ἀγαθόν. διωρισμένης δὲ τῆς θέσεως
οὔσης, διχῶς ἀναιρεῖν ἔσται, οἷον εἰ τεθείη τινὶ
μὲν ὑπάρχειν ἡδονῇ ἀγαθῷ εἶναι, τινὶ δ᾽ οὐχ
ὑπάρχειν· εἴτε γὰρ πᾶσα δειχθείη ἡδονὴ ἀγαθὸν

hypothesis makes the problem universal, though it is posited in a particular form; for he demands that the maker of a particular admission should make a universal admission, since he demands that, if an attribute belongs in a particular case, it belongs in like manner to all.

When the problem is indefinite, there is only one way of demolishing a statement, for example, if someone has said that pleasure is good or is not good, and has added nothing by way of definition. If he meant that a certain pleasure is good, it must be shown universally that no pleasure is good, if the proposition is to be destroyed. Similarly, if he meant that some particular pleasure is not good, it must be shown universally that every pleasure is good; it is impossible to destroy the proposition in any other way. For if we show that a particular pleasure is not good or is good, the proposition is not yet destroyed. It is clear, then, that there is only one method of destruction but two of construction; for the proposition will have been demonstrated both if we show universally that all pleasure is good, and also if we show that some particular pleasure is good. Similarly, when one has to argue that a particular pleasure is not good, if we show that no pleasure is good or that a particular pleasure is not good, we shall have argued in two ways, universally and particularly, that a particular pleasure is not good. On the other hand, when the thesis is definite, it will be possible to destroy it by two methods, for example, if it be laid down that it is the attribute of some particular pleasure to be good, but not of another; for whether it be shown that all pleasure is good or that none is good, the

(c) The effect of the definiteness and indefiniteness of the problem on proof and disproof.

415

120 a

εἴτε μηδεμία, ἀνηρημένον ἔσται τὸ προκείμενον.

25 εἰ δὲ μίαν ἡδονὴν μόνην ἀγαθὸν ἔθηκεν εἶναι,
τριχῶς ἐνδέχεται ἀναιρεῖν· δείξαντες γὰρ ὅτι πᾶσα
ἢ ὅτι οὐδεμία ἢ ὅτι πλείους μιᾶς ἀγαθόν, ἀνηρη-
κότες ἐσόμεθα τὸ προκείμενον. ἐπὶ πλεῖον δὲ τῆς
θέσεως διορισθείσης, οἷον ὅτι ἡ φρόνησις μόνη
τῶν ἀρετῶν ἐπιστήμη, τετραχῶς ἔστιν ἀναιρεῖν·
δειχθέντος γὰρ ὅτι πᾶσα ἀρετὴ ἐπιστήμη ἢ ὅτι
30 οὐδεμία ἢ ὅτι καὶ ἄλλη τις, οἷον ἡ δικαιοσύνη,
ἢ ὅτι αὐτὴ ἡ φρόνησις οὐκ ἐπιστήμη, ἀνηρημένον
ἔσται τὸ προκείμενον.

Χρήσιμον δὲ καὶ τὸ ἐπιβλέπειν ἐπὶ τὰ καθ᾿
ἕκαστα, ἐν οἷς ὑπάρχειν τι ἢ μὴ εἴρηται, καθάπερ
ἐν τοῖς καθόλου προβλήμασιν. ἔτι δ᾿ ἐν τοῖς
35 γένεσιν ἐπιβλεπτέον, διαιροῦντα κατ᾿ εἴδη μέχρι
τῶν ἀτόμων, καθὰ προείρηται· ἄν τε γὰρ παντὶ
φαίνηται ὑπάρχον ἄν τε μηδενί, πολλὰ προενέγ-
καντι ἀξιωτέον καθόλου ὁμολογεῖν ἢ φέρειν ἔνστασιν ἐπὶ τίνος οὐχ οὕτως. ἔτι ἐφ᾿ ὧν ἔστιν ἢ
εἴδει ἢ ἀριθμῷ διορίσαι τὸ συμβεβηκός, σκεπτέον
120 b εἰ μηδὲν τούτων ὑπάρχει, οἷον ὅτι ὁ χρόνος οὐ
κινεῖται οὐδ᾿ ἐστὶ κίνησις, καταριθμησάμενον πόσα
εἴδη κινήσεως· εἰ γὰρ μηδὲν τούτων ὑπάρχει τῷ
χρόνῳ, δῆλον ὅτι οὐ κινεῖται οὐδ᾿ ἐστὶ κίνησις.

416

proposition will have been destroyed. If, however, our opponent has stated that one pleasure alone is good, it is possible to destroy the proposition in three ways; for if we show that all pleasure, or no pleasure, or more than one pleasure, is good, we shall have destroyed the proposition. If the thesis is still more strictly defined—for example, that prudence alone of the virtues is knowledge—four ways of destroying it are possible; for if it has been shown that all virtue is knowledge, or that no virtue is knowledge, or that some other virtue (for example, justice) is knowledge, or that prudence itself is not knowledge, the proposition will have been destroyed.

It is useful to look at particular instances where *(d)* Various it has been stated that some attribute belongs or further rules. does not belong, as in the case of universal problems. Further, you must look within the genera, dividing them according to their species until you reach the indivisible, as has already been described.[a] For whether the attribute is shown to be present in all or in none, you should, after bringing forward numerous cases, claim that your contention should be admitted universally or else an objection should be made stating in what instance it does not hold good. Further, where it is possible to define the accident either by species or by number, you must see whether none of them belongs, showing, for example, that time does not move and that it is not a form of motion, by enumerating all the different kinds of motion; for if none of these belongs to time, it is clear that it does not move and is not a form of motion. Similarly, too, you can

[a] 109 b 15.

ὁμοίως δὲ καὶ ὅτι ἡ ψυχὴ οὐκ ἀριθμός, διελόμενον
ὅτι πᾶς ἀριθμὸς ἢ περιττὸς ἢ ἄρτιος· εἰ γὰρ ἡ
5 ψυχὴ μήτε περιττὸν μήτε ἄρτιον, δῆλον ὅτι οὐκ
ἀριθμός.

Πρὸς μὲν οὖν τὸ συμβεβηκὸς διὰ τῶν τοιούτων
καὶ οὕτως ἐπιχειρητέον.

show that the soul is not a number by distinguishing all numbers as either odd or even ; for if the soul is neither odd nor even, clearly it is not a number.

As regards accident, then, such are the means and such the methods which you should employ.

Δ

I. Μετὰ δὲ ταῦτα περὶ τῶν πρὸς τὸ γένος καὶ τὸ ἴδιον ἐπισκεπτέον. ἔστι δὲ ταῦτα στοιχεῖα τῶν πρὸς τοὺς ὅρους· περὶ αὐτῶν δὲ τούτων ὀλιγάκις 15 αἱ σκέψεις γίνονται τοῖς διαλεγομένοις. ἂν δὴ τεθῇ γένος τινὸς τῶν ὄντων, πρῶτον μὲν ἐπι- βλέπειν ἐπὶ πάντα τὰ συγγενῆ τῷ λεχθέντι, εἴ τινος μὴ κατηγορεῖται, καθάπερ ἐπὶ τοῦ συμ- βεβηκότος, οἷον εἰ τῆς ἡδονῆς τἀγαθὸν γένος κεῖται, εἴ τις ἡδονὴ μὴ ἀγαθόν· εἰ γὰρ τοῦτο, δῆλον ὅτι οὐ γένος τἀγαθὸν τῆς ἡδονῆς· τὸ γὰρ 20 γένος κατὰ πάντων τῶν ὑπὸ τὸ αὐτὸ εἶδος κατ- ηγορεῖται. εἶτα εἰ μὴ ἐν τῷ τί ἐστι κατηγορεῖται, ἀλλ' ὡς συμβεβηκός, καθάπερ τὸ λευκὸν τῆς χιόνος, ἢ ψυχῆς τὸ κινούμενον ὑφ' αὑτοῦ. οὔτε γὰρ ἡ χιὼν ὅπερ λευκόν, διόπερ οὐ γένος τὸ λευκὸν τῆς χιόνος, οὔθ' ἡ ψυχὴ ὅπερ κινούμενον· συμ- 25 βέβηκε δ' αὐτῇ κινεῖσθαι, καθάπερ καὶ τῷ ζῴῳ πολλάκις βαδίζειν τε καὶ βαδίζοντι εἶναι. ἔτι τὸ κινούμενον οὐ τί ἐστιν, ἀλλά τι ποιοῦν ἢ πάσχον σημαίνειν ἔοικεν. ὁμοίως δὲ καὶ τὸ λευκόν· οὐ

BOOK IV

I. The next questions which we must examine are those which relate to genus and property. These are elements in questions relating to definitions, but in themselves are seldom the subject of inquiries by disputants. If, then, a genus is asserted of something which exists, you must first examine all the things which are related to the subject in question and see whether it fails to be predicated of one of them, as was done in the case of the accident. For example, when it is stated that 'good' is a genus of pleasure, you must see whether some particular pleasure is not good; for, if so, clearly 'good' is not the genus of pleasure, for the genus is predicated of everything which falls under the same species. Next, you must see whether it is predicated, not in the category of essence, but as an accident, as 'white' is predicated of 'snow' or 'self-moved' of the soul. For neither is 'snow' 'that which is white,' [a] and therefore 'white' is not the genus of snow, nor is the 'soul' 'that which moves'; for it is an accident that it moves, just as it is often an accident of an animal that it walks or is walking. Further, 'moving' does not seem to signify the essence of a thing but that it does something or has something done to it. Similarly also 'white'; for it does not signify the

(B) Of Genus (Book IV). *Various rules:*

(a) The genus must include all members of the same species as that of which it is predicated.

---

[a] *i.e.* a species of white.

120 b γὰρ τί ἐστιν ἡ χιών, ἀλλὰ ποιόν τι δηλοῖ. ὥστ᾽
οὐδέτερον αὐτῶν ἐν τῷ τί ἐστι κατηγορεῖται.

30 Μάλιστα δ᾽ ἐπὶ τὸν τοῦ συμβεβηκότος ὁρισμὸν
ἐπιβλέπειν, εἰ ἐφαρμόττει ἐπὶ τὸ ῥηθὲν γένος,
οἷον καὶ τὰ νῦν εἰρημένα. ἐνδέχεται γὰρ κινεῖν τι
αὐτὸ ἑαυτὸ καὶ μή, ὁμοίως δὲ καὶ λευκὸν εἶναι
καὶ μή. ὥστ᾽ οὐδέτερον αὐτῶν γένος ἀλλὰ συμβεβηκός, ἐπειδὴ συμβεβηκὸς ἐλέγομεν ὃ ἐνδέχεται
35 ὑπάρχειν τινὶ καὶ μή.

Ἔτι εἰ μὴ ἐν τῇ αὐτῇ διαιρέσει τὸ γένος καὶ τὸ
εἶδος, ἀλλὰ τὸ μὲν οὐσία τὸ δὲ ποιόν, ἢ τὸ μὲν
πρός τι τὸ δὲ ποιόν, οἷον ἡ μὲν χιὼν καὶ ὁ κύκνος
οὐσία, τὸ δὲ λευκὸν οὐκ οὐσία ἀλλὰ ποιόν, ὥστ᾽
οὐ γένος τὸ λευκὸν τῆς χιόνος οὐδὲ τοῦ κύκνου.
121 a πάλιν ἡ μὲν ἐπιστήμη τῶν πρός τι, τὸ δ᾽ ἀγαθὸν
καὶ τὸ καλὸν ποιόν, ὥστ᾽ οὐ γένος τὸ ἀγαθὸν ἢ
τὸ καλὸν τῆς ἐπιστήμης· τὰ γὰρ τῶν πρός τι γένη
καὶ αὐτὰ τῶν πρός τι δεῖ εἶναι, καθάπερ ἐπὶ τοῦ
5 διπλασίου· καὶ γὰρ τὸ πολλαπλάσιον, ὂν γένος
τοῦ διπλασίου, καὶ αὐτὸ τῶν πρός τί ἐστιν. καθόλου δ᾽ εἰπεῖν, ὑπὸ τὴν αὐτὴν διαίρεσιν δεῖ τὸ γένος
τῷ εἴδει εἶναι· εἰ γὰρ τὸ εἶδος οὐσία, καὶ τὸ γένος,
καὶ εἰ ποιὸν τὸ εἶδος, καὶ τὸ γένος ποιόν τι, οἷον
εἰ τὸ λευκὸν ποιόν τι, καὶ τὸ χρῶμα. ὁμοίως δὲ
καὶ ἐπὶ τῶν ἄλλων.

10 Πάλιν εἰ ἀνάγκη ἢ ἐνδέχεται τοῦ τεθέντος ἐν
τῷ γένει μετέχειν τὸ γένος. ὅρος δὲ τοῦ μετέχειν

ᵃ 102 b 6.

essence of snow, but its possession of a certain quality. So neither ' white ' nor ' moving ' is predicated in the category of essence.

You should look particularly at the definition of the accident and see whether it fits the asserted genus, as, for example, in the instances just mentioned. For it is possible for a thing to be and not to be self-moved, and similarly for it to be and not to be white ; so that neither attribute is a genus but both are accidents, since we said [a] that an accident is something which can and also can not belong to something. *(b) Accident is distinguished from genus by being an attribute which can belong or not belong.*

Further, you must see whether the genus and the species are not in the same division, but the one is a substance and the other a quality, or the one is a relative and the other a quality, as, for example, ' snow ' and ' swan ' are substance, but ' white ' is not a substance but a quality ; so that ' white ' is not the genus of ' snow ' or of ' swan.' Again, ' knowledge ' is a relative, whereas ' good ' and ' noble ' are qualities, so that ' good ' and ' noble ' are not genera of knowledge. For the genera of relatives must themselves be relatives, as is true of ' double '; for ' multiple,' which is the genus of ' double,' is itself also a relative. To put the matter generally, the genus must fall under the same division as the species ; for, if the species is a substance, so also is the genus, and if the species is a quality, the genus also is a quality ; for example, if white is a quality, so also is colour. Similarly also with the other instances. *(c) The genus and the species must fall in the same category.*

Again, you must see whether it is necessary or possible for the genus to partake of that which has been placed in the genus. (The definition of *(d) Species partake of genera, but not genera of species.*

121 a

τὸ ἐπιδέχεσθαι τὸν τοῦ μετεχομένου λόγον. δῆλον
οὖν ὅτι τὰ μὲν εἴδη μετέχει τῶν γενῶν, τὰ δὲ γένη
τῶν εἰδῶν οὔ· τὸ μὲν γὰρ εἶδος ἐπιδέχεται τὸν
τοῦ γένους λόγον, τὸ δὲ γένος τὸν τοῦ εἴδους οὔ.

15 σκεπτέον οὖν εἰ μετέχει ἢ ἐνδέχεται μετέχειν τοῦ
εἴδους τὸ ἀποδοθὲν γένος, οἷον εἴ τις τοῦ ὄντος ἢ
τοῦ ἑνὸς γένος τι ἀποδοίη· συμβήσεται γὰρ μετέχειν τὸ γένος τοῦ εἴδους· κατὰ πάντων γὰρ τῶν
ὄντων τὸ ὂν καὶ τὸ ἓν κατηγορεῖται, ὥστε καὶ
ὁ λόγος αὐτῶν.

20 Ἔτι εἰ κατά τινος τὸ ἀποδοθὲν εἶδος ἀληθεύεται,
τὸ δὲ γένος μή, οἷον εἰ τὸ ὂν ἢ τὸ ἐπιστητὸν τοῦ
δοξαστοῦ γένος τεθείη. κατὰ γὰρ τοῦ μὴ ὄντος
τὸ δοξαστὸν κατηγορηθήσεται· πολλὰ γὰρ τῶν
μὴ ὄντων δοξαστά. ὅτι δὲ τὸ ὂν ἢ τὸ ἐπιστητὸν
οὐ κατηγορεῖται κατὰ τοῦ μὴ ὄντος, δῆλον. ὥστ᾽

25 οὐ γένος τὸ ὂν οὐδὲ τὸ ἐπιστητὸν τοῦ δοξαστοῦ·
καθ᾽ ὧν γὰρ τὸ εἶδος κατηγορεῖται, καὶ τὸ γένος
δεῖ κατηγορεῖσθαι.

Πάλιν εἰ μηδενὸς τῶν εἰδῶν ἐνδέχεται μετέχειν
τὸ τεθὲν ἐν τῷ γένει· ἀδύνατον γὰρ τοῦ γένους
μετέχειν μηδενὸς τῶν εἰδῶν μετέχον, ἂν μή τι

30 τῶν κατὰ τὴν πρώτην διαίρεσιν εἰδῶν ᾖ· ταῦτα
δὲ τοῦ γένους μόνον μετέχει. ἂν οὖν ἡ κίνησις
γένος τῆς ἡδονῆς τεθῇ, σκεπτέον εἰ μήτε φορὰ
μήτ᾽ ἀλλοίωσις ἡ ἡδονὴ μήτε τῶν λοιπῶν τῶν

'partaking' is 'admitting the definition of that which is partaken.') It is obvious, therefore, that the species partake of the genera, whereas the genera do not partake of the species; for the species admits the definition of the genus, whereas the genus does not admit the definition of the species. You must, therefore, look and see whether the genus assigned partakes, or can partake of the species; for example, if one were to assign something as the genus of 'being' or of 'oneness,' for the result will be that the genus partakes of the species, for 'being' and 'oneness' are predicated of everything which exists, and therefore so is their definition also.

Further, you must look whether there is any case *(e)* If the in which the species assigned is true but the genus species is predicated, is not true, for example, if 'being' or 'knowable' the genus were given as the genus of 'conjectural.' For 'con- also will be jectural' will be predicated of that which does not predicated. exist; for many things which do not exist are subjects of conjecture. But it is obvious that 'being' and 'knowable' are not predicated of that which does not exist. And so neither 'being' nor 'knowable' is the genus of 'conjectural'; for of things of which the species is predicated, the genus also must be predicated.

Again, you must see whether that which is placed *(f)* A pre- in the genus cannot possibly partake of any of its dicate can- not partake species; for it is impossible for it to partake of the of the genus genus if it does not partake of any of its species, if it par- takes of unless it is one of the species obtained at the first none of its division, which do partake of the genus only. If, species. therefore, 'motion' is laid down as the genus of pleasure, you must examine whether pleasure is neither locomotion nor alteration nor any of the

ARISTOTLE

121 a

ἀποδοθεισῶν κινήσεων μηδεμία· δῆλον γὰρ ὅτι
οὐδενὸς ἂν τῶν εἰδῶν μετέχοι· ὥστ' οὐδὲ τοῦ
γένους, ἐπειδὴ ἀναγκαῖόν ἐστι τὸ τοῦ γένους
35 μετέχον καὶ τῶν εἰδῶν τινος μετέχειν· ὥστ' οὐκ
ἂν εἴη εἶδος ἡ ἡδονὴ κινήσεως, οὐδὲ τῶν ἀτόμων
οὐδὲν[1] τῶν ὑπὸ τὸ γένος[2] τὸ τῆς κινήσεως ὄντων.
καὶ γὰρ τὰ ἄτομα μετέχει τοῦ γένους καὶ τοῦ
εἴδους, οἷον ὁ τὶς ἄνθρωπος καὶ ἀνθρώπου μετέχει
καὶ ζῴου.

121 b

Ἔτι εἰ ἐπὶ πλέον λέγεται τοῦ γένους τὸ ἐν τῷ
γένει τεθέν, οἷον τὸ δοξαστὸν τοῦ ὄντος· καὶ γὰρ
τὸ ὂν καὶ τὸ μὴ ὂν δοξαστόν, ὥστ' οὐκ ἂν εἴη
τὸ δοξαστὸν εἶδος τοῦ ὄντος· ἐπὶ πλέον γὰρ ἀεὶ τὸ
γένος τοῦ εἴδους λέγεται. πάλιν εἰ ἐπ' ἴσων τὸ
5 εἶδος καὶ τὸ γένος λέγεται, οἷον εἰ τῶν πᾶσιν
ἑπομένων τὸ μὲν εἶδος τὸ δὲ γένος τεθείη, καθάπερ
τὸ ὂν καὶ τὸ ἕν· παντὶ γὰρ τὸ ὂν καὶ τὸ ἕν, ὥστ'
οὐδέτερον οὐδετέρου γένος, ἐπειδὴ ἐπ' ἴσων λέγεται. ὁμοίως δὲ καὶ εἰ τὸ πρῶτον καὶ ἡ ἀρχὴ
ὑπ'[3] ἄλληλα τεθείη· ἥ τε γὰρ ἀρχὴ πρῶτον καὶ τὸ
10 πρῶτον ἀρχή, ὥστ' ἢ ἀμφότερα τὰ εἰρημένα
ταὐτόν ἐστιν ἢ οὐδέτερον οὐδετέρου γένος. στοιχεῖον δὲ πρὸς ἅπαντα τὰ τοιαῦτα τὸ ἐπὶ πλέον τὸ
γένος ἢ τὸ εἶδος καὶ τὴν διαφορὰν λέγεσθαι· ἐπ'
ἔλαττον γὰρ καὶ ἡ διαφορὰ τοῦ γένους λέγεται.

---

[1] Reading οὐδὲν with Wallies for οὐδὲ.
[2] γένος W. S. Maguinness, εἶδος codd.
[3] Reading ὑπ' with Waitz for ἐπ'.

---

[a] εἶδος, ' species,' which the mss. read here, is quite contrary to the argument, which requires γένος, ' genus.'

other generally assigned modes of motion; for, then, obviously it would not partake of any of the species, and, therefore, cannot partake of the genus either, since that which partakes of the genus must necessarily partake of one of the species also. So pleasure cannot be a species of motion nor any of the individual things which fall under the genus [a] of motion. For the individuals also partake of the genus and of the species; for example, the individual man partakes both of ' man ' and ' animal.'

Further, you must see whether that which is placed in the genus has a wider application than the genus as, for example, ' an object of conjecture ' is wider than ' being '; for both that which is and that which is not are objects of conjecture, so that ' object of conjecture ' could not be a species of ' being '; for the genus is always applied more widely than the species. Again, you must see whether the species and its genus are applied to an equal number of things; for example, if, of the attributes which accompany everything, one were to be put down as a species and the other as a genus, for example, ' being ' and ' oneness '; for everything possesses ' being ' and ' oneness,' so that neither is the genus of the other, since they are applied to an equal number of things. Similarly, too, if the ' first ' and the ' beginning ' were to be placed one under the other; for the ' beginning ' is ' first ' and the ' first ' is a ' beginning,' so that either the two terms are identical or neither is the genus of the other. In all such cases the basic principle is that the genus has a wider application than the species and its differentia; for the differentia also has a narrower application than the genus.

(g) The genus has a wider application than the species.

427

15 Ὁρᾶν δὲ καὶ εἴ τινος τῶν ἀδιαφόρων εἴδει μή
ἐστι τὸ εἰρημένον γένος ἢ μὴ δόξειεν ἄν, κατασκευάζοντι δέ, εἰ ἔστι τινός. ταὐτὸν γὰρ πάντων
τῶν ἀδιαφόρων εἴδει γένος. ἂν οὖν ἑνὸς δειχθῇ,
δῆλον ὅτι πάντων, κἂν ἑνὸς μή, δῆλον ὅτι οὐδενός,
οἷον εἴ τις ἀτόμους τιθέμενος γραμμὰς τὸ ἀδι-
20 αίρετον γένος αὐτῶν φήσειεν εἶναι. τῶν γὰρ διαίρεσιν ἐχουσῶν γραμμῶν οὐκ ἔστι τὸ εἰρημένον
γένος, ἀδιαφόρων οὐσῶν κατὰ τὸ εἶδος· ἀδιάφοροι
γὰρ ἀλλήλαις κατὰ τὸ εἶδος αἱ εὐθεῖαι γραμμαὶ
πᾶσαι.

II. Σκοπεῖν δὲ καὶ εἴ τι ἄλλο γένος ἐστὶ τοῦ
25 ἀποδοθέντος εἴδους, ὃ μήτε περιέχει τὸ ἀποδοθὲν
γένος μήθ' ὑπ' ἐκεῖνό ἐστιν, οἷον εἴ τις τῆς δικαιοσύνης τὴν ἐπιστήμην θείη γένος. ἔστι γὰρ καὶ
ἡ ἀρετὴ γένος, καὶ οὐδέτερον τῶν γενῶν τὸ λοιπὸν
περιέχει, ὥστ' οὐκ ἂν εἴη ἡ ἐπιστήμη γένος τῆς
δικαιοσύνης· δοκεῖ γάρ, ὅταν ἓν εἶδος ὑπὸ δύο
30 γένη ᾖ, τὸ ἕτερον ὑπὸ τοῦ ἑτέρου περιέχεσθαι.
ἔχει δ' ἀπορίαν ἐπ' ἐνίων τὸ τοιοῦτο. δοκεῖ γὰρ
ἐνίοις ἡ φρόνησις ἀρετή τε καὶ ἐπιστήμη εἶναι,
καὶ οὐδέτερον τῶν γενῶν ὑπ' οὐδετέρου περι-
έχεσθαι· οὐ μὴν ὑπὸ πάντων γε συγχωρεῖται τὴν
φρόνησιν ἐπιστήμην εἶναι. εἰ δ' οὖν τις συγ-
35 χωροίη τὸ λεγόμενον ἀληθὲς εἶναι, ἀλλὰ τό γε
ὑπ' ἄλληλα ἢ ὑπὸ ταὐτὸ ἄμφω γίγνεσθαι τὰ τοῦ
αὐτοῦ γένη τῶν ἀναγκαίων δόξειεν ἂν εἶναι,
καθάπερ καὶ ἐπὶ τῆς ἀρετῆς καὶ τῆς ἐπιστήμης

You must also see whether the genus stated is inapplicable, or would be generally held to be inapplicable, to something which is not specifically different from the thing under discussion; or, if you are arguing constructively, whether it *is* applicable. For the genus of all things which are not specifically different is the same. If, therefore, it is shown to be the genus of one, obviously it is the genus also of all, and if it is shown not to be the genus of one, obviously it is not the genus of any, for example, if anyone positing ' indivisible lines ' were to assert that ' the indivisible ' is their genus. For the genus stated is inapplicable to divisible lines, which in species do not differ from indivisible lines; for all straight lines show no difference from one another in species.

(h) The genus of things not specifically different is the same.

II. You must also examine whether there is any other genus of the species assigned which neither includes the genus assigned nor falls under it, for example, if someone were to lay down that knowledge is the genus of justice. For virtue is also its genus and neither of the genera includes the other, so that knowledge could not be the genus of justice; for it is generally held that, when one species falls under two genera, the one is included in the other. But such a principle sometimes involves a difficulty. For, in the view of some people, prudence is both virtue and knowledge and neither of its genera is included in the other; it is not, however, universally agreed that prudence is knowledge. If, therefore, one were to agree that this statement is true, it would nevertheless be generally held as necessary that the genera of the same thing must at least be subaltern either the one to the other or both of them to the same thing. This happens in the case

(i) When one species falls under two genera, the one is embraced by the other.

121 b

συμβαίνει· ἄμφω γὰρ ὑπὸ τὸ αὐτὸ γένος ἐστίν·
ἑκάτερον γὰρ αὐτῶν ἕξις καὶ διάθεσίς ἐστιν.
σκεπτέον οὖν εἰ μηδέτερον ὑπάρχει τῷ ἀποδοθέντι
122 a γένει. εἰ γὰρ μήθ᾿ ὑπ᾿ ἀλλήλά ἐστι τὰ γένη μήθ᾿
ὑπὸ ταὐτὸν ἄμφω, οὐκ ἂν εἴη τὸ ἀποδοθὲν γένος.

Σκοπεῖν δὲ δεῖ καὶ τὸ γένος τοῦ ἀποδοθέντος
γένους, καὶ οὕτως ἀεὶ τὸ ἐπάνω γένος, εἰ πάντα
5 κατηγορεῖται τοῦ εἴδους καὶ εἰ ἐν τῷ τί ἐστι
κατηγορεῖται· πάντα γὰρ τὰ ἐπάνω γένη κατηγορεῖσθαι δεῖ τοῦ εἴδους ἐν τῷ τί ἐστιν. εἰ οὖν
που διαφωνεῖ, δῆλον ὅτι οὐ γένος τὸ ἀποδοθέν.
πάλιν εἰ μετέχει τὸ γένος τοῦ εἴδους, ἢ αὐτὸ ἢ
τῶν ἐπάνω τι γενῶν· οὐδενὸς γὰρ τῶν ὑποκάτω
10 τὸ ἐπάνω μετέχει. ἀνασκευάζοντι μὲν οὖν καθάπερ εἴρηται χρηστέον· κατασκευάζοντι δέ, ὁμο-
λογουμένου μὲν ὑπάρχειν τῷ εἴδει τοῦ ῥηθέντος
γένους, ὅτι δ᾿ ὡς γένος ὑπάρχει ἀμφισβητουμένου,
ἀπόχρη τὸ δεῖξαί τι τῶν ἐπάνω γενῶν ἐν τῷ τί
ἐστι τοῦ εἴδους κατηγορούμενον. ἑνὸς γὰρ ἐν τῷ
τί ἐστι κατηγορουμένου, πάντα καὶ τὰ ἐπάνω
15 τούτου καὶ τὰ ὑποκάτω, ἄν περ κατηγορῆται τοῦ
εἴδους, ἐν τῷ τί ἐστι κατηγορηθήσεται· ὥστε
καὶ τὸ ἀποδοθὲν γένος ἐν τῷ τί ἐστι κατηγορεῖται.
ὅτι δ᾿ ἑνὸς ἐν τῷ τί ἐστι κατηγορουμένου πάντα
τὰ λοιπά, ἄν περ κατηγορῆται, ἐν τῷ τί ἐστι
κατηγορηθήσεται, δι᾿ ἐπαγωγῆς ληπτέον. εἰ δ᾿
20 ἁπλῶς ὑπάρχειν ἀμφισβητεῖται τὸ ἀποδοθὲν γένος,

of virtue and knowledge, for both of them fall under the same genus, each of them being a state and a disposition. You must, therefore, examine whether neither of these things belongs to the genus assigned ; for, if the genera are subaltern neither the one to the other nor both of them to the same thing, then what was assigned could not be the real genus.

You must also examine the genus of the assigned genus and so in succession the genus next above, and see if they are all predicated of the species and predicated in the category of essence ; for all the higher genera must be predicated of the species in the category of essence. If, then, there is a discrepancy anywhere, it is clear that what was assigned is not the genus. Again, you must see whether the genus itself, or one of its higher genera, partakes of the species ; for the higher genus does not partake of any of the lower. For destructive purposes, then, you must employ the above method ; for constructive purposes, if the asserted genus is admitted to belong to the species but it is a matter of dispute whether it belongs as a genus, then it is enough to show that one of its higher genera is predicated of the species in the category of essence. For, if one genus is predicated in the category of essence, all of them, both higher and lower than this one, if they *are* predicated of the species, will be predicated in the category of essence ; so that the genus assigned is also predicated in the category of essence. The fact that, if one genus is predicated in the category of essence, all the rest, if they *are* predicated, will be predicated in the category of essence, must be obtained by induction. But, if it is disputed whether the assigned genus belongs at all, it is not enough

(j) All higher genera must be predicated of the species in the category of essence.

431

οὐκ ἀπόχρη τὸ δεῖξαι τῶν ἐπάνω τι γενῶν ἐν τῷ
τί ἐστι τοῦ εἴδους κατηγορούμενον. οἷον εἴ τις
τῆς βαδίσεως γένος ἀπέδωκε τὴν φοράν, οὐκ
ἀπόχρη τὸ δεῖξαι διότι κίνησίς ἐστιν ἡ βάδισις
πρὸς τὸ δεῖξαι ὅτι φορά ἐστιν, ἐπειδὴ καὶ ἄλλαι
25 κινήσεις εἰσίν, ἀλλὰ προσδεικτέον ὅτι οὐδενὸς
μετέχει ἡ βάδισις τῶν κατὰ τὴν αὐτὴν διαίρεσιν
εἰ μὴ τῆς φορᾶς. ἀνάγκη γὰρ τὸ τοῦ γένους
μετέχον καὶ τῶν εἰδῶν τινος μετέχειν τῶν κατὰ
τὴν πρώτην διαίρεσιν. εἰ οὖν ἡ βάδισις μήτ'
αὐξήσεως μήτε μειώσεως μήτε τῶν ἄλλων κινήσεων μετέχει, δῆλον ὅτι τῆς φορᾶς ἂν μετέχοι,
30 ὥστ' εἴη ἂν γένος ἡ φορὰ τῆς βαδίσεως.

Πάλιν ἐφ' ὧν τὸ εἶδος τὸ τεθὲν ὡς γένος κατηγορεῖται, σκοπεῖν εἰ καὶ τὸ ἀποδοθὲν γένος ἐν τῷ
τί ἐστιν αὐτῶν τούτων κατηγορεῖται ὧνπερ τὸ
εἶδος, ὁμοίως δὲ καὶ εἰ τὰ ἐπάνω τοῦ γένους
35 πάντα. εἰ γάρ που διαφωνεῖ, δῆλον ὅτι οὐ γένος
τὸ ἀποδοθέν· εἰ γὰρ ἦν γένος, ἅπαντ' ἂν καὶ τὰ
ἐπάνω τούτου καὶ αὐτὸ τοῦτο ἐν τῷ τί ἐστι κατ-
ηγορεῖτο, ὥσπερ καὶ τὸ εἶδος ἐν τῷ τί ἐστι
κατηγορεῖται. ἀνασκευάζοντι μὲν οὖν χρήσιμον, εἰ
μὴ κατηγορεῖται τὸ γένος ἐν τῷ τί ἐστιν ὧνπερ
καὶ τὸ εἶδος κατηγορεῖται· κατασκευάζοντι δ', εἰ
122 b κατηγορεῖται ἐν τῷ τί ἐστι, χρήσιμον. συμβήσεται
γὰρ τὸ γένος καὶ τὸ εἶδος τοῦ αὐτοῦ ἐν τῷ τί ἐστι

to show that one of the higher genera is predicated in the category of essence. For example, if someone has assigned 'impulsion' as the genus of 'walking,' it is not enough to show that walking is 'motion' in order to show that it is 'impulsion,' since there are other forms of motion also ; but it must be further shown that walking partakes of none of the other forces of motion which result from the same division except 'impulsion.' For that which partakes of the genus must necessarily also partake of one of the species resulting from the first division of it. If, therefore, walking partakes neither of increase or decrease nor of any of the other kinds of motion, obviously it would partake of impulsion, so that impulsion would be the genus of walking.

Again, in cases where the species asserted is predicated as genus, you must look and see whether that which is assigned as genus is also predicated in the category of essence of the very things of which the species is predicated, and likewise, whether the same is also true of all the genera higher than this genus. For, if there is any discrepancy anywhere, obviously what has been assigned is not the genus ; for, if it were genus, all the genera higher than it and this genus itself would be predicated in the category of essence of all those things of which the species also is predicated in the category of essence. For destructive criticism, then, it is useful to see whether the genus is not predicated in the category of essence of those things of which the species is also predicated. For constructive purposes, on the other hand, it is useful to see whether it *is* predicated in the category of essence ; for then the result will be that the genus and the species are predicated of the

(k) The genus is predicated in the category of essence of those things of which the species is predicated.

433

κατηγορεῖσθαι, ὥστε τὸ αὐτὸ ὑπὸ δύο γένη γίνεται.
ἀναγκαῖον οὖν ὑπ᾿ ἄλληλα τὰ γένη εἶναι. ἂν οὖν
5 δειχθῇ, ὃ βουλόμεθα γένος κατασκευάσαι, μὴ ὂν
ὑπὸ τὸ εἶδος, δῆλον ὅτι τὸ εἶδος ὑπὸ·τοῦτ᾿ ἂν εἴη,
ὥστε δεδειγμένον ἂν εἴη ὅτι γένος τοῦτο.

Σκοπεῖν δὲ καὶ τοὺς λόγους τῶν γενῶν, εἰ ἐφαρμόττουσιν ἐπί τε τὸ ἀποδοθὲν εἶδος καὶ τὰ μετέχοντα τοῦ εἴδους. ἀνάγκη γὰρ τοὺς τῶν γενῶν
10 λόγους κατηγορεῖσθαι τοῦ εἴδους καὶ τῶν μετ-
εχόντων τοῦ εἴδους· εἰ οὖν που διαφωνεῖ, δῆλον
ὅτι οὐ γένος τὸ ἀποδοθέν.

Πάλιν εἰ τὴν διαφορὰν ὡς γένος ἀπέδωκεν,
οἷον εἰ τὸ ἀθάνατον γένος θεοῦ. διαφορὰ γάρ ἐστι
ζῴου τὸ ἀθάνατον, ἐπειδὴ τῶν ζῴων τὰ μὲν θνητὰ
15 τὰ δ᾿ ἀθάνατα. δῆλον οὖν ὅτι διημάρτηται· οὐδενὸς γὰρ ἡ διαφορὰ γένος ἐστίν. ὅτι δὲ τοῦτ᾿
ἀληθές, δῆλον· οὐδεμία γὰρ διαφορὰ σημαίνει τί
ἐστιν, ἀλλὰ μᾶλλον ποιόν τι, καθάπερ τὸ πεζὸν
καὶ τὸ δίπουν.

Καὶ εἰ τὴν διαφορὰν εἰς τὸ γένος ἔθηκεν, οἷον
τὸ περιττὸν ὅπερ ἀριθμόν. διαφορὰ γὰρ ἀριθμοῦ
20 τὸ περιττόν, οὐκ εἶδός ἐστιν. οὐδὲ δοκεῖ μετέχειν
ἡ διαφορὰ τοῦ γένους· πᾶν γὰρ τὸ μετέχον τοῦ
γένους ἢ εἶδος ἢ ἄτομόν ἐστιν, ἡ δὲ διαφορὰ οὔτε
εἶδος οὔτε ἄτομόν ἐστιν. δῆλον οὖν ὅτι οὐ μετέχει

same thing in the category of essence, so that the same object falls under two genera; the genera, therefore, must necessarily fall one under the other, and so, if it has been shown that what we wish to establish as a genus does not fall under the species, it is obvious that the species would fall under it, so that it would have been shown that it is the genus.

You must also examine the definitions of the genera to see if they fit both the species assigned and the things which partake of the species. For the definitions of the genera must also be predicated of the species and of the things which partake of the species. If, therefore, there is a discrepancy anywhere, it is obvious that what has been assigned is not the genus. *(l) The definitions of the genera must suit the species and the things which partake of it.*

Again, you must see whether your opponent has assigned the differentia as the genus, for example, 'immortal' as the genus of 'God.' For 'immortal' is a differentia of 'living creature'; for some living creatures are mortal and some immortal. It is, therefore, obvious that an error has been committed; for the differentia is never the genus of anything. This is clearly true; for no differentia indicates the essence, but rather some quality, such as 'pedestrian' and 'biped.' *(m) The differentia must not be assigned as genus.*

Also, you must see whether he has put the differentia inside the genus, for example, whether he has given 'odd' as a 'number,' for 'odd' is a differentia of number, not a species. Nor is the differentia generally held to partake of the genus; for everything which partakes of the genus is either a species or an individual, but the differentia is neither a species nor an individual. It is obvious, therefore, that the differentia does not partake of *(n) The differentia must not be placed within the genus.*

435

122 b

τοῦ γένους ἡ διαφορά, ὥστ' οὐδὲ τὸ περιττὸν
εἶδος ἂν εἴη ἀλλὰ διαφορά, ἐπειδὴ οὐ μετέχει τοῦ
γένους.

25 Ἔτι εἰ τὸ γένος εἰς τὸ εἶδος ἔθηκεν, οἷον τὴν
ἄψιν ὅπερ συνοχὴν ἢ τὴν μίξιν ὅπερ κρᾶσιν, ἢ
ὡς Πλάτων ὁρίζεται φορὰν τὴν κατὰ τόπον κίνησιν. οὐ γὰρ ἀναγκαῖον τὴν ἄψιν συνοχὴν εἶναι,
ἀλλ' ἀνάπαλιν τὴν συνοχὴν ἄψιν· οὐ γὰρ πᾶν τὸ
30 ἁπτόμενον συνέχεται, ἀλλὰ τὸ συνεχόμενον ἅπ-
τεται. ὁμοίως δὲ καὶ ἐπὶ τῶν λοιπῶν· οὔτε γὰρ
ἡ μίξις ἅπασα κρᾶσις (ἡ γὰρ τῶν ξηρῶν μίξις οὐκ
ἔστι κρᾶσις) οὔθ' ἡ κατὰ τόπον μεταβολὴ πᾶσα
φορά· ἡ γὰρ βάδισις οὐ δοκεῖ φορὰ εἶναι· σχεδὸν
γὰρ ἡ φορὰ ἐπὶ τῶν ἀκουσίως τόπον ἐκ τόπου
35 μεταβαλλόντων λέγεται, καθάπερ ἐπὶ τῶν ἀψύχων
συμβαίνει. δῆλον δ' ὅτι καὶ ἐπὶ πλέον λέγεται τὸ
εἶδος τοῦ γένους ἐν τοῖς ἀποδοθεῖσι, δέον ἀνάπαλιν
γίνεσθαι.

Πάλιν εἰ τὴν διαφορὰν εἰς τὸ εἶδος ἔθηκεν, οἷον
τὸ ἀθάνατον ὅπερ θεόν. συμβήσεται γὰρ [ἐπ'
ἴσης ἢ][1] ἐπὶ πλεῖον τὸ εἶδος λέγεσθαι· ἀεὶ γὰρ ἡ
123 a διαφορὰ ἐπ' ἴσης ἢ ἐπὶ πλεῖον τοῦ εἴδους λέγεται.
ἔτι εἰ τὸ γένος εἰς τὴν διαφοράν, οἷον τὸ χρῶμα
ὅπερ συγκριτικὸν ἢ τὸν ἀριθμὸν ὅπερ περιττόν.
καὶ εἰ τὸ γένος ὡς διαφορὰν εἶπεν· ἐγχωρεῖ γάρ

---

[1] Omitting ἐπ' ἴσης ἢ with Strache.

the genus; so that 'odd' too cannot be a species but must be a differentia, since it does not partake of the genus.

Further, you must see whether your opponent has placed the genus inside the species, taking, for example, 'contact' as 'conjunction' or 'mixture' as 'fusion,' or, according to Plato's definition,[a] 'locomotion' as 'impulsion.' For 'contact' is not necessarily 'conjunction,' but the converse is true namely, that 'conjunction' is 'contact'; for what is in contact is not always conjoined, but that which is conjoined is always in contact. Similarly also with the other instances; for 'mixture' is not always 'fusion' (for the mixture of dry substances is not fusion) nor is 'locomotion' always 'impulsion.' For walking is not generally held to be 'impulsion'; for 'impulsion' is generally used of objects which change their position involuntarily, as happens to inanimate things. It is obvious, also, that the species is used in a wider sense than the genus in the above examples, whereas the converse ought to be true.

Again, you must see whether he has placed the differentia within the species, for example, if he has taken 'immortal' as what 'God' is. For this will result in the species being used in a greater number of cases; for it is the differentia which is always used in an equal number of cases or in a greater number of cases than the species. Again, you must see whether he has put the genus within the differentia; for example, if he has taken 'colour' as that which is 'compressive'[b] or 'number' as 'odd.' You must also see if he has stated the genus as the differentia; for it is possible to produce a thesis of this kind also,

(o) The genus must not be placed within the species.

(p) The differentia must not be placed within the species nor the genus within the differentia.

---

[a] *Theaet.* 181 D 5.   [b] *Cf.* 107 b 30 and note.

τινα καὶ τοιαύτην κομίσαι θέσιν, οἷον κράσεως τὴν
5 μίξιν διαφορὰν ἢ φορᾶς τὴν κατὰ τόπον μεταβολήν.
σκεπτέον δὲ πάντα τὰ τοιαῦτα διὰ τῶν αὐτῶν·
ἐπικοινωνοῦσι γὰρ οἱ τόποι· ἐπὶ πλέον τε γὰρ τὸ
γένος τῆς διαφορᾶς δεῖ λέγεσθαι, καὶ μὴ μετέχειν
τῆς διαφορᾶς. οὕτω δ' ἀποδοθέντος οὐδέτερον
τῶν εἰρημένων δυνατὸν συμβαίνειν· ἐπ' ἔλαττόν
10 τε γὰρ ῥηθήσεται, καὶ μεθέξει τὸ γένος τῆς
διαφορᾶς.

Πάλιν εἰ μηδεμία διαφορὰ κατηγορεῖται τῶν τοῦ
γένους κατὰ τοῦ ἀποδοθέντος εἴδους, οὐδὲ τὸ
γένος κατηγορηθήσεται, οἷον ψυχῆς οὔτε τὸ περιττὸν οὔτε τὸ ἄρτιον κατηγορεῖται, ὥστ' οὐδ'
ἀριθμός. ἔτι εἰ πρότερον φύσει τὸ εἶδος καὶ
15 συναναιρεῖ τὸ γένος· δοκεῖ γὰρ τὸ ἐναντίον. ἔτι
εἰ ἐνδέχεται ἀπολιπεῖν τὸ εἰρημένον γένος ἢ τὴν
διαφοράν, οἷον ψυχὴν τὸ κινεῖσθαι ἢ δόξαν τὸ
ἀληθὲς καὶ ψεῦδος, οὐκ ἂν εἴη τῶν εἰρημένων
οὐδέτερον γένος οὐδὲ διαφορά· δοκεῖ γὰρ τὸ γένος
καὶ ἡ διαφορὰ παρακολουθεῖν, ἕως ἂν ᾖ τὸ εἶδος.
20 III. Σκοπεῖν δὲ καὶ εἰ τὸ ἐν τῷ γένει κείμενον
μετέχει τινὸς ἐναντίου τῷ γένει ἢ εἰ ἐνδέχεται
μετέχειν· τὸ γὰρ αὐτὸ τῶν ἐναντίων ἅμα μεθέξει,
ἐπειδὴ τὸ μὲν γένος οὐδέποτ' ἀπολείπει, μετέχει
δὲ καὶ τοὐναντίου ἢ ἐνδέχεται μετέχειν. ἔτι εἴ
τινος κοινωνεῖ τὸ εἶδος, ὃ ἀδύνατον ὅλως ὑπάρχειν
25 τοῖς ὑπὸ τὸ γένος. οἷον εἰ ἡ ψυχὴ τῆς ζωῆς

---

for example, making 'mixture' the differentia of 'fusion' or 'locomotion' of 'impulsion.' All such cases must be examined by the same methods (for the commonplaces are inter-related); for the genus must both be used in a wider sense than its differentia and not partake of its differentia. But, if the genus is assigned as differentia, neither of the above conditions can occur; for the genus will be used in a narrower sense and will partake of the differentia.

Again, if no differentia belonging to the genus is predicated of the species assigned, neither will the genus be predicated of it; for example, neither 'odd' nor 'even' is predicated of 'soul,' and so 'number' is not predicated of it either. Further, you must see whether the species is prior by nature and destroys the genus along with itself[a]; for the contrary view is generally held. Further, if it is possible for the genus stated or its differentia to be separated from the species, for example, 'motion' from the 'soul' or 'truth and falsehood' from 'opinion,' then neither of the said terms would be the genus or its differentia; for it is generally held that the genus and its differentia attend the species as long as it exists. *(q)* If no differentia of the genus is predicated of the species, the genus cannot be predicated of it. *(r)* The genus is prior to the species. *(s)* The genus and its differentia accompany the species.

III. You must also see whether what is placed in the genus partakes, or could possibly partake, of something contrary to the genus; for then the same thing will partake of contraries at the same time, since the genus never leaves it, and it also partakes, or can possibly partake, of its contrary. Further, you must see whether the species participates in anything which cannot by any possibility belong to anything which falls under the genus. For example, if the soul participates in life, and it is impossible *(t)* What is placed in the genus cannot partake of anything contrary to the genus.

439

123 a

κοινωνεῖ, τῶν δ' ἀριθμῶν μηδένα δυνατὸν ζῆν, οὐκ ἂν εἴη εἶδος ἀριθμοῦ ἡ ψυχή.

Σκεπτέον δὲ καὶ εἰ ὁμώνυμον τὸ εἶδος τῷ γένει, στοιχείοις χρώμενον τοῖς εἰρημένοις πρὸς τὸ ὁμώνυμον· συνώνυμον γὰρ τὸ γένος καὶ τὸ εἶδος.

30 Ἐπεὶ δὲ παντὸς γένους εἴδη πλείω, σκοπεῖν εἰ μὴ ἐνδέχεται ἕτερον εἶδος εἶναι τοῦ εἰρημένου γένους· εἰ γὰρ μή ἐστι, δῆλον ὅτι οὐκ ἂν εἴη ὅλως γένος τὸ εἰρημένον.

Σκοπεῖν δὲ καὶ εἰ τὸ μεταφορᾷ λεγόμενον ὡς γένος ἀποδέδωκεν, οἷον τὴν σωφροσύνην συμφω-
35 νίαν· πᾶν γὰρ γένος κυρίως κατὰ τῶν εἰδῶν κατηγορεῖται, ἡ δὲ συμφωνία κατὰ τῆς σωφροσύνης οὐ κυρίως ἀλλὰ μεταφορᾷ· πᾶσα γὰρ συμφωνία ἐν φθόγγοις.

123 b Ἔτι ἂν ᾖ ἐναντίον τι τῷ εἴδει, σκοπεῖν. ἔστι δὲ πλεοναχῶς ἡ σκέψις, πρῶτον μὲν εἰ ἐν τῷ αὐτῷ γένει καὶ τὸ ἐναντίον, μὴ ὄντος ἐναντίου τῷ γένει· δεῖ γὰρ τὰ ἐναντία ἐν τῷ αὐτῷ γένει εἶναι,
5 ἂν μηδὲν ἐναντίον τῷ γένει ᾖ. ὄντος δ' ἐναντίου τῷ γένει, σκοπεῖν εἰ τὸ ἐναντίον ἐν τῷ ἐναντίῳ· ἀνάγκη γὰρ τὸ ἐναντίον ἐν τῷ ἐναντίῳ εἶναι, ἅπερ ᾖ ἐναντίον τι τῷ γένει. φανερὸν δὲ τούτων ἕκαστον διὰ τῆς ἐπαγωγῆς. πάλιν εἰ ὅλως ἐν μηδενὶ γένει τὸ τῷ εἴδει ἐναντίον, ἀλλ' αὐτὸ γένος,
10 οἷον τἀγαθόν· εἰ γὰρ τοῦτο μὴ ἐν γένει, οὐδὲ τὸ ἐναντίον τούτου ἐν γένει ἔσται, ἀλλ' αὐτὸ γένος,

---

^a 106 a 9 ff.

for any number to live, the soul could not be a species of number.

You must also see whether the species is used equivocally of the genus, employing the principles already laid down for dealing with the equivocals [a] for the genus and the species are synonymous. *(u)* The species must not be used equivocally of the genus.

Since of every genus there are always several species, you must see whether it is impossible for there to be another species of the genus stated; for if there is none, it is obvious that what has been stated could not be a genus at all. *(v)* A genus cannot exist of only one species.

You must also see whether your opponent has assigned as a genus a term used metaphorically, speaking, for example, of ' temperance ' as a ' harmony '; for every genus is predicated of its species in its proper sense, but ' harmony ' is predicated of temperance not in its proper sense but metaphorically; for a harmony consists always of sounds. *(w)* The use of metaphorical language is misleading.

Further, you must examine any contrary that there may be of the species. This examination may take several forms, the first being to see whether the contrary also exists in the same genus, the genus itself having no contrary; for contraries must of necessity be in the same genus, if there is no contrary to the genus. If, however, there is a contrary to the genus, you must see whether the contrary of the species is in the contrary genus; for the contrary species must necessarily be in the contrary genus if the genus has a contrary. Each of these points is made clear by induction. Again, you must see whether the contrary of the species is not found in any genus at all, but is itself a genus, for example, ' good '; for if this is not found in any genus, neither will its contrary be found in any genus, but will itself *Rules drawn from: (a)* Contraries.

441

καθάπερ ἐπὶ τοῦ ἀγαθοῦ καὶ τοῦ κακοῦ συμβαίνει·
οὐδέτερον γὰρ τούτων ἐν γένει, ἀλλ' ἑκάτερον
αὐτῶν γένος. ἔτι εἰ ἐναντίον τινὶ καὶ τὸ γένος
καὶ τὸ εἶδος, καὶ τῶν μὲν ἔστι τι μεταξύ, τῶν δὲ
15 μή. εἰ γὰρ τῶν γενῶν ἔστι τι μεταξύ, καὶ τῶν
εἰδῶν, καὶ εἰ τῶν εἰδῶν, καὶ τῶν γενῶν, καθάπερ
ἐπ' ἀρετῆς καὶ κακίας καὶ δικαιοσύνης καὶ ἀδι-
κίας· ἑκατέρων γὰρ ἔστι τι μεταξύ. ἔνστασις
τούτου ὅτι ὑγιείας καὶ νόσου οὐδὲν μεταξύ, κακοῦ
δὲ καὶ ἀγαθοῦ. ἢ εἰ ἔστι μέν τι ἀμφοῖν ἀνὰ μέσον,
καὶ τῶν εἰδῶν καὶ τῶν γενῶν, μὴ ὁμοίως δέ, ἀλλὰ
20 τῶν μὲν κατὰ ἀπόφασιν τῶν δ' ὡς ὑποκείμενον.
ἔνδοξον γὰρ τὸ ὁμοίως ἀμφοῖν, καθάπερ ἐπ' ἀρετῆς
καὶ κακίας καὶ δικαιοσύνης καὶ ἀδικίας· ἀμφοῖν
γὰρ κατὰ ἀπόφασιν τὰ ἀνὰ μέσον. ἔτι ὅταν μὴ
ᾖ ἐναντίον τῷ γένει, σκοπεῖν μὴ μόνον εἰ τὸ ἐναν-
25 τίον ἐν τῷ αὐτῷ γένει, ἀλλὰ καὶ τὸ ἀνὰ μέσον· ἐν
ᾧ γὰρ τὰ ἄκρα, καὶ τὰ ἀνὰ μέσον, οἷον ἐπὶ λευκοῦ
καὶ μέλανος· τὸ γὰρ χρῶμα γένος τούτων τε καὶ
τῶν ἀνὰ μέσον χρωμάτων ἁπάντων. ἔνστασις ὅτι
ἡ μὲν ἔνδεια καὶ ὑπερβολὴ ἐν τῷ αὐτῷ γένει (ἐν
τῷ κακῷ γὰρ ἄμφω), τὸ δὲ μέτριον ἀνὰ μέσον ὂν
30 τούτων οὐκ ἐν τῷ κακῷ ἀλλ' ἐν τῷ ἀγαθῷ. σκοπεῖν δὲ καὶ εἰ τὸ μὲν γένος ἐναντίον τινί, τὸ δὲ

be a genus, as happens with 'good' and 'evil'; for neither of them is found in a genus, but each of them is a genus. Further, you must see whether both genus and species are contrary to something, and whether there is an intermediate between one pair of contraries but not between the other. For, if there is an intermediate between the genera, there will also be one between the species, and, if between the species, likewise also between the genera, as in the case of virtue and vice and justice and injustice; for each pair has an intermediate. (It may be objected here that there is no intermediate between health and disease as there is between evil and good.) Or, again, you must see whether, though there is an intermediate between both pairs, that is, between the species and between the genera, yet not in a similar way, but in one case negatively and in the others as a subject. For it is generally held that the intermediate is of a similar kind in both cases, as happens with virtue and vice, and justice and injustice; for between both of these pairs the intermediates are purely negative. Further, when there is no contrary to the genus, you must see not only whether the contrary is in the same genus, but whether the intermediate is so also; for the intermediates are in the same genus as the extremes, in the case, for example, of black and white, for colour is the genus of both of these and of all the intermediate colours. (It may be objected that 'defect' and 'excess' are in the same genus—for both are in the genus of 'evil'—whereas 'what is moderate,' which is intermediate between them, is not in the genus of 'evil,' but in that of 'good.') You must also see whether, whereas the genus is contrary to

123 b

εἶδος μηδενί. εἰ γὰρ τὸ γένος ἐναντίον τινί, καὶ
τὸ εἶδος, καθάπερ ἀρετὴ κακίᾳ καὶ δικαιοσύνη
ἀδικίᾳ. ὁμοίως δὲ καὶ ἐπὶ τῶν ἄλλων σκοποῦντι
φανερὸν ἂν δόξειεν εἶναι τὸ τοιοῦτον. ἔνστασις
35 ἐπὶ τῆς ὑγιείας καὶ νόσου· ἁπλῶς μὲν γὰρ πᾶσα
ὑγίεια νόσῳ ἐναντίον, ἡ δέ τις νόσος εἶδος ὂν νόσου
οὐδενὶ ἐναντίον, οἷον ὁ πυρετὸς καὶ ἡ ὀφθαλμία
καὶ τῶν ἄλλων ἕκαστον.

124 a

Ἀναιροῦντι μὲν οὖν τοσαυταχῶς ἐπισκεπτέον·
εἰ γὰρ μὴ ὑπάρχει τὰ εἰρημένα, δῆλον ὅτι οὐ γένος
τὸ ἀποδοθέν· κατασκευάζοντι δὲ τριχῶς, πρῶτον
μὲν εἰ τὸ ἐναντίον τῷ εἴδει ἐν τῷ εἰρημένῳ γένει,
5 μὴ ὄντος ἐναντίου τῷ γένει· εἰ γὰρ τὸ ἐναντίον
ἐν τούτῳ, δῆλον ὅτι καὶ τὸ προκείμενον. ἔτι εἰ
τὸ ἀνὰ μέσον ἐν τῷ εἰρημένῳ γένει· ἐν ᾧ γὰρ τὸ
ἀνὰ μέσον, καὶ τὰ ἄκρα. πάλιν ἂν ᾖ ἐναντίον τι
τῷ γένει, σκοπεῖν εἰ καὶ τὸ ἐναντίον ἐν τῷ ἐναντίῳ·
ἂν γὰρ ᾖ, δῆλον ὅτι καὶ τὸ προκείμενον ἐν τῷ
προκειμένῳ.

10 Πάλιν ἐπὶ τῶν πτώσεων καὶ ἐπὶ τῶν συστοίχων,
εἰ ὁμοίως ἀκολουθοῦσι, καὶ ἀναιροῦντι καὶ κατασκευάζοντι. ἅμα γὰρ ἑνὶ καὶ πᾶσιν ὑπάρχει ἢ
οὐχ ὑπάρχει, οἷον εἰ ἡ δικαιοσύνη ἐπιστήμη τις,

444

something, the species is not contrary to anything; for, if the genus is contrary to something, so also is the species, as virtue is the contrary of vice, and justice of injustice. Similarly, if one examines the other cases also, such a view would appear evident. (There is an objection with regard to health and disease; for health, generally speaking, is always contrary to disease, yet a particular disease, which is a species of disease, for example, a fever or ophthalmia or any other specific disease, is not the contrary of anything.)

Such then are the various inquiries which should be made when one is seeking to demolish an opinion; for, if the conditions mentioned above are not present, it is clear that what has been assigned is not the genus. For constructive argument, on the other hand, there are three methods of procedure. Firstly, you must see whether the contrary of the species is found in the genus named when there is no contrary to the genus; for, if the contrary is found in it, obviously the proposed species is also found there. Further, you must see whether the intermediate is found in the genus named; for the extremes are found in the same genus as the intermediates. Again, if there is a contrary to the genus, you must see whether the contrary species is also found in the contrary genus; for, if it is, clearly the proposed species is also found in the proposed genus. *(The use of contraries in constructive argument.)*

Again, you must take the inflexions and the co-ordinates and see if they follow similarly, both in destructive and constructive argument. For whatever belongs or does not belong to one, at the same time belongs or does not belong to all; for example, if justice is a kind of knowledge, then also, 'justly' *(b) Inflexions and co-ordinates.*

124 a

καὶ τὸ δικαίως ἐπιστημόνως καὶ ὁ δίκαιος ἐπιστή-
μων· εἰ δὲ τούτων τι μή, οὐδὲ τῶν λοιπῶν οὐδέν.

15 IV. Πάλιν ἐπὶ τῶν ὁμοίως ἐχόντων πρὸς ἄλληλα,
οἷον τὸ ἡδὺ ὁμοίως ἔχει πρὸς τὴν ἡδονὴν καὶ τὸ
ὠφέλιμον πρὸς τἀγαθόν· ἑκάτερον γὰρ ἑκατέρου
ποιητικόν. εἰ οὖν ἐστὶν ἡ ἡδονὴ ὅπερ ἀγαθόν,
καὶ τὸ ἡδὺ ὅπερ ὠφέλιμον ἔσται· δῆλον γὰρ ὅτι
20 ἀγαθοῦ ἂν εἴη ποιητικόν, ἐπειδὴ ἡ ἡδονὴ ἀγαθόν.
ὡσαύτως δὲ καὶ ἐπὶ τῶν γενέσεων καὶ φθορῶν,
οἷον εἰ τὸ οἰκοδομεῖν ἐνεργεῖν, τὸ ᾠκοδομηκέναι
ἐνηργηκέναι, καὶ εἰ τὸ μανθάνειν ἀναμιμνήσκεσθαι,
καὶ τὸ μεμαθηκέναι ἀναμεμνῆσθαι, καὶ εἰ τὸ
διαλύεσθαι φθείρεσθαι, τὸ διαλελύσθαι ἐφθάρθαι
25 καὶ ἡ διάλυσις φθορά τις. καὶ ἐπὶ τῶν γενητικῶν
δὲ καὶ φθαρτικῶν ὡσαύτως, καὶ ἐπὶ τῶν δυνάμεων καὶ χρήσεων, καὶ ὅλως καθ᾽ ὁποιανοῦν
ὁμοιότητα καὶ ἀναιροῦντι καὶ κατασκευάζοντι
σκεπτέον, καθάπερ ἐπὶ τῆς γενέσεως καὶ φθορᾶς
ἐλέγομεν. εἰ γὰρ τὸ φθαρτικὸν διαλυτικόν, καὶ
τὸ φθείρεσθαι διαλύεσθαι· καὶ εἰ τὸ γενητικὸν
30 ποιητικόν, τὸ γίνεσθαι ποιεῖσθαι καὶ ἡ γένεσις
ποίησις. ὁμοίως δὲ καὶ ἐπὶ τῶν δυνάμεων καὶ
χρήσεων· εἰ γὰρ ἡ δύναμις διάθεσις, καὶ τὸ δύνασθαι διακεῖσθαι, καὶ εἴ τινος ἡ χρῆσις ἐνέργεια,
τὸ χρῆσθαι ἐνεργεῖν καὶ τὸ κεχρῆσθαι ἐνηργηκέναι.
35 Ἂν δὲ στέρησις ᾖ τὸ ἀντικείμενον τῷ εἴδει,
διχῶς ἔστιν ἀνελεῖν, πρῶτον μὲν εἰ ἐν τῷ ἀπο-

is ' knowingly,' and ' the just man ' is ' the man of knowledge '; but if one of these things is not true, none of the rest is true either.

IV. Again, you must take things which stand in a similar relation to one another. For example, the pleasant stands in the same relation to pleasure as the beneficial to the good; for in each case the one is productive of the other. If, therefore, pleasure is what is good, then the pleasant will be what is beneficial; for it is clear that it would be productive of good, since pleasure is a good. So likewise with the processes of generation and destruction; if, for example, to build is to be active, to have built is to have been active, and, if to learn is to remember, to have learnt is to have remembered, and, if to be dissolved is to be destroyed, to have been dissolved is to have been destroyed, and dissolution is a kind of destruction. You must deal in the same way with the agents of generation and destruction and with the capacities and uses of things, and, in short, both in destructive and constructive argument, you must make your examination in the light of any possible likeness, as we stated in dealing with generation and destruction. For, if what is destructive is dissolvent, then to be destroyed is to be dissolved; and if what is generative is productive, then to be generated is to be produced, and generation is production. So, also, with capacities and uses; if capacity is a disposition, then to be capable of something is to be disposed to it, and, if the use of something is an activity, then to use is to be active, and to have used is to have been active.

If the opposite of the species is a privation, we can demolish an argument in two ways, firstly, by seeing

(c) Similarity of relation.

(d) Generation and destruction.

(e) Capacities and uses of things.

(f) Opposition between states

124 a

δοθέντι γένει τὸ ἀντικείμενον· ἢ γὰρ ἁπλῶς ἐν
οὐδενὶ γένει τῷ αὐτῷ ἡ στέρησις, ἢ οὐκ ἐν τῷ
ἐσχάτῳ, οἷον εἰ ἡ ὄψις ἐν ἐσχάτῳ γένει τῇ αἰσθήσει, ἡ τυφλότης οὐκ ἔσται αἴσθησις. δεύτερον

124 b δ᾽ εἰ καὶ τῷ γένει καὶ τῷ εἴδει ἀντίκειται στέρησις,
μή ἐστι δὲ τὸ ἀντικείμενον ἐν τῷ ἀντικειμένῳ,
οὐδ᾽ ἂν τὸ ἀποδοθὲν ἐν τῷ ἀποδοθέντι εἴη. ἀναιροῦντι μὲν οὖν καθάπερ εἴρηται χρηστέον, κατασκευάζοντι δὲ μοναχῶς· εἰ γὰρ τὸ ἀντικείμενον

5 ἐν τῷ ἀντικειμένῳ, καὶ τὸ προκείμενον ἐν τῷ
προκειμένῳ ἂν εἴη, οἷον εἰ ἡ τυφλότης ἀναισθησία
τις, ἡ ὄψις αἴσθησίς τις.

Πάλιν ἐπὶ τῶν ἀποφάσεων σκοπεῖν ἀνάπαλιν,
καθάπερ ἐπὶ τοῦ συμβεβηκότος ἐλέγετο, οἷον εἰ
τὸ ἡδὺ ὅπερ ἀγαθόν, τὸ μὴ ἀγαθὸν οὐχ ἡδύ. εἰ

10 γὰρ μὴ οὕτως ἔχοι, εἴη ἄν τι καὶ οὐκ ἀγαθὸν ἡδύ.
ἀδύνατον δέ, εἴπερ τὸ ἀγαθὸν γένος τοῦ ἡδέος,
εἶναί τι μὴ ἀγαθὸν ἡδύ· ὧν γὰρ τὸ γένος μὴ κατηγορεῖται, οὐδὲ τῶν εἰδῶν οὐδέν. καὶ κατασκευάζοντι δὲ ὡσαύτως σκεπτέον· εἰ γὰρ τὸ μὴ ἀγαθὸν
οὐχ ἡδύ, τὸ ἡδὺ ἀγαθόν, ὥστε γένος τὸ ἀγαθὸν
τοῦ ἡδέος.

15 Ἐὰν δ᾽ ᾖ πρός τι τὸ εἶδος, σκοπεῖν εἰ καὶ τὸ
γένος πρός τι· εἰ γὰρ τὸ εἶδος τῶν πρός τι, καὶ
τὸ γένος, καθάπερ ἐπὶ τοῦ διπλασίου καὶ πολλα-
πλασίου· ἑκάτερον γὰρ τῶν πρός τι. εἰ δὲ τὸ

ᵃ 113 b 15 ff.

whether the opposite is found in the genus assigned ; and their for either the privation is not found anywhere at all privations. in the same genus or not in the ultimate genus ; for example, if sight is found in sensation as the ultimate genus, blindness will not be a sensation. Secondly, if a privation is opposed both to the genus and to the species, but the opposite of the species is not found in the opposite of the genus, then neither can the species assigned be in the genus assigned. For destructive criticism, then, you should use the above two methods ; but for constructive argument there is only one method. If the opposite species is found in the opposite genus, then the proposed species would be found in the proposed genus ; for example, if blindness is a kind of insensibility, then sight is a kind of sensation.

Again, you must take the negations and examine (g) Contra-them, reversing the order of the terms, as was dictory op-positions. described in dealing with the accident [a] ; for example, if the pleasant is what is good, what is not good is not pleasant, for otherwise something not good would also be pleasant. Now it is impossible, if good is the genus of pleasant, that anything not good would be pleasant ; for, where the genus is not predicated, neither can any of the species be predicated. For constructive argument a similar examination must be made ; for, if what is not good is not pleasant, the pleasant is good, and so ' good ' is the genus of ' pleasant.'

If the species is a relative term, you must see (h) Relative whether the genus is also a relative term ; for, if opposi-tions. the species is a relative term, so also is the genus, for example, ' double ' and ' multiple ' ; for each is a relative term. If, however, the genus is a rela-

449

γένος τῶν πρός τι, οὐκ ἀνάγκη καὶ τὸ εἶδος· ἡ
μὲν γὰρ ἐπιστήμη τῶν πρός τι, ἡ δὲ γραμματικὴ
20 οὔ. ἢ οὐδὲ τὸ πρότερον ῥηθὲν ἀληθὲς ἂν δόξειεν·
ἡ γὰρ ἀρετὴ ὅπερ καλὸν καὶ ὅπερ ἀγαθόν, καὶ ἡ
μὲν ἀρετὴ τῶν πρός τι, τὸ δ' ἀγαθὸν καὶ τὸ καλὸν
οὐ τῶν πρός τι ἀλλὰ ποιά.

Πάλιν εἰ μὴ πρὸς ταὐτὸ λέγεται τὸ εἶδος καθ'
αὑτό τε καὶ κατὰ τὸ γένος, οἷον εἰ τὸ διπλάσιον
25 ἡμίσεος λέγεται διπλάσιον, καὶ τὸ πολλαπλάσιον
ἡμίσεος δεῖ λέγεσθαι. εἰ δὲ μή, οὐκ ἂν εἴη τὸ
πολλαπλάσιον γένος τοῦ διπλασίου.

Ἔτι εἰ μὴ πρὸς ταὐτὸ κατά τε τὸ γένος λέγεται
καὶ κατὰ πάντα τὰ τοῦ γένους γένη. εἰ γὰρ τὸ
30 διπλάσιον ἡμίσεος πολλαπλάσιόν ἐστι, καὶ τὸ
ὑπερέχον ἡμίσεος ῥηθήσεται, καὶ ἁπλῶς κατὰ
πάντα τὰ ἐπάνω γένη πρὸς τὸ ἥμισυ ῥηθήσεται.
ἔνστασις ὅτι οὐκ ἀνάγκη καθ' αὑτὸ καὶ κατὰ τὸ
γένος πρὸς ταὐτὸ λέγεσθαι· ἡ γὰρ ἐπιστήμη ἐπιστητοῦ λέγεται, ἕξις δὲ καὶ διάθεσις οὐκ ἐπιστητοῦ
ἀλλὰ ψυχῆς.

35 Πάλιν εἰ ὡσαύτως λέγεται τὸ γένος καὶ τὸ εἶδος
κατὰ τὰς πτώσεις, οἷον εἰ τινὶ ἢ τινὸς ἢ ὁσαχῶς
ἄλλως. ὡς γὰρ τὸ εἶδος, καὶ τὸ γένος, καθάπερ
ἐπὶ τοῦ διπλασίου καὶ τῶν ἐπάνω· τινὸς γὰρ καὶ
450

tive term, it does not necessarily follow that the species is so also; for 'knowledge' is a relative term, but 'grammar' is not. Or, possibly, it might be held that not even the first assertion is true; for 'virtue' is something 'honourable' and something 'good,' and yet, though 'virtue' is a relative term, 'good' and 'honourable' are not relative terms but qualities.

Again, you must see whether the species is not being used in the same relation both *per se* and in respect of the genus. For example, if 'double' is used in the sense of double of a half, then also 'multiple' ought to be used in the sense of multiple of a half; otherwise 'multiple' would not be the genus of 'double.'

Again, you must see whether the species is not being used in the same relation in respect of the genus and in respect of all the genera of the genus. For if the double is a multiple of the half, that which is 'in excess of' will also be used of the half, and in general it will be used in respect of all the higher genera in relation to the half. (An objection may be raised that a term is not necessarily referred to the same thing when it is used *per se* and when it is used in respect of the genus; for 'knowledge' is said to be of the 'knowable,' but is a 'state' or 'disposition' not of the 'knowable' but of the 'soul').

Again, you must see whether the genus and (i) In-species are used in the same manner in respect of flexions the inflexions which follow them, for example, as pertaining 'to' something, or predicated as being 'of' something, or in the other possible ways. For, as the species is predicated, so also is the genus, as, for example, in the case of the double and its higher

124 b

τὸ διπλάσιον καὶ τὸ πολλαπλάσιον. ὁμοίως δὲ

125 a καὶ ἐπὶ τῆς ἐπιστήμης· τινὸς γὰρ καὶ αὐτὴ καὶ τὰ γένη, οἷον ἥ τε διάθεσις καὶ ἡ ἕξις. ἔνστασις ὅτι ἐνιαχοῦ οὐχ οὕτως· τὸ μὲν γὰρ διάφορον καὶ τὸ ἐναντίον τινί, τὸ δ' ἕτερον, γένος ὂν τούτων, οὐ τινὶ ἀλλὰ τινός· ἕτερον γάρ τινος λέγεται.

5 Πάλιν εἰ ὁμοίως τὰ πρός τι κατὰ τὰς πτώσεις λεγόμενα μὴ ὁμοίως ἀντιστρέφει, καθάπερ ἐπὶ τοῦ διπλασίου καὶ τοῦ πολλαπλασίου. ἑκάτερον γὰρ τούτων τινὸς καὶ αὐτὸ καὶ κατὰ τὴν ἀντιστροφὴν λέγεται· τινὸς γὰρ καὶ τὸ ἥμισυ καὶ τὸ πολλοστημόριον. ὡσαύτως δὲ καὶ ἐπὶ τῆς ἐπι-

10 στήμης καὶ τῆς ὑπολήψεως· αὗται γάρ τινος, καὶ ἀντιστρέφει ὁμοίως τό τε ἐπιστητὸν καὶ τὸ ὑποληπτὸν τινί. εἰ οὖν ἐπί τινων μὴ ὁμοίως ἀντιστρέφει, δῆλον ὅτι οὐ γένος θάτερον θατέρου.

Πάλιν εἰ μὴ πρὸς ἴσα τὸ εἶδος καὶ τὸ γένος

15 λέγεται. ὁμοίως γὰρ καὶ ἰσαχῶς ἑκάτερον δοκεῖ λέγεσθαι, καθάπερ ἐπὶ τῆς δωρεᾶς καὶ τῆς δόσεως. ἥ τε γὰρ δωρεὰ τινὸς ἢ τινὶ λέγεται, καὶ ἡ δόσις τινὸς καὶ τινί. ἔστι δὲ ἡ δόσις γένος τῆς δωρεᾶς· ἡ γὰρ δωρεὰ δόσις ἐστὶν ἀναπόδοτος. ἐπ' ἐνίων δ' οὐ συμβαίνει πρὸς ἴσα λέγεσθαι· τὸ μὲν γὰρ

452

genera; for both the double and the multiple are predicated 'of' something. Similarly, too, in the case of 'knowledge'; for both 'knowledge' itself and its genera, for example, 'disposition' and 'state,' are said to be 'of' something. It may be objected that sometimes this is not true; for we say 'alien *to*' and 'contrary *to*,' but when we use 'different,' which is a genus of these terms, we add '*from*,' not '*to*'; for we say 'different *from*.'

Again, you must see whether terms which are used in the same manner in respect of the inflexions which follow them do not take the same cases when they are converted, as is the case with 'double' and 'multiple'; for each of these is said to be '*of*' something both in its original and in its converted form; for one thing is both 'a half of' and 'a fraction of' something else. Likewise with 'knowledge' and 'conception'; for these are followed by the genitive, and in the converted form 'knowable' and 'conceivable' are both alike followed by the dative. If, therefore, in any instance the converted forms do not take the same case, clearly the one is not the genus of the other.

Again, you must see whether the relative applica- (*j*) Equality tion of the species and of the genus extends to an of content equal number of things; for it is generally held that and genus. the relative application of each is similar and co-extensive as in the case of 'gift' and 'giving.' For we speak of a gift *of* something or *to* someone, and of a giving *of* something and *to* someone; and 'giving' is the genus of 'gift,' for a 'gift' is a 'giving which needs no giving in return.' But some-times the relative applications do not extend to an equal number of things; for double is double *of*

453

20 διπλάσιον τινὸς διπλάσιον, τὸ δ' ὑπερέχον καὶ τὸ
μεῖζον τινὸς καὶ τινί· πᾶν γὰρ τὸ ὑπερέχον καὶ
τὸ μεῖζον τινὶ ὑπερέχει καὶ τινὸς ὑπερέχει. ὥστ'
οὐ γένη τὰ εἰρημένα τοῦ διπλασίου, ἐπειδὴ οὐ
πρὸς ἴσα τῷ εἴδει λέγεται. ἢ οὐ καθόλου ἀληθὲς
τὸ πρὸς ἴσα τὸ εἶδος καὶ τὸ γένος λέγεσθαι.

25 Ὁρᾶν δὲ καὶ εἰ τοῦ ἀντικειμένου τὸ ἀντικείμενον
γένος, οἷον εἰ τοῦ διπλασίου τὸ πολλαπλάσιον καὶ
τοῦ ἡμίσεος τὸ πολλοστημόριον· δεῖ γὰρ τὸ ἀντικείμενον τοῦ ἀντικειμένου γένος εἶναι.. εἰ οὖν τις
θείη τὴν ἐπιστήμην ὅπερ αἴσθησιν, δεήσει καὶ τὸ
ἐπιστητὸν ὅπερ αἰσθητὸν εἶναι. οὐκ ἔστι δέ· οὐ
30 γὰρ πᾶν τὸ ἐπιστητὸν αἰσθητόν· καὶ γὰρ τῶν
νοητῶν ἔνια ἐπιστητά. ὥστ' οὐ γένος τὸ αἰσθητὸν
τοῦ ἐπιστητοῦ. εἰ δὲ τοῦτο μή, οὐδ' αἴσθησις
ἐπιστήμης.

Ἐπεὶ δὲ τῶν πρός τι λεγομένων τὰ μὲν ἐξ
ἀνάγκης ἐν ἐκείνοις ἢ περὶ ἐκεῖνά ἐστι πρὸς ἃ
35 ποτε τυγχάνει λεγόμενα, οἷον ἡ διάθεσις καὶ ἡ
ἕξις καὶ ἡ συμμετρία (ἐν ἄλλῳ γὰρ οὐδενὶ δυνατὸν
ὑπάρχειν τὰ εἰρημένα ἢ ἐν ἐκείνοις πρὸς ἃ λέγεται),
τὰ δ' οὐκ ἀνάγκη μὲν ἐν ἐκείνοις ὑπάρχειν πρὸς

something, but we speak of ' in excess ' (or ' greater ')
' of ' (or ' *than* ') something else ; and ' *in* ' something ;
for what is ' in excess ' (or ' greater ') is always in
excess *in* something as well as in excess *of* something.[a] So the above terms are not the genera of
' double,' since their relative application is not co-
extensive with that of the species. Or perhaps it is
not universally true that the relative application of
the species and the genus extends to an equal number
of things.

You must also see whether the opposite of the (k) The
genus is the genus of the opposite of the species, for opposite of
the genus is
example, whether, if ' multiple ' is the genus of the genus of
' double,' ' fraction ' is also the genus of ' half ' ; the opposite
of the
for the opposite of the genus must be the genus of species.
the opposite species. If, therefore, someone were to
lay it down that knowledge is a kind of sense-perception, then also the object of knowledge will
necessarily be a kind of object of sense-perception.
But this is not so ; for not every object of knowledge
is an object of sensation, for some of the objects
of intelligence are objects of knowledge. And so
' object of sensation ' is not the genus of ' object
of knowledge ' ; and, if this is true, neither is
' sensation ' the genus of ' knowledge.'

Since of relative terms (a) some are necessarily (l) The mis-
found in, or employed about, those things in relation use of
certain
to which they happen at any time to be employed, relative
for example, ' disposition,' ' state ' and ' proportion ' terms.
(for these terms cannot possibly exist anywhere else
except in the things in relation to which they are
employed), and (b) others do not necessarily exist in

---

[a] For the cases used with the verb ὑπερέχειν cf. Plato, *Tim.*
24 D πάντων . . . ὑπερέχει μεγέθει καὶ ἀρετῇ.

125 a

ἅ ποτε λέγεται, ἐνδέχεται δέ (οἷον εἰ ἐπιστητὸν
ἡ ψυχή· οὐδὲν γὰρ κωλύει τὴν αὑτῆς ἐπιστήμην
ἔχειν τὴν ψυχήν, οὐκ ἀναγκαῖον δέ· δυνατὸν γὰρ

125 b καὶ ἐν ἄλλῳ ὑπάρχειν τὴν αὐτὴν ταύτην), τὰ δ'
ἁπλῶς οὐκ ἐνδέχεται ἐν ἐκείνοις ὑπάρχειν πρὸς ἅ
ποτε τυγχάνει λεγόμενα (οἷον τὸ ἐναντίον ἐν τῷ
ἐναντίῳ οὐδὲ τὴν ἐπιστήμην ἐν τῷ ἐπιστητῷ, ἐὰν
μὴ τυγχάνῃ τὸ ἐπιστητὸν ψυχὴ ἢ ἄνθρωπος ὄν).

5 σκοπεῖν οὖν χρή, ἐάν τις εἰς γένος θῇ τὸ τοιοῦτον,
⟨εἰ⟩[1] εἰς τὸ μὴ τοιοῦτον, οἷον εἰ τὴν μνήμην μονὴν
ἐπιστήμης εἶπεν. πᾶσα γὰρ μονὴ ἐν τῷ μένοντι
καὶ περὶ ἐκεῖνο, ὥστε καὶ ἡ τῆς ἐπιστήμης μονὴ
ἐν τῇ ἐπιστήμῃ. ἡ μνήμη ἄρα ἐν τῇ ἐπιστήμῃ,
ἐπειδὴ μονὴ τῆς ἐπιστήμης ἐστίν. τοῦτο δ' οὐκ

10 ἐνδέχεται· μνήμη γὰρ πᾶσα ἐν ψυχῇ. ἔστι δ' ὁ
εἰρημένος τόπος καὶ πρὸς τὸ συμβεβηκὸς κοινός·
οὐδὲν γὰρ διαφέρει τῆς μνήμης γένος τὴν μονὴν
εἰπεῖν ἢ συμβεβηκέναι φάσκειν αὐτῇ τοῦτο· εἰ
γὰρ ὁπωσοῦν ἐστὶν ἡ μνήμη μονὴ ἐπιστήμης, ὁ
αὐτὸς ἁρμόσει περὶ αὐτῆς λόγος.

15 V. Πάλιν εἰ τὴν ἕξιν εἰς τὴν ἐνέργειαν ἔθηκεν
ἢ τὴν ἐνέργειαν εἰς τὴν ἕξιν, οἷον τὴν αἴσθησιν
κίνησιν διὰ σώματος· ἡ μὲν γὰρ αἴσθησις ἕξις, ἡ
δὲ κίνησις ἐνέργεια. ὁμοίως δὲ καὶ εἰ τὴν μνήμην

[1] εἰ added by W. S. Maguinness.

those things in relation to which they are employed
at any particular time, though they *may* so exist (for
example, if the soul be called an ' object of knowledge '; for there is nothing to prevent the soul
from having knowledge of itself, though it does not
necessarily possess it, for it is possible for this same
knowledge to exist elsewhere), and (c) others simply
cannot exist in those things in relation to which
they happen to be employed at any particular time,
for example, the contrary cannot exist in the contrary
nor knowledge in the object of knowledge, unless the
object of knowledge happens to be a soul or a man.
If, therefore, someone places a term of a certain kind
within a genus, you must look and see whether he
has placed it within a genus which is not of that
kind, for example, if it has been stated that ' memory '
is the ' permanency of knowledge.' For ' permanency ' always exists in, and is concerned with, that
which is permanent, so that the permanency of
knowledge also exists in knowledge. Memory, then,
exists in knowledge, since it is the permanency of
knowledge ; but this is impossible, for memory
always exists in the soul. The above commonplace
is common also to accident ; for it makes no difference whether we say that permanency is the genus
of memory or call it accidental to it ; for, if memory
is in any way the permanency of knowledge, the
same argument about it will be applicable.

V. Again, you must see whether your opponent *Some com-*
has placed a ' state ' in the genus of ' activity ' or *mon errors*
in predica-
an ' activity ' in the genus of ' state,' for example, *tion:*
calling ' sensation ' ' movement through the body ' ; *(a)* Confu-
sion of
for sensation is a ' state ' while movement is an ' state ' and
' activity.' Likewise, too, if he has made ' memory ' *' activity '*
and ' state '
and
' capacity.'

ARISTOTLE

125 b ἕξιν καθεκτικὴν ὑπολήψεως εἶπεν· οὐδεμία γὰρ
μνήμη ἕξις, ἀλλὰ μᾶλλον ἐνέργεια.

20 Διαμαρτάνουσι δὲ καὶ οἱ τὴν ἕξιν εἰς τὴν ἀκο-
λουθοῦσαν δύναμιν τάττοντες, οἷον τὴν πρᾳότητα
ἐγκράτειαν ὀργῆς καὶ τὴν ἀνδρίαν καὶ τὴν δικαιοσύνην φόβων καὶ κερδῶν· ἀνδρεῖος μὲν γὰρ καὶ
πρᾷος ὁ ἀπαθὴς λέγεται, ἐγκρατὴς δ' ὁ πάσχων
καὶ μὴ ἀγόμενος. ἴσως μὲν οὖν ἀκολουθεῖ δύναμις
25 ἑκατέρῳ τοιαύτη, ὥστ' εἰ πάθοι, μὴ ἄγεσθαι ἀλλὰ
κρατεῖν· οὐ μὴν τοῦτό γ' ἐστὶ τῷ μὲν ἀνδρείῳ τῷ
δὲ πρᾴῳ εἶναι, ἀλλὰ τὸ ὅλως μὴ πάσχειν ὑπὸ τῶν
τοιούτων μηδέν.

Ἐνίοτε δὲ καὶ τὸ παρακολουθοῦν ὁπωσοῦν ὡς
γένος τιθέασιν, οἷον τὴν λύπην τῆς ὀργῆς καὶ τὴν
30 ὑπόληψιν τῆς πίστεως. ἄμφω γὰρ τὰ εἰρημένα
παρακολουθεῖ μὲν τρόπον τινὰ τοῖς ἀποδοθεῖσιν
εἴδεσιν, οὐδέτερον δ' αὐτῶν γένος ἐστίν· ὁ μὲν
γὰρ ὀργιζόμενος λυπεῖται προτέρας ἐν αὐτῷ τῆς
λύπης γενομένης· οὐ γὰρ ἡ ὀργὴ τῆς λύπης, ἀλλ'
ἡ λύπη τῆς ὀργῆς αἰτία, ὥσθ' ἁπλῶς ἡ ὀργὴ οὐκ
35 ἔστι λύπη. κατὰ ταῦτα δ' οὐδ' ἡ πίστις ὑπόληψις·
ἐνδέχεται γὰρ τὴν αὐτὴν ὑπόληψιν καὶ μὴ πι-
στεύοντα ἔχειν. οὐκ ἐνδέχεται δ', εἴπερ εἶδος
ἡ πίστις ὑπολήψεως· οὐ γὰρ ἐνδέχεται τὸ αὐτὸ
ἔτι διαμένειν, ἄνπερ ἐκ τοῦ εἴδους ὅλως μεταβάλῃ,
καθάπερ οὐδὲ τὸ αὐτὸ ζῷον ὁτὲ μὲν ἄνθρωπον
40 εἶναι ὁτὲ δὲ μή. ἂν δέ τις φῇ ἐξ ἀνάγκης τὸν
126 a ὑπολαμβάνοντα καὶ πιστεύειν, ἐπ' ἴσον ἡ ὑπό-

458

' a state which can retain a conception '; for memory
is never a ' state ' but rather an ' activity.'

They also err who range a ' state ' in the ' capacity '
which accompanies it, for example, making ' mild-
ness ' ' the controlling of anger,' and ' courage ' and
' justice ' ' the controlling of fears ' and of ' gains '
respectively; for ' courageous ' and ' mild ' are used
of one who is free from passion, whereas a ' self-
controlled ' man is one who is subject to passion but
is not carried away by it. Now, perhaps each of the
former is attended by a capacity of such a kind that,
if he is subjected to a passion, he is not carried away
by it but can control it; this, however, is not to
be ' courageous ' in the one case and ' mild ' in the
other, but to be absolutely free from any such passion.

Sometimes also, people put down as genus that
which is in any manner attendant on the species,
making, for example, ' pain ' the genus of ' anger '
and ' conception ' the genus of ' belief '; for both
in a sense are attendant on the species assigned, but
neither of them is its genus. For when the angry
man is pained, the pain has been produced in him
before he is angry; for the anger is not the cause
of the pain but the pain of the anger; so that anger
simply is not pain. On this principle neither is belief
conception; for it is possible to have the same conception even without believing in it, whereas this is
impossible if belief is a species of conception. For
it is impossible for a thing still to remain the same
if it is entirely removed from its species, just as
neither can the same animal be a man at one time
and not at another. But if anyone asserts that the
man who has a conception must necessarily also
believe in it, then conception and belief will be used

(b) Mis-
taken as-
sumption
that what is
consequent
upon species
is genus.

459

λῆψις καὶ ἡ πίστις ῥηθήσεται, ὥστ' οὐδ' ἂν οὕτως
εἴη γένος· ἐπὶ πλέον γὰρ δεῖ λέγεσθαι τὸ γένος.

Ὁρᾶν δὲ καὶ εἰ ἔν τινι τῷ αὐτῷ πέφυκεν ἄμφω
γίνεσθαι· ἐν ᾧ γὰρ τὸ εἶδος, καὶ τὸ γένος, οἷον
5 ἐν ᾧ τὸ λευκόν, καὶ τὸ χρῶμα, καὶ ἐν ᾧ γραμματική, καὶ ἐπιστήμη. ἐὰν οὖν τις τὴν αἰσχύνην
φόβον εἴπῃ ἢ τὴν ὀργὴν λύπην, οὐ συμβήσεται ἐν
τῷ αὐτῷ τὸ εἶδος καὶ τὸ γένος ὑπάρχειν· ἡ μὲν
γὰρ αἰσχύνη ἐν τῷ λογιστικῷ, ὁ δὲ φόβος ἐν τῷ
θυμοειδεῖ, καὶ ἡ μὲν λύπη ἐν τῷ ἐπιθυμητικῷ
10 (ἐν τούτῳ γὰρ καὶ ἡ ἡδονή), ἡ δὲ ὀργὴ ἐν τῷ
θυμοειδεῖ, ὥστ' οὐ γένη τὰ ἀποδοθέντα, ἐπειδὴ
οὐκ ἐν τῷ αὐτῷ τοῖς εἴδεσι πέφυκε γίνεσθαι.
ὁμοίως δὲ καὶ εἰ ἡ φιλία ἐν τῷ ἐπιθυμητικῷ, οὐκ
ἂν εἴη βούλησίς τις· πᾶσα γὰρ βούλησις ἐν τῷ
λογιστικῷ. χρήσιμος δ' ὁ τόπος καὶ πρὸς τὸ
15 συμβεβηκός· ἐν τῷ αὐτῷ γὰρ τὸ συμβεβηκὸς καὶ
ᾧ συμβέβηκεν, ὥστ' ἂν μὴ ἐν τῷ αὐτῷ φαίνηται,
δῆλον ὅτι οὐ συμβέβηκεν.

Πάλιν εἰ κατά τι τὸ εἶδος τοῦ εἰρημένου γένους
μετέχει· οὐ δοκεῖ γὰρ κατά τι μετέχεσθαι τὸ γένος·
οὐ γάρ ἐστιν ὁ ἄνθρωπος κατά τι ζῷον, οὐδ' ἡ
20 γραμματικὴ κατά τι ἐπιστήμη· ὁμοίως δὲ καὶ ἐπὶ
τῶν ἄλλων. σκοπεῖν οὖν εἰ ἐπί τινων κατά τι
μετέχεται τὸ γένος, οἷον εἰ τὸ ζῷον ὅπερ αἰσθητὸν

to cover the same ground, so that not even so could the one be the genus of the other, since the genus must cover a wider field of predication.

You must also see whether it is the nature of both to come into being in some one and the same thing; for where the species is, there also is the genus; for example, where there is 'whiteness,' there is also 'colour,' and, where there is the 'science of grammar,' there is also 'knowledge.' If, therefore, anyone says that ' shame ' is ' fear ' or that ' anger ' is ' pain,' the result will be that the species and the genus do not exist in the same thing; for shame exists in the ' reasoning ' faculty of the soul, fear in the ' spirited ' faculty, and ' pain ' in the ' appetitive ' faculty (for pleasure is also in this), anger in the ' spirited ' faculty, so that the terms assigned are not genera, since it is not their nature to come into being in the same thing as the species. Similarly, too, if ' friendship ' is in the ' appetitive ' faculty, it cannot be a kind of ' wish '; for a ' wish ' is always in the ' reasoning ' faculty. This commonplace is also useful in dealing with the accident; for the accident and that of which it is an accident are both in the same thing, so that, if they do not appear in the same thing, it is obviously not a case of accident. *(c) Erroneous assumption of things which fall under different faculties as genus and species.*

Again, you must see whether the species partakes only partially of the genus assigned; for it is generally held that genus is not partially imparted; for a man is not merely partially an animal nor is the science of grammar partially knowledge, and so likewise in the other instances. You must examine, therefore, whether in some cases the genus is only partially imparted, for example, if ' animal ' has been described as an ' object of sensation ' or an ' object *(d) Error of making the species partake only partially of the genus.*

126 a

ἢ ὁρατὸν εἴρηται. κατά τι γὰρ αἰσθητὸν ἢ ὁρατὸν
τὸ ζῷον· κατὰ τὸ σῶμα γὰρ αἰσθητὸν καὶ ὁρατόν,
κατὰ δὲ τὴν ψυχὴν οὔ, ὥστ᾿ οὐκ ἂν εἴη γένος τὸ
25 ὁρατὸν καὶ τὸ αἰσθητὸν τοῦ ζῴου.

Λανθάνουσι δ᾿ ἐνίοτε καὶ τὸ ὅλον εἰς τὸ μέρος
τιθέντες, οἷον τὸ ζῷον σῶμα ἔμψυχον. οὐδαμῶς
δὲ τὸ μέρος τοῦ ὅλου κατηγορεῖται, ὥστ᾿ οὐκ ἂν
εἴη τὸ σῶμα γένος τοῦ ζῴου, ἐπειδὴ μέρος ἐστίν.
30 Ὁρᾶν δὲ καὶ εἴ τι τῶν ψεκτῶν ἢ φευκτῶν εἰς
δύναμιν ἢ τὸ δυνατὸν ἔθηκεν, οἷον τὸν σοφιστὴν
ἢ διάβολον ἢ κλέπτην τὸν δυνάμενον λάθρα ἀλλότρια
κλέπτειν.[1] οὐδεὶς γὰρ τῶν εἰρημένων τῷ δυνατὸς
εἶναί τι τούτων τοιοῦτος λέγεται· δύναται μὲν
35 γὰρ καὶ ὁ θεὸς καὶ ὁ σπουδαῖος τὰ φαῦλα δρᾶν,
ἀλλ᾿ οὐκ εἰσὶ τοιοῦτοι· πάντες γὰρ οἱ φαῦλοι κατὰ
προαίρεσιν λέγονται. ἔτι πᾶσα δύναμις τῶν
αἱρετῶν· καὶ γὰρ αἱ τῶν φαύλων δυνάμεις αἱρεταί,
διὸ καὶ τὸν θεὸν καὶ τὸν σπουδαῖον ἔχειν φαμὲν
αὐτάς· δυνατοὺς γὰρ εἶναι τὰ φαῦλα πράσσειν.
126 b ὥστ᾿ οὐδενὸς ἂν εἴη ψεκτοῦ γένος ἡ δύναμις. εἰ
δὲ μή, συμβήσεται τῶν ψεκτῶν τι αἱρετὸν εἶναι·
ἔσται γάρ τις δύναμις ψεκτή.

Καὶ εἴ τι τῶν δι᾿ αὐτὸ τιμίων ἢ αἱρετῶν εἰς
5 δύναμιν ἢ τὸ δυνατὸν ἢ τὸ ποιητικὸν ἔθηκεν. πᾶσα

---

[1] Reading with AB δυνάμενον λάθρα ἀλλότρια κλέπτειν.

of sight.' For an animal is only in part an object
of sensation or of sight ; for it is an object of sensation
and sight as regards its body but not as regards its
soul ; so that 'object of sight' and 'object of
sensation' cannot be the genus of 'animal.'

Sometimes too people unobservedly put the whole (e) Error of
within the part, describing, for example, 'animal' taking part
as 'animated body.' But the part is not in any way species
predicable of the whole, so that 'body' cannot be as genus.
the genus of 'animal,' for it is a part only.

You must also see whether your opponent has put
anything blameworthy or to be avoided in the (f) Error of
category of 'capacity' or 'capable,' for example, what is
in his definition of a sophist or a slanderer, or a thief blame-
whom he describes as capable of secretly stealing capacity.
the good of others. For none of the above is
described by his particular name because he is
'capable' in one of these respects ; for even God
and the good man are capable of doing bad deeds,
but God and man are not of that character ; for the
wicked are always so called because of their deliberate
choice of evil. Furthermore, a capacity is always
among the things worthy of choice, for even capacities
for evil are worthy of choice ; and so we say that
God and the good man possess them, for we say
that they are capable of doing evil. Therefore
capacity cannot be the genus of anything blameworthy ; otherwise the result will be that something
blameworthy is an object of choice, for there will
be a kind of capacity which is blameworthy.

You must also see whether he has placed anything (g) Placing
which is in itself valuable or worthy of choice in the in the cate-
category of 'capacity' or 'the capable' or 'the pacity what
productive.' For every capacity and everything is in itself
desirable.

126 b

γὰρ δύναμις καὶ πᾶν τὸ δυνατὸν ἢ τὸ ποιητικὸν
δι' ἄλλο αἱρετόν.

Ἢ εἴ τι τῶν ἐν δύο γένεσιν ἢ πλείοσιν εἰς
θάτερον ἔθηκεν. ἔνια γὰρ οὐκ ἔστιν εἰς ἓν γένος
θεῖναι, οἷον τὸν φένακα καὶ τὸν διάβολον· οὔτε
10 γὰρ ὁ προαιρούμενος ἀδυνατῶν δέ, οὔθ' ὁ δυνάμενος μὴ προαιρούμενος δὲ διάβολος ἢ φέναξ,
ἀλλ' ὁ ἄμφω ταῦτα ἔχων. ὥστ' οὐ θετέον εἰς ἓν
γένος ἀλλ' εἰς ἀμφότερα τὰ εἰρημένα.

Ἔτι ἐνίοτε ἀνάπαλιν τὸ μὲν γένος ὡς διαφορὰν
τὴν δὲ διαφορὰν ὡς γένος ἀποδιδόασιν, οἷον τὴν
15 ἔκπληξιν ὑπερβολὴν θαυμασιότητος καὶ τὴν πίστιν
σφοδρότητα ὑπολήψεως. οὔτε γὰρ ἡ ὑπερβολὴ
οὔθ' ἡ σφοδρότης γένος, ἀλλὰ διαφορά· δοκεῖ γὰρ
ἡ ἔκπληξις θαυμασιότης εἶναι ὑπερβάλλουσα καὶ
ἡ πίστις ὑπόληψις σφοδρά, ὥστε γένος ἡ θαυμασιότης καὶ ἡ ὑπόληψις, ἡ δ' ὑπερβολὴ καὶ ἡ σφο-
20 δρότης διαφορά. ἔτι εἴ τις τὴν ὑπερβολὴν καὶ
σφοδρότητα ὡς γένος ἀποδώσει, τὰ ἄψυχα πιστεύσει καὶ ἐκπλαγήσεται. ἡ γὰρ ἑκάστου σφοδρότης καὶ ὑπερβολὴ πάρεστιν ἐκείνῳ οὗ ἐστὶ
σφοδρότης καὶ ὑπερβολή. εἰ οὖν ἡ ἔκπληξις
ὑπερβολή ἐστι θαυμασιότητος, παρέσται τῇ θαυ-
25 μασιότητι ἡ ἔκπληξις, ὥσθ' ἡ θαυμασιότης
ἐκπλαγήσεται. ὁμοίως δὲ καὶ ἡ πίστις παρέσται
τῇ ὑπολήψει, εἴπερ σφοδρότης ὑπολήψεώς ἐστιν,
ὥστε ἡ ὑπόληψις πιστεύσει. ἔτι συμβήσεται τῷ
464

capable or productive is worthy of choice for the sake of something else.

Or again, you must see whether he has placed something which falls under two or more genera in one of them only. For there are some things which cannot be placed in one genus only, for example, the 'imposter' and the 'slanderer.' For neither is he who possesses the inclination but not the ability, nor he who possesses the ability but not the inclination, a slanderer or an imposter, but he who has the ability and the inclination. He must, therefore, be placed not in one genus only but in both the above genera. *(h) Placing in only one genus that which falls under several genera.*

Moreover, by a process of inversion, people sometimes assign genus as differentia and differentia as genus, calling, for example, 'amazement' an 'excess of astonishment' and 'belief' an 'intensification of opinion.' For 'excess' and 'intensification' are not the genus but the differentia; for amazement is generally regarded as excessive astonishment and belief as intensified opinion, so that astonishment and opinion are the genus, while excess and intensification are the differentia. Further, if excess and intensification are to be assigned as genus, inanimate things will believe and be amazed. For the intensification and excess of any particular thing are present in that of which they are the intensification and excess. If, therefore, amazement is an excess of astonishment, the amazement will be present in the astonishment, so that the astonishment will be amazed. Similarly also the belief will be present in the opinion, since it is the intensification of the opinion; and so the opinion will believe. Further, the result of making an assertion of this kind will *(i) Error of assigning genus as differentia and vice versa.*

465

126 b

οὕτως ἀποδιδόντι σφοδρότητα σφοδρὰν λέγειν καὶ
ὑπερβολὴν ὑπερβάλλουσαν. ἔστι γὰρ πίστις σφο-
30 δρά· εἰ οὖν ἡ πίστις σφοδρότης ἐστί, σφοδρότης
ἂν εἴη σφοδρά. ὁμοίως δὲ καὶ ἔκπληξίς ἐστιν
ὑπερβάλλουσα· εἰ οὖν ἡ ἔκπληξις ὑπερβολή ἐστιν,
ὑπερβολὴ ἂν εἴη ὑπερβάλλουσα. οὐ δοκεῖ δ᾽
οὐδέτερον τούτων, ὥσπερ οὐδ᾽ ἐπιστήμη ἐπιστῆμον[1]
οὐδὲ κίνησις κινούμενον.

Ἐνίοτε δὲ διαμαρτάνουσι καὶ τὸ πάθος εἰς γένος
35 τὸ πεπονθὸς τιθέντες, οἷον ὅσοι τὴν ἀθανασίαν
ζωὴν ἀΐδιόν φασιν εἶναι· πάθος γάρ τι ζωῆς ἢ
σύμπτωμα ἡ ἀθανασία ἔοικεν εἶναι. ὅτι δ᾽ ἀληθὲς
τὸ λεγόμενον, δῆλον ἂν γένοιτο, εἴ τις συγχωρήσειεν
ἐκ θνητοῦ τινα ἀθάνατον γίνεσθαι· οὐδεὶς γὰρ φήσει
ἑτέραν αὐτὸν ζωὴν λαμβάνειν, ἀλλὰ σύμπτωμά τι
127 a ἢ πάθος αὐτῇ ταύτῃ παραγενέσθαι. ὥστ᾽ οὐ γένος
ἡ ζωὴ τῆς ἀθανασίας.

Πάλιν εἰ τοῦ πάθους, οὗ ἐστὶ πάθος, ἐκεῖνο γένος
φασὶν εἶναι, οἷον τὸ πνεῦμα ἀέρα κινούμενον.
5 μᾶλλον γὰρ κίνησις ἀέρος τὸ πνεῦμα· ὁ γὰρ αὐτὸς
ἀὴρ διαμένει, ὅταν τε κινῆται καὶ ὅταν μένῃ. ὥστ᾽
οὐκ ἔστιν ὅλως ἀὴρ τὸ πνεῦμα· ἦν γὰρ ἂν καὶ
μὴ κινουμένου τοῦ ἀέρος πνεῦμα, εἴπερ ὁ αὐτὸς
ἀὴρ διαμένει ὅσπερ ἦν πνεῦμα. ὁμοίως δὲ καὶ
ἐπὶ τῶν ἄλλων τῶν τοιούτων. εἰ δ᾽ ἄρα καὶ ἐπὶ
10 τούτου δεῖ συγχωρῆσαι ὅτι ἀήρ ἐστι κινούμενος
τὸ πνεῦμα, ἀλλ᾽ οὔτι κατὰ πάντων τὸ τοιοῦτον
ἀποδεκτέον καθ᾽ ὧν μὴ ἀληθεύεται τὸ γένος, ἀλλ᾽
ἐφ᾽ ὅσων ἀληθῶς κατηγορεῖται τὸ ἀποδοθὲν γένος.
ἐπ᾽ ἐνίων γὰρ οὐ δοκεῖ ἀληθεύεσθαι, οἷον ἐπὶ τοῦ

---

[1] Reading ἐπιστῆμον with C.

be to call intensification intensified and excess
excessive. For belief is intensified; if, therefore,
belief is intensification, intensification would be
intensified. Similarly, too, amazement is excessive;
if, therefore, amazement is excess, excess would be
excessive. But neither of these things accords with
current belief any more than that knowledge is a
knowing thing or motion a moving thing.

Sometimes too, people err in placing an affection *(j)* Error of
in that which has been affected, as its genus, for making the
example, those who say that immortality is ever- affected the
lasting life; for immortality seems to be an affection genus of the
or accidental property of life. That this description
is true would be clearly seen if one were to concede
that a man can become immortal after having been
mortal; for no one will say that he is taking on
another life, but that an accidental property or
affection is added to life as it is. Life, therefore, is
not the genus of immortality.

Again, you must see whether they are asserting *(k)* Error of
that the genus of an affection is that of which it is making the
an affection, for example, when they say that the affected the
wind is ' air in motion.' For wind is rather ' motion genus of the
of air,' for the same air remains both when it is in
motion and when it is at rest. And so wind is not
air at all; otherwise there would be wind even
when the air was not in motion, since the same air
which was wind still remains. Similarly, too, in the
other cases of this kind. But if after all we must
in this case concede that the wind is air in motion,
yet we ought not to accept such a statement with
regard to everything of which the genus is not truly
asserted but only where the genus assigned is truly
predicated. For in some cases, for example ' mud '

467

127 a

πηλοῦ καὶ τῆς χιόνος. τὴν μὲν γὰρ χιόνα φασὶν
15 ὕδωρ εἶναι πεπηγός, τὸν δὲ πηλὸν γῆν ὑγρῷ
πεφυραμένην· ἔστι δ' οὔθ' ἡ χιὼν ὕδωρ οὔθ' ὁ
πηλὸς γῆ, ὥστ' οὐκ ἂν εἴη γένος οὐδέτερον τῶν
ἀποδοθέντων· δεῖ γὰρ τὸ γένος ἀληθεύεσθαι ἀεὶ
κατὰ τῶν εἰδῶν. ὁμοίως δ' οὐδ' ὁ οἶνός ἐστιν
ὕδωρ σεσηπός, καθάπερ Ἐμπεδοκλῆς φησὶ σαπὲν
ἐν ξύλῳ ὕδωρ· ἁπλῶς γὰρ οὐκ ἔστιν ὕδωρ.
20 VI. Ἔτι εἰ ὅλως τὸ ἀποδοθὲν μηδενός ἐστι
γένος· δῆλον γὰρ ὡς οὐδὲ τοῦ λεχθέντος. σκοπεῖν
δ' ἐκ τοῦ μηδὲν διαφέρειν εἴδει τὰ μετέχοντα τοῦ
ἀποδοθέντος γένους, οἷον τὰ λευκά· οὐδὲν γὰρ
διαφέρει τῷ εἴδει ταῦτ' ἀλλήλων. παντὸς δὲ
γένους ἐστὶ τὰ εἴδη διάφορα, ὥστ' οὐκ ἂν εἴη τὸ
25 λευκὸν γένος οὐδενός.

Πάλιν εἰ τὸ πᾶσιν ἀκολουθοῦν γένος ἢ διαφορὰν
εἶπεν. πλείω γὰρ τὰ πᾶσιν ἑπόμενα, οἷον τὸ
ὂν καὶ τὸ ἓν τῶν πᾶσιν ἑπομένων ἐστίν. εἰ οὖν
τὸ ὂν γένος ἀπέδωκε, δῆλον ὅτι πάντων ἂν εἴη
30 γένος, ἐπειδὴ κατηγορεῖται αὐτῶν· κατ' οὐδενὸς
γὰρ τὸ γένος ἀλλ' ἢ κατὰ τῶν εἰδῶν κατηγορεῖται.
ὥστε καὶ τὸ ἓν εἶδος ἂν εἴη τοῦ ὄντος. συμβαίνει
οὖν κατὰ πάντων, ὧν τὸ γένος κατηγορεῖται, καὶ
τὸ εἶδος κατηγορεῖσθαι, ἐπειδὴ τὸ ὂν καὶ τὸ ἓν

and 'snow,' it does not seem to be truly asserted. For they describes now as 'congealed water,' and mud as 'earth mingled with moisture'; but neither is snow water nor mud earth, so that neither of the terms assigned could be the genus; for the genus must always be truly asserted of every species. Similarly, neither is wine 'putrefied water,' as Empedocles speaks of 'water putrefied in wood'[a]; for it simply is not water at all.

VI. Furthermore, you must see whether the term assigned is not the genus of anything at all; for then obviously it is not the genus of the species named. You must make your examination on the basis of an absence of any difference in species between the things which partake of the genus assigned, for example, white objects; for these do not differ at all from one another specifically, whereas the species of a genus are always different from one another; so that 'white' could not be the genus of anything. *Various Rules:* (a) The proposed genus must contain subject species.

Again, you must see whether your opponent has asserted that some attribute which accompanies everything is genus or differentia. For there are several attributes which accompany everything; 'being,' for example, and 'oneness' are among the attributes which accompany everything. If, then, he has assigned 'being' as a genus, obviously it would be the genus of everything, since it is predicated of everything; for the genus is not predicated of anything except its species. Hence 'oneness' too would be a species of 'being.' It results, therefore, that the species also is predicated of everything of which the genus is predicated, since 'being' and 'oneness' are predicated of absolutely everything, *(b)* An attribute which is universally present cannot be taken as genus or differentia.

127 a

κατὰ πάντων ἁπλῶς κατηγορεῖται, δέον ἐπ' ἔλατ-
35 τον τὸ εἶδος κατηγορεῖσθαι. εἰ δὲ τὸ πᾶσιν
ἑπόμενον διαφορὰν εἶπε, δῆλον ὅτι ἐπ' ἴσον ἢ ἐπὶ
πλέον ἡ διαφορὰ τοῦ γένους ῥηθήσεται. εἰ μὲν
γὰρ καὶ τὸ γένος τῶν πᾶσιν ἑπομένων, ἐπ' ἴσον,
εἰ δὲ μὴ πᾶσιν ἕπεται τὸ γένος, ἐπὶ πλέον ἡ
διαφορὰ λέγοιτ' ἂν αὐτοῦ.

127 b Ἔτι εἰ ἐν ὑποκειμένῳ τῷ εἴδει τὸ ἀποδοθὲν
γένος λέγεται, καθάπερ τὸ λευκὸν ἐπὶ τῆς χιόνος,
ὥστε δῆλον ὅτι οὐκ ἂν εἴη γένος· καθ' ὑποκειμένου
γὰρ τοῦ εἴδους μόνον τὸ γένος λέγεται.

5 Σκοπεῖν δὲ καὶ εἰ μὴ συνώνυμον τὸ γένος τῷ
εἴδει· κατὰ πάντων γὰρ τῶν εἰδῶν συνωνύμως τὸ
γένος κατηγορεῖται.

Ἔτι ὅταν ὄντος καὶ τῷ εἴδει καὶ τῷ γένει
ἐναντίου τὸ βέλτιον τῶν ἐναντίων εἰς τὸ χεῖρον
10 γένος θῇ· συμβήσεται γὰρ τὸ λοιπὸν ἐν τῷ λοιπῷ
εἶναι, ἐπειδὴ τἀναντία ἐν τοῖς ἐναντίοις γένεσιν,
ὥστε τὸ βέλτιον ἐν τῷ χείρονι ἔσται καὶ τὸ χεῖρον
ἐν τῷ βελτίονι· δοκεῖ δὲ τοῦ βελτίονος καὶ τὸ
γένος βέλτιον εἶναι. καὶ εἰ τοῦ αὐτοῦ εἴδους
ὁμοίως πρὸς ἄμφω ἔχοντος εἰς τὸ χεῖρον καὶ μὴ
15 εἰς τὸ βέλτιον γένος ἔθηκεν, οἷον τὴν ψυχὴν ὅπερ
κίνησιν ἢ κινούμενον. ὁμοίως γὰρ ἡ αὐτὴ στατικὴ

whereas the species ought to be less widely predicated. If, however, he has asserted that the attribute which accompanies everything is a differentia, it is obvious that the differentia will be predicated to an extent equal to, or greater than, the genus. For if the genus also is one of the attributes which accompany everything, the differentia would be predicated to an equal extent, but, if the genus does not accompany everything, to a greater extent than the genus.

Furthermore, you must see whether the genus assigned is said to be inherent in the subject species as ' white ' is in the case of snow, so that it is obvious that it cannot be the genus ; for the genus is only predicated of the subject species. *(c) The genus cannot be inherent in the subject species.*

You must also see whether the genus is not synonymous with the species ; for the genus is always predicated of the species synonymously. *(d) The genus and the species are predicated synonymously.*

Further, there is the case when, both the species and the genus having a contrary, your opponent places the better of the contrary species in the worse genus ; for this will result in the other species being placed in the other genus, since contraries are found in contrary genera, so that the better species will be found in the worse genus and the worse species in the better genus, whereas it is generally held that the genus of the better species is also better. You must also see whether, when the same species is similarly related to both, your opponent has placed it in the worse and not in the better genus, saying, for example, that the ' soul ' is ' a kind of motion ' or ' a moving thing.' For the same soul is generally regarded as being in like manner a principle of rest and a principle of motion ; *(e) The better of two contraries must not be assigned to the worse genus.*

471

127 b

καὶ κινητικὴ δοκεῖ εἶναι, ὥστ' εἰ βέλτιον ἡ στάσις,
εἰς τοῦτο ἔδει τὸ γένος θεῖναι.

Ἔτι ἐκ τοῦ μᾶλλον καὶ ἧττον, ἀνασκευάζοντι
μέν, εἰ τὸ γένος δέχεται τὸ μᾶλλον, τὸ δ' εἶδος
20 μὴ δέχεται μήτ' αὐτὸ μήτε τὸ κατ' ἐκεῖνο λεγόμενον. οἷον εἰ ἡ ἀρετὴ δέχεται τὸ μᾶλλον, καὶ ἡ
δικαιοσύνη καὶ ὁ δίκαιος· λέγεται γὰρ δικαιότερος
ἕτερος ἑτέρου. εἰ οὖν τὸ μὲν ἀποδοθὲν γένος τὸ
μᾶλλον δέχεται, τὸ δ' εἶδος μὴ δέχεται μήτ' αὐτὸ
μήτε τὸ κατ' ἐκεῖνο λεγόμενον, οὐκ ἂν εἴη γένος
25 τὸ ἀποδοθέν.

Πάλιν εἰ τὸ μᾶλλον δοκοῦν ἢ ὁμοίως μή ἐστι
γένος, δῆλον ὅτι οὐδὲ τὸ ἀποδοθέν. χρήσιμος δ'
ὁ τόπος ἐπὶ τῶν τοιούτων μάλιστα ἐφ' ὧν πλείω
φαίνεται τοῦ εἴδους ἐν τῷ τί ἐστι κατηγορούμενα,
30 καὶ μὴ διώρισται, μηδ' ἔχομεν εἰπεῖν ποῖον αὐτῶν
γένος, οἷον τῆς ὀργῆς καὶ ἡ λύπη καὶ ἡ ὑπόληψις
ὀλιγωρίας ἐν τῷ τί ἐστι κατηγορεῖσθαι δοκεῖ·
λυπεῖταί τε γὰρ ὁ ὀργιζόμενος καὶ ὑπολαμβάνει
ὀλιγωρεῖσθαι. ἡ αὐτὴ δὲ σκέψις καὶ ἐπὶ τοῦ εἴδους
πρὸς ἄλλο τι συγκρίνοντι· εἰ γὰρ τὸ μᾶλλον ἢ τὸ
35 ὁμοίως δοκοῦν εἶναι ἐν τῷ ἀποδοθέντι γένει μή
ἐστιν ἐν τῷ γένει, δῆλον ὅτι οὐδὲ τὸ ἀποδοθὲν εἶδος
εἴη ἂν ἐν τῷ γένει.

Ἀναιροῦντι μὲν οὖν καθάπερ εἴρηται χρηστέον·
κατασκευάζοντι δέ, εἰ μὲν ἐπιδέχεται τὸ μᾶλλον
128 a τό τε ἀποδοθὲν γένος καὶ τὸ εἶδος, οὐ χρήσιμος

so that, if rest is better, it ought to have been placed in this as its genus.

Further, you must argue from the greater and less degrees. For destructive criticism, you should see whether the genus admits of the greater degree, while neither the species itself nor anything which is named after it does so. For example, if virtue admits of the greater degree, 'justice' and 'the just man' do so also; for one man is called 'more just' than another. If, therefore, the genus assigned admits of the greater degree but neither the species itself nor anything which is named after it admits of it, the term assigned cannot be the genus.

Again, if what is more generally or equally generally held to be the genus is not the genus, obviously neither is the term assigned the genus. This commonplace is useful especially when several things are clearly predicable of the species in the category of essence and no distinction has been made between them and we cannot say which of them is genus. For example, both 'pain' and the 'conception of contempt' are generally regarded as predicates of 'anger' in the category of essence; for the angry man both feels pain and conceives that he is contemned. The same inquiry is also applicable in the case of the species by means of a comparison with some other species; for, if what is more generally or equally generally held to be in the assigned genus is not present in the genus, obviously neither could the species assigned be present in the genus.

In destructive criticism, then, the above method should be employed; but for constructive purposes the commonplace of seeing whether both the assigned genus and the species admit of the greater

(f) Arguments from the greater or less and equal degrees.

(1) In destructive criticism.

(2) In constructive argument.

ὁ τόπος· οὐδὲν γὰρ κωλύει ἀμφοτέρων ἐπιδεχο-
μένων μὴ εἶναι θάτερον θατέρου γένος. τό τε
γὰρ καλὸν καὶ τὸ λευκὸν ἐπιδέχεται τὸ μᾶλλον,
καὶ οὐδέτερον οὐδετέρου γένος. ἡ δὲ τῶν γενῶν
5 καὶ τῶν εἰδῶν πρὸς ἄλληλα σύγκρισις χρήσιμος,
οἷον εἰ ὁμοίως τόδε καὶ τόδε γένος, εἰ θάτερον
γένος, καὶ θάτερον. ὁμοίως δὲ καὶ εἰ τὸ ἧττον
καὶ τὸ μᾶλλον, οἷον εἰ τῆς ἐγκρατείας μᾶλλον ἡ
δύναμις ἢ ἡ ἀρετὴ γένος, ἡ δ' ἀρετὴ γένος, καὶ
ἡ δύναμις. τὰ δ' αὐτὰ καὶ ἐπὶ τοῦ εἴδους ἁρμόσει
10 λέγεσθαι. εἰ γὰρ ὁμοίως τόδε καὶ τόδε τοῦ προκειμένου εἶδος, εἰ θάτερον εἶδος, καὶ τὸ λοιπόν·
καὶ εἰ τὸ ἧττον δοκοῦν εἶδός ἐστι, καὶ τὸ μᾶλλον.

"Ἔτι πρὸς τὸ κατασκευάζειν σκεπτέον εἰ καθ'
ὧν ἀπεδόθη τὸ γένος, ἐν τῷ τί ἐστι κατηγορεῖται,
15 μὴ ὄντος ἑνὸς τοῦ ἀποδοθέντος εἴδους, ἀλλὰ
πλειόνων καὶ διαφόρων· δῆλον γὰρ ὅτι γένος ἔσται.
εἰ δ' ἓν τὸ ἀποδοθὲν εἶδός ἐστι, σκοπεῖν εἰ καὶ
κατ' ἄλλων εἰδῶν τὸ γένος ἐν τῷ τί ἐστι κατη-
γορεῖται· πάλιν γὰρ συμβήσεται κατὰ πλειόνων
καὶ διαφόρων αὐτὸ κατηγορεῖσθαι.

20 Ἐπεὶ δὲ δοκεῖ τισὶ καὶ ἡ διαφορὰ ἐν τῷ τί ἐστι
τῶν εἰδῶν κατηγορεῖσθαι, χωριστέον τὸ γένος

degree is of no use ; for, even though they both
admit of it, there is nothing to prevent one not
being the genus of the other. For both ' beautiful '
and ' white ' admit of the greater degree, and
neither is the genus of the other. The comparison,
however, of the genera and the species with one
another is useful ; for example, if A and B have
equal claim to be regarded as genera, then, if one
is a genus, so also is the other. Similarly, too, if
the less degree is a genus, so also is the greater
degree ; for example, if ' capacity ' has more claim
than ' virtue ' to be considered the genus of ' self
control,' and ' virtue ' is the genus, so also is
' capacity.' The same considerations will be sui-
tably applied also to the species. For if A and B
have equal claim to be regarded as species of the
proposed genus, then, if one is a species, so also is
the other ; also, if that which is less generally held
to be a species, is a species, so also is that which is
more generally held to be so.

Further, for constructive purposes, you must (g) The
examine whether the genus has been predicated genus must
be predi-
in the category of essence of those things to which cated in the
it has been assigned, in the case where the species essence.
category of
assigned is not a single species but there are several
different species ; for then it will obviously be the
genus. If, however, the species assigned is a single
species, you must examine whether the genus is
predicated in the category of essence of other
species also ; for then, again, the result will be that
it is predicated of several different species.

Since some people hold that the differentia also (h) Method
is predicated of the species in the category of of distinguishing
essence, the genus must be distinguished from the genus and
differentia

475

128 a

ἀπὸ τῆς διαφορᾶς χρώμενον τοῖς εἰρημένοις
στοιχείοις, πρῶτον μὲν ὅτι τὸ γένος ἐπὶ πλέον
λέγεται τῆς διαφορᾶς· εἶθ' ὅτι κατὰ τὴν τοῦ τί
ἐστιν ἀπόδοσιν μᾶλλον ἁρμόττει τὸ γένος ἢ τὴν
25 διαφορὰν εἰπεῖν· ὁ γὰρ ζῷον εἴπας τὸν ἄνθρωπον
μᾶλλον δηλοῖ τί ἐστιν ὁ ἄνθρωπος ἢ ὁ πεζόν· καὶ
ὅτι ἡ μὲν διαφορὰ ποιότητα τοῦ γένους ἀεὶ σημαίνει, τὸ δὲ γένος τῆς διαφορᾶς οὔ· ὁ μὲν γὰρ
εἴπας πεζὸν ποιόν τι ζῷον λέγει, ὁ δὲ ζῷον εἴπας
οὐ λέγει ποιόν τι πεζόν.

30   Τὴν μὲν οὖν διαφορὰν ἀπὸ τοῦ γένους οὕτω
χωριστέον. ἐπεὶ δὲ δοκεῖ ⟨εἰ⟩[1] τὸ μουσικόν, ᾗ
μουσικόν ἐστιν, ἐπιστῆμόν τί ἐστι[2] καὶ ἡ μουσικὴ
ἐπιστήμη τις εἶναι, καὶ εἰ τὸ βαδίζον τῷ βαδίζειν
κινεῖται, ἡ βάδισις κίνησίς τις εἶναι, σκοπεῖν ἐν
ᾧ ἂν γένει βούλῃ τι κατασκευάσαι, τὸν εἰρημένον
35 τρόπον, οἷον εἰ τὴν ἐπιστήμην ὅπερ πίστιν, εἰ ὁ
ἐπιστάμενος ᾗ ἐπίσταται πιστεύει· δῆλον γὰρ ὅτι
ἡ ἐπιστήμη πίστις ἄν τις εἴη. τὸν αὐτὸν δὲ τρόπον
καὶ ἐπὶ τῶν ἄλλων τῶν τοιούτων.

Ἔτι ἐπεὶ τὸ παρεπόμενόν τινι ἀεὶ καὶ μὴ ἀντι-
στρέφον χαλεπὸν χωρίσαι τοῦ μὴ γένος εἶναι, ἂν
128 b τόδε μὲν τῷδ' ἔπηται παντί, τόδε δὲ τῷδε μὴ
παντί, οἷον τῇ νηνεμίᾳ ἡ ἠρεμία καὶ τῷ ἀριθμῷ

---

[1] εἰ add. Imelmann.
[2] Reading τί ἐστι for τι εἶναι with Imelmann.

differentia by the use of the elementary principles already mentioned, namely, (1) that the genus is more widely predicated than the differentia ; (2) that, in assigning the essence, it is more appropriate to state the genus than the differentia ; for he who describes ' man ' as an ' animal ' indicates his essence better than he who describes him as ' pedestrian ' ; and (3) that the differentia always indicates a quality of the genus, whereas the genus does not describe a quality of the differentia ; for he who uses the term ' pedestrian ' describes a certain kind of animal, but he who uses the term ' animal ' does not describe a certain kind of ' pedestrian.'

This, then, is how the differentia must be distinguished from the genus. Now, since it is generally *Practical examples.* held that, if that which is musical, in as much as it is musical, possesses a certain kind of knowledge, then also ' music ' is a kind of ' knowledge,' and that if that which walks moves by walking, then ' walking ' is a kind of ' motion '—you should examine on the principle described above any genus in which you wish to confirm the presence of something ; for example, if you wish to confirm that ' knowledge ' is a kind of ' belief,' you must see whether the man who knows, in as much as he knows, believes ; for then it is obvious that knowledge would be a kind of belief. And you must use the same method in the other cases of this kind.

Further, since it is difficult to distinguish that which always accompanies a thing and is not convertible with it and to show that it is not its genus —if A always accompanies B whereas B does not always accompany A ; for example, ' rest ' always accompanies ' calm,' and ' divisibility ' accompanies

τὸ διαιρετόν, ἀνάπαλιν δ' οὔ (τὸ γὰρ διαιρετὸν οὐ
πᾶν ἀριθμός, οὐδ' ἡ ἠρεμία νηνεμία), αὐτὸν μὲν
χρῆσθαι ὡς γένους ὄντος τοῦ ἀεὶ ἀκολουθοῦντος,
5 ὅταν μὴ ἀντιστρέφῃ θάτερον, ἄλλου δὲ προτείνοντος μὴ ἐπὶ πάντων ὑπακούειν. ἔνστασις δ'
αὐτοῦ ὅτι τὸ μὴ ὂν ἕπεται παντὶ τῷ γινομένῳ
(τὸ γὰρ γινόμενον οὐκ ἔστι) καὶ οὐκ ἀντιστρέφει
(οὐ γὰρ πᾶν τὸ μὴ ὂν γίνεται), ἀλλ' ὅμως οὐκ
ἔστι γένος τὸ μὴ ὂν τοῦ γιγομένου· ἁπλῶς γὰρ
οὐκ ἔστι τοῦ μὴ ὄντος εἴδη.

10 Περὶ μὲν οὖν τοῦ γένους, καθάπερ εἴρηται,
μετιτέον.

' number,' but the converse is not true (for the
divisible is not always a number, nor is rest always
a calm)—you should yourself deal with the matter
on the principle that what always accompanies a
thing is the genus whenever the other is not convertible with it ; but, when someone else makes the
proposition, you should not admit it in every case.
To this it may be objected that ' not-being ' always
accompanies ' that which is coming into being ' (for
that which is coming into being does not exist) and
is not convertible with it (for what does not exist
is not always coming into being), but that, nevertheless, ' not-being ' is not the genus of ' that which
is coming into being,' for ' not-being ' has no species
at all.

Such, then, are the methods which must be
followed in dealing with genus.

E

Ι. Πότερον δ' ἴδιον ἢ οὐκ ἴδιόν ἐστι τὸ εἰρημένον,
15 διὰ τῶνδε σκεπτέον.

Ἀποδίδοται δὲ τὸ ἴδιον ἢ καθ' αὑτὸ καὶ ἀεὶ ἢ
πρὸς ἕτερον καὶ ποτέ, οἷον καθ' αὑτὸ μὲν ἀνθρώπου τὸ ζῷον ἥμερον φύσει, πρὸς ἕτερον δὲ οἷον
ψυχῆς πρὸς σῶμα, ὅτι τὸ μὲν προστακτικὸν τὸ
δ' ὑπηρετικόν ἐστιν, ἀεὶ δὲ οἷον θεοῦ τὸ ζῷον
20 ἀθάνατον, ποτὲ δ' οἷον τοῦ τινὸς ἀνθρώπου τὸ
περιπατεῖν ἐν τῷ γυμνασίῳ.

Ἔστι δὲ τὸ πρὸς ἕτερον ἴδιον ἀποδιδόμενον ἢ
δύο προβλήματα ἢ τέτταρα. ἐὰν μὲν γὰρ τοῦ μὲν
ἀποδῷ τοῦ δ' ἀρνήσηται ταὐτὸ τοῦτο, δύο μόνον
προβλήματα γίνονται, καθάπερ τὸ ἀνθρώπου πρὸς
25 ἵππον ἴδιον ὅτι δίπουν ἐστίν. καὶ γὰρ ὅτι ἄνθρωπος
οὐ δίπουν ἐστὶν ἐπιχειροίη τις ἄν, καὶ ὅτι ὁ ἵππος
δίπουν· ἀμφοτέρως δ' ἂν κινοῖ τὸ ἴδιον. ἐὰν δ'
ἑκατέρου ἑκάτερον ἀποδῷ καὶ ἑκατέρου ἀπαρνηθῇ,
τέτταρα προβλήματα ἔσται, καθάπερ τὸ ἀνθρώπου
30 ἴδιον πρὸς ἵππον, ὅτι τὸ μὲν δίπουν τὸ δὲ τετράπουν ἐστίν. καὶ γὰρ ὅτι ἄνθρωπος οὐ δίπουν
καὶ ὅτι τετράπουν πέφυκεν ἔστιν ἐπιχειρεῖν, καὶ
480

BOOK V

I. WHETHER the attribute assigned is a *property* or not must be examined on the following principles :

Property is assigned either *essentially and permanently* or *relatively and temporarily*. For example, it is an essential property of man to be ' by nature a civilized animal.' A relative property may be exemplified by the relation of the soul to the body, namely, that the former gives orders and the latter obeys. An example of a permanent property is that of God as ' an immortal living being,' of a temporary property that of a particular man as ' walking about in a gymnasium.'

The assignment of a property relatively produces either two or four problems. If the disputant assigns it to one thing and denies it of another, two problems only arise ; for example, when it is stated as the property of a man in relation to a horse that he is a biped. For someone might argue that man is not a biped and that a horse is a biped ; by both these statements he would seek to remove the property. But if he assigns one of two attributes to each of two things and denies it of the other, there will be four problems ; for example, when he says that the property of a man in relation to a horse is that one is a biped and the other a quadruped. For then it is possible to argue that man is not a biped and that it is his nature to be

481

128 b

διότι ὁ ἵππος δίπουν καὶ διότι οὐ τετράπουν οἷόν
τ᾽ ἐπιχειρεῖν. ὅπως δ᾽ οὖν δειχθέντος ἀναιρεῖται
τὸ προκείμενον.

Ἔστι δὲ τὸ μὲν καθ᾽ αὑτὸ ἴδιον ὃ πρὸς ἅπαντα
35 ἀποδίδοται καὶ παντὸς χωρίζει, καθάπερ ἀνθρώπου
τὸ ζῷον θνητὸν ἐπιστήμης δεκτικόν. τὸ δὲ πρὸς
ἕτερον ὃ μὴ ἀπὸ παντὸς ἀλλ᾽ ἀπό τινος τακτοῦ
διορίζει, καθάπερ ἀρετῆς πρὸς ἐπιστήμην, ὅτι τὸ
μὲν ἐν πλείοσι, τὸ δ᾽ ἐν λογιστικῷ μόνον καὶ τοῖς
ἔχουσι λογιστικὸν πέφυκε γίνεσθαι. τὸ δ᾽ ἀεὶ ὃ
129 a κατὰ πάντα χρόνον ἀληθεύεται καὶ μηδέποτ᾽
ἀπολείπεται, καθάπερ τοῦ ζῴου τὸ ἐκ ψυχῆς καὶ
σώματος συγκείμενον. τὸ δὲ ποτὲ ὃ κατά τινα
χρόνον ἀληθεύεται καὶ μὴ ἐξ ἀνάγκης ἀεὶ παρέπε-
5 ται, καθάπερ τοῦ τινὸς ἀνθρώπου τὸ περιπατεῖν
ἐν ἀγορᾷ.

Ἔστι δὲ τὸ πρὸς ἄλλο ἴδιον ἀποδοῦναι τὸ διαφορὰν εἰπεῖν ἢ ἐν ἅπασι καὶ ἀεὶ ἢ ὡς ἐπὶ τὸ
πολὺ καὶ ἐν τοῖς πλείστοις, οἷον ἐν ἅπασι μὲν
καὶ ἀεί, καθάπερ τὸ ἀνθρώπου ἴδιον πρὸς ἵππον
10 ὅτι δίπουν· ἄνθρωπος μὲν γὰρ καὶ ἀεὶ καὶ πᾶς
ἐστὶ δίπους, ἵππος δ᾽ οὐδείς ἐστι δίπους οὐδέποτε.
ὡς ἐπὶ τὸ πολὺ δὲ καὶ ἐν τοῖς πλείστοις, καθάπερ
τὸ λογιστικοῦ ἴδιον πρὸς ἐπιθυμητικὸν καὶ θυμικὸν
τῷ τὸ μὲν προστάττειν τὸ δ᾽ ὑπηρετεῖν· οὔτε γὰρ
482

a quadruped, and it is also open to him to argue that the horse is a biped and that it is not a quadruped. If he can prove any one of these statements, the proposed attribute is destroyed.

An *essential* property is one which is assigned to something in contrast to everything else and sets a thing apart from everything else, for example, the property of man as ' a mortal living creature receptive of knowledge.' A *relative* property is one which distinguishes a thing not from everything else but from some specified thing ; for example, the property of virtue in relation to knowledge is that it is the nature of the former to come into being in a number of faculties, of the latter to come into being in the reasoning faculty only and in creatures possessing that faculty. A *permanent* property is one which is true at all times and never fails ; for example, that of a living creature that it is ' composed of soul and body.' A *temporary* property is one which is true at a particular time and is not always a necessary accompaniment, for example, that of a particular man as ' walking about in the market-place.'

To assign a property to something relatively to something else is to assert a difference between them either universally and permanently or usually and in the majority of cases. As an example of a universal and permanent difference we may take the property of man in relation to a horse, that he is a biped ; for man is always and in every case a biped, whereas no horse is ever a biped. A difference which is found usually and in most cases is exemplified in the property possessed by the reasoning faculty in relation to the appetitive and spirited faculty, namely, that the former commands while the latter serves ; for

483

129 a

τὸ λογιστικὸν πάντοτε προστάττει, ἀλλ' ἐνίοτε
καὶ προστάττεται, οὔτε τὸ ἐπιθυμητικὸν καὶ θυ-
15 μικὸν ἀεὶ προστάττεται, ἀλλὰ καὶ προστάττει
ποτέ, ὅταν ᾖ μοχθηρὰ ἡ ψυχὴ τοῦ ἀνθρώπου.

Τῶν δ' ἰδίων ἐστὶ λογικὰ μάλιστα τά τε καθ'
αὑτὰ καὶ ἀεὶ καὶ τὰ πρὸς ἕτερον. τὸ μὲν γὰρ πρὸς
ἕτερον ἴδιον πλείω προβλήματά ἐστι, καθάπερ
20 εἴπομεν καὶ πρότερον· ἢ γὰρ δύο ἢ τέτταρα ἐξ
ἀνάγκης γίνονται τὰ προβλήματα· πλείους οὖν οἱ
λόγοι γίνονται πρὸς ταῦτα. τὸ δὲ καθ' αὑτὸ καὶ
τὸ ἀεὶ πρὸς πολλὰ ἔστιν ἐπιχειρεῖν ἢ πρὸς πλείους
χρόνους παρατηρεῖν, τὸ μὲν καθ' αὑτὸ πρὸς πολλά·
πρὸς ἕκαστον γὰρ τῶν ὄντων δεῖ ὑπάρχειν αὐτῷ
25 τὸ ἴδιον, ὥστ' εἰ μὴ πρὸς ἅπαντα χωρίζεται, οὐκ
ἂν εἴη καλῶς ἀποδεδομένον τὸ ἴδιον. τὸ δ' ἀεὶ
πρὸς πολλοὺς χρόνους τηρεῖν· κἂν γὰρ εἰ μὴ
ὑπάρχει κἂν εἰ μὴ ὑπῆρξε κἂν εἰ μὴ ὑπάρξει, οὐκ
ἔσται ἴδιον. τὸ δὲ ποτὲ οὐκ ἐν ἄλλοις ἢ πρὸς τὸν
νῦν λεγόμενον χρόνον ἐπισκοποῦμεν· οὔκουν εἰσὶ
30 λόγοι πρὸς αὐτὸ πολλοί. λογικὸν δὲ τοῦτ' ἐστὶ
πρόβλημα πρὸς ὃ λόγοι γένοιντ' ἂν καὶ συχνοὶ
καὶ καλοί.

Τὸ μὲν οὖν πρὸς ἕτερον ἴδιον ῥηθὲν ἐκ τῶν περὶ
τὸ συμβεβηκὸς τόπων ἐπισκεπτέον ἐστίν, εἰ τῷ
μὲν συμβέβηκε τῷ δὲ μὴ συμβέβηκεν· περὶ δὲ
35 τῶν ἀεὶ καὶ τῶν καθ' αὑτὸ διὰ τῶνδε θεωρητέον.

ᵃ See 128 b 22 ff.

neither does the reasoning faculty always command but is also sometimes commanded, nor is the appetitive and spirited faculty always commanded but also sometimes commands, when a man's soul is depraved.

Of properties those which are most suitable for arguments are the essential and the permanent and the relative. For a relative property, as we have already said,[a] produces several problems; for the problems which arise are necessarily either two or four in number and, therefore, the arguments which arise in connexion with them are several. The essential and the permanent can be discussed in relation to a number of things and can be observed in relation to several periods of time. The essential can be discussed in contrast with a number of things; for the property must necessarily belong to it as contrasted with everything else that exists, and so, if the subject is not set apart by it in relation to everything else, the property cannot have been duly assigned. The permanent must be observed in relation to many periods of time; for if it does not at present exist, or, if it has not existed in the past, or if it is not going to exist in the future, it will not be a property at all. On the other hand, we examine the temporary only in relation to what we call present time; there are not, therefore, many arguments about it, whereas a problem suitable for argument is one about which numerous good arguments may arise.

What, then, has been called a relative property must be examined by means of the commonplaces about accident, to see whether it has happened to one thing but not to another; but permanent and essential properties must be viewed on the principles which now follow.

Suitability of each of the four kinds of property for discussion:

129 b II. Πρῶτον μὲν εἰ μὴ καλῶς ἀποδέδοται τὸ
ἴδιον ἢ καλῶς. τοῦ δὲ μὴ καλῶς ἢ καλῶς ἐστὶν
ἓν μέν, εἰ μὴ διὰ γνωριμωτέρων ἢ γνωριμωτέρων
κεῖται τὸ ἴδιον, ἀνασκευάζοντα μὲν εἰ μὴ διὰ
5 γνωριμωτέρων, κατασκευάζοντα δὲ εἰ διὰ γνωριμωτέρων. τοῦ δὲ μὴ διὰ γνωριμωτέρων ἐστὶ τὸ
μέν, εἰ ὅλως ἀγνωστότερόν ἐστι τὸ ἴδιον ὃ ἀποδίδωσι τούτου οὗ τὸ ἴδιον εἴρηκεν· οὐ γὰρ ἔσται
καλῶς κείμενον τὸ ἴδιον. γνώσεως γὰρ ἕνεκα τὸ
ἴδιον ποιούμεθα· διὰ γνωριμωτέρων οὖν ἀποδοτέον·
οὕτω γὰρ ἔσται κατανοεῖν ἱκανῶς μᾶλλον. οἷον
10 ἐπεὶ ὁ θεὶς πυρὸς ἴδιον εἶναι τὸ ὁμοιότατον ψυχῇ
ἀγνωστοτέρῳ κέχρηται τοῦ πυρὸς τῇ ψυχῇ (μᾶλλον γὰρ ἴσμεν τί ἐστι πῦρ ἢ ψυχή), οὐκ ἂν εἴη
καλῶς κείμενον ἴδιον πυρὸς τὸ ὁμοιότατον ψυχῇ.
τὸ δ᾽, εἰ μὴ γνωριμώτερόν ἐστι τόδε τῷδ᾽ ὑπάρχον.
δεῖ γὰρ μὴ μόνον εἶναι γνωριμώτερον τοῦ πράγ-
15 ματος, ἀλλὰ καὶ ὅτι τῷδ᾽ ὑπάρχει[1] γνωριμώτερον
ὑπάρχειν.[2] ὁ γὰρ μὴ εἰδὼς εἰ τῷδ᾽ ὑπάρχει, οὐδ᾽
εἰ τῷδ᾽ ὑπάρχει μόνῳ γνωριεῖ, ὥσθ᾽ ὁποτέρου
τούτων συμβάντος ἀσαφὲς γίνεται τὸ ἴδιον. οἷον
ἐπεὶ ὁ θεὶς πυρὸς ἴδιον τὸ ἐν ᾧ πρώτῳ ψυχὴ

[1] Reading ὑπάρχει with Wallies.
[2] Reading ὑπάρχειν with Wallies.

II. First, you must see whether the property has been rightly or wrongly assigned. One criterion of the rightness or wrongness of its assignment is to see whether the property is stated in terms which are less comprehensible or more comprehensible—in destructive criticism whether they are less comprehensible, in constructive argument whether they are more so. To prove that the terms are less comprehensible, one method is to see whether in general the property which your opponent assigns is less comprehensible than the subject of which he has stated it to be the property ; for then the property will not have been rightly stated. For it is for the sake of comprehension that we introduce the property ; therefore it must be assigned in more comprehensible terms, for it will thus be possible to understand it more adequately. For example, a man who has asserted that it is a property of ' fire ' ' to be very like the soul,' in using the term ' soul ' has employed something which is less comprehensible than fire (for we know better what ' fire ' is than what ' soul ' is), and so it would not be a correct statement of the property of fire to say that it is ' very like the soul.' Another method is to see whether the property is not more comprehensibly attributed to the subject ; for not only ought the property to be more comprehensible than the subject, but it ought to be more comprehensible that it is attributed to the subject. For anyone who does not know whether it is an attribute of the subject, will also not know whether it is the attribute of that subject alone, so that, whichever of these two things occurs, the property becomes a matter of obscurity. For example, a man who has stated that it is a property of ' fire '

Methods of testing whether a property has been correctly assigned : (a) The property must be more evident than its subject.

487

129 b

πέφυκεν εἶναι ἀγνωστοτέρῳ κέχρηται τοῦ πυρὸς
20 τῷ εἰ ἐν τούτῳ ὑπάρχει ψυχὴ καὶ εἰ ἐν πρώτῳ
ὑπάρχει, οὐκ ἂν εἴη καλῶς κείμενον ἴδιον πυρὸς
τὸ ἐν ᾧ πρώτῳ ψυχὴ πέφυκεν εἶναι. κατασκευάζοντα δὲ εἰ διὰ γνωριμωτέρων κεῖται τὸ ἴδιον, καὶ
εἰ διὰ γνωριμωτέρων καθ' ἑκάτερον τῶν τρόπων.
ἔσται γὰρ καλῶς κατὰ τοῦτο κείμενον τὸ ἴδιον·
25 τῶν γὰρ κατασκευαστικῶν τόπων τοῦ καλῶς οἱ
μὲν κατὰ τοῦτο μόνον οἱ δ' ἁπλῶς δείξουσιν ὅτι
καλῶς. οἷον ἐπεὶ ὁ εἴπας ζῴου ἴδιον τὸ αἴσθησιν
ἔχειν διὰ γνωριμωτέρων καὶ γνωριμώτερον ἀποδέδωκε τὸ ἴδιον καθ' ἑκάτερον τῶν τρόπων, εἴη
ἂν καλῶς ἀποδεδομένον κατὰ τοῦτο τοῦ ζῴου
ἴδιον τὸ αἴσθησιν ἔχειν.

30 Ἔπειτ' ἀνασκευάζοντα μὲν εἴ τι τῶν ὀνομάτων
τῶν ἐν τῷ ἰδίῳ ἀποδεδομένων πλεοναχῶς λέγεται
ἢ καὶ ὅλος ὁ λόγος πλείω σημαίνει· οὐ γὰρ ἔσται
καλῶς κείμενον τὸ ἴδιον. οἷον ἐπεὶ τὸ αἰσθάνεσθαι
πλείω σημαίνει, ἓν μὲν τὸ αἴσθησιν ἔχειν ἓν δὲ τὸ
35 αἰσθήσει χρῆσθαι, οὐκ ἂν εἴη τοῦ ζῴου ἴδιον καλῶς
130 a κείμενον τὸ αἰσθάνεσθαι πεφυκός. διὰ τοῦτο δ'
οὐ χρηστέον ἐστὶν οὔτ' ὀνόματι πλεοναχῶς λεγο-

to be 'that in which the soul by nature primarily exists' has brought in a consideration which is less comprehensible than fire, by raising the question whether the soul exists in it and whether it exists in it primarily; and so it could not have been rightly asserted as a property of fire that it is 'that in which the soul by nature primarily exists.' For constructive argument, on the other hand, you must see whether the property is stated in terms which are more comprehensible and whether they are more comprehensible in each of the two ways. For then the property will have been correctly stated in this respect; for of the commonplaces used to support the correctness of the assignment, some will show that it is correctly assigned in this respect only, others that it is correctly assigned absolutely. For example, the man who has asserted as the property of a 'living creature' that it is 'possessed of sensation' has both employed more comprehensible terms and made the property more comprehensible in each of the two ways; and so to be 'possessed of sensation' would in this respect have been correctly assigned as a property of 'living creature.'

In the next place, for destructive argument, you must see whether any of the terms assigned in the property is employed in several senses, or whether the whole expression also has more than one signification; for if so, the property will not have been correctly stated. For example, since 'to be sentient' signifies more than one thing, namely, (a) 'to be possessed of sensation' and (b) 'to exercise sensation,' 'to be by nature sentient' would not be correctly assigned as a property of 'living creature.' Therefore, one must not use as signifying property either a word or an

(b) The assignment of a property is subverted: (1) If the term used has several significations.

489

130 a

μένῳ οὔτε λόγῳ τῷ τὸ ἴδιον σημαίνοντι, διότι τὸ
πλεοναχῶς λεγόμενον ἀσαφὲς ποιεῖ τὸ ῥηθέν,
ἀποροῦντος τοῦ μέλλοντος ἐπιχειρεῖν πότερον λέγει
5 τῶν πλεοναχῶς λεγομένων· τὸ γὰρ ἴδιον τοῦ
μαθεῖν χάριν ἀποδίδοται. ἔτι δὲ πρὸς τούτοις
ἀναγκαῖόν ἐστιν ἔλεγχόν τινα γίνεσθαι τοῖς οὕτως
ἀποδιδοῦσι τὸ ἴδιον, ὅταν ἐπὶ τοῦ διαφωνοῦντός
τις ποιῇ τὸν συλλογισμὸν τοῦ πλεοναχῶς λεγομένου.
κατασκευάζοντα δὲ εἰ μὴ πλείω σημαίνει μήτε
10 τῶν ὀνομάτων μηδὲν μήθ᾽ ὅλος ὁ λόγος· ἔσται
γὰρ καλῶς κατὰ τοῦτο κείμενον τὸ ἴδιον. οἷον
ἐπεὶ οὔτε τὸ σῶμα πολλὰ δηλοῖ οὔτε τὸ εὐκινητότατον εἰς τὸν ἄνω τόπον οὔτε τὸ σύνολον τὸ ἐκ
τούτων συντιθέμενον, εἴη ἂν καλῶς κείμενον κατὰ
τοῦτο πυρὸς ἴδιον σῶμα τὸ εὐκινητότατον εἰς
τὸν ἄνω τόπον.

15 Ἔπειτ᾽ ἀνασκευάζοντα μὲν εἰ πλεοναχῶς λέγεται τοῦτο οὗ τὸ ἴδιον ἀποδίδωσι, μὴ διώρισται
δὲ τὸ τίνος αὐτῶν ἴδιον τίθησιν· οὐ γὰρ ἔσται
καλῶς ἀποδεδομένον τὸ ἴδιον. δι᾽ ἃς δ᾽ αἰτίας,
οὐκ ἄδηλόν ἐστιν ἐκ τῶν πρότερον εἰρημένων·
τὰ γὰρ αὐτὰ συμβαίνειν ἀναγκαῖόν ἐστιν. οἷον
20 ἐπεὶ τὸ ἐπίστασθαι τοῦτο πολλὰ σημαίνει (τὸ μὲν
γὰρ ἐπιστήμην ἔχειν αὐτό, τὸ δ᾽ ἐπιστήμῃ χρῆσθαι
αὐτό, τὸ δ᾽ ἐπιστήμην εἶναι αὐτοῦ, τὸ δ᾽ ἐπιστήμῃ
χρῆσθαι αὐτοῦ), οὐκ ἂν εἴη τοῦ ἐπίστασθαι τοῦτο

490

expression which is used with several meanings, because anything which has several meanings renders the statement obscure, since he who is about to argue is doubtful which of the various meanings his opponent is using ; for the property is assigned in order to promote understanding. Further, besides this, an opportunity is necessarily offered to refute those who assign the property in this way, by basing one's syllogism on the irrelevant meaning of a term used in several senses. In constructive argument, on the other hand, you must see whether any of the terms or the expression as a whole does not bear more than one meaning ; for the property will then be correctly asserted in this respect. For example, since neither ' body,' nor ' that which most easily moves upwards,' nor the whole expression made up by putting the two terms together has more than one meaning, it would be correct in this respect to assert that it is a property of fire that it is ' the body which most easily moves upwards.'

In the next place, for destructive criticism, you must see whether the term to which your opponent is assigning the property is used in several senses but no distinction has been made as to which of them it is whose property he asserts it to be ; for then the property will not have been correctly assigned. The reason for this is quite obvious from what has already been said ; for the results must necessarily be the same. For example, since ' knowledge of this ' signifies several different things—for it means (a) that it has knowledge, (b) that it uses knowledge, (c) that there is knowledge of it and (d) that there is use of the knowledge of it—no property of ' knowledge of this ' could be correctly assigned unless it has been

(2) If there is a multifarious predication of the subject.

130 a

καλῶς ἴδιον ἀποδεδομένον μὴ διορισθέντος τοῦ
τίνος τίθησιν αὐτῶν τὸ ἴδιον. κατασκευάζοντα
25 δὲ εἰ μὴ λέγεται πολλαχῶς τοῦτο οὗ τὸ ἴδιον
τίθησιν, ἀλλ' ἔστιν ἓν καὶ ἁπλοῦν· ἔσται γὰρ
καλῶς κατὰ τοῦτο κείμενον τὸ ἴδιον. οἷον ἐπεὶ ὁ
ἄνθρωπος λέγεται ἕν, εἴη ἂν καλῶς κείμενον κατὰ
τοῦ ἀνθρώπου ἴδιον τὸ ζῷον ἥμερον φύσει.

Ἔπειτ' ἀνασκευάζοντα μὲν εἰ πλεονάκις εἴρηται
30 τὸ αὐτὸ ἐν τῷ ἰδίῳ. πολλάκις γὰρ λανθάνουσι
τοῦτο ποιοῦντες καὶ ἐν τοῖς ἰδίοις, καθάπερ καὶ
ἐν τοῖς ὅροις. οὐκ ἔσται δὲ καλῶς κείμενον τὸ
τοῦτο πεπονθὸς ἴδιον· ταράττει γὰρ τὸν ἀκούοντα
πλεονάκις λεχθέν· ἀσαφὲς οὖν ἀναγκαῖόν ἐστι γίνεσθαι, καὶ πρὸς τούτοις ἀδολεσχεῖν δοκοῦσιν.
35 ἔσται δὲ συμπῖπτον τὸ πλεονάκις εἰπεῖν τὸ αὐτὸ
κατὰ δύο τρόπους, καθ' ἕνα μὲν ὅταν ὀνομάσῃ
πλεονάκις τὸ αὐτό, καθάπερ εἴ τις ἴδιον ἀποδοίη
πυρὸς σῶμα τὸ λεπτότατον τῶν σωμάτων (οὗτος
γὰρ πλεονάκις εἴρηκε τὸ σῶμα), δεύτερον δ' ἂν
τις μεταλαμβάνῃ τοὺς λόγους ἀντὶ τῶν ὀνομάτων,
130 b καθάπερ εἴ τις ἀποδοίη γῆς ἴδιον οὐσία ἡ μάλιστα
κατὰ φύσιν φερομένη τῶν σωμάτων εἰς τὸν κάτω
τόπον, ἔπειτα μεταλάβοι ἀντὶ τῶν σωμάτων τὸ
οὐσιῶν τοιωνδί· ἓν γὰρ καὶ ταὐτόν ἐστι σῶμα
καὶ οὐσία τοιαδί. ἔσται γὰρ οὗτος τὸ οὐσία
5 πλεονάκις εἰρηκώς, ὥστ' οὐδέτερον ἂν εἴη καλῶς
κείμενον τῶν ἰδίων. κατασκευάζοντα δὲ εἰ μηδενὶ
χρῆται πλεονάκις ὀνόματι τῷ αὐτῷ· ἔσται γὰρ

definitely stated of which of these meanings the property is being asserted. For constructive argument one must see if that of which one is stating the property does not bear several meanings, but is one and single; for then the property will be correctly stated in this respect. For example, since 'man' is used in only one sense, 'animal by nature civilized' would be correctly stated as a property in the case of 'man.'

Next, for destructive criticism, you must see whether the same term has been used more than once in describing the property; for, without it being noticed, people often do this in describing properties, just as they do in definitions also. A property to which this has occurred will not be correctly stated; for frequent repetition confuses the hearer, and this necessarily causes obscurity, and, besides, an impression of nonsense is created. Repetition will be likely to occur in two ways; firstly, when a man uses the same word more than once—for example, when he assigns to 'fire' the property of being 'the body which is lightest of bodies' (for he has used the word body more than once)—; secondly, when he puts definitions in place of words; for instance if he were to assign to 'earth' the property of being 'the substance which most of all bodies tends by its nature to be carried downwards' and were then to replace 'bodies' by 'substances of a certain kind'; for 'body' and 'substance of a certain kind' are one and the same thing. He will thus have repeated the term 'substance,' and so neither of the properties would be correctly stated. For constructive argument, on the other hand, one must see whether he avoids using the same term more than once; for

(3) If the same term is used more than once in describing the property.

493

κατὰ τοῦτο καλῶς ἀποδεδομένον τὸ ἴδιον. οἷον
ἐπεὶ ὁ εἴπας ἀνθρώπου ἴδιον ζῷον ἐπιστήμης
δεκτικὸν οὐ κέχρηται τῷ αὐτῷ πολλάκις ὀνόματι,
10 εἴη ἂν κατὰ τοῦτο καλῶς ἀποδεδομένον τοῦ ἀνθρώπου τὸ ἴδιον.

Ἔπειτ' ἀνασκευάζοντα μὲν εἰ τοιοῦτόν τι ἀποδέδωκεν ἐν τῷ ἰδίῳ ὄνομα, ὃ πᾶσιν ὑπάρχει. ἀ-
χρεῖον γὰρ ἔσται τὸ μὴ χωρίζον ἀπό τινων, τὸ δ'
ἐν τοῖς ἰδίοις λεγόμενον χωρίζειν δεῖ, καθάπερ
15 καὶ τὰ ἐν τοῖς ὅροις· οὔκουν ἔσται καλῶς κείμενον
τὸ ἴδιον. οἷον ἐπεὶ ὁ θεὶς ἐπιστήμης ἴδιον ὑπόληψιν ἀμετάπειστον ὑπὸ λόγου, ἓν ὄν, τοιούτῳ
τινὶ κέχρηται ἐν τῷ ἰδίῳ τῷ ἑνὶ ὃ πᾶσιν ὑπάρχει,
οὐκ ἂν εἴη καλῶς κείμενον τὸ τῆς ἐπιστήμης
ἴδιον. κατασκευάζοντα δὲ εἰ μηδενὶ κέχρηται
κοινῷ, ἀλλ' ἀπό τινος χωρίζοντι· ἔσται γὰρ καλῶς
20 κείμενον κατὰ τοῦτο τὸ ἴδιον. οἷον ἐπεὶ ὁ εἴπας
ζῴου ἴδιον τὸ ψυχὴν ἔχειν οὐδενὶ κέχρηται κοινῷ,
εἴη ἂν κατὰ τοῦτο καλῶς κείμενον ζῴου ἴδιον τὸ
ψυχὴν ἔχειν.

Ἔπειτ' ἀνασκευάζοντα μὲν εἰ πλείω ἴδια ἀποδίδωσι τοῦ αὐτοῦ, μὴ διορίσας ὅτι πλείω τίθησιν·
25 οὐ γὰρ ἔσται καλῶς κείμενον τὸ ἴδιον. καθάπερ

then the property will have been correctly assigned in this respect. For example, he who has stated as a property of man that he is ' a living creature receptive of knowledge ' has not used the same word more than once, and so the property of man would be in this respect correctly assigned.

Next, for destructive criticism, you must see whether he has assigned in the property any term which has a universal application, (for anything which does not distinguish the subject from any other things will be useless, but what is stated in properties, like what is stated in definitions, must make a distinction) and so the property will not be correctly assigned. For example, he who has laid down as a property of ' knowledge ' that it is ' a conception which cannot be changed by argument, because it is one,' has made use in the property of a term, namely, the ' one,' of such a kind as to be universally applicable, and so the property of knowledge cannot have been correctly assigned. For constructive purposes, on the other hand, you must see if he has used, not a common term, but one which distinguishes the subject from something else ; for then the property will have been correctly assigned in this respect. For example, he who has said that ' the possession of a soul ' is a property of ' living creature ' has not used any common term, and so ' the possession of a soul ' would in this respect be correctly assigned as a property of ' living creature.' *(4) If the term assigned has universal application.*

Next, for destructive criticism, see whether your opponent assigns more than one property to the same thing without definitely stating that he is laying down more than one ; for then the property will not have been correctly stated. For, just as in definitions *(5) If many properties are assigned to the same thing without distinction.*

γὰρ οὐδ' ἐν τοῖς ὅροις δεῖ παρὰ τὸν δηλοῦντα λόγον
τὴν οὐσίαν προσκεῖσθαί τι πλέον, οὕτως οὐδ' ἐν
τοῖς ἰδίοις παρὰ τὸν ποιοῦντα λόγον ἴδιον τὸ ῥηθὲν
οὐδὲν προσαποδοτέον· ἀχρεῖον γὰρ γίνεται τὸ
τοιοῦτον. οἷον ἐπεὶ ὁ εἴπας ἴδιον πυρὸς σῶμα τὸ
30 λεπτότατον καὶ κουφότατον πλείω ἀποδέδωκεν
ἴδια (ἑκάτερον γὰρ κατὰ μόνου τοῦ πυρὸς ἀληθές
ἐστιν εἰπεῖν), οὐκ ἂν εἴη καλῶς κείμενον ἴδιον
πυρὸς σῶμα τὸ λεπτότατον καὶ κουφότατον.
κατασκευάζοντα δ' εἰ μὴ πλείω τοῦ αὐτοῦ τὰ
ἴδια ἀποδέδωκεν, ἀλλ' ἕν· ἔσται γὰρ κατὰ τοῦτο
35 καλῶς κείμενον τὸ ἴδιον. οἷον ἐπεὶ ὁ εἴπας ὑγροῦ
ἴδιον σῶμα τὸ εἰς ἅπαν σχῆμα ἀγόμενον ἓν ἀποδέδωκε τὸ ἴδιον ἀλλ' οὐ πλείω, εἴη ἂν κατὰ τοῦτο
καλῶς κείμενον τὸ τοῦ ὑγροῦ ἴδιον.

III. Ἔπειτ' ἀνασκευάζοντα μὲν εἰ αὐτῷ προσκέχρηται οὗ τὸ ἴδιον ἀποδίδωσιν, ἢ τῶν αὐτοῦ
131 a τινί· οὐ γὰρ ἔσται καλῶς κείμενον τὸ ἴδιον. τοῦ
γὰρ μαθεῖν χάριν ἀποδίδοται τὸ ἴδιον· αὐτὸ μὲν
οὖν αὑτῷ ὁμοίως ἄγνωστόν ἐστι, τὸ δέ τι τῶν
αὐτοῦ ὕστερον· οὔκουν ἐστὶ γνωριμώτερον. ὥστ'
οὐ γίνεται διὰ τούτων μᾶλλόν τι μαθεῖν. οἷον
5 ἐπεὶ ὁ εἴπας ζῴου ἴδιον οὐσίαν ἧς εἶδός ἐστιν

also nothing more ought to be added beyond the
expression which shows the essence, so too in properties nothing ought to be assigned beyond the
expression which makes up the property which is
asserted; for such a proceeding proves useless. For
example, a man who has said that it is a property of
'fire' to be 'the most subtle and lightest body' has
assigned more than one property (for it is true to
predicate each of these terms of fire alone), and so
'the most subtle and lightest body' would not be
correctly stated as a property of fire. For constructive
argument, on the other hand, you must see if the
properties which your opponent has assigned to the
same thing are not several but he has assigned only
one; for then the property will be correctly stated
in this respect. For example, a man who has said
that it is a property of 'liquid' to be 'a body which
can be induced to assume any shape' has assigned
one thing and not more than one as its property, and
so the property of liquid would in this respect be
correctly stated.

III. Next, for destructive criticism, you must see (6) If the
whether he has introduced either the actual subject actual sub-
whose property he is rendering or something be- tained in
longing to it; for then the property will not be property.
correctly stated. For the property is assigned to
promote understanding; the subject, then, itself
is as incomprehensible as ever, while anything that
belongs to it is posterior to it and, therefore, not more
comprehensible, and so the result of this method is
not to understand the subject any better. For
example, he who has said that it is a property of
'living creature' to be 'a substance of which man
is a species' has introduced something which belongs

ἄνθρωπος τινὶ προσκέχρηται τῶν τούτου, οὐκ ἂν
εἴη καλῶς κείμενον τὸ ἴδιον. κατασκευάζοντα δὲ
εἰ μήτε αὐτῷ μήτε τῶν αὐτοῦ μηδενὶ χρῆται.
ἔσται γὰρ καλῶς κατὰ τοῦτο κείμενον τὸ ἴδιον.
οἷον ἐπεὶ ὁ θεὶς ζῴου ἴδιον τὸ ἐκ ψυχῆς καὶ σώματος συγκείμενον οὔτε αὐτῷ οὔτε τῶν αὐτοῦ
10 οὐδενὶ προσκέχρηται, εἴη ἂν καλῶς κατὰ τοῦτο
ἀποδεδομένον τὸ τοῦ ζῴου ἴδιον.

Τὸν αὐτὸν δὲ τρόπον καὶ ἐπὶ τῶν ἄλλων σκεπτέον
ἐστὶ τῶν μὴ ποιούντων ἢ ποιούντων γνωριμώτερον,
ἀνασκευάζοντα μὲν εἴ τινι προσκέχρηται ἢ ἀντι-
15 κειμένῳ ἢ ὅλως ἅμα τῇ φύσει ἢ ὑστέρῳ τινί· οὐ
γὰρ ἔσται καλῶς κείμενον τὸ ἴδιον. τὸ μὲν γὰρ
ἀντικείμενον ἅμα τῇ φύσει, τὸ δ' ἅμα τῇ φύσει
καὶ τὸ ὕστερον οὐ ποιεῖ γνωριμώτερον. οἷον ἐπεὶ
ὁ εἴπας ἀγαθοῦ ἴδιον ὃ κακῷ μάλιστ' ἀντίκειται,
τῷ ἀντικειμένῳ προσκέχρηται τοῦ ἀγαθοῦ, οὐκ
20 ἂν εἴη τοῦ ἀγαθοῦ καλῶς ἀποδεδομένον τὸ ἴδιον.
κατασκευάζοντα δὲ εἰ μηδενὶ προσκέχρηται μήτ'
ἀντικειμένῳ μήτε ὅλως ἅμα τῇ φύσει μήθ' ὑστέρῳ·
ἔσται γὰρ κατὰ τοῦτο καλῶς ἀποδεδομένον τὸ
ἴδιον. οἷον ἐπεὶ ὁ θεὶς ἐπιστήμης ἴδιον ὑπόληψιν
τὴν πιστοτάτην οὐδενὶ προσκέχρηται οὔτ' ἀντι-

to 'living creature,' and so the property cannot be correctly stated. For constructive purposes you must see whether he avoids introducing either the subject itself or anything belonging to it; for then the property will be correctly stated in this respect. For example, he who has stated that it is a property of ' living creature ' to be ' composed of soul and body ' has not introduced the subject itself nor anything which belongs to it, and so the property of living creature would in this respect have been correctly assigned.

In the same manner inquiry must be made regarding the other terms which do or do not make the subject more comprehensible. For destructive criticism, you must see whether your opponent has introduced anything either opposite to the subject or, in general, naturally simultaneous with it or posterior to it; for then the property will not be correctly stated. For the opposite of a thing is naturally simultaneous with it, and what is naturally simultaneous and what is posterior to a thing do not make it more comprehensible. For example, he who has said that it is a property of ' good ' to be ' that which is most opposed to bad ' has introduced the opposite of ' good,' and so the property of ' good ' could not have been correctly assigned. For constructive argument, on the other hand, you must see whether he has avoided introducing anything which is either opposite to the subject, or naturally simultaneous with it, or posterior to it; for then the property will have been correctly assigned in this respect. For example, he who has stated that it is a property of ' knowledge ' to be ' the most trustworthy conception ' has not introduced anything either opposite

(7) If the opposite of the subject, or something less clear than it, is assigned as a property.

499

25 κειμένῳ οὔθ' ἅμα τῇ φύσει οὔθ' ὑστέρῳ, εἴη ἂν
κατὰ τοῦτο καλῶς κείμενον τὸ τῆς ἐπιστήμης
ἴδιον.

Ἔπειτ' ἀνασκευάζοντα μὲν εἰ τὸ μὴ ἀεὶ παρεπόμενον ἴδιον ἀποδέδωκεν, ἀλλὰ τοῦτο ὃ γίνεταί
ποτε μὴ ἴδιον· οὐ γὰρ ἔσται καλῶς εἰρημένον τὸ
30 ἴδιον. οὔτε γὰρ ἐφ' ᾧ καταλαμβάνομεν ὑπάρχον
αὐτό, κατὰ τούτου καὶ τοὔνομα ἐξ ἀνάγκης ἀλη-
θεύεται· οὔτ' ἐφ' ᾧ καταλαμβάνεται μὴ ὑπάρχον,
κατὰ τούτου ἐξ ἀνάγκης οὐ ῥηθήσεται τοὔνομα.
ἔτι δὲ πρὸς τούτοις οὐδ' ὅτε ἀποδέδωκε τὸ ἴδιον,
ἔσται φανερὸν εἰ ὑπάρχει, εἴπερ τοιοῦτόν ἐστιν
35 οἷον ἀπολείπειν. οὔκουν ἔσται σαφὲς τὸ ἴδιον· οἷον
ἐπεὶ ὁ θεὶς ζῴου ἴδιον τὸ κινεῖσθαί ποτε καὶ ἑστάναι τοιοῦτον ἀποδέδωκε τὸ ἴδιον ὃ οὐ γίνεταί ποτε
ἴδιον, οὐκ ἂν εἴη καλῶς κείμενον τὸ ἴδιον. κατασκευάζοντα δὲ εἰ τὸ ἐξ ἀνάγκης ἀεὶ ὂν ἴδιον ἀπο-
131 b δέδωκεν· ἔσται γὰρ καλῶς κείμενον τὸ ἴδιον
κατὰ τοῦτο. οἷον ἐπεὶ ὁ θεὶς ἀρετῆς ἴδιον ὃ τὸν
ἔχοντα ποιεῖ σπουδαῖον τὸ ἀεὶ παρεπόμενον ἴδιον
ἀποδέδωκεν, εἴη ἂν κατὰ τοῦτο καλῶς ἀποδεδομένον τὸ τῆς ἀρετῆς ἴδιον.

5 Ἔπειτ' ἀνασκευάζοντα μὲν εἰ τὸ νῦν ἴδιον
ἀποδιδοὺς μὴ διωρίσατο ὅτι τὸ νῦν ἴδιον ἀπο-
δίδωσιν· οὐ γὰρ ἔσται καλῶς κείμενον τὸ ἴδιον.

to the subject, or naturally simultaneous with it, or posterior to it, and so the property of knowledge will be correctly stated in this respect.

Next, for destructive criticism, you must see whether he has assigned as a property something which does not always accompany the subject but sometimes ceases to be a property; for then the property will not have been correctly asserted. For neither is the name of the subject necessarily true of that to which we find that the property belongs, nor will it necessarily not be applied to that to which we find that the property does not belong. Further, besides this, even when he has assigned the property, it will not be clear whether it belongs, since it is of such a kind as to fail; and so the property will not be clear. For example, he who has stated that it is a property of 'living creature' 'sometimes to move and sometimes to stand still' has assigned the kind of property which is sometimes not a property; and so the property would not be correctly stated. For constructive argument, on the other hand, you must see if he has assigned what must of necessity always be a property; for then the property will be correctly stated in this respect. For example, he who has stated that it is a property of ' virtue ' to be ' that which makes its possessor good ' has assigned as a property that which always accompanies its subject, and so the property of virtue would have been correctly assigned in this respect. *(8) If the property assigned does not always accompany the subject.*

Next, for destructive criticism, you must see whether, in assigning what is a property at the present moment, he has omitted to state definitely that he is assigning what is a property at the moment; for then the property will not be correctly stated. For, *(9) If the assigner of a present property does not distinguish the time.*

πρῶτον μὲν γὰρ τὸ παρὰ τὸ ἔθος γινόμενον ἅπαν
διορισμοῦ προσδεῖται· εἰώθασι δ᾽ ὡς ἐπὶ τὸ πολὺ
πάντες τὸ ἀεὶ παρακολουθοῦν ἴδιον ἀποδιδόναι.
10 δεύτερον δὲ ἄδηλός ἐστιν ὁ μὴ διορισάμενος εἰ
τὸ νῦν ἴδιον ἐβούλετο θεῖναι· οὔκουν δοτέον ἐστὶν
ἐπιτιμήσεως σκῆψιν. οἷον ἐπεὶ ὁ θέμενος τοῦ τινὸς ἀνθρώπου ἴδιον τὸ καθῆσθαι μετά τινος τὸ νῦν
ἴδιον τίθησιν, οὐκ ἂν εἴη καλῶς τὸ ἴδιον ἀποδε-
δωκώς, εἴπερ μὴ διορισάμενος εἶπεν. κατασκευά-
15 ζοντα δ᾽ εἰ τὸ νῦν ἴδιον ἀποδιδοὺς διορισάμενος
ἔθηκεν ὅτι τὸ νῦν ἴδιον τίθησιν· ἔσται γὰρ καλῶς
κείμενον κατὰ τοῦτο τὸ ἴδιον. οἷον ἐπεὶ ὁ εἴπας
τοῦ τινὸς ἀνθρώπου ἴδιον τὸ περιπατεῖν νῦν δια-
στειλάμενος ἔθηκε τοῦτο, καλῶς ἂν εἴη κείμενον
τὸ ἴδιον.

Ἔπειτ᾽ ἀνασκευάζοντα μὲν εἰ τοιοῦτο ἀποδέδωκε
20 τὸ ἴδιον, ὃ φανερὸν μή ἐστιν ἄλλως ὑπάρχον ἢ
αἰσθήσει· οὐ γὰρ ἔσται καλῶς κείμενον τὸ ἴδιον.
ἅπαν γὰρ τὸ αἰσθητὸν ἔξω γινόμενον τῆς αἰσθήσεως
ἄδηλον γίνεται· ἀφανὲς γάρ ἐστιν εἰ ἔτι ὑπάρχει,
διὰ τὸ τῇ αἰσθήσει μόνον γνωρίζεσθαι. ἔσται δ᾽
ἀληθὲς τοῦτο ἐπὶ τῶν μὴ ἐξ ἀνάγκης ἀεὶ παρακο-
25 λουθούντων. οἷον ἐπεὶ ὁ θέμενος ἡλίου ἴδιον ἄστρον
φερόμενον ὑπὲρ γῆς τὸ λαμπρότατον τοιούτῳ
κέχρηται ἐν τῷ ἰδίῳ τῷ ὑπὲρ γῆς φέρεσθαι, ὃ τῇ

in the first place, any departure from custom needs to be definitely indicated, and men are usually accustomed to assign as property that which always accompanies the subject. Secondly, anyone who has not definitely laid down whether it was his intention to state what is a property at the moment, is obscure ; no pretext, therefore, should be given for criticism. For example, he who has stated that it is a property of a certain man to be sitting with someone, states what is a property at the moment, and so he would not have assigned the property correctly, since he spoke without any definite indication. For constructive argument, you must see whether, in assigning what is a property at the moment, he stated definitely that he was laying down what was a property *at the moment* ; for then the property will be correctly stated in this respect. For instance, he who has said that it is a property of a particular man to be walking about *at the moment*, has made this distinction in his statement, and so the property would be correctly stated.

Next, for destructive criticism, you should see whether the property which he has assigned is of such a kind that its presence is manifest only to sensation ; for then the property will not be correctly stated. For every object of sensation, when it passes outside the range of sensation, becomes obscure ; for it is not clear whether it still exists, because it is comprehended only by sensation. This will be true of such attributes as do not necessarily and always attend upon the subject. For example, he who has stated that it is a property of the sun to be ' the brightest star that moves above the earth ' has employed in the property something of a kind which

(10) If the property assigned is evident only to the senses.

ARISTOTLE

αἰσθήσει γνωρίζεται, οὐκ ἂν εἴη καλῶς τὸ τοῦ ἡλίου
ἀποδεδομένον ἴδιον· ἄδηλον γὰρ ἔσται, ὅταν δύῃ

30 ὁ ἥλιος, εἰ φέρεται ὑπὲρ γῆς, διὰ τὸ τὴν αἴσθησιν
τότε ἀπολείπειν ἡμᾶς. κατασκευάζοντα δ᾽ εἰ
τοιοῦτον ἀποδέδωκε τὸ ἴδιον, ὃ μὴ τῇ αἰσθήσει
φανερόν ἐστιν ἢ ὃ αἰσθητὸν ὂν ἐξ ἀνάγκης ὑπάρχον
δηλόν ἐστιν· ἔσται γὰρ κατὰ τοῦτο καλῶς κείμενον
τὸ ἴδιον. οἷον ἐπεὶ ὁ θέμενος ἐπιφανείας ἴδιον ὃ
πρῶτον κέχρωσται αἰσθητῷ μέν τινι προσκέχρηται

35 τῷ κεχρῶσθαι, τοιούτῳ δ᾽ ὃ φανερόν ἐστιν ὑπάρχον ἀεί, εἴη ἂν κατὰ τοῦτο καλῶς ἀποδεδομένον
τὸ τῆς ἐπιφανείας ἴδιον.

Ἔπειτ᾽ ἀνασκευάζοντα μὲν εἰ τὸν ὅρον ὡς ἴδιον
ἀποδέδωκεν· οὐ γὰρ ἔσται καλῶς κείμενον τὸ

132 a ἴδιον· οὐ γὰρ δεῖ δηλοῦν τὸ τί ἦν εἶναι τὸ ἴδιον.
οἷον ἐπεὶ ὁ εἴπας ἀνθρώπου ἴδιον ζῷον πεζὸν
δίπουν τὸ τί ἦν εἶναι σημαῖνον ἀποδέδωκε τοῦ
ἀνθρώπου ἴδιον, οὐκ ἂν εἴη τὸ τοῦ ἀνθρώπου ἴδιον
καλῶς ἀποδεδομένον. κατασκευάζοντα δὲ εἰ ἀντι-

5 κατηγορούμενον μὲν ἀποδέδωκε τὸ ἴδιον, μὴ τὸ
τί ἦν εἶναι δὲ δηλοῦν. ἔσται γὰρ κατὰ τοῦτο
καλῶς ἀποδεδομένον τὸ ἴδιον. οἷον ἐπεὶ ὁ θεὶς
ἀνθρώπου ἴδιον ζῷον ἥμερον φύσει ἀντικατηγορούμενον μὲν ἀποδέδωκε τὸ ἴδιον, οὐ τὸ τί ἦν

504

is comprehensible only by sensation, namely, 'moving above the earth'; and so the property of the sun would not have been correctly assigned, for it will not be manifest, when the sun sets, whether it is still moving above the earth, because sensation then fails us. For constructive argument, on the other hand, you must see whether the property which he has assigned is such that it is not manifest to the sensation, or, being sensible, obviously belongs of necessity to the subject; for then the property will be in this respect correctly stated. For example, he who has stated that it is a property of 'surface' to be 'that which is the first thing to be coloured,' has employed a sensible attribute, namely 'to be coloured,' but an attribute which obviously is always present, and so the property of 'surface' will in this respect have been correctly assigned.

Next, for destructive criticism, you must see whether he has assigned the definition as a property; for then the property will not be correctly stated, for the property ought not to show the essence. For example, he who has said that it is a property of man to be 'a pedestrian biped animal' has assigned as a property of man that which signifies his essence, and so the man's property will not have been correctly assigned. For constructive argument, on the other hand, you must see whether he has assigned as the property a predicate which is convertible with the subject but does not signify the essence; for then the property will have been correctly assigned in this respect. For example, he who has stated that it is a property of man to be 'by nature a civilized animal' has assigned a property which is convertible with the subject but does not signify the essence; and so the

(11) If what is assigned as a property is the definition.

505

εἶναι δὲ δηλοῦν, εἴη ἂν κατὰ τοῦτο καλῶς ἀποδεδομένον τὸ ἴδιον τοῦ ἀνθρώπου.

10 Ἔπειτ᾽ ἀνασκευάζοντα μὲν εἰ μὴ εἰς τὸ τί ἐστι
θεὶς[1] ἀποδέδωκε τὸ ἴδιον. δεῖ γὰρ τῶν ἰδίων,
καθάπερ καὶ τῶν ὅρων, τὸ πρῶτον ἀποδίδοσθαι
γένος, ἔπειθ᾽ οὕτως ἤδη προσάπτεσθαι τὰ λοιπά,
καὶ χωρίζειν. ὥστε τὸ μὴ τοῦτον τὸν τρόπον
κείμενον ἴδιον οὐκ ἂν εἴη καλῶς ἀποδεδομένον.
15 οἷον ἐπεὶ ὁ εἴπας ζῴου ἴδιον τὸ ψυχὴν ἔχειν οὐκ
ἔθηκεν εἰς τὸ τί ἐστι τὸ ζῷον, οὐκ ἂν εἴη καλῶς
κείμενον τὸ τοῦ ζῴου ἴδιον. κατασκευάζοντα δὲ
εἴ τις εἰς τὸ τί ἐστι θεὶς οὗ τὸ ἴδιον ἀποδίδωσι, τὰ
λοιπὰ προσάπτει· ἔσται γὰρ κατὰ τοῦτο καλῶς
ἀποδεδομένον τὸ ἴδιον. οἷον ἐπεὶ ὁ θεὶς ἀνθρώπου
20 ἴδιον ζῷον ἐπιστήμης δεκτικὸν εἰς τὸ τί ἐστι θεὶς
ἀπέδωκε τὸ ἴδιον, εἴη ἂν κατὰ τοῦτο καλῶς
κείμενον τὸ ἴδιον τοῦ ἀνθρώπου.

IV. Πότερον μὲν οὖν καλῶς ἢ οὐ καλῶς ἀποδέδοται τὸ ἴδιον, διὰ τῶνδε σκεπτέον. πότερον
δ᾽ ἴδιόν ἐστιν ὅλως τὸ εἰρημένον ἢ οὐκ ἴδιον, ἐκ
25 τῶνδε θεωρητέον. οἱ γὰρ ἁπλῶς κατασκευάζοντες
τὸ ἴδιον ὅτι καλῶς κεῖται τόποι οἱ αὐτοὶ ἔσονται
τοῖς ἴδιον ὅλως ποιοῦσιν· ἐν ἐκείνοις οὖν ῥηθή-
σονται.

---

[1] Reading ἐστι θεὶς with Dennison for ἐστιν ὁ θεὶς.

[a] i.e. from other members of the same genus.

property of man will have been correctly assigned in this respect.

Next, for destructive criticism, you must see whether he has assigned the property without placing the subject in its essence ; for in properties, as in definitions, the first term to be assigned ought to be the genus, and then, and not till then, the other terms should be added and should distinguish the subject.[a] The property, therefore, which is not stated in this manner will not have been correctly assigned. For example, he who has said that it is a property of 'living creature' 'to possess a soul' has not placed 'living creature' in its essence, and so the property of 'living creature' would not be correctly stated. For constructive argument, on the other hand, you must see if he has placed the subject, whose property he is assigning, in its essence and then adds the other terms ; for then the property will have been correctly assigned in this respect. For example, he who has stated as a property of 'man' that he is 'a living creature receptive of knowledge' has placed the subject in its essence and then assigned the property, and so the property of 'man' would be correctly stated in this respect.

(12) If the property is assigned without mentioning the essence of the subject.

IV. It is by these methods, then, that examination should be made to see whether the property has been correctly or incorrectly assigned. Whether that which is asserted to be a property is really a property or not a property at all, must be considered on the following principles ; for the commonplaces which confirm absolutely that the property is correctly stated will be the same as those which make it a property at all, and will, therefore, be included in the statement of them.

Rules for testing whether a term belongs as a property at all :

507

132 a

Πρῶτον μὲν οὖν ἀνασκευάζοντα ἐπιβλέπειν ἐφ'
ἕκαστον οὗ τὸ ἴδιον ἀποδέδωκεν, [οἷον] εἰ μηδενὶ
ὑπάρχει, ἢ εἰ μὴ κατὰ τοῦτο ἀληθεύεται, ἢ εἰ μή
30 ἐστιν ἴδιον ἑκάστου αὐτῶν κατ' ἐκεῖνο οὗ τὸ ἴδιον
ἀποδέδωκεν· οὐ γὰρ ἔσται ἴδιον τὸ κείμενον εἶναι
ἴδιον. οἷον ἐπεὶ κατὰ τοῦ γεωμετρικοῦ οὐκ ἀληθεύεται τὸ ἀνεξαπάτητον εἶναι ὑπὸ λόγου (ἀπα-
τᾶται γὰρ ὁ γεωμετρικὸς ἐν τῷ ψευδογραφεῖσθαι),
35 ὑπὸ λόγου. κατασκευάζοντα δ' εἰ κατὰ παντὸς
ἀληθεύεται καὶ κατὰ τοῦτ' ἀληθεύεται· ἔσται γὰρ
ἴδιον τὸ κείμενον ⟨μὴ⟩ εἶναι[1] ἴδιον. οἷον ἐπεὶ τὸ
132 b ζῷον ἐπιστήμης δεκτικὸν κατὰ παντὸς ἀνθρώπου
ἀληθεύεται καὶ ᾗ ἄνθρωπος, εἴη ἂν ἀνθρώπου ἴδιον
τὸ ζῷον ἐπιστήμης δεκτικόν. ἔστι δ' ὁ τόπος
οὗτος ἀνασκευάζοντι μέν, εἰ μὴ καθ' οὗ τοὔνομα,
5 καὶ ὁ λόγος ἀληθεύεται, καὶ εἰ μὴ καθ' οὗ ὁ λόγος,
καὶ τοὔνομα ἀληθεύεται· κατασκευάζοντι δέ, εἰ
καθ' οὗ τοὔνομα, καὶ ὁ λόγος, καὶ εἰ καθ' οὗ ὁ
λόγος, καὶ τοὔνομα κατηγορεῖται.

Ἔπειτ' ἀνασκευάζοντα μὲν εἰ μὴ καθ' οὗ τοὔνομα, καὶ ὁ λόγος, καὶ εἰ μὴ καθ' οὗ ὁ λόγος, καὶ

---

[1] Reading ⟨μὴ⟩ εἶναι with Pacius, Waitz and Strache.

[a] i.e. that given in the property.
[b] i.e. that of the subject.

First of all, then, for destructive criticism, you must look at each subject of which he has assigned the property, and see whether it does not belong to any of them, or whether it is not true in the particular respect in question, or whether it is not a property of each of them as regards that of which he has assigned the property ; for then that which is stated to be a property will not be a property. For example, seeing that it is not true to say about a geometrician that he is ' not liable to be deceived by argument ' (for he is deceived when a false figure is drawn), it could not be a property of a scientific man ' not to be deceived by argument.' For constructive purposes, on the other hand, you must see whether the property is true in every case and in the particular respect in question ; for then what is stated not to be a property will be a property. For example, seeing that ' a living creature receptive of knowledge ' is a true description of every man and true *qua* man, it would be a property of man to be ' a living creature receptive of knowledge.' The object of this commonplace is, for destructive criticism, to see whether the description [a] is untrue of that of which the name [b] is true, and whether the name is untrue of that of which the description is true ; on the other hand, in constructive argument, the object is to see whether the description also is predicated of that of which the name is predicated, and whether the name also is predicated of that of which the description is predicated.

Next, for destructive criticism, you must see whether the description is not asserted of that of which the name is asserted, and if the name is not asserted of that of which the description is asserted ;

It is not a property (a) if it does not concur with each individual.

(b) If the description is not asserted of that of which the

509

10 τοὔνομα λέγεται· οὐ γὰρ ἔσται ἴδιον τὸ κείμενον
ἴδιον εἶναι. οἷον ἐπεὶ τὸ μὲν ζῷον ἐπιστήμης
μετέχον ἀληθεύεται κατὰ τοῦ θεοῦ, ὁ δ᾽ ἄνθρωπος
οὐ κατηγορεῖται, οὐκ ἂν εἴη τοῦ ἀνθρώπου ἴδιον
ζῷον ἐπιστήμης μετέχον. κατασκευάζοντα δὲ εἰ
καθ᾽ οὗ ὁ λόγος, καὶ τοὔνομα κατηγορεῖται, καὶ
15 καθ᾽ οὗ τοὔνομα, καὶ ὁ λόγος κατηγορεῖται· ἔσται
γὰρ ἴδιον τὸ κείμενον μὴ εἶναι ἴδιον. οἷον ἐπεὶ
καθ᾽ οὗ τὸ ψυχὴν ἔχειν, τὸ ζῷον ἀληθεύεται, καὶ
καθ᾽ οὗ τὸ ζῷον, τὸ ψυχὴν ἔχειν, εἴη ἂν τὸ ψυχὴν
ἔχειν τοῦ ζῴου ἴδιον.

Ἔπειτ᾽ ἀνασκευάζοντα μὲν εἰ τὸ ὑποκείμενον
20 ἴδιον ἀπέδωκε τοῦ ἐν τῷ ὑποκειμένῳ λεγομένου·
οὐ γὰρ ἔσται ἴδιον τὸ κείμενον ἴδιον. οἷον ἐπεὶ
ὁ ἀποδοὺς ἴδιον τοῦ λεπτομερεστάτου σώματος τὸ
πῦρ τὸ ὑποκείμενον ἀποδέδωκε τοῦ κατηγορουμένου ἴδιον, οὐκ ἂν εἴη τὸ πῦρ σώματος τοῦ
λεπτομερεστάτου ἴδιον. διὰ τοῦτο δ᾽ οὐκ ἔσται
25 τὸ ὑποκείμενον τοῦ ἐν τῷ ὑποκειμένῳ ἴδιον, ὅτι
τὸ αὐτὸ πλειόνων ἔσται καὶ διαφόρων τῷ εἴδει
ἴδιον. τῷ γὰρ αὐτῷ πλείω τινὰ διάφορα τῷ
εἴδει ὑπάρχει κατὰ μόνου λεγόμενα, ὧν ἔσται
πάντων ἴδιον τὸ ὑποκείμενον, ἐάν τις οὕτω τιθῆται
τὸ ἴδιον. κατασκευάζοντα δ᾽ εἰ τὸ ἐν τῷ ὑπο-

for then the property which is stated will not be a property. For example, since a ' living creature which partakes of knowledge ' is true of ' God ' but ' man ' is not predicated of ' God,' a ' living creature which partakes of knowledge ' would not be a property of man. For constructive argument, on the other hand, you must see whether the name also is predicated of that of which the description is predicated, and whether the description also is predicated of that of which the name is predicated ; for then that which is asserted not to be a property will be a property. For example, since ' living creature ' is true of that of which ' possessing a soul ' is true, and ' possessing a soul ' is true of that of which ' living creature ' is true, ' possessing a soul ' would be a property of ' living being.'

Next, for destructive criticism, you must see whether he has assigned the subject as a property of that which is said to be ' in the subject ' ; for then what is stated to be a property will not be a property. For example, he who has assigned ' fire ' as a property of ' the body consisting of the most subtle particles,' has assigned the subject as a property of its predicate, and so ' fire ' could not be a property of ' the body consisting of the most subtle particles.' The subject will not be a property of that which is in the subject for this reason, namely, that the same thing will then be the property of a number of specifically different things. For a number of specifically different things belong to the same thing, being asserted to belong to it alone, of all of which the subject will be a property, if one states the property in this manner. For constructive argument, on the other hand, you must see whether he assigned what

511

30 κειμένῳ ἀπέδωκεν ἴδιον τοῦ ὑποκειμένου. ἔσται
γὰρ ἴδιον τὸ κείμενον μὴ εἶναι ἴδιον, ἐάνπερ κατὰ
μόνων κατηγορῆται, ὧν εἴρηται τὸ ἴδιον. οἷον
ἐπεὶ ὁ εἴπας γῆς ἴδιον σῶμα τὸ βαρύτατον τῷ
εἴδει τοῦ ὑποκειμένου ἀπέδωκε τὸ ἴδιον κατὰ
μόνου λεγόμενον τοῦ πράγματος, καὶ ὡς τὸ ἴδιον
κατηγορεῖται, εἴη ἂν τὸ τῆς γῆς ἴδιον ὀρθῶς
κείμενον.

35 Ἔπειτ᾿ ἀνασκευάζοντα μὲν εἰ κατὰ μέθεξιν
ἀπέδωκε τὸ ἴδιον· οὐ γὰρ ἔσται ἴδιον τὸ κείμενον
133 a εἶναι ἴδιον. τὸ γὰρ κατὰ μέθεξιν ὑπάρχον εἰς τὸ
τί ἦν εἶναι συμβάλλεται· εἴη δ᾿ ἂν τὸ τοιοῦτο
διαφορά τις κατά τινος ἑνὸς εἴδους λεγομένη.
οἷον ἐπεὶ ὁ εἴπας ἀνθρώπου ἴδιον τὸ πεζὸν δίπουν
κατὰ μέθεξιν ἀπέδωκε τὸ ἴδιον, οὐκ ἂν εἴη τἀν-
5 θρώπου ἴδιον τὸ πεζὸν δίπουν. κατασκευάζοντα
δὲ εἰ μὴ κατὰ μέθεξιν ἀπέδωκε τὸ ἴδιον, μηδὲ τὸ
τί ἦν εἶναι δηλοῦν, ἀντικατηγορουμένου τοῦ πράγ-
ματος· ἔσται γὰρ ἴδιον τὸ κείμενον μὴ εἶναι ἴδιον.
οἷον ἐπεὶ ὁ θεὶς ζῴου ἴδιον τὸ αἰσθάνεσθαι πεφυκὸς
οὔτε κατὰ μέθεξιν ἀπέδωκεν ἴδιον οὔτε τὸ τί ἦν
10 εἶναι δηλοῦν, ἀντικατηγορουμένου τοῦ πράγματος,
εἴη ἂν ζῴου ἴδιον τὸ αἰσθάνεσθαι πεφυκός.

Ἔπειτ᾿ ἀνασκευάζοντα μὲν εἰ μὴ ἐνδέχεται ἅμα

512

is in the subject as a property of the subject; for then what is stated not to be a property will be a property, if it is predicated only of those things of which it has been asserted to be the property. For example, he who has said that it is a property of ' earth ' to be ' specifically the heaviest body ' has assigned as a property of the subject something which is asserted of that thing alone, and it is predicated as the property; and so the property of ' earth ' would be correctly stated.

Next, for destructive criticism, you must see whether he assigned the property as something of which the subject partakes; for then that which is stated to be a property will not be a property. For that which belongs because the subject partakes of it is a contribution to its essence, and, as such, would be a differentia attributed to some one species. For example, he who has said that it is a property of ' man ' to be a ' pedestrian biped ' has assigned the property as something of which the subject partakes, and so ' pedestrian biped ' could not be a property of ' man.' For constructive argument, on the other hand, you must see whether he has failed to assign the property as something of which the subject partakes, or as showing the essence, the subject being convertible; for then what is stated not to be a property will be a property. For example, he who has stated that it is a property of ' living creature ' to be ' naturally possessed of sensation ' has assigned a property neither as partaken of by the subject nor as showing its essence, the subject being convertible; and so to be ' naturally possessed of sensation ' would be a property of ' living creature.'

Next, for destructive criticism, you must see

(d) If that is assigned as a property which belongs to the subject as a differentia.

(e) If that is assigned

513

133 a

ὑπάρχειν τὸ ἴδιον, ἀλλ' ἢ ὕστερον ἢ πρότερον ἢ
οὗ τοὔνομα· οὐ γὰρ ἔσται ἴδιον τὸ κείμενον εἶναι
15 ἴδιον, ἢ οὐδέποτε ἢ οὐκ ἀεί. οἷον ἐπεὶ ἐνδέχεται
καὶ πρότερόν τινι ὑπάρξαι καὶ ὕστερον τὸ βαδίζειν
διὰ τῆς ἀγορᾶς ἢ τὸ ἄνθρωπος, οὐκ ἂν εἴη τὸ
βαδίζειν διὰ τῆς ἀγορᾶς τοῦ ἀνθρώπου ἴδιον, ἢ
οὐδέποτ' ἢ οὐκ ἀεί. κατασκευάζοντα δὲ εἰ ἅμα
ἐξ ἀνάγκης ἀεὶ ὑπάρχει, μήτε ὅρος ὂν μήτε δια-
20 φορά· ἔσται γὰρ ἴδιον τὸ κείμενον μὴ εἶναι ἴδιον.
οἷον ἐπεὶ τὸ ζῷον ἐπιστήμης δεκτικὸν ἅμα ἐξ
ἀνάγκης ἀεὶ ὑπάρχει καὶ τὸ ἄνθρωπος, οὔτε διαφορὰ ὂν οὔθ' ὅρος, εἴη ἂν τὸ ζῷον ἐπιστήμης
δεκτικὸν τοῦ ἀνθρώπου ἴδιον.

Ἔπειτ' ἀνασκευάζοντα μὲν εἰ τῶν αὐτῶν, ἢ
25 ταὐτά ἐστι, μή ἐστι τὸ αὐτὸ ἴδιον· οὐ γὰρ ἔσται
ἴδιον τὸ κείμενον εἶναι ἴδιον. οἷον ἐπεὶ οὐκ ἔστι
διωκτοῦ τὸ φαίνεσθαί τισιν ἀγαθὸν ἴδιον, οὐδ' ἂν
αἱρετοῦ εἴη ἴδιον τὸ φαίνεσθαί τισιν ἀγαθόν·
ταὐτὸν γάρ ἐστι τὸ διωκτὸν καὶ τὸ αἱρετόν.
κατασκευάζοντα δ' εἰ τοῦ αὐτοῦ, ἢ ταὐτό ἐστι,
30 ταὐτὸ ἴδιον· ἔσται γὰρ ἴδιον τὸ κείμενον μὴ εἶναι

514

whether the property cannot possibly belong simul- as a pro-
taneously but must belong as something posterior or perty which is prior or
prior to that to which the name belongs ; for then posterior to
that which is stated to be a property will not be a the subject.
property, that is to say, it will be either never or
not always a property. For example, since it is possible for ' walking through the market-place ' to be
an attribute of something as both prior and posterior
to the attribute ' man,' ' walking through the market-
place ' could not be a property of ' man,' that is to
say, it would be either never or not always a property.
For constructive argument you must see whether the
property always belongs of necessity simultaneously,
being neither a definition nor a differentia ; for then
what is stated not to be a property will be a property.
For example, ' animal receptive of knowledge ' always belongs of necessity simultaneously with ' man '
and is neither a differentia nor a definition, and so
' animal receptive of knowledge ' would be a property
of ' man.'

Next, for destructive criticism, you must see whether (f) If the
the same thing fails to be a property of things which same thing fails to be
are the same as the subject, in so far as they are the the pro-
same ; for then what is stated to be a property will not perty of the same things,
be a property. For example, since it is not a property in so far as
of an ' object of pursuit ' to ' appear good to certain they are the
people,' neither could it be a property of an ' object same.
of choice ' to ' appear good to certain people ' ;
for ' object of pursuit ' and ' object of choice ' are the
same thing. For constructive argument, on the
other hand, you must see whether the same thing is
a property of something which is the same as the
subject, in so far as it is the same ; for then what is
stated not to be a property will be a property. For

133 a

ἴδιον. οἷον ἐπεὶ ἀνθρώπου, ᾗ ἄνθρωπός ἐστι,
λέγεται ἴδιον τὸ τριμερῆ ψυχὴν ἔχειν, καὶ βροτοῦ,
ᾗ βροτός ἐστιν, εἴη ἂν ἴδιον τὸ τριμερῆ ψυχὴν
ἔχειν. χρήσιμος δ' ὁ τόπος οὗτος καὶ ἐπὶ τοῦ
συμβεβηκότος· τοῖς γὰρ αὐτοῖς, ᾗ ταὐτά ἐστι,
ταὐτὰ δεῖ ὑπάρχειν ἢ μὴ ὑπάρχειν.

35 Ἔπειτ' ἀνασκευάζοντα μὲν εἰ τῶν αὐτῶν τῷ εἴδει μὴ ταὐτὸν ἀεὶ τῷ εἴδει τὸ ἴδιόν ἐστιν· οὐδὲ γὰρ
133 b τοῦ εἰρημένου ἔσται ἴδιον τὸ κείμενον εἶναι ἴδιον.
οἷον ἐπεὶ ταὐτόν ἐστι τῷ εἴδει ἄνθρωπος καὶ ἵππος, οὐκ ἀεὶ δὲ τοῦ ἵππου ἐστὶν ἴδιον τὸ ἑστάναι
ὑφ' αὑτοῦ, οὐκ ἂν εἴη τοῦ ἀνθρώπου ἴδιον τὸ κινεῖσθαι ὑφ' αὑτοῦ· ταὐτὸν γάρ ἐστι τῷ εἴδει τὸ
5 κινεῖσθαι καὶ ἑστάναι ὑφ' αὑτοῦ, ᾗ ζῷον δ' ἐστὶν
ἑκάτερον αὐτῶν συμβέβηκεν.[1] κατασκευάζοντα δ'
εἰ τῶν αὐτῶν τῷ εἴδει ταὐτὸν ἀεὶ τὸ ἴδιον· ἔσται
γὰρ ἴδιον τὸ κείμενον μὴ εἶναι ἴδιον. οἷον ἐπεὶ
ἀνθρώπου ἐστὶν ἴδιον τὸ εἶναι πεζὸν δίπουν, καὶ
ὄρνιθος ἂν εἴη ἴδιον τὸ εἶναι πτηνὸν δίπουν· ἑκά-
10 τερον γὰρ τούτων ἐστὶ ταὐτὸν τῷ εἴδει, ᾗ τὰ μὲν
ὡς ὑπὸ τὸ αὐτὸ γένος ἐστὶν εἴδη, ὑπὸ τὸ ζῷον
ὄντα, τὰ δὲ ὡς γένους διαφοραί, τοῦ ζῴου. οὗτος
δ' ὁ τόπος ψευδής ἐστιν, ὅταν τὸ μὲν ἕτερον τῶν
λεχθέντων ἑνί τινι μόνῳ ὑπάρχῃ εἴδει, τὸ δ' ἕτερον
πολλοῖς, καθάπερ τὸ πεζὸν τετράπουν.

15 Ἐπεὶ δὲ τὸ ταὐτὸν καὶ τὸ ἕτερον πολλαχῶς

---

[1] ᾗ ζῷον ⟨δ'⟩ ἐστὶν ἑκάτερον αὐτῶν συμβέβηκεν˙ Strache-
Wallies.

---

[a] Plato, *Republic* iv. 435 b ff.
[b] *i.e.* there are many pedestrian quadrupeds besides the
horse, but man is the only pedestrian biped.

example, since it is said to be a property of ' man,'
qua man, ' to possess a tripartite soul,' [a] it would also
be a property of ' mortal,' *qua* mortal, ' to possess a
tripartite soul.' This commonplace is useful also in
dealing with an accident; for the same things must
necessarily belong or not belong to the same things
in so far as they are the same.

Next, for destructive criticism you must see
whether the property of things which are the same
in kind are not always the same in kind; for then
neither will that which is stated to be a property be
a property of the proposed subject. For example,
since man and horse are the same in kind and it is not
always a property of a horse to stand still of his own
accord, neither could it be a property of a man to
move of his own accord, since to stand still and to
move of one's own accord are the same in kind and
have occurred in as much as each of them is an animal.
For constructive argument, on the other hand, you
must see whether the property of things which are
the same in kind is always the same; for then what
is stated not to be a property will be a property. For
example, since it is a property of ' man ' to be a
' pedestrian biped,' it would also be a property of
' bird ' to be a ' winged biped '; for each of these is
the same in kind, in as much as ' man ' and ' bird '
are the same, being species falling under the same
genus, namely ' animal,' while ' pedestrian ' and
' winged ' are the same, being differentiae of the
genus, namely ' animal.' This commonplace is misleading when one of the properties mentioned belongs
to one species only, while the other belongs to many,
as, for instance, ' pedestrian quadruped.' [b]

Now, since ' same ' and ' different ' have several

(*g*) If the
property of
things
which are
specifically
the same is
not always
specifically
the same.

(*h*) If wha
is the pro

133 b
λέγεται, ἔργον ἐστὶ σοφιστικῶς λαμβάνοντι ἑνὸς
ἀποδοῦναι καὶ μόνου τινὸς τὸ ἴδιον. τὸ γὰρ
ὑπάρχον τινὶ ᾧ συμβέβηκέ τι, καὶ τῷ συμβεβηκότι
ὑπάρξει λαμβανομένῳ μετὰ τοῦ ᾧ συμβέβηκεν,
οἷον τὸ ὑπάρχον ἀνθρώπῳ καὶ λευκῷ ἀνθρώπῳ
20 ὑπάρξει, ἂν ᾖ λευκὸς ἄνθρωπος, καὶ τὸ λευκῷ δὲ
ἀνθρώπῳ ὑπάρχον καὶ ἀνθρώπῳ ὑπάρξει. δια-
βάλλοι δ᾽ ἄν τις τὰ πολλὰ τῶν ἰδίων, τὸ ὑποκείμενον ἄλλο μὲν καθ᾽ αὑτὸ ποιῶν ἄλλο δὲ μετὰ τοῦ
συμβεβηκότος, οἷον ἄλλο μὲν ἄνθρωπον εἶναι
25 λέγων ἄλλο δὲ λευκὸν ἄνθρωπον, ἔτι δὲ ἕτερον
ποιῶν τὴν ἕξιν καὶ τὸ κατὰ τὴν ἕξιν λεγόμενον.
τὸ γὰρ τῇ ἕξει ὑπάρχον καὶ τῷ κατὰ τὴν ἕξιν
λεγομένῳ ὑπάρξει, καὶ τὸ τῷ κατὰ τὴν ἕξιν λεγομένῳ ὑπάρχον καὶ τῇ ἕξει ὑπάρξει. οἷον ἐπεὶ ὁ
ἐπιστήμων κατὰ τὴν ἐπιστήμην λέγεται διακεῖ-
30 σθαι, οὐκ ἂν εἴη τῆς ἐπιστήμης ἴδιον τὸ ἀμετάπειστον ὑπὸ λόγου· καὶ γὰρ ὁ ἐπιστήμων ἔσται
ἀμετάπειστος ὑπὸ λόγου. κατασκευάζοντα δὲ
ῥητέον ὅτι οὐκ ἔστιν ἕτερον ἁπλῶς τὸ ᾧ συμβέβηκε καὶ τὸ συμβεβηκὸς μετὰ τοῦ ᾧ συμβέβηκε
λαμβανόμενον, ἀλλ᾽ ἄλλο λέγεται τῷ ἕτερον εἶναι
αὐτοῖς τὸ εἶναι· οὐ ταὐτὸν γάρ ἐστιν ἀνθρώπῳ τε
35 τὸ εἶναι ἀνθρώπῳ καὶ λευκῷ ἀνθρώπῳ τὸ εἶναι
ἀνθρώπῳ λευκῷ. ἔτι δὲ θεωρητέον ἐστὶ παρὰ τὰς
134 a πτώσεις, λέγοντα διότι οὔθ᾽ ὁ ἐπιστήμων ἔσται
τὸ ἀμετάπειστον ὑπὸ λόγου ἀλλ᾽ ὁ ἀμετάπειστος
ὑπὸ λόγου, οὔθ᾽ ἡ ἐπιστήμη τὸ ἀμετάπειστον ὑπὸ

meanings, it is a difficult task with a sophistical opponent to assign the property of some one thing taken by itself. For that which belongs to something to which an accident is attached will also belong to the accident taken with the subject to which it is attached. For example, what belongs to 'man' will also belong to 'white man,' if there is a white man, and what belongs to 'white man' will also belong to 'man.' One might, therefore, misrepresent the majority of properties by making the subject one thing when taken by itself and another thing when taken with its accident, saying, for example, that 'man' is one thing and 'white man' another thing, and, further, by making a difference between the state and that which is described in the terms of the state. For that which belongs to the state will belong also to that which is described in the terms of the state, and that which belongs to what is described in the terms of the state will belong also to the state. For example, since the condition of a scientist is described in the terms of his science, it cannot be a property of 'science' to be 'proof against the persuasion of argument,' for then the scientist also will be 'proof against the persuasion of argument.' For constructive purposes you should say that that to which the accident belongs is not absolutely different from the accident taken with that to which it is accidental, but is called 'other than it' because their kind of being is different; for it is not the same thing for a 'man' to be a 'man' and for a 'white man' to be a 'white man.' Further, you should look at the inflexions, maintaining that the scientist is not 'that which' but 'he who' is proof against the persuasion of argument, while Science is

perty of the subject alone is not the property when joined to an accident and vice versa.

519

ARISTOTLE

134 a

λόγου ἀλλ' ἡ ἀμετάπειστος ὑπὸ λόγου· πρὸς γὰρ
τὸν πάντως ἐνιστάμενον πάντως ἀντιτακτέον ἐστίν.

5 V. Ἔπειτ' ἀνασκευάζοντα μὲν εἰ τὸ φύσει ὑπάρχον βουλόμενος ἀποδοῦναι τοῦτον τὸν τρόπον
τίθησι τῇ λέξει, ὥστε τὸ ἀεὶ ὑπάρχον σημαίνειν·
δόξειε γὰρ ἂν κινεῖσθαι τὸ κείμενον εἶναι ἴδιον.
οἷον ἐπεὶ ὁ εἴπας ἀνθρώπου ἴδιον τὸ δίπουν βούλεται μὲν τὸ φύσει ὑπάρχον ἀποδιδόναι, σημαίνει
10 δὲ τῇ λέξει τὸ ἀεὶ ὑπάρχον, οὐκ ἂν εἴη ἀνθρώπου
ἴδιον τὸ δίπουν· οὐ γὰρ πᾶς ἄνθρωπός ἐστι δύο
πόδας ἔχων. κατασκευάζοντα δ' εἰ βούλεται τὸ
φύσει ὑπάρχον ἴδιον ἀποδιδόναι καὶ τῇ λέξει τοῦτον τὸν τρόπον σημαίνει· οὐ γὰρ κινήσεται κατὰ
τοῦτο τὸ ἴδιον. οἷον ἐπεὶ ὁ ἀνθρώπου ἴδιον ἀπο-
15 διδοὺς τὸ ζῷον ἐπιστήμης δεκτικὸν καὶ βούλεται
καὶ τῇ λέξει σημαίνει τὸ φύσει ὑπάρχον ἴδιον,
οὐκ ἂν κινοῖτο κατὰ τοῦτο, ὡς οὐκ ἔστιν ἀνθρώπου ἴδιον τὸ ζῷον ἐπιστήμης δεκτικόν.

Ἔτι ὅσα λέγεται ὡς κατ' ἄλλο τι πρῶτον ἢ ὡς
πρῶτον αὐτό, ἔργον ἐστὶν ἀποδοῦναι τῶν τοιούτων
20 τὸ ἴδιον· ἐὰν μὲν γὰρ τοῦ κατ' ἄλλο τι ἴδιον
ἀποδῷς, καὶ κατὰ τοῦ πρώτου ἀληθεύσεται, ἐὰν
δὲ τοῦ πρώτου θῇς, καὶ τοῦ κατ' ἄλλο κατηγο-

---

[a] Scientist being masculine and Science feminine in Greek.

520

not 'that which' but 'she who'[a] is proof against the persuasion of argument; for against the man who uses every kind of objection, you should use every kind of opposition.

V. Next, for destructive criticism, you should see whether your opponent, while he intends to assign to the subject an attribute which naturally belongs, expresses himself in such language as to signify one which always belongs; for then that which is stated to be a property would seem to be subverted. For example, he who has said that 'biped' is a property of man intends to assign an attribute which belongs by nature, but, by the language which he uses, signifies an attribute which always belongs; and so 'biped' could not be a property of man, since every man is not in possession of two feet. For constructive purposes, on the other hand, you must see whether he intends to assign as a property that which belongs by nature and signifies this by the language which he uses; for then the property will not be subverted in this respect. For example, he who assigns as a property of man that he is 'an animal receptive of knowledge.' both has the intention and succeeds in signifying by his language the property which belongs by nature, and so 'an animal receptive of knowledge' cannot be subverted in this respect on the ground that it is not a property of man.

Various rules for subverting a proposition: (a) Observe whether an attribute which belongs naturally is assigned as always belonging.

Further, it is a difficult task to assign the property of such things as are described primarily in the terms of something else or primarily in themselves; for if you assign a property of that which is described in the terms of something else, it will be true also of that which is primary; whereas if you state it of something which is primary, it will also be predicated of

[Note on the difficulty of rendering things which are called as they are primarily after something else,

521

ῥηθήσεται. οἷον ἐὰν μέν τις ἐπιφανείας ἴδιον
ἀποδῷ τὸ κεχρῶσθαι, καὶ κατὰ σώματος ἀληθεύσεται τὸ κεχρῶσθαι, ἐὰν δὲ σώματος, καὶ
25 κατ' ἐπιφανείας κατηγορηθήσεται. ὥστε οὐ καθ' οὗ
ὁ λόγος, καὶ τοὔνομα ἀληθεύσεται.

Συμβαίνει δ' ἐν ἐνίοις τῶν ἰδίων ὡς ἐπὶ τὸ πολὺ
γίνεσθαί τινα ἁμαρτίαν παρὰ τὸ μὴ διορίζεσθαι
πῶς καὶ τίνων τίθησι τὸ ἴδιον. ἅπαντες γὰρ ἐπι-
χειροῦσιν ἀποδιδόναι τὸ ἴδιον ἢ τὸ φύσει ὑπάρ-
30 χον, καθάπερ ἀνθρώπου τὸ δίπουν, ἢ τὸ ὑπάρχον,
καθάπερ ἀνθρώπου τινὸς τὸ τέτταρας δακτύλους
ἔχειν, ἢ εἴδει, καθάπερ πυρὸς τὸ λεπτομερέστατον, ἢ ἁπλῶς, καθάπερ ζῴου τὸ ζῆν, ἢ κατ'
ἄλλο, καθάπερ ψυχῆς τὸ φρόνιμον, ἢ ὡς τὸ πρῶτον, καθάπερ λογιστικοῦ τὸ φρόνιμον, ἢ ὡς τῷ
35 ἔχειν, καθάπερ ἐπιστήμονος τὸ ἀμετάπειστον ὑπὸ
λόγου (οὐδὲν γὰρ ἕτερον ἢ τῷ ἔχειν τι ἔσται ἀ-
134 b μετάπειστος ὑπὸ λόγου), ἢ τῷ ἔχεσθαι, καθάπερ
ἐπιστήμης τὸ ἀμετάπειστον ὑπὸ λόγου, ἢ τῷ
μετέχεσθαι, καθάπερ ζῴου τὸ αἰσθάνεσθαι (αἰσθάνεται μὲν γὰρ καὶ ἄλλο τι, οἷον ἄνθρωπος, ἀλλὰ
μετέχων[1] ἤδη τούτου[2] αἰσθάνεται), ἢ τῷ μετέχειν,
5 καθάπερ τοῦ τινὸς ζῴου τὸ ζῆν. μὴ προσθεὶς
μὲν οὖν τὸ φύσει ἁμαρτάνει, διότι ἐνδέχεται τὸ
φύσει ὑπάρχον μὴ ὑπάρχειν ἐκείνῳ ᾧ φύσει

---

[1] Reading μετέχων for μετέχον.
[2] Reading τούτου for τοῦτο.

---

[a] i.e. ' surface ' will not be applicable to everything which
can be described as ' coloured,' since a body is coloured but
is not a surface. ' Body ' will not be applicable to everything
which can be described as ' coloured,' since a surface is
coloured but is not a body.

that which is described in the terms of something else. *or primarily in themselves.]* For example, if one assigns ' coloured ' as a property of ' surface,' ' coloured ' will also be true of ' body,' but if one assigns it as a property of ' body,' it will also be predicated of ' surface,' so that the name also will not be true of that of which the description is true.[a]

With some properties it usually happens that an error arises from lack of a definite statement how and of what the property is stated. For everyone attempts to assign as the property of a thing either that which belongs by nature, as ' biped ' belongs to man, or that which actually belongs, as ' possessing four fingers ' belongs to a particular man, or specifically, as ' consisting of the most subtle particles ' belongs to ' fire,' or absolutely, as ' life ' belongs to ' living creature,' or in virtue of something else, as ' prudence ' belongs to the ' soul,' or primarily, as ' prudence ' belongs to the ' faculty of reason,' or owing to something being in a certain state, as ' proof against the persuasion of argument ' belongs to the ' scientist ' (for it is only because he is in a certain state that he will be ' proof against the persuasion of argument '), or because it is a state possessed by something, as ' proof against the persuasion of argument ' belongs to ' science,' or because it is partaken of, as ' sensation ' belongs to ' living creature ' (for something else also possesses sensation, *e.g.* ' man,' but he does so because he already partakes of ' living creature '), or because it partakes of something, as ' life ' belongs to a particular ' living creature.' A man, therefore, errs if he does not add the words ' by nature,' for it is possible for that which belongs by nature not actually to belong to that to

(b) Observe whether the manner and subject of the property are accurately defined.

134 b

ὑπάρχει, καθάπερ ἀνθρώπῳ τὸ δύο πόδας ἔχειν.
μὴ διορίσας δ᾽ ὅτι τὸ ὑπάρχον ἀποδίδωσιν, ὅτι
οὐκ ἔσται τοιοῦτον οἷον νῦν ὑπάρχει ἐκείνῳ,[1] καθά-
10 περ τὸ τέτταρας δακτύλους ἔχειν τὸν ἄνθρωπον.
μὴ δηλώσας δὲ διότι ὡς πρῶτον ἢ ὡς κατ᾽ ἄλλο
τίθησιν, ὅτι οὐ καθ᾽ οὗ ὁ λόγος, καὶ τοὔνομα ἀληθεύσεται, καθάπερ τὸ κεχρῶσθαι, εἴτε τῆς ἐπιφανείας εἴτε τοῦ σώματος ἀποδοθὲν ἴδιον. μὴ
προείπας δὲ διότι ἢ τῷ ἔχειν ἢ τῷ ἔχεσθαι τὸ
15 ἴδιον ἀποδέδωκε, διότι οὐκ ἔσται ἴδιον· ὑπάρξει
γάρ, ἐὰν μὲν τῷ ἔχεσθαι ἀποδιδῷ τὸ ἴδιον, τῷ
ἔχοντι, ἐὰν δὲ τῷ ἔχοντι, τῷ ἐχομένῳ, καθάπερ
τὸ ἀμετάπειστον ὑπὸ λόγου τῆς ἐπιστήμης ἢ τοῦ
ἐπιστήμονος τεθὲν ἴδιον. μὴ προσσημήνας δὲ τῷ
μετέχειν ἢ τῷ μετέχεσθαι, ὅτι καὶ ἄλλοις τισὶν
20 ὑπάρξει τὸ ἴδιον· ἐὰν μὲν γὰρ τῷ μετέχεσθαι
ἀποδῷ, τοῖς μετέχουσιν, ἐὰν δὲ τῷ μετέχειν,
τοῖς μετεχομένοις, καθάπερ εἰ τοῦ τινὸς ζῴου ἢ
τοῦ ζῴου τιθείη τὸ ζῆν ἴδιον. μὴ διαστείλας δὲ
τὸ τῷ εἴδει, ὅτι ἑνὶ μόνῳ ὑπάρξει τῶν ὑπὸ τοῦτο

[1] Reading ἐκείνῳ for ἐκεῖνο with Waitz.

which it belongs by nature ; for example, it belongs
to man by nature to possess two feet. He also errs
if he does not state definitely that he is assigning
what actually belongs, because it will not always
belong, as it now does, to that particular subject,
for example, the man's possession of four fingers. He
also errs if he has not made it clear that he is stating
it as being primary or as being called as it is in virtue
of something else, because then the name also will
not be true of that of which the description is true, for
example ' coloured ' whether assigned as a property
of ' surface ' or of ' body.' He also errs if he has not
stated beforehand that he has assigned the property
because something is in a certain state or because it
is possessed by something as a state ; for then it will
not be a property. For if he assigns the property as
a state possessed by something, it will belong to that
which possesses the state, while, if he assigns it to the
possessor of the state, it will belong to the state which
is possessed, as ' proof against the persuasion of
argument ' when assigned as a property of ' science '
or of the ' scientist.' He also errs if he has not signified in addition that he assigns the property because
the subject partakes of, or is partaken of by, something, since then the property will belong to some
other things also. For if he assigns it because it is
partaken of, it will belong to the things which partake of it, while if he assigns it because the subject
partakes of it, it will belong to the things partaken
of, for example, if ' life ' be stated to be a property
of a particular ' living creature ' or merely of ' living
creature.' He also errs if he has not distinguished
the property as belonging specifically, because then
it will belong to one only of those things which come

134 b

ὄντων οὗ τὸ ἴδιον τίθησι· τὸ γὰρ καθ' ὑπερβολὴν
25 ἑνὶ μόνῳ ὑπάρχει, καθάπερ τοῦ πυρὸς τὸ κουφότατον. ἐνίοτε δὲ καὶ τὸ τῷ εἴδει προσθεὶς δι-
ήμαρτεν. δεήσει γὰρ ἓν εἶδος εἶναι τῶν λεχθέντων
ὅταν τὸ τῷ εἴδει προστεθῇ· τοῦτο δ' ἐπ' ἐνίων οὐ
συμπίπτει, καθάπερ οὐδ' ἐπὶ τοῦ πυρός. οὐ γάρ
ἐστιν ἓν εἶδος τοῦ πυρός· ἕτερον γάρ ἐστι τῷ εἴδει
30 ἄνθραξ καὶ φλὸξ καὶ φῶς, ἕκαστον αὐτῶν πῦρ ὄν.
διὰ τοῦτο δ' οὐ δεῖ, ὅταν τὸ τῷ[1] εἴδει προστεθῇ,
ἕτερον εἶναι εἶδος τοῦ λεχθέντος, ὅτι τοῖς μὲν μᾶλλον τοῖς δ' ἧττον ὑπάρξει τὸ λεχθὲν ἴδιον, καθάπερ
ἐπὶ τοῦ πυρὸς τὸ λεπτομερέστατον· λεπτομερέ-
στερον γάρ ἐστι τὸ φῶς τοῦ ἄνθρακος καὶ τῆς
φλογός. τοῦτο δ' οὐ δεῖ γίνεσθαι, ὅταν μὴ καὶ
35 τὸ ὄνομα μᾶλλον κατηγορῆται, καθ' οὗ ὁ λόγος
μᾶλλον ἀληθεύεται· εἰ δὲ μή, οὐκ ἔσται, καθ' οὗ
135 a ὁ λόγος μᾶλλον, καὶ τοὔνομα μᾶλλον. ἔτι δὲ πρὸς
τούτοις ταὐτὸν εἶναι συμβήσεται τὸ ἴδιον τοῦ τε
ἁπλῶς καὶ τοῦ μάλιστα ὄντος ἐν τῷ ἁπλῶς τοιούτου,[2] καθάπερ ἐπὶ τοῦ πυρὸς ἔχει τὸ λεπτομερέ-
στατον· καὶ γὰρ τοῦ φωτὸς ἔσται ταὐτὸ τοῦτο
5 ἴδιον· λεπτομερέστατον γάρ ἐστι τὸ φῶς. ἄλλου
μὲν οὖν οὕτως ἀποδιδόντος τὸ ἴδιον ἐπιχειρητέον,
αὐτῷ δ' οὐ δοτέον ἐστὶ ταύτην τὴν ἔνστασιν, ἀλλ'
εὐθὺς τιθέμενον τὸ ἴδιον διοριστέον ὃν τρόπον τίθησι τὸ ἴδιον.

---

[1] Reading τὸ τῷ with D.
[2] Reading τοιούτου with AB.

under the term of which he is stating the property ; for the superlative degree belongs to one only of them, for example, ' lightest ' when used of ' fire.' Sometimes also he has erred even when he has added the word ' specifically ' ; for the things mentioned will have to be of one species when ' specifically ' is added ; but this does not occur in some cases, for example, in the case of ' fire.' For there is not one species only of fire, since a burning coal, a flame and light are different in species, though each of them is ' fire.' It is necessary when ' specifically ' is added that there should not be a species other than that stated, for the reason that the property mentioned will belong to some things in a greater and to others in a less degree, for example ' consisting of the subtlest particles ' as applied to ' fire ' ; for light consists of subtler particles than a burning coal or a flame. But this ought not to occur unless the name is predicated in a greater degree of that of which the description is true to a greater degree ; otherwise the name will not be truer when applied to that of which the description is truer. Further, besides this, the same thing will happen to be the property both of that which possesses it absolutely and of that which possesses it in the highest degree in that which possesses it absolutely, as in the case of ' consisting of the subtlest particles ' when used of ' fire ' ; for this same thing will be a property of ' light,' for ' light ' ' consists of the subtlest particles.' If, therefore, someone else assigns the property in this manner, one ought to argue against it, but one ought not oneself to give an opening for this objection, but one ought to define in what manner one is stating the property immediately when one is stating it.

527

135 a

Ἔπειτ᾽ ἀνασκευάζοντα μὲν εἰ αὐτὸ αὑτοῦ ἴδιον
10 ἔθηκεν· οὐ γὰρ ἔσται ἴδιον τὸ κείμενον εἶναι ἴδιον.
αὐτὸ γὰρ αὑτοῦ[1] πᾶν τὸ εἶναι δηλοῖ, τὸ δὲ τὸ εἶναι
δηλοῦν οὐκ ἴδιον ἀλλ᾽ ὅρος ἐστίν. οἷον ἐπεὶ ὁ
εἴπας καλοῦ τὸ πρέπον ἴδιον εἶναι αὐτὸ ἑαυτοῦ
ἴδιον ἀπέδωκε (ταὐτὸν γὰρ ἐστι τὸ καλὸν καὶ
πρέπον), οὐκ ἂν εἴη τὸ πρέπον τοῦ καλοῦ ἴδιον.
15 κατασκευάζοντα δὲ εἰ μὴ αὐτὸ μὲν αὑτοῦ ἴδιον
ἀπέδωκεν, ἀντικατηγορούμενον δ᾽ ἔθηκεν· ἔσται
γὰρ ἴδιον τὸ κείμενον μὴ εἶναι ἴδιον. οἷον ἐπεὶ
ὁ θεὶς ζῴου ἴδιον τὸ οὐσία ἔμψυχος οὐκ αὐτὸ μὲν
αὑτοῦ ἴδιον ἔθηκεν, ἀντικατηγορούμενον δ᾽ ἀποδέδωκεν, εἴη ἂν ἴδιον τοῦ ζῴου τὸ οὐσία ἔμψυχος.
20 Ἔπειτ᾽ ἐπὶ τῶν ὁμοιομερῶν σκεπτέον ἐστὶν
ἀνασκευάζοντα μὲν εἰ τὸ τοῦ συνόλου ἴδιον μὴ
ἀληθεύεται κατὰ τοῦ μέρους, ἢ εἰ τὸ τοῦ μέρους
μὴ λέγεται κατὰ·τοῦ σύμπαντος· οὐ γὰρ ἔσται
ἴδιον τὸ κείμενον ἴδιον εἶναι. συμβαίνει δ᾽ ἐπ᾽
ἐνίων τοῦτο γίνεσθαι· ἀποδοίη γὰρ ἄν τις ἐπὶ τῶν
25 ὁμοιομερῶν ἴδιον ἐνίοτε μὲν ἐπὶ τὸ σύμπαν βλέψας,
ἐνίοτε δ᾽ ἐπὶ τὸ κατὰ μέρος λεγόμενον αὐτὸς αὑτὸν
ἐπιστήσας· ἔσται δ᾽ οὐδέτερον ὀρθῶς ἀποδεδομένον. οἷον ἐπὶ μὲν τοῦ σύμπαντος, ἐπεὶ ὁ εἴπας

---

[1] Reading αὑτοῦ for αὑτῷ.

Next, for destructive criticism, you must see whether your opponent has stated a thing itself as a property of itself; for then what is stated to be a property will not be a property. For a thing itself always shows its own essence, and that which shows the essence is not a property but a definition. For example, a man who has said that ' decorous ' is a property of ' beautiful ' has assigned the thing itself as its own property (for ' beautiful ' and ' decorous ' are the same thing), and so ' decorous ' cannot be a property of ' beautiful.' For constructive argument you must see whether, though he has not assigned the thing itself as a property of itself, he has nevertheless stated a convertible predicate; for then what has been stated not to be the property will be the property. For example, a man who has stated that ' animate substance ' is a property of ' living creature,' though he has not stated that the thing itself is a property of itself, has nevertheless assigned a convertible predicate, and so ' animate substance ' would be a property of ' living creature.'

(c) Observe whether the thing itself is assigned as its own property.

Next, in dealing with things which have like parts, for destructive criticism you must see whether the property of the whole is untrue of the part or if the property of the part is not predicated of the whole; for then what is stated to be a property will not be a property. This may happen in some cases; for a man might, in dealing with things which have like parts, assign a property sometimes looking at the whole and sometimes directing his attention to what is predicated of a part; and so in neither case will the property have been correctly assigned. For example, in the case of the whole, the man who has said that it is a property of ' sea ' to be ' the greatest

(d) Observe whether, in things which consist of similar parts, the property of the whole is untrue of the parts, or that of the parts not predicated of the whole.

135 a

θαλάττης ἴδιον τὸ πλεῖστον ὕδωρ ἁλμυρὸν ὁμοιομεροῦς μέν τινος ἔθηκε τὸ ἴδιον, τοιοῦτον δ᾽ ἀπ-
30 έδωκεν ὃ οὐκ ἀληθεύεται κατὰ τοῦ μέρους (οὐ γάρ
ἐστιν ἡ τὶς θάλαττα τὸ πλεῖστον ὕδωρ ἁλμυρόν),
οὐκ ἂν εἴη τῆς θαλάττης ἴδιον τὸ πλεῖστον ὕδωρ
ἁλμυρόν. ἐπὶ δὲ τοῦ μέρους, οἷον ἐπεὶ ὁ θεὶς
ἀέρος ἴδιον τὸ ἀναπνευστὸν ὁμοιομεροῦς μέν τινος
εἴρηκε τὸ ἴδιον, τοιοῦτον δ᾽ ἀπέδωκεν ὃ κατὰ τοῦ
35 τινὸς ἀέρος ἀληθεύεται, κατὰ δὲ τοῦ σύμπαντος
οὐ λέγεται (οὐ γάρ ἐστιν ὁ σύμπας ἀναπνευστός),
135 b οὐκ ἂν εἴη τοῦ ἀέρος ἴδιον τὸ ἀναπνευστόν. κατασκευάζοντα δὲ εἰ ἀληθεύεται μὲν καθ᾽ ἑκάστου
τῶν ὁμοιομερῶν, ἔστι δ᾽ ἴδιον αὐτῶν κατὰ τὸ
σύμπαν· ἔσται γὰρ ἴδιον τὸ κείμενον μὴ εἶναι ἴδιον.
οἷον ἐπεὶ ἀληθεύεται κατὰ πάσης γῆς[1] τὸ κάτω
5 φέρεσθαι κατὰ φύσιν, ἔστι δὲ τοῦτο ἴδιον καὶ τῆς
τινὸς γῆς κατὰ τὴν γῆν, εἴη ἂν τῆς γῆς ἴδιον τὸ
κάτω φέρεσθαι κατὰ φύσιν.

VI. Ἔπειτ᾽ ἐκ τῶν ἀντικειμένων σκεπτέον ἐστὶ
πρῶτον μὲν ἐκ τῶν ἐναντίων ἀνασκευάζοντα μὲν
εἰ τοῦ ἐναντίου μή ἐστι τὸ ἐναντίον ἴδιον· οὐδὲ
10 γὰρ τοῦ ἐναντίου ἔσται τὸ ἐναντίον ἴδιον. οἷον
ἐπεὶ ἐναντίον ἐστὶ δικαιοσύνῃ μὲν ἀδικία, τῷ
βελτίστῳ δὲ τὸ χείριστον, οὐκ ἔστι δὲ τῆς δικαιοσύνης ἴδιον τὸ βέλτιστον, οὐκ ἂν εἴη τῆς
ἀδικίας ἴδιον τὸ χείριστον. κατασκευάζοντα δὲ εἰ

---

[1] Omitting τῆς before γῆς with Waitz.

mass of salt-water ' has stated the property of something which has like parts, but he has assigned an
attribute of such a kind that it is not true of the part
(for a particular sea is not ' the greatest mass of salt-
water '), and so ' the greatest mass of salt-water '
could not be a property of ' sea.' So too in the case
of the part ; for example, the man who has stated
that ' respirable ' is a property of ' air ' has asserted
the property of something which has like parts, but
has assigned an attribute of such a kind that it is true
of some air but is not predicable of the whole (for the
whole air is not respirable), and so ' respirable ' could
not be a property of the air. For constructive argument, on the other hand, you must see whether, while
it is true of each of the things which have like parts, it
is a property of them taken as a whole ; for then
what is stated not to be a property will be a property.
For example, while it is true of all earth that it is
carried naturally downwards, and this is also a property of a certain portion of earth as forming part of
' the earth,' it would be a property of ' earth ' ' to be
carried naturally downwards.'

VI. Next, you must examine on the basis of *Rules*
opposites and, in the first place, of *contraries* and, for *drawn from*
destructive criticism, see whether the contrary of the *modes of*
term fails to be a property of the contrary subject ; *opposition :*
for then neither will the contrary of the former be a *trary op-*
property of the contrary of the latter. For example, *position.*
since injustice is contrary to justice, and the greatest
evil is contrary to the greatest good, but it is not a
property of ' justice ' to be ' the greatest good,' then
the ' greatest evil ' would not be a property of ' injustice.' For constructive argument, on the other
hand, you must see whether the contrary is a pro-

35 b

τοῦ ἐναντίου τὸ ἐναντίον ἴδιόν ἐστιν· καὶ γὰρ τοῦ
ἐναντίου τὸ ἐναντίον ἴδιον ἔσται. οἷον ἐπεὶ ἐναντίον
15 ἐστὶν ἀγαθῷ μὲν κακόν, αἱρετῷ δὲ φευκτόν, ἔστι
δὲ τοῦ ἀγαθοῦ ἴδιον τὸ αἱρετόν, εἴη ἂν κακοῦ ἴδιον
τὸ φευκτόν.

Δεύτερον δ' ἐκ τῶν πρός τι ἀνασκευάζοντα μὲν
εἰ τὸ πρός τι τοῦ πρός τι μή ἐστιν ἴδιον· οὐδὲ γὰρ
τὸ πρός τι τοῦ πρός τι ἔσται ἴδιον. οἷον ἐπεὶ
20 λέγεται διπλάσιον μὲν πρὸς ἥμισυ, ὑπερέχον δὲ
πρὸς ὑπερεχόμενον, οὐκ ἔστι δὲ τοῦ διπλασίου
τὸ ὑπερέχον ἴδιον, οὐκ ἂν εἴη τοῦ ἡμίσεος τὸ
ὑπερεχόμενον ἴδιον. κατασκευάζοντα δὲ εἰ τοῦ
πρός τι τὸ πρός τί ἐστιν ἴδιον· καὶ γὰρ τοῦ πρός
τι τὸ πρός τι ἔσται ἴδιον. οἷον ἐπεὶ λέγεται τὸ
25 μὲν διπλάσιον πρὸς τὸ ἥμισυ, τὸ δὲ δύο πρὸς ἕν
⟨πρὸς τὸ ἓν πρὸς δύο⟩,[1] ἔστι δὲ τοῦ διπλασίου ἴδιον
τὸ ὡς δύο πρὸς ἕν, εἴη ἂν τοῦ ἡμίσεος ἴδιον τὸ ὡς
ἓν πρὸς δύο.

Τρίτον ἀνασκευάζοντα μὲν εἰ τῆς ἕξεως τὸ καθ'
ἕξιν λεγόμενον μή ἐστιν ἴδιον· οὐδὲ γὰρ τῆς στερήσεως τὸ κατὰ στέρησιν λεγόμενον ἔσται ἴδιον. κἂν
30 εἰ δὲ τῆς στερήσεως τὸ κατὰ στέρησιν λεγόμενον
μή ἐστιν ἴδιον, οὐδὲ τῆς ἕξεως τὸ κατὰ τὴν ἕξιν

---

[1] Reading with Strache-Wallies τὸ δὲ δύο πρὸς ἕν ⟨πρὸς τὸ ἓν
πρὸς δύο⟩, ἔστι.

perty of the contrary ; for then the contrary too of the former will be a property of the contrary of the latter. For example, since ' evil ' is contrary to ' good ' and ' object of avoidance ' contrary to ' object of choice,' and ' object of choice ' is a property of ' good,' ' object of avoidance ' would be a property of ' evil.'

Secondly, you must examine on the basis of *relative* (2) Relative *opposites*, and see, for destructive criticism, whether opposition. one correlative of the term fails to be the property of the correlatives of the subject ; for then neither will the correlative of the former be a property of the correlative of the latter. For example, ' double ' is described as relative to ' half,' and ' exceeding ' to ' exceeded,' but ' exceeding ' is not a property of ' double,' and so ' exceeded ' could not be a property of ' half.' For constructive argument on the other hand you must see whether the correlative of the property is a property of the correlative of the subject ; for then too the correlative of the former will be a property of the correlative of the latter. For example, ' double ' is described as relative to ' half,' and the proportion 2 : 1 as relative to the proportion 1 : 2, and it is a property of ' double ' to be in the proportion of 2 : 1 ; it would, therefore, be a property of ' half ' to be in the proportion of 1 : 2.

Thirdly, for destructive criticism, you must see (3) The whether what is described in the terms of a state (A) opposition is not a property of the state (B), for then neither of a state will what is described in the terms of the privation and its (of A) be a property of the privation (of B). Also, privation. if what is described in the terms of a privation (of A) is not a property of the privation (of B), neither will what is described in the terms of the state (A) be a

λεγόμενον ἴδιον ἔσται. οἷον ἐπεὶ οὐ λέγεται τῆς
κωφότητος ἴδιον τὸ ἀναισθησίαν εἶναι, οὐδ' ἂν
τῆς ἀκούσεως εἴη ἴδιον τὸ αἴσθησιν εἶναι. κατασκευάζοντα δὲ εἰ τὸ καθ' ἕξιν λεγόμενόν ἐστι τῆς
35 ἕξεως ἴδιον· καὶ γὰρ τῆς στερήσεως τὸ κατὰ
στέρησιν λεγόμενον ἔσται ἴδιον. κἂν εἰ τῆς στερήσεως τὸ κατὰ στέρησιν λεγόμενον ἔστιν ἴδιον,
136 a καὶ τῆς ἕξεως τὸ καθ' ἕξιν λεγόμενον ἔσται ἴδιον.
οἷον ἐπεὶ τῆς ὄψεώς ἐστιν ἴδιον τὸ βλέπειν, καθὸ
ἔχομεν ὄψιν, εἴη ἂν τῆς τυφλότητος ἴδιον τὸ μὴ
βλέπειν, καθὸ οὐκ ἔχομεν ὄψιν πεφυκότες ἔχειν.

5 Ἔπειτα ἐκ τῶν φάσεων καὶ τῶν ἀποφάσεων,
πρῶτον μὲν ἐξ αὐτῶν τῶν κατηγορουμένων. ἔστι
δ' ὁ τόπος οὗτος χρήσιμος ἀνασκευάζοντι μόνον.
οἷον εἰ ἡ φάσις ἢ τὸ κατὰ τὴν φάσιν λεγόμενον
αὐτοῦ ἴδιόν ἐστιν· οὐ γὰρ ἔσται αὐτοῦ ἡ ἀπόφασις
οὐδὲ τὸ κατὰ τὴν ἀπόφασιν λεγόμενον ἴδιον. κἂν
10 εἰ δ' ἡ ἀπόφασις ἢ τὸ κατὰ τὴν ἀπόφασιν λεγόμενόν
ἐστιν αὐτοῦ ἴδιον, οὐκ ἔσται ἡ φάσις οὐδὲ τὸ κατὰ
τὴν φάσιν λεγόμενον ἴδιον· οἷον ἐπεὶ τοῦ ζῴου
ἐστὶν ἴδιον τὸ ἔμψυχον, οὐκ ἂν εἴη τοῦ ζῴου ἴδιον
τὸ οὐκ ἔμψυχον.

Δεύτερον δ' ἐκ τῶν κατηγορουμένων ἢ μὴ
15 κατηγορουμένων, καὶ καθ' ὧν κατηγορεῖται ἢ μὴ
κατηγορεῖται, ἀνασκευάζοντα μὲν εἰ ἡ φάσις τῆς

---

[a] It is not a property of deafness, because it can also be
predicated of, for example, blindness.

property of the state (B). For example, since 'absence of sensation' is not predicated as a property of deafness,'[a] neither would 'sensation' be a property of 'hearing.' For constructive argument, on the other hand, you must see whether what is described in the terms of a state (A) is a property of the state (B); for then what is described in the terms of a privation (of A) will be a property of the privation (of B). And, again, if what is described in the terms of a privation (of A) is a property of the privation (of B), then, too, what is described in the term of the state (A) will be a property of the state (B). For example, since 'to see' is a property of 'vision,' in as far as we possess 'vision,' 'inability to see' would be a property of 'blindness,' in as much as we do not possess vision, though it is our nature to possess it.

Next, you must argue from affirmations and negation, and first from the predicates themselves. This commonplace is useful only for destructive criticism. For example, you must see whether the affirmation or the attribute predicated affirmatively is a property of the subject; for then neither the negation nor the attribute predicated negatively will be a property of the subject. Also, if the negation or the attribute predicated negatively is a property of the subject, then neither the affirmation nor the attribute predicated affirmatively will be a property of the subject. For example, since 'animate' is a property of 'living creature,' 'not animate' could not be a property of it. (4) Contradictory opposition applied to predicates only.

Secondly, you must argue from the things which are predicated or not predicated and from the subjects of which they are or are not predicated, and, for destructive criticism, see whether the affirmative (5) Contradictory opposition applied both to predicates

535

φάσεως μή ἐστιν ἴδιον· οὐδὲ γὰρ ἡ ἀπόφασις τῆς
ἀποφάσεως ἔσται ἴδιον. κἂν εἰ δ' ἡ ἀπόφασις
τῆς ἀποφάσεως μή ἐστιν ἴδιον, οὐδ' ἡ φάσις τῆς
φάσεως ἔσται ἴδιον. οἷον ἐπεὶ οὐκ ἔστι τοῦ ἀν-
20 θρώπου ἴδιον τὸ ζῷον, οὐδ' ἂν τοῦ μὴ ἀνθρώπου εἴη ἴδιον τὸ μὴ ζῷον. κἂν εἰ δὲ τοῦ μὴ
ἀνθρώπου φαίνηται μὴ ἴδιον τὸ μὴ ζῷον, οὐδὲ τοῦ
ἀνθρώπου ἔσται ἴδιον τὸ ζῷον. κατασκευάζοντα δ'
εἰ τῆς φάσεως ἡ φάσις ἐστὶν ἴδιον· καὶ γὰρ τῆς
ἀποφάσεως ἡ ἀπόφασις ἔσται ἴδιον. κἂν εἰ δὲ
25 τῆς ἀποφάσεως ἡ ἀπόφασίς ἐστιν ἴδιον, καὶ ἡ
φάσις τῆς φάσεως ἔσται ἴδιον. οἷον ἐπεὶ τοῦ μὴ
ζῴου ἴδιόν ἐστι τὸ μὴ ζῆν, εἴη ἂν τοῦ ζῴου ἴδιον
τὸ ζῆν· κἂν εἰ δὲ τοῦ ζῴου φαίνηται ἴδιον τὸ ζῆν,
καὶ τοῦ μὴ ζῴου φανεῖται ἴδιον τὸ μὴ ζῆν.

Τρίτον δὲ ἐξ αὐτῶν τῶν ὑποκειμένων ἀνασκευ-
30 άζοντα μὲν εἰ τὸ ἀποδεδομένον ἴδιον τῆς φάσεώς
ἐστιν ἴδιον· οὐ γὰρ ἔσται τὸ αὐτὸ καὶ τῆς ἀποφάσεως ἴδιον. κἂν εἰ δὲ τῆς ἀποφάσεως ἴδιον τὸ
ἀποδοθέν, οὐκ ἔσται τῆς φάσεως ἴδιον. οἷον ἐπεὶ
τοῦ ζῴου ἴδιον τὸ ἔμψυχον, οὐκ ἂν εἴη τοῦ μὴ
ζῴου ἴδιον τὸ ἔμψυχον. κατασκευάζοντα δὲ εἰ τὸ

predicate is not a property of the affirmative subject ; for then neither will the negative predicate be a property of the negative subject. Also if the negative predicate fails to be a property of the negative subject, neither will the affirmative predicate be a property of the affirmative subject. For example, since 'living creature' is not a property of 'man,' neither could 'not-living-creature' be a property of 'not-man.' Again, if 'not-living-creature' appears not to be a property of 'not-man,' neither will 'living creature' be a property of 'man.' For constructive argument, on the other hand, you must see whether the affirmative predicate is a property of the affirmative subject ; for then, too, the negative predicate will be a property of the negative subject. And if the negative predicate is a property of the negative subject, the affirmative predicate also will be a property of the affirmative subject. For example, since 'not to live' is a property of a 'not-living-creature,' 'to live' would be a property of 'living-creature,' and, if 'to live' appears to be a property of 'living-creature,' 'not-to-live' will appear to be a property of 'not-living-creature.'

Thirdly, you must argue from the subjects themselves and, for destructive criticism, see whether the property assigned is a property of the affirmative subject ; for then the same thing will not be a property of the negative subject also. And if the property assigned is a property of the negative subject, it will not be a property of the affirmative subject. For example, since 'animate' is a property of 'living-creature,' 'animate' could not be a property of 'not-living-creature.' For constructive argument, you must see whether the property assigned fails to be a

136 a

35 ἀποδοθὲν μὴ τῆς φάσεως ἴδιον· ⟨εἰ γὰρ μὴ τῆς
φάσεως, ἴδιον⟩¹ εἴη ἂν τῆς ἀποφάσεως. οὗτος δ᾽
ὁ τόπος ψευδής ἐστιν· φάσις γὰρ ἀποφάσεως καὶ
ἀπόφασις φάσεως οὐκ ἔστιν ἴδιον. φάσις μὲν

136 b γὰρ ἀποφάσει οὐδ᾽ ὅλως ὑπάρχει, ἀπόφασις δὲ φά-
σει ὑπάρχει μέν, οὐχ ὡς ἴδιον δὲ ὑπάρχει.

Ἔπειτα δ᾽ ἐκ τῶν ἀντιδιῃρημένων ἀνασκευάζοντα
μὲν εἰ τῶν ἀντιδιῃρημένων μηδὲν μηδενὸς τῶν
5 λοιπῶν ἀντιδιῃρημένων ἐστὶν ἴδιον· οὐδὲ γὰρ τὸ
κείμενον ἔσται ἴδιον τούτου οὗ κεῖται ἴδιον. οἷον
ἐπεὶ ζῷον αἰσθητὸν οὐδενὸς τῶν ἄλλων² ζῴων
ἐστὶν ἴδιον, οὐκ ἂν εἴη τὸ ζῷον νοητὸν τοῦ θεοῦ
ἴδιον. κατασκευάζοντα δ᾽ εἰ τῶν λοιπῶν τῶν
ἀντιδιῃρημένων ὁτιοῦν ἐστιν ἴδιον τούτων ἑκάστου
10 τῶν ἀντιδιῃρημένων· καὶ γὰρ τὸ λοιπὸν ἔσται
τούτου ἴδιον, οὗ κεῖται μὴ εἶναι ἴδιον. οἷον ἐπεὶ
φρονήσεώς ἐστιν ἴδιον τὸ καθ᾽ αὑτὸ πεφυκέναι
λογιστικοῦ ἀρετὴν εἶναι, καὶ τῶν ἄλλων ἀρετῶν
οὕτως ἑκάστης λαμβανομένης, εἴη ἂν σωφροσύνης
ἴδιον τὸ καθ᾽ αὑτὸ πεφυκέναι ἐπιθυμητικοῦ ἀρετὴν
εἶναι.

15 VII. Ἔπειτ᾽ ἐκ τῶν πτώσεων, ἀνασκευάζοντα
μὲν εἰ ἡ πτῶσις τῆς πτώσεως μή ἐστιν ἴδιον· οὐδὲ
γὰρ ἡ πτῶσις τῆς πτώσεως ἔσται ἴδιον. οἷον

---

¹ εἰ γὰρ μὴ τῆς φάσεως, ἴδιον add. Wallies.
² Omitting θνητῶν with B²DP.

ᵃ A B C D are members of one division which have corresponding predicates a b c d. If any one of b, c or d is a property of any one of B, C or D other than that to which it
corresponds, then a cannot be a property of A.

ᵇ It has been alleged that a is not a property of A ; but,
if b, c and d are properties respectively of B, C and D, then
a must be a property of A.

property of the affirmative subject; for, if it is not a property of the affirmative subject, it would be a property of the negative subject. But this common-place is misleading; for an affirmative term is not a property of a negative subject, nor a negative term of a positive subject; for an affirmative term does not belong to a negative subject at all, while a negative term does belong to an affirmative subject, but not as a property.

Next, you can take the opposite members of corresponding divisions and see, for destructive criticism, whether no member of one division is a property of any opposite member of the other division; for then neither will the term stated be a property of that of which it is stated to be a property.[a] For example, since 'sensible living creature' is a property of none of the other living creatures, 'intelligible living creature' could not be a property of God. For constructive argument, on the other hand, you must see whether any one of the other opposite members is a property of each of the opposite members; for then the remaining one too will be a property of that of which it has been stated not to be a property.[b] For example, since it is a property of 'prudence' to be 'in itself naturally the virtue of the reasoning faculty,' then, if each of the other virtues is treated similarly, it would be the property of 'temperance' to be 'in itself naturally the virtue of the appetitive faculty.' *Rules drawn from the co-ordinate members of a division.*

VII. Next, you can take the inflexions and see, for destructive criticism, whether one inflexion fails to be a property of another inflexion; for then neither will one changed inflexion be a property of the other changed inflexion. For example, since *Rules drawn (a) from inflexions.*

ἐπεὶ οὐκ ἔστι τοῦ δικαίως ἴδιον τὸ καλῶς, οὐδ᾿
ἂν τοῦ δικαίου εἴη ἴδιον τὸ καλόν. κατασκευάζοντα
δὲ εἰ ἡ πτῶσις τῆς πτώσεώς ἐστιν ἴδιον· καὶ γὰρ
20 ἡ πτῶσις τῆς πτώσεως ἔσται ἴδιον. οἷον ἐπεὶ
τοῦ ἀνθρώπου ἐστὶν ἴδιον τὸ πεζὸν δίπουν, καὶ
τῷ ἀνθρώπῳ εἴη ἂν ἴδιον τὸ πεζῷ δίποδι λέγεσθαι.
οὐ μόνον δ᾿ ἐπ᾿ αὐτοῦ τοῦ εἰρημένου κατὰ τὰς
πτώσεις ἐστὶ σκεπτέον, ἀλλὰ καὶ ἐπὶ τῶν ἀντικειμένων, καθάπερ καὶ ἐπὶ τῶν πρότερον τόπων
25 εἴρηται, ἀνασκευάζοντα μὲν εἰ ἡ τοῦ ἀντικειμένου
πτῶσις μή ἐστιν ἴδιον τῆς τοῦ ἀντικειμένου πτώ-
σεως· οὐδὲ γὰρ ἡ τοῦ ἀντικειμένου πτῶσις ἔσται
ἴδιον τῆς τοῦ ἀντικειμένου πτώσεως. οἷον ἐπεὶ
οὐκ ἔστι τοῦ δικαίως ἴδιον τὸ ἀγαθῶς, οὐδ᾿ ἂν
τοῦ ἀδίκως εἴη ἴδιον τὸ κακῶς. κατασκευάζοντα
δὲ εἰ ἡ τοῦ ἀντικειμένου πτῶσίς ἐστιν ἴδιον τῆς
30 τοῦ ἀντικειμένου πτώσεως· καὶ γὰρ ἡ τοῦ ἀντικειμένου πτῶσις ἔσται ἴδιον τῆς τοῦ ἀντικειμένου
πτώσεως. οἷον ἐπεὶ τοῦ ἀγαθοῦ ἐστιν ἴδιον τὸ
βέλτιστον, καὶ τοῦ κακοῦ ἂν εἴη ἴδιον τὸ χείριστον.

Ἔπειτ᾿ ἐκ τῶν ὁμοίως ἐχόντων, ἀνασκευάζοντα
35 μὲν εἰ τὸ ὁμοίως ἔχον τοῦ ὁμοίως ἔχοντος μή
ἐστιν ἴδιον· οὐδὲ γὰρ τὸ ὁμοίως ἔχον τοῦ ὁμοίως
ἔχοντος ἔσται ἴδιον. οἷον ἐπεὶ ὁμοίως ἔχει ὁ
οἰκοδόμος πρὸς τὸ ποιεῖν οἰκίαν καὶ ὁ ἰατρὸς πρὸς

---

[a] The datives here used cannot be satisfactorily rendered
in English. They can be expressed in Latin; Pacius renders:
'*homini proprium est dici pedestri bipedi.*'

[b] *Cf.* 114 b 6 ff.

'honourably' is not a property of 'justly,' neither could 'honourable' be a property of 'just.' For constructive argument, you must see whether one inflexion is a property of the other inflexion; for then one changed inflexion will be a property of the other changed inflexion. For example, since 'pedestrian biped' is a property of 'man,' the description 'of pedestrian biped' would be the property 'of man.'[a] You must examine the inflexions not only in the actual term assigned but also in its opposites, as has been said in the earlier commonplaces also,[b] and, for destructive criticism, see whether the inflexion of one opposite fails to be a property of the inflexion of the other opposite; for then neither will the changed inflexion of one opposite be a property of the changed inflexion of the other opposite. For example, since 'well' is not a property of 'justly,' neither could 'badly' be a property of 'unjustly.' For constructive argument, you must see whether the inflexion of one opposite is a property of the inflexion of the other opposite; for then the changed inflexion of one opposite will be also a property of the changed inflexion of the other opposite. For example, since 'best' is a property of 'the good,' 'worst' also would be a property of 'the bad.'

Next, you must argue from things which stand in a similar relation, and, for destructive criticism, see whether an attribute which is similarly related fails to be a property of the similarly related subject; for then neither will that which is related like the former be a property of that which is related like the latter. For example, since the builder stands in a similar relation for the production of a house to that in which the doctor stands for the production of

(b) From relations like the relation asserted to be a property.

541

136 b

τὸ ποιεῖν ὑγίειαν, οὐκ ἔστι δὲ ἰατροῦ ἴδιον τὸ ποι-
137 a εῖν ὑγίειαν, οὐκ ἂν εἴη οἰκοδόμου ἴδιον τὸ ποιεῖν
οἰκίαν. κατασκευάζοντα δὲ εἰ τὸ ὁμοίως ἔχον τοῦ
ὁμοίως ἔχοντός ἐστιν ἴδιον· καὶ γὰρ τὸ ὁμοίως
ἔχον τοῦ ὁμοίως ἔχοντος ἔσται ἴδιον. οἷον ἐπεὶ
ὁμοίως ἔχει ἰατρός τε πρὸς τὸ ποιητικὸς ὑγιείας
5 εἶναι καὶ γυμναστὴς πρὸς τὸ ποιητικὸς εὐεξίας, ἔστι
δ᾽ ἴδιον γυμναστοῦ τὸ ποιητικὸν εἶναι εὐεξίας, εἴη
ἂν ἴδιον ἰατροῦ τὸ ποιητικὸν εἶναι ὑγιείας.

Ἔπειτ᾽ ἐκ τῶν ὡσαύτως ἐχόντων, ἀνασκευάζοντα
μὲν εἰ τὸ ὡσαύτως ἔχον τοῦ ὡσαύτως ἔχοντος μή
10 ἐστιν ἴδιον· οὐδὲ γὰρ τὸ ὡσαύτως ἔχον τοῦ ὡσαύτως ἔχοντος ἔσται ἴδιον. εἰ δ᾽ ἔστι τοῦ ὡσαύτως
ἔχοντος τὸ ὡσαύτως ἔχον ἴδιον, τούτου οὐκ ἔσται
ἴδιον οὗ κεῖται εἶναι ἴδιον. οἷον ἐπεὶ ὡσαύτως
ἔχει φρόνησις πρὸς τὸ καλὸν καὶ τὸ αἰσχρὸν τῷ
ἐπιστήμη ἑκατέρου αὐτῶν εἶναι, οὐκ ἔστι δ᾽ ἴδιον
15 φρονήσεως τὸ ἐπιστήμην εἶναι καλοῦ, οὐκ ἂν εἴη
ἴδιον φρονήσεως τὸ ἐπιστήμην εἶναι αἰσχροῦ. εἰ
δ᾽ ἔστιν ἴδιον φρονήσεως τὸ ἐπιστήμην εἶναι καλοῦ, οὐκ ἂν εἴη ἴδιον αὐτῆς τὸ ἐπιστήμην εἶναι
αἰσχροῦ· ἀδύνατον γὰρ εἶναι τὸ αὐτὸ πλειόνων ἴδιον.
κατασκευάζοντι δὲ οὐδὲν οὗτος ὁ τόπος ἐστὶ χρή-
20 σιμος· τὸ γὰρ ὡσαύτως ἔχον ἓν πρὸς πλείω συγκρίνεται.

---

[a] Let *a* and *b* be identically related to A ; if A is not a
property of *a*, neither will it be a property of *b*.

[b] If A is a property of *a*, it cannot be a property of *b*,
because the same thing cannot be a property of more than
one subject.

health, but it is not a property of a doctor to produce health, it would not be a property of a builder to produce a house. For constructive argument, you must see whether a similarly related attribute is a property of the similarly related subject; for then an attribute which is related like the former will be a property of a subject which is related like the latter. For example, since a doctor stands in a similar relation as productive of health to that in which a trainer stands as productive of good condition, and it is a property of the trainer to be productive of good condition, it would be a property of the doctor to be productive of health.

Next, you must argue from things which stand in identical relations and see, for destructive criticism, whether what is identically related to two things fails to be a property of one of these things, for then it will not be the property of the other either [a]; but if what is identically related to two things is a property of one of them, it will not be a property of that of which it is stated to be a property.[b] For example, since prudence is identically related to the honourable and the disgraceful, since it is a knowledge of each of them, and it is not a property of prudence to be a knowledge of the honourable, it would not be a property of prudence to be a knowledge of the disgraceful. But if a knowledge of the honourable is a property of prudence, a knowledge of the disgraceful could not be a property of prudence; for it is impossible for the same thing to be a property of more than one thing. For constructive argument this commonplace is of no use; for what is identically related is one thing brought into comparison with more than one thing.

(c) From identity of relations between the property and two subjects.

Ἔπειτ᾽ ἀνασκευάζοντα μὲν εἰ τὸ κατὰ τὸ εἶναι
λεγόμενον μή ἐστι τοῦ κατὰ τὸ εἶναι λεγομένου
ἴδιον· οὐδὲ γὰρ τὸ φθείρεσθαι τοῦ κατὰ τὸ φθείρεσθαι, οὐδὲ τὸ γίνεσθαι τοῦ κατὰ τὸ γίνεσθαι
λεγομένου ἔσται ἴδιον. οἷον ἐπεὶ οὐκ ἔστιν ἀν-
25 θρώπου ἴδιον τὸ εἶναι ζῷον, οὐδ᾽ ἂν τοῦ ἄνθρωπον
γίνεσθαι εἴη ἴδιον τὸ γίνεσθαι ζῷον· οὐδ᾽ ἂν τοῦ
ἄνθρωπον φθείρεσθαι εἴη ἴδιον τὸ φθείρεσθαι ζῷον.
τὸν αὐτὸν δὲ τρόπον ληπτέον ἐστὶ καὶ ἐκ τοῦ
γίνεσθαι πρὸς τὸ εἶναι καὶ φθείρεσθαι καὶ ἐκ τοῦ
φθείρεσθαι πρὸς τὸ εἶναι καὶ πρὸς τὸ γίνεσθαι,
30 καθάπερ εἴρηται νῦν ἐκ τοῦ εἶναι πρὸς τὸ γίνεσθαι
καὶ φθείρεσθαι. κατασκευάζοντα δὲ εἰ τοῦ κατὰ
τὸ εἶναι τεταγμένου ἐστὶ τὸ κατ᾽ αὐτὸ τεταγμένον
ἴδιον· καὶ γὰρ τοῦ κατὰ τὸ γίνεσθαι λεγομένου
ἔσται τὸ κατὰ τὸ γίνεσθαι λεγόμενον ἴδιον καὶ
τοῦ κατὰ τὸ φθείρεσθαι τὸ κατὰ τοῦτο ἀποδιδό-
35 μενον. οἷον ἐπεὶ τοῦ ἀνθρώπου ἐστὶν ἴδιον τὸ
εἶναι βροτόν, καὶ τοῦ γίνεσθαι ἄνθρωπον εἴη ἂν
ἴδιον τὸ γίνεσθαι βροτὸν καὶ τοῦ φθείρεσθαι
ἄνθρωπον τὸ φθείρεσθαι βροτόν. τὸν αὐτὸν δὲ
137 b τρόπον ληπτέον ἐστὶ καὶ ἐκ τοῦ γίνεσθαι καὶ
φθείρεσθαι πρός τε τὸ εἶναι καὶ πρὸς τὰ ἐξ αὐτῶν,
καθάπερ καὶ ἀνασκευάζοντι εἴρηται.

Ἔπειτ᾽ ἐπιβλέπειν ἐπὶ τὴν ἰδέαν τοῦ κειμένου,

Next, for destructive criticism, you must see *(d) From the processes of coming into being and destruction.* whether the predicate which is said 'to be' is *not a* property of the subject which is said 'to be'; for then neither will the predicate which is said 'to be destroyed' be a property of the subject which is said 'to be destroyed,' nor will the predicate which is said 'to be becoming' be a property of the subject which is said 'to be becoming.' For example, since it is not the property of man to be an animal, neither could 'becoming an animal' be a property of 'becoming a man'; nor could the 'destruction of an animal' be a property of the 'destruction of a man.' In the same way you must make the assumption from 'becoming' to 'being' and 'being destroyed,' and from 'being destroyed' to 'being' and 'becoming,' by the process of argument just described from 'being' to 'becoming' and 'being destroyed.' For constructive argument, on the other hand, you must see whether the predicate which is laid down as 'being' is a property of the subject laid down as 'being'; for then also the predicate which is described as 'becoming' will be a property of the subject which is described as 'becoming,' and the predicate assigned in virtue of destruction will be a property of the subject which is said to 'be destroyed.' For example, since it is a property of man to be mortal, 'becoming mortal' would be a property of 'becoming a man,' and the 'destruction of a mortal' would be a property of the 'destruction of a man.' In the same way you must make the assumption also from 'becoming' and 'being destroyed' to 'being' and to the other consequences which are derived from them, as was described for destructive criticism.

Next you must look at the idea of that which is *(e) From reference of*

ἀνασκευάζοντα μὲν εἰ τῇ ἰδέᾳ μὴ ὑπάρχει, ἢ εἰ
5 μὴ κατὰ τοῦτο καθ' ὃ λέγεται τοῦτο οὗ τὸ ἴδιον
ἀπεδόθη· οὐ γὰρ ἔσται ἴδιον τὸ κείμενον εἶναι
ἴδιον. οἷον ἐπεὶ αὐτοανθρώπῳ οὐχ ὑπάρχει τὸ
ἠρεμεῖν, ᾗ ἄνθρωπός ἐστιν, ἀλλ' ᾗ ἰδέα, οὐκ ἂν
εἴη ἀνθρώπου ἴδιον τὸ ἠρεμεῖν. κατασκευάζοντα
δὲ εἰ τῇ ἰδέᾳ ὑπάρχει, καὶ κατὰ τοῦτο ὑπάρχει,
10 ᾗ λέγεται κατ' αὐτοῦ ἐκεῖνο οὗ κεῖται μὴ εἶναι
ἴδιον· ἔσται γὰρ ἴδιον τὸ κείμενον μὴ εἶναι ἴδιον.
οἷον ἐπεὶ ὑπάρχει τῷ αὐτοζῴῳ τὸ ἐκ ψυχῆς καὶ
σώματος συγκεῖσθαι, καὶ ᾗ ζῷον αὐτῷ ὑπάρχει
τοῦτο, εἴη ἂν ζῴου ἴδιον τὸ ἐκ ψυχῆς καὶ σώματος
συγκεῖσθαι.

VIII. Ἔπειτα ἐκ τοῦ μᾶλλον καὶ ἧττον, πρῶτον
15 μὲν ἀνασκευάζοντα εἰ τὸ μᾶλλον τοῦ μᾶλλον μή
ἐστιν ἴδιον· οὐδὲ γὰρ τὸ ἧττον τοῦ ἧττον ἔσται
ἴδιον, οὐδὲ τὸ ἥκιστα τοῦ ἥκιστα, οὐδὲ τὸ μάλιστα
τοῦ μάλιστα, οὐδὲ τὸ ἁπλῶς τοῦ ἁπλῶς. οἷον ἐπεὶ
οὐκ ἔστι τὸ μᾶλλον κεχρῶσθαι τοῦ μᾶλλον σώματος ἴδιον, οὐδὲ τὸ ἧττον κεχρῶσθαι τοῦ ἧττον
20 σώματος εἴη ἂν ἴδιον, οὐδὲ τὸ κεχρῶσθαι σώματος
ὅλως. κατασκευάζοντα δὲ εἰ τὸ μᾶλλον τοῦ
μᾶλλόν ἐστιν ἴδιον· καὶ γὰρ τὸ ἧττον τοῦ ἧττον

stated, and, for destructive criticism, see whether the *the property* property fails to belong to the idea, or whether *asserted to* it fails to belong in virtue of that which causes that *of the* of which the property was assigned to be so described; *subject.* for then what was stated to be a property will not be a property. For example, since 'being at rest' does not belong to 'man-himself' as 'man' but as 'idea,' 'to be at rest' could not be a property of 'man.' For constructive argument, you must see whether the property belongs to the idea and belongs to it in virtue of this, namely, in as much as that is predicated of it of which it is stated not to be a property ; for then what was stated to be a property will not be a property. For example, since it belongs to 'animal-itself' to be composed of soul and body and it belongs to it as animal, to be composed of soul and body would be a property of 'animal.'

VIII. Next, you can argue from the greater and *Rules* less degrees and, first of all, for destructive criticism, *drawn (a)* see whether the greater degree of the predicate fails *from the* to be a property of the greater degree of subject; for *greater and* then neither will the less degree of the predicate be *less degrees.* a property of the less degree of the subject, nor the least degree of the least degree, nor the greatest degree of the greatest degree, nor the predicate simply of the subject simply. For example, since to be more coloured is not a property of what is more a body, neither would to be less coloured be a property of what is less a body, nor would colour be a property of body at all. For constructive argument, on the other hand, you must see whether a greater degree of the predicate is a property of a greater degree of the subject ; for then a less degree of the predicate will be a property of a less degree of

547

ἔσται ἴδιον, καὶ τὸ ἥκιστα τοῦ ἥκιστα, καὶ τὸ
μάλιστα τοῦ μάλιστα, καὶ τὸ ἁπλῶς τοῦ ἁπλῶς.
οἷον ἐπεὶ τοῦ μᾶλλον ζῶντος τὸ μᾶλλον αἰσθά-
25 νεσθαί ἐστιν ἴδιον, καὶ τοῦ ἧττον ζῶντος τὸ ἧττον
αἰσθάνεσθαι εἴη ἂν ἴδιον, καὶ τοῦ μάλιστα δὲ τὸ
μάλιστα, καὶ τοῦ ἥκιστα τὸ ἥκιστα, καὶ τοῦ
ἁπλῶς τὸ ἁπλῶς.

Καὶ ἐκ τοῦ ἁπλῶς δὲ πρὸς ταὐτὰ σκεπτέον
ἐστὶν ἀνασκευάζοντα μὲν εἰ τὸ ἁπλῶς τοῦ ἁπλῶς
30 μή ἐστιν ἴδιον· οὐδὲ γὰρ τὸ μᾶλλον τοῦ μᾶλλον,
οὐδὲ τὸ ἧττον τοῦ ἧττον, οὐδὲ τὸ μάλιστα τοῦ
μάλιστα, οὐδὲ τὸ ἥκιστα τοῦ ἥκιστα ἔσται ἴδιον.
οἷον ἐπεὶ οὐκ ἔστι τοῦ ἀνθρώπου τὸ σπουδαῖον
ἴδιον, οὐδ' ἂν τοῦ μᾶλλον ἀνθρώπου τὸ μᾶλλον
σπουδαῖον ἴδιον εἴη. κατασκευάζοντα δὲ εἰ τὸ
35 ἁπλῶς τοῦ ἁπλῶς ἐστιν ἴδιον· καὶ γὰρ τὸ μᾶλλον
τοῦ μᾶλλον καὶ τὸ ἧττον τοῦ ἧττον καὶ τὸ ἥκιστα
τοῦ ἥκιστα καὶ τὸ μάλιστα τοῦ μάλιστα ἔσται
ἴδιον. οἷον ἐπεὶ τοῦ πυρός ἐστιν ἴδιον τὸ ἄνω
138 a φέρεσθαι κατὰ φύσιν, καὶ τοῦ μᾶλλον πυρὸς εἴη
ἂν ἴδιον τὸ μᾶλλον ἄνω φέρεσθαι κατὰ φύσιν.
τὸν αὐτὸν δὲ τρόπον σκεπτέον ἐστὶ καὶ ἐκ τῶν
ἄλλων πρὸς ἅπαντα ταῦτα.

Δεύτερον δ' ἀνασκευάζοντα μὲν εἰ τὸ μᾶλλον
5 τοῦ μᾶλλον μή ἐστιν ἴδιον· οὐδὲ γὰρ τὸ ἧττον τοῦ

---

^a i.e. the more, the less, etc.

the subject, and the least degree of the least degree and the greatest degree of the greatest degree, and the predicate simply of the subject simply. For example, since a higher degree of sensation is a property of a higher degree of living thing, a lower degree of sensation would be a property of a lower degree of living thing, and the highest degree of the highest degree, and the lowest degree of the lowest degree, and sensation simply of living thing simply.

Next, you can argue from the simple predication to these same kinds of predication,[a] and, for destructive criticism, see whether the predicate simply is not a property of the subject simply ; for then neither will the greater degree of the predicate be a property of the greater degree of the subject, nor the less degree of the less degree, nor the greatest degree of the greatest degree, nor the least degree of the least degree. For example, since ' virtuous ' is not a property of ' man,' ' more virtuous ' could not be a property of ' more-man.' For constructive argument, on the other hand, you must see whether the predicate simply is a property of the subject simply ; for then also the greater degree of the predicate will be a property of the greater degree of the subject, and the less degree of the less degree, and the least degree of the least degree, and the greatest degree of the greatest degree. For example, since it is a property of ' fire ' ' to be carried naturally upwards,' it would be a property of ' a greater degree of fire ' ' to be carried naturally upwards to a greater degree.' In the same manner also one must examine these things from the point of view of the other degrees also.

Secondly, for destructive argument, you must see whether the more fails to be a property of the more ;

ἧττον ἔσται ἴδιον. οἷον ἐπεὶ μᾶλλόν ἐστιν ἴδιον
ζώου τὸ αἰσθάνεσθαι ἢ ἀνθρώπου τὸ ἐπίστασθαι,
οὐκ ἔστι δὲ ζώου ἴδιον τὸ αἰσθάνεσθαι, οὐκ ἂν
εἴη ἀνθρώπου ἴδιον τὸ ἐπίστασθαι. κατασκευάζοντα δ' εἰ τὸ ἧττον τοῦ ἧττόν ἐστιν ἴδιον· καὶ
10 γὰρ τὸ μᾶλλον τοῦ μᾶλλον ἔσται ἴδιον. οἷον ἐπεὶ
ἧττόν ἐστιν ἴδιον ἀνθρώπου τὸ ἥμερον φύσει ἢ
ζώου τὸ ζῆν, ἔστι δ' ἀνθρώπου ἴδιον τὸ ἥμερον
φύσει, εἴη ἂν ζώου ἴδιον τὸ ζῆν.

Τρίτον δ' ἀνασκευάζοντα μὲν εἰ οὗ μᾶλλόν ἐστιν
ἴδιον, μή ἐστιν ἴδιον· οὐδὲ γὰρ οὗ ἧττόν ἐστιν ἴδιον,
15 ἔσται τούτου ἴδιον. εἰ δ' ἐκείνου ἐστὶν ἴδιον, οὐκ
ἔσται τούτου ἴδιον. οἷον ἐπεὶ τὸ κεχρῶσθαι μᾶλλον τῆς ἐπιφανείας ἢ τοῦ σώματός ἐστιν ἴδιον,
οὐκ ἔστι δὲ τῆς ἐπιφανείας ἴδιον, οὐκ ἂν εἴη τοῦ
σώματος ἴδιον τὸ κεχρῶσθαι. εἰ δ' ἐστὶ τῆς
ἐπιφανείας ἴδιον, οὐκ ἂν εἴη τοῦ σώματος ἴδιον.
20 κατασκευάζοντι δὲ ὁ τόπος οὗτος οὐκ ἔστι χρήσι-
μος· ἀδύνατον γάρ ἐστι ταὐτὸ πλειόνων ἴδιον εἶναι.

Τέταρτον δ' ἀνασκευάζοντα μὲν εἰ τὸ μᾶλλον
αὐτοῦ ἴδιον μή ἐστιν ἴδιον· οὐδὲ γὰρ τὸ ἧττον
αὐτοῦ ἴδιον ἔσται ἴδιον. οἷον ἐπεὶ μᾶλλόν ἐστι
25 τοῦ ζώου ἴδιον τὸ αἰσθητὸν ἢ τὸ μεριστόν, οὐκ
ἔστι δὲ τοῦ ζώου τὸ αἰσθητὸν ἴδιον, οὐκ ἂν εἴη
τοῦ ζώου τὸ μεριστὸν ἴδιον. κατασκευάζοντα δὲ

for then neither will the less be a property of the less.
For example, since 'perceiving' is more a property
of 'animal' than 'knowing' is a property of 'man,'
and 'perceiving' is not a property of 'animal,'
'knowing' would not be a property of 'man.' For
constructive argument, on the other hand, you must
see whether the less is a property of the less, for then
the more will also be a property of the more. For
example, since 'to be naturally civilized' is less a
property of 'man' than 'living' is a property of 'animal,' and it is a property of 'man' 'to be naturally
civilized,' 'living' would be a property of 'animal.'

Thirdly, for destructive criticism, you must see
whether a predicate fails to be a property of that of
which it is to a greater degree a property; for then
neither will it be a property of that of which it is to a
less degree a property; and if it is a property of the
former, it will not be a property of the latter. For
example, since 'to be coloured' is to a greater degree
a property of 'surface' than of 'body,' and it is not a
property of 'surface,' 'to be coloured' could not
be a property of 'body'; and if it is a property of
'surface,' it could not be a property of 'body.' This
commonplace is of no use for constructive argument;
for the same thing cannot possibly be a property of
more than one thing.

Fourthly, for destructive criticism, you must see
whether what is to a greater degree a property of the
subject fails to be its property; for then neither will
what is to a less degree a property be its property.
For example, since 'sensible' is to a greater degree
a property of 'animal' than 'divisible,' and 'sensible'
is not a property of 'animal,' 'divisible' could not
be a property of 'animal.' For constructive argu

138 a

εἰ τὸ ἧττον αὐτοῦ ὂν ἴδιον ἔστιν ἴδιον· καὶ γὰρ τὸ
μᾶλλον αὐτοῦ ὂν ἴδιον ἔσται ἴδιον. οἷον ἐπεὶ ἧττόν
ἐστιν ἴδιον ζώου τὸ αἰσθάνεσθαι ἢ τὸ ζῆν, ἔστι
δὲ τοῦ ζώου τὸ αἰσθάνεσθαι ἴδιον, εἴη ἂν τοῦ ζώου
τὸ ζῆν ἴδιον.

30 Ἔπειτ᾽ ἐκ τῶν ὁμοίως ὑπαρχόντων πρῶτον μὲν
ἀνασκευάζοντα εἰ τὸ ὁμοίως ὂν ἴδιον μή ἐστιν
ἴδιον τούτου οὗ ὁμοίως ἐστὶν ἴδιον· οὐδὲ γὰρ τὸ
ὁμοίως ὂν ἴδιον ἔσται ἴδιον τούτου οὗ ὁμοίως ἐστὶν
ἴδιον. οἷον ἐπεὶ ὁμοίως ἐστὶν ἴδιον ἐπιθυμητικοῦ
τὸ ἐπιθυμεῖν καὶ λογιστικοῦ τὸ λογίζεσθαι, οὐκ
35 ἔστι δ᾽ ἴδιον ἐπιθυμητικοῦ τὸ ἐπιθυμεῖν, οὐκ ἂν
εἴη ἴδιον λογιστικοῦ τὸ λογίζεσθαι. κατασκευάζοντα δὲ εἰ τὸ ὁμοίως ὂν ἴδιον ἔστι τούτου ἴδιον
οὗ ὁμοίως ἐστὶν ἴδιον· ἔσται γὰρ καὶ τὸ ὁμοίως ὂν
138 b ἴδιον τούτου ἴδιον οὗ ὁμοίως ἐστὶν ἴδιον. οἷον
ἐπεὶ ὁμοίως ἐστὶν ἴδιον λογιστικοῦ τὸ πρῶτον
φρόνιμον καὶ ἐπιθυμητικοῦ τὸ πρῶτον σῶφρον,
ἔστι δὲ τοῦ λογιστικοῦ ἴδιον τὸ πρῶτον φρόνιμον,
5 εἴη ἂν τοῦ ἐπιθυμητικοῦ ἴδιον τὸ πρῶτον σῶφρον.

Δεύτερον δ᾽ ἀνασκευάζοντα μὲν εἰ τὸ ὁμοίως ὂν
ἴδιον μή ἐστιν ἴδιον αὐτοῦ· οὐδὲ γὰρ τὸ ὁμοίως

ment you must see whether what is to a less degree
a property of the subject is a property; for then
what is to a greater degree a property will be a
property. For example, since 'sensation' is to a less
degree a property of 'animal' than 'life,' and 'sensation' is a property of 'animal,' 'life' would be a
property of 'animal.'

Next, you can argue from attributes which belong
in an equal degree and first, for destructive criticism,
see whether what is to an equal degree a property fails
to be a property of that which is an equal degree a
property; for then neither will what is a property
in an equal degree be a property of that of which
it is in an equal degree a property. For example,
since 'appetite' is a property of 'the appetitive
faculty' in a degree equal to that in which 'reason'
is a property of the 'reasoning faculty,' and 'appetitive' is not a property of the 'appetitive faculty,'
'reason' could not be a property of the 'reasoning
faculty.' For constructive argument, you must see
whether what is in an equal degree a property is a
property of that of which it is in an equal degree
a property; for then also what is to an equal degree a property will be a property of that of which it
is in an equal degree a property. For example, since
'primary wisdom' is a property of the 'reasoning
faculty' in a degree equal to that in which 'primary temperance' is a property of the 'appetitive
faculty,' and 'primary wisdom' is a property of the
'reasoning faculty,' 'primary temperance' would be
a property of the 'appetitive faculty.'

(b) From a comparison of an attri-bute-relation which re-sembles the alleged property-relation (1) between a different attribute and a different subject.

Secondly, for destructive criticism, you must see
whether what is in an equal degree a property of a
subject fails to be a property of it; for then neither will

(2) Between the subject of the alleged property and a different attribute.

138 b

ὂν ἴδιον ἔσται ἴδιον αὐτοῦ. οἷον ἐπεὶ ὁμοίως ἐστὶν
ἴδιον ἀνθρώπου τὸ ὁρᾶν καὶ τὸ ἀκούειν, οὐκ ἔστι
10 δ' ἀνθρώπου ἴδιον τὸ ὁρᾶν, οὐκ ἂν εἴη ἀνθρώπου
ἴδιον τὸ ἀκούειν. κατασκευάζοντα δὲ εἰ τὸ ὁμοίως
αὐτοῦ ὂν ἴδιον ἔστιν ἴδιον· καὶ γὰρ τὸ ὁμοίως
αὐτοῦ ὂν ἴδιον ἔσται ἴδιον. οἷον ἐπεὶ ὁμοίως ἐστὶν
ἴδιον ψυχῆς τὸ μέρος αὐτῆς ἐπιθυμητικὸν εἶναι
καὶ λογιστικὸν πρώτου, ἔστι δὲ ψυχῆς ἴδιον τὸ
μέρος αὐτῆς εἶναι ἐπιθυμητικὸν πρώτου, εἴη ἂν
15 ἴδιον ψυχῆς τὸ μέρος αὐτῆς εἶναι λογιστικὸν
πρώτου.

Τρίτον δ' ἀνασκευάζοντα μὲν εἰ οὗ ὁμοίως ἐστὶν
ἴδιον, μή ἐστιν ἴδιον· οὐδὲ γὰρ οὗ ὁμοίως ἐστὶν
ἴδιον, ἔσται ἴδιον. εἰ δ' ἐκείνου ἐστὶν ἴδιον, οὐκ
ἔσται θατέρου ἴδιον. οἷον ἐπεὶ ὁμοίως ἐστὶν ἴδιον
τὸ καίειν φλογὸς καὶ ἄνθρακος, οὐκ ἔστι δ' ἴδιον
20 φλογὸς τὸ καίειν, οὐκ ἂν εἴη ἴδιον ἄνθρακος τὸ
καίειν. εἰ δ' ἐστὶ φλογὸς ἴδιον, οὐκ ἂν εἴη ἄνθρακος ἴδιον. κατασκευάζοντι δὲ οὐδὲν οὗτος ὁ
τόπος ἐστὶ χρήσιμος.

Διαφέρει δ' ὁ ἐκ τῶν ὁμοίως ἐχόντων τοῦ ἐκ
τῶν ὁμοίως ὑπαρχόντων, ὅτι τὸ μὲν κατ' ἀνα-

what is in an equal degree a property be a property of it. For example, since 'sight' and 'hearing' are in an equal degree properties of 'man,' and 'sight' is not a property of 'man,' neither could 'hearing' be a property of 'man.' For constructive argument you must see whether what is in an equal degree a property of the subject is a property; for then what is in an equal degree a property will be a property. For example, since it is a property of 'soul,' as something primary, for part of it to be 'appetitive' in a degree equal to that in which part of it is part 'reasoning,' and it is a property of 'soul,' as something primary, for part of it to be 'appetitive,' it would be a property of 'soul,' as something primary, for part of it to be 'reasoning.'

Thirdly, for destructive criticism, you must see whether it is *not* a property of that of which it is in an equal degree a property; for then neither will it be a property of that of which it is in an equal degree a property; and, if it is a property of the former, it will not be a property of the latter. For example, since 'to cause burning' is in an equal degree a property of 'flame' and of 'live-coal,' and 'to cause burning' is not a property of 'flame,' 'to cause burning' could not be a property of 'live-coal'; and if it *is* a property of 'flame,' it could not be a property of 'live-coal.' For constructive argument, however, this commonplace is of no use. *(3) Between the alleged property and a different subject.*

The commonplace based on things which stand in a similar relation [a] differs from that based on things which belong in an equal degree,[b] because the former case is derived by analogy and not from a considera-

---

[a] See 136 b 33 ff.
[b] See 138 a 30 ff.

25 λογίαν λαμβάνεται, οὐκ ἐπὶ τοῦ ὑπάρχειν τι θεω-
ρούμενον, τὸ δ' ἐκ τοῦ ὑπάρχειν τι συγκρίνεται.

IX. Ἔπειτ' ἀνασκευάζοντα μὲν εἰ δυνάμει τὸ
ἴδιον ἀποδιδοὺς καὶ πρὸς μὴ ὂν ἀποδέδωκε τὸ
ἴδιον τῇ δυνάμει, μὴ ἐνδεχομένης τῆς δυνάμεως
30 ὑπάρχειν τῷ μὴ ὄντι· οὐ γὰρ ἔσται ἴδιον τὸ κείμενον εἶναι ἴδιον. οἷον ἐπεὶ ὁ εἴπας ἀέρος ἴδιον
τὸ ἀναπνευστὸν τῇ δυνάμει μὲν ἀπέδωκε τὸ ἴδιον
(τὸ γὰρ τοιοῦτον οἷον ἀναπνεῖσθαι ἀναπνευστόν
ἐστιν), ἀποδέδωκε δὲ καὶ πρὸς τὸ μὴ ὂν τὸ ἴδιον·
καὶ γὰρ μὴ ὄντος ζῴου, οἷον ἀναπνεῖν πέφυκε τὸ
ἀέρα, ἐνδέχεται ἀέρα εἶναι· οὐ μέντοι μὴ ὄντος
35 ζῴου δυνατόν ἐστιν ἀναπνεῖν· ὥστ' οὐδ' ἀέρος
ἔσται ἴδιον τὸ τοιοῦτον οἷον ἀναπνεῖσθαι, τότε ὅτε
ζῷον οὐκ ἔσται τοιοῦτον οἷον ἀναπνεῖν. οὐκ ἂν
οὖν εἴη ἀέρος ἴδιον τὸ ἀναπνευστόν.

139 a Κατασκευάζοντα δὲ εἰ τῇ δυνάμει ἀποδιδοὺς τὸ
ἴδιον ἢ πρὸς ὂν ἀποδίδωσι τὸ ἴδιον ἢ πρὸς μὴ ὄν,
ἐνδεχομένης τῆς δυνάμεως τῷ μὴ ὄντι ὑπάρχειν·
ἔσται γὰρ ἴδιον τὸ κείμενον μὴ εἶναι ἴδιον. οἷον
5 ἐπεὶ ὁ ἀποδιδοὺς ἴδιον τοῦ ὄντος τὸ δυνατὸν παθεῖν
ἢ ποιῆσαι, δυνάμει ἀποδιδοὺς τὸ ἴδιον, πρὸς ὂν
ἀπέδωκε τὸ ἴδιον· ὅτε γὰρ ὄν ἐστι, καὶ δυνατὸν

tion about some attribute belonging, while the latter involves a comparison based on the fact that some attribute belongs.

IX. Next, for destructive criticism, you must see whether, in assigning the property potentially, your opponent has also through the potentiality assigned the property in relation to something which does not exist, since the potentiality cannot possibly belong to something which does not exist; for then what is stated to be a property will not be a property. For example, the man who has said that 'respirable' is a property of 'air' has, on the one hand, assigned the property in virtue of a potentiality (for that is 'respirable' which is of such a kind as to be respired), while, on the other hand, he has also assigned the property in relation to what does not exist. For air can exist even if no animal exists of such a kind as to respire it; but it is impossible to respire it, if no animal exists. And so it will not be a property of air to be such as to be respired at a time when no animal will exist of such a kind as to respire it. Therefore 'respirable' could not be a property of air.

Two further rules: (a) A property is subverted when assigned potentially to something which does not exist, and confirmed *vice versa.*

For constructive argument, you must see whether in assigning the property potentially he assigns the property in relation either to something which exists or to something which does not exist, when the potentiality can belong to what does exist; for then what is stated not to be a property will be a property. For example, he who assigns 'able to affect, or be affected by, something' as a property of 'being,' by assigning the property potentially, has assigned it in relation to what exists (for, when 'being' exists, it will also be 'able to be affected by, or to affect

ARISTOTLE

139 a

παθεῖν τι ἢ ποιῆσαι ἔσται· ὥστε εἴη ἂν ἴδιον τοῦ
ὄντος τὸ δυνατὸν παθεῖν ἢ ποιῆσαι.

Ἔπειτ᾽ ἀνασκευάζοντα μὲν εἰ ὑπερβολῇ τέθεικε
10 τὸ ἴδιον· οὐ γὰρ ἔσται ἴδιον τὸ κείμενον εἶναι ἴδιον.
συμβαίνει γὰρ τοῖς οὕτως ἀποδιδοῦσι τὸ ἴδιον οὐ
καθ᾽ οὗ τὸν λόγον τοὔνομα ἀληθεύεσθαι· φθαρέντος
γὰρ τοῦ πράγματος οὐδὲν ἧττον ἔσται ὁ λόγος·
τῶν γὰρ ὄντων τινὶ μάλιστα ὑπάρχει. οἷον εἴ
15 τις ἀποδοίη τοῦ πυρὸς ἴδιον σῶμα τὸ κουφότατον·
φθαρέντος γὰρ τοῦ πυρὸς ἔσται τι τῶν σωμάτων
ὃ κουφότατον ἔσται, ὥστ᾽ οὐκ ἂν εἴη τοῦ πυρὸς
ἴδιον σῶμα τὸ κουφότατον. κατασκευάζοντα δὲ
εἰ μὴ ὑπερβολῇ τέθεικε τὸ ἴδιον· ἔσται γὰρ κατὰ
τοῦτο καλῶς κείμενον τὸ ἴδιον. οἷον ἐπεὶ ὁ θεὶς
ἀνθρώπου ἴδιον ζῷον ἥμερον φύσει οὐχ ὑπερβολῇ
20 ἀποδέδωκε τὸ ἴδιον, εἴη ἂν κατὰ τοῦτο καλῶς
κείμενον τὸ ἴδιον.

something else '), and so to be ' able to be affected by, or to affect, something else ' would be a property of ' being.'

Next, for destructive criticism, you must see whether he has stated the property in a superlative degree ; for then what is stated to be a property will not be a property. For the result of stating the property in this manner is that the name is not true of that of which the description is true ; for, if the thing itself has perished, the description will none the less exist, for it belongs in the greatest degree to something which exists. For example, if one were to assign as a property of ' fire ' that it is ' the lightest of bodies '; for, though the fire has perished, there will still be some body which will be the lightest ; and so ' the lightest body ' could not be a property of ' fire.' For constructive argument, on the other hand, you must see whether he failed to state the property in a superlative degree ; for then the property will be correctly stated in this respect. For example, since he who has stated that it is a property of ' man ' that he is ' by nature a civilized animal,' has not assigned the property in a superlative degree, the property would be correctly stated in this respect.

(b) A property is subverted if stated in the superlative.

Z

I. Τῆς δὲ περὶ τοὺς ὅρους πραγματείας μέρη
25 πέντε ἐστίν. ἢ γὰρ ὅτι ὅλως οὐκ ἀληθὲς εἰπεῖν,
καθ' οὗ τοὔνομα, καὶ τὸν λόγον (δεῖ γὰρ τὸν τοῦ
ἀνθρώπου ὁρισμὸν κατὰ παντὸς ἀνθρώπου ἀληθεύεσθαι), ἢ ὅτι ὄντος γένους οὐκ ἔθηκεν εἰς τὸ
γένος ἢ οὐκ εἰς τὸ οἰκεῖον γένος ἔθηκεν (δεῖ γὰρ
τὸν ὁριζόμενον εἰς τὸ γένος θέντα τὰς διαφορὰς
30 προσάπτειν· μάλιστα γὰρ τῶν ἐν τῷ ὁρισμῷ τὸ
γένος δοκεῖ τὴν τοῦ ὁριζομένου οὐσίαν σημαίνειν),
ἢ ὅτι οὐκ ἴδιος ὁ λόγος (δεῖ γὰρ τὸν ὁρισμὸν ἴδιον
εἶναι, καθάπερ καὶ πρότερον εἴρηται), ἢ εἰ πάντα
τὰ εἰρημένα πεποιηκὼς μὴ ὥρισται μηδ' εἴρηκε
τὸ τί ἦν εἶναι τῷ ὁριζομένῳ. λοιπὸν δὲ παρὰ τὰ
35 εἰρημένα, εἰ ὥρισται μέν, μὴ καλῶς δ' ὥρισται.

Εἰ μὲν οὖν μὴ ἀληθεύεται, καθ' οὗ τοὔνομα, καὶ
ὁ λόγος, ἐκ τῶν πρὸς τὸ συμβεβηκὸς τόπων
ἐπισκεπτέον. καὶ γὰρ ἐκεῖ, πότερον ἀληθὲς ἢ οὐκ
139 b ἀληθές, πᾶσα ἡ σκέψις γίνεται· ὅταν μὲν γὰρ ὅτι

BOOK VI

I. Of the discussion of definitions there are five parts. You must prove [a] either (1) that it is quite untrue to use the description also about the subject to which the name is given (for the definition of 'man' must be true of every man); or (2) that, though the subject has a genus, your opponent has not put it into its genus or has not put it into its proper genus (for he who defines must put the subject into its genus and then add the differentiae; for, more than any of the other component parts of a definition, the genus is generally regarded as indicating the essence of the subject of the definition); or (3) that the description is not peculiar to the subject (for the definition must be peculiar, as has been already remarked [b]); or (4) that, although he has satisfied all the above requirements, he has not given a definition, that is, he has not stated the essence of the subject which he is defining. Apart from the above conditions, (5) it still remains to see whether, although he has given a definition, he has failed to give a correct definition.

The question whether the description is not also true about the subject to which the name is given must be examined on the basis of the commonplaces relating to accident. For there also the question always asked is, 'Is it true or not?' For, when we are

(D) OF DEFINI-TION (BOOKS VI AND VII).

General division of problems dealing with definition, some of which have been already treated.

561

ὑπάρχει τὸ συμβεβηκὸς διαλεγώμεθα, ὅτι ἀληθὲς
λέγομεν, ὅταν δ' ὅτι οὐχ ὑπάρχει, ὅτι οὐκ ἀληθές. εἰ δὲ μὴ ἐν τῷ οἰκείῳ γένει ἔθηκεν, ἢ εἰ μὴ
ἴδιος ὁ ἀποδοθεὶς λόγος, ἐκ τῶν πρὸς τὸ γένος
5 καὶ τὸ ἴδιον ῥηθέντων τόπων ἐπισκεπτέον.

Λοιπὸν δ', εἰ μὴ ὥρισται ἢ εἰ μὴ καλῶς ὥρισται,
πῶς μετιτέον, εἰπεῖν. πρῶτον μὲν οὖν ἐπισκεπτέον
εἰ μὴ καλῶς ὥρισται. ῥᾷον γὰρ ὁτιοῦν ποιῆσαι
ἢ καλῶς ποιῆσαι. δῆλον οὖν ὅτι ἡ ἁμαρτία περὶ
10 τοῦτο πλείων, ἐπειδὴ ἐργωδέστερον, ὥσθ' ἡ ἐπιχείρησις ῥᾴων ἡ περὶ τοῦτο ἢ ἡ περὶ ἐκεῖνο γίνεται.

Ἔστι δὲ τοῦ μὴ καλῶς μέρη δύο, ἓν μὲν τὸ
ἀσαφεῖ τῇ ἑρμηνείᾳ κεχρῆσθαι (δεῖ γὰρ τὸν ὁριζόμενον ὡς ἐνδέχεται σαφεστάτῃ τῇ ἑρμηνείᾳ
15 κεχρῆσθαι, ἐπειδὴ τοῦ γνωρίσαι χάριν ἀποδίδοται
ὁ ὁρισμός), δεύτερον δ', εἰ ἐπὶ πλεῖον εἴρηκε τὸν
λόγον τοῦ δέοντος· πᾶν γὰρ τὸ προσκείμενον ἐν τῷ
ὁρισμῷ περίεργον. πάλιν δ' ἑκάτερον τῶν εἰρημένων εἰς πλείω μέρη διείληπται.

II. Εἷς μὲν οὖν τόπος τοῦ ἀσαφῶς, εἰ ὁμώνυμόν
20 ἐστί τινι τὸ εἰρημένον, οἷον ὅτι ἡ γένεσις ἀγωγὴ
εἰς οὐσίαν ἢ ὅτι ἡ ὑγίεια συμμετρία θερμῶν καὶ
ψυχρῶν. ὁμώνυμος γὰρ ἡ ἀγωγὴ καὶ ἡ συμμετρία·
ἄδηλον οὖν ὁπότερον βούλεται λέγειν τῶν δηλου-

arguing that the accident belongs, we assert that it is true; when we are arguing that it does not belong, we assert that it is untrue. If your opponent has failed to put the subject in its proper genus, or if the description assigned is not peculiar to the subject, we must make our inquiry on the basis of the commonplaces relating to genus and property already mentioned.

It remains to state how we ought to proceed to inquire whether the subject has not been defined or whether it has been incorrectly defined. First, then, we must examine whether it has been incorrectly defined; for it is easier to do anything, no matter what, than to do it correctly. It is obvious, then, that error is more frequent in the latter task (for it is more laborious), and so the attack is made more easily in the latter than in the former case.

Incorrectness in definition falls under two headings: The first is the use of obscure language (for the framer of a definition ought to use the clearest possible language, since the definition is assigned in order to make the subject known). The second is whether he has used a description which is unnecessarily long; for anything additional is superfluous in a definition. Each of these two headings is divided into several parts.

II. One commonplace regarding obscurity is that you should see whether what is stated is equivocal with something else, as, for example, in the statement that ' coming-to-be is a channel towards being ' or that ' health is a balancing of hot and cold.' The words ' channel ' and ' balancing ' are equivocal; it is, therefore, obscure which of the significations of a word which has more than one meaning the dis-

How to avoid obscurity.

μένων ὑπὸ τοῦ πλεοναχῶς λεγομένου. ὁμοίως δὲ
καὶ εἰ τοῦ ὁριζομένου πλεοναχῶς λεγομένου μὴ
25 διελὼν εἶπεν· ἄδηλον γὰρ ὁποτέρου τὸν ὅρον
ἀποδέδωκεν, ἐνδέχεταί τε συκοφαντεῖν ὡς οὐκ
ἐφαρμόττοντος τοῦ λόγου ἐπὶ πάντα ὧν τὸν ὁρισμὸν
ἀποδέδωκεν. μάλιστα δ᾿ ἐνδέχεται τὸ τοιοῦτον
ποιεῖν λανθανούσης τῆς ὁμωνυμίας. ἐνδέχεται δὲ
καὶ διελόμενον αὐτόν, ποσαχῶς λέγεται τὸ ἐν τῷ
30 ὁρισμῷ ἀποδοθέν, συλλογισμὸν ποιῆσαι· εἰ γὰρ
κατὰ μηδένα τῶν τρόπων ἱκανῶς εἴρηται, δῆλον
ὅτι οὐκ ἂν ὡρισμένος εἴη κατὰ τρόπον.

Ἄλλος, εἰ κατὰ μεταφορὰν εἴρηκεν, οἷον εἰ τὴν
ἐπιστήμην ἀμετάπτωτον ἢ τὴν γῆν τιθήνην ἢ
τὴν σωφροσύνην συμφωνίαν. πᾶν γὰρ ἀσαφὲς τὸ
35 κατὰ μεταφορὰν λεγόμενον. ἐνδέχεται δὲ τὸν
κατὰ μεταφορὰν[1] εἰπόντα συκοφαντεῖν ὡς κυρίως
εἰρηκότα· οὐ γὰρ ἐφαρμόσει ὁ λεχθεὶς ὅρος, οἷον
ἐπὶ τῆς σωφροσύνης· πᾶσα γὰρ συμφωνία ἐν
φθόγγοις. ἔτι εἰ γένος ἡ συμφωνία τῆς σωφρο-
140 a σύνης, ἐν δύο γένεσιν ἔσται ταὐτὸν οὐ περιέχουσιν
ἄλληλα· οὔτε γὰρ ἡ συμφωνία τὴν ἀρετὴν οὔθ᾿
ἡ ἀρετὴ τὴν συμφωνίαν περιέχει.

Ἔτι εἰ μὴ κειμένοις ὀνόμασι χρῆται, οἷον Πλάτων ὀφρυόσκιον τὸν ὀφθαλμόν, ἢ τὸ φαλάγγιον
5 σηψιδακές, ἢ τὸν μυελὸν ὀστεογενές· πᾶν γὰρ
ἀσαφὲς τὸ μὴ εἰωθός.

Ἔνια δ᾿ οὔτε καθ᾿ ὁμωνυμίαν οὔτε κατὰ μετα-

---

[1] Reading τὸν κατὰ μεταφορὰν with P.

---

[a] Presumably the reference is to Plato Comicus, since these words do not occur in the extant works of the philosopher.

putant wishes to convey. Similarly, too, if he has made a statement, when the subject which is being defined bears several senses, without distinguishing them; for then it is uncertain of which sense he has given the definition, and it is possible to make a quibbling objection on the ground that the description does not fit everything of which he has given the definition. Such a proceeding is especially possible if the equivocation is not detected. Again, it is open to his opponent himself to distinguish the various meanings of the subject rendered in the definition and argue accordingly; for, if the description is not adequate in respect of any of the various senses, obviously he cannot have given a proper description.

Another commonplace is to see whether he has spoken metaphorically, as, for example, if he has described knowledge as 'unshakeable,' or the earth as a 'nurse,' or temperance as a 'harmony'; for metaphorical expressions are always obscure. Also, it is possible to quibble against one who has spoken metaphorically, representing him as having used the word in its proper sense; for then the definition given will not fit, as in the case of 'temperance,' for 'harmony' is always used of sounds. Further, if harmony is the genus of temperance, the same thing will be found in two genera neither of which includes the other; for neither does harmony include virtue, nor virtue harmony.

Further, you must see if he uses terms of which the use is not well established, as Plato [a] calls the eye 'brow-shaded' or the poison-spider 'bite-mortifying,' or 'marrow' as 'bone-begotten'; for unusual words are always obscure.

Words are sometimes used neither equivocally, nor

140 a

φορὰν οὔτε κυρίως εἴρηται, οἷον ὁ νόμος μέτρον
ἢ εἰκὼν τῶν φύσει δικαίων. ἔστι δὲ τὰ τοιαῦτα
χείρω τῆς μεταφορᾶς· ἡ μὲν γὰρ μεταφορὰ ποιεῖ
10 πως γνώριμον τὸ σημαινόμενον διὰ τὴν ὁμοιότητα·
πάντες γὰρ οἱ μεταφέροντες κατά τινα ὁμοιότητα
μεταφέρουσιν· τὸ δὲ τοιοῦτον οὐ ποιεῖ γνώριμον·
οὔτε γὰρ ἡ ὁμοιότης ὑπάρχει, καθ᾽ ἣν μέτρον ἢ
εἰκὼν ὁ νόμος ἐστίν, οὔτε κυρίως εἴωθε λέγεσθαι.
ὥστε εἰ μὲν κυρίως μέτρον ἢ εἰκόνα τὸν νόμον
15 φησὶν εἶναι, ψεύδεται· εἰκὼν γάρ ἐστιν οὗ ἡ γένεσις
διὰ μιμήσεως, τοῦτο δ᾽ οὐχ ὑπάρχει τῷ νόμῳ·
εἰ δὲ μὴ κυρίως, δῆλον ὅτι ἀσαφῶς εἴρηκε καὶ
χεῖρον ὁποιουοῦν τῶν κατὰ μεταφορὰν λεγομένων.

Ἔτι εἰ μὴ δῆλος ὁ τοῦ ἐναντίου λόγος ἐκ τοῦ
λεχθέντος· οἱ γὰρ καλῶς ἀποδεδομένοι καὶ τοὺς
20 ἐναντίους προσσημαίνουσιν. ἢ εἰ καθ᾽ αὑτὸν
λεχθεὶς μὴ φανερὸς εἴη τίνος ἐστὶν ὁρισμός, ἀλλὰ
καθάπερ τὰ τῶν ἀρχαίων γραφέων, εἰ μή τις
ἐπιγράψαι, οὐκ ἐγνωρίζετο τί ἐστιν ἕκαστον.

III. Εἰ μὲν οὖν μὴ σαφῶς, ἐκ τῶν τοιούτων
ἐστὶν ἐπισκεπτέον. εἰ δ᾽ ἐπὶ πλεῖον εἴρηκε τὸν
25 ὅρον, πρῶτον μὲν σκοπεῖν εἴ τινι κέχρηται ὃ πᾶσιν
ὑπάρχει, ἢ ὅλως τοῖς οὖσιν ἢ τοῖς ὑπὸ ταὐτὸ γένος

metaphorically, nor in their proper sense; for example, the law is said to be the 'measure' or 'image' of things naturally just. Such phrases are worse than metaphors; for a metaphor in a way adds to our knowledge of what is indicated on account of the similarity, for those who use metaphors always do so on account of some similarity. But the kind of phrase of which we are speaking does not add to our knowledge; for no similarity exists in virtue of which the law is a 'measure' or an 'image,' nor is the law usually described by these words in their proper sense. So, if anyone says that the law is a 'measure' or an 'image' in the proper sense of these words, he is lying; for an image is something whose coming into being is due to imitation, and this does not apply to the law. If, however, he is not using the word in its proper sense, obviously he has spoken obscurely, and with worse effect than any kind of metaphorical language.

Further, you must see whether the definition of the contrary fails to be clear from the description given; for correctly assigned definitions also indicate their contraries. Or, again, you must see whether, when it is stated by itself, it fails to show clearly what it is that it defines, just as in the works of the early painters, unless they were inscribed, it was impossible to recognize what each figure represented.

III. If, then, the definition is not clearly rendered, it should be examined by the methods described above. If, however, he has stated the definition in too many words, you must first see if he has made use of any attribute universally applicable, that is, either generally to existing things, or to things which fall under the same genus as the subject of the defini-

How to avoid redundancy.

140 a

τῷ ὁριζομένῳ· ἐπὶ πλεῖον γὰρ εἰρῆσθαι ἀναγκαῖον
τοῦτο. δεῖ γὰρ τὸ μὲν γένος ἀπὸ τῶν ἄλλων
χωρίζειν, τὴν δὲ διαφορὰν ἀπό τινος τῶν ἐν τῷ
αὐτῷ γένει. τὸ μὲν οὖν πᾶσιν ὑπάρχον ἁπλῶς
30 ἀπ' οὐδενὸς χωρίζει, τὸ δὲ τοῖς ὑπὸ ταὐτὸ γένος
πᾶσιν ὑπάρχον οὐ χωρίζει ἀπὸ τῶν ἐν ταὐτῷ γένει,
ὥστε μάταιον τὸ τοιοῦτον προσκείμενον.

Ἢ εἰ ἔστι μὲν ἴδιον τὸ προσκείμενον, ἀφαιρεθέντος δὲ τούτου καὶ ὁ λοιπὸς λόγος ἴδιός ἐστι
35 καὶ δηλοῖ τὴν οὐσίαν. οἷον ἐν τῷ τοῦ ἀνθρώπου
λόγῳ τὸ ἐπιστήμης δεκτικὸν προστεθὲν περίεργον·
καὶ γὰρ ἀφαιρεθέντος τούτου ὁ λοιπὸς λόγος
ἴδιος καὶ δηλοῖ τὴν οὐσίαν. ἁπλῶς δ' εἰπεῖν,
140 b ἅπαν περίεργον οὗ ἀφαιρεθέντος τὸ λοιπὸν δῆλον
ποιεῖ τὸ ὁριζόμενον. τοιοῦτος δὲ καὶ ὁ τῆς ψυχῆς
ὅρος, εἰ ἀριθμὸς αὐτὸς αὑτὸν κινῶν ἐστίν· καὶ γὰρ
τὸ αὐτὸ αὑτὸ κινοῦν ψυχή, καθάπερ Πλάτων
5 ὥρισται. ἢ ἴδιον μέν ἐστι τὸ εἰρημένον, οὐ δηλοῖ
δὲ τὴν οὐσίαν ἀφαιρεθέντος τοῦ ἀριθμοῦ. ποτέρως
μὲν οὖν ἔχει, χαλεπὸν διασαφῆσαι· χρηστέον δ'
ἐπὶ πάντων τῶν τοιούτων πρὸς τὸ συμφέρον.
οἷον ὅτι ὁ τοῦ φλέγματος ὅρος ὑγρὸν πρῶτον
ἀπὸ τροφῆς ἄπεπτον. ἓν γὰρ τὸ πρῶτον, οὐ
πολλά, ὥστε περίεργον τὸ ἄπεπτον προσκείμενον·
10 καὶ γὰρ τούτου ἀφαιρεθέντος ὁ λοιπὸς ἔσται ἴδιος
λόγος· οὐ γὰρ ἐνδέχεται ἀπὸ τῆς τροφῆς καὶ τοῦτο

---

a Xenocrates, fr. 60 (Heinze) ; de Anim. 404 b 29.

tion ; for then there must necessarily be redundancy in the statement. For the genus ought to separate the subject from all other things, and the differentia from something in the same genus. Now what is universally applicable does not separate the subject from anything at all, and what belongs to everything which falls under the same genus does not separate it from the other things which fall under the same genus ; and so such an addition has no point.

Or, again, you must see whether, though the addition is peculiar to the subject, yet its removal still leaves the rest of the description peculiar to the subject and demonstrates the essence. For example, in the description of ' man ' the addition of ' receptive of knowledge ' is superfluous ; for, if it is removed, the rest of the description is still peculiar and demonstrates the essence. In a word, anything is superfluous the removal of which leaves a clear statement of the subject of the definition. The definition of the soul, if stated as a ' number moving itself,'[a] is a case in point ; for the soul is ' that which moves itself,' according to Plato's definition.[b] Or, perhaps, the statement, though it is peculiar to the subject, does not demonstrate the essence if the word ' number ' is removed. Which of the two statements is true, it is difficult to determine ; but in all such cases our procedure must be guided by expediency. For example, take the definition of phlegm as ' the first unconcocted moisture from food.' Here that which is ' first ' is one and not many, so that the addition of ' unconcocted ' is superfluous ; for, if it is removed, the rest of the description will be peculiar to the subject ; for it is not possible for both phlegm and

[b] *Phaedr.* 245 E.

καὶ ἄλλο τι πρῶτον εἶναι. ἢ οὐχ ἁπλῶς πρῶτον
ἀπὸ τροφῆς τὸ φλέγμα, ἀλλὰ τῶν ἀπέπτων πρῶτον,
ὥστε προσθετέον τὸ ἄπεπτον· ἐκείνως μὲν γὰρ
ῥηθέντος οὐκ ἀληθὴς ὁ λόγος, εἴπερ μὴ πάντων
15 πρῶτόν ἐστιν.

Ἔτι εἴ τι τῶν ἐν τῷ λόγῳ μὴ πᾶσιν ὑπάρχει
τοῖς ὑπὸ ταὐτὸ εἶδος· ὁ γὰρ τοιοῦτος χεῖρον
ὥρισται τῶν χρωμένων ὃ πᾶσιν ὑπάρχει τοῖς
οὖσιν. ἐκείνως μὲν γὰρ ἂν ὁ λοιπὸς ἴδιος ᾖ λόγος,
20 καὶ ὁ πᾶς ἴδιος ἔσται· ἁπλῶς γὰρ πρὸς τὸ ἴδιον
ὁτουοῦν προστεθέντος ἀληθοῦς ὅλος ἴδιος γίνεται.
εἰ δέ τι τῶν ἐν τῷ λόγῳ μὴ πᾶσιν ὑπάρχει τοῖς
ὑπὸ ταὐτὸ εἶδος, ἀδύνατον ὅλον τὸν λόγον ἴδιον
εἶναι· οὐ γὰρ ἀντικατηγορηθήσεται τοῦ πράγματος.
οἷον τὸ ζῷον πεζὸν δίπουν τετράπηχυ· ὁ γὰρ
25 τοιοῦτος λόγος οὐκ ἀντικατηγορεῖται τοῦ πράγματος διὰ τὸ μὴ πᾶσιν ὑπάρχειν τοῖς ὑπὸ ταὐτὸν
εἶδος τὸ τετράπηχυ.

Πάλιν εἰ ταὐτὸν πλεονάκις εἴρηκεν, οἷον τὴν ἐπιθυμίαν ὄρεξιν ἡδέος εἰπών· πᾶσα γὰρ ἐπιθυμία ἡδέος
ἐστίν, ὥστε καὶ τὸ ταὐτὸν τῇ ἐπιθυμίᾳ ἡδέος ἔσται.
30 γίνεται οὖν ὅρος τῆς ἐπιθυμίας ὄρεξις ἡδέος
ἡδέος· οὐδὲν γὰρ διαφέρει ἐπιθυμίαν εἰπεῖν ἢ ὄρεξιν ἡδέος, ὥσθ᾽ ἑκάτερον αὐτῶν ἡδέος ἔσται. ἢ

something else as well to be the first thing produced from food. Or, possibly, phlegm is not the first thing produced from food, but only the first of things un-concocted, so that the word ' unconcocted ' must be added ; for according to the other statement the description is untrue unless phlegm is the first product of all.

Moreover, you must see whether anything in the description fails to belong to everything which falls under the same species ; for a definition of this kind is worse than one which employs an attribute which is universally applicable. For, in that case, if the rest of the description is peculiar to the subject, the whole definition too will be peculiar ; for, without exception, if anything at all which is true is added to what is peculiar, the whole becomes peculiar. If, on the other hand, anything in the description does not belong to everything which falls under the same species, the description as a whole cannot be peculiar; for it will not be predicated convertibly with the subject. Take, for example, the definition ' pedestrian biped animal four cubits high ' ; such a description is not predicated convertibly with the subject, because ' four cubits high ' does not belong to everything which falls under the same species.

Again, you must see whether he has said the same thing more than once, as, for example, if he declares that ' desire ' is an ' appetite for the pleasant ' ; for all ' desire ' is ' for the pleasant,' so that what is the same as desire will also be ' for the pleasant.' The result then is a definition of ' desire ' as ' an appetite-for-the-pleasant for the pleasant ' ; for there is no difference between saying ' desire ' and ' appetite for the pleasant,' so that both will be ' for the pleasant.'

140 b

τοῦτο μὲν οὐδὲν ἄτοπον· καὶ γὰρ ὁ ἄνθρωπος δι
πουν ἐστίν, ὥστε καὶ τὸ ταὐτὸν τῷ ἀνθρώπῳ δίπουν
ἔσται. ἔστι δὲ ταὐτὸν τῷ ἀνθρώπῳ ζῷον πεζὸν δίπουν, ὥστε ζῷον πεζὸν δίπουν δίπουν ἐστίν.
35 ἀλλ' οὐ διὰ τοῦτο ἄτοπόν τι συμβαίνει· οὐ γὰρ
κατὰ ζῴου πεζοῦ τὸ δίπουν κατηγορεῖται (οὕτω
μὲν γὰρ ἂν δὶς περὶ τοῦ αὐτοῦ τὸ δίπουν ἂν κατ-
141 a ηγοροῖτο), ἀλλὰ περὶ ζῴου πεζοῦ δίποδος τὸ
δίπουν λέγεται, ὥστε ἅπαξ μόνον τὸ δίπουν
κατηγορεῖται. ὁμοίως δὲ καὶ ἐπὶ τῆς ἐπιθυμίας·
οὐ γὰρ κατὰ τῆς ὀρέξεως τὸ ἡδέος εἶναι κατηγορεῖται, ἀλλὰ κατὰ τοῦ σύμπαντος, ὥστε ἅπαξ
5 καὶ ἐνταῦθα ἡ κατηγορία γίνεται. οὐκ ἔστι δὲ
τὸ δὶς φθέγξασθαι ταὐτὸν ὄνομα τῶν ἀτόπων,
ἀλλὰ τὸ πλεονάκις περί τινος τὸ αὐτὸ κατηγο-
ρῆσαι, οἷον ὡς Ξενοκράτης τὴν φρόνησιν ὁρι-
στικὴν καὶ θεωρητικὴν τῶν ὄντων φησὶν εἶναι. ἡ
γὰρ ὁριστικὴ θεωρητική τίς ἐστιν, ὥστε δὶς τὸ
αὐτὸ λέγει προσθεὶς πάλιν καὶ θεωρητικήν.
10 ὁμοίως δὲ καὶ ὅσοι τὴν κατάψυξιν στέρησιν τοῦ
κατὰ φύσιν θερμοῦ φασιν εἶναι· πᾶσα γὰρ στέρησίς
ἐστι τοῦ κατὰ φύσιν ὑπάρχοντος, ὥστε περίεργον
τὸ προσθεῖναι τοῦ κατὰ φύσιν, ἀλλ' ἱκανὸν ἦν
εἰπεῖν στέρησιν θερμοῦ, ἐπειδὴ αὐτὴ ἡ στέρησις
γνώριμον ποιεῖ ὅτι τοῦ κατὰ φύσιν λέγεται.
15 Πάλιν εἰ τοῦ καθόλου εἰρημένου προσθείη καὶ
ἐπὶ μέρους, οἷον εἰ τὴν ἐπιείκειαν ἐλάττωσιν τῶν
συμφερόντων καὶ δικαίων· τὸ γὰρ δίκαιον συμφέρον τι, ὥστε περιέχεται ἐν τῷ συμφέροντι.

Or, perhaps, there is no absurdity here. Take the statement, ' man is a biped '; then, what is the same as man will be a ' biped '; but ' pedestrian biped animal ' is the same as man, and, therefore, ' pedestrian biped animal ' is a ' biped.' But no absurdity really arises here ; for ' biped ' is not *predicated* of ' pedestrian animal ' (for then ' biped ' would be predicated twice of the same thing), but ' biped ' is used in the description of ' pedestrian biped animal,' so that ' biped ' is *predicated* only once. So likewise with ' desire ' too ; for that it is ' for the pleasant ' is predicated not of appetite but of the whole phrase,[a] and so here too the predication occurs only once. The absurdity consists not in uttering the same word twice but in *predicating* the same thing more than once of anything ; for example, when Xenocrates says that prudence is ' definitive and contemplative of things which exist '; for what is ' definitive ' is in a way ' contemplative,' so that when he adds ' and contemplative ' he is saying the same things twice. So, too, with those who say that ' cooling ' is a ' privation of natural heat '; for all privation is a privation of that which is natural, so that it is superfluous to add ' natural,' but it would be enough to say ' privation of heat,' since the term ' privation ' itself makes it known that the heat referred to is ' natural.'

Again, you must see whether, after a universal has been stated, he adds a particular as well, for example, if he has said that ' equity is a diminution of the expedient and the just '; for the just is something expedient, so that it is included in the expedient.

---

[a] *i.e.* of the phrase ' appetite for the pleasant.' If we predicate ' is for the pleasant ' of this, only the second ' for the pleasant ' is in the predicate.

141 a

περιττὸν οὖν τὸ δίκαιον, ὥστε καθόλου εἴπας ἐπὶ
μέρους προσέθηκεν. καὶ εἰ τὴν ἰατρικὴν ἐπι-
20 στήμην τῶν ὑγιεινῶν ζῴῳ καὶ ἀνθρώπῳ, ἢ τὸν
νόμον εἰκόνα τῶν φύσει καλῶν καὶ δικαίων· τὸ
γὰρ δίκαιον καλόν τι, ὥστε πλεονάκις τὸ αὐτὸ
λέγει.

IV. Πότερον μὲν οὖν καλῶς ἢ οὐ καλῶς, διὰ
τούτων καὶ τῶν τοιούτων ἐπισκεπτέον· πότερον
25 δ᾽ εἴρηκε καὶ ὥρισται τὸ τί ἦν εἶναι ἢ οὐχί, ἐκ
τῶνδε.

Πρῶτον μὲν εἰ μὴ διὰ προτέρων καὶ γνωριμωτέρων πεποίηται τὸν ὁρισμόν. ἐπεὶ γὰρ ὁ
ὅρος ἀποδίδοται τοῦ γνωρίσαι χάριν τὸ λεχθέν,
γνωρίζομεν δ᾽ οὐκ ἐκ τῶν τυχόντων ἀλλ᾽ ἐκ τῶν
προτέρων καὶ γνωριμωτέρων, καθάπερ ἐν ταῖς
30 ἀποδείξεσιν (οὕτω γὰρ πᾶσα διδασκαλία καὶ
μάθησις ἔχει), φανερὸν ὅτι ὁ μὴ διὰ τοιούτων
ὁριζόμενος οὐχ ὥρισται. εἰ δὲ μή, πλείους ἔσονται
τοῦ αὐτοῦ ὁρισμοί. δῆλον γὰρ ὅτι καὶ ὁ διὰ
προτέρων καὶ γνωριμωτέρων βέλτιον ὥρισται,
ὥστε ἀμφότεροι ἂν εἶησαν ὅροι τοῦ αὐτοῦ. τὸ
35 δὲ τοιοῦτον οὐ δοκεῖ· ἑκάστῳ γὰρ τῶν ὄντων ἕν
ἐστι τὸ εἶναι ὅπερ ἐστίν· ὥστ᾽ εἰ πλείους ἔσονται
τοῦ αὐτοῦ ὁρισμοί, ταὐτὸν ἔσται τῷ ὁριζομένῳ
τὸ εἶναι ὅπερ καθ᾽ ἑκάτερον τῶν ὁρισμῶν δηλοῦται,
141 b ταῦτα δ᾽ οὐ ταὐτά ἐστιν, ἐπειδὴ οἱ ὁρισμοὶ ἕτεροι.

'The just' is, therefore, superfluous, and so after stating the universal he has added the particular. So too in the definition of 'medicine' as 'knowledge of things healthful for animal and man,' or 'law' as 'the image of things naturally noble and just'; for the just is something noble, so that he is saying the same thing more than once.

IV. Whether your opponent has made a correct or an incorrect definition should be examined by these and similar methods; but whether he has stated and defined the essence or not, should be examined in the following manner :

First, you must see whether he has failed to make the definition by means of prior and more intelligible terms. For the object in assigning the definition is to make known the meaning of the subject, and we make things known by using, not any chance terms, but those which are prior and more intelligible, as we do in demonstrations (for this is true of every kind of teaching and learning) ; it is, therefore, obvious that the man who does not define by means of such terms has not defined at all. With any other method, there will be more than one definition of the same thing ; for clearly he who has used terms which are prior and more intelligible has given another and a better definition, so that both would be definitions of the same thing. But this is not the view generally held ; for everything that is has one single essence, and so, if there is to be more than one definition of the same thing, the essence, which is demonstrated in accordance with each of the definitions, will be the same for the framer of the definition ; but the demonstrations of it are not the same since the definitions are different. It is, therefore, obvious

Rules for testing whether the alleged definition really defines the essence :

The terms of a definition should be prior and more intelligible.

575

141 b

δῆλον οὖν ὅτι οὐχ ὥρισται ὁ μὴ διὰ προτέρων
καὶ γνωριμωτέρων ὁρισάμενος.

Τὸ μὲν οὖν μὴ διὰ γνωριμωτέρων εἰρῆσθαι τὸν
ὅρον διχῶς ἔστιν ἐκλαβεῖν· ἢ γὰρ εἰ ἁπλῶς ἐξ
5 ἀγνωστοτέρων ἢ εἰ ἡμῖν ἀγνωστοτέρων· ἐνδέχεται
γὰρ ἀμφοτέρως. ἁπλῶς μὲν οὖν γνωριμώτερον
τὸ πρότερον τοῦ ὑστέρου, οἷον στιγμὴ γραμμῆς
καὶ γραμμὴ ἐπιπέδου καὶ ἐπίπεδον στερεοῦ, καθάπερ καὶ μονὰς ἀριθμοῦ· πρότερον γὰρ καὶ ἀρχὴ
παντὸς ἀριθμοῦ. ὁμοίως δὲ καὶ στοιχεῖον συλ-
10 λαβῆς. ἡμῖν δ' ἀνάπαλιν ἐνίοτε συμβαίνει· μάλιστα
γὰρ τὸ στερεὸν ὑπὸ τὴν αἴσθησιν πίπτει, τὸ δ'
ἐπίπεδον μᾶλλον τῆς γραμμῆς, γραμμὴ δὲ σημείου
μᾶλλον. οἱ πολλοὶ γὰρ τὰ τοιαῦτα προγνωρί-
ζουσιν· τὰ μὲν γὰρ τῆς τυχούσης τὰ δ' ἀκριβοῦς
καὶ περιττῆς διανοίας καταμαθεῖν ἐστιν.

15 Ἁπλῶς μὲν οὖν βέλτιον τὸ διὰ τῶν πρότερον τὰ
ὕστερα πειρᾶσθαι γνωρίζειν· ἐπιστημονικώτερον
γὰρ τὸ τοιοῦτόν ἐστιν. οὐ μὴν ἀλλὰ πρὸς τοὺς
ἀδυνατοῦντας γνωρίζειν διὰ τῶν τοιούτων ἀναγκαῖον ἴσως διὰ τῶν ἐκείνοις γνωρίμων ποιεῖσθαι
τὸν λόγον. εἰσὶ δὲ τῶν τοιούτων ὁρισμῶν ὅ τε
20 τῆς στιγμῆς καὶ ὁ τῆς γραμμῆς καὶ ὁ τοῦ ἐπι-
πέδου· πάντες γὰρ διὰ τῶν ὑστέρων τὰ πρότερα
δηλοῦσιν· τὸ μὲν γὰρ γραμμῆς, τὸ δ' ἐπιπέδου,
τὸ δὲ στερεοῦ φασὶ πέρας εἶναι. οὐ δεῖ δὲ λανθάνειν ὅτι τοὺς οὕτως ὁριζομένους οὐκ ἐνδέχεται τὸ

that anyone who has not framed his definition by means of prior and more intelligible terms has not given a definition.

That the definition has not been stated in more intelligible terms can be taken in two senses, namely, that it is composed either of terms which are less intelligible absolutely or of terms which are less intelligible to us; for both meanings are possible. Thus absolutely the prior is more intelligible than the posterior; for example, a point is more intelligible than a line, a line than a plane, and a plane than a solid, just as also a unit is more intelligible than a number, since it is prior to and the starting-point of all number. Similarly a letter is more intelligible than a syllable. To us, however, the converse sometimes happens; for a solid falls most under our perception, and a plane more than a line, and a line more than a point. For most people recognize such things as solids and planes before they recognize lines and points; for the former can be grasped by an ordinary understanding, the latter only by one which is accurate and superior.

How to detect the failure to use more intelligible terms of definition.

Absolutely, then, it is better to aim at knowledge of the posterior by means of what is prior; for such a method is more scientific. Nevertheless, for the benefit of those who are incapable of acquiring knowledge by such means, it is perhaps necessary to frame the description by means of terms which are intelligible to them. Among definitions of this kind are those of the point, the line and the plane; for all these demonstrate the prior by means of the posterior —the point being called the limit of the line, the line that of the plane, and the plane that of the solid. We must not, however, fail to notice that it is impossible

141 b

τί ἦν εἶναι τῷ ὁριζομένῳ δηλοῦν, ἐὰν μὴ τυγχάνῃ
25 ταὐτὸν ἡμῖν τε γνωριμώτερον καὶ ἁπλῶς γνωριμώτερον, εἴπερ δεῖ μὲν διὰ τοῦ γένους καὶ τῶν
διαφορῶν ὁρίζεσθαι τὸν καλῶς ὁριζόμενον, ταῦτα
δὲ τῶν ἁπλῶς γνωριμωτέρων καὶ προτέρων τοῦ
εἴδους ἐστίν. συναναιρεῖ γὰρ τὸ γένος καὶ ἡ
διαφορὰ τὸ εἶδος, ὥστε πρότερα ταῦτα τοῦ εἴδους.
30 ἔστι δὲ καὶ γνωριμώτερα· τοῦ μὲν γὰρ εἴδους
γνωριζομένου ἀνάγκη καὶ τὸ γένος καὶ τὴν διαφορὰν γνωρίζεσθαι (ὁ γὰρ ἄνθρωπον γνωρίζων
καὶ ζῷον καὶ πεζὸν γνωρίζει), τοῦ δὲ γένους ἢ
τῆς διαφορᾶς γνωριζομένης οὐκ ἀνάγκη καὶ τὸ
εἶδος γνωρίζεσθαι, ὥστε ἀγνωστότερον τὸ εἶδος.
ἔτι τοῖς κατ' ἀλήθειαν τοὺς τοιούτους ὁρισμοὺς
35 φάσκουσιν εἶναι, τοὺς ἐκ τῶν ἑκάστῳ γνωρίμων,
πολλοὺς τοῦ αὐτοῦ συμβήσεται λέγειν ὁρισμοὺς
εἶναι· ἕτερα γὰρ ἑτέροις καὶ οὐ ταὐτὰ πᾶσι τυγχάνει γνωριμώτερα ὄντα, ὥστε πρὸς ἕκαστον
142 a ἕτερος ἂν εἴη ὁρισμὸς ἀποδοτέος, εἴπερ ἐκ τῶν
ἑκάστοις γνωριμωτέρων τὸν ὁρισμὸν ποιεῖσθαι
χρή. ἔτι τοῖς αὐτοῖς ἄλλοτ' ἄλλα μᾶλλον γνώριμα,
ἐξ ἀρχῆς μὲν τὰ αἰσθητά, ἀκριβεστέροις δὲ γινο-
5 μένοις ἀνάπαλιν, ὥστ' οὐδὲ πρὸς τὸν αὐτὸν ἀεὶ
ὁ αὐτὸς ὁρισμὸς ἀποδοτέος τοῖς διὰ τῶν ἑκάστοις
γνωριμωτέρων τὸν ὁρισμὸν φάσκουσιν ἀποδοτέον

for those who define in this way to show the essence
of the subject of their definition, unless it so happens
that the same thing is both more intelligible to us
and also more intelligible absolutely ; for the framer
of a good definition must define by means of the
genus and the differentiae, and these are among the
things which are more intelligible absolutely than
the species and prior to it ; for the genus and the
differentia cancel the species and therefore are prior
to it. They are also more intelligible ; for, if the
species is known, both the genus and the differentia
must also be known (for he who has knowledge of
' man ' has also knowledge of ' animal ' and ' pedestrian '). On the other hand, if the genus and the
differentia are known, it does not necessarily follow
that the species is also known ; the species, therefore,
is less intelligible. Furthermore, those who declare
that such definitions, namely, those which are based on
what is known to individual persons, accord with the
truth, will, as a result, have to say that there are
many definitions of the same thing ; for different
things are more intelligible to different people, and
not the same things equally intelligible to all ; and so
a different definition would have to be given to each
individual, if the definition has to be framed as the
basis of what is more intelligible to each of them.
Furthermore, to the same persons different things
are more intelligible at different times—first of all
the objects of sense-perception, and then, when their
knowledge becomes more accurate, the converse
occurs ; and so neither would the same definition
always have to be given to the same person by those
who say that a definition ought to be given by means
of what is more intelligible to each individual. It

εἶναι. δῆλον οὖν ὅτι οὐχ ὁριστέον διὰ τῶν τοιούτων, ἀλλὰ διὰ τῶν ἁπλῶς γνωριμωτέρων· μόνως
γὰρ ἂν οὕτως εἷς καὶ ὁ αὐτὸς ὁρισμὸς ἀεὶ γίνοιτο.
ἴσως δὲ καὶ τὸ ἁπλῶς γνώριμον οὐ τὸ πᾶσι
10 γνώριμόν ἐστιν, ἀλλὰ τὸ τοῖς εὖ διακειμένοις τὴν
διάνοιαν, καθάπερ καὶ τὸ ἁπλῶς ὑγιεινὸν τὸ τοῖς
εὖ ἔχουσι τὸ σῶμα. δεῖ μὲν οὖν ἕκαστα τῶν
τοιούτων ἐξακριβοῦν, χρῆσθαι δὲ διαλεγομένους
πρὸς τὸ συμφέρον. μάλιστα δ' ὁμολογουμένως
15 ἀναιρεῖν ἐνδέχεται τὸν ὁρισμόν, ἐὰν μήτ' ἐκ τῶν
ἁπλῶς γνωριμωτέρων μήτ' ἐκ τῶν ἡμῖν τυγχάνῃ
τὸν λόγον πεποιημένος.

Εἷς μὲν οὖν τρόπος τοῦ μὴ διὰ γνωριμωτέρων
ἐστὶ τὸ διὰ τῶν ὑστέρων τὰ πρότερα δηλοῦν,
καθάπερ πρότερον εἴπαμεν· ἄλλος, εἰ τοῦ ἐν
ἠρεμίᾳ καὶ τοῦ ὡρισμένου διὰ τοῦ ἀορίστου καὶ
20 τοῦ ἐν κινήσει ἀποδέδοται ὁ λόγος· πρότερον γὰρ
τὸ μένον καὶ τὸ ὡρισμένον τοῦ ἀορίστου καὶ ἐν
κινήσει ὄντος.

Τοῦ δὲ μὴ ἐκ προτέρων τρεῖς εἰσι τρόποι, πρῶτος μὲν εἰ διὰ τοῦ ἀντικειμένου τὸ ἀντικείμενον
ὥρισται, οἷον διὰ τοῦ κακοῦ τὸ ἀγαθόν· ἅμα γὰρ
25 τῇ φύσει τὰ ἀντικείμενα. ἐνίοις δὲ καὶ ἡ αὐτὴ
ἐπιστήμη ἀμφοτέρων δοκεῖ εἶναι, ὥστ' οὐδὲ
γνωριμώτερον τὸ ἕτερον τοῦ ἑτέρου. δεῖ δὲ μὴ
λανθάνειν ὅτι ἔνια ἴσως οὐκ ἔστιν ὁρίσασθαι
ἄλλως, οἷον τὸ διπλάσιον ἄνευ τοῦ ἡμίσεος, καὶ
ὅσα καθ' αὑτὰ πρός τι λέγεται· πᾶσι γὰρ τοῖς

---

a 141 a 26 f.

is obvious, therefore, that definitions ought not to be made by means of terms of this kind but by means of those which are more intelligible absolutely; for only thus could one and the same definition be always produced. Perhaps, also, what is intelligible absolutely is what is intelligible not to everyone but only to those who are intellectually in a sound condition, just as also what is healthy absolutely is what is healthy to those who are physically in a sound condition. All such points must be accurately observed and used in discussion as circumstances demand. But the subversion of a definition is most generally admitted to be possible, if the definer happens to have framed his description neither from what is more intelligible absolutely nor from what is more intelligible to us.

One way, then, of not defining by means of more intelligible terms is to demonstrate the prior by means of the posterior, as we said before.[a] Another way consists in having rendered the description of what is at rest and definite by means of what is indefinite and in motion; for what stays still and is definite is prior to what is indefinite and in motion.

There are three ways of failing to define by means of prior terms. (a) The first is when an opposite has been defined by means of its opposite, for example, good by means of evil; for opposites are naturally simultaneous. In the view of some people, too, there is the same knowledge of both, so that the one is not more intelligible than the other. We must not, however, fail to notice that it is perhaps impossible to define some things in any other way. We cannot, for example, define the double without the half, and the same is true also of things which are described as

How to detect the failure to use prior terms of definition.

581

142 a

τοιούτοις ταὐτὸν τὸ εἶναι τῷ πρός τί πως ἔχειν,
30 ὥστ' ἀδύνατον ἄνευ θατέρου θάτερον γνωρίζειν,
διόπερ ἀναγκαῖον ἐν τῷ τοῦ ἑτέρου λόγῳ συμ-
περιειλῆφθαι καὶ θάτερον. γνωρίζειν μὲν οὖν
δεῖ τὰ τοιαῦτα πάντα, χρῆσθαι δ' αὐτοῖς ὡς ἂν
δοκῇ συμφέρειν.

Ἄλλος, εἰ αὐτῷ κέχρηται τῷ ὁριζομένῳ. λαν-
35 θάνει δ', ὅταν μὴ αὐτῷ τῷ τοῦ ὁριζομένου ὀνόματι
142 b χρήσηται, οἷον εἰ τὸν ἥλιον ἄστρον ἡμεροφανὲς
ὡρίσατο· ὁ γὰρ ἡμέρᾳ χρώμενος ἡλίῳ χρῆται. δεῖ
δ' ὅπως φωραθῇ τὰ τοιαῦτα μεταλαμβάνειν ἀντὶ
τοῦ ὀνόματος τὸν λόγον, οἷον ὅτι ἡμέρα ἡλίου
φορὰ ὑπὲρ γῆς ἐστίν· δῆλον γὰρ ὅτι ὁ τὴν φορὰν
5 ἡλίου ὑπὲρ γῆς εἰρηκὼς τὸν ἥλιον εἴρηκεν, ὥστε
κέχρηται τῷ ἡλίῳ ὁ τῇ ἡμέρᾳ χρησάμενος.

Πάλιν εἰ τῷ ἀντιδιῃρημένῳ τὸ ἀντιδιῃρημένον
ὥρισται, οἷον περιττὸν τὸ μονάδι μεῖζον ἀρτίου.
ἅμα γὰρ τῇ φύσει τὰ ἐκ τοῦ αὐτοῦ γένους ἀντιδι-
10 ῃρημένα, τὸ δὲ περιττὸν καὶ ἄρτιον ἀντιδιῄρηται·
ἄμφω γὰρ ἀριθμοῦ διαφοραί.

Ὁμοίως δὲ καὶ εἰ διὰ τῶν ὑποκάτω τὸ ἐπάνω
ὥρισται, οἷον ἄρτιον ἀριθμὸν τὸν δίχα διαιρούμενον

---

^a See 136 b 3 ff.

in themselves relative; for in all such things their being is the same as a certain relation in which they stand to something, so that it is impossible to recognize the one without the other and, therefore, necessary that the one should also be included in the description of the other. We must, therefore, take cognizance of all such facts and make use of them as seems expedient.

(b) Another way is when the term which is being defined is used in the definition itself. This passes unobserved when the actual name of the object which is being defined is not employed, for example, if one has defined the sun as ' a star appearing by day '; for in introducing the day one introduces the sun. For the detection of this kind of practice we must substitute the description for the name, saying, for example, that ' day ' is ' the passage of the sun over the earth '; for it is obvious that a man who has spoken of ' the passage of the sun over the earth ' has spoken of ' the sun,' so he who has introduced ' the day ' has introduced ' the sun.'

(c) Again, you must see whether your opponent has defined one of the opposite members of corresponding divisions [a] by means of another, for example, if he has defined ' an odd number ' as ' one which is greater by a unit than an even number.' For the opposite numbers of corresponding divisions taken from the same genus are by nature simultaneous, and ' odd ' and ' even ' are opposite members of corresponding divisions, for both are differentiae of number.

(d) Similarly also, you must see whether he has defined a superior by means of subordinates, for example, if he has defined an ' even number ' as ' a number divisible into two parts ' or ' the good ' as ' a

ἢ τὸ ἀγαθὸν ἕξιν ἀρετῆς· τό τε γὰρ δίχα ἀπὸ
τῶν δύο εἴληπται, ἀρτίων ὄντων, καὶ ἡ ἀρετὴ ἀγα-
15 θόν τί ἐστιν, ὥσθ' ὑποκάτω ταῦτα ἐκείνων ἐστίν.
ἔτι δ' ἀνάγκη τὸν τῷ ὑποκάτω χρώμενον καὶ αὐτῷ χρῆσθαι. ὅ τε γὰρ τῇ ἀρετῇ χρώμενος χρῆται
τῷ ἀγαθῷ, ἐπειδὴ ἀγαθόν τι ἡ ἀρετή· ὁμοίως
δὲ καὶ ὁ τῷ δίχα χρώμενος τῷ ἀρτίῳ χρῆται,
ἐπειδὴ εἰς δύο διῃρῆσθαι σημαίνει τὸ δίχα, τὰ δὲ
δύο ἄρτιά ἐστιν.

20 V. Καθόλου μὲν οὖν εἰπεῖν εἷς ἐστι τόπος τὸ μὴ
διὰ προτέρων καὶ γνωριμωτέρων ποιήσασθαι τὸν
λόγον, μέρη δ' αὐτοῦ τὰ εἰρημένα. δεύτερος, εἰ
ἐν γένει τοῦ πράγματος ὄντος μὴ κεῖται ἐν γένει.
ἐν ἅπασι δὲ τὸ τοιοῦτον ἁμάρτημά ἐστιν, ἐν οἷς οὐ
πρόκειται τοῦ λόγου τὸ τί ἐστιν, οἷον ὁ τοῦ σώ-
25 ματος ὁρισμός, τὸ ἔχον τρεῖς διαστάσεις, ἢ εἴ
τις τὸν ἄνθρωπον ὁρίσαιτο τὸ ἐπιστάμενον ἀριθμεῖν.
οὐ γὰρ εἴρηται τί ὂν τρεῖς ἔχει διαστάσεις ἢ τί ὂν
ἐπίσταται ἀριθμεῖν· τὸ δὲ γένος βούλεται τὸ τί
ἐστι σημαίνειν, καὶ πρῶτον ὑποτίθεται τῶν ἐν τῷ
ὁρισμῷ λεγομένων.

30 Ἔτι εἰ πρὸς πλείω λεγομένου τοῦ ὁριζομένου
μὴ πρὸς πάντα ἀποδέδωκεν, οἷον εἰ τὴν γραμματικὴν ἐπιστήμην τοῦ γράψαι τὸ ὑπαγορευθέν·
προσδεῖται γὰρ ὅτι καὶ τοῦ ἀναγνῶναι· οὐδὲν γὰρ

state of virtue.' For the expression 'into two parts' is taken from 'two,' which is an even number, and virtue is a kind of good ; so that the former terms are subordinate to the latter. Further, in introducing the subordinate term, one is obliged to introduce the term itself also ; for he who introduces the term 'virtue' introduces 'the good,' since virtue is a kind of good ; and similarly, too, he who introduces the phrase 'into two parts' introduces 'even,' for division 'into two parts' signifies division by two, and two is an even number.

V. Speaking generally, then, one commonplace concerns the failure to frame the description by means of prior and more intelligible terms, and the above are the divisions into which it falls. A second commonplace is to see whether, though the subject of the definition falls under a genus, it has not been placed in a genus. This kind of error always occurs in cases where the essence is not put first in the description, for example, in the definition of 'body' as 'that which has three dimensions,' or the definition of 'man,' if it were to be given as 'that which knows how to count.' For no statement has been given what it is that has three dimensions or what it is that knows how to count ; whereas the genus aims at signifying what it is and is the first thing to be laid down in the description contained in the definition.

Rules as to the use of genus in definition:

(a) Observe whether the genus is omitted.

Furthermore, you must see whether, though the term which is being defined applies to a number of things, your opponent has failed to apply it to all of them ; for example, if he has defined 'grammar' as 'the knowledge of writing from dictation' ; for he ought to add that it is also the knowledge of reading.

(b) Observe whether the definition is applied to everything which comes under the subject of the definition.

585

142 b

μᾶλλον τοῦ γράψαι ἢ τοῦ ἀναγνῶναι ἀποδοὺς ὥρισται, ὥστ' οὐδέτερος, ἀλλ' ὁ ἄμφω ταῦτ' εἰπών,
35 ἐπειδὴ πλείους οὐκ ἐνδέχεται ταὐτοῦ ὁρισμοὺς
143 a εἶναι. ἐπ' ἐνίων μὲν οὖν κατ' ἀλήθειαν ἔχει καθάπερ εἴρηται, ἐπ' ἐνίων δ' οὔ, οἷον ἐφ' ὅσων μὴ
καθ' αὑτὸ πρὸς ἄμφω λέγεται, καθάπερ ἰατρικὴ
τοῦ νόσον καὶ ὑγίειαν ποιῆσαι· τοῦ μὲν γὰρ καθ'
αὑτὴν λέγεται, τοῦ δὲ κατὰ συμβεβηκός· ἁπλῶς
5 γὰρ ἀλλότριον τῆς ἰατρικῆς τὸ νόσον ποιεῖν. ὥστ'
οὐδὲν μᾶλλον ὥρισται ὁ πρὸς ἄμφω ἀποδοὺς τοῦ
πρὸς θάτερον, ἀλλ' ἴσως καὶ χεῖρον, ἐπειδὴ καὶ
τῶν λοιπῶν ὁστισοῦν δυνατός ἐστι νόσον ποιῆσαι.

Ἔτι εἰ μὴ πρὸς τὸ βέλτιον ἀλλὰ πρὸς τὸ χεῖρον
10 ἀποδέδωκε, πλειόνων ὄντων πρὸς ἃ λέγεται τὸ
ὁριζόμενον· πᾶσα γὰρ ἐπιστήμη καὶ δύναμις τοῦ
βελτίστου δοκεῖ εἶναι.

Πάλιν εἰ μὴ κεῖται ἐν τῷ οἰκείῳ γένει τὸ λεχθέν,
σκοπεῖν ἐκ τῶν περὶ τὰ γένη στοιχείων, καθάπερ
πρότερον εἴρηται.

15 Ἔτι εἰ ὑπερβαίνων[1] λέγει τὰ γένη, οἷον ὁ τὴν
δικαιοσύνην ἕξιν ἰσότητος ποιητικὴν ἢ διανεμη-
τικὴν τοῦ ἴσου. ὑπερβαίνει γὰρ οὕτως ὁριζόμενος

[1] Bekker's ὑπερβαίνειν a misprint for ὑπερβαίνων.

586

For in describing it as 'a knowledge of writing' he has no more given a definition than he who has called it 'a knowledge of reading,' so that neither of them has given a definition, but only he who makes both these statements, since there cannot be more than one definition of the same thing. In some cases, to be sure, the above statement accords with the truth but not in others, for example, where the term is not essentially applicable to both things, for instance in the definition of medicine as concerned with the production of disease and health. For it is said to do the latter essentially, the former only accidentally, since it is absolutely foreign to medicine to produce disease. So he who has described medicine in reference to both health and disease has given no better a definition than he who has done so in reference to one of them only; nay, he has perhaps even given a worse definition, since anyone else who is not a doctor is capable of producing disease.

Furthermore, when there are more things than one to which the term which is being defined is applicable, you must see whether he has assigned it in reference not to the better but to the worse; for every kind of knowledge and capacity is generally regarded as concerned with the best. *(c) Observe whether the subject of the definition is referred not to the better but to the worse.*

Again, if the term which has been described is not placed in its appropriate genus, you must examine it according to the elementary rules regarding genera, as has been said above.[a] *(d) Observe whether the genus is not rightly constituted.*

Furthermore, you must see whether in his description he passes over the genera, for example, when he defines justice as 'a state productive of equality,' or 'distributive of what is equal'; for by such a defini- *(e) Observe whether there is a failure to put the subject in*

---

[a] 139 b 3.

143 a

τὴν ἀρετήν. ἀπολιπὼν οὖν τὸ τῆς δικαιοσύνης
γένος οὐ λέγει τὸ τί ἦν εἶναι· ἡ γὰρ οὐσία ἑκάστῳ
μετὰ τοῦ γένους. ἔστι δὲ τοῦτο ταὐτὸν τῷ μὴ εἰς
20 τὸ ἐγγυτάτω γένος θεῖναι· ὁ γὰρ εἰς τὸ ἐγγυτάτω
θεὶς πάντα τὰ ἐπάνω εἴρηκεν, ἐπειδὴ πάντα
τὰ ἐπάνω γένη τῶν ὑποκάτω κατηγορεῖται. ὥστ'
ἢ εἰς τὸ ἐγγυτάτω γένος θετέον, ἢ πάσας τὰς
διαφορὰς τῷ ἐπάνω γένει προσαπτέον, δι' ὧν
ὁρίζεται τὸ ἐγγυτάτω γένος. οὕτω γὰρ οὐδὲν
25 ἂν εἴη παραλελοιπώς, ἀλλ' ἀντ' ὀνόματος λόγῳ
εἰρηκὼς ἂν εἴη τὸ ὑποκάτω γένος. ὁ δ' αὐτὸ μόνον τὸ ἐπάνω γένος εἴπας οὐ λέγει καὶ τὸ ὑποκάτω γένος· ὁ γὰρ φυτὸν εἴπας οὐ λέγει δένδρον.

VI. Πάλιν ἐπὶ τῶν διαφορῶν ὁμοίως σκεπτέον
30 εἰ καὶ τὰς διαφορὰς εἶπε τὰς τοῦ γένους. εἰ γὰρ
μὴ ταῖς τοῦ πράγματος ἰδίαις ὥρισται διαφοραῖς,
ἢ καὶ παντελῶς τοιοῦτον εἴρηκεν ὃ μηδενὸς ἐνδέχεται διαφορὰν εἶναι, οἷον τὸ ζῷον ἢ τὴν οὐσίαν,
δῆλον ὅτι οὐχ ὥρισται· οὐδενὸς γὰρ διαφοραὶ τὰ
εἰρημένα. ὁρᾶν δὲ καὶ εἰ ἔστιν ἀντιδιῃρημένον
35 τι τῇ εἰρημένῃ διαφορᾷ. εἰ γὰρ μή ἐστι, δῆλον
ὅτι οὐκ ἂν εἴη ἡ εἰρημένη τοῦ γένους διαφορά·
143 b πᾶν γὰρ γένος ταῖς ἀντιδιῃρημέναις διαφοραῖς
διαιρεῖται, καθάπερ τὸ ζῷον τῷ πεζῷ καὶ τῷ
πτηνῷ καὶ τῷ ἐνύδρῳ καὶ τῷ δίποδι. ἢ εἰ ἔστι
μὲν ἡ ἀντιδιῃρημένη διαφορά, μὴ ἀληθεύεται δὲ

tion he passes over virtue, and so by omitting the its nearest genus. genus of justice he fails to state its essence; for the essence of a thing involves its genus. This amounts to the same thing as not putting the subject into its nearest genus; for he who has put it into the nearest genus has stated all the higher genera, since all the higher genera are predicated of the lower. Either, therefore, it ought to put into the nearest genus, or else all the differentiae, through which the nearest genus is defined, ought to be added to the higher genus. By so doing he would not have omitted anything, but would have stated the lower genus instead of mentioning the name. But he who has merely stated the higher genus by itself does not state the lower genus also; for he who calls a thing a 'plant' does not call it a 'tree.'

VI. Again, you must, in like manner, consider, as Rules as to the use of differentiae in defini-tion: (a) The ratio of difference must be considered. regards differentiae, whether he has stated the differentiae too as those of the genus. For, if he has not framed his definition by means of the differentiae peculiar to the subject, or else has stated something such as cannot possibly be a differentia of anything at all (for example 'animal' or 'substance'), it is obvious that he has not given a definition; for the above terms are not differentiae of anything. Also you must see whether there is an opposite member of a division corresponding to the differentia stated; for, if not, obviously the differentia stated could not be a differentia of the genus; for every genus is distinguished by differentiae which are the opposite members of a corresponding division, for example, 'animal' by the terms 'pedestrian,' 'winged,' 'aquatic' and 'biped.' Or else you must see whether the corresponding differentia exists but is not true of the

κατὰ τοῦ γένους. δῆλον γὰρ ὅτι οὐδετέρα ἂν εἴη
5 τοῦ γένους διαφορά· πᾶσαι γὰρ αἱ ἀντιδιῃρημέναι
διαφοραὶ ἀληθεύονται κατὰ τοῦ οἰκείου γένους.
ὁμοίως δὲ καὶ εἰ ἀληθεύεται μέν, μὴ ποιεῖ δὲ
προστιθεμένη τῷ γένει εἶδος. δῆλον γὰρ ὅτι οὐκ
ἂν εἴη αὕτη εἰδοποιὸς διαφορὰ τοῦ γένους· πᾶσα
γὰρ εἰδοποιὸς διαφορὰ μετὰ τοῦ γένους εἶδος
10 ποιεῖ. εἰ δ᾽ αὕτη μή ἐστι διαφορά, οὐδ᾽ ἡ λεχθεῖσα,
ἐπεὶ ταύτῃ ἀντιδιῄρηται.

Ἔτι ἐὰν ἀποφάσει διαιρῇ τὸ γένος, καθάπερ οἱ
τὴν γραμμὴν ὁριζόμενοι μῆκος ἀπλατὲς εἶναι.
οὐδὲν γὰρ ἄλλο σημαίνει ἢ ὅτι οὐκ ἔχει πλάτος.
συμβήσεται οὖν τὸ γένος μετέχειν τοῦ εἴδους·
15 πᾶν γὰρ μῆκος ἢ ἀπλατὲς ἢ πλάτος ἔχον ἐστίν,
ἐπεὶ κατὰ παντὸς ἢ ἡ κατάφασις ἢ ἡ ἀπόφασις
ἀληθεύεται, ὥστε καὶ τὸ γένος τῆς γραμμῆς μῆκος
ὂν ἢ ἀπλατὲς ἢ πλάτος ἔχον ἔσται. μῆκος δ᾽
ἀπλατὲς εἴδους ἐστὶ λόγος, ὁμοίως δὲ καὶ μῆκος
πλάτος ἔχον· τὸ γὰρ ἀπλατὲς καὶ πλάτος ἔχον
20 διαφοραί εἰσιν, ἐκ δὲ τῆς διαφορᾶς καὶ τοῦ γένους
ὁ τοῦ εἴδους ἐστὶ λόγος, ὥστε τὸ γένος ἐπιδέχοιτ᾽
ἂν τὸν τοῦ εἴδους λόγον. ὁμοίως δὲ καὶ τὸν τῆς
διαφορᾶς, ἐπειδὴ ἡ ἑτέρα τῶν εἰρημένων διαφορῶν
ἐξ ἀνάγκης κατηγορεῖται τοῦ γένους. ἔστι δ᾽
ὁ εἰρημένος τόπος χρήσιμος πρὸς τοὺς τιθεμένους
25 ἰδέας εἶναι. εἰ γάρ ἐστιν αὐτὸ μῆκος, πῶς κατηγορηθήσεται κατὰ τοῦ γένους ὅτι πλάτος ἔχον
ἐστὶν ἢ ἀπλατές ἐστιν; δεῖ γὰρ κατὰ παντὸς

genus; for then obviously neither of them could be a
differentia of the genus; for all the corresponding
differentiae are true of the proper genus. In like
manner, too, you must see whether, though it is true,
yet its addition to the genus does not make a species.
For then it is obvious that this could not be a specific
differentia of the genus; for a specific differentia,
combined with the genus, always makes a species.
But, if this is not a differentia, neither is the one
which has been stated, since it is an opposite member
of a division corresponding with this.

Furthermore, you must see whether he divides the (b) Observe
genus by means of a negation, as do those who define whether the
'line' as 'length without breadth'; for this simply divided by
signifies that it has not breadth. The result, there-negation.
fore, will be that the genus partakes of its species;
for, since either the affirmation or the negation is
true of everything, length must always either be
without breadth or possess breadth, and so the genus
of 'line,' which is 'length,' will also either be without
breadth or possess breadth. But 'length without
breadth' is a description of a species, as similarly also
is 'length with breadth'; for 'without breadth'
and 'with breadth' are differentiae, and the description of the species is made up of the differentia
and the genus; and so the genus would admit of the
description of the species. Similarly, too, it would
admit of the description of the differentia, since one
of the above differentiae is necessarily predicated of
the genus. The above commonplace is useful in
dealing with those who assert that 'ideas' exist;
for, if absolute length exists, how is it to be predicated
of the genus that it is possessed of breadth or that
it is without breadth? For one of these two state-

143 b

μήκους τὸ ἕτερον αὐτῶν ἀληθεύεσθαι, εἴπερ κατὰ
τοῦ γένους ἀληθεύεσθαι μέλλει. τοῦτο δ' οὐ συμ-
βαίνει· ἔστι γὰρ ἁπλᾶ καὶ πλάτος ἔχοντα μήκη.
30 ὥστε πρὸς ἐκείνους μόνους χρήσιμος ὁ τόπος,
οἳ πᾶν[1] γένος ἐν ἀριθμῷ φασὶν εἶναι. τοῦτο δὲ
ποιοῦσιν οἱ τὰς ἰδέας τιθέμενοι· αὐτὸ γὰρ μῆκος
καὶ αὐτὸ ζῷον γένος φασὶν εἶναι.

Ἴσως δ' ἐπ' ἐνίων ἀναγκαῖον καὶ ἀποφάσει
χρῆσθαι τὸν ὁριζόμενον, οἷον ἐπὶ τῶν στερήσεων·
35 τυφλὸν γάρ ἐστι τὸ μὴ ἔχον ὄψιν, ὅτε πέφυκεν
ἔχειν. διαφέρει δ' οὐδὲν ἀποφάσει διελεῖν τὸ γέ-
144 a νος, ἢ τοιαύτῃ καταφάσει ᾗ ἀπόφασιν ἀναγκαῖον
ἀντιδιαιρεῖσθαι, οἷον εἰ μῆκος πλάτος ἔχον ὥρι-
σται· τῷ γὰρ πλάτος ἔχοντι τὸ μὴ ἔχον πλάτος
ἀντιδιῄρηται, ἄλλο δ' οὐδέν, ὥστε ἀποφάσει πάλιν
διαιρεῖται τὸ γένος.

5   Πάλιν εἰ τὸ εἶδος ὡς διαφορὰν ἀπέδωκε, καθάπερ οἱ τὸν προπηλακισμὸν ὕβριν μετὰ χλευασίας
ὁριζόμενοι· ἡ γὰρ χλευασία ὕβρις τις, ὥστ' οὐ
διαφορὰ ἀλλ' εἶδος ἡ χλευασία.

Ἔτι εἰ τὸ γένος ὡς διαφορὰν εἴρηκεν, οἷον τὴν
10 ἀρετὴν ἕξιν ἀγαθὴν ἢ σπουδαίαν· γένος γὰρ
τἀγαθὸν τῆς ἀρετῆς ἐστίν. ἢ οὐ γένος τἀγαθόν,
ἀλλὰ διαφορά, εἴπερ ἀληθὲς ὅτι οὐκ ἐνδέχεται
ταὐτὸν ἐν δύο γένεσιν εἶναι μὴ περιέχουσιν
ἄλληλα. οὔτε γὰρ τἀγαθὸν τὴν ἕξιν περιέχει οὔθ'

---

[1] Reading πᾶν with AB for τό.

592

ments must be true of every length, if it is going to be true of the genus. This, however, does not happen; for there are lengths without breadth and lengths possessing breadth. This commonplace, therefore, is useful only in dealing with those who say that every genus is numerically one ; and this is what those do who assert the existence of ' ideas ' ; for they say that absolute length and absolute animal are the genus.

Perhaps in some cases the definer must necessarily use negation, for example, in defining privations. For ' blind ' is that which does not possess sight when it is its nature to possess it. But there is no difference between dividing the genus by means of a negation and by means of such an affirmation as must necessarily have a negation in the opposite member of a corresponding division, for example, when a definition has been given as ' length possessing breadth ' ; for the opposite member of the corresponding division to that which possesses breadth is that which does not possess breadth, and nothing else, so that again the genus is divided by a negation. *[Note on an exceptional case.]*

Again, you must see whether he has assigned the species as a differentia, as do those who define ' contumely ' as ' insolence combined with scoffing ' ; for scoffing is a kind of insolence, and so scoffing is not a differentia but a species. *(c) Observe whether the species or the genus is assigned as a differentia.*

Moreover, you must see whether he has stated the genus as a differentia, saying, for example, that ' virtue is a good or worthy state ' ; for ' good ' is the genus of ' virtue.' Or perhaps ' good ' is not the genus but the differentia, if indeed it is true that it is impossible for the same thing to be in two genera one of which does not include the other ; for ' good ' does not include ' state,' nor does ' state ' include

144 a

ἡ ἕξις τἀγαθόν· οὐ γὰρ πᾶσα ἕξις ἀγαθόν, οὐδὲ
15 πᾶν ἀγαθὸν ἕξις, ὥστ' οὐκ ἂν εἴη γένη ἀμφότερα.
εἰ οὖν ἡ ἕξις τῆς ἀρετῆς γένος, δῆλον ὅτι τἀγαθὸν
οὐ γένος, ἀλλὰ μᾶλλον διαφορά. ἔτι ἡ μὲν ἕξις
τί ἐστι σημαίνει ἡ ἀρετή, τὸ δ' ἀγαθὸν οὐ τί ἐστιν
ἀλλὰ ποιόν· δοκεῖ δ' ἡ διαφορὰ ποιόν τι σημαίνειν.
20   Ὁρᾶν δὲ καὶ εἰ μὴ ποιόν τι ἀλλὰ τόδε σημαίνει
ἡ ἀποδοθεῖσα διαφορά· δοκεῖ γὰρ ποιόν τι πᾶσα
διαφορὰ δηλοῦν.

Σκοπεῖν δὲ καὶ εἰ κατὰ συμβεβηκὸς ὑπάρχει τῷ
ὁριζομένῳ ἡ διαφορά. οὐδεμία γὰρ διαφορὰ τῶν
25 κατὰ συμβεβηκὸς ὑπαρχόντων ἐστί, καθάπερ οὐδὲ
τὸ γένος· οὐ γὰρ ἐνδέχεται τὴν διαφορὰν ὑπάρχειν
τινὶ καὶ μὴ ὑπάρχειν.

Ἔτι εἰ κατηγορεῖται τοῦ γένους ἡ διαφορὰ ἢ
τὸ εἶδος ἢ τῶν κάτωθέν τι τοῦ εἴδους, οὐκ ἂν εἴη
30 ὡρισμένος· οὐδὲν γὰρ τῶν εἰρημένων ἐνδέχεται τοῦ
γένους κατηγορεῖσθαι, ἐπειδὴ τὸ γένος ἐπὶ πλεῖστον
πάντων λέγεται. πάλιν εἰ κατηγορεῖται τὸ γένος
τῆς διαφορᾶς· οὐ γὰρ κατὰ τῆς διαφορᾶς, ἀλλὰ
καθ' ὧν ἡ διαφορά, τὸ γένος δοκεῖ κατηγορεῖσθαι,
οἷον τὸ ζῷον κατὰ τοῦ ἀνθρώπου καὶ τοῦ βοὸς
35 καὶ τῶν ἄλλων πεζῶν ζῴων, οὐκ αὐτῆς τῆς διαφορᾶς τῆς κατὰ τοῦ εἴδους λεγομένης. εἰ γὰρ
καθ' ἑκάστης τῶν διαφορῶν τὸ ζῷον κατηγορηθήσεται, πολλὰ ζῷα τοῦ εἴδους ἂν κατηγοροῖτο·
144 b αἱ γὰρ διαφοραὶ τοῦ εἴδους κατηγοροῦνται. ἔτι

'good,' for not every 'state' is 'good' nor every 'good' a 'state.' They could not, therefore, both be genera, and so, if 'state' is the genus of virtue, obviously 'good' is not its genus but rather a differentia. Furthermore, a 'state' indicates the essence of virtue, whereas 'good' indicates not the essence but a quality; and it is generally held that it is the differentia which indicates a quality.

You must also see whether the differentia assigned indicates not a quality but a particular thing; for it is generally held that the differentia always signifies a quality. *(d)* Observe whether the differentia signifies a particular thing, or

You must also consider whether the differentia belongs accidentally to the subject of the definition. For no differentia is of the number of things which belong accidentally, as neither is the genus; for it is impossible for the differentia to belong to something and also not to belong. has the notion of an accident.

Furthermore, if the differentia or the species or anything that falls under the species is predicated of the genus, the definer cannot have given a definition; for none of the above can be predicated of the genus, since the genus has the widest field of all. Again, you must see whether the genus is predicated of the differentia; for it is generally held that the genus is predicated, not of the differentia, but of the things of which the differentia is predicated. For example, 'animal' is predicated of 'man' and of 'ox' and of the other pedestrian animals, not of the differentia itself, which is predicated of the species. For, if 'animal' is going to be predicated of each of the differentiae, a number of animals would be predicated of the species; for the differentiae are predicated of the species. Further, all differentiae *(e)* Observe whether differentia or species be predicated of genus or genus of differentia, or species of differentia.

595

διαφοραὶ πᾶσαι ἢ εἴδη ἢ ἄτομα ἔσται, εἴπερ ζῷα·
ἕκαστον γὰρ τῶν ζῴων ἢ εἶδός ἐστιν ἢ ἄτομον.
Ὁμοίως δὲ σκεπτέον καὶ εἰ τὸ εἶδος ἢ τῶν
5 ὑποκάτω τι τοῦ εἴδους τῆς διαφορᾶς κατηγορεῖται·
ἀδύνατον γάρ, ἐπειδὴ ἐπὶ πλέον ἡ διαφορὰ τῶν
εἰδῶν λέγεται. ἔτι συμβήσεται τὴν διαφορὰν εἶδος εἶναι, εἴπερ κατηγορεῖταί τι αὐτῆς τῶν εἰδῶν·
εἰ γὰρ κατηγορεῖται ἄνθρωπος, δῆλον ὅτι ἡ διαφορὰ ἄνθρωπός ἐστιν. πάλιν εἰ μὴ πρότερον ἡ
10 διαφορὰ τοῦ εἴδους· τοῦ μὲν γὰρ γένους ὕστερον,
τοῦ δ᾿ εἴδους πρότερον τὴν διαφορὰν δεῖ εἶναι.

Σκοπεῖν δὲ καὶ εἰ ἑτέρου γένους ἡ ῥηθεῖσα διαφορὰ μὴ περιεχομένου μηδὲ περιέχοντος. οὐ
δοκεῖ γὰρ ἡ αὐτὴ διαφορὰ δύο γενῶν εἶναι μὴ
15 περιεχόντων ἄλληλα. εἰ δὲ μή, συμβήσεται καὶ
εἶδος τὸ αὐτὸ ἐν δύο γένεσιν εἶναι μὴ περιέχουσιν
ἄλληλα· ἐπιφέρει γὰρ ἑκάστη τῶν διαφορῶν τὸ
οἰκεῖον γένος, καθάπερ τὸ πεζὸν καὶ τὸ δίπουν
τὸ ζῷον συνεπιφέρει. ὥστε εἰ καθ᾿ οὗ ἡ διαφορά,
καὶ τῶν γενῶν ἑκάτερον, δῆλον [οὖν] ὅτι τὸ εἶδος
20 ἐν δύο γένεσιν οὐ περιέχουσιν ἄλληλα. ἢ οὐκ
ἀδύνατον τὴν αὐτὴν διαφορὰν δύο γενῶν εἶναι
μὴ περιεχόντων ἄλληλα, ἀλλὰ προσθετέον μηδ᾿
ἄμφω ὑπὸ ταὐτὸν ὄντων. τὸ γὰρ πεζὸν ζῷον
καὶ τὸ πτηνὸν ζῷον γένη ἐστὶν οὐ περιέχοντα
ἄλληλα, καὶ ἀμφοτέρων αὐτῶν ἐστι τὸ δίπουν
25 διαφορά. ὥστε προσθετέον ὅτι μηδ᾿ ὑπὸ ταὐτὸ

will be either species or individuals, if they are animals; for each animal is either a species or an individual.

In like manner you must consider also whether the species or any of the things which come under the species is predicated of the differentia; for this is impossible, since the differentia is used over a wider field than the species. Furthermore, if any of the species is predicated of it, the result will be that the differentia is a species; for if ' man ' is predicated, obviously the differentia is man. Again, you must see whether the differentia fails to be prior to the species; for the differentia ought to be posterior to the genus but prior to the species.

You must consider also whether the differentia stated is of a different genus, neither contained by nor containing it. For it is generally held that the same differentia cannot attach to two genera neither of which contains the other; otherwise it will result that the same species also is in two genera neither of which includes the other; for each of the differentiae involves its own genus, for example ' pedestrian ' and ' winged ' involve ' animal.' If, therefore, each of the genera, too, is predicated of that of which the differentia is predicated, it is obvious that the species falls under two genera neither of which contains the other. Or, perhaps, it is not impossible that the same differentia should belong to two genera neither of which contains the other, and we ought to add ' if they do not fall under the same genus.' For ' pedestrian animal ' and ' winged animal ' are genera neither of which contains the other, and ' biped ' is a differentia of both of them, so that ' if they do not fall under the same genus ' ought to be added; *(f)* Observe whether the same differentia belongs to another genus.

597

144 b

ὄντων ἄμφω· ταῦτα γὰρ ἄμφω ὑπὸ τὸ ζῷόν ἐστιν.
δῆλον δὲ καὶ ὅτι οὐκ ἀνάγκη τὴν διαφορὰν πᾶν
τὸ οἰκεῖον ἐπιφέρειν γένος, ἐπειδὴ ἐνδέχεται τὴν
αὐτὴν δύο γενῶν εἶναι μὴ περιεχόντων ἄλληλα·
ἀλλὰ τὸ ἕτερον μόνον ἀνάγκη συνεπιφέρειν καὶ
30 τὰ ἐπάνω τούτου, καθάπερ τὸ δίπουν τὸ πτηνὸν
ἢ τὸ πεζὸν συνεπιφέρει ζῷον.

Ὁρᾶν δὲ καὶ εἰ τὸ ἔν τινι διαφορὰν ἀποδέδωκεν
οὐσίας· οὐ δοκεῖ γὰρ διαφέρειν οὐσία οὐσίας τῷ
ποῦ εἶναι. διὸ καὶ τοῖς τῷ πεζῷ καὶ τῷ ἐνύδρῳ
διαιροῦσι τὸ ζῷον ἐπιτιμῶσιν ὡς τὸ πεζὸν καὶ
35 τὸ ἔνυδρον ποῦ σημαῖνον. ἢ ἐπὶ μὲν τούτων οὐκ
ὀρθῶς ἐπιτιμῶσιν· οὐ γὰρ ἔν τινι οὐδὲ ποῦ σημαίνει
τὸ ἔνυδρον, ἀλλὰ ποιόν τι· καὶ γὰρ ἂν ᾖ ἐν τῷ
ξηρῷ, ὁμοίως ἔνυδρον· ὁμοίως δὲ τὸ χερσαῖον,
145 a κἂν ἐν ὑγρῷ, χερσαῖον ἀλλ᾽ οὐκ ἔνυδρον ἔσται.
ἀλλ᾽ ὅμως ἐάν ποτε σημαίνῃ τὸ ἔν τινι ἡ διαφορά,
δῆλον ὅτι διημαρτηκὼς ἔσται.

Πάλιν εἰ τὸ πάθος διαφορὰν ἀποδέδωκεν. πᾶν
γὰρ πάθος μᾶλλον γινόμενον ἐξίστησι τῆς οὐσίας,
5 ἡ δὲ διαφορὰ οὐ τοιοῦτον· μᾶλλον γὰρ σῴζειν
δοκεῖ ἡ διαφορὰ οὗ ἐστι διαφορά, καὶ ἁπλῶς
ἀδύνατον εἶναι ἄνευ τῆς οἰκείας διαφορᾶς ἕκαστον·
πεζοῦ γὰρ μὴ ὄντος οὐκ ἔσται ἄνθρωπος. ἁπλῶς
δ᾽ εἰπεῖν, καθ᾽ ὅσα ἀλλοιοῦται τὸ ἔχον, οὐδὲν

598

for they both fall under 'animal.' It is obvious also
that, since it is possible for the same differentia to
attach to two genera neither of which contains the
other, it does not necessarily follow that the differentia
involves every appropriate genus, but it need only
involve one or other of them and the genera which
are higher than it, as 'biped' involves 'winged
animal' or 'walking animal.'

You must also see whether the definer has assigned
existence 'in' something as a differentia of the
essence; for it is generally held that one essence does
not differ from another in respect of locality. Hence
arises the criticism of those who divide animals by
the term 'pedestrian' and 'aquatic,' on the ground
that 'pedestrian' and 'aquatic' signify locality. Or
perhaps the criticism is not justified; for 'aquatic'
does not signify existence 'in' something nor
locality, but a certain quality; for even though it
be on dry land, an aquatic animal is equally aquatic,
and likewise the land animal, even though it be in
the water, will still be a land and not an aquatic
animal. But, for all that, if ever the differentia
signifies existence 'in' something, obviously he will
have committed a serious error.

Again, you must see whether he has assigned an
affection as a differentia; for every affection, if it is
intensified, causes a departure from the essence,
whereas a differentia is not of this kind. For it is
generally held that the differentia tends rather to
preserve that of which it is the differentia and that
it is absolutely impossible for an individual thing to
exist without its appropriate differentia; for if
'pedestrian' does not exist, 'man' will not exist.
To put the matter generally, nothing in respect of

(g) Observe
whether
locality or
an affection
is assigned
as the dif-
ferentia of
the essence.

599

τούτων διαφορὰ ἐκείνου· ἅπαντα γὰρ τὰ τοιαῦτα
10 μᾶλλον γινόμενα ἐξίστησι τῆς οὐσίας. ὥστ᾽ εἴ
τινα τοιαύτην διαφορὰν ἀπέδωκεν, ἡμάρτηκεν·
ἁπλῶς γὰρ οὐκ ἀλλοιούμεθα κατὰ τὰς διαφοράς.

Καὶ εἴ τινος τῶν πρός τι μὴ πρὸς ἄλλο τὴν
διαφορὰν ἀποδέδωκεν· τῶν γὰρ πρός τι καὶ αἱ δια-
15 φοραὶ πρός τι, καθάπερ καὶ τῆς ἐπιστήμης· θεωρητικὴ γὰρ καὶ πρακτικὴ καὶ ποιητικὴ λέγεται,
ἕκαστον δὲ τούτων πρός τι σημαίνει· θεωρητικὴ
γάρ τινος καὶ ποιητική τινος καὶ πρακτική.

Σκοπεῖν δὲ καὶ εἰ πρὸς ὃ πέφυκεν ἕκαστον τῶν
20 πρός τι ἀποδίδωσιν ὁ ὁριζόμενος. ἐνίοις μὲν γὰρ
πρὸς ὃ πέφυκεν ἕκαστον τῶν πρός τι μόνον ἔστι
χρῆσθαι, πρὸς ἄλλο δ᾽ οὐδέν, ἐνίοις δὲ καὶ πρὸς
ἄλλο, οἷον τῇ ὄψει πρὸς τὸ ἰδεῖν μόνον, τῇ δὲ
στλεγγίδι κἂν ἀρύσαιτό τις· ἀλλ᾽ ὅμως εἴ τις
25 ὁρίσαιτο τὴν στλεγγίδα ὄργανον πρὸς τὸ ἀρύειν,
ἡμάρτηκεν· οὐ γὰρ πρὸς τοῦτο πέφυκεν. ὅρος
δὲ τοῦ πρὸς ὃ πέφυκεν, ἐφ᾽ ὃ ἂν χρήσαιτο ὁ
φρόνιμος ᾗ φρόνιμος, καὶ ἡ περὶ ἕκαστον οἰκεία
ἐπιστήμη.

Ἢ εἰ μὴ τοῦ πρώτου ἀπέδωκεν, ὅταν τυγχάνῃ
πρὸς πλείω λεγόμενον, οἷον τὴν φρόνησιν ἀρετὴν

which its possessor undergoes alteration is a differentia of its possessor; for all things of this kind, if they are intensified, cause a departure from the essence. If, therefore, the definer has assigned any differentia of this kind, he has made a mistake; for we undergo absolutely no alteration in respect of our differentiae.

You must also see whether he has failed to assign the differentia of a relative term as relative to something else; for the differentiae of relative terms are also relative, for example, those of knowledge. For it is said to be theoretical, practical and creative, and each of these terms signifies a relation; for it theorizes about something or creates something or does something. *(h) Observe whether the differentia of relatives fails to be relative, and whether the relation is apt.*

You must also see whether the definer assigns each relative term relatively to that for which it is naturally adapted; for some things can be used for that for which each of them is naturally adapted and for nothing else, while other things can be used also for some other purpose; for example, sight can only be used for seeing, whereas one can use a strigil for drawing off liquid.[a] Nevertheless if a man should define a strigil as an instrument for drawing off liquid, he has made a mistake; for this is not its natural purpose. The definition of the natural purpose of an object is ' that for which the prudent man, in virtue of his prudence, and the science which is appropriate to the object would employ it.'

Or, again, you must see whether, when a term happens to be applied in several relations, he has failed to assign it in its primary relation; for example, *(i) Observe whether the definition is assigned in its primary relation.*

[a] In Aristoph. *Thesm.* 556 the word is actually used of an instrument for drawing off wine from a cask.

145 a

30 ἀνθρώπου ἢ ψυχῆς καὶ μὴ τοῦ λογιστικοῦ· πρώτου
γὰρ τοῦ λογιστικοῦ ἀρετὴ ἡ φρόνησις· κατὰ γὰρ
τοῦτο καὶ ἡ ψυχὴ καὶ ὁ ἄνθρωπος φρονεῖν λέγεται.
Ἔτι εἰ μὴ δεκτικόν ἐστιν οὗ εἴρηται τὸ ὡρισμένον πάθος ἢ¹ διάθεσις ἢ ὁτιοῦν ἄλλο, ἡμάρτηκεν.
35 πᾶσα γὰρ διάθεσις καὶ πᾶν πάθος ἐν ἐκείνῳ πέφυκε γίνεσθαι οὗ ἐστι διάθεσις ἢ πάθος, καθάπερ
καὶ ἡ ἐπιστήμη ἐν ψυχῇ διάθεσις οὖσα ψυχῆς.
ἐνίοτε δὲ διαμαρτάνουσιν ἐν τοῖς τοιούτοις, οἷον
145 b ὅσοι λέγουσιν ὅτι ὕπνος ἐστὶν ἀδυναμία αἰσθήσεως,
καὶ ἡ ἀπορία ἰσότης ἐναντίων λογισμῶν, καὶ ἡ
ἀλγηδὼν διάστασις τῶν συμφύτων μερῶν μετὰ
βίας· οὔτε γὰρ ὁ ὕπνος ὑπάρχει τῇ αἰσθήσει, ἔδει
δ᾽, εἴπερ ἀδυναμία αἰσθήσεώς ἐστιν. ὁμοίως δ᾽
5 οὐδ᾽ ἡ ἀπορία ὑπάρχει τοῖς ἐναντίοις λογισμοῖς,
οὐδ᾽ ἡ ἀλγηδὼν τοῖς συμφύτοις μέρεσιν· ἀλγήσει
γὰρ τὰ ἄψυχα, εἴπερ ἀλγηδὼν αὐτοῖς παρέσται.
τοιοῦτος δὲ καὶ ὁ τῆς ὑγιείας ὁρισμός, εἴπερ συμμετρία θερμῶν καὶ ψυχρῶν ἐστίν· ἀνάγκη γὰρ
ὑγιαίνειν τὰ θερμὰ καὶ ψυχρά· ἡ γὰρ ἑκάστου
10 συμμετρία ἐν ἐκείνοις ὑπάρχει ὧν ἐστι συμμετρία,
ὥσθ᾽ ἡ ὑγίεια ὑπάρχοι ἂν αὐτοῖς. ἔτι τὸ ποιούμενον εἰς τὸ ποιητικὸν ἢ ἀνάπαλιν συμβαίνει
τιθέναι τοῖς οὕτως ὁριζομένοις. οὐ γάρ ἐστιν
ἀλγηδὼν ἡ διάστασις τῶν συμφύτων μερῶν, ἀλλὰ
ποιητικὸν ἀλγηδόνος· οὐδ᾽ ἡ ἀδυναμία τῆς αἰ-
15 σθήσεως ὕπνος, ἀλλὰ ποιητικὸν θάτερον θατέρου·

¹ Deleting ἡ after ἢ.

if he has defined ' wisdom ' as the virtue of ' man '
or of the ' soul ' and not of the ' reasoning faculty ' ;
for wisdom is primarily the virtue of the reasoning
faculty, for it is in respect of this that both ' soul '
and ' man ' are said to be wise.

Moreover, he has made a mistake, if that of which (j) Observe
the term which has been defined has been said to be affection
an affection or disposition or whatever else it may be, affects that
which it is
does not admit of it. For every disposition and every defined as
affection naturally comes into being in that of which affecting.
it is a disposition or affection, for example, knowledge in the soul, since it is a disposition of soul. But
sometimes people make mistakes in such matters, for
example, those who say that ' sleep ' is ' impotence
of sensation ' and ' perplexity ' an ' equality of contrary reasonings,' and ' pain ' a ' separation of conjoined parts accompanied by violence.' For neither
is sleep an attribute of sensation, though it ought to
be if it is an impotence of sensation. Similarly neither
is perplexity an attribute of contrary reasonings nor
pain an attribute of conjoined parts ; for, if it were
so, inanimate things will be in pain, since pain will
be present in them. Of like character is the definition of ' health,' if it is stated to be a ' balance of
things hot and cold ' ; for then things hot and cold
must have health ; for the balance of anything
exists in those things of which it is the balance, and
so health would exist in them. Moreover, the result
produced by those who frame definitions in this way
is to put the effect in place of the cause and vice
versa. For the separation of the conjoined parts is
not pain, but a cause of pain, and impotence of
sensation is not sleep, but one is the cause of the
other ; for either we go to sleep owing to impotence

ARISTOTLE

ἤτοι γὰρ διὰ τὴν ἀδυναμίαν ὑπνοῦμεν, ἢ διὰ τὸν
ὕπνον ἀδυνατοῦμεν. ὁμοίως δὲ καὶ τῆς ἀπορίας
δόξειεν ἂν ποιητικὸν εἶναι ἡ τῶν ἐναντίων ἰσότης
λογισμῶν· ὅταν γὰρ ἐπ᾽ ἀμφότερα λογιζομένοις
ἡμῖν ὁμοίως ἅπαντα φαίνηται καθ᾽ ἑκάτερον
20 γίνεσθαι, ἀποροῦμεν ὁπότερον πράξωμεν.

Ἔτι κατὰ τοὺς χρόνους πάντας ἐπισκοπεῖν εἴ
που διαφωνεῖ, οἷον εἰ τὸ ἀθάνατον ὡρίσατο ζῷον
ἄφθαρτον νῦν εἶναι· τὸ γὰρ νῦν ἄφθαρτον ζῷον
νῦν ἀθάνατον ἔσται. ἢ ἐπὶ μὲν τούτου οὐ συμ-
25 βαίνει· ἀμφίβολον γὰρ τὸ νῦν ἄφθαρτον εἶναι· ἢ
γὰρ ὅτι οὐκ ἔφθαρται νῦν σημαίνει, ἢ ὅτι οὐ δυνατὸν φθαρῆναι νῦν, ἢ ὅτι τοιοῦτόν ἐστι νῦν οἷον
μηδέποτε φθαρῆναι. ὅταν οὖν λέγωμεν ὅτι ἄφθαρτον νῦν ἐστι ζῷον, τοῦτο λέγομεν ὅτι νῦν τοιοῦτόν
ἐστι ζῷον οἷον μηδέποτε φθαρῆναι. τοῦτο δὲ τῷ
ἀθανάτῳ τὸ αὐτὸ ἦν, ὥστ᾽ οὐ συμβαίνει νῦν
30 αὐτὸ ἀθάνατον εἶναι. ἀλλ᾽ ὅμως ἂν συμβαίνῃ τὸ
μὲν κατὰ τὸν λόγον ἀποδοθὲν ὑπάρχειν νῦν ἢ
πρότερον, τὸ δὲ κατὰ τοὔνομα μὴ ὑπάρχειν, οὐκ
ἂν εἴη ταὐτόν. χρηστέον οὖν τῷ τόπῳ καθάπερ
εἴρηται.

VII. Σκεπτέον δὲ καὶ εἰ καθ᾽ ἕτερόν τι μᾶλλον
35 λέγεται τὸ ὁρισθὲν ἢ κατὰ τὸν ἀποδοθέντα λόγον,
οἷον εἰ ἡ δικαιοσύνη δύναμις τοῦ ἴσου διανεμητική.
604

of sensation, or we lose the power of sensation owing to sleep. Similarly, too, it would be generally held that the equality of contrary reasonings is a cause of perplexity ; for, when we are reasoning on both sides of a question and everything appears to have equal weight on either side, we are perplexed which of the two courses we are to adopt.

Furthermore, you must consider all the possible periods of time and look for any discrepancy. Take, for example, the definition of ' immortal ' as ' a living creature at present immune from destruction '; for a living creature ' at present ' immune from destruction will be ' at present ' immortal. Or, possibly, it does not follow in this case ; for ' at present immune from destruction ' is ambiguous, since it can mean either that it has not been destroyed at present, or that it cannot be destroyed at present, or that is at present such as never to be destroyed. When, therefore, we say that a living creature is at present immune from destruction, we mean that it is at present a living creature such as never to be destroyed; and this is the same as saying that it is immortal, so that it does not follow that it is immortal only at present. But, nevertheless, if that which is assigned in the description happens to belong only in the present or in the past, whereas that which is expressed by the name does not so belong, they could not be the same thing. The commonplace, therefore, ought to be employed as described above. *(k)* Observe whether the ratio of time concurs with the subject of definition.

VII. You should also consider whether the term defined is rather applied in virtue of something other than what is expressed in the description assigned. Take, for example, the definition of ' justice ' as ' a capacity for distributing what is equal '; for a just *Various ways of testing a definition : (a)* Is there any better definition ?

δίκαιος γὰρ μᾶλλον ὁ προαιρούμενος τὸ ἴσον
146 a διανεῖμαι τοῦ δυναμένου, ὥστ' οὐκ ἂν εἴη ἡ δικαιοσύνη δύναμις τοῦ ἴσου διανεμητική· καὶ γὰρ
δίκαιος εἴη ἂν μάλιστα ὁ δυνάμενος μάλιστα τὸ
ἴσον διανεῖμαι.

Ἔτι εἰ τὸ μὲν πρᾶγμα δέχεται τὸ μᾶλλον, τὸ
δὲ κατὰ τὸν λόγον ἀποδοθὲν μὴ δέχεται, ἢ ἀνά-
5 παλιν τὸ μὲν κατὰ τὸν λόγον ἀποδοθὲν δέχεται,
τὸ δὲ πρᾶγμα μή. δεῖ γὰρ ἀμφότερα δέχεσθαι ἢ
μηδέτερον, εἴπερ δὴ ταὐτόν ἐστι τὸ κατὰ τὸν
λόγον ἀποδοθὲν τῷ πράγματι. ἔτι εἰ δέχεται
μὲν ἀμφότερα τὸ μᾶλλον, μὴ ἅμα δὲ τὴν ἐπίδοσιν
ἀμφότερα λαμβάνει, οἷον εἰ ὁ ἔρως ἐπιθυμία
10 συνουσίας ἐστίν· ὁ γὰρ μᾶλλον ἐρῶν οὐ μᾶλλον
ἐπιθυμεῖ τῆς συνουσίας, ὥστ' οὐχ ἅμα ἀμφότερα
τὸ μᾶλλον ἐπιδέχεται· ἔδει δέ γε, εἴπερ ταὐτὸν
ἦν.

Ἔτι εἰ δύο τινῶν προτεθέντων, καθ' οὗ τὸ
πρᾶγμα μᾶλλον λέγεται, τὸ κατὰ τὸν λόγον ἧττον
15 λέγεται, οἷον εἰ τὸ πῦρ ἐστι σῶμα τὸ λεπτομερέ-
στατον· πῦρ μὲν γὰρ μᾶλλον ἡ φλὸξ ἐστι τοῦ
φωτός, σῶμα δὲ τὸ λεπτομερέστατον ἧττον ἢ[1]
φλὸξ τοῦ φωτός· ἔδει δ' ἀμφότερα μᾶλλον τῷ αὐτῷ
ὑπάρχειν, εἴπερ ταὐτὰ ἦν. πάλιν εἰ τὸ μὲν ὁμοίως

[1] Reading ⟨ἡ⟩ φλόξ.

man is rather he who deliberately chooses to distribute what is equal than he who has the capacity for doing so : so that justice could not be a capacity for distributing what is equal; for then a man would be most just who has the greatest capacity for distributing what is equal.

Furthermore, you must see whether the subject of the definition admits of a greater degree, whereas that which is assigned by the terms of the description does not ; or, on the contrary, whether that which is assigned by the terms of the description admits of a greater degree, whereas what is assigned by the terms of the definition does not. For either both must admit of it or neither, if that which is assigned by the terms of the description is the same as the subject of the definition. Further, you must see whether both admit of a greater degree while both do not experience the increase at the same time. The definition of ' love ' as ' a desire for sexual intercourse ' is a case in point ; for he who is more in love has not more desire for intercourse, so that both feelings do not admit of a greater degree at the same time, whereas they should do so if they were the same thing. *(b) Does the definition admit of degrees while its subject does not ?*

Furthermore, when alternatives are proposed, you must see whether, where the subject of the definition applies in a greater degree, what is assigned by the definition applies in a less degree. Take, for example, the definition of ' fire ' as ' a body consisting of the most subtle parts ' ; for ' fire ' is ' flame ' rather than ' light,' on the other hand ' the body consisting of the most subtle parts ' is less ' flame ' than ' light,' whereas both ought to belong in a greater degree to the same thing, if they were the same. Again, *(c) In the case of alternatives where the subject of the definition is more applicable, is its content less so ?*

607

ἀμφοτέροις ὑπάρχει τοῖς προτεθεῖσι, τὸ δ' ἕτερον
20 μὴ ὁμοίως ἀμφοτέροις, ἀλλὰ τῷ ἑτέρῳ μᾶλλον.

Ἔτι ἐὰν πρὸς δύο τὸν ὁρισμὸν ἀποδῷ καθ' ἑκάτερον, οἷον τὸ καλὸν τὸ δι' ὄψεως ἢ τὸ δι' ἀκοῆς
ἡδύ, καὶ τὸ ὂν τὸ δυνατὸν παθεῖν ἢ ποιῆσαι· ἅμα
γὰρ ταὐτὸν καλόν τε καὶ οὐ καλὸν ἔσται, ὁμοίως
25 δὲ καὶ ὄν τε καὶ οὐκ ὄν. τὸ γὰρ δι' ἀκοῆς ἡδὺ
ταὐτὸν τῷ καλῷ ἔσται, ὥστε τὸ μὴ ἡδὺ δι' ἀκοῆς
τῷ μὴ καλῷ ταὐτόν· τοῖς γὰρ αὐτοῖς καὶ τὰ
ἀντικείμενα ταὐτά, ἀντίκειται δὲ τῷ μὲν καλῷ
τὸ οὐ καλόν, τῷ δὲ δι' ἀκοῆς ἡδεῖ τὸ οὐχ ἡδὺ δι'
ἀκοῆς. δῆλον οὖν ὅτι ταὐτὸν τὸ οὐχ ἡδὺ δι' ἀκοῆς
30 τῷ οὐ καλῷ. εἰ οὖν τι ἐστὶ δι' ὄψεως μὲν ἡδὺ
δι' ἀκοῆς δὲ μή, καλόν τε καὶ οὐ καλὸν ἔσται.
ὁμοίως δὲ δείξομεν καὶ διότι ταὐτὸν ὄν τε καὶ οὐκ
ὄν ἐστιν.

Ἔτι καὶ τῶν γενῶν καὶ τῶν διαφορῶν καὶ τῶν
ἄλλων ἁπάντων τῶν ἐν τοῖς ὁρισμοῖς ἀποδιδομέ-
35 νων λόγους ἀντὶ τῶν ὀνομάτων ποιοῦντα σκοπεῖν
εἴ τι διαφωνεῖ.

VIII. Ἐὰν δ' ᾖ πρός τι τὸ ὁριζόμενον ἢ καθ'
αὑτὸ ἢ κατὰ τὸ γένος, σκοπεῖν εἰ μὴ εἴρηται ἐν
146 b τῷ ὁρισμῷ πρὸς ὃ λέγεται ἢ αὐτὸ ἢ κατὰ τὸ
γένος, οἷον εἰ τὴν ἐπιστήμην ὡρίσατο ὑπόληψιν
ἀμετάπειστον ἢ τὴν βούλησιν ὄρεξιν ἄλυπον. παν-

you must see whether one belongs similarly to the
terms proposed, while the other does not belong
similarly to both, but in a greater degree to one of
them.

Furthermore, you must see if he renders the defini- *(d)* Is the
tion in relation to two things separately, for example definition
when he defines ' the beautiful ' as ' what is pleasant relation to
to the sight or to the hearing,' or ' the existent ' as taken
' what is capable of being affected or of affecting separately ?
something else '; for then the same thing will
be both beautiful and not beautiful, and likewise also
both existent and non-existent. For ' pleasant to
the hearing ' will be the same as ' beautiful,' and so
' not pleasant to the hearing ' will be the same as
' not beautiful '; for the opposites of identical things
too are identical, and ' not beautiful ' is the opposite
of ' beautiful,' while ' not pleasant to the hearing '
is the opposite of ' pleasant to the hearing.' Obviously, therefore, ' not pleasant to the hearing ' is the
same as ' not beautiful.' If, therefore, a thing is
pleasant to the sight but not to the hearing, it will
be both beautiful and not beautiful. And, similarly,
we shall show also that the same thing is both
existent and non-existent.

Furthermore, you should frame descriptions of both *(e)* Is there
the genera and the differentiae and everything else any dis-
assigned in the definitions to take the place of the genera and
names and see whether there is any discrepancy. differentiae?

VIII. If what is being defined is relative, either in *Rules for*
itself or in its genus, you must examine whether there *testing the*
has been a failure in the definition to mention to what *a relative*
it is relative, either in itself or in its genus; for *term:*
example, if the definer has defined ' knowledge ' as *(a)* If the
an ' incontrovertible conception,' or ' wish ' as a tion is rela-

609

146 b

τὸς γὰρ τοῦ πρός τι ἡ οὐσία πρὸς ἕτερον, ἐπειδὴ
ταὐτὸν ἦν ἑκάστῳ τῶν πρός τι τὸ εἶναι ὅπερ
5 τὸ πρός τί πως ἔχειν. ἔδει οὖν τὴν ἐπιστήμην εἰπεῖν ὑπόληψιν ἐπιστητοῦ καὶ τὴν βούλησιν ὄρεξιν
ἀγαθοῦ. ὁμοίως δὲ καὶ εἰ τὴν γραμματικὴν
ὡρίσατο ἐπιστήμην γραμμάτων· ἔδει γὰρ ἢ πρὸς
ὃ αὐτὸ λέγεται ἢ πρὸς ὅ ποτε τὸ γένος ἐν τῷ
διορισμῷ ἀποδίδοσθαι. ἢ εἰ πρός τι εἰρημένον
10 μὴ πρὸς τὸ τέλος ἀποδέδοται. τέλος δ' ἐν ἑκάστῳ
τὸ βέλτιστον ἢ οὗ χάριν τἆλλα. ῥητέον δὴ ἢ τὸ
βέλτιστον ἢ τὸ ἔσχατον, οἷον τὴν ἐπιθυμίαν οὐχ
ἡδέος ἀλλ' ἡδονῆς· ταύτης γὰρ χάριν καὶ τὸ ἡδὺ
αἱρούμεθα.

Σκοπεῖν δὲ καὶ εἰ γένεσίς ἐστι πρὸς ὃ ἀποδέδωκεν ἢ ἐνέργεια· οὐδὲν γὰρ τῶν τοιούτων
15 τέλος· μᾶλλον γὰρ τὸ ἐνηργηκέναι καὶ γεγενῆσθαι
τέλος ἢ τὸ γίνεσθαι καὶ ἐνεργεῖν. ἢ οὐκ ἐπὶ
πάντων ἀληθὲς τὸ τοιοῦτον· σχεδὸν γὰρ οἱ πλεῖστοι
ἥδεσθαι μᾶλλον βούλονται ἢ πεπαῦσθαι ἡδόμενοι,
ὥστε τὸ ἐνεργεῖν μᾶλλον τέλος ἂν ποιοῖντο τοῦ
ἐνηργηκέναι.

20 Πάλιν ἐπ' ἐνίων εἰ μὴ διώρικε τοῦ πόσου ἢ
ποίου ἢ ποῦ ἢ κατὰ τὰς ἄλλας διαφοράς, οἷον
φιλότιμος ὁ ποίας καὶ ὁ πόσης ὀρεγόμενος τιμῆς·

'painless desire.' For the essence of anything that is relative is relative to something, since the being of every relative term is the same as the being in some relation to something. He ought, therefore, to have described knowledge as 'conception of an object of knowledge,' and wish as 'desire of the good.' Similarly, also, if he has defined 'grammar' as a 'knowledge of letters,' whereas either that to which the term itself is relative or that to whichsoever its genus is relative ought to have been assigned in the definition. Or, again, you ought to see whether a term mentioned in relation to something has not been assigned in relation to its end; for the end in any particular case is that which is best or that for the sake of which all else exists. What is best, then, or ultimate should be stated; for example, desire should be described as not for the pleasant but for pleasure, for it is for the sake of pleasure that we also choose what is pleasant.

You must also examine whether that in relation to which he has assigned the term is a coming-into-being or an activity; for none of such things is an end to have completed an activity or a coming-into-being is an end rather than the actual coming-into-being and activity. Or, possibly, such a statement is not invariably true; for almost everyone wishes to be delighted rather than to have ceased to be delighted, so that people apparently would account the actual activity as an end rather than the completion of it.

Again, cases occur in which you must see whether he has failed to define the quantity or quality or place, or the other differentiae which are involved, for example, what is the quality and quantity of the honour which he desires that makes a man ambitious;

(marginal notes)
tive, is it stated to what it is relative?

(b) Is any relation to coming-into-being or activity stated?

(c) Is there any failure to define quantity or quality or place?

πάντες γὰρ ὀρέγονται τιμῆς, ὥστ' οὐκ ἀπόχρη
φιλότιμον εἰπεῖν τὸν ὀρεγόμενον τιμῆς, ἀλλὰ
προσθετέον τὰς εἰρημένας διαφοράς. ὁμοίως δὲ
25 καὶ φιλοχρήματος ὁ πόσων ὀρεγόμενος χρημάτων
ἢ ἀκρατὴς ὁ περὶ ποίας ἡδονάς· οὐ γὰρ ὁ ὑφ'
οἱασποτοῦν ἡδονῆς κρατούμενος ἀκρατὴς λέγεται,
ἀλλ' ὁ ὑπό τινος. ἢ πάλιν, ὡς ὁρίζονται τὴν νύκτα
σκιὰν γῆς, ἢ τὸν σεισμὸν κίνησιν γῆς, ἢ τὸ νέφος
πύκνωσιν ἀέρος, ἢ τὸ πνεῦμα κίνησιν ἀέρος·
30 προσθετέον γὰρ πόσου καὶ ποίου καὶ ὑπὸ τίνος.
ὁμοίως δὲ καὶ ἐπὶ τῶν ἄλλων τῶν τοιούτων·
ἀπολείπων γὰρ διαφορὰν ἡντινοῦν οὐ λέγει τὸ τί
ἦν εἶναι. δεῖ δ' ἀεὶ πρὸς τὸ ἐνδεὲς ἐπιχειρεῖν· οὐ
γὰρ ὁπωσοῦν γῆς κινηθείσης οὐδ' ὁποσησοῦν σει-
σμὸς ἔσται, ὁμοίως δ' οὐδ' ἀέρος ὁπωσοῦν οὐδ'
35 ὁποσουοῦν κινηθέντος πνεῦμα.

Ἔτι ἐπὶ τῶν ὀρέξεων εἰ μὴ πρόσκειται τὸ
φαινόμενον, καὶ ἐφ' ὅσων ἄλλων ἁρμόττει, οἷον
147 a ὅτι ἡ βούλησις ὄρεξις ἀγαθοῦ, ἡ δ' ἐπιθυμία
ὄρεξις ἡδέος, ἀλλὰ μὴ φαινομένου ἀγαθοῦ ἢ ἡδέος.
πολλάκις γὰρ λανθάνει τοὺς ὀρεγομένους ὅ τι
ἀγαθὸν ἢ ἡδύ ἐστιν, ὥστ' οὐκ ἀναγκαῖον ἀγαθὸν
ἢ ἡδὺ εἶναι, ἀλλὰ φαινόμενον μόνον. ἔδει οὖν
5 οὕτω καὶ τὴν ἀπόδοσιν ποιήσασθαι. ἐὰν δὲ καὶ
ἀποδῷ τὸ εἰρημένον, ἐπὶ τὰ εἴδη ἀκτέον τὸν τιθέμενον ἰδέας εἶναι· οὐ γάρ ἐστιν ἰδέα φαινομένου

612

for all men desire honour, and so it is not enough to say that the man who desires honour is ambitious, but the above-mentioned differentiae must be added. Similarly, too, we must state what quantity of money which he desires makes a man avaricious and what quality of pleasures which he desires makes a man incontinent; for a man is not called incontinent who is the slave of any kind of pleasure whatsoever, but only if he is the slave of a particular kind. Or, again, when people define ' night ' as ' a shadow over the earth,' or an ' earthquake ' as ' movement of the earth,' or ' a cloud ' as ' condensation of air,' or ' wind ' as ' movement of the air,' the quality and quantity and cause must be added. And, similarly, in all cases of this kind; for the omission of any differentia whatever involves a failure to state the essence. One should always deal with the deficiency; for an earthquake will not result from *any* kind or *any* extent whatsoever of movement of the earth, nor a wind from *any* kind or extent whatsoever of movement of the air.

Furthermore, in dealing with desires, and in any other case where it is fitting, you must see whether there is a failure to add the qualification ' apparent,' for example in the definitions ' wish is a desire for the good,' or ' appetite is a desire for the pleasant ' instead of ' the apparently good or pleasant.' For often those who feel desire fail to perceive what is good or pleasant, so that the object of their desire is not necessarily good or pleasant, but only apparently so. One ought, therefore, to have assigned the definition with this qualification. He, however, who asserts the existence of ' ideas,' if he *does* assign the above qualification, must be confronted with his ' ideas '; for there can be no ' idea ' of what is only

(d) In the definition of appetites, is the object of desire qualified as ' apparent ' ?

613

οὐδενός, τὸ δ' εἶδος πρὸς τὸ εἶδος δοκεῖ λέγεσθαι,
οἷον αὐτὴ ἐπιθυμία αὐτοῦ ἡδέος καὶ αὐτὴ βούλησις
αὐτοῦ ἀγαθοῦ. οὐκ ἔστιν οὖν φαινομένου ἀγαθοῦ
10 οὐδὲ φαινομένου ἡδέος· ἄτοπον γὰρ τὸ εἶναι αὐτὸ
φαινόμενον ἀγαθὸν ἢ ἡδύ.

IX. Ἔτι ἐὰν μὲν ᾖ τῆς ἕξεως ὁ ὁρισμός, σκοπεῖν
ἐπὶ τοῦ ἔχοντος, ἐὰν δὲ τοῦ ἔχοντος, ἐπὶ τῆς ἕξεως·
ὁμοίως δὲ καὶ ἐπὶ τῶν ἄλλων τῶν τοιούτων. οἷον
15 εἰ τὸ ἡδὺ ὅπερ ὠφέλιμον, καὶ ὁ ἡδόμενος ὠφελού-
μενος. καθόλου δ' εἰπεῖν, ἐν τοῖς τοιούτοις ὁρισμοῖς τρόπον τινὰ πλείω ἑνὸς συμβαίνει τὸν
ὁριζόμενον ὁρίζεσθαι· ὁ γὰρ τὴν ἐπιστήμην ὁριζόμενος τρόπον τινὰ καὶ τὴν ἄγνοιαν ὁρίζεται,
ὁμοίως δὲ καὶ τὸ ἐπιστῆμον καὶ τὸ ἀνεπιστῆμον
20 καὶ τὸ ἐπίστασθαι καὶ τὸ ἀγνοεῖν· τοῦ γὰρ πρώτου
δήλου γενομένου τρόπον τινὰ καὶ τὰ λοιπὰ δῆλα
γίνονται. σκεπτέον οὖν ἐπὶ πάντων τῶν τοιούτων
μή τι διαφωνῇ, στοιχείοις χρώμενον τοῖς ἐκ τῶν
ἐναντίων καὶ τῶν συστοίχων.

Ἔτι ἐπὶ τῶν πρός τι σκοπεῖν εἰ πρὸς ὃ τὸ γένος
ἀποδίδοται, τὸ εἶδος πρὸς ἐκεῖνό τι ἀποδίδοται, οἷον
25 εἰ ἡ ὑπόληψις πρὸς ὑποληπτόν, ἢ τὶς ὑπόληψις
πρὸς ⟨τὸ⟩[1] τὶ ὑποληπτόν, καὶ εἰ τὸ πολλαπλάσιον
πρὸς τὸ πολλοστημόριον, τὸ τὶ πολλαπλάσιον πρὸς

apparent, but an ' idea ' is generally held to be used
in relation to another ' idea.' For example, absolute
appetite is for the absolutely pleasant, and absolute
wish for the absolutely good, and so they are not for
the apparently good or the apparently pleasant, for
it is absurd to suppose that an absolutely-apparently-
good or pleasant can exist.

IX. Furthermore, if the definition is of the state *Rules for*
of anything, you must examine the possessor of the *defining*
state, or, if the definition is of the possessor of the *(a) a state.*
state, you must examine the state, and so likewise
in all such cases. For example, if the pleasant is
what is beneficial, he who feels pleasure is benefited.
To put the matter generally, in definitions of this
kind it happens that the framer of the definition in
a way defines more than one thing ; for he who
defines knowledge in a way defines ignorance also,
and likewise also what possesses and what does not
possess knowledge, and what it is to know and to
be ignorant. For when the first of these things is
clear, the rest also in a way become clear also. You
must be careful then in all such cases that there is
no discrepancy, using the elementary principles
derived from contraries and corresponding terms.

Furthermore, in dealing with relatives, you must *(b) A rela-*
examine whether the species is assigned as relative *tive term.*
to a species of that to which the genus is assigned as
relative. For example, if ' conception ' is relative
to ' object of conception,' you must see whether a particular conception is assigned relative to a particular
object of conception, and, if a multiple is relative to
a fraction, whether a particular multiple is assigned

---

¹ τὸ added by Wallies.

147 a

τὸ τὶ πολλοστημόριον· εἰ γὰρ μὴ οὕτως ἀποδίδοται,
δῆλον ὅτι ἡμάρτηται.

Ὁρᾶν δὲ καὶ εἰ τοῦ ἀντικειμένου ὁ ἀντικείμενος
30 λόγος, οἷον τοῦ ἡμίσεος ὁ ἀντικείμενος τῷ τοῦ
διπλασίου· εἰ γὰρ διπλάσιον τὸ ἴσῳ ὑπερέχον,
ἥμισυ τὸ ἴσῳ ὑπερεχόμενον. καὶ ἐπὶ τῶν ἐναντίων
δ' ὡσαύτως. ὁ γὰρ ἐναντίος τοῦ ἐναντίου λόγος
ἔσται κατὰ μίαν τινὰ συμπλοκὴν τῶν ἐναντίων,
οἷον εἰ ὠφέλιμον τὸ ποιητικὸν ἀγαθοῦ, βλαβερὸν
35 τὸ ποιητικὸν κακοῦ ἢ τὸ φθαρτικὸν ἀγαθοῦ· θά-
147 b τερον γὰρ τούτων ἀναγκαῖον ἐναντίον εἶναι τῷ ἐξ
ἀρχῆς ῥηθέντι. εἰ οὖν μηδέτερον ἐναντίον τῷ ἐξ ἀρχῆς ῥηθέντι, δῆλον ὅτι οὐδέτερος ἂν εἴη τῶν ὕστερον ἀποδοθέντων τοῦ ἐναντίου λόγος, ὥστ' οὐδ'
ἐξ ἀρχῆς ἀποδοθεὶς ὀρθῶς ἀποδέδοται. ἐπεὶ δ'
5 ἔνια τῶν ἐναντίων στερήσει θατέρου λέγεται,—
οἷον ἡ ἀνισότης στέρησις ἰσότητος δοκεῖ εἶναι
(ἄνισα γὰρ τὰ μὴ ἴσα λέγεται),—δῆλον ὅτι τὸ μὲν
κατὰ στέρησιν λεγόμενον ἐναντίον ἀναγκαῖον ὁρίζεσθαι διὰ θατέρου, τὸ δὲ λοιπὸν οὐκέτι διὰ τοῦ
κατὰ στέρησιν λεγομένου· συμβαίνοι γὰρ ἂν
ἑκάτερον δι' ἑκατέρου γνωρίζεσθαι. ἐπισκεπτέον
10 οὖν ἐν τοῖς ἐναντίοις τὴν τοιαύτην ἁμαρτίαν, οἷον
εἴ τις ὁρίσαιτο τὴν ἰσότητα εἶναι τὸ ἐναντίον ἀν-
ισότητι· διὰ γὰρ τοῦ κατὰ στέρησιν λεγομένου

616

as relative to a particular fraction ; for if it has not to be so assigned, obviously a mistake has been made.

You must also see whether the opposite of the description describes the opposite of the term, for example, whether the opposite of the description of 'double' is the description of 'half'; for if 'double' is 'that which exceeds by an equal amount,' 'half' is 'that which is exceeded by an equal amount.' So likewise in the case of contraries also ; for the description which is contrary according to one of the modes of conjunction of contraries will describe the contrary term. For example, if 'beneficial' is 'productive of good,' 'harmful' is 'productive of evil' or 'destructive of good'; for one of these must necessarily be the contrary of the original term. If, then, neither of them is the contrary of the original term, obviously neither of the descriptions assigned later could be the description of the contrary of that term, and so neither has the description originally assigned been assigned correctly. Now since some contraries derive their names from the privation of another contrary—for example, inequality is generally regarded as a privation of equality, for things which are not equal are called 'unequal'—it is obvious that the contrary whose name takes the form of a privation must necessarily be defined by means of the other contrary, but the other contrary cannot then be defined by means of the contrary whose name takes the form of a privation ; for then the result would be that each was known through the other. We must, therefore, be on our guard against this mistake in dealing with contraries, for example, if one were to define equality as the contrary of inequality ; for he is defining by

(c) Opposites and contraries.

617

ὁρίζεται. ἔτι τὸν οὕτως ὁριζόμενον ἀναγκαῖον
αὐτῷ τῷ ὁριζομένῳ χρῆσθαι. δῆλον δὲ τοῦτο,
ἐὰν μεταληφθῇ ἀντὶ τοῦ ὀνόματος ὁ λόγος· εἰπεῖν
15 γὰρ ἢ ἀνισότητα οὐδὲν διαφέρει ἢ στέρησιν ἰσότητος. ἔσται οὖν ἡ ἰσότης τὸ ἐναντίον στερήσει
ἰσότητος, ὥστ᾿ αὐτῷ ἂν εἴη κεχρημένος. ἂν δὲ
μηδέτερον τῶν ἐναντίων κατὰ στέρησιν λέγηται,
ἀποδοθῇ δ᾿ ὁ λόγος ὁμοίως, οἷον ἀγαθὸν τὸ ἐναντίον κακῷ, δῆλον ὅτι κακὸν τὸ ἐναντίον ἀγαθῷ
20 ἔσται (τῶν γὰρ οὕτως ἐναντίων ὁμοίως ὁ λόγος
ἀποδοτέος), ὥστε πάλιν αὐτῷ τῷ ὁριζομένῳ συμβαίνει χρῆσθαι· ἐνυπάρχει γὰρ ἐν τῷ τοῦ κακοῦ
λόγῳ τὸ ἀγαθόν. ὥστ᾿ εἰ ἀγαθόν ἐστι τὸ κακῷ
ἐναντίον, τὸ δὲ κακὸν οὐδὲν διαφέρει ἢ τὸ τῷ
ἀγαθῷ ἐναντίον, ἔσται ἀγαθὸν τὸ ἐναντίον τῷ τοῦ
25 ἀγαθοῦ ἐναντίῳ. δῆλον οὖν ὅτι αὐτῷ κέχρηται.

Ἔτι εἰ τὸ κατὰ στέρησιν λεγόμενον ἀποδιδοὺς
μὴ ἀποδέδωκεν οὗ ἐστι στέρησις, οἷον τῆς ἕξεως
ἢ τοῦ ἐναντίου ἢ ὁτουοῦν ἐστὶν ἡ στέρησις· καὶ
εἰ μὴ ἐν ᾧ πέφυκε γίνεσθαι προσέθηκεν, ἢ ἁπλῶς
30 ἢ ἐν ᾧ πρώτῳ πέφυκε γίνεσθαι, οἷον εἰ τὴν ἄγνοιαν
εἰπὼν στέρησιν μὴ ἐπιστήμης στέρησιν εἶπεν, ἢ
μὴ προσέθηκεν ἐν ᾧ πέφυκε γίνεσθαι, ἢ προσθεὶς

means of a term which takes the form of a privation. Moreover, he who defines in this way must necessarily employ the very term which he is defining ; and this becomes obvious if the description is substituted for the name ; for it makes no difference whether we say 'inequality' or 'privation of equality.' Equality, therefore, will be ' the contrary of the privation of equality,' so that he would have used the actual term. If, however, neither of the contraries is named in the form of a privation but the description is assigned in the same manner, for example in the definition of ' good ' as ' the contrary of evil,' it is obvious that ' evil ' will be ' the contrary of good ' (for the description of things which are contrary in this way must be assigned in a similar manner), and so the result again is that he uses the actual term which is being defined ; for ' good ' is inherent in the description of ' evil.' If, then, ' good ' is ' the contrary of evil,' and ' evil ' is indistinguishable from ' the contrary of good,' ' good ' will be ' the contrary of the contrary of good ' ; it is obvious, therefore, that he has made use of the actual term.

Furthermore, you must see whether, in assigning a *(d) Priva-* term named in the form of a privation, he has failed *tions.* to assign that of which it is a privation, for example, the state, or the contrary, or whatever else it is of which it is the privation ; and also whether he has failed to add what it is in which it naturally comes into being absolutely or in which it naturally comes into being primarily ; for example, if, in calling ' ignorance ' a privation, he has failed to call it a privation of ' knowledge,' or has failed to add what it is in which it naturally comes into being, or, though he has added this, has not assigned that in which it

ARISTOTLE

147 b

μὴ ἐν ᾧ πρώτῳ ἀπέδωκεν, οἷον ὅτι οὐκ ἐν τῷ
λογιστικῷ ἀλλ' ἐν ἀνθρώπῳ ἢ ψυχῇ· ἐὰν γὰρ ὁτιοῦν
τούτων μὴ ποιήσῃ, ἡμάρτηκεν. ὁμοίως δὲ καὶ εἰ
35 τὴν τυφλότητα μὴ ὄψεως στέρησιν ἐν ὀφθαλμῷ
148 a εἶπεν· δεῖ γὰρ τὸν καλῶς ἀποδιδόντα τὸ τί ἐστι,
καὶ τίνος ἐστὶν ἡ στέρησις ἀποδοῦναι καὶ τί ἐστι
τὸ ἐστερημένον.

Ὁρᾶν δὲ καὶ εἰ μὴ λεγομένου κατὰ στέρησιν
στερήσει ὡρίσατο, οἷον καὶ ἐπὶ τῆς ἀγνοίας δόξειεν
5 ἂν ὑπάρχειν ἡ τοιαύτη ἁμαρτία τοῖς μὴ κατ'
ἀπόφασιν τὴν ἄγνοιαν λέγουσιν. τὸ γὰρ μὴ ἔχον
ἐπιστήμην οὐ δοκεῖ ἀγνοεῖν, ἀλλὰ μᾶλλον τὸ
διηπατημένον, διὸ οὔτε τὰ ἄψυχα οὔτε τὰ παιδία
φαμὲν ἀγνοεῖν, ὥστ' οὐ κατὰ στέρησιν ἐπιστήμης
ἡ ἄγνοια λέγεται.

10 X. Ἔτι εἰ ⟨ἐπὶ⟩[1] τῶν ὁμοίων τοῦ ὀνόματος πτώσεων αἱ ὅμοιαι τοῦ λόγου πτώσεις ἐφαρμόττουσιν,
οἷον εἰ ὠφέλιμον τὸ ποιητικὸν ὑγιείας, ὠφελίμως
τὸ ποιητικῶς ὑγιείας καὶ ὠφεληκὸς τὸ πεποιη-
κὸς ὑγίειαν.

Σκοπεῖν δὲ καὶ ἐπὶ τὴν ἰδέαν εἰ ἐφαρμόσει ὁ
15 λεχθεὶς ὅρος. ἐπ' ἐνίων γὰρ οὐ συμβαίνει, οἷον
ὡς Πλάτων ὁρίζεται τὸ θνητὸν προσάπτων ἐν
τοῖς τῶν ζῴων ὁρισμοῖς· ἡ γὰρ ἰδέα οὐκ ἔσται
θνητή, οἷον αὐτοάνθρωπος, ὥστ' οὐκ ἐφαρμόσει
ὁ λόγος ἐπὶ τὴν ἰδέαν. ἁπλῶς δ' οἷς πρόσκειται
τὸ ποιητικὸν ἢ παθητικόν, ἀνάγκη διαφωνεῖν

[1] ἐπὶ add. Wallies.

620

naturally comes in being primarily, assigning it, for
example, to 'man' or 'the soul' instead of to 'the
reasoning faculty'; for if he has failed to do any of
these things, he has made a mistake. Similarly, also,
if he has failed to call 'blindness' 'a privation of
sight in *the eye*'; for he who is stating the essence
correctly must state both what it is of which there
is privation and what it is which is deprived.

You must also see whether, when a term is not (e) *Priva-*
used as a privation, he has defined it as a privation. *tions*
For example, a mistake of this kind would be gener- *called.*
ally held to be committed in the case of 'ignorance'
by those who do not use ignorance as a merely
negative term. For what is regarded as ignorant is
not that which does not possess knowledge but rather
that which is deceived. Therefore we do not speak
of inanimate things or children as 'ignorant,' and
so 'ignorance' is not used for a mere privation of
knowledge.

X. Furthermore, you must see whether the simi- *Rules*
lar inflexions in the description apply to the similar *drawn* (a)
inflexions of the term; for example, whether, if *inflexions.*
'beneficial' means 'productive of health,' 'benefi-
cially' means 'in a manner productive of health' and
'having benefited' means 'having produced health.'

You must also consider whether the definition (b) *From*
given will fit the 'idea' also. In some cases this does *reference of*
not occur, for example, when Plato in his definitions *tion to the*
of living creatures inserts the term 'mortal' in his *idea of the*
definition; for the 'idea,' for example 'absolute *defined.*
man,' will not be mortal, so that the definition will
not fit the 'idea.' Also, where the terms 'capable
of affecting' or 'of being affected by' are added,
there is necessarily an absolute discrepancy between

148 a

20 ἐπὶ τῆς ἰδέας τὸν ὅρον· ἀπαθεῖς γὰρ καὶ ἀκίνητοι
δοκοῦσιν αἱ ἰδέαι τοῖς λέγουσιν ἰδέας εἶναι. πρὸς
δὲ τούτους καὶ οἱ τοιοῦτοι λόγοι χρήσιμοι.

Ἔτι εἰ τῶν καθ' ὁμωνυμίαν λεγομένων ἕνα
λόγον ἁπάντων κοινὸν ἀπέδωκεν. συνώνυμα γὰρ
25 ὧν εἷς ὁ κατὰ τοὔνομα λόγος, ὥστ' οὐδενὸς τῶν
ὑπὸ τοὔνομα ὁ ἀποδοθεὶς ὅρος, εἰ δὴ ὁμοίως ἐπὶ
πᾶν τὸ ὁμώνυμον ἐφαρμόττει. πέπονθε δὲ τοῦτο
καὶ ὁ Διονυσίου τῆς ζωῆς ὅρος, εἴπερ ἐστὶ κίνησις
γένους θρεπτοῦ σύμφυτος παρακολουθοῦσα· οὐδὲν
γὰρ μᾶλλον τοῦτο τοῖς ζῴοις ἢ τοῖς φυτοῖς ὑπάρχει·
30 ἡ δὲ ζωὴ οὐ καθ' ἓν εἶδος δοκεῖ λέγεσθαι, ἀλλ'
ἑτέρα μὲν τοῖς ζῴοις ἑτέρα δὲ τοῖς φυτοῖς ὑπάρχειν.
ἐνδέχεται μὲν οὖν καὶ κατὰ προαίρεσιν οὕτως
ἀποδοῦναι τὸν ὅρον ὡς συνωνύμου καὶ καθ' ἓν
εἶδος πάσης τῆς ζωῆς λεγομένης· οὐδὲν δὲ κωλύει
καὶ συνορῶντα τὴν ὁμωνυμίαν, καὶ θατέρου βου-
35 λόμενον τὸν ὁρισμὸν ἀποδοῦναι, λαθεῖν μὴ ἴδιον
ἀλλὰ κοινὸν ἀμφοῖν λόγον ἀποδόντα. ἀλλ' οὐδὲν
ἧττον, εἰ ὁποτερωσοῦν πεποίηκεν, ἡμάρτηκεν.

148 b ἐπεὶ δ' ἔνια λανθάνει τῶν ὁμωνύμων, ἐρωτῶντι
μὲν ὡς συνωνύμοις χρηστέον (οὐ γὰρ ἐφαρμόσει
ὁ θατέρου ὅρος ἐπὶ θάτερον, ὥστε δόξει οὐχ
ὡρίσθαι κατὰ τρόπον· δεῖ γὰρ ἐπὶ πᾶν τὸ συνώνυμον ἐφαρμόττειν), αὐτῷ δ' ἀποκρινομένῳ διαι-

the definition and the 'idea'; for 'ideas,' in the view
of those who hold that they exist, are not liable to
any affection or to motion. In dealing with such
persons such arguments, amongst others, are useful.

Furthermore, you must see whether he has given *Rules for* one common description of terms used equivocally. *testing the definition of* For terms of which the description corresponding *equivocal* with the name is one and the same, are synonymous, *terms.* and so, if the definition assigned fits the equivocal term equally well in all its senses, it cannot apply to any one of the meanings which fall under the name. This is the defect of Dionysius' definition of 'life,' which he describes as 'innate and accompanying movement of an organism nourished by food'; for this applies not less to plants than to animals, whereas it is generally held that the term 'life' is not used of one kind of thing only, but that there is one life of animals and another of plants. It is possible, however, also deliberately to assign the definition in this way on the ground that life as a whole is a synonymous term and applied to one kind of thing only; but there is no reason why a man, though he both sees the equivocation and wishes to assign the definition of one meaning only, should yet unconsciously assign a description which is not peculiar to one of two meaning but common to both. Nevertheless, whichever of these two courses he has adopted, he is equally in error. Since equivocal terms sometimes pass unnoticed, you should, when you are questioning, treat them as synonymous (for the definition of one meaning will not fit the other, so that the definition will be generally regarded as incorrect, for it ought to fit every instance of the synonymous term); on the other hand, you yourself, when answering, ought to

ρετέον. ἐπεὶ δ' ἔνιοι τῶν ἀποκρινομένων τὸ μὲν
5 συνώνυμον ὁμώνυμόν φασιν εἶναι, ὅταν μὴ ἐφαρμόττῃ ἐπὶ πᾶν ὁ ἀποδοθεὶς λόγος, τὸ δ' ὁμώνυμον
συνώνυμον, ἐὰν ἐπ' ἄμφω ἐφαρμόττῃ, προδιομολογητέον ὑπὲρ τῶν τοιούτων ἢ προσυλλογιστέον
ὅτι ὁμώνυμον ἢ συνώνυμον, ὁπότερον ἂν ᾖ· μᾶλλον
10 γὰρ συγχωροῦσιν οὐ προορῶντες τὸ συμβησόμενον. ἂν δὲ μὴ γενομένης ὁμολογίας φῇ τις τὸ
συνώνυμον ὁμώνυμον εἶναι διὰ τὸ μὴ ἐφαρμόττειν
καὶ ἐπὶ τοῦτο τὸν ἀποδοθέντα λόγον, σκοπεῖν εἰ
ὁ τούτου λόγος ἐφαρμόττει καὶ ἐπὶ τὰ λοιπά·
δῆλον γὰρ ὅτι συνώνυμον ἂν εἴη τοῖς λοιποῖς. εἰ
δὲ μή, πλείους ἔσονται ὁρισμοὶ τῶν λοιπῶν· δύο
15 γὰρ οἱ κατὰ τοὔνομα λόγοι ἐφαρμόττουσιν ἐπ'
αὐτά, ὅ τε πρότερον ἀποδοθεὶς καὶ ὁ ὕστερον·
πάλιν εἴ τις ὁρισάμενος τῶν πολλαχῶς τι λεγομένων, καὶ τοῦ λόγου μὴ ἐφαρμόττοντος ἐπὶ
πάντα, ὅτι μὲν ὁμώνυμον μὴ λέγοι, τὸ δ' ὄνομα
μὴ φαίη ἐπὶ πάντα ἐφαρμόττειν, ὅτι οὐδ' ὁ λόγος,
20 ῥητέον πρὸς τὸν τοιοῦτον ὅτι τῇ μὲν ὀνομασίᾳ δεῖ
χρῆσθαι τῇ παραδεδομένῃ καὶ παρεπομένῃ καὶ μὴ
κινεῖν τὰ τοιαῦτα, ἔνια δ' οὐ λεκτέον ὁμοίως τοῖς
πολλοῖς.

XI. Ἐὰν δὲ τῶν συμπεπλεγμένων τινὸς ἀποδοθῇ ὅρος, σκοπεῖν ἀφαιροῦντα τὸν θατέρου τῶν
25 συμπεπλεγμένων λόγον, εἰ καὶ ὁ λοιπὸς τοῦ λοι-

distinguish the various meanings. Since some answerers call a term 'equivocal' which is really synonymous whenever the description assigned does not fit all its meanings, and call a term 'synonymous' which is really equivocal if the description fits both meanings, you must obtain a previous agreement on such points or else prove in advance that the term is 'equivocal' or 'synonymous,' whichever it may be ; for people concur more readily when they do not foresee what will be the result. If, on the other hand, when there has been no agreement, a man declares that a synonymous term is equivocal because the description assigned does not fit a particular meaning of it, you must see whether the description of this meaning fits the other meanings also ; for then it is obvious that it must be synonymous with the other meanings. If this is not so, there will be more than one definition of the other meanings; for there are two descriptions applied to the term which fit them, namely, the one originally assigned and the one subsequently assigned. Again, if a man were to define a term used in several meanings, and then, when the description did not fit all the meanings, were not to say that it is equivocal but were to assert that the term does not fit all the meanings just because the description does not fit them either, you must say to such a person that, though sometimes one ought not to use the same language as the multitude, yet one ought to employ the traditional and received terminology and not disturb things of that kind.

XI. If a definition has been given of some complex term, you must take away the description of one part of the complex and see whether the remainder of the definition is a description of the remainder of it ; *Rules for the definition of a complex term: (a) Does the*

148 b

ποῦ· εἰ γὰρ μή, δῆλον ὅτι οὐδ' ὁ ὅλος τοῦ ὅλου. οἷον εἰ ὡρίσατο γραμμὴν πεπερασμένην εὐθεῖαν πέρας ἐπιπέδου ἔχοντος πέρατα, οὗ τὸ μέσον ἐπιπροσθεῖ τοῖς πέρασιν, εἰ τῆς πεπερασμένης γραμμῆς ὁ λόγος ἐστὶ πέρας ἐπιπέδου ἔχοντος
30 πέρατα, τοῦ εὐθέος δεῖ εἶναι τὸ λοιπόν, οὗ τὸ μέσον ἐπιπροσθεῖ τοῖς πέρασιν. ἀλλ' ἡ ἄπειρος οὔτε μέσον οὔτε πέρατα ἔχει, εὐθεῖα δ' ἐστίν, ὥστ' οὐκ ἔστιν ὁ λοιπὸς τοῦ λοιποῦ λόγος.

Ἔτι εἰ συνθέτου ὄντος τοῦ ὁριζομένου ἰσόκωλος ὁ λόγος ἀπεδόθη τῷ ὁριζομένῳ. ἰσόκωλος δὲ
35 λέγεται ὁ λόγος εἶναι, ὅταν ὅσαπερ ἂν ᾖ τὰ συγκείμενα, τοσαῦτα καὶ ἐν τῷ λόγῳ ὀνόματα καὶ ῥήματα ᾖ. ἀνάγκη γὰρ αὐτῶν τῶν[1] ὀνομάτων ἐν τοῖς τοιούτοις μεταλλαγὴν γίνεσθαι, ἢ πάντων ἢ
149 a τινῶν, ἐπειδὴ οὐδὲν πλείω νῦν ἢ πρότερον ὀνόματα εἴρηται· δεῖ δὲ τὸν ὁριζόμενον λόγον ἀντὶ τῶν ὀνομάτων ἀποδοῦναι, μάλιστα μὲν πάντων, εἰ δὲ μή, τῶν πλείστων. οὕτω γὰρ καὶ ἐπὶ τῶν ἁπλῶν ὁ τοὔνομα μεταλαβὼν ὡρισμένος ἂν εἴη, οἷον ἀντὶ λωπίου ἱμάτιον.

5 Ἔτι δὲ μείζων ἁμαρτία, εἰ καὶ ἀγνωστοτέρων ὀνομάτων τὴν μετάληψιν ἐποιήσατο, οἷον ἀντὶ ἀνθρώπου λευκοῦ βροτὸν ἀργόν· οὔτε γὰρ ὥρισται ἧττόν τε σαφὲς οὕτω ῥηθέν.

Σκοπεῖν δὲ καὶ ἐν τῇ μεταλλαγῇ τῶν ὀνομάτων

---

[1] Reading αὐτῶν τῶν with BC.

if not, it is obvious that neither does the whole defini- definition describe the whole complex ? tion describe the whole complex. Suppose, for example, someone has defined a ' finite straight line ' as the ' limit of a finite plane, such that its centre is directly between its extremities '; if the description of a ' finite line ' is the ' limit of a finite plane,' the remainder, namely, ' such that its centre is directly between its extremities ' ought to be the description of ' straight.' But an infinite line has neither extremities nor a centre and is nevertheless straight, so that the remaining part of the definition does not describe the remainder of the term.

Furthermore, when that which is being defined is (b) Does the definition consist of as many parts as the complex which is its subject ? compound, you must see whether the description assigned possesses the same number of members as that which is being defined. The description is said to contain the same number of members when the nouns and verbs in the description are equal in number to the component parts of the subject of the definition. For in such cases there must be a change of all or some of the terms themselves, since no more terms are used now than before, whereas he who is giving a definition must assign a description in place of all the terms, if possible, or, failing this, of most of them. For on that principle, in dealing with simple terms also, he who has simply changed the name would have given a definition, for example, if he substituted ' cloak ' for ' mantle.'

The error is still greater if what is substituted con- (c) Are the terms used more obscure ? sists of terms which are even less intelligible, for example, ' gleaming mortal ' in place of ' white man '; for it forms no definition and is less intelligible when stated in this way.

You must also consider whether in the change of (d) Are

εἰ οὐ ταὐτὸν ἔτι σημαίνει, οἷον ὁ τὴν θεωρητικὴν
10 ἐπιστήμην ὑπόληψιν θεωρητικὴν εἰπών. ἡ γὰρ
ὑπόληψις τῇ ἐπιστήμῃ οὐ ταὐτόν, δεῖ δέ γε, εἴπερ
μέλλει καὶ τὸ ὅλον ταὐτὸν εἶναι· τὸ μὲν γὰρ θεω-
ρητικὸν κοινὸν ἐν ἀμφοτέροιν τοῖν λόγοιν ἐστί,
τὸ δὲ λοιπὸν διάφορον.

Ἔτι εἰ θατέρου τῶν ὀνομάτων τὴν μετάληψιν
15 ποιούμενος μὴ τῆς διαφορᾶς ἀλλὰ τοῦ γένους τὴν
μεταλλαγὴν ἐποιήσατο, καθάπερ ἐπὶ τοῦ ἀρτίως
ῥηθέντος. ἀγνωστότερον γὰρ ἡ θεωρητικὴ τῆς
ἐπιστήμης· τὸ μὲν γὰρ γένος, τὸ δὲ διαφορά,
πάντων δὲ γνωριμώτατον τὸ γένος· ὥστ᾽ οὐ τοῦ
γένους ἀλλὰ τῆς διαφορᾶς ἔδει τὴν μετάληψιν
20 ποιήσασθαι, ἐπειδὴ ἀγνωστότερόν ἐστιν. ἢ τοῦτο
μὲν γελοῖον τὸ ἐπιτίμημα· οὐδὲν γὰρ κωλύει τὴν
μὲν διαφορὰν τῷ γνωριμωτάτῳ ὀνόματι εἰρῆσθαι,
τὸ δὲ γένος μή· οὕτω δ᾽ ἐχόντων δῆλον ὅτι τοῦ
γένους καὶ οὐ τῆς διαφορᾶς κατὰ τοὔνομα καὶ τὴν
μετάληψιν ποιητέον. εἰ δὲ μὴ ὄνομα ἀντ᾽ ὀνό-
25 ματος ἀλλὰ λόγον ἀντ᾽ ὀνόματος μεταλαμβάνει,
δῆλον ὅτι τῆς διαφορᾶς μᾶλλον ἢ τοῦ γένους
ὁρισμὸν ἀποδοτέον, ἐπειδὴ τοῦ γνωρίσαι χάριν
ὁ ὁρισμὸς ἀποδίδοται· ἧττον γὰρ ἡ διαφορὰ τοῦ
γένους γνώριμον.

XII. Εἰ δὲ τῆς διαφορᾶς τὸν ὅρον ἀποδέδωκε,
30 σκοπεῖν εἰ καὶ ἄλλου τινὸς κοινὸς ὁ ἀποδοθεὶς
ὅρος, οἷον ὅταν περιττὸν ἀριθμὸν ἀριθμὸν μέσον
ἔχοντα εἴπῃ, ἐπιδιοριστέον τὸ πῶς μέσον ἔχοντα.
ὁ μὲν γὰρ ἀριθμὸς κοινὸς ἐν ἀμφοτέροις τοῖς
λόγοις ὑπάρχει, τοῦ δὲ περιττοῦ μετείληπται ὁ

terms the significance is no longer the same, for example, when 'speculative knowledge' is called 'speculative conception.' For 'conception' is not the same as 'knowledge,' and yet it ought to be the same if the whole phrase too is to be the same; for, while 'speculative' is common to both phrases, the remainder is different.

Furthermore, you must see whether, in the sub- stitution of one of the terms, the change is made not of the differentia but of the genus, as in the example just given. For 'speculative' is less familiar than 'knowledge'; for the latter is a genus, the former a differentia, and the genus is always the most intelligible of all terms. The substitution ought, therefore, to have taken place not in the genus but in the differentia, since the latter is less intelligible. Or, possibly, this criticism is ridiculous; for there is no reason why the differentia rather than the genus should be described by the most familiar term, and, if so, obviously the change ought to be made in the term expressing not the differentia but the genus. But if it is a question of substituting not term for term but phrase for term, obviously a definition should be given of the differentia rather than of the genus, since a definition is given to make something intelligible; for the differentia is less intelligible than the genus.

XII. If the definer has given the definition of the differentia, you must see whether the definition given is common to something else also. For example, when an odd number is described as a 'number which has a middle,' a further definition must be given to show in what sense it has a middle; for the word 'number' is common to both expressions, but the

149 a

λόγος. ἔχει δὲ καὶ γραμμὴ καὶ σῶμα μέσον, οὐ
35 περιττὰ ὄντα. ὥστ' οὐκ ἂν εἴη ὁρισμὸς οὗτος
τοῦ περιττοῦ. εἰ δὲ πολλαχῶς λέγεται τὸ μέσον
ἔχον, διοριστέον τὸ πῶς μέσον ἔχον. ὥστ' ἢ ἐπιτίμησις ἔσται, ἢ συλλογισμὸς ὅτι οὐχ ὥρισται.

Πάλιν εἰ οὗ μὲν τὸν λόγον ἀποδίδωσι τῶν ὄντων
ἐστί, τὸ δ' ὑπὸ τὸν λόγον μὴ τῶν ὄντων, οἷον εἰ
149 b τὸ λευκὸν ὡρίσατο χρῶμα πυρὶ μεμιγμένον· ἀδύνατον γὰρ τὸ ἀσώματον μεμῖχθαι σώματι, ὥστ' οὐκ
ἂν εἴη χρῶμα πυρὶ μεμιγμένον· λευκὸν δ' ἔστιν.

Ἔτι ὅσοι μὴ διαιροῦσιν ἐν τοῖς πρός τι πρὸς ὃ
5 λέγεται, ἀλλ' ἐν πλείοσι περιλαβόντες εἶπαν, ἢ
ὅλως ἢ ἐπί τι ψεύδονται, οἷον εἴ τις τὴν ἰατρικὴν
ἐπιστήμην ὄντος εἶπεν. εἰ μὲν γὰρ μηδενὸς τῶν
ὄντων ἡ ἰατρικὴ ἐπιστήμη, δῆλον ὅτι ὅλως ἔψευ-
σται, εἰ δὲ τινὸς μὲν τινὸς δὲ μή, ἐπί τι ἔψευσται·
δεῖ γὰρ παντός, εἴπερ καθ' αὑτὸ καὶ μὴ κατὰ
10 συμβεβηκὸς ὄντος εἶναι λέγεται, καθάπερ ἐπὶ
τῶν ἄλλων ἔχει τῶν πρός τι· πᾶν γὰρ ἐπιστητὸν
πρὸς ἐπιστήμην λέγεται. ὁμοίως δὲ καὶ ἐπὶ τῶν
ἄλλων, ἐπειδὴ ἀντιστρέφει πάντα τὰ πρός τι.
ἔτι εἴπερ ὁ μὴ καθ' αὑτὸ ἀλλὰ κατὰ συμβεβηκὸς
τὴν ἀπόδοσιν ποιούμενος ὀρθῶς ἀποδίδωσιν, οὐ
15 πρὸς ἓν ἀλλὰ πρὸς πλείω ἕκαστον ἂν τῶν πρός

new expression has been substituted for ' odd.' Now thing else also ?
a line and a body also have a middle, though they
are not ' odd,' so that this could not be a definition
of ' odd.' But if the expression ' having a middle '
is used in several senses, the sense in which ' having
a middle ' is used must be defined. This will either
result in the destructive criticism of the definition
or prove that no definition has been given.

Again, you must see whether the term of which (b) Is the subject to be defined existent, but the description non-existent ?
he is giving the description has a real existence,
whereas what is given in the description has not. An
example of this is the definition of ' white ' as ' colour
mixed with fire '; for it is impossible for that which
is without body to be mixed with a body, so that
' colour ' ' mixed with fire ' could not exist, whereas
' white ' does exist.

Furthermore, those who, in dealing with relative (c) When a relation is defined, is that to which the subject is related too wide in extent ?
terms, fail to distinguish what it is to which the
subject is related, but, in describing it, include it
amongst a number of things, are either wholly or
partly in error ; for example, if one described ' medicine ' as a ' science of reality.' For, if medicine is not
a science of anything real, he is wholly wrong, but,
if it is a science of something which is real but not
of something else which is real, he is partly wrong ;
for it ought to be a science of all reality, if it is
described as being a science of reality essentially
and not accidentally (as is true of all the other relative terms) ; for every ' object of science ' is used
in relation to science. So likewise with the other
relative terms, since they are all convertible. Furthermore, if he who gives an account of anything not as
it really is but as it is accidentally, is giving a correct
account, every relative term would be employed in

631

τι λέγοιτο. οὐδὲν γὰρ κωλύει τὸ αὐτὸ καὶ ὂν καὶ
λευκὸν καὶ ἀγαθὸν εἶναι, ὥστε πρὸς ὁποιονοῦν
τούτων ἀποδιδοὺς ὀρθῶς ἂν εἴη ἀποδιδούς, εἴπερ
ὁ κατὰ συμβεβηκὸς ἀποδιδοὺς ὀρθῶς ἀποδίδωσιν.
ἔτι δ' ἀδύνατον τὸν τοιοῦτον λόγον ἴδιον τοῦ
20 ἀποδοθέντος εἶναι· οὐ γὰρ μόνον ἡ ἰατρικὴ ἀλλὰ
καὶ τῶν ἄλλων ἐπιστημῶν αἱ πολλαὶ πρὸς ὂν λέγονται, ὥσθ' ἑκάστη ὄντος ἐπιστήμη ἔσται. δῆλον
οὖν ὅτι ὁ τοιοῦτος οὐδεμιᾶς ἐστὶν ἐπιστήμης ὁρι-
σμός· ἴδιον γὰρ καὶ οὐ κοινὸν δεῖ τὸν ὁρισμὸν
εἶναι.

Ἐνίοτε δ' ὁρίζονται οὐ τὸ πρᾶγμα, ἀλλὰ τὸ
25 πρᾶγμα εὖ ἔχον ἢ τετελεσμένον. τοιοῦτος δ' ὁ
τοῦ ῥήτορος καὶ ὁ τοῦ κλέπτου ὅρος, εἴπερ ἐστὶ
ῥήτωρ μὲν ὁ δυνάμενος τὸ ἐν ἑκάστῳ πιθανὸν
θεωρεῖν καὶ μηδὲν παραλείπειν, κλέπτης δ' ὁ λάθρᾳ
λαμβάνων· δῆλον γὰρ ὅτι τοιοῦτος ὢν ἑκάτερος
ὁ μὲν ἀγαθὸς ῥήτωρ ὁ δ' ἀγαθὸς κλέπτης ἔσται·
30 οὐ γὰρ ὁ λάθρᾳ λαμβάνων ἀλλ' ὁ βουλόμενος
λάθρᾳ λαμβάνειν κλέπτης ἐστίν.

Πάλιν εἰ τὸ δι' αὑτὸ αἱρετὸν ὡς ποιητικὸν ἢ
πρακτικὸν ἢ ὁπωσοῦν δι' ἄλλο αἱρετὸν ἀποδέδωκεν,
οἷον τὴν δικαιοσύνην νόμων σωστικὴν εἰπὼν ἢ
τὴν σοφίαν ποιητικὴν εὐδαιμονίας· τὸ γὰρ ποιη-
35 τικὸν ἢ σωστικὸν τῶν δι' ἄλλο αἱρετῶν. ἢ οὐδὲν
μὲν κωλύει τὸ δι' αὑτὸ αἱρετὸν καὶ δι' ἄλλο εἶναι

relation not to one thing but to many things. For there is nothing to prevent the same thing being both real and white and good ; so that, if to give an account of a thing as it is accidentally is the correct method, one would be giving a correct account if one gave it in relation to any one of these. Furthermore, it is impossible for such a description to be peculiar to that of which the account has been given ; for not only medicine but most of the sciences also are employed in relation to something real, so that each of them will be a science of reality. Obviously, therefore, such a definition is not a definition of any science ; for the definition ought to be peculiar to one thing, not common to many.

Sometimes men define not the thing, but the thing *(d)* Is the in a good and perfect state. Examples of this are definition the definitions of an ' orator ' as ' he who can see what the subject is a plausible argument on any occasion and omit as it is, but nothing,' and of a ' thief ' as ' he who takes something of a perfect by stealth ' ; for obviously, if they each act thus, form of it ? the former will be a good orator, the latter a good thief ; for it is not he who actually takes something by stealth, but he who wishes to do so, that is really a thief.

Again, you must see whether the definer has repre- *(e)* Is what sented what is worthy of choice for its own sake as is eligible being so because it produces or effects something *per se* or for some other reason, describing, for example, it were ' justice ' as ' preservative of the laws ' or ' wisdom ' *propter* as ' productive of happiness ' ; for what is preservative *aliud* ? or productive is among the things which are worthy of choice for the sake of something else. Or, possibly, there is nothing to prevent what is worthy of choice for its own sake being also worthy of choice for some

αἱρετόν, οὐ μὴν ἀλλ' οὐδὲν ἧττον ἡμάρτηκεν ὁ
οὕτως ὁρισάμενος τὸ δι' αὐτὸ αἱρετόν· ἑκάστου
γὰρ τὸ βέλτιστον ἐν τῇ οὐσίᾳ μάλιστα, βέλτιον
δὲ τὸ δι' αὐτὸ αἱρετὸν εἶναι τοῦ δι' ἕτερον, ὥστε
τοῦτο καὶ τὸν ὁρισμὸν ἔδει μᾶλλον σημαίνειν.

XIII. Σκοπεῖν δὲ καὶ εἴ τινος ὁρισμὸν ἀποδιδοὺς τάδε ἢ τὸ ἐκ τούτων ἢ τόδε μετὰ τοῦδε
ὡρίσατο. εἰ μὲν γὰρ τάδε, συμβήσεται ἀμφοῖν
καὶ μηδετέρῳ ὑπάρχειν, οἷον εἰ τὴν δικαιοσύνην
σωφροσύνην καὶ ἀνδρίαν ὡρίσατο· δύο γαρ ὄντων
5 ἐὰν ἑκάτερος θάτερον ἔχῃ, ἀμφότεροι δίκαιοι
ἔσονται καὶ οὐδέτερος, ἐπειδὴ ἀμφότεροι μὲν
ἔχουσι δικαιοσύνην, ἑκάτερος δ' οὐκ ἔχει. εἰ δὲ
μήπω τὸ εἰρημένον σφόδρα ἄτοπον διὰ τὸ καὶ ἐπ'
ἄλλων συμβαίνειν τὸ τοιοῦτον (οὐδὲν γὰρ κωλύει
ἀμφοτέρους ἔχειν μνᾶν μηδετέρου ἔχοντος), ἀλλ'
10 οὖν τό γε τἀναντία ὑπάρχειν αὐτοῖς παντελῶς
ἄτοπον ἂν δόξειεν εἶναι. συμβήσεται δὲ τοῦτο,
ἐὰν ὁ μὲν αὐτῶν σωφροσύνην καὶ δειλίαν ἔχῃ, ὁ
δὲ ἀνδρίαν καὶ ἀκολασίαν· ἄμφω γὰρ δικαιοσύνην
καὶ ἀδικίαν ἕξουσιν. εἰ γὰρ ἡ δικαιοσύνη σωφροσύνη καὶ ἀνδρία ἐστίν, ἡ ἀδικία δειλία καὶ ἀκο-
15 λασία ἔσται. ὅλως τε ὅσα ἔστιν ἐπιχειρεῖν ὅτι οὐ
ταὐτόν ἐστι τὰ μέρη καὶ τὸ ὅλον, πάντα χρήσιμα
πρὸς τὸ νῦν εἰρημένον· ἔοικε γὰρ ὁ οὕτως ὁριζόμενος

other reason ; but he who has thus defined what is worthy of choice for its own sake has nevertheless made a mistake ; for what is best in any particular thing is what is most inherent in its essence, and what is worthy of choice for its own sake is better than what is worthy of choice for some other reason, and it is this, therefore, which the definition ought to have signified.

XIII. You must also examine whether the definer *How to deal* in giving a definition of anything has defined it as *with defini-* either (1) ' A and B,' or (2) ' made up of A and B,' *take the* or (3) ' A plus B.' (1) If he defines it as ' A and B,' the *following* result will be that it applies to both and neither, for *(a) X is ' A* example, if he has defined ' justice ' as ' temperance *and B.'* and courage.' For if there are two persons each of whom has one of these qualities, the two together will be ' just,' but neither singly so, since both together they possess justice but each taken singly does not do so. If the above statement is not utterly ridiculous at first sight owing to the fact that this sort of thing occurs in other instances (*e.g.* there is nothing to prevent two persons together possessing a mina, though neither singly possesses it), yet at any rate it would be generally regarded as totally absurd that they should have contrary qualities ; and this will happen if one of them has temperance and cowardice, and the other justice and incontinence, for taken together they will have justice and injustice ; for, if justice is temperance and courage, injustice will be cowardice and incontinence. To speak generally, all the arguments that can be used to prove that the whole and its parts are not the same are useful for countering the statement made just now ; for he who defines in this manner appears to state that the

τὰ μέρη τῷ ὅλῳ ταὐτὰ φάσκειν εἶναι. μάλιστα
δ᾽ οἰκεῖοι γίνονται οἱ λόγοι, ἐφ᾽ ὅσων κατάδηλός
ἐστιν ἡ τῶν μερῶν σύνθεσις, καθάπερ ἐπ᾽ οἰκίας
20 καὶ τῶν ἄλλων τῶν τοιούτων· δῆλον γὰρ ὅτι τῶν
μερῶν ὄντων οὐδὲν κωλύει τὸ ὅλον μὴ εἶναι, ὥστ᾽
οὐ ταὐτὸν τὰ μέρη τῷ ὅλῳ.

Εἰ δὲ μὴ ταῦτα ἀλλὰ τὸ ἐκ τούτων ἔφησεν εἶναι
τὸ ὁριζόμενον, πρῶτον μὲν ἐπισκοπεῖν εἰ μὴ
πέφυκεν ἓν γίνεσθαι ἐκ τῶν εἰρημένων· ἔνια γὰρ
25 οὕτως ἔχει πρὸς ἄλληλα ὥστε μηδὲν ἐξ αὐτῶν
γίνεσθαι, οἷον γραμμὴ καὶ ἀριθμός. ἔτι εἰ τὸ μὲν
ὡρισμένον ἐν ἑνί τινι πέφυκε τῷ πρώτῳ γίνεσθαι,
ἐξ ὧν δ᾽ ἔφησεν αὐτὸ εἶναι, μὴ ἐν ἑνὶ τῷ πρώτῳ,
ἀλλ᾽ ἑκάτερον ἐν ἑκατέρῳ· δῆλον γὰρ ὅτι οὐκ ἂν
εἴη ἐκ τούτων ἐκεῖνο· ἐν οἷς γὰρ τὰ μέρη, καὶ τὸ
30 ὅλον ἀνάγκη ὑπάρχειν, ὥστ᾽ οὐκ ἐν ἑνὶ τὸ ὅλον
πρώτῳ, ἀλλ᾽ ἐν πλείοσιν. εἰ δὲ καὶ τὰ μέρη καὶ
τὸ ὅλον ἐν ἑνί τινι πρώτῳ, σκοπεῖν εἰ μὴ ἐν τῷ
αὐτῷ ἀλλ᾽ ἐν ἑτέρῳ τὸ ὅλον καὶ ἐν ἑτέρῳ τὰ μέρη.
πάλιν εἰ τῷ ὅλῳ συμφθείρεται τὰ μέρη· ἀνάπαλιν
γὰρ δεῖ συμβαίνειν, τῶν μερῶν φθαρέντων φθεί-
35 ρεσθαι τὸ ὅλον· τοῦ δ᾽ ὅλου φθαρέντος οὐκ ἀναγκαῖον καὶ τὰ μέρη ἐφθάρθαι. ἢ εἰ τὸ μὲν ὅλον
ἀγαθὸν ἢ κακόν, τὰ δὲ μηδέτερα, ἢ ἀνάπαλιν τὰ

parts are the same as the whole. But these arguments are specially appropriate when the process of compounding the parts is obvious, as in a house and all other such things ; for here it is obvious that, though the parts exist, there is no reason why the whole should not be non-existent, and so the parts are not the same as the whole.

(2) If, however, he has asserted that that which is *(b) X is being defined is not ' A and B ' but ' made up of A made up of A and B.' and B,'* you must first of all consider whether it is unnatural for a single product to come into being from the said component parts ; for some things are so constituted in relation to one another that nothing can come into being from them, for example, a line and a number. Moreover, you must see whether what has been defined naturally comes into being primarily in some single thing, whereas those things which, according to his account, produce it, do not come into being primarily in any single thing but each in a different thing. For then obviously it could not come into being from these things ; for the whole must necessarily exist in those things in which the parts exist, so that the whole does not exist primarily in one thing only but in many. If, however, both the parts and the whole exist primarily in some single thing, you must see whether they exist in the same thing and not the whole in one thing and the parts in another. Again, you must see whether the parts perish when the whole perishes ; for the converse ought to happen, namely, that the whole perishes when the parts do so, and it does not necessarily follow that the parts also have perished when the whole has perished. Or, again, you must see whether the whole is good or bad, and the parts neither, or,

150 a

μὲν ἀγαθὰ ἢ κακά, τὸ δ' ὅλον μηδέτερον· οὔτε γὰρ
150 b ἐκ μηδετέρου δυνατὸν ἢ ἀγαθόν τι ἢ κακὸν γενέσθαι,
οὔτ' ἐκ κακῶν ἢ ἀγαθῶν μηδέτερον. ἢ εἰ μᾶλλον
μὲν θάτερον ἀγαθὸν ἢ θάτερον κακόν, τὸ δ' ἐκ
τούτων μὴ μᾶλλον ἀγαθὸν ἢ κακόν, οἷον εἰ ἡ
ἀναίδεια ἐξ ἀνδρίας καὶ ψευδοῦς δόξης. μᾶλλον
5 γὰρ ἀγαθὸν ἡ ἀνδρία ἢ κακὸν ἡ ψευδὴς δόξα· ἔδει
οὖν καὶ τὸ ἐκ τούτων ἀκολουθεῖν τῷ μᾶλλον,
καὶ εἶναι ἢ ἁπλῶς ἀγαθὸν ἢ μᾶλλον ἀγαθὸν ἢ
κακόν. ἢ τοῦτο μὲν οὐκ ἀναγκαῖον, ἐὰν μὴ ἑκάτερον ᾖ καθ' αὑτὸ ἀγαθὸν ἢ κακόν· πολλὰ γὰρ
τῶν ποιητικῶν καθ' αὑτὰ μὲν οὐκ ἔστιν ἀγαθά,
10 μιχθέντα δέ, ἢ ἀνάπαλιν, ἑκάτερον μὲν ἀγαθόν, μιχθέντα δὲ κακὸν ἢ οὐδέτερον. μάλιστα δὲ καταφανὲς τὸ νῦν ῥηθὲν ἐπὶ τῶν ὑγιεινῶν καὶ νοσωδῶν·
ἔνια γὰρ τῶν φαρμάκων οὕτως ἔχει ὥσθ' ἑκάτερον μὲν εἶναι ἀγαθόν, ἐὰν δ' ἄμφω δοθῇ μιχθέντα,
κακόν.

Πάλιν εἰ ἐκ βελτίονος καὶ χείρονος ὂν μή ἐστι
15 τὸ ὅλον τοῦ μὲν βελτίονος χεῖρον, τοῦ δὲ χείρονος
βέλτιον. ἢ οὐδὲ τοῦτ' ἀναγκαῖον, ἐὰν μὴ καθ'
αὑτὰ ᾖ τὰ ἐξ ὧν σύγκειται ἀγαθά, ἀλλ' οὐδὲν
κωλύει τὸ ὅλον μὴ γίνεσθαι ἀγαθόν, καθάπερ ἐπὶ
τῶν ἀρτίως ῥηθέντων.

Ἔτι εἰ συνώνυμον τὸ ὅλον θατέρῳ· οὐ δεῖ γάρ,
20 καθάπερ οὐδ' ἐπὶ τῶν συλλαβῶν· οὐδενὶ γὰρ τῶν
στοιχείων ἐξ ὧν σύγκειται ἡ συλλαβὴ συνώνυμός
ἐστιν.

638

conversely, whether the parts are good or bad and the whole neither ; for it is impossible that anything either good or bad should come into being from something which is neither, or anything which is neither from things which are good or bad. Or, again, you must see whether the one thing has more good in it than the other has evil, and yet the product of the two has not more good in it than evil, as, for example, in the definition of ' shamelessness ' as ' made up of courage and false opinion.' For courage has more good in it than false opinion has evil, and so their product ought to maintain this excess and be either good absolutely or good rather than bad. Or, perhaps this does not necessarily follow, unless each is in itself good or bad ; for many of the things which produce effects are not good in themselves but only when mingled together, or, conversely, are good separately but either good or neither good nor bad when mingled together. The state of affairs just described is best seen in things which produce health and disease ; for some drugs are so constituted as each separately to be good whereas they are bad if given in a mixture.

Again, you must see whether the whole, when it is made up of a better and a worse, fails to be worse than the better and better than the worse. Perhaps this too does not necessarily follow, unless the component parts are themselves good ; but there is nothing to prevent the whole being good, as in the cases just mentioned.

Furthermore, you must see whether the whole is synonymous with one of the parts ; for it ought not to be so, any more than occurs in the case of syllables, for the syllable is not synonymous with any of the letters of which it is composed.

Ἔτι εἰ μὴ εἴρηκε τὸν τρόπον τῆς συνθέσεως. οὐ γὰρ αὔταρκες πρὸς τὸ γνωρίσαι τὸ εἰπεῖν ἐκ τούτων· οὐ γὰρ τὸ ἐκ τούτων, ἀλλὰ τὸ οὕτως ἐκ

25 τούτων ἑκάστου τῶν συνθέτων ἡ οὐσία, καθάπερ ἐπ' οἰκίας· οὐ γὰρ ἂν ὁπωσοῦν συντεθῇ ταῦτα, οἰκία ἐστίν.

Εἰ δὲ τόδε μετὰ τοῦδε ἀποδέδωκε, πρῶτον μὲν ῥητέον ὅτι τόδε μετὰ τοῦδε ἢ τοῖσδε ταὐτὸν ἢ τῷ ἐκ τῶνδε· ὁ γὰρ λέγων μέλι μεθ' ὕδατος ἤτοι

30 μέλι καὶ ὕδωρ λέγει ἢ τὸ ἐκ μέλιτος καὶ ὕδατος, ὥστ' ἐὰν ὁποτερῳοῦν τῶν εἰρημένων ταὐτὸν ὁμο- λογήσῃ εἶναι τὸ τόδε μετὰ τοῦδε, ταὐτὰ ἁρμόσει λέγειν ἅπερ πρὸς ἑκάτερον τούτων ἔμπροσθεν εἴρηται. ἔτι διελόμενον ὁσαχῶς λέγεται ἕτερον μεθ' ἑτέρου, σκοπεῖν εἰ μηδαμῶς τόδε μετὰ τοῦδε.

35 οἷον εἰ λέγεται ἕτερον μεθ' ἑτέρου ἢ ὡς ἔν τινι ταὐτῷ δεκτικῷ, καθάπερ ἡ δικαιοσύνη καὶ ἡ ἀνδρία ἐν ψυχῇ, ἢ ἐν τόπῳ τῷ αὐτῷ ἢ ἐν χρόνῳ τῷ αὐτῷ, μηδαμῶς δ' ἀληθὲς τὸ εἰρημένον ἐπὶ τούτων, δῆλον ὅτι οὐδενὸς ἂν εἴη ὁ ἀποδοθεὶς

151 a ὁρισμός, ἐπειδὴ οὐδαμῶς τόδε μετὰ τοῦδέ ἐστιν. εἰ δὲ τῶν διαιρεθέντων ἀληθὲς τὸ ἐν ταὐτῷ χρόνῳ ἑκάτερον ὑπάρχειν, σκοπεῖν εἰ ἐνδέχεται μὴ πρὸς ταὐτὸν λέγεσθαι ἑκάτερον. οἷον εἰ τὴν ἀνδρίαν ὡρίσατο τόλμαν μετὰ διανοίας ὀρθῆς· ἐνδέχεται

Furthermore, you must see whether he has omitted to state the method of their composition ; for merely to say that something is made up of this and that is not enough to make the matter clear. For the essence of each compound is not merely that it is made up of this and that, but that it is made up of this and that compounded in a particular way, as in the case of a house ; for this and that material put together anyhow does not constitute a house.

(3) If he has given a definition of something in the form of ' A plus B,' the first thing that must be stated is that ' A plus B ' is equivalent to either ' A and B ' or ' made up of A and B.' For he who speaks of ' honey plus water ' means either ' honey and water ' or else something ' made up of honey and water.' If, therefore, he admits that ' A plus B ' is the same as either of the above, it will be relevant to use the same arguments as have been employed before against each of them. Furthermore, you must distinguish the various senses in which something is said to be ' plus ' something else, and see whether it is impossible for A to be in any sense ' plus B.' For example, if it means that A is plus B in the sense either that they are contained in an identical receptacle (like justice and courage in the soul), or in the same place or time, whereas the sense assigned is in no way true of A and B, it is obvious that the definition given could not apply to anything, since in no possible way can A be ' plus B.' If, however, among the various senses which we have distinguished, it is true that A and B each exist at the same time, you must look whether it is possible that each is used in a different relation. Suppose, for example, that ' daring plus right opinion' has been given as the definition of ' courage';

(c) X is ' A plus B.'

641

151 a

5 γὰρ τόλμαν μὲν ἔχειν τοῦ ἀποστερεῖν, ὀρθὴν δὲ
διάνοιαν περὶ τὰ ὑγιεινά· ἀλλ' οὐδέπω ἀνδρεῖος
ὁ ἐν τῷ αὐτῷ χρόνῳ τόδε μετὰ τοῦδε ἔχων. ἔτι
εἰ καὶ πρὸς ταὐτὸν ἄμφω λέγεται, οἷον πρὸς τὰ
ἰατρικά· οὐδὲν γὰρ κωλύει καὶ τόλμαν καὶ ὀρθὴν
διάνοιαν ἔχειν πρὸς τὰ ἰατρικά· ἀλλ' ὅμως οὐδ'
10 οὗτος ἀνδρεῖος ὁ τόδε μετὰ τοῦδε ἔχων. οὔτε
γὰρ πρὸς ἕτερον αὐτῶν ἑκάτερον δεῖ λέγεσθαι οὔτε
πρὸς ταὐτὸν τὸ τυχόν, ἀλλὰ πρὸς τὸ τῆς ἀνδρίας
τέλος, οἷον πρὸς τοὺς πολεμικοὺς κινδύνους ἢ εἴ
τι μᾶλλον τούτου τέλος.

Ἔνια δὲ τῶν οὕτως ἀποδιδομένων οὐδαμῶς
15 ὑπὸ τὴν εἰρημένην πίπτει διαίρεσιν, οἷον εἰ ἡ
ὀργὴ λύπη μεθ' ὑπολήψεως τοῦ ὀλιγωρεῖσθαι.
ὅτι γὰρ διὰ τὴν ὑπόληψιν τὴν τοιαύτην ἡ λύπη
γίνεται, τοῦτο βούλεται δηλοῦν· τὸ δὲ διὰ τόδε
γίνεσθαί τι οὐκ ἔστι ταὐτὸν τῷ μετὰ τούτου τόδ'
εἶναι κατ' οὐδένα τῶν εἰρημένων τρόπων.

20 XIV. Πάλιν εἰ τὴν τούτων σύνθεσιν εἴρηκε τὸ
ὅλον, οἷον τῆς ψυχῆς καὶ τοῦ σώματος σύνθεσιν
ζῷον, πρῶτον μὲν σκοπεῖν εἰ μὴ εἴρηκε ποία
σύνθεσις, καθάπερ εἰ σάρκα ὁριζόμενος ἢ ὀστοῦν
τὴν πυρὸς καὶ γῆς καὶ ἀέρος εἶπε σύνθεσιν. οὐ
γὰρ ἀπόχρη τὸ σύνθεσιν εἰπεῖν, ἀλλὰ καὶ ποία
25 τις προσδιοριστέον· οὐ γὰρ ὁπωσοῦν συντεθέντων
τούτων σὰρξ γίνεται, ἀλλ' οὑτωσὶ μὲν συντεθέντων
σάρξ, οὑτωσὶ δ' ὀστοῦν. ἔοικε δ' οὐδ' εἶναι τὸ

it is possible for a man to show daring in committing robbery, and right opinion about matters of health, but he who possesses the former plus the latter at the same time is far from being courageous. Moreover, even if both are used in the same relation, for example, in matters of health (for there is no reason why a man should not show both daring and right opinion in matters of health), yet, for all that, the man who possesses the one plus the other is not 'brave.' For each must be related neither to some different object nor to some chance object which is identical, but to the true function of courage, for example, facing the dangers of war or anything which is a still more characteristic function of courage.

Some of the definitions given in this manner do not fall under the above division at all, for example, that of 'anger' as 'pain plus an idea that one is slighted.' For the purpose of the definition is to show that the pain is caused by an idea of this kind; but to say that it is 'caused by' a thing is not the same as saying that it is 'plus' that thing in any of the senses mentioned.

XIV. Again, if he has described the whole as a composition of such and such things, for example, a 'living creature' as a 'composition of soul and body,' you must, first of all, see whether he has failed to state the kind of composition, as, for example, in the definition of 'flesh' or 'bone' as a 'composition of fire, earth and air.' For it is not enough to speak of composition, but the kind of composition must be further defined; for flesh is not formed of these components put together anyhow, but there is one form of composition for flesh and another for bone. Now it seems likely that neither of the said substances

Various rules : (a) When something has been defined as a compound whole, insist on a statement of the nature of the composition.

643

151 a

παράπαν συνθέσει ταὐτὸν οὐδέτερον τῶν εἰρη-
μένων· συνθέσει μὲν γὰρ πάσῃ διάλυσις ἐναντίον,
τῶν δ' εἰρημένων οὐδετέρῳ οὐδέν. ἔτι εἰ ὁμοίως
30 πιθανὸν πᾶν τὸ σύνθετον σύνθεσιν εἶναι ἢ μηδέν,
τῶν δὲ ζῴων ἕκαστον σύνθετον ὂν μή ἐστι σύνθεσις, οὐδὲ τῶν ἄλλων οὐδὲν τῶν συνθέτων
σύνθεσις ἂν εἴη.

Πάλιν εἰ ὁμοίως ἔν τινι πέφυκεν ὑπάρχειν
τἀναντία, ὥρισται δὲ διὰ θατέρου, δῆλον ὅτι οὐχ
ὥρισται. εἰ δὲ μή, πλείους τοῦ αὐτοῦ συμβήσεται
35 ὁρισμοὺς εἶναι· τί γὰρ μᾶλλον ὁ διὰ τούτου ἢ ὁ
διὰ τοῦ ἑτέρου ὁρισάμενος εἴρηκεν, ἐπειδὴ ὁμοίως
ἀμφότερα πέφυκε γίνεσθαι ἐν αὐτῷ; τοιοῦτος δ'
151 b ὁ τῆς ψυχῆς ὅρος, εἰ ἔστιν οὐσία ἐπιστήμης
δεκτική· ὁμοίως γὰρ καὶ ἀγνοίας ἐστὶ δεκτική.

Δεῖ δὲ καὶ ἐὰν μὴ πρὸς ὅλον ἔχῃ τις ἐπιχειρεῖν
τὸν ὁρισμὸν διὰ τὸ μὴ γνώριμον εἶναι τὸ ὅλον,
5 πρὸς τῶν μερῶν τι ἐπιχειρεῖν, ἐὰν ᾖ γνώριμον
καὶ μὴ καλῶς ἀποδεδομένον φαίνηται· τοῦ γὰρ
μέρους ἀναιρεθέντος καὶ ὁ πᾶς ὁρισμὸς ἀναιρεῖται.
ὅσοι τ' ἀσαφεῖς τῶν ὁρισμῶν, συνδιορθώσαντα
καὶ συσχηματίσαντα πρὸς τὸ δηλοῦν τι καὶ ἔχειν
ἐπιχείρημα, οὕτως ἐπισκοπεῖν· ἀναγκαῖον γὰρ τῷ
10 ἀποκρινομένῳ ἢ δέχεσθαι τὸ ἐκλαμβανόμενον ὑπὸ
τοῦ ἐρωτῶντος, ἢ αὐτὸν διασαφῆσαι τί ποτε
τυγχάνει τὸ δηλούμενον ὑπὸ τοῦ λόγου. ἔτι καθάπερ ἐν ταῖς ἐκκλησίαις νόμον εἰώθασιν ἐπεισφέρ-
ειν, κἂν ᾖ βελτίων ὁ ἐπεισφερόμενος, ἀναιροῦσι
τὸν ἔμπροσθεν, οὕτω καὶ ἐπὶ τῶν ὁρισμῶν ποιητέον

is at all the same as a 'composition'; for every 'composition' has as its contrary a 'decomposition,' and neither flesh nor bone has a contrary. Further, if it is probable that every compound alike is a composition or else that none is so, and every living creature, though it is a compound, is not a composition, then neither could any other compound be a composition.

Again, if it is natural for contraries to have an equal existence in a thing, and it has been defined by means of one of them, clearly it has not really been defined; for else the result will be that there is more than one definition of the same thing. For in what respect has he who has given a definition by means of one contrary described it better than he who has defined by means of the other, since both are equally likely to occur in it? The definition of 'soul' as 'substance receptive of knowledge' is a case in point; for it is equally also receptive of ignorance. *(b) Observe whether that which has been defined by one contrary is capable of both.*

Also, even though one cannot attack the definition as a whole, because one is not familiar with it as a whole, yet one ought to attack a part of it, if one is familiar with that part and it has obviously been incorrectly assigned; for if part is subverted, the whole definition is subverted also. When definitions are obscure, you should correct and remodel them so as to make some part clear and have something to attack, and then make your examination; for the answerer must either accept the interpretation suggested by the questioner or himself make clear what is indicated by the description. Furthermore, just as in public assemblies it is customary to introduce a new law and, if the newly introduced law is better, to abrogate the old one, so one ought to deal with *(c) If you cannot attack the definition as whole, attack part of it, or emend it.*

15 καὶ αὐτὸν ὁρισμὸν ἕτερον οἰστέον· ἐὰν γὰρ φαίνηται
βελτίων καὶ μᾶλλον δηλῶν τὸ ὁριζόμενον, δῆλον
ὅτι ἀνηρημένος ἔσται ὁ κείμενος, ἐπειδὴ οὐκ εἰσὶ
πλείους τοῦ αὐτοῦ ὁρισμοί.

Πρὸς ἅπαντας δὲ τοὺς ὁρισμοὺς οὐκ ἐλάχιστον
στοιχεῖον τὸ πρὸς ἑαυτὸν εὐστόχως ὁρίσασθαι τὸ
20 προκείμενον ἢ καλῶς εἰρημένον ὅρον ἀναλαβεῖν·
ἀνάγκη γάρ, ὥσπερ πρὸς παράδειγμα θεώμενον,
τό τ' ἐλλεῖπον ὧν προσῆκεν ἔχειν τὸν ὁρισμὸν
καὶ τὸ προσκείμενον περιέργως καθορᾶν, ὥστε
μᾶλλον ἐπιχειρημάτων εὐπορεῖν.

Τὰ μὲν οὖν περὶ τοὺς ὁρισμοὺς ἐπὶ τοσοῦτον
εἰρήσθω.

definitions, too, and oneself bring forward another one ; for, if it is obviously a better definition and gives a better indication of the object defined, clearly the definition already laid down will have been subverted, since there is never more than one definition of the same thing.

In dealing with any definition, it is a most important elementary principle to make a shrewd guess in one's own mind at the definition of the object before one or else to take over some happily expressed definition. For it necessarily follows that, with a model, as it were, before one, one can see anything that is lacking which the definition ought to contain and any needless addition, and thus be better provided in the points for attack.

(d) It is advantageous to make a definition of one's own.

Let so much, therefore, suffice for our treatment of definitions.

Η

151 b 28   Ι. Πότερον δὲ ταὐτὸν ἢ ἕτερον κατὰ τὸν κυριώτατον τῶν ῥηθέντων περὶ ταὐτοῦ τρόπων (ἐλέγετο
30 δὲ κυριώτατα ταὐτὸν τὸ τῷ ἀριθμῷ ἕν) σκοπεῖν
ἔκ τε τῶν πτώσεων καὶ τῶν συστοίχων καὶ τῶν
ἀντικειμένων. εἰ γὰρ ἡ δικαιοσύνη ταὐτὸν τῇ
ἀνδρίᾳ, καὶ ὁ δίκαιος τῷ ἀνδρείῳ καὶ τὸ δικαίως
τῷ ἀνδρείως. ὁμοίως δὲ καὶ ἐπὶ τῶν ἀντικειμένων·
εἰ γὰρ τάδε ταὐτά, καὶ τὰ ἀντικείμενα τούτοις
35 ταὐτὰ καθ᾽ ὁποιανοῦν τῶν λεγομένων ἀντιθέσεων.
οὐδὲν γὰρ διαφέρει τὸ τούτῳ ἢ τούτῳ ἀντικείμενον
λαβεῖν, ἐπειδὴ ταὐτόν ἐστιν. πάλιν ἐκ τῶν ποιη-
152 a τικῶν καὶ φθαρτικῶν καὶ γενέσεως καὶ φθορῶν
καὶ ὅλως τῶν ὁμοίως ἐχόντων πρὸς ἑκάτερον.
ὅσα γὰρ ἁπλῶς ταὐτά, καὶ αἱ γενέσεις αὐτῶν
καὶ αἱ φθοραὶ αἱ αὐταί, καὶ τὰ ποιητικὰ καὶ
φθαρτικά.

5   Σκοπεῖν δὲ καὶ ὧν θάτερον μάλιστα λέγεται
ὁτιοῦν, εἰ καὶ θάτερον τῶν αὐτῶν τούτων κατὰ
τὸ αὐτὸ μάλιστα λέγεται, καθάπερ Ξενοκράτης

BOOK VII

I. WHETHER things are 'the same' or 'different' in the strictest verbal sense of the term 'same'—and we said [a] that sameness in its strictest sense is numerical oneness—should be examined from the point of view of their inflexions and co-ordinates and opposites. For if justice is the same as courage, then also the just man is the same as the courageous, and 'justly' the same as 'courageously.' So likewise with opposites also; for, if two things are the same, their opposites, in accordance with any of the so-called oppositions, are also the same. For it makes no difference whether one takes the opposite of the one or of the other, since they are the same. Again, an examination should be made from the point of view of the agents of their production or destruction and their coming-into-being and destruction, and generally, of anything which stands in a similar relation to each of them; for, when things are absolutely the same, their coming-into-being and destruction are also the same and so are the agents of their production and destruction.

You must also examine, when one of two things is said to be something in a superlative degree, whether the other of these same things also attains a superlative degree in the same respect. For

Rules for dealing with things which are said to be 'the same': (a) Identity can be proved by looking at their inflexions, co-ordinates and opposites; also at the agents of their production and destruction.

(b) When one of two same things is said to have some quality in a superlative

[a] 103 a 23.

152 a

τὸν εὐδαίμονα βίον καὶ τὸν σπουδαῖον ἀποδείκνυσι
τὸν αὐτόν, ἐπειδὴ πάντων τῶν βίων αἱρετώτατος
ὁ σπουδαῖος καὶ ὁ εὐδαίμων· ἓν γὰρ τὸ αἱρετώτα-
10 τον καὶ μέγιστον. ὁμοίως δὲ καὶ ἐπὶ τῶν ἄλλων
τῶν τοιούτων. δεῖ δ' ἑκάτερον ἓν ἀριθμῷ εἶναι
τὸ λεγόμενον μέγιστον ἢ αἱρετώτατον. εἰ δὲ μή,
οὐκ ἔσται δεδειγμένον ὅτι ταὐτόν· οὐ γὰρ ἀναγκαῖον, εἰ ἀνδρειότατοι τῶν Ἑλλήνων Πελοποννήσιοι
καὶ Λακεδαιμόνιοι, τοὺς αὐτοὺς εἶναι Πελο-
15 ποννησίους Λακεδαιμονίοις, ἐπειδὴ οὐχ εἷς ἀριθμῷ
Πελοποννήσιος οὐδὲ Λακεδαιμόνιος. ἀλλὰ περιέχεσθαι μὲν τὸν ἕτερον ὑπὸ τοῦ ἑτέρου ἀναγκαῖον,
καθάπερ οἱ Λακεδαιμόνιοι ὑπὸ τῶν Πελοποννη-
σίων. εἰ δὲ μή, συμβήσεται ἀλλήλων εἶναι
βελτίους, ἐὰν μὴ περιέχωνται οἱ ἕτεροι ὑπὸ τῶν
20 ἑτέρων. ἀναγκαῖον γὰρ τοὺς Πελοποννησίους βελτίους εἶναι τῶν Λακεδαιμονίων, εἴπερ μὴ περι-
έχονται οἱ ἕτεροι ὑπὸ τῶν ἑτέρων· πάντων γὰρ
τῶν λοιπῶν εἰσὶ βελτίους. ὁμοίως δὲ καὶ τοὺς Λα-
κεδαιμονίους ἀνάγκη βελτίους εἶναι τῶν Πελο-
ποννησίων· καὶ γὰρ καὶ οὗτοι πάντων τῶν λοιπῶν
25 εἰσὶ βελτίους. ὥστε ἀλλήλων βελτίους γίνονται.
δῆλον οὖν ὅτι ἓν ἀριθμῷ δεῖ εἶναι τὸ βέλτιστον
καὶ μέγιστον λεγόμενον, εἰ μέλλει ὅτι ταὐτὸν
ἀποδείκνυσθαι. διὸ καὶ Ξενοκράτης οὐκ ἀπο-
δείκνυσιν· οὐ γὰρ εἷς ἀριθμῷ ὁ εὐδαίμων οὐδ' ὁ
σπουδαῖος βίος, ὥστ' οὐκ ἀναγκαῖον τὸν αὐτὸν
εἶναι, διότι ἄμφω αἱρετώτατοι, ἀλλὰ τὸν ἕτερον
30 ὑπὸ τὸν ἕτερον.

ᵃ Fr. 82 (Heinze).

instance, Xenocrates [a] tries to show that the happy life and the good life are the same, since of all lives the good life and the happy life are most worthy of choice; for only one thing can be characterized as 'the most worthy of choice' and 'the greatest.' So likewise with all other such things also. But each of two things which is described as 'greatest' or 'most worthy of choice' must be numerically one, otherwise it will not have been shown that they are the same; for it does not necessarily follow that, if the Peloponnesians and the Lacedaemonians are the bravest of the Greeks, the Peloponnesians are the same as the Lacedaemonians, since neither 'Peloponnesian' nor 'Lacedaemonian' is a numerically single thing; but it merely follows that the one group must be included in the other, just as the Lacedaemonians are included in the Peloponnesians. Otherwise, if one group is not included in the other, the result will be that each is better than the other. For it necessarily follows that the Peloponnesians are better than the Lacedaemonians, if the one group is not included in the other; for they are both better than any-one else. Similarly, too, the Lacedaemonians must be better than the Peloponnesians; for they also are better than anyone else. Thus they are each better than the other. It is obvious, therefore, that what is described as 'best' and 'greatest' must be numerically one if it is going to be shown to be 'the same' as something else. For this reason, too, Xeno-crates does not prove his contention; for neither the happy life nor the good life is numerically one, so that they are not necessarily the same because they are both most worthy of choice, but only that one must fall under the other.

degree, or whether this is true of the other.

651

Πάλιν σκοπεῖν εἰ ᾧ θάτερον ταὐτόν, καὶ θάτερον·
εἰ γὰρ μὴ ἀμφότερα τῷ αὐτῷ ταὐτά, δῆλον ὅτι
οὐδ' ἀλλήλοις.

Ἔτι ἐκ τῶν τούτοις συμβεβηκότων, καὶ οἷς
ταῦτα συμβέβηκεν, ἐπισκοπεῖν· ὅσα γὰρ θατέρῳ
35 συμβέβηκε, καὶ θατέρῳ δεῖ συμβεβηκέναι, καὶ
οἷς θάτερον αὐτῶν συμβέβηκε, καὶ θάτερον δεῖ
συμβεβηκέναι. εἰ δέ τι τούτων διαφωνεῖ, δῆλον
ὅτι οὐ ταὐτά.

Ὁρᾶν δὲ καὶ εἰ μὴ ἐν ἑνὶ γένει κατηγορίας
ἀμφότερα, ἀλλὰ τὸ μὲν ποιὸν τὸ δὲ ποσὸν ἢ πρός
152 b τι δηλοῖ. πάλιν εἰ τὸ γένος ἑκατέρου μὴ ταὐτόν,
ἀλλὰ τὸ μὲν ἀγαθὸν τὸ δὲ κακόν, ἢ τὸ μὲν ἀρετὴ
τὸ δ' ἐπιστήμη. ἢ εἰ τὸ μὲν γένος ταὐτόν, αἱ
διαφοραὶ δὲ μὴ αἱ αὐταὶ ἑκατέρου κατηγοροῦνται,
ἀλλὰ τοῦ μὲν ὅτι θεωρητικὴ ἐπιστήμη, τοῦ δ'
5 ὅτι πρακτική. ὁμοίως δὲ καὶ ἐπὶ τῶν ἄλλων.

Ἔτι ἐκ τοῦ μᾶλλον, εἰ τὸ μὲν δέχεται τὸ μᾶλλον
τὸ δὲ μή, ἢ εἰ ἄμφω μὲν δέχεται, μὴ ἅμα δέ,
καθάπερ ὁ μᾶλλον ἐρῶν οὐ μᾶλλον ἐπιθυμεῖ τῆς
συνουσίας, ὥστ' οὐ ταὐτὸν ἔρως καὶ ἐπιθυμία
συνουσίας.

10 Ἔτι ἐκ τῆς προσθέσεως, εἰ τῷ αὐτῷ ἑκάτερον
προστιθέμενον μὴ ποιεῖ τὸ ὅλον ταὐτόν. ἢ εἰ τοῦ
αὐτοῦ ἀφ' ἑκατέρου ἀφαιρεθέντος τὸ λοιπὸν ἕτε-

652

Again, you must see whether, when the one of two things is the same as a third thing, the other is also the same as it; for, if they are not the same as the same thing, obviously they are not the same as one another either. *(c) See whether each of two same things is the same as a third thing.*

Furthermore, you must examine them from the point of view of their accidents or of the things of which they are accidents; for any accident of the one must also be an accident of the other, and, if the one of them is an accident of something else, so must the other be also. For, if there is any discrepancy on these points, obviously they are not the same. *(d) Observe whether their accidents are the same.*

You must also see whether they fail both to fall in the same class of predicates, but one signifies a quality, the other a quantity or a relation; again, whether the genus of each fails to be the same, the one being 'good' and the other 'evil,' or the one 'virtue' and the other 'knowledge'; or whether, though the genus is the same, the differentiae predicated of either of them are not the same, that of one being 'speculative' and that of the other 'practical' knowledge. And so likewise with the other instances. *(e) See whether both are in the same category and genus, and have the same differentiae.*

Furthermore, from the point of view of the greater degree, you must see whether the one admits of the greater degree while the other does not, or whether both admit of it but not at the same time; for example, he who is more in love has not a greater desire for intercourse, and so love and the desire for intercourse are not the same thing. *(f) See whether both simultaneously increase and diminish.*

Furthermore, you must note the result of an addition and see whether each added to the same thing fails to produce the same whole; or whether the subtraction of the same thing from each leaves the remainder different. Suppose, for example, someone *(g) Observe the effect of an addition on each of them.*

ρον, οἷον εἰ διπλάσιον ἡμίσεος καὶ πολλαπλάσιον
ἡμίσεος ταὐτὸν ἔφησεν εἶναι. ἀφαιρεθέντος γὰρ
ἀφ᾿ ἑκατέρου τοῦ ἡμίσεος τὰ λοιπὰ ταὐτὸν ἔδει
15 δηλοῦν, οὐ δηλοῖ δέ· τὸ γὰρ διπλάσιον καὶ πολλαπλάσιον οὐ ταὐτὸν δηλοῖ.

Σκοπεῖν δὲ μὴ μόνον εἰ ἤδη τι συμβαίνει ἀδύνατον διὰ τῆς θέσεως, ἀλλὰ καὶ εἰ δυνατὸν ἐξ
ὑποθέσεως ὑπάρξαι, καθάπερ τοῖς τὸ κενὸν καὶ
20 τὸ πλῆρες ἀέρος ταὐτὸν φάσκουσιν. δῆλον γὰρ
ὅτι ἐὰν ἐξέλθῃ ὁ ἀήρ, κενὸν μὲν οὐχ ἧσσον ἀλλὰ
μᾶλλον ἔσται, πλῆρες δ᾿ ἀέρος οὐκέτι ἔσται.
ὥστε ὑποτεθέντος τινὸς εἴτε ψευδοῦς εἴτ᾿ ἀληθοῦς
(οὐδὲν γὰρ διαφέρει) τὸ μὲν ἕτερον ἀναιρεῖται
αὐτῶν, τὸ δ᾿ ἕτερον οὔ. ὥστ᾿ οὐ ταὐτόν.

25 Καθόλου δ᾿ εἰπεῖν, ἐκ τῶν ὁπωσοῦν ἑκατέρου
κατηγορουμένων, καὶ ὧν ταῦτα κατηγορεῖται,
σκοπεῖν εἴ που διαφωνεῖ· ὅσα γὰρ θατέρου κατηγορεῖται, καὶ θατέρου κατηγορεῖσθαι δεῖ, καὶ
ὧν θάτερον κατηγορεῖται, καὶ θάτερον κατηγορεῖσθαι δεῖ.

30 Ἔτι ἐπεὶ πολλαχῶς ταὐτὸν λέγεται, σκοπεῖν εἰ
καὶ καθ᾿ ἕτερόν τινα τρόπον ταὐτά ἐστιν· τὰ γὰρ
εἴδει ἢ γένει ταὐτὰ ἢ οὐκ ἀνάγκη ἢ οὐκ ἐνδέχεται
ἀριθμῷ ταὐτὰ εἶναι, ἐπισκοποῦμεν δὲ πότερον
οὕτω ταὐτὰ ἢ οὐχ οὕτως.

Ἔτι εἰ δυνατὸν θάτερον ἄνευ θατέρου εἶναι· οὐ
35 γὰρ ἂν εἴη ταὐτόν.

has stated that a 'double of a half' and a 'multiple of a half' are the same thing; then, if 'of a half' has been subtracted from each, the remainders ought to signify the same thing, which they do not; for 'double' and 'multiple' do not signify the same thing.

You must also look not only whether some impossibility immediately follows from the statement that two things are the same, but also whether it can result from a supposition, as, for example, when it is asserted that 'empty' and 'full of air' are the same thing. For it is obvious that, if the air has been expelled, the space will not be less but more empty, though it will be no longer full of air. So by a supposition, whether false or true (for it makes no difference), one of the two terms is subverted, while the other is not; and so they cannot be the same. *(h) Observe whether, as the result of a supposition, one of two same things is subverted, but not the other.*

To speak generally, you should look at every possible predicate of each of the two terms and at the things of which they are predicated and see whether there is any discrepancy anywhere; for anything which is predicated of the one ought also to be predicated of the other, and of anything of which the one is a predicate the other also ought to be a predicate. *(i) Observe whether the same things may be predicated of both.*

Furthermore, since 'sameness' is used in several senses, you should look whether things are the same in some different way also; for things which are the same specifically or generically are not necessarily the same or cannot possibly be the same numerically, and we examine whether they are or are not the same in this sense. *(j) Observe whether they are the same generically or specifically, but not numerically.*

Furthermore, you must see whether the one can exist without the other; for then they cannot be the same.

II. Οἱ μὲν οὖν πρὸς ταὐτὸν τόποι τοσοῦτοι λέγονται. δῆλον δ᾽ ἐκ τῶν εἰρημένων ὅτι ἅπαντες οἱ πρὸς ταὐτὸν ἀνασκευαστικοὶ τόποι καὶ πρὸς ὅρον χρήσιμοι, καθάπερ ἔμπροσθεν εἴρηται· εἰ γὰρ μὴ ταὐτὸν δηλοῖ τό τ᾽ ὄνομα καὶ ὁ λόγος,

153 a δῆλον ὅτι οὐκ ἂν εἴη ὁρισμὸς ὁ ἀποδοθεὶς λόγος. τῶν δὲ κατασκευαστικῶν τόπων οὐδεὶς χρήσιμος πρὸς ὅρον· οὐ γὰρ ἀπόχρη δεῖξαι ταὐτὸν τὸ ὑπὸ τὸν λόγον καὶ τοὔνομα πρὸς τὸ κατασκευάσαι ὅτι

5 ὁρισμός, ἀλλὰ καὶ τὰ ἄλλα πάντα δεῖ ἔχειν τὰ παρηγγελμένα τὸν ὁρισμόν.

III. Ἀναιρεῖν μὲν οὖν ὅρον οὕτως καὶ διὰ τούτων ἀεὶ πειρατέον· ἐὰν δὲ κατασκευάζειν βουλώμεθα, πρῶτον μὲν εἰδέναι δεῖ ὅτι οὐδεὶς ἢ ὀλίγοι τῶν διαλεγομένων ὅρον συλλογίζονται, ἀλλὰ πάντες ἀρχὴν τὸ τοιοῦτον λαμβάνουσιν, οἷον οἵ τε περὶ

10 γεωμετρίαν καὶ ἀριθμοὺς καὶ τὰς ἄλλας τὰς τοιαύτας μαθήσεις· εἶθ᾽ ὅτι δι᾽ ἀκριβείας μὲν ἄλλης ἐστὶ πραγματείας ἀποδοῦναι καὶ τί ἐστιν ὅρος καὶ πῶς ὁρίζεσθαι δεῖ, νῦν δ᾽ ὅσον ἱκανὸν πρὸς τὴν παροῦσαν χρείαν, ὥστε τοσοῦτον μόνον λεκτέον ὅτι δυνατὸν γενέσθαι ὁρισμοῦ καὶ τοῦ τι

15 ἦν εἶναι συλλογισμόν. εἰ γάρ ἐστιν ὅρος λόγος ὁ τὸ τί ἦν εἶναι τῷ πράγματι δηλῶν, καὶ δεῖ τὰ ἐν τῷ ὅρῳ κατηγορούμενα καὶ ἐν τῷ τί ἐστι τοῦ πράγματος μόνα κατηγορεῖσθαι, κατηγορεῖται δ᾽ ἐν τῷ τί ἐστι τὰ γένη καὶ αἱ διαφοραί, φανερὸν ὡς

ᵃ 102 a 11.   ᵇ 139 a 24 ff.
ᶜ An. Post. II. iii-xiii.

II. These, then, are the various commonplaces relating to 'sameness.' It is obvious from what has been said that all the destructive commonplaces dealing with sameness are also useful for dealing with definition, as has already been remarked *a* ; for, if the term and the description do not signify the same thing, it is obvious that the description assigned cannot be a definition. On the other hand, none of the constructive commonplaces are useful for definition ; for it is not enough to show that the content of the description and the term are the same in order to establish that the description is a definition, but the definition must possess also all the other characteristics which have been laid down.*b*

The rules given in the last chapter are useful for subverting but not for confirming a definition.

III. In this way and by these methods we must always try to destroy a definition ; but, if we wish to construct one, in the first place, we must realize that few if any of those who hold discussions reason out a definition, but all take as their starting-point some such assumption as those take who deal with geometry and numbers and all other such studies. Secondly, we must realize that it belongs to another inquiry *c* to lay down accurately both what a definition is and how we must frame it, and that for the moment we need only go as far as is requisite for our present task and, therefore, we only need state that it is possible that there should be reasoning about a definition and the essence of a thing. For if a definition is a description which indicates the essence of a thing, and the predicates in the definition ought also to be the only ones to be predicated of the thing in the category of essence (and the genera and differentiae are predicated in the category of essence), it is obvious that, if one were to assume that A and

Rules for establishing a definition: (a) Method of confirming a definition.

657

153 a

εἴ τις λάβοι ταῦτα μόνα[1] ἐν τῷ τί ἐστι τοῦ πράγ-
20 ματος κατηγορεῖσθαι,[2] ὁ ταῦτα ἔχων λόγος ὅρος
ἐξ ἀνάγκης ἂν εἴη· οὐ γὰρ ἐνδέχεται ἕτερον εἶναι
ὅρον, ἐπειδὴ οὐδὲν ἕτερον ἐν τῷ τί ἐστι τοῦ πράγματος κατηγορεῖται.

Ὅτι μὲν οὖν ἐγχωρεῖ συλλογισμὸν ὅρου γενέσθαι,
φανερόν· ἐκ τίνων δὲ δεῖ κατασκευάζειν, διώρισται
25 μὲν ἐν ἑτέροις ἀκριβέστερον, πρὸς δὲ τὴν προκειμένην μέθοδον οἱ αὐτοὶ τόποι χρήσιμοι. σκεπτέον
γὰρ ἐπὶ τῶν ἐναντίων καὶ τῶν ἄλλων τῶν ἀντικειμένων, καὶ ὅλους τοὺς λόγους καὶ κατὰ μέρος
ἐπισκοποῦντα· εἰ γὰρ ὁ ἀντικείμενος τοῦ ἀντικειμένου, καὶ τὸν εἰρημένον τοῦ προκειμένου ἀνάγκη
30 εἶναι. ἐπεὶ δὲ τῶν ἐναντίων πλείους συμπλοκαί,
ληπτέον τῶν ἐναντίων, ὁποίου ἂν μάλιστα φανῇ
ὁ ἐναντίος ὁρισμός. ὅλους μὲν οὖν τοὺς λόγους
καθάπερ εἴρηται σκεπτέον, κατὰ μέρος δ' ὧδε.
πρῶτον μὲν οὖν ὅτι τὸ ἀποδοθὲν γένος ὀρθῶς
ἀποδέδοται. εἰ γὰρ τὸ ἐναντίον ἐν τῷ ἐναντίῳ,
35 τὸ δὲ προκείμενον μή ἐστιν ἐν τῷ αὐτῷ, δῆλον
ὅτι ἐν τῷ ἐναντίῳ ἂν εἴη, ἐπειδὴ ἀνάγκη τὰ ἐναντία
ἐν τῷ αὐτῷ ἢ ἐν τοῖς ἐναντίοις γένεσιν εἶναι. καὶ
τὰς διαφορὰς δὲ τὰς ἐναντίας τῶν ἐναντίων ἀξιοῦμεν κατηγορεῖσθαι, καθάπερ λευκοῦ καὶ μέλανος·
153 b τὸ μὲν γὰρ διακριτικὸν τὸ δὲ συγκριτικὸν ὄψεως.
ὥστ' εἰ τοῦ ἐναντίου αἱ ἐναντίαι κατηγοροῦνται,
τοῦ προκειμένου αἱ ἀποδοθεῖσαι κατηγοροῖντ' ἄν.

---

[1] Reading μόνα with Wallies for μόνον.
[2] Deleting ὅτι before ὁ ταῦτα.

[a] *An. Post.* II. xiii, xiv.

B were the only attributes predicated of the thing in the category of essence, then the description containing A and B would necessarily be a definition; for nothing else can possibly be a definition, since nothing else is a predicate of the thing in the category of essence.

It is clear, then, that it is possible to reason about a definition. Of what materials definitions should be constructed has been determined more precisely elsewhere,[a] but the same commonplaces are useful for the inquiry now before us. You must look at the contraries and the other opposites, examining the descriptions both as wholes and in detail; for if the opposite description is a definition of the opposite term, the description given must necessarily be a definition of the term under consideration. Since, however, there are several possible conjunctions of the contraries, you must choose from among the contraries the one whose contrary definition is most plain. The descriptions, then, as a whole must be examined in the manner described, and in detail in the following manner. First of all, you must see that the genus assigned has been assigned correctly. For, if the contrary is placed in the contrary genus, and the term under consideration is not in the same genus, it is obvious that it would be in the contrary genus, since contraries must necessarily be in the same genus or in contrary genera. Also, we hold that the contrary differentiae should be predicated of contraries, as, for example, of black and white; for the one tends to penetrate, the one to compress, the vision. So, if contrary differentiae are predicated of the contrary term, the differentiae assigned would be predicated of the term under consideration. Since,

(b) Method of eliciting genus and differentia from a contrary and so constructing a definition from the definition of the contrary.

659

ὥστ' ἐπεὶ καὶ τὸ γένος καὶ αἱ διαφοραὶ ὀρθῶς
ἀποδέδονται, δῆλον ὅτι ὁρισμὸς ἂν εἴη ὁ ἀπο-
5 δοθείς. ἢ οὐκ ἀναγκαῖον τῶν ἐναντίων τὰς ἐναντίας διαφορὰς κατηγορεῖσθαι, ἂν μὴ ἐν τῷ αὐτῷ
γένει ᾖ τὰ ἐναντία· ὧν δὲ τὰ γένη ἐναντία, οὐδὲν
κωλύει τὴν αὐτὴν διαφορὰν κατ' ἀμφοῖν λέγεσθαι,
οἷον κατὰ δικαιοσύνης καὶ ἀδικίας· τὸ μὲν γὰρ
ἀρετὴ τὸ δὲ κακία ψυχῆς, ὥστε τὸ ψυχῆς διαφορὰ
10 ἐν ἀμφοῖν λέγεται, ἐπειδὴ καὶ σώματός ἐστι ἀρετὴ καὶ κακία. ἀλλ' οὖν τοῦτό γ' ἀληθές, ὅτι
τῶν ἐναντίων ἢ ἐναντίαι ἢ αἱ αὐταὶ διαφοραί
εἰσιν. εἰ οὖν τοῦ ἐναντίου ἡ ἐναντία κατηγορεῖται,
τούτου δὲ μή, δῆλον ὅτι ἡ εἰρημένη τούτου ἂν
κατηγοροῖτο. καθόλου δ' εἰπεῖν, ἐπεὶ ὁ ὁρισμός
15 ἐστιν ἐκ γένους καὶ διαφορῶν, ἂν ὁ τοῦ ἐναντίου
ὁρισμὸς φανερὸς ᾖ, καὶ ὁ τοῦ προκειμένου ὁρισμὸς
φανερὸς ἔσται. ἐπεὶ γὰρ τὸ ἐναντίον ἐν τῷ αὐτῷ
γένει ἢ ἐν τῷ ἐναντίῳ, ὁμοίως δὲ καὶ αἱ διαφοραὶ
ἢ ἐναντίαι τῶν ἐναντίων ἢ αἱ αὐταὶ κατηγοροῦνται,
δῆλον ὅτι τοῦ προκειμένου ἤτοι τὸ αὐτὸ γένος ἂν
20 κατηγοροῖτο ὅπερ καὶ τοῦ ἐναντίου, αἱ δὲ διαφοραὶ
ἐναντίαι, ἢ ἅπασαι ἢ τινές, αἱ δὲ λοιπαὶ αἱ αὐταί·
ἢ ἀνάπαλιν αἱ μὲν διαφοραὶ αἱ αὐταὶ τὰ δὲ γένη
ἐναντία· ἢ ἄμφω ἐναντία, καὶ τὰ γένη καὶ αἱ διαφοραί. ἀμφότερα γὰρ ταὐτὰ εἶναι οὐκ ἐνδέχεται·
εἰ δὲ μή, ὁ αὐτὸς ὁρισμὸς τῶν ἐναντίων ἔσται.

25 Ἔτι ἐκ τῶν πτώσεων καὶ τῶν συστοίχων·

therefore, both the genus and the differentiae have been correctly assigned, it is obvious that the description assigned would be a definition. But, possibly, it does not necessarily follow that the contrary differentiae are predicated of contraries, unless the contraries are in the same genus; but where the genera are contrary, there is no reason why the same differentia should not be predicated of both, for example, of justice and injustice, for the one is a virtue and the other a vice, of the soul; and so ' of the soul ' is employed as a differentia in both cases, since there is a virtue and a vice of the body also. This, however, at any rate is true, that the differentiae of contraries are either contrary or the same. If, therefore, the contrary differentia is predicated of the contrary term and not of the term in question, it is obvious that the stated differentia would be predicated of the latter. To put the matter generally, since the definition is composed of genus and differentia, if the definition of the contrary is clear, the definition also of the term under consideration will be clear also. For, since the contrary is either in the same or in the contrary genus, and likewise too the differentiae predicated of contraries are either contrary or the same, obviously either (a) the same genus would be predicated of the term under consideration as of its contrary, whereas the differentiae are either all contrary or else some of them contrary and the rest the same, or, (b) conversely the differentiae are the same and the genera contrary, or (c) both the genera and the differentiae are contrary. For it is not possible that both should be the same; otherwise contraries will have the same definition.

Furthermore, you must judge from inflexions and (c) Employ-

ἀνάγκη γὰρ ἀκολουθεῖν τὰ γένη τοῖς γένεσι καὶ
τοὺς ὅρους τοῖς ὅροις. οἷον εἰ ἡ λήθη ἐστὶν ἀποβολὴ ἐπιστήμης, καὶ τὸ ἐπιλανθάνεσθαι ἀποβάλλειν
ἐπιστήμην ἔσται καὶ τὸ ἐπιλελῆσθαι ἀποβεβλη-
κέναι ἐπιστήμην. ἑνὸς οὖν ὁποιουοῦν τῶν εἰρη-
30 μένων ὁμολογηθέντος ἀνάγκη καὶ τὰ λοιπὰ
ὁμολογεῖσθαι. ὁμοίως δὲ καὶ εἰ ἡ φθορὰ διάλυσις
οὐσίας, καὶ τὸ φθείρεσθαι διαλύεσθαι οὐσίαν καὶ
τὸ φθαρτικῶς διαλυτικῶς, εἴ τε τὸ φθαρτικὸν
διαλυτικὸν οὐσίας, καὶ ἡ φθορὰ διάλυσις οὐσίας.
ὁμοίως δὲ καὶ ἐπὶ τῶν ἄλλων. ὥσθ' ἑνὸς ὁποιουοῦν
35 ληφθέντος καὶ τὰ λοιπὰ πάντα ὁμολογεῖται.

Καὶ ἐκ τῶν ὁμοίως δ' ἐχόντων πρὸς ἄλληλα.
εἰ γὰρ τὸ ὑγιεινὸν ποιητικὸν ὑγιείας, καὶ τὸ
εὐεκτικὸν ποιητικὸν εὐεξίας ἔσται καὶ τὸ ὠφέλιμον
154 a ποιητικὸν ἀγαθοῦ. ὁμοίως γὰρ ἕκαστον τῶν
εἰρημένων πρὸς τὸ οἰκεῖον τέλος ἔχει, ὥστ' εἰ
ἑνὸς αὐτῶν ὁ ὁρισμός ἐστι τὸ ποιητικὸν εἶναι τοῦ
τέλους, καὶ τῶν λοιπῶν ἑκάστου οὗτος ἂν εἴη
ὁρισμός.

Ἔτι ἐκ τοῦ μᾶλλον καὶ τοῦ ὁμοίως, ὁσαχῶς
5 ἐνδέχεται κατασκευάσαι δύο πρὸς δύο συγκρίνοντα,
οἷον εἰ μᾶλλον ὅδε τοῦδε ἢ ὅδε τοῦδε ὁρισμός,
ὁ δὲ ἧττον ὁρισμός, καὶ ὁ μᾶλλον. καὶ εἰ ὁμοίως
ὅδε τοῦδε καὶ ὅδε τοῦδε, εἰ ὁ ἕτερος τοῦ ἑτέρου,

co-ordinates ; for here genus must follow genus and definition follow definition. For example, if ' forget-fulness ' is ' a loss of knowledge,' ' to forget ' is ' to lose knowledge,' and ' to have forgotten ' is ' to have lost knowledge.' If, therefore, any one of these things is admitted, the rest also must necessarily also be admitted. Similarly, too, if ' destruction ' is ' a dissolution of essence,' then ' to be destroyed ' is ' to have one's essence dissolved,' and ' destructively ' means ' in such a way as to dissolve the essence '; and if ' destructive ' means ' tending to destroy the essence,' ' destruction ' is ' the dissolution of the essence.' So likewise with the other inflexions ; if any one of them is assumed, all the others also are admitted. ment of inflexions and co-ordinates for the construction of a definition.

You must also judge from things which are related in the same way to one another. For if ' healthy ' means ' productive of health,' ' invigorating ' also will mean ' productive of vigour ' and ' beneficial ' will mean ' productive of good.' For each of the above is similarly related to its own particular end, so that, if the definition of one of them is that it is ' productive of ' its end, this would also be the definition of each of the others. (d) Argument from things which stand in similar relation.

Furthermore, you must judge from the greater and the similar degrees, in all the various ways in which it is possible to be constructive by comparing two things with two other things. For example, if one thing is to a greater degree the definition of another than something else is of something else, and the latter is a definition, then so also is the former. Also, if one thing is a definition of another and something else a definition of something else in a similar degree, if the latter is a definition of (e) Formation of a definition by the comparison of other definitions.

καὶ ὁ λοιπὸς τοῦ λοιποῦ. ἑνὸς δ' ὁρισμοῦ πρὸς
δύο συγκρινομένου, ἢ δύο ὁρισμῶν πρὸς ἕνα,
10 οὐδὲν χρήσιμος ἡ ἐκ τοῦ μᾶλλον ἐπίσκεψις· οὔτε
γὰρ ἕνα δυοῖν οὔτε δύο τοῦ αὐτοῦ ὅρους δυνατόν
ἐστιν εἶναι.

IV. Εἰσὶ δὲ καὶ ἐπικαιρότατοι τῶν τόπων οἵ
τε νῦν εἰρημένοι καὶ οἱ ἐκ τῶν συστοίχων καὶ οἱ
ἐκ τῶν πτώσεων. διὸ καὶ δεῖ μάλιστα κατέχειν
15 καὶ προχείρους ἔχειν τούτους· χρησιμώτατοι γὰρ
πρὸς πλεῖστα. καὶ τῶν ἄλλων δὲ τοὺς μάλιστα
κοινούς· οὗτοι γὰρ ἐνεργότατοι τῶν λοιπῶν, οἷον
τό τ' ἐπιβλέπειν ἐπὶ τὰ¹ καθ' ἕκαστα, καὶ ἐπὶ τῶν
εἰδῶν σκοπεῖν εἰ ἐφαρμόττει ὁ λόγος, ἐπειδὴ
συνώνυμον τὸ εἶδος. ἔστι δὲ χρήσιμον τὸ τοιοῦτον
20 πρὸς τοὺς τιθεμένους ἰδέας εἶναι, καθάπερ πρότερον
εἴρηται. ἔτι εἰ μεταφέρων εἴρηκε τοὔνομα, ἢ
αὐτὸ αὑτοῦ κατηγόρηκεν ὡς ἕτερον. καὶ εἴ τις
ἄλλος κοινὸς καὶ ἐνεργὸς τῶν τόπων ἐστί, τούτῳ
χρηστέον.

V. Ὅτι δὲ χαλεπώτερον κατασκευάζειν ἢ ἀνασκευάζειν ὅρον, ἐκ τῶν μετὰ ταῦτα ῥηθησομένων
25 φανερόν. καὶ γὰρ ἰδεῖν αὐτὸν καὶ λαβεῖν παρὰ
τῶν ἐρωτωμένων τὰς τοιαύτας προτάσεις οὐκ
εὐπετές, οἷον ὅτι τῶν ἐν τῷ ἀποδοθέντι λόγῳ
τὸ μὲν γένος τὸ δὲ διαφορά, καὶ ὅτι ἐν τῷ τί ἐστι
τὸ γένος καὶ αἱ διαφοραὶ κατηγοροῦνται. ἄνευ
δὲ τούτων ἀδύνατον ὁρισμοῦ γένεσθαι συλλογισμόν·
30 εἰ γάρ τινα καὶ ἄλλα ἐν τῷ τί ἐστι τοῦ πράγματος

---

¹ τὸ in Bekker's text is a misprint for τά.

the latter, then the former is also a definition of the former. The examination on the basis of the greater degree is of no use when one definition is compared with two things or two definitions with one thing; for there cannot possibly be one definition of two things or two definitions of the same thing.

IV. The most convenient of the commonplaces are those just mentioned and those based on co-ordinates and inflexions. It is, therefore, particularly necessary to grasp these and have them ready for use; for they are most often useful. Of the rest you must employ those which are most widely applicable (for they are the most efficacious of the remainder), for example, the consideration of individual cases and the examination of the species to see whether the description fits; for the species is synonymous with its members. Such a procedure is useful against those who assume the existence of 'ideas,' as has been said before.[a] Further, you must see whether a term has been used metaphorically or has been predicated of itself as though it were something different. Also any other commonplace ought to be used if it is widely applicable and efficacious. [Note on what are the most useful commonplaces.]

V. That it is more difficult to construct than to destroy a definition is obvious for reasons which are to be next set forth. For oneself to discern, and to secure from those who are being questioned, the sort of premisses which one requires is far from easy, for example, that the constituent parts of the description given are, firstly, genus and, secondly, differentia, and that the genus and differentiae are predicated in the category of essence. But without these premisses it is impossible to reason out a definition; for, if other things also are predicated of the thing [Notes on the construction and destruction of definitions and their component parts. (a) Definitions are more easily destroyed than constructed.]

154 a

κατηγορεῖται, ἄδηλον πότερον ὁ ῥηθεὶς ἢ ἕτερος
αὐτοῦ ὁρισμός ἐστιν, ἐπειδὴ ὁρισμός ἐστι λόγος
ὁ τὸ τί ἦν εἶναι σημαίνων. δῆλον δὲ καὶ ἐκ τῶνδε.
ῥᾷον γὰρ ἓν συμπεράνασθαι ἢ πολλά. ἀναιροῦντι
μὲν οὖν ἀπόχρη πρὸς ἓν[1] διαλεγῆναι (ἓν γὰρ ὁποι-
35 ονοῦν ἀνασκευάσαντες ἀνῃρηκότες ἐσόμεθα τὸν
ὅρον), κατασκευάζοντι δὲ πάντα ἀνάγκη συμβιβά-
ζειν ὅτι ὑπάρχει τὰ ἐν τῷ ὅρῳ. ἔτι κατασκευάζοντι μὲν καθόλου οἰστέον συλλογισμόν· δεῖ γὰρ
154 b κατὰ παντὸς οὗ τοὔνομα κατηγορεῖσθαι τὸν ὅρον,
καὶ ἔτι πρὸς τούτοις ἀντιστρέφειν, εἰ μέλλει ἴδιος
εἶναι ὁ ἀποδοθεὶς ὅρος. ἀνασκευάζοντα δ' οὐκέτι
ἀνάγκη δεῖξαι τὸ καθόλου· ἀπόχρη γὰρ τὸ δεῖξαι
5 ὅτι οὐκ ἀληθεύεται περί τινος τῶν ὑπὸ τοὔνομα
ὁ λόγος. εἴ τε καὶ καθόλου δέοι ἀνασκευάσαι, οὐδ'
ὡς τὸ ἀντιστρέφειν ἀναγκαῖον ἐπὶ τοῦ ἀνασκευά-
ζειν· ἀπόχρη γὰρ ἀνασκευάζοντι καθόλου τὸ
δεῖξαι ὅτι κατά τινος ὧν τοὔνομα κατηγορεῖται
ὁ λόγος οὐ κατηγορεῖται. τὸ δ' ἀνάπαλιν οὐκ
ἀναγκαῖον πρὸς τὸ δεῖξαι, ὅτι καθ' ὧν ὁ λόγος
10 μὴ κατηγορεῖται τοὔνομα κατηγορεῖται. ἔτι εἰ
καὶ παντὶ ὑπάρχει τῷ ὑπὸ τοὔνομα, μὴ μόνῳ δέ,
ἀνῃρημένος γίνεται ὁ ὁρισμός.

Ὁμοίως δὲ καὶ περὶ τὸ ἴδιον καὶ τὸ γένος ἔχει·
ἐν ἀμφοτέροις γὰρ ἀνασκευάζειν ἢ κατασκευάζειν
15 ῥᾷον. περὶ μὲν οὖν τοῦ ἰδίου φανερὸν ἐκ τῶν

---

[1] Reading ἓν with C.

in the category of essence, it is obscure whether the description given or some other description is the definition of the thing ; for a definition is a description which signifies the essence of a thing. This is also clear from the following considerations. It is easier to come to one conclusion than to many ; when, therefore, one is destroying a definition, it is enough to argue against a single point (for, if we have destroyed any one point whatsoever, we shall have destroyed the definition), but for constructive purposes it is necessary to establish that everything in the definition is applicable. Further, for constructive purposes, reasoning of universal application must be adduced ; for the definition must be predicated of everything of which the term is predicated, and, besides this, it must be convertible, if the definition assigned is to be peculiar to the subject. On the other hand, for destructive purposes, it is no longer necessary to prove universality ; for it is enough to show that the description is untrue of some one thing which falls under the term. Also, if it were necessary to destroy the definition universally, even so there is no need for the proposition to be convertible in order to destroy it ; for it is enough, for its destruction universally, to show that the description is not predicated of any one of things of which the term is predicated ; and the converse of this is not necessary in order to show that the term is predicated of those things of which the description is not predicated. Furthermore, if it belongs to everything which falls under the term, but not to it alone, the definition is destroyed.

A similar thing happens also in respect of the property and the genus ; ⸀for in both cases to destroy is easier than to confirm. The case of the property is *(b)* The same is true of property and genus.

667

εἰρημένων· ὡς γὰρ ἐπὶ τὸ πολὺ ἐν συμπλοκῇ τὸ
ἴδιον ἀποδίδοται, ὥστ' ἀνασκευάζειν μὲν ἔστιν
ἓν ἀνελόντα, κατασκευάζοντι δὲ ἀνάγκη πάντα
συλλογίζεσθαι. σχεδὸν δὲ καὶ τὰ λοιπὰ πάντα,
ὅσα πρὸς τὸν ὁρισμόν, καὶ πρὸς τὸ ἴδιον ἁρμόσει
20 λέγεσθαι· παντί τε γὰρ δεῖ τῷ ὑπὸ τοὔνομα τὸν
κατασκευάζοντα δεικνύναι ὅτι ὑπάρχει, ἀνασκευάζοντι δ' ἀπόχρη ἑνὶ δεῖξαι μὴ ὑπάρχον· εἴ τε καὶ
παντὶ ὑπάρχει, μὴ μόνῳ δέ, καὶ οὕτως ἀνεσκευα-
σμένον γίνεται, καθάπερ ἐπὶ τοῦ ὁρισμοῦ λέγεται. περὶ δὲ τοῦ γένους, ὅτι κατασκευάζειν
25 μὲν ἀνάγκη μοναχῶς παντὶ δείξαντα ὑπάρχειν,
ἀνασκευάζοντι δὲ διχῶς· καὶ γὰρ εἰ μηδενὶ καὶ
εἰ τινὶ δέδεικται μὴ ὑπάρχον, ἀνήρηται τὸ ἐν ἀρχῇ.
ἔτι κατασκευάζοντι μὲν οὐκ ἀπόχρη ὅτι ὑπάρχει
δεῖξαι, ἀλλὰ καὶ διότι ὡς γένος ὑπάρχει δεικτέον·
ἀνασκευάζοντι δ' ἱκανὸν τὸ δεῖξαι μὴ ὑπάρχον ἢ τινὶ
30 ἢ παντί. ἔοικε δ', ὥσπερ καὶ ἐν τοῖς ἄλλοις τὸ
διαφθεῖραι τοῦ ποιῆσαι ῥᾷον, οὕτω καὶ ἐπὶ τούτων
τὸ ἀνασκευάσαι τοῦ κατασκευάσαι.

Ἐπὶ δὲ τοῦ συμβεβηκότος τὸ μὲν καθόλου ῥᾷον
ἀνασκευάζειν ἢ κατασκευάζειν· κατασκευάζοντι μὲν
35 γὰρ δεικτέον ὅτι παντί, ἀνασκευάζοντι δ' ἀπόχρη
ἑνὶ δεῖξαι μὴ ὑπάρχον. τὸ δ' ἐπὶ μέρους ἀνάπαλιν
ῥᾷον κατασκευάσαι ἢ ἀνασκευάσαι· κατασκευά-

---

clear from what has been said; for the property is usually assigned in a complex expression, so that it is possible to destroy it by demolishing one element in it, whereas in confirming it is necessary to establish all the elements by reasoning. Also, almost all the other things which can be said of the definition can be fittingly said of the property also; for he who is confirming a property must show that it belongs to everything which falls under the term, whereas it is enough for destructive purposes to show that it fails to belong to one of them. Also, even it if belongs to every one of them but not exclusively, in these circumstances too the property is demolished, as was observed[a] about definition. As regards the genus, it is clear that there is only one course for you to follow when confirming it, namely, to show that it belongs in every case, whereas for demolishing it there are two possible courses; for the original assumption is destroyed both if it has been shown never to belong and also if it has been shown not to belong in a particular case. Further, in confirming a genus, it is not enough to show that it belongs, but you must also show that it belongs as a genus, whereas, in demolishing it, it suffices to show that it fails to belong either in a particular case or in every case. Indeed it looks as if just as in everything else to destroy is easier than to create, so also here to demolish is easier than to confirm.

In the case of the accident it is easier to demolish than confirm the universal; for, to confirm it, you must show that it belongs in every case, but to demolish it, it is enough to show that it does not belong in a particular instance. The particular, on the contrary, is easier to confirm than to demolish;

(c) Accident is more easily demolished if it is universal, confirmed if it is particular.

ARISTOTLE

155 a ζῶντι μὲν γὰρ ἀπόχρη δεῖξαι τινὶ ὑπάρχον, ἀνασκευάζοντι δὲ δεικτέον ὅτι οὐδενὶ ὑπάρχει.

Φανερὸν δὲ καὶ διότι πάντων ῥᾷστον ὅρον ἀνα-
σκευάσαι· πλεῖστα γὰρ ἐν αὐτῷ τὰ δεδομένα
5 πολλῶν εἰρημένων, ἐκ δὲ τῶν πλειόνων θᾶττον
γίνεται συλλογισμός. εἰκὸς γὰρ ἐν τοῖς πολλοῖς
μᾶλλον ἢ ἐν τοῖς ὀλίγοις ἁμάρτημα γίνεσθαι. ἔτι
πρὸς μὲν ὅρον ἐνδέχεται καὶ διὰ τῶν ἄλλων ἐπι-
χειρεῖν· εἴτε γὰρ μὴ ἴδιος ὁ λόγος, εἴτε μὴ γένος
τὸ ἀποδοθέν, εἴτε μὴ ὑπάρχει τι τῶν ἐν τῷ λόγῳ,
10 ἀνῃρημένος γίνεται ὁ ὁρισμός· πρὸς δὲ τἆλλα οὔτε
τὰ ἐκ τῶν ὅρων οὔτε τἆλλα ἐνδέχεται πάντ᾽ ἐπι-
χειρεῖν· μόνα γὰρ τὰ πρὸς τὸ συμβεβηκὸς κοινὰ
πάντων τῶν εἰρημένων ἐστίν. ὑπάρχειν μὲν γὰρ
δεῖ ἕκαστον τῶν εἰρημένων· εἰ δὲ μὴ ὡς ἴδιον
ὑπάρχει τὸ γένος, οὐδέπω ἀνῄρηται τὸ γένος.
15 ὁμοίως δὲ καὶ τὸ ἴδιον οὐκ ἀναγκαῖον ὡς γένος,
οὐδὲ τὸ συμβεβηκὸς ὡς γένος ἢ ἴδιον, ἀλλ᾽ ὑπάρχειν μόνον. ὥστ᾽ οὐ δυνατὸν ἐκ τῶν ἑτέρων πρὸς
τὰ ἕτερα ἐπιχειρεῖν ἀλλ᾽ ἢ ἐπὶ τοῦ ὁρισμοῦ. δῆλον
οὖν ὅτι ῥᾷστον πάντων ὅρον ἀναιρεῖν, κατασκευάζειν δὲ χαλεπώτατον· ἐκεῖνά τε γὰρ δεῖ πάντα
20 συλλογίσασθαι (καὶ γὰρ ὅτι ὑπάρχει τὰ εἰρημένα
καὶ ὅτι γένος τὸ ἀποδοθὲν καὶ ὅτι ἴδιος ὁ λόγος),
καὶ ἔτι παρὰ ταῦτα, ὅτι δηλοῖ τὸ τί ἦν εἶναι ὁ
λόγος, καὶ τοῦτο καλῶς δεῖ πεποιηκέναι.

---

for, to confirm it, it is enough to show that it belongs in one instance, but, to demolish it, you must show that it never belongs.

It is clear also that a definition is the easiest of all things to destroy ; for, since it contains many assertions, the opportunities which it offers are very numerous, and the more abundant the material, the more quickly can reasoning set to work ; for it is more likely that error should occur when the material is copious than when it is scanty. Moreover, it is possible also to attack a definition by means of the other attributes [a] ; for if the description is not peculiar, or if that which is assigned is not genus, or if something in the description does not belong, the definition is demolished. On the other hand, against the others it is impossible to argue with all the material derived from definitions nor can the rest of the others be used ; for only those which relate to accident are common to all the said attributes. For each of the said attributes must belong to the subject, but, if the genus does not belong as a property, the genus is not yet destroyed. Similarly, too, the property does not necessarily belong as a genus, nor the accident as a genus or a property, but they may merely belong. It is, therefore, impossible to use one set against the other except where definition is concerned. It is obvious, then, that a definition is the easiest of all things to destroy but the most difficult to confirm ; for one has to establish all the other points by reasoning (namely, that the attributes asserted belong, and that what has been assigned is a true genus, and that the description is peculiar), and, besides this, that the description shows the essence of the thing ; and this must be done properly.

(d) Definition is of all things the most easy to destroy, the most difficult to confirm.

671

ARISTOTLE

Τῶν δ' ἄλλων τὸ ἴδιον μάλιστα τοιοῦτον· ἀναιρεῖν μὲν γὰρ ῥᾷον διὰ τὸ ἐκ πολλῶν ὡς ἐπὶ
25 τὸ πολύ, κατασκευάζειν δὲ χαλεπώτατον, ὅτι τε
πολλὰ δεῖ συμβιβάσαι, καὶ πρὸς τούτῳ ὅτι μόνῳ
ὑπάρχει καὶ ἀντικατηγορεῖται τοῦ πράγματος.

Ῥᾷστον δὲ πάντων κατασκευάσαι τὸ συμβεβηκός·
ἐν μὲν γὰρ τοῖς ἄλλοις οὐ μόνον ὑπάρχον, ἀλλὰ
30 καὶ ὅτι οὕτως ὑπάρχει, δεικτέον· ἐπὶ δὲ τοῦ συμβεβηκότος, ὅτι ὑπάρχει μόνον, ἱκανὸν δεῖξαι.
ἀνασκευάζειν δὲ χαλεπώτατον τὸ συμβεβηκός, ὅτι
ἐλάχιστα ἐν αὐτῷ δέδοται· οὐ γὰρ προσσημαίνει
ἐν τῷ συμβεβηκότι πῶς ὑπάρχει, ὥστ' ἐπὶ μὲν
τῶν ἄλλων διχῶς ἔστιν ἀνελεῖν, ἢ δείξαντα ὅτι
35 οὐχ ὑπάρχει ἢ ὅτι οὐχ οὕτως ὑπάρχει, ἐπὶ δὲ τοῦ
συμβεβηκότος οὐκ ἔστιν ἀνελεῖν ἀλλ' ἢ δείξαντα
ὅτι οὐχ ὑπάρχει.

Οἱ μὲν οὖν τόποι δι' ὧν εὐπορήσομεν πρὸς ἕκαστα τῶν προβλημάτων ἐπιχειρεῖν, σχεδὸν ἱκανῶς
ἐξηρίθμηνται.

Of the rest, the property most merely resembles the definition; for it is easier to destroy, because it is usually composed of a number of terms, and most difficult to confirm, because a number of points must be brought together, and, besides this, because it belongs to the subject alone and is predicated convertibly with it. *(e) Property is the next easiest to destroy.*

The accident is the easiest thing of all to confirm; for in the other cases it must be shown not only that the attribute belongs but also that it belongs in a particular way, whereas in the case of the accident it is enough to show only that it belongs. On the other hand, the accident is most difficult to destroy, because it offers the fewest opportunities; for in stating an accident one does not add any indication of the manner in which it belongs, so that in the other cases it is possible to destroy the statement in two ways, by showing either that it does not belong or that it does not belong in a particular way, but in the case of the accident it is impossible to destroy it except by showing that it does not belong. *(f) Accident is the most difficult to destroy and the easiest to confirm.]*

The commonplaces which will provide us with abundant means of attacking each kind of problem have now been more or less adequately enumerated.

155 b 3   I. Μετὰ δὲ ταῦτα περὶ τάξεως, καὶ πῶς δεῖ
ἐρωτᾶν, λεκτέον. δεῖ δὲ πρῶτον μὲν ἐρωτηματίζειν
5 μέλλοντα τὸν τόπον εὑρεῖν ὅθεν ἐπιχειρητέον,
δεύτερον δὲ ἐρωτηματίσαι καὶ τάξαι καθ᾽ ἕκαστα
πρὸς ἑαυτόν, τὸ δὲ λοιπὸν καὶ τρίτον εἰπεῖν ταῦτα
ἤδη πρὸς ἕτερον. μέχρι μὲν οὖν τοῦ εὑρεῖν τὸν
τόπον ὁμοίως τοῦ φιλοσόφου καὶ τοῦ διαλεκτικοῦ
ἡ σκέψις, τὸ δ᾽ ἤδη ταῦτα τάττειν καὶ ἐρωτη-
10 ματίζειν ἴδιον τοῦ διαλεκτικοῦ· πρὸς ἕτερον γὰρ
πᾶν τὸ τοιοῦτον, τῷ δὲ φιλοσόφῳ καὶ ζητοῦντι
καθ᾽ ἑαυτὸν οὐδὲν μέλει, ἐὰν ἀληθῆ μὲν ᾖ καὶ
γνώριμα δι᾽ ὧν ὁ συλλογισμός, μὴ θῇ δ᾽ αὐτὰ ὁ
ἀποκρινόμενος διὰ τὸ σύνεγγυς εἶναι τοῦ ἐξ ἀρχῆς
καὶ προορᾶν τὸ συμβησόμενον· ἀλλ᾽ ἴσως κἂν
15 σπουδάσειεν ὅτι μάλιστα γνώριμα καὶ σύνεγγυς
εἶναι τὰ ἀξιώματα· ἐκ τούτων γὰρ οἱ ἐπιστη-
μονικοὶ συλλογισμοί.

Τοὺς μὲν οὖν τόπους ὅθεν δεῖ λαμβάνειν, εἴρηται
πρότερον· περὶ τάξεως δὲ καὶ τοῦ ἐρωτηματίσαι
λεκτέον διελόμενον τὰς προτάσεις, ὅσαι ληπτέαι

---

a Bks. II-VII.

BOOK VIII

I. NEXT we must speak about arrangement and the way to ask questions. He who is about to ask questions must, first of all, choose the ground from which he must make his attack ; secondly, he must formulate his questions and arrange them separately in his own mind ; thirdly and lastly, he must go on to address them to another person. As far as the choice of ground goes, the philosopher and the dialectician are making a similar inquiry, but the subsequent arrangement of material and the framing of questions are the peculiar province of the dialectician ; for such a proceeding always involves a relation with another party. On the other hand, the philosopher and individual seeker does not care if, though the premisses by means of which his reasoning proceeds are true and familiar, the answerer refuses to admit them because they are too close to the point of departure and he foresees what will result from his admission ; indeed the philosopher may perhaps even be eager that his axioms should be as familiar and as near to his starting-point as possible ; for it is of this material that scientific reasonings are constructed.

The sources from which the commonplaces should be derived have already been stated.[a] We must now deal with arrangement and the framing of questions, after having first distinguished the premisses which

ARISTOTLE

20 παρὰ τὰς ἀναγκαίας. ἀναγκαῖαι δὲ λέγονται δι'
ὧν ὁ συλλογισμὸς γίνεται. αἱ δὲ παρὰ ταύτας
λαμβανόμεναι τέτταρές εἰσιν· ἢ γὰρ ἐπαγωγῆς
χάριν τοῦ δοθῆναι τὸ καθόλου, ἢ εἰς ὄγκον τοῦ
λόγου, ἢ πρὸς κρύψιν τοῦ συμπεράσματος, ἢ πρὸς
τὸ σαφέστερον εἶναι τὸν λόγον. παρὰ δὲ ταύτας
25 οὐδεμίαν ληπτέον πρότασιν, ἀλλὰ διὰ τούτων
αὔξειν καὶ ἐρωτηματίζειν πειρατέον. εἰσὶ δ' αἱ
πρὸς κρύψιν ἀγῶνος χάριν· ἀλλ' ἐπειδὴ πᾶσα ἡ
τοιαύτη πραγματεία πρὸς ἕτερόν ἐστιν, ἀνάγκη
καὶ ταύταις χρῆσθαι.

Τὰς μὲν οὖν ἀναγκαίας, δι' ὧν ὁ συλλογισμός,
30 οὐκ εὐθὺς αὐτὰς¹ προτατέον, ἀλλ' ἀποστατέον ὅτι
ἀπωτάτω,² οἷον μὴ τῶν ἐναντίων ἀξιοῦντα τὴν
αὐτὴν ἐπιστήμην, ἂν τοῦτο βούληται λαβεῖν, ἀλλὰ
τῶν ἀντικειμένων· τεθέντος γὰρ τούτου, καὶ ὅτι
τῶν ἐναντίων ἡ αὐτὴ συλλογιεῖται, ἐπειδὴ ἀντικείμενα τὰ ἐναντία. ἂν δὲ μὴ τιθῇ, δι' ἐπαγωγῆς
35 ληπτέον, προτείνοντα ἐπὶ τῶν κατὰ μέρος ἐναντίων.
ἢ γὰρ διὰ συλλογισμοῦ ἢ δι' ἐπαγωγῆς τὰς ἀναγκαίας ληπτέον, ἢ τὰς μὲν ἐπαγωγῇ τὰς δὲ συλλογισμῷ, ὅσαι δὲ λίαν προφανεῖς εἰσί, καὶ αὐτὰς
προτείνοντα· ἀδηλότερόν τε γὰρ ἀεὶ ἐν τῇ ἀπο-
156 a στάσει καὶ τῇ ἐπαγωγῇ τὸ συμβησόμενον, καὶ ἅμα

¹ Inserting αὐτὰς with AB.

676

have to be obtained, other than those which are (a) *Neces-*
necessary. What are called necessary premises are *sary and other*
those by means of which reasoning proceeds. Those *premisses.*
which are obtained other than these fall into four
classes ; they are used either (1) for the sake of in
duction, so that the universal may be granted, or
(2) to add weight to the argument, or (3) to conceal
the conclusion, or (4) to give greater clearness to the
argument. Besides these no other premiss needs to
be provided, but by means of them we must try to
amplify and frame our questions. Those which are
used for concealment are for contentious purposes ;
but, since this kind of proceeding is always directed
against another party, these also must be employed.

The necessary premises, then, by means of which *How to*
reasoning proceeds, ought not to be advanced im- *employ necessary*
mediately in their original form, but you must keep *premisses.*
as far away from them as you can ; for example, if
you wish to establish that the knowledge of contraries
is the same, you should make the claim not for contraries but for opposites ; for, if this is granted, you
will then argue that the knowledge of contraries is
also the same, since contraries are opposites. If, on
the other hand, the answerer refuses to admit this,
you should then establish it by induction, making a
proposition dealing with particular contraries. For
you must secure the necessary premises either by
reasoning or by induction, or else partly by induction
and partly by reasoning, though you can advance in
their original form any premisses which are clear
beyond all doubt ; for the conclusion which will
follow is always less obvious when it is still far off and
being reached by induction, and at the same time,

---

² Reading ἀπωτάτω for ἀνωτάτω.

τὸ αὐτὰς τὰς χρησίμους προτεῖναι καὶ μὴ δυνάμενον ἐκείνως λαβεῖν ἕτοιμον. τὰς δὲ παρὰ
ταύτας εἰρημένας ληπτέον μὲν τούτων χάριν,
5 ἑκάστῃ δ' ὧδε χρηστέον, ἐπάγοντα μὲν ἀπὸ τῶν
καθ' ἕκαστον ἐπὶ τὸ καθόλου καὶ τῶν γνωρίμων
ἐπὶ τὰ ἄγνωστα· γνώριμα δὲ μᾶλλον τὰ κατὰ τὴν
αἴσθησιν, ἢ ἁπλῶς ἢ τοῖς πολλοῖς. κρύπτοντα
δὲ προσυλλογίζεσθαι δι' ὧν ὁ συλλογισμὸς τοῦ
ἐξ ἀρχῆς μέλλει γίνεσθαι, καὶ ταῦτα ὡς πλεῖστα.
10 εἴη δ' ἂν τοῦτο, εἴ τις μὴ μόνον τὰς ἀναγκαίας
ἀλλὰ καὶ τῶν πρὸς ταύτας χρησίμων τινὰ συλ-
λογίζοιτο. ἔτι τὰ συμπεράσματα μὴ λέγειν,
ἀλλ' ὕστερον ἀθρόα συλλογίζεσθαι· οὕτω γὰρ ἂν
πορρωτάτω ἀποστήσειε τῆς ἐξ ἀρχῆς θέσεως.
καθόλου δ' εἰπεῖν, οὕτω δεῖ ἐρωτᾶν τὸν κρυπτικῶς
πυνθανόμενον, ὥστ' ἠρωτημένου τοῦ παντὸς λόγου
15 καὶ εἰπόντος τὸ συμπέρασμα ζητεῖσθαι τὸ διὰ
τί. τοῦτο δ' ἔσται μάλιστα διὰ τοῦ λεχθέντος
ἔμπροσθεν τρόπου· μόνου γὰρ τοῦ ἐσχάτου ῥηθέντος συμπεράσματος ἄδηλον πῶς συμβαίνει, διὰ
τὸ μὴ προορᾶν τὸν ἀποκρινόμενον ἐκ τίνων
συμβαίνει, μὴ διαρθρωθέντων τῶν πρότερον συλ-
20 λογισμῶν. ἥκιστα δ' ἂν διαρθροῖτο ὁ συλλογισμὸς τοῦ συμπεράσματος μὴ τὰ τούτου λήμματα
ἡμῶν τιθέντων, ἀλλ' ἐκεῖνα ὑφ' ὧν ὁ συλλογισμὸς
γίνεται.

if you cannot establish the requisite premisses in the above manner, it is still feasible to advance them in their original form. The premisses, other than *How to* these, already mentioned, must be established for *employ premisses* the sake of the latter, and must each be used as fol- *other than* lows, namely, by induction from the particulars to the *necessary* universal and from the known to the unknown ; and *inductions.* the objects of sense-perception are better known ab- solutely or at any rate to most people. For the con- *(2) For* cealment of your conclusion, you should establish by *concealing one's con-* previous reasonings the premisses through which the *clusion :* reasoning of your original proposition is to proceed, and they should be as numerous as possible. This would best be achieved if one were to establish by reasoning not only the necessary premisses but also some of those which are requisite for obtaining them. Further, you should not state the conclusions, but *a. Postpone* establish them by reasoning all at the same time at *the state- ment of* a later stage ; for them you would keep the answerer *your con-* as far as possible from the original proposition. To *clusion.* put the matter generally, he who wishes to conceal his purpose while eliciting answers should frame his questions in such a way that, when the whole argu- ment has been the subject of questions and he has stated the conclusion, it should still be asked " Why is it so ? " This will be best achieved by following the above method ; for, if only the final conclusion is stated, it is not clear how it comes about, because the answerer cannot foresee the basis on which it rests, because the preliminary reasonings have not formed an organic whole, and the reasoning-out of the conclusion would least form an organic whole, if we set forth not the admitted premisses but only those by which the reasoning proceeds.

156 a

Χρήσιμον δὲ καὶ τὸ μὴ συνεχῆ τὰ ἀξιώματα λαμβάνειν ἐξ ὧν οἱ συλλογισμοί, ἀλλ' ἐναλλὰξ τὸ 25 πρὸς ἕτερον καὶ ἕτερον συμπέρασμα· τιθεμένων γὰρ τῶν οἰκείων παρ' ἄλληλα μᾶλλον τὸ συμβησόμενον ἐξ αὐτῶν προφανές.

Χρὴ δὲ καὶ ὁρισμῷ λαμβάνειν, ἐφ' ὧν ἐνδέχεται, τὴν καθόλου πρότασιν, μὴ ἐπ' αὐτῶν ἀλλ' ἐπὶ τῶν συστοίχων· παραλογίζονται γὰρ ἑαυτούς, ὅταν 30 ἐπὶ συστοίχου ληφθῇ ὁ ὁρισμός, ὡς οὐ τὸ καθόλου συγχωροῦντες, οἷον εἰ δέοι λαβεῖν ὅτι ὁ ὀργιζόμενος ὀρέγεται τιμωρίας διὰ φαινομένην ὀλιγωρίαν, ληφθείη δ' ἡ ὀργὴ ὄρεξις εἶναι τιμωρίας διὰ φαινομένην ὀλιγωρίαν· δῆλον γὰρ ὅτι τούτου ληφθέντος ἔχοιμεν ἂν καθόλου ὃ προαιρούμεθα. 35 τοῖς δ' ἐπ' αὐτῶν προτείνουσι πολλάκις ἀνανεύειν συμβαίνει τὸν ἀποκρινόμενον διὰ τὸ μᾶλλον ἔχειν ἐπ' αὐτοῦ τὴν ἔνστασιν, οἷον ὅτι ὁ ὀργιζόμενος οὐκ ὀρέγεται τιμωρίας· τοῖς γὰρ γονεῦσιν ὀργιζόμεθα μέν, οὐκ ὀρεγόμεθα δὲ τιμωρίας. ἴσως μὲν οὖν οὐκ ἀληθὴς ἡ ἔνστασις· παρ' ἐνίων γὰρ 156 b ἱκανὴ τιμωρία τὸ λυπῆσαι μόνον καὶ ποιῆσαι μεταμέλεσθαι· οὐ μὴν ἀλλ' ἔχει τι πιθανὸν πρὸς τὸ μὴ δοκεῖν ἀλόγως ἀρνεῖσθαι τὸ προτεινόμενον. ἐπὶ δὲ τοῦ τῆς ὀργῆς ὁρισμοῦ οὐχ ὁμοίως ῥᾴδιόν ἐστιν εὑρεῖν ἔνστασιν.

It is also a useful practice not to establish the *b.* Vary the admitted propositions on which the reasonings are order in based in their natural order but to alternate one which you which leads to one conclusion with another which the various leads to another conclusion ; for, if those which are arguments. closely related are set side by side with one another, the conclusion which will result from them is more clearly foreseen.

You should also, whenever possible, establish the *c.* Establish universal premiss in the form of a definition relating a universal not to the actual terms in question but to co-ordinates a definition of them ; for people let themselves be deceived when a co-a definition is established dealing with a co-ordinate, ordinate of imagining that they are not making the admission term. universally. This would happen, for example, if it were necessary to establish that the angry man is desirous of revenge for a fancied slight, and it were to be established that anger is a desire for revenge for a fancied slight ; for, obviously, if this were established, we should have the universal admission which we require. On the other hand, it often happens, when people make propositions dealing with the actual term, that the answerer refuses his assent, because he objects more readily when the actual term is used, saying, for example, that the angry man is not desirous of revenge, for though we become angry with our parents, yet we are not desirous of revenge. Possibly, the objection is not a true one ; for with some people merely to cause pain and induce repentance is sufficient revenge. However, it tends to create an impression that the denial of the proposition is not unreasonable. But as regards the definition of anger it is not so easy to find an objection as in some other cases.

Ἔτι τὸ προτείνειν μὴ ὡς δι᾽ αὐτὸ ἀλλ᾽ ἄλλου
5 χάριν προτείνοντα· εὐλαβοῦνται γὰρ τὰ πρὸς τὴν
θέσιν χρήσιμα. ἁπλῶς δ᾽ εἰπεῖν, ὅτι μάλιστα
ποιεῖν ἄδηλον πότερον τὸ προτεινόμενον ἢ τὸ
ἀντικείμενον βούλεται λαβεῖν· ἀδήλου γὰρ ὄντος
τοῦ πρὸς τὸν λόγον χρησίμου μᾶλλον τὸ δοκοῦν
αὐτοῖς τιθέασιν.

10 Ἔτι διὰ τῆς ὁμοιότητος πυνθάνεσθαι· καὶ γὰρ
πιθανὸν καὶ λανθάνει μᾶλλον τὸ καθόλου. οἷον
ὅτι ὥσπερ ἐπιστήμη καὶ ἄγνοια τῶν ἐναντίων ἡ
αὐτή, οὕτω καὶ αἴσθησις τῶν ἐναντίων ἡ αὐτή, ἢ
ἀνάπαλιν, ἐπειδὴ αἴσθησις ἡ αὐτή, καὶ ἐπιστήμη.
τοῦτο δ᾽ ἐστὶν ὅμοιον ἐπαγωγῇ, οὐ μὴν ταὐτόν
15 γε· ἐκεῖ μὲν γὰρ ἀπὸ τῶν καθ᾽ ἕκαστα τὸ καθόλου
λαμβάνεται, ἐπὶ δὲ τῶν ὁμοίων οὐκ ἔστι τὸ
λαμβανόμενον τὸ καθόλου, ὑφ᾽ ὃ πάντα τὰ ὅμοιά
ἐστιν.

Δεῖ δὲ καὶ αὐτόν ποτε αὐτῷ ἔνστασιν φέρειν·
ἀνυπόπτως γὰρ ἔχουσιν οἱ ἀποκρινόνενοι πρὸς
20 τοὺς δοκοῦντας δικαίως ἐπιχειρεῖν. χρήσιμον δὲ
καὶ τὸ ἐπιλέγειν ὅτι σύνηθες καὶ λεγόμενον τὸ
τοιοῦτον· ὀκνοῦσι γὰρ κινεῖν τὸ εἰωθὸς ἔνστασιν
μὴ ἔχοντες. ἅμα δὲ καὶ τῷ χρῆσθαι καὶ αὐτοὶ τοῖς
τοιούτοις φυλάττονται κινεῖν αὐτά. ἔτι τὸ μὴ
σπουδάζειν, κἂν ὅλως χρήσιμον ᾖ· πρὸς γὰρ τοὺς
25 σπουδάζοντας μᾶλλον ἀντιτείνουσιν. καὶ τὸ ὡς
ἐν παραβολῇ προτείνειν· τὸ γὰρ δι᾽ ἄλλο προτεινό-

Furthermore, you should state your proposition *d.* Conceal as if you were doing so not for its own sake but the object of the with some other object; for people are on the watch desired against what is useful for the thesis. In a word, the concession. questioner should leave it obscure whether he wishes to establish what he is really proposing or its opposite; for if what is useful to the argument is obscure, people are more likely to state what they really think.

Further, you should carry on your questioning by *e.* Secure means of similarity; for this is a plausible method, the admis- sions by and the universal is less obvious. For example, you means of should argue that, as knowledge and ignorance of likeness. contraries is the same thing, so is the perception of contraries the same thing, or, conversely, since the perception of them is the same, so also is the know- ledge. This method resembles induction but is not the same thing; for, in induction, the universal is established from the particulars, whereas, in dealing with similars, what is established is not the universal under which all the similars fall.

You should, also, yourself sometimes bring an *f.* Various objection against yourself; for answerers are un- other de- vices: *e.g.* suspicious when dealing with those who appear to self-objec- them to be arguing fairly. It is useful also to add: tion, indif- ference and " Such and such a view is that generally held and irrelevant expressed "; for people shrink from trying to upset amplifica- customary opinions unless they have some objection tion. to bring, and they are wary of trying to upset them at the same time as they are themselves also making use of such things. Further, you should not be too zealous, even though it is entirely to your advantage to be so; for people offer more opposition to the zealous. Further, you should put forward your pro- position as if it were an illustration; for people

μενον καὶ μὴ δι᾽ αὐτὸ χρήσιμον τιθέασι μᾶλλον.
ἔτι μὴ αὐτὸ προτείνειν ὃ δεῖ ληφθῆναι, ἀλλ᾽ ᾧ
τοῦτο ἕπεται ἐξ ἀνάγκης· μᾶλλόν τε γὰρ συγχωροῦσι διὰ τὸ μὴ ὁμοίως ἐκ τούτου φανερὸν
30 εἶναι τὸ συμβησόμενον, καὶ ληφθέντος τούτου
εἴληπται κἀκεῖνο. καὶ τὸ ἐπ᾽ ἐσχάτῳ ἐρωτᾶν ὃ
μάλιστα βούλεται λαβεῖν· μάλιστα γὰρ τὰ πρῶτα
ἀνανεύουσι διὰ τὸ τοὺς πλείστους τῶν ἐρωτώντων
πρῶτα λέγειν περὶ ἃ μάλιστα σπουδάζουσιν. πρὸς
ἐνίους δὲ πρῶτα τὰ τοιαῦτα προτείνειν· οἱ γὰρ
35 δύσκολοι τὰ πρῶτα μάλιστα συγχωροῦσιν, ἂν μὴ
παντελῶς φανερὸν ᾖ τὸ συμβησόμενον, ἐπὶ τελευτῆς
δὲ δυσκολαίνουσιν. ὁμοίως δὲ καὶ ὅσοι οἴονται
δριμεῖς εἶναι ἐν τῷ ἀποκρίνεσθαι· θέντες γὰρ τὰ
πλεῖστα ἐπὶ τέλους τερθρεύονται ὡς οὐ συμ-
βαίνοντος ἐκ τῶν κειμένων· τιθέασι δὲ προχείρως,
157 a πιστεύοντες τῇ ἕξει καὶ ὑπολαμβάνοντες οὐδὲν
πείσεσθαι. ἔτι τὸ μηκύνειν καὶ παρεμβάλλειν
τὰ μηδὲν χρήσιμα πρὸς τὸν λόγον, καθάπερ οἱ
ψευδογραφοῦντες· πολλῶν γὰρ ὄντων ἄδηλον ἐν
ὁποίῳ τὸ ψεῦδος. διὸ καὶ λανθάνουσιν ἐνίοτε οἱ
5 ἐρωτῶντες ἐν παραβύστῳ προστιθέντες ἃ καθ᾽
αὑτὰ προτεινόμενα οὐκ ἂν τεθείη.

Εἰς μὲν οὖν κρύψιν τοῖς εἰρημένοις χρηστέον, εἰς

more readily admit what is proposed for some other purpose and is not useful for its own sake. Further, you should not put forward the actual proposition which has to be established, but something from which it necessarily follows; for people are more likely to concede the latter because what will follow from it is less obvious, and when it has been established, the other has also been established. Also you should keep for the last question the point which you most wish to establish; for people are most apt to deny the first questions asked because most questioners put first the points on which they set most store. But in dealing with some people you should put forward such propositions first; for bad-tempered people most readily concede the first points, if what is going to result is not absolutely obvious, and indulge their bad temper at the end. Something of the same kind occurs with those who think that they are clever at answering; for, after admitting most of the points, they finally indulge in quibbling, saying that the conclusion does not result from what has been admitted, yet they make admissions readily, trusting to their habitual practice and conceiving that they will suffer no defeat. Further, it is a good thing to prolong the argument and to introduce into it points which are of no practical good, just as those do who construct false geometrical figures; for, when the material is abundant, it is less obvious where the fallacy lies. It is for this reason also that those who are asking questions escape detection by introducing in a hole-and-corner fashion things which, if proposed separately, would not be admitted.

For concealing your purpose, then, the above (3) *For* mentioned methods should be used; for ornament, *ornament.*

157 a

δὲ κόσμον ἐπαγωγῇ καὶ διαιρέσει τῶν συγγενῶν.
ἡ μὲν οὖν ἐπαγωγὴ ὁποῖον τί ἐστι δῆλον, τὸ δὲ
διαιρεῖσθαι τοιοῦτον οἷον ὅτι ἐπιστήμη ἐπιστήμης
10 βελτίων ἢ τῷ ἀκριβεστέρα εἶναι ἢ τῷ βελτιόνων,
καὶ ὅτι τῶν ἐπιστημῶν αἱ μὲν θεωρητικαὶ αἱ δὲ
πρακτικαὶ αἱ δὲ ποιητικαί. τῶν γὰρ τοιούτων
ἕκαστον συνεπικοσμεῖ μὲν τὸν λόγον, οὐκ ἀναγκαῖα
δὲ ῥηθῆναι πρὸς τὸ συμπέρασμα.

Εἰς δὲ σαφήνειαν παραδείγματα καὶ παραβολὰς
15 οἰστέον, παραδείγματα δὲ οἰκεῖα καὶ ἐξ ὧν ἴσμεν,
οἷα Ὅμηρος, μὴ οἷα Χοιρίλος· οὕτω γὰρ ἂν σαφέστερον εἴη τὸ προτεινόμενον.

II. Χρηστέον δ' ἐν τῷ διαλέγεσθαι τῷ μὲν
συλλογισμῷ πρὸς τοὺς διαλεκτικοὺς μᾶλλον ἢ
20 πρὸς τοὺς πολλούς, τῇ δ' ἐπαγωγῇ τοὐναντίον
πρὸς τοὺς πολλοὺς μᾶλλον· εἴρηται δ' ὑπὲρ τούτων
καὶ πρότερον. ἔστι δὲ ἐπ' ἐνίων μὲν ἐπάγοντα
δυνατὸν ἐρωτῆσαι τὸ καθόλου, ἐπ' ἐνίων δ' οὐ
ῥάδιον διὰ τὸ μὴ κεῖσθαι ταῖς ὁμοιότησιν ὄνομα
πάσαις κοινόν· ἀλλ' ὅταν δέῃ τὸ καθόλου λαβεῖν,
οὕτως ἐπὶ πάντων τῶν τοιούτων φασίν· τοῦτο
25 δὲ διορίσαι τῶν χαλεπωτάτων, ὁποῖα τῶν προ-
φερομένων τοιαῦτα καὶ ποῖα οὔ. καὶ παρὰ τοῦτο
πολλάκις ἀλλήλους παρακρούονται κατὰ τοὺς
λόγους, οἱ μὲν φάσκοντες ὅμοια εἶναι τὰ μὴ ὄντα
ὅμοια, οἱ δ' ἀμφισβητοῦντες τὰ ὅμοια μὴ εἶναι
ὅμοια. διὸ πειρατέον ἐπὶ πάντων τῶν τοιούτων
30 ὀνοματοποιεῖν αὐτόν, ὅπως μήτε τῷ ἀποκρινομένῳ

---

[a] An epic poet of Iasos in Asia Minor who attached himself
to Alexander the Great (Horace, *A.P.* 357, *Epp.* ii. 1. 233).
[b] 105 a 16-19.

you should employ induction and the distinction of things of a closely similar kind. What induction is, is obvious ; distinction is attained by statements such as that one science is better than another, either because it is more exact or because it is concerned with better objects, and that some sciences are theoretical, others practical and others creative. Every distinction of this kind helps to adorn your argument, though its introduction is not necessary to the conclusion.

For clearness, examples and illustrations should be adduced, the examples being to the point and drawn from things which are familiar to us, of the kind which Homer uses and not of the kind that Choerilus [a] employs ; for thus the proposition would be rendered clearer. *(4) For clearness.*

II. In dialectical argument, the syllogism should be used against dialecticians rather than against the multitude ; on the contrary, induction should rather be used against the multitide ; this matter has been dealt with before.[b] When you are using induction, it is possible sometimes to put the question in a general form, but sometimes it is not easy to do so, because there is no common term laid down which applies to all the similarities ; but, when it is necessary to establish the universal, people use the expression "So in all cases of this kind." But it is one of the most difficult of tasks to define which of the terms proposed are ' of this kind ' and which are not. Because of this, people often mislead one another in their discussions, some alleging that things are similar which are not similar, others arguing that similar things are not similar. Therefore, you must try to invent a term which will apply to all things of a certain kind, in order that it may be impossible *(b) Inductions.*

687

157 a

ἐξῇ ἀμφισβητεῖν ὡς οὐχ ὁμοίως τὸ ἐπιφερόμενον λέγεται, μήτε τῷ ἐρωτῶντι συκοφαντεῖν ὡς ὁμοίως λεγομένου, ἐπειδὴ πολλὰ τῶν οὐχ ὁμοίως λεγομένων ὁμοίως φαίνεται λέγεσθαι.

Ὅταν δ' ἐπάγοντος ἐπὶ πολλῶν μὴ διδῷ τὸ
35 καθόλου, τότε δίκαιον ἀπαιτεῖν ἔνστασιν. μὴ εἰπόντα δ' αὐτὸν ἐπὶ τίνων οὕτως, οὐ δίκαιον ἀπαιτεῖν ἐπὶ τίνων οὐχ οὕτως· δεῖ γὰρ ἐπάγοντα πρότερον οὕτω τὴν ἔνστασιν ἀπαιτεῖν. ἀξιωτέον τε τὰς ἐνστάσεις μὴ ἐπ' αὐτοῦ τοῦ προτεινομένου φέρειν, ἐὰν μὴ ἓν μόνον ᾖ τὸ τοιοῦτον, καθάπερ
157 b ἡ δυὰς τῶν ἀρτίων μόνος ἀριθμὸς πρῶτος· δεῖ γὰρ τὸν ἐνιστάμενον ἐφ' ἑτέρου τὴν ἔνστασιν φέρειν, ἢ λέγειν ὅτι τοῦτο μόνον τοιοῦτο. πρὸς δὲ τοὺς ἐνισταμένους τῷ καθόλου, μὴ ἐν αὐτῷ δὲ τὴν ἔνστασιν φέροντας ἀλλ' ἐν τῷ ὁμωνύμῳ, οἷον
5 ὅτι ἔχοι ἄν τις τὸ μὴ αὑτοῦ χρῶμα ἢ πόδα ἢ χεῖρα (ἔχοι γὰρ ἂν ὁ ζωγράφος χρῶμα καὶ ὁ μάγειρος πόδα τὸν μὴ αὑτοῦ) διελόμενον οὖν ἐπὶ τῶν τοιούτων ἐρωτητέον· λανθανούσης γὰρ τῆς ὁμωνυμίας εὖ δόξει ἐνστῆναι τῇ προτάσει. ἐὰν δὲ μὴ ἐν τῷ ὁμωνύμῳ ἀλλ' ἐν αὐτῷ ἐνιστάμενος
10 κωλύῃ τὴν ἐρώτησιν, ἀφαιροῦντα δεῖ ἐν ᾧ ἡ ἔνστασις προτείνειν τὸ λοιπὸν καθόλου ποιοῦντα, ἕως ἂν λάβῃς¹ τὸ χρήσιμον. οἷον ἐπὶ τῆς λήθης

¹ Reading λάβῃς with C.

either for the answerer to argue that what is being proposed is not used similarly, or for the questioner falsely to represent it as used similarly when it is not so, since many things seem to be used similarly when they are not really so.

When one makes an induction on the basis of a *(c) Objec-* number of particulars and the answerer refuses to *tions.* admit the universal, one is justified in demanding his objection. If, on the other hand, one has not oneself stated the cases in which something is so, one is not justified in demanding from him the cases in which it is not so ; one ought to make the induction first and then demand the objection. Also, one ought to demand that objections should not be brought against the actual thing proposed unless it is the only one thing of its kind, as, for example, two is the only even number which is a prime number ; for the objector ought either to make his objection with regard to another instance or else assert that the instance in question is the only one of its kind. When people object to a universal proposition, bringing their objection not against the thing itself but against something homonymous with it—saying, for example, that a man could not have a colour or a foot or a hand which was not his own (for a painter could have a colour and a cook could have a foot which was not his own)—you should make a distinction in such cases and then ask your question ; for, if the homonym is not exposed, the objection to the proposition will appear valid. If, however, he stops your questioning by objecting not to a homonym but to the thing itself, you should omit the point to which the objection is made and bring forward the remainder, putting it in the form of a universal, until you have got what you require. For

689

καὶ τοῦ ἐπιλελῆσθαι· οὐ γὰρ συγχωροῦσι τὸν
ἀποβεβληκότα ἐπιστήμην ἐπιλελῆσθαι, διότι μετα-
πεσόντος τοῦ πράγματος ἀποβέβληκε μὲν τὴν
ἐπιστήμην, ἐπιλέλησται δ' οὔ. ῥητέον οὖν ἀφε-
15 λόντα ἐν ᾧ ἡ ἔνστασις τὸ λοιπόν, οἷον εἰ διαμέ-
νοντος τοῦ πράγματος ἀποβέβληκε τὴν ἐπιστήμην,
διότι ἐπιλέλησται. ὁμοίως δὲ καὶ πρὸς τοὺς
ἐνισταμένους διότι τῷ μείζονι ἀγαθῷ μεῖζον
ἀντίκειται κακόν· προφέρουσι γὰρ ὅτι τῇ ὑγιείᾳ,
ἐλάττονι ὄντι ἀγαθῷ τῆς εὐεξίας, μεῖζον κακὸν
20 ἀντίκειται· τὴν γὰρ νόσον μεῖζον κακὸν εἶναι τῆς
καχεξίας. ἀφαιρετέον οὖν καὶ ἐπὶ τούτου ἐν ᾧ
ἡ ἔνστασις· ἀφαιρεθέντος γὰρ μᾶλλον ἂν θείη,
οἷον ὅτι τῷ μείζονι ἀγαθῷ μεῖζον κακὸν ἀντίκειται, ἐὰν μὴ συνεπιφέρῃ θάτερον θάτερον, καθάπερ
ἡ εὐεξία τὴν ὑγίειαν. οὐ μόνον δ' ἐνισταμένου
25 τοῦτο ποιητέον, ἀλλὰ κἂν ἄνευ ἐνστάσεως ἀρνῆται
διὰ τὸ προορᾶν τι τῶν τοιούτων· ἀφαιρεθέντος
γὰρ ἐν ᾧ ἡ ἔνστασις, ἀναγκασθήσεται τιθέναι διὰ
τὸ μὴ προορᾶν ἐν τῷ λοιπῷ ἐπὶ τίνος οὐχ οὕτως·
ἐὰν δὲ μὴ τιθῇ, ἀπαιτούμενος ἔνστασιν οὐ μὴ
ἔχῃ ἀποδοῦναι. εἰσὶ δὲ τοιαῦται τῶν προτάσεων
30 αἱ ἐπὶ τὶ μὲν ψευδεῖς ἐπὶ τὶ δ' ἀληθεῖς· ἐπὶ τούτων
γὰρ ἔστιν ἀφελόντα τὸ λοιπὸν ἀληθὲς καταλιπεῖν.

example, in the case of forgetfulness and having forgotten, people do not concede that the man who has lost the knowledge of something has forgotten it, because, if the thing changes, he has lost knowledge of it but has not forgotten it. You must, therefore, omit the point to which the objection is made and assert the remainder, saying, for example, that if he has lost the knowledge of the thing while it still remains, he has then forgotten it. You must deal similarly with those who object to the statement that a greater evil is the opposite of the greater good ; for they advance the argument that health, which is a lesser good than sound bodily condition, has a greater evil as its opposite, since disease is a greater evil than unsound bodily condition. You must, therefore, omit in this instance also the point to which the objection is made ; for, if this is omitted, your opponent would more readily make an admission such as that " the greater evil is the opposite of the greater good, unless one good entails the other also," as sound bodily condition entails health. This course should be followed, not only when he offers an objection, but also if he denies your proposition without making an objection, because he foresees something of this kind ; for, if that to which the objection is made is omitted, he will be forced to admit your proposition because he cannot foresee any case in which it is not true in the future course of the argument. If he does not admit it, he will be quite unable to assign an objection when asked to do so. Propositions of this kind are those which are partly false and partly true. In dealing with these it is possible to omit something and leave the remainder true. If you make a proposition based on

157 b

ἐὰν δ' ἐπὶ πολλῶν προτείνοντος μὴ φέρῃ ἔνστασιν,
ἀξιωτέον τιθέναι· διαλεκτικὴ γάρ ἐστι πρότασις
πρὸς ἣν οὕτως ἐπὶ πολλῶν ἔχουσαν μὴ ἔστιν
ἔνστασις.

Ὅταν δ' ἐνδέχηται τὸ αὐτὸ ἄνευ τε τοῦ ἀδυνάτου
35 καὶ διὰ τοῦ ἀδυνάτου συλλογίσασθαι, ἀποδεικνύντι
μὲν καὶ μὴ διαλεγομένῳ οὐδὲν διαφέρει οὕτως ἢ
ἐκείνως συλλογίσασθαι, διαλεγομένῳ δὲ πρὸς
ἄλλον οὐ χρηστέον τῷ διὰ τοῦ ἀδυνάτου συλλογισμῷ. ἄνευ μὲν γὰρ τοῦ ἀδυνάτου συλλογισα-
μένῳ οὐκ ἔστιν ἀμφισβητεῖν· ὅταν δὲ τὸ ἀδύνατον
158 a συλλογίσηται, ἂν μὴ λίαν ᾖ περιφανὲς ψεῦδος ὄν,
οὐκ ἀδύνατόν φασιν εἶναι, ὥστ' οὐ γίνεται τοῖς
ἐρωτῶσιν ὃ βούλονται.

Δεῖ δὲ προτείνειν ὅσα ἐπὶ πολλῶν μὲν οὕτως
5 ἔχει, ἔνστασις δὲ ἢ ὅλως μὴ ἔστιν ἢ μὴ ἐπιπολῆς
τὸ συνιδεῖν· μὴ δυνάμενοι γὰρ συνορᾶν ἐφ' ὧν οὐχ
οὕτως, ὡς ἀληθὲς ὂν τιθέασιν.

Οὐ δεῖ δὲ τὸ συμπέρασμα ἐρώτημα ποιεῖν· εἰ
δὲ μή, ἀνανεύσαντος οὐ δοκεῖ γεγονέναι συλλο-
10 γισμός. πολλάκις γὰρ καὶ μὴ ἐρωτῶντος ἀλλ'
ὡς συμβαῖνον ἐπιφέροντος ἀρνοῦνται, καὶ τοῦτο
ποιοῦντες οὐ δοκοῦσιν ἐλέγχεσθαι τοῖς μὴ συνο-
ρῶσιν ὅτι συμβαίνει ἐκ τῶν τεθέντων. ὅταν οὖν
μηδὲ φήσας συμβαίνειν ἐρωτήσῃ, ὁ δ' ἀρνηθῇ,
παντελῶς οὐ δοκεῖ γεγονέναι συλλογισμός.

a number of instances and he offers no objection, you must claim that he admits it; for a dialectical proposition is one which thus rests on a number of instances and against which there is no objection.

When it is possible to establish the same point *(d) The argument per impossible.* either without or by means of the impossible, if one is demonstrating and not arguing dialectically, it does not matter whether one reasons by the former or the latter method; but if one is arguing dialectically with another person, reasoning by means of the impossible must not be employed. For if one has reasoned without the impossible, no dispute can arise; but when one establishes the impossible by reasoning, unless the fallacy is too obvious, people declare that there is no impossibility, so that the questioners do not achieve their object.

One ought to advance all the propositions which are true in a number of instances and to which there is no objection at all, or at any rate none to be seen on the surface; for if men can see no instances in which the proposition does not hold good, they admit it as true.

One ought not to put the conclusion in the form *(e) Various recommendations on the putting of questions.* of a question; otherwise one's opponent shakes his head and the reasoning appears to have been unsuccessful. For often, even if one does not put it in the form of a question but advances it as a consequence, people deny it, and by so doing avoid appearing to be refuted in the eyes of those who fail to see that the conclusion follows from the admissions which have been made. Whenever, therefore, one puts the conclusion in the form of a question, without even saying that it follows as a consequence, and the other party denies it, the reasoning has the appearance of having failed utterly.

Οὐ δοκεῖ δὲ πᾶν τὸ καθόλου διαλεκτικὴ πρό-
15 τασις εἶναι οἷον τί ἐστιν ἄνθρωπος, ἢ ποσαχῶς
λέγεται τἀγαθόν; ἔστι γὰρ πρότασις διαλεκτικὴ
πρὸς ἣν ἔστιν ἀποκρίνασθαι ναί ἢ οὔ· πρὸς δὲ
τὰς εἰρημένας οὐκ ἔστιν. διὸ οὐ διαλεκτικά ἐστι
τὰ τοιαῦτα τῶν ἐρωτημάτων, ἂν μὴ αὐτὸς διορίσας ἢ διελόμενος εἴπῃ, οἷον ἆρά γε τἀγαθὸν οὕτως
20 ἢ οὕτως λέγεται; πρὸς γὰρ τὰ τοιαῦτα ῥᾳδία ἡ
ἀπόκρισις ἢ καταφήσαντι ἢ ἀποφήσαντι. διὸ πειρατέον οὕτω προτείνειν τὰς τοιαύτας τῶν προτάσεων. ἅμα δὲ καὶ δίκαιον ἴσως παρ᾿ ἐκείνου
ζητεῖν ποσαχῶς λέγεται τἀγαθόν, ὅταν αὐτοῦ διαιρουμένου καὶ προτείνοντος μηδαμῶς συγχωρῇ.

25 Ὅστις δ᾿ ἕνα λόγον πολὺν χρόνον ἐρωτᾷ, κακῶς
πυνθάνεται. εἰ μὲν γὰρ ἀποκρινομένου τοῦ ἐρω-
τωμένου τὸ ἐρωτώμενον, δῆλον ὅτι πολλὰ ἐρωτήματα ἐρωτᾷ ἢ πολλάκις ταὐτά, ὥστε ἢ ἀδολεσχεῖ
ἢ οὐκ ἔχει συλλογισμόν· ἐξ ὀλίγων γὰρ πᾶς συλ-
λογισμός· εἰ δὲ μὴ ἀποκρινομένου, διὰ τί[1] οὐκ
30 ἐπιτιμᾷ ἢ ἀφίσταται;

III. Ἔστι δ᾿ ἐπιχειρεῖν τε χαλεπὸν καὶ ὑπέχειν
ῥᾴδιον τὰς αὐτὰς ὑποθέσεις. ἔστι δὲ τοιαῦτα τά
τε φύσει πρῶτα καὶ τὰ ἔσχατα. τὰ μὲν γὰρ
πρῶτα ὅρου δεῖται, τὰ δ᾿ ἔσχατα διὰ πολλῶν
35 περαίνεται βουλομένῳ τὸ συνεχὲς λαμβάνειν ἀπὸ

---

[1] Reading διὰ τί for ὅτι.

It is generally agreed that not every universal can form a dialectical proposition, for example " What is man ? " or " In what various senses can ' the good ' be used ? " For a dialectical proposition is one to which it is possible to answer ' yes ' or ' no,' whereas to the above questions this is impossible. Therefore such questions are not dialectical unless the questioner himself makes divisions or distinctions before he asks them, saying, for example, " Is ' the good ' used in this or in that sense ? " To such questions the answer can easily be given by affirmation or denial. So you must try to advance such propositions in this form. At the same time it is also perhaps justifiable to inquire from the answerer what are the various senses in which ' the good ' is used, when you have yourself distinguished and formulated them, and he absolutely refuses to agree.

Anyone who goes on asking one question for a long time is a bad interrogator. For, if the person questioned keeps on answering his question, obviously he asks a number of questions or asks the same thing time after time, so that either he is babbling or else he has no reasoned argument to offer ; for reasoning is always based on a few premisses only. On the other hand, if he goes on asking questions because the other party does not answer, why does he not reprove him or else stop asking questions ?

III. The same hypotheses may be both difficult to attack and easy to defend. Both things which are by nature primary and things which are by nature ultimate are of this kind. For things which are primary require definition and things which are ultimate are reached by many stages if one wishes to establish a continuous train of proof from primary [Notes on various degrees of difficulty in dialectic arguments : (a) Things which are primary and which are ultimate

158 a

τῶν πρώτων, ἢ σοφισματώδη φαίνεται τὰ ἐπι-
χειρήματα· ἀδύνατον γὰρ ἀποδεῖξαί τι μὴ ἀρξάμενον ἀπὸ τῶν οἰκείων ἀρχῶν καὶ συνείραντα
μέχρι τῶν ἐσχάτων. ὁρίζεσθαι μὲν οὖν οὔτ᾽
ἀξιοῦσιν οἱ ἀποκρινόμενοι, οὔτ᾽ ἂν ὁ ἐρωτῶν ὁρί-
ζηται προσέχουσιν· μὴ γενομένου δὲ φανεροῦ τί
158 b ποτ᾽ ἐστὶ τὸ προκείμενον, οὐ ῥᾴδιον ἐπιχειρεῖν.
μάλιστα δὲ τὸ τοιοῦτον περὶ τὰς ἀρχὰς συμβαίνει·
τὰ μὲν γὰρ ἄλλα διὰ τούτων δείκνυται, ταῦτα δ᾽
οὐκ ἐνδέχεται δι᾽ ἑτέρων, ἀλλ᾽ ἀναγκαῖον ὁρισμῷ
τῶν τοιούτων ἕκαστον γνωρίζειν.

5 Ἔστι δὲ δυσεπιχείρητα καὶ τὰ λίαν ἐγγὺς τῆς
ἀρχῆς· οὐ γὰρ ἐνδέχεται πολλοὺς πρὸς αὐτὰ λόγους
πορίσασθαι, ὀλίγων ὄντων τῶν ἀνὰ μέσον αὐτοῦ
τε καὶ τῆς ἀρχῆς, δι᾽ ὧν ἀνάγκη δείκνυσθαι τὰ
μετὰ ταῦτα. τῶν δὲ ὅρων δυσεπιχειρητότατοι
10 πάντων εἰσὶν ὅσοι κέχρηνται τοιούτοις ὀνόμασιν,
ἃ πρῶτον μὲν ἄδηλά ἐστιν εἴτε ἁπλῶς εἴτε πολλαχῶς λέγεται, πρὸς δὲ τούτοις μηδὲ γνώριμα
πότερον κυρίως ἢ κατὰ μεταφορὰν ὑπὸ τοῦ ὁρισα-
μένου λέγεται. διὰ μὲν γὰρ τὸ ἀσαφῆ εἶναι οὐκ
ἔχει ἐπιχειρήματα, διὰ δὲ τὸ ἀγνοεῖσθαι εἰ παρὰ
τὸ κατὰ μεταφορὰν λέγεσθαι τοιαῦτ᾽ ἐστίν, οὐκ
15 ἔχει ἐπιτίμησιν.

Ὅλως δὲ πᾶν πρόβλημα, ὅταν ᾖ δυσεπιχείρητον,
ἢ ὅρου δεῖσθαι ὑποληπτέον, ἢ τῶν πολλαχῶς ἢ
τῶν κατὰ μεταφορὰν εἶναι λεγομένων, ἢ οὐ πόρρω

principles, or else the arguments have the appearance of being sophistical; for it is impossible to demonstrate anything without starting from the appropriate first principles and keeping up a connected argument until ultimate principles are reached. Now those who are being questioned do not want to give definitions nor do they take any notice if the questioner gives them; and yet it is difficult to argue if what is proposed is not made clear. This kind of thing is most likely to happen in the matter of first principles; for, whereas it is through them that everything else is made clear, they cannot be made clear through anything else, but everything of that kind must be made known by definition. *are difficult to overthrow but easy to establish.*

Things which lie very close to a first principle are also difficult to attack; for it is not possible to supply many arguments against them, since the stages between them and the first principle, through which it is necessary to prove what is to follow, are few. Of definitions the most difficult to attack are those which employ terms about which, firstly, it is not clear whether they are used in one sense only or in several senses, and, besides this, it is not known whether they are used in their original sense or metaphorically by the framer of the definition. For, because of their obscurity, they do not offer points of attack, and, because one does not know whether they are obscure from being used metaphorically, they do not offer matter for criticism. *(b) Inferences which lie very near a first principle are difficult to attack.*

To speak generally, any problem, when it proves difficult to attack, may be supposed either to require definition, or to be one of those which bear several meanings or are couched in metaphorical language, or else to be not far removed from first principles; *(c) Various difficulties which hinder the confutation of an opponent.*

τῶν ἀρχῶν, ἢ διὰ τὸ μὴ φανερὸν εἶναι πρῶτον
20 ἡμῖν τοῦτ᾽ αὐτό, κατὰ τίνα ποτὲ τῶν εἰρημένων
τρόπον ἐστὶν ὃ τὴν ἀπορίαν παρέχεται· φανεροῦ
γὰρ ὄντος τοῦ τρόπου δῆλον ὅτι ἢ ὁρίζεσθαι ἂν
δέοι ἢ διαιρεῖσθαι ἢ τὰς ἀνὰ μέσον προτάσεις
πορίζεσθαι· διὰ τούτων γὰρ δείκνυται τὰ ἔσχατα.

Πολλαῖς τε τῶν θέσεων μὴ καλῶς ἀποδιδομένου
25 τοῦ ὁρισμοῦ οὐ ῥᾴδιον διαλέγεσθαι καὶ ἐπιχειρεῖν,
οἷον πότερον ἓν ἑνὶ ἐναντίον ἢ πλείω· ὁρισθέντων
δὲ τῶν ἐναντίων κατὰ τρόπον ῥᾴδιον συμβιβάσαι
πότερον ἐνδέχεται πλείω τῷ αὐτῷ εἶναι ἐναντία
ἢ οὔ. τὸν αὐτὸν δὲ τρόπον καὶ ἐπὶ τῶν ἄλλων
τῶν ὁρισμοῦ δεομένων. ἔοικε δὲ καὶ ἐν τοῖς
30 μαθήμασιν ἔνια δι᾽ ὁρισμοῦ ἔλλειψιν οὐ ῥᾳδίως
γράφεσθαι, οἷον καὶ ὅτι ἡ παρὰ τὴν πλευρὰν
τέμνουσα τὸ ἐπίπεδον ὁμοίως διαιρεῖ τήν τε γραμμὴν καὶ τὸ χωρίον. τοῦ δὲ ὁρισμοῦ ῥηθέντος
εὐθέως φανερὸν τὸ λεγόμενον· τὴν γὰρ αὐτὴν
ἀνταναίρεσιν ἔχει τὰ χωρία καὶ αἱ γραμμαί· ἔστι
35 δ᾽ ὁρισμὸς τοῦ αὐτοῦ λόγου οὗτος. ἁπλῶς δὲ τὰ
πρῶτα τῶν στοιχείων τιθεμένων μὲν τῶν ὁρισμῶν,
οἷον τί γραμμὴ καὶ τί κύκλος, ῥᾷστα δεῖξαι, πλὴν
οὐ πολλά γε πρὸς ἕκαστον ἔστι τούτων ἐπιχειρεῖν
διὰ τὸ μὴ πολλὰ τὰ ἀνὰ μέσον εἶναι· ἂν δὲ μὴ
τιθῶνται οἱ τῶν ἀρχῶν ὁρισμοί, χαλεπόν, τάχα δ᾽

or it may be because at first this point is not clear to us, namely, in which of the above-mentioned ways the cause of our difficulty arises ; for, when the manner in which it arises is plain, it is obvious that it would be necessary either to give a definition, or to make a distinction, or to supply the intervening premisses ; for it is by these means that the ultimate conclusions are shown.

There are many theses which are not easily discussed and dealt with unless the definition is correctly assigned, for example, the question whether one thing has one contrary or many. If a proper definition has been given of ' contraries,' it is easy to make people see whether the same thing can have more than one contrary or not. The other terms which need definition can be dealt with in the same way. It seems likely that in mathematics also the construction of geometrical figures is sometimes rendered difficult through lack of definition, for example, in the proof that the line cutting the superficies parallel to the side of a parallelogram divides both the line and the area 'similarly.' [a] If the definition of ' similarly ' is stated, the meaning immediately becomes clear ; for the areas and lines undergo the same corresponding diminution, and this is the definition of ' in the same ratio.' To speak generally, it is very easy to make clear the most primary of the elementary principles, such as the meaning of a line or a circle, if their definitions are laid down, except that it is not possible to advance numerous arguments about any one of them because the intervening stages are not many. If, however, the definitions of the first principles are not laid down, it is difficult and perhaps

(d) Difficulties from a badly enunciated definition.

---

[a] This is intepreted in l. 35 to mean ' in the same ratio.'

159 a ὅλως ἀδύνατον. ὁμοίως δὲ τούτοις καὶ ἐπὶ τῶν κατὰ τοὺς λόγους ἔχει.

Οὔκουν δεῖ λανθάνειν, ὅταν δυσεπιχείρητος ᾖ ἡ θέσις, ὅτι πέπονθέ τι τῶν εἰρημένων. ὅταν δ'
5 ᾖ πρὸς τὸ ἀξίωμα καὶ τὴν πρότασιν μεῖζον ἔργον διαλεγῆναι ἢ τὴν θέσιν, διαπορήσειεν ἄν τις πότερον θετέον τὰ τοιαῦτα ἢ οὔ. εἰ γὰρ μὴ θήσει ἀλλ' ἀξιώσει καὶ πρὸς τοῦτο διαλέγεσθαι, μεῖζον προστάξει τοῦ ἐν ἀρχῇ κειμένου· εἰ δὲ θήσει, πιστεύσει ἐξ ἧττον πιστῶν. εἰ μὲν οὖν δεῖ μὴ
10 χαλεπώτερον τὸ πρόβλημα ποιεῖν, θετέον, εἰ δὲ διὰ γνωριμωτέρων συλλογίζεσθαι, οὐ θετέον· ἢ τῷ μὲν μανθάνοντι οὐ θετέον, ἂν μὴ γνωριμώτερον ᾖ, τῷ δὲ γυμναζομένῳ θετέον, ἂν ἀληθὲς μόνον φαίνηται. ὥστε φανερὸν ὅτι οὐχ ὁμοίως ἐρωτῶντί τε καὶ διδάσκοντι ἀξιωτέον τιθέναι.

15 IV. Πῶς μὲν οὖν ἐρωτηματίζειν καὶ τάττειν δεῖ, σχεδὸν ἱκανὰ τὰ εἰρημένα· περὶ δ' ἀποκρίσεως πρῶτον μὲν διοριστέον τί ἐστιν ἔργον τοῦ καλῶς ἀποκρινομένου, καθάπερ τοῦ καλῶς ἐρωτῶντος. ἔστι δὲ τοῦ μὲν ἐρωτῶντος τὸ ˙οὕτως ἐπαγαγεῖν τὸν λόγον ὥστε ποιῆσαι τὸν ἀποκρινόμενον τὰ
20 ἀδοξότατα λέγειν τῶν διὰ τὴν θέσιν ἀναγκαίων, τοῦ δ' ἀποκρινομένου τὸ μὴ δι' αὐτὸν φαίνεσθαι συμβαίνειν τὸ ἀδύνατον ἢ τὸ παράδοξον, ἀλλὰ διὰ

<hr>

^a 158 b 16-21.

wholly impossible. There is a close resemblance
between dialectical and geometrical processes.

We must then carefully note that, when a thesis
is hard to deal with, it is because one of the above-
mentioned circumstances [a] has arisen in connexion
with it. When, however, it is a harder task to discuss
the assumed principle which forms the premiss than
the thesis, one might well doubt whether such assumption should be made or not. For if your opponent
will not admit the assumption and is going to demand
that you shall discuss it as well, he will be prescribing
a greater task than was originally proposed, whereas,
if he is going to admit the assumption, he will be
founding his belief on a less credible basis. If, therefore, one ought not to increase the difficulty of the
problem, the admission ought to be made ; but, if
one ought to reason through premisses which are
more certain, it should not be made, or, to put the
matter differently, one who is seeking knowledge
ought not to make the admission unless it is more
certain than the conclusion, but he who is only
practising discussion ought to make the admission if
it merely appears to be true. It is clear, then, that a
mere questioner and a man who is imparting knowledge have not the same right to claim an admission.

(e) Should assumptions be made which are more difficult than the thesis itself ?]

IV. The formulation and arrangement of questions
have now been more or less adequately treated. As
regards answering, the function of the good answerer
must first be defined, as also that of the good questioner. The function of the questioner is so to direct
the discussion as to make the answerer give the most
paradoxical replies that necessarily result because of
the thesis. The function of the answerer is to make
it seem that the impossible or paradoxical is not his

How to ANSWER QUESTIONS. The rôles of questioner and answerer.

ARISTOTLE

159 a

τὴν θέσιν· ἑτέρα γὰρ ἴσως ἁμαρτία τὸ θέσθαι
πρῶτον ὃ μὴ δεῖ καὶ τὸ θέμενον μὴ φυλάξαι κατὰ
τρόπον.

25 V. Ἐπεὶ δ' ἐστὶν ἀδιόριστα τοῖς γυμνασίας καὶ
πείρας ἕνεκα τοὺς λόγους ποιουμένοις· (οὐ γὰρ
οἱ αὐτοὶ σκοποὶ τοῖς διδάσκουσιν ἢ μανθάνουσι
καὶ τοῖς ἀγωνιζομένοις, οὐδὲ τούτοις τε καὶ τοῖς
διατρίβουσι μετ' ἀλλήλων σκέψεως χάριν. τῷ
μὲν γὰρ μανθάνοντι θετέον ἀεὶ τὰ δοκοῦντα· καὶ
30 γὰρ οὐδ' ἐπιχειρεῖ ψεῦδος οὐδεὶς διδάσκειν· τῶν
δ' ἀγωνιζομένων τὸν μὲν ἐρωτῶντα φαίνεσθαί τι
δεῖ ποιεῖν πάντως, τὸν δ' ἀποκρινόμενον μηδὲν
φαίνεσθαι πάσχειν· ἐν δὲ ταῖς διαλεκτικαῖς συνόδοις
τοῖς μὴ ἀγῶνος χάριν ἀλλὰ πείρας καὶ σκέψεως
τοὺς λόγους ποιουμένοις οὐ διήρθρωταί πω τίνος
35 δεῖ στοχάζεσθαι τὸν ἀποκρινόμενον καὶ ὁποῖα
διδόναι καὶ ποῖα μὴ πρὸς τὸ καλῶς ἢ μὴ καλῶς φυλάττειν τὴν θέσιν)· ἐπεὶ οὖν οὐδὲν ἔχομεν
παραδεδομένον ὑπ' ἄλλων, αὐτοί τι πειραθῶμεν
εἰπεῖν.

Ἀνάγκη δὴ τὸν ἀποκρινόμενον ὑπέχειν λόγον
θέμενον ἤτοι ἔνδοξον ἢ ἄδοξον θέσιν ἢ μηδέτερον,
159 b καὶ ἤτοι ἁπλῶς ἔνδοξον ἢ ἄδοξον ἢ ὡρισμένως,
οἷον τῳδί τινι ἢ αὐτῷ ἢ ἄλλῳ. διαφέρει δ' οὐδὲν
ὁπωσοῦν ἐνδόξου ἢ ἀδόξου οὔσης· ὁ γὰρ αὐτὸς
τρόπος ἔσται τοῦ καλῶς ἀποκρίνεσθαι, καὶ δοῦναι
ἢ μὴ δοῦναι τὸ ἐρωτηθέν. ἀδόξου μὲν οὖν οὔσης

702

fault but is due to the thesis ; for, possibly, to lay down the wrong thesis originally is a different kind of mistake from not maintaining it properly after one has laid it down.

V. Now since there are no definite principles for those who discuss for the sake of practice and experiment—for those who teach or learn and those who compete with one another have not the same aim, and the aim of the latter differs from that of those who discuss for the sake of inquiry ; for he who is learning must always state what he thinks, since no one even attempts to teach a lie ; on the other hand, when men are competing with one another, the questioner must by some means or other appear to be producing some effect, while the answerer must appear to be unaffected ; but in meetings held for discussion, where the disputants argue not in competition but for the sake of experiment and inquiry, no formal rules have yet been laid down as to the aim which the answerer ought to seek and what sort of things he must offer and what not, so as to maintain his thesis properly or otherwise—since, then, we have no traditions handed down by others, let us try to say something ourselves on the subject. [Note on the absence of definite rules for discussions held for practice and experiment.]

The answerer must of necessity carry on the argument by taking up a position which is either generally accepted, or generally rejected, or neither accepted nor rejected, or which is accepted or rejected either absolutely or conditionally, for instance by some particular person or by the speaker himself or by someone else. But the way in which it is accepted or rejected makes no difference ; for the proper mode of answering will be the same, namely, to accede to or reject what has been asked. If the The answerer's procedure depends on the nature (a) of his own thesis, which may be either

5 τῆς θέσεως ἔνδοξον ἀνάγκη τὸ συμπέρασμα
γίνεσθαι, ἐνδόξου δ᾽ ἄδοξον· τὸ γὰρ ἀντικείμενον
ἀεὶ τῇ θέσει ὁ ἐρωτῶν συμπεραίνεται. εἰ δὲ μήτ᾽
ἄδοξον μήτ᾽ ἔνδοξον τὸ κείμενον, καὶ τὸ συμπέρασμα ἔσται τοιοῦτον. ἐπεὶ δ᾽ ὁ καλῶς συλλογιζόμενος ἐξ ἐνδοξοτέρων καὶ γνωριμωτέρων τὸ
προβληθὲν ἀποδείκνυσι, φανερὸν ὡς ἀδόξου μὲν
10 ὄντος ἁπλῶς τοῦ κειμένου οὐ δοτέον τῷ ἀποκρινομένῳ οὔθ᾽ ὃ μὴ δοκεῖ ἁπλῶς, οὔθ᾽ ὃ δοκεῖ μὲν
ἧττον δὲ τοῦ συμπεράσματος δοκεῖ. ἀδόξου γὰρ
οὔσης τῆς θέσεως ἔνδοξον τὸ συμπέρασμα, ὥστε
δεῖ τὰ λαμβανόμενα ἔνδοξα πάντ᾽ εἶναι καὶ μᾶλλον
ἔνδοξα τοῦ προκειμένου, εἰ μέλλει διὰ τῶν γνωρι-
15 μωτέρων τὸ ἧττον γνώριμον περαίνεσθαι. ὥστ᾽
εἴ τι μὴ τοιοῦτόν ἐστι τῶν ἐρωτωμένων, οὐ θετέον
τῷ ἀποκρινομένῳ. εἰ δ᾽ ἔνδοξος ἁπλῶς ἡ θέσις,
δῆλον ὅτι τὸ συμπέρασμα ἁπλῶς ἄδοξον. θετέον
οὖν τά τε δοκοῦντα πάντα, καὶ τῶν μὴ δοκούντων
ὅσα ἧττόν ἐστιν ἄδοξα τοῦ συμπεράσματος·
20 ἱκανῶς γὰρ ἂν δόξειε διειλέχθαι. ὁμοίως δὲ εἰ
μήτ᾽ ἄδοξος μήτ᾽ ἔνδοξός ἐστιν ἡ θέσις· καὶ γὰρ

position taken up by the answerer is one which is generally rejected, the conclusion must be one which is generally accepted, and *vice versa*; for the questioner always tries to elicit the conclusion which is the opposite of the answerer's position. If, however, his position is one which is neither generally accepted nor generally rejected, the conclusion will also be of this kind. Now since he who reasons well demonstrates his proposition from more generally accepted and more familiar premisses, (1) it is obvious that, if the questioner's proposition is one which is generally rejected absolutely, the answerer ought not to concede what is thus absolutely rejected, or what is accepted indeed, but less generally than the conclusion aimed at. For, if the answerer's position is one which is generally rejected, the conclusion will be one which is generally accepted, so that the premisses which the questioner tries to secure must all be generally accepted and more so than the conclusion, if the less familiar is to be reached through the more familiar. Therefore, if any of the questions asked are not of this kind, the answerer ought not to agree to them. (2) If, however, the position taken up by the answerer is one generally accepted absolutely, obviously the conclusion aimed at by the questioner will be one which is generally rejected absolutely. The answerer, therefore, should concede all points which are generally accepted and all those not generally accepted which are less generally rejected than the conclusion aimed at; for then he would be thought to have argued adequately. (3) So likewise if the answerer's position is one which is neither generally rejected nor generally accepted; for in these circumstances, too, whatever seems true

(1) Generally rejected.

(2) Generally accepted.

(3) Neither generally accepted nor rejected.

159 b

οὕτως τά τε φαινόμενα ἅπαντα δοτέον, καὶ τῶν
μὴ δοκούντων ὅσα μᾶλλον ἔνδοξα τοῦ συμπερά-
σματος· οὕτω γὰρ ἐνδοξοτέρους συμβήσεται τοὺς
λόγους γίνεσθαι. εἰ μὲν οὖν ἁπλῶς ἔνδοξον ἢ
25 ἄδοξον τὸ κείμενον, πρὸς τὰ δοκοῦντα ἁπλῶς τὴν
σύγκρισιν ποιητέον· εἰ δὲ μὴ ἁπλῶς ἔνδοξον ἢ
ἄδοξον τὸ κείμενον ἀλλὰ τῷ ἀποκρινομένῳ, πρὸς
αὐτὸν[1] τὸ δοκοῦν καὶ μὴ δοκοῦν κρίνοντα θετέον
ἢ οὐ θετέον. ἂν δ᾿ ἑτέρου δόξαν διαφυλάττῃ ὁ
ἀποκρινόμενος, δῆλον ὅτι πρὸς τὴν ἐκείνου διάνοιαν
30 ἀποβλέποντα θετέον ἕκαστα καὶ ἀρνητέον. διὸ
καὶ οἱ κομίζοντες ἀλλοτρίας δόξας, οἷον ἀγαθὸν
καὶ κακὸν εἶναι ταὐτόν, καθάπερ Ἡράκλειτός
φησιν, οὐ διδόασι μὴ παρεῖναι ἅμα τῷ αὐτῷ
τἀναντία, οὐχ ὡς οὐ δοκοῦν αὐτοῖς τοῦτο, ἀλλ᾿
ὅτι καθ᾿ Ἡράκλειτον οὕτω λεκτέον. ποιοῦσι δὲ
τοῦτο καὶ οἱ παρ᾿ ἀλλήλων δεχόμενοι τὰς θέσεις·
35 στοχάζονται γὰρ ὡς ἂν εἴπειεν ὁ θέμενος.

VI. Φανερὸν οὖν τίνων στοχαστέον τῷ ἀποκρινομένῳ, εἴτε ἁπλῶς ἔνδοξον εἴτε τινὶ τὸ κείμενόν
ἐστιν. ἐπεὶ δ᾿ ἀνάγκη πᾶν τὸ ἐρωτώμενον ἢ
ἔνδοξον εἶναι ἢ ἄδοξον ἢ μηδέτερον, καὶ ἢ πρὸς
τὸν λόγον ἢ μὴ πρὸς τὸν λόγον εἶναι τὸ ἐρωτώ-
160 a μενον, ἐὰν μὲν ᾖ δοκοῦν καὶ μὴ πρὸς τὸν λόγον,
δοτέον φήσαντα δοκεῖν, ἐὰν δὲ μὴ δοκοῦν καὶ μὴ

---

[1] Reading αὐτὸν for αὑτὸν with Pickard-Cambridge.

[a] Frags. 58 and 102 (Diels).

should be conceded, and also of the points not generally accepted those which are more generally accepted than the conclusion ; for the result of this is that the arguments will be more generally accepted. If, then, the answerer's proposition is one which is generally accepted or generally rejected absolutely, the comparison must be made with reference to what is generally accepted ; but, if the proposition is not generally accepted or rejected absolutely, but only by the answerer, then it must be conceded or not conceded with reference to his own personal judgement of what is generally accepted or not. If, however, the answerer is defending someone else's opinion, obviously he must concede or reject each point in accordance with that person's judgement. It is for this reason too that those who bring in other people's opinions—for example, Heracleitus' statement that good and evil are the same thing [a]—refuse to concede that it is impossible for contraries to belong to the same thing at the same time, not because this is not their view, but because, according to Heracleitus, they must say so. This is also the practice of those who take over positions from one another ; for they aim at saying what the man who took up the position in question would say.

VI. It is now clear what should be the aims of the answerer, whether the position adopted is generally accepted absolutely or only by some individual. Now, every question asked must be either generally accepted or generally rejected or neither accepted nor rejected, and what is asked must be either relevant or irrelevant to the argument ; if it is generally accepted and irrelevant, the answerer should admit its general acceptance and concede it. If, however,

(b) Of the particular question asked, which (1) should be generally acceptable and relevant.

πρὸς τὸν λόγον, δοτέον μέν, ἐπισημαντέον δὲ τὸ
μὴ δοκοῦν πρὸς εὐλάβειαν εὐηθείας. ὄντος δὲ πρὸς
τὸν λόγον καὶ δοκοῦντος λεκτέον ὅτι δοκεῖ μέν,
5 ἀλλὰ λίαν σύνεγγυς τοῦ ἐν ἀρχῇ ἐστι καὶ ἀναιρεῖται
τούτου τεθέντος τὸ κείμενον. εἰ δὲ πρὸς τὸν
λόγον, λίαν δ' ἄδοξον τὸ ἀξίωμα, συμβαίνειν μὲν
φατέον τούτου τεθέντος, ἀλλὰ λίαν εὔηθες εἶναι
τὸ προτεινόμενον. εἰ δὲ μήτ' ἄδοξον μήτ' ἔνδοξον,
εἰ μὲν μηδὲν πρὸς τὸν λόγον, δοτέον μηδὲν διορί-
10 σαντι, εἰ δὲ πρὸς τὸν λόγον, ἐπισημαντέον ὅτι
ἀναιρεῖται τεθέντος τὸ ἐν ἀρχῇ. οὕτω γὰρ ὅ τ'
ἀποκρινόμενος οὐδὲν δόξει δι' αὑτὸν πάσχειν, ἐὰν
προορῶν ἕκαστα τιθῇ, ὅ τ' ἐρωτῶν τεύξεται συλλογισμοῦ τιθεμένων αὐτῷ πάντων τῶν ἐνδοξοτέρων τοῦ συμπεράσματος. ὅσοι δ' ἐξ ἀδοξοτέρων
15 τοῦ συμπεράσματος ἐπιχειροῦσι συλλογίζεσθαι,
δῆλον ὡς οὐ καλῶς συλλογίζονται· διὸ τοῖς ἐρωτῶσιν οὐ θετέον.

VII. Ὁμοίως δὲ καὶ ἐπὶ τῶν ἀσαφῶς καὶ
πλεοναχῶς λεγομένων ἀπαντητέον. ἐπεὶ γὰρ
δέδοται τῷ ἀποκρινομένῳ μὴ μανθάνοντι εἰπεῖν
20 ὅτι οὐ μανθάνω, καὶ πλεοναχῶς λεγομένου μὴ ἐξ
ἀνάγκης ὁμολογῆσαι ἢ ἀρνήσασθαι, δῆλον ὡς πρῶτον μέν, ἂν μὴ σαφὲς ᾖ τὸ ῥηθέν, οὐκ ἀποκνη-

it is not generally accepted and irrelevant, he should
concede it but put in a remark that it is not generally
accepted, as a precaution against appearing to be
simple minded. If, on the other hand, it is relevant
and generally accepted, he should remark that it is
generally accepted but that it is too near to the
original view and say that, if it is conceded, the
proposition falls to the ground. If what the questioner claims is relevant to the argument but too
generally rejected, he should say that, if this concession is made, the conclusion results, but that what
is proposed is too silly to be accepted. When it is
neither generally rejected nor generally accepted,
if it is not relevant to the argument, it should be
conceded without qualification, but, if it is relevant,
a remark should be added that, if it is conceded, the
original proposition falls to the ground. In this way
the answerer will not be thought to suffer through
his own fault, since he foresees the result of his
various concessions, and the questioner will carry
through his reasoning with all the premisses which
are more generally accepted than the conclusion
conceded to him. Those who attempt to reason from
premisses less generally accepted than the conclusion obviously do not reason properly ; therefore
such premisses should not be conceded to questioners.

VII. The situation must be met in a similar way
when terms are used obscurely and have more than
one meaning. For, since the answerer is always
allowed, if he does not understand, to say, " I don't
understand," and, if the question has more than one
meaning, he need not necessarily assent or deny, it is
obvious, in the first place, that, if what is said is not
clear, he must not shrink from saying that he does

(2) Should
be stated
clearly and
unequivo-
cally.

160 a

τέον τὸ φάναι μὴ συνιέναι· πολλάκις γὰρ ἐκ τοῦ
μὴ σαφῶς ἐρωτηθέντας διδόναι ἀπαντᾷ τι δυσχερές.
ἂν δὲ γνώριμον μὲν ᾖ πλεοναχῶς δὲ λεγόμενον,
25 ἐὰν μὲν ἐπὶ πάντων ἀληθὲς ἢ ψεῦδος ᾖ τὸ λεγόμενον, δοτέον ἁπλῶς ἢ ἀρνητέον, ἐὰν δ' ἐπὶ τὶ
μὲν ψεῦδος ᾖ ἐπὶ τὶ δ' ἀληθές, ἐπισημαντέον
ὅτι πλεοναχῶς λέγεται καὶ διότι τὸ μὲν ψεῦδος
τὸ δ' ἀληθές· ὕστερον γὰρ διαιρουμένου ἄδηλον
εἰ καὶ ἐν ἀρχῇ συνεώρα τὸ ἀμφίβολον. ἐὰν δὲ μὴ
προΐδῃ τὸ ἀμφίβολον ἀλλ' εἰς θάτερον βλέψας θῇ,
30 ῥητέον πρὸς τὸν ἐπὶ θάτερον ἄγοντα ὅτι οὐκ εἰς
τοῦτο βλέπων ἔδωκα ἀλλ' εἰς θάτερον αὐτῶν.
πλειόνων γὰρ ὄντων τῶν ὑπὸ ταὐτὸν ὄνομα ἢ
λόγον ῥᾳδία ἡ ἀμφισβήτησις. ἐὰν δὲ καὶ σαφὲς
ᾖ καὶ ἁπλοῦν τὸ ἐρωτώμενον, ἢ ναί ἢ οὒ ἀποκριτέον.

35 VIII. Ἐπεὶ δὲ πᾶσα πρότασις συλλογιστικὴ ἢ
τούτων τίς ἐστιν ἐξ ὧν ὁ συλλογισμὸς ἤ τινος
τούτων ἕνεκα (δῆλον δ' ὅταν ἑτέρου χάριν λαμβάνηται τῷ πλείω τὰ ὅμοια ἐρωτᾶν· ἢ γὰρ δι'
ἐπαγωγῆς ἢ δι' ὁμοιότητος ὡς ἐπὶ τὸ πολὺ τὸ
καθόλου λαμβάνουσιν), τὰ μὲν οὖν καθ' ἕκαστα
160 b πάντα θετέον, ἂν ᾖ ἀληθῆ καὶ ἔνδοξα, πρὸς δὲ τὸ
καθόλου πειρατέον ἔνστασιν φέρειν· τὸ γὰρ ἄνευ
ἐνστάσεως, ἢ οὔσης ἢ δοκούσης, κωλύειν τὸν
λόγον δυσκολαίνειν ἐστίν. εἰ οὖν ἐπὶ πολλῶν
φαινομένων μὴ δίδωσι τὸ καθόλου μὴ ἔχων ἔν-
5 στασιν, φανερὸν ὅτι δυσκολαίνει. ἔτι εἰ μηδ'

not comprehend; for a difficulty often confronts people if they assent when questions have not been clearly put to them. When the question is intelligible but can bear more than one meaning, then, supposing what it says is true or false in every case, he must assent or deny absolutely, but, if it is partly true and partly false, he must add the remark that it has several meanings and that in one meaning it is false, in the other true; for, if he makes this distinction only at a later stage, it is not clear whether originally he noticed the ambiguity. If he did not foresee the ambiguity but assents when he has only seen one meaning, he must say to the questioner when he leads on to the other meaning, " It was not that meaning that I had in view but the other one, when I gave my assent "; for, when several things fall under the same term or expression, disagreement easily arises. If, on the other hand, the question asked is plain and simple, the answer must be ' yes ' or ' no.'

VIII. Now since every premiss used in reasoning is either one of the constituent parts of the reasoning or else is assumed for the sake of one of these parts (and it is obvious when it is assumed for the sake of something else from the asking of many similar questions; for people usually secure the universal either by induction or by similarity), all the several particulars must be admitted if they are true and generally accepted. But against the universal one must try to bring an objection; for to hold up the argument without an objection, either real or apparent, is to behave peevishly. If, therefore, a man refuses to concede the universal, in a case where many instances are displayed, without having any objection to offer, he is clearly behaving peevishly. Further, if

(3) Should not admit of objection or counterargument.

711

ἀντεπιχειρεῖν ἔχει ὅτι οὐκ ἀληθές, πολλῷ μᾶλλον
ἂν δόξειε δυσκολαίνειν. καίτοι οὐδὲ τοῦθ᾽ ἱκανόν·
πολλοὺς γὰρ λόγους ἔχομεν ἐναντίους ταῖς δόξαις,
οὓς χαλεπὸν λύειν, καθάπερ τοῦ[1] Ζήνωνος ὅτι οὐκ
ἐνδέχεται κινεῖσθαι οὐδὲ τὸ στάδιον διελθεῖν· ἀλλ᾽
10 οὐ διὰ τοῦτο ἀντικείμενα τούτοις οὐ θετέον. εἰ
οὖν μήτ᾽ ἐνίστασθαι μήτ᾽ ἀντεπιχειρεῖν ἔχων μὴ
τίθησι, δῆλον ὅτι δυσκολαίνει· ἔστι γὰρ ἡ ἐν
λόγοις δυσκολία ἀπόκρισις παρὰ τοὺς εἰρημένους
τρόπους, συλλογισμοῦ φθαρτική.

IX. Ὑπέχειν δὲ καὶ θέσιν καὶ ὁρισμὸν αὐτὸν
15 αὑτῷ δεῖ προεγχειρήσαντα· ἐξ ὧν γὰρ ἀναιροῦσιν
οἱ πυνθανόμενοι τὸ κείμενον, δῆλον ὅτι τούτοις
ἐναντιωτέον.

Ἄδοξον δ᾽ ὑπόθεσιν εὐλαβητέον ὑπέχειν. εἴη
δ᾽ ἂν ἄδοξος διχῶς· καὶ γὰρ ἐξ ἧς ἄτοπα συμβαίνει λέγειν, οἷον εἰ πάντα φαίη τις κινεῖσθαι ἢ
20 μηδέν, καὶ ὅσα χείρονος ἤθους ἑλέσθαι καὶ ὑπ-
εναντία ταῖς βουλήσεσιν, οἷον ὅτι ἡδονὴ τἀγαθὸν
καὶ τὸ ἀδικεῖν βέλτιον τοῦ ἀδικεῖσθαι. οὐ γὰρ
ὡς λόγου χάριν ὑπέχοντα ἀλλ᾽ ὡς τὰ δοκοῦντα
λέγοντα μισοῦσιν.

X. Ὅσοι δὲ τῶν λόγων ψεῦδος συλλογίζονται,
λυτέον ἀναιροῦντα παρ᾽ ὃ γίνεται τὸ ψεῦδος. οὐ

---

[1] τοῦ is omitted by Bekker in error.

[a] *Phys.* 233 a 21 ff. ; 239 b 9 ff.

he cannot even advance a counter-argument to prove that it is not true, he would be regarded as much more peevish. Yet even this is not enough ; for we get many arguments which are contrary to accepted opinions and yet are difficult to solve, for example, that of Zeno [a] that motion or traversing the stadium is impossible ; but we ought not on this account to refuse to assert the opposites of these views. If, therefore, a man refuses to make an admission when he has no objection or counter-argument to advance, he is obviously acting peevishly ; for peevishness in argument is answering otherwise than in the ways mentioned above, with the object of destroying the reasoning.

IX. Before he upholds a thesis or a definition, a man ought to argue against it by himself ; for obviously he must oppose the grounds on which the questioners seek to subvert the position which he has taken up. *Rules for the defence of a thesis.*

Care must be taken not to uphold a hypothesis which is generally unacceptable. There are two ways in which it may be unacceptable. It may be one which leads to the making of absurd statements, for example, if one were to say that everything or nothing is in motion ; on the other hand, it may be one of those which a bad character would choose or which are contrary to our wishes, for example, that pleasure is the good and that to commit injustice is better than to suffer it. For men hate him who makes such assertions, regarding him not as maintaining them for the sake of argument but as saying what he really thinks.

X. Of arguments which reason to establish a falsehood, a solution must be provided by demolishing that from which the falsehood arises. For a man has *The solution of false arguments.*

25 γὰρ ὁτιοῦν ἀνελὼν λέλυκεν, οὐδ᾿ εἰ ψεῦδός ἐστι
τὸ ἀναιρούμενον. ἔχοι γὰρ ἂν πλείω ψεύδη ὁ
λόγος, οἷον ἐάν τις λάβῃ τὸν καθήμενον γράφειν,
Σωκράτη δὲ καθῆσθαι· συμβαίνει γὰρ ἐκ τούτων
Σωκράτη γράφειν. ἀναιρεθέντος οὖν τοῦ Σωκράτη
καθῆσθαι οὐδὲν μᾶλλον λέλυται ὁ λόγος· καίτοι
30 ψεῦδος τὸ ἀξίωμα. ἀλλ᾿ οὐ παρὰ τοῦτο ὁ λόγος
ψευδής· ἂν γάρ τις τύχῃ καθήμενος μὲν μὴ γράφων
δέ, οὐκέτι ἐπὶ τοῦ τοιούτου ἡ αὐτὴ λύσις ἁρμόσει.
ὥστε οὐ τοῦτο ἀναιρετέον, ἀλλὰ τὸ τὸν καθήμενον
γράφειν· οὐ γὰρ πᾶς ὁ καθήμενος γράφει. λέλυκε
μὲν οὖν πάντως ὁ ἀνελὼν παρ᾿ ὃ γίνεται τὸ ψεῦδος,
35 οἶδε δὲ τὴν λύσιν ὁ εἰδὼς ὅτι παρὰ τοῦτο ὁ λόγος,
καθάπερ ἐπὶ τῶν ψευδογραφουμένων· οὐ γὰρ
ἀπόχρη τὸ ἐνστῆναι, οὐδ᾿ ἂν ψεῦδος ᾖ τὸ ἀναιρούμενον, ἀλλὰ καὶ διότι ψεῦδος ἀποδεικτέον· οὕτω
γὰρ ἂν εἴη φανερὸν πότερον προορῶν τι ἢ οὒ
ποιεῖται τὴν ἔνστασιν.

Ἔστι δὲ λόγον κωλῦσαι συμπεράνασθαι τετραχῶς. ἢ γὰρ ἀνελόντα παρ᾿ ὃ γίνεται τὸ ψεῦδος,
ἢ πρὸς τὸν ἐρωτῶντα ἔνστασιν εἰπόντα· πολλάκις
γὰρ οὐδὲ λέλυκεν, ὁ μέντοι πυνθανόμενος οὐ
5 δύναται πορρωτέρω προαγαγεῖν. τρίτον δὲ πρὸς
τὰ ἠρωτημένα· συμβαίη γὰρ ἂν ἐκ μὲν τῶν
ἠρωτημένων μὴ γίνεσθαι ὃ βούλεται διὰ τὸ κακῶς
ἠρωτῆσθαι, προστεθέντος δέ τινος γίνεσθαι τὸ

not reached a solution by demolishing any chance point, even though what is demolished is false. For the argument might contain several falsehoods, for example, if one were to assume that ' he who sits, writes ' and ' Socrates is sitting '; for the result of these premisses is that ' Socrates is writing.' If the statement that ' Socrates is sitting ' is demolished, the argument is no nearer a solution, and yet what was claimed is false, but the argument is not false in respect of this ; for if a man happened to be sitting but not writing, then the same solution would be no longer applicable. And so this is not the point which must be demolished, but that ' he who sits, writes '; for not everyone who sits is writing. The man who has demolished that on which the falsehood depends has provided a complete solution, and he who knows that the argument depends on a particular point, knows the solution, just as in the case of false geometrical figures ; for it is not enough to make an objection even if what is demolished is false, but why it is false must also be demonstrated ; for thus it would be clear whether or no he makes his objection with an object in view.

There are four ways in which it is possible to prevent a man from bringing his argument to a con-clusion, firstly, by demolishing that on which the falsehood depends, or, secondly, by bringing an objection against the questioner ; for often the answerer has provided no solution, but nevertheless the questioner can proceed no further. Thirdly, an objection can be made to the questions ; for it might so happen that what the questioner wants does not follow as a result of his questions because they have been badly asked, but, if something is added, the

Four methods of preventing an argu- ment from reaching a conclusion.

715

161 a

συμπέρασμα. εἰ μὲν οὖν μηκέτι δύναται προάγειν
ὁ ἐρωτῶν, πρὸς τὸν ἐρωτῶντα εἴη ἂν ἔνστασις,
εἰ δὲ δύναται, πρὸς τὰ ἠρωτημένα. τετάρτη δὲ
10 καὶ χειρίστη τῶν ἐνστάσεων ἡ πρὸς τὸν χρόνον·
ἔνιοι γὰρ τοιαῦτα ἐνίστανται πρὸς ἃ διαλεχθῆναι
πλείονός ἐστι χρόνου ἢ τῆς παρούσης διατριβῆς.

Αἱ μὲν οὖν ἐνστάσεις, καθάπερ εἴπαμεν, τετραχῶς γίνονται· λύσις δ᾽ ἐστὶ τῶν εἰρημένων ἡ
15 πρώτη μόνον, αἱ δὲ λοιπαὶ κωλύσεις τινὲς καὶ
ἐμποδισμοὶ τῶν συμπερασμάτων.

XI. Ἐπιτίμησις δὲ λόγου κατ᾽ αὐτόν τε τὸν
λόγον, καὶ ὅταν ἐρωτᾶται, οὐχ ἡ αὐτή· πολλάκις
γὰρ τοῦ μὴ καλῶς διειλέχθαι τὸν λόγον ὁ ἐρωτώ-
μενος αἴτιος διὰ τὸ μὴ συγχωρεῖν ἐξ ὧν ἦν δια-
20 λεχθῆναι καλῶς πρὸς τὴν θέσιν· οὐ γὰρ ἔστιν ἐπὶ
θατέρῳ μόνον τὸ καλῶς ἐπιτελεσθῆναι τὸ κοινὸν
ἔργον. ἀναγκαῖον οὖν ἐνίοτε πρὸς τὸν λέγοντα
καὶ μὴ πρὸς τὴν θέσιν ἐπιχειρεῖν, ὅταν ὁ ἀποκρινόμενος τἀναντία τῷ ἐρωτῶντι παρατηρῇ προσ-
επηρεάζων. δυσκολαίνοντες οὖν ἀγωνιστικὰς καὶ
οὐ διαλεκτικὰς ποιοῦνται τὰς διατριβάς. ἔτι δ᾽
25 ἐπεὶ γυμνασίας καὶ πείρας χάριν ἀλλ᾽ οὐ διδα-
σκαλίας οἱ τοιοῦτοι τῶν λόγων, δῆλον ὡς οὐ μόνον
τἀληθῆ συλλογιστέον ἀλλὰ καὶ ψεῦδος, οὐδὲ δι᾽
ἀληθῶν ἀεὶ ἀλλ᾽ ἐνίοτε καὶ ψευδῶν. πολλάκις
γὰρ ἀληθοῦς τεθέντος ἀναιρεῖν ἀνάγκη τὸν διαλεγόμενον, ὥστε προτατέον τὰ ψευδῆ. ἐνίοτε δὲ

conclusion results. If, therefore, he cannot advance his argument any further, an objection could be raised against the questioner, but, if he can still advance his argument, against his questions. The fourth and worst form of objection is that which relates to the time available ; for some people bring forward objections which take longer to deal with than the present discussion allows.

The kinds of objection, then, as we have said, are four in number ; but of those mentioned the first only is a solution, the others are merely hindrances and impediments in the path to conclusions.

XI. Criticism of an argument when it is taken by itself is not the same thing as when it forms the subject of questions ; for often the person questioned is the cause of the argument not being properly discussed, because he does not concede the points which would have enabled the argument against his thesis to have been properly carried out ; for it is not within the power of one party only to ensure the proper accomplishment of the common task. It is, therefore, necessary sometimes to attack the speaker and not his thesis, when the answerer is on the watch for points against the questioner and also employs abuse. By behaving peevishly, then, people make their discussions contentious instead of dialectical. Furthermore, since such arguments are carried on for the sake of practice and experiment rather than instruction, it is obvious that people must argue to establish not only the truth but also falsehood, and not always by means of what is true but also sometimes by means of what is false. For often, when what is true has been asserted, the dialectician has to demolish it and so false views have to be put forward. Sometimes,

Various points concerning arguments and conclusions : (a) Adverse criticism of an argument and of a person arguing is not the same thing.

717

161 a

30 καὶ ψεύδους τεθέντος ἀναιρετέον διὰ ψευδῶν·
οὐδὲν γὰρ κωλύει τινὶ δοκεῖν τὰ μὴ ὄντα μᾶλλον
τῶν ἀληθῶν, ὥστ' ἐκ τῶν ἐκείνῳ δοκούντων τοῦ
λόγου γινομένου μᾶλλον ἔσται πεπεισμένος ἢ
ὠφελημένος. δεῖ δὲ τὸν καλῶς μεταβιβάζοντα
διαλεκτικῶς καὶ μὴ ἐριστικῶς μεταβιβάζειν, καθ-
35 άπερ τὸν γεωμέτρην γεωμετρικῶς, ἄν τε ψεῦδος
ἄν τ' ἀληθὲς ᾖ τὸ συμπεραινόμενον· ποῖοι δὲ
διαλεκτικοὶ συλλογισμοί, πρότερον εἴρηται. ἐπεὶ
δὲ φαῦλος κοινωνὸς ὁ ἐμποδίζων τὸ κοινὸν ἔργον,
δῆλον ὅτι καὶ ἐν λόγῳ. κοινὸν γάρ τι καὶ ἐν τούτοις προκείμενόν ἐστι, πλὴν τῶν ἀγωνιζομένων.
40 τούτοις δ' οὐκ ἔστιν ἀμφοτέροις τυχεῖν τοῦ αὐτοῦ

161 b τέλους· πλείους γὰρ ἑνὸς ἀδύνατον νικᾶν. διαφέρει
δ' οὐδὲν ἄν τε διὰ τοῦ ἀποκρίνεσθαι ἄν τε διὰ τοῦ
ἐρωτᾶν ποιῇ τοῦτο· ὅ τε γὰρ ἐριστικῶς ἐρωτῶν
φαύλως διαλέγεται, ὅ τ' ἐν τῷ ἀποκρίνεσθαι μὴ
διδοὺς τὸ φαινόμενον μηδ' ἐκδεχόμενος ὅ τί ποτε
5 βούλεται ὁ ἐρωτῶν πυθέσθαι. δῆλον οὖν ἐκ τῶν
εἰρημένων ὅτι οὐχ ὁμοίως ἐπιτιμητέον καθ' αὑτόν
τε τῷ λόγῳ καὶ τῷ ἐρωτῶντι· οὐδὲν γὰρ κωλύει
τὸν μὲν λόγον φαῦλον εἶναι, τὸν δ' ἐρωτῶντα ὡς
ἐνδέχεται βέλτιστα πρὸς τὸν ἀποκρινόμενον διειλέχθαι. πρὸς γὰρ τοὺς δυσκολαίνοντας οὐ δυνατὸν
10 ἴσως εὐθὺς οἵους τις βούλεται ἀλλ' οἵους ἐνδέχεται
ποιεῖσθαι τοὺς συλλογισμούς.

Ἐπεὶ δ' ἐστὶν ἀδιόριστον πότε τἀναντία καὶ
πότε τὰ ἐν ἀρχῇ λαμβάνουσιν οἱ ἄνθρωποι (πολ-

718

too, when what is false has been asserted, it has to be demolished by means of falsehoods; for there is nothing to prevent a man accepting what are not facts rather than the truth; and so, if the argument is based on what he accepts, he will be persuaded rather than benefited. The man, however, who is seeking to convert another in the proper manner should do so in a dialectical and not in a contentious way, just as a geometrician reasons geometrically, whether the conclusion aimed at is false or true. The nature of dialectical reasonings has already been described. Now in business he who hinders the common task is a bad partner, and the same is true in argument; for here, too, there is a common purpose, unless the parties are merely competing against one another; for then they cannot both reach the same goal, since more than one cannot be victorious. It makes no difference whether a man acts like this in his answers or in his questions; for he who asks questions in a contentious spirit and he who in replying refuses to admit what is apparent and to accept whatever question the questioner wishes to put, are both of them bad dialecticians. It is clear, therefore, from what has been said that the argument by itself and the questioner by himself are not open to the same sort of criticism; for there is no reason why, though the argument is bad, the questioner should not have argued with the answerer in the best possible manner. Against those who shew peevishness it is not perhaps possible immediately to employ such reasonings as one wishes, but one only employs such as one can.

Since it cannot be determined when men are assuming contraries and when they are assuming

(b) Contentious argument should be avoided.

(c) How arguments become vitiated.

161 b

λάκις γὰρ καθ᾽ αὑτοὺς λέγοντες τὰ ἐναντία λέγουσι,
καὶ ἀνανεύσαντες πρότερον διδόασιν ὕστερον·
διόπερ ἐρωτώμενοι τἀναντία καὶ τὸ ἐν ἀρχῇ
15 πολλάκις ὑπακούουσιν), ἀνάγκη φαύλους γίνεσθαι
τοὺς λόγους. αἴτιος δ᾽ ὁ ἀποκρινόμενος, τὰ μὲν
οὐ διδούς, τὰ δὲ τοιαῦτα διδούς. φανερὸν οὖν ὡς
οὐχ ὁμοίως ἐπιτιμητέον τοῖς ἐρωτῶσι καὶ τοῖς
λόγοις.

Καθ᾽ αὑτὸν δὲ τῷ λόγῳ πέντ᾽ εἰσὶν ἐπιτιμήσεις,
20 πρώτη μὲν ὅταν ἐκ τῶν ἐρωτωμένων μὴ συμπεραίνηται μήτε τὸ προτεθὲν μήτε ὅλως μηδὲν
ὄντων ψευδῶν ἢ ἀδόξων, ἢ ἁπάντων ἢ τῶν πλείστων, ἐν οἷς τὸ συμπέρασμα, καὶ μήτ᾽ ἀφαιρεθέντων
τινῶν μήτε προστεθέντων μηδὲ τῶν μὲν ἀφαιρεθέντων τῶν δὲ προστεθέντων γίνηται τὸ συμπέρασμα.
25 δευτέρα δὲ εἰ πρὸς τὴν θέσιν μὴ γίνοιτο ὁ συλλογισμὸς ἐκ τοιούτων τε καὶ οὕτως ὡς εἴρηται
πρότερον. τρίτη δ᾽ εἰ προστεθέντων τινῶν γίνοιτο
συλλογισμός, ταῦτα δ᾽ εἴη χείρω τῶν ἐρωτηθέντων
καὶ ἧττον ἔνδοξα τοῦ συμπεράσματος. πάλιν εἰ
ἀφαιρεθέντων τινῶν· ἐνίοτε γὰρ πλείω λαμβάνουσι
30 τῶν ἀναγκαίων, ὥστε οὐ τῷ ταῦτ᾽ εἶναι γίνεται
ὁ συλλογισμός. ἔτι εἰ ἐξ ἀδοξοτέρων καὶ ἧττον
πιστῶν τοῦ συμπεράσματος, ἢ εἰ ἐξ ἀληθῶν ἀλλὰ
πλείονος ἔργου δεομένων ἀποδεῖξαι τοῦ προβλήματος.

720

the original contention—for often when they are speaking by themselves they assert contraries and, after first denying something, afterwards admit it (hence, when they are questioned, they often assent to contraries and to the original contention)—arguments necessarily deteriorate. But it is the answerer who is responsible since he refuses to grant some points but grants others of the same kind. It is obvious, therefore, that the questioners and the arguments are not open to the same kind of criticism.

The argument in itself is open to criticism under (d) Five five different conditions : (1) when as a result of the ways in which an questions neither the conclusion proposed, nor any argument conclusion at all, is reached, because all or most of is in itself the premisses on which the conclusion depends are criticism. either false or not generally accepted, and when neither the suppression nor the addition of any premisses makes the conclusion possible ; (2) if the reasoning, based on the premisses in the manner described above, were not to be applicable to the thesis ; (3) if reasoning were to proceed as a result of certain additional premisses, but yet these were to be inferior to those contained in the questions and less generally accepted than the conclusion ; again (4) if the reasoning were to proceed as the result of certain suppressions : for sometimes people assume more premisses than are necessary, and so it is not their presence which allows the reasoning to proceed ; furthermore (5) if the reasoning were to proceed from premisses less generally accepted and less credible than the conclusion, or if it were to proceed from premisses which, though true, require more labour to demonstrate than the problem.

161 b

Οὐ δεῖ δὲ πάντων τῶν προβλημάτων ὁμοίως
35 ἀξιοῦν τοὺς συλλογισμοὺς ἐνδόξους εἶναι καὶ
πιθανούς· φύσει γὰρ εὐθὺς ὑπάρχει τὰ μὲν ῥάω
τὰ δὲ χαλεπώτερα τῶν ζητουμένων, ὥστε ἂν ἐξ
ὧν ἐνδέχεται μάλιστα ἐνδόξων συμβιβάσῃ, διείλεκται καλῶς. φανερὸν οὖν ὅτι οὐδὲ λόγῳ ἡ αὐτὴ
ἐπιτίμησις πρός τε τὸ προβληθὲν καὶ καθ᾿ αὑτόν.
40 οὐδὲν γὰρ κωλύει καθ᾿ αὑτὸν μὲν εἶναι τὸν λόγον
162 a ψεκτόν, πρὸς δὲ τὸ πρόβλημα ἐπαινετόν, καὶ
πάλιν ἀντεστραμμένως καθ᾿ αὑτὸν μὲν ἐπαινετόν,
πρὸς δὲ τὸ πρόβλημα ψεκτόν, ὅταν ἐκ πολλῶν ᾖ
ῥᾴδιον ἐνδόξων συμπεράνασθαι καὶ ἀληθῶν. εἴη
δ᾿ ἄν ποτε λόγος καὶ συμπεπερασμένος μὴ συμ-
5 πεπερασμένου χείρων, ὅταν ὁ μὲν ἐξ εὐήθων
συμπεραίνηται μὴ τοιούτου τοῦ προβλήματος
ὄντος, ὁ δὲ προσδέηται τοιούτων ἅ ἐστιν ἔνδοξα
καὶ ἀληθῆ, καὶ μὴ ἐν τοῖς προσλαμβανομένοις ᾖ
ὁ λόγος. τοῖς δὲ διὰ ψευδῶν ἀληθὲς συμπεραι-
νομένοις οὐ δίκαιον ἐπιτιμᾶν· ψεῦδος μὲν γὰρ ἀεὶ
10 ἀνάγκη διὰ ψεύδους συλλογίζεσθαι, τὸ δ᾿ ἀληθὲς
ἔστι καὶ διὰ ψευδῶν ποτὲ συλλογίζεσθαι. φανερὸν
δ᾿ ἐκ τῶν Ἀναλυτικῶν.[a]

Ὅταν δ᾿ ἀπόδειξις ᾖ τινὸς ὁ εἰρημένος λόγος,
εἰ τί ἐστιν ἄλλο πρὸς τὸ συμπέρασμα μηδαμῶς

---

[a] *An. Pr.* 53 b 26 ff.

One ought not to demand that the reasoning of every problem should meet with the same general acceptance and be equally convincing; for it is an immediate result of the nature of things that some subjects of inquiry are easier and some more difficult, so that, if a man carries conviction by means of views which meet with the widest acceptance possible, he has argued well. It is clear, therefore, that the same criticism does not apply to an argument when viewed in relation to the proposition and when taken by itself. For there is no reason why the argument should not be reprehensible in itself but commendable when viewed in relation to the proposition, and again, conversely, commendable in itself but reprehensible when viewed in relation to the proposition, when it is easy to draw a conclusion from a number of premisses which are generally accepted and true. It may also be that sometimes an argument even though brought to a conclusion is inferior to one which is not brought to a conclusion, when the former is concluded from premisses which are foolish, though the proposition is not foolish, whereas the latter requires additional premisses which are generally accepted and true but the argument does not depend on these additional assumptions. It is unjust to criticize those who draw true conclusions from false premisses; for a false conclusion must necessarily be always argued by means of a false premiss, whereas the truth may sometimes be argued even by means of false premisses. This is clearly shown in the *Analytics.*[a]

When the argument stated is a demonstration of something, but it is something irrelevant which has nothing to do with the conclusion, no inference will

(e) An argument may be open to criticism in itself but commendable in relation to the proposition, and vice versa.

(f) Philosopheme, epicheireme, sophism and aporeme.

ἔχον, οὐκ ἔσται περὶ¹ ἐκείνου συλλογισμός· ἂν δὲ
15 φαίνηται, σόφισμα ἔσται, οὐκ ἀπόδειξις. ἔστι
δὲ φιλοσόφημα μὲν συλλογισμὸς ἀποδεικτικός,
ἐπιχείρημα δὲ συλλογισμὸς διαλεκτικός, σόφισμα
δὲ συλλογισμὸς ἐριστικός, ἀπόρημα δὲ συλλογισμὸς
διαλεκτικὸς ἀντιφάσεως.

Εἰ δ' ἐξ ἀμφοτέρων τι δοκούντων δειχθείη, μὴ
20 ὁμοίως δὲ δοκούντων, οὐδὲν κωλύει τὸ δειχθὲν
μᾶλλον ἑκατέρου δοκεῖν. ἀλλ' εἰ τὸ μὲν δοκοίη
τὸ δὲ μηδετέρως, ἢ εἰ τὸ μὲν δοκοίη τὸ δὲ μὴ
δοκοίη, εἰ μὲν ὁμοίως, ὁμοίως ἂν εἴη καὶ μή, εἰ
δὲ μᾶλλον θάτερον, ἀκολουθήσει τῷ μᾶλλον.

Ἔστι δέ τις ἁμαρτία καὶ αὕτη περὶ τοὺς συλ-
25 λογισμούς, ὅταν δείξῃ διὰ μακροτέρων, ἐνὸν δι'
ἐλαττόνων καὶ ἐν τῷ λόγῳ ὑπαρχόντων, οἷον ὅτι
ἐστὶ δόξα μᾶλλον ἑτέρα ἑτέρας, εἴ τις αἰτήσαιτο
αὐτοέκαστον μάλιστ' εἶναι, εἶναι δὲ δοξαστὸν
ἀληθῶς αὐτό, ὥστε τῶν τινῶν μᾶλλον εἶναι αὐτό·
πρὸς δὲ τὸ μᾶλλον μᾶλλον τὸ λεγόμενον εἶναι· εἶναι
30 δὲ καὶ αὐτοδόξαν ἀληθῆ, ἢ ἔσται μᾶλλον ἀκριβὴς
τῶν τινῶν· ᾔτηται δὲ καὶ αὐτοδόξαν ἀληθῆ εἶναι
καὶ αὐτοέκαστον μάλιστ' εἶναι· ὥστε αὕτη ἡ δόξα²

¹ Reading περὶ for παρὰ with Strache-Wallies.
² Omitting ἡ μάλιστα ἀληθὴς with the best mss.

be drawn from it about the latter ; if there appears
to be such an inference, it will be a sophism not a
demonstration. A philosopheme is a demonstrative
inference, an epichireme is a dialectical inference,
a sophism is a contentious inference, and an aporeme
is a contentious inference of contradiction.

If something were to be shown from two premisses, (g) Conclu-
both of them generally accepted but not equally sions which follow cer-
accepted, there is no reason why what is shown should tain com-
not be more generally accepted than either of them. binations of premisses.
But if one premiss were to be generally accepted and
the other neither accepted nor rejected, or if one
were to be accepted and the other rejected, then, if
the acceptance and the rejection were equal, the conclusion would also be equally accepted and rejected.
If, however, either acceptance or rejection is more
general, the conclusion will follow the more general.

An error in reasoning also occurs when a man (h) The
shows something by a longer process, when he might error of proving
employ a shorter process, using material which is something
already existent in the argument, for example, when by an unnecessarily
he is showing that one opinion is more truly an long process.
opinion than another ; if he were to claim (a) that
' a thing-in-itself is most completely that thing,' and
(b) that ' an object-of-opinion-in-itself really exists,' so
that ' it is more completely an object of opinion than
the individual objects of opinion,' and were to claim
that ' when a thing-in-itself admits of a greater degree, that which is referred to it also admits of a
greater degree,' and ' opinion-in-itself, which is more
accurate than the individual objects of opinion, is
true,' and it has been claimed that ' there is a true
opinion-in-itself ' and that ' a thing-in-itself is most
completely that thing, it follows that this particular

725

162 a

ἀκριβεστέρα ἐστίν. τίς δὲ ἡ μοχθηρία; ἢ ὅτι
ποιεῖ, παρ' ὃ ὁ λόγος, λανθάνειν τὸ αἴτιον;

35 XII. Λόγος δ' ἐστὶ δῆλος ἕνα μὲν τρόπον καὶ
δημοσιώτατον, ἐὰν συμπεπερασμένος οὕτως ὥστε
μηδὲν δεῖν ἐπερωτῆσαι· ἕνα δέ, καὶ ὃς μάλιστα
162 b λέγεται, ὅταν εἰλημμένα μὲν ᾖ ἐξ ὧν ἀναγκαῖον
εἶναι, ᾖ δὲ διὰ συμπερασμάτων συμπεραινόμενος[1]·
ἔτι εἰ ἐλλείπει σφόδρα ἐνδόξων.

Ψευδὴς δὲ λόγος καλεῖται τετραχῶς, ἕνα μὲν
τρόπον ὅταν φαίνηται συμπεραίνεσθαι μὴ συμ-
5 περαινόμενος, ὃς καλεῖται ἐριστικὸς συλλογισμός·
ἄλλον δὲ ὅταν συμπεραίνηται μὲν μὴ μέντοι πρὸς
τὸ προκείμενον, ὅπερ συμβαίνει μάλιστα τοῖς
εἰς τὸ ἀδύνατον ἄγουσιν· ἢ πρὸς τὸ προκείμενον
μὲν συμπεραίνηται, μὴ μέντοι κατὰ τὴν οἰκείαν
μέθοδον. τοῦτο δ' ἐστίν, ὅταν μὴ ὢν ἰατρικὸς
10 δοκῇ ἰατρικὸς εἶναι ἢ γεωμετρικὸς μὴ ὢν γεωμετρικὸς ἢ διαλεκτικὸς μὴ ὢν διαλεκτικός, ἄν τε
ψεῦδος ἄν τ' ἀληθὲς ᾖ τὸ συμβαῖνον. ἄλλον δὲ
τρόπον ἐὰν διὰ ψευδῶν συμπεραίνηται. τούτου
δ' ἔσται ποτὲ μὲν τὸ συμπέρασμα ψεῦδος, ποτὲ
δ' ἀληθές· τὸ μὲν γὰρ ψεῦδος ἀεὶ διὰ ψευδῶν
15 περαίνεται, τὸ δ' ἀληθὲς ἐγχωρεῖ καὶ μὴ ἐξ
ἀληθῶν, ὥσπερ εἴρηται καὶ πρότερον.

Τὸ μὲν οὖν ψευδῆ τὸν λόγον εἶναι τοῦ λέγοντος
ἁμάρτημα μᾶλλον ἢ τοῦ λόγου, καὶ οὐδὲ τοῦ
λέγοντος ἀεί, ἀλλ' ὅταν λανθάνῃ αὐτόν, ἐπεὶ καθ'
αὑτόν γε πολλῶν ἀληθῶν ἀποδεχόμεθα μᾶλλον,

---

[1] Reading συμπειραινόμενος with A B and Ca[1].

opinion is more accurate.' What is objectionable in this? Is it not that it causes the ground on which the argument rests to be hidden?

XII. An argument is clear in one sense (and this is the most popular one), if it is brought to a conclusion in such a way that it is unnecessary to ask any further questions; and in another sense (and it is in this sense that the term is most often used) when the results are obtained from premises from which they must necessarily follow and the argument is concluded by means of conclusions, and if, moreover, there is a marked absence of popular opinions. *Clearness in argument: its three kinds.*

An argument is called fallacious in four different senses: (a) when it seems to be brought to a conclusion when it is not really so (the so-called contentious reasoning); (b) when it reaches a conclusion, but not the proposed conclusion (this happens most frequently in *reductiones ad impossibile*); (c) when it comes to the proposed conclusion but not by the appropriate method (that is, when a non-medical argument appears to be medical, or a non-geometrical to be geometrical, or a non-dialectical to be dialectical, whether the result be true or false); and (d) when the conclusion is reached by means of false premises (here the conclusion will be sometimes false and sometimes true; for a false conclusion is always reached through false premises, but a true conclusion may be reached even from false premises, as has been already stated[a]). *Fallacy in argument: (a) Its four kinds.*

The fallaciousness of an argument is the fault of the arguer rather than of the argument itself; but it is not always the fault of the arguer either, but only when he fails to observe its fallaciousness; for we often accept a fallacious argument for its own sake *(b) How far does it deserve censure?*

162 b

20 ἂν ἐξ ὅτι μάλιστα δοκούντων ἀναιρῇ τι τῶν ἀληθῶν. τοιοῦτος γὰρ ὢν ἑτέρων ἀληθῶν ἀπόδειξίς
ἐστιν· δεῖ γὰρ τῶν κειμένων τι μὴ εἶναι παντελῶς,
ὥστ' ἔσται τούτου ἀπόδειξις. εἰ δ' ἀληθὲς συμ-
περαίνοιτο διὰ ψευδῶν καὶ λίαν εὐήθων, πολλῶν
ἂν εἴη χείρων ψεῦδος συλλογιζομένων· εἴη δ' ἂν
25 τοιοῦτος καὶ ψεῦδος συμπεραινόμενος. ὥστε δῆλον
ὅτι πρώτη μὲν ἐπίσκεψις λόγου καθ' αὑτὸν εἰ
συμπεραίνεται, δευτέρα δὲ πότερον ἀληθὲς ἢ
ψεῦδος, τρίτη δ' ἐκ ποίων τινῶν. εἰ μὲν γὰρ ἐκ
ψευδῶν ἐνδόξων δέ, λογικός, εἰ δ' ἐξ ὄντων μὲν
ἀδόξων δέ, φαῦλος. εἰ δὲ καὶ ψευδῆ καὶ λίαν
ἄδοξα, δῆλον ὅτι φαῦλος, ἢ ἁπλῶς ἢ τοῦ πρά-
30 γματος.

XIII. Τὸ δ' ἐν ἀρχῇ καὶ τὰ ἐναντία πῶς αἰτεῖται
ὁ ἐρωτῶν, κατ' ἀλήθειαν μὲν ἐν τοῖς Ἀναλυτικοῖς
εἴρηται, κατὰ δόξαν δὲ νῦν λεκτέον.

Αἰτεῖσθαι δὲ φαίνονται τὸ ἐν ἀρχῇ πενταχῶς,
35 φανερώτατα μὲν καὶ πρῶτον εἴ τις αὐτὸ τὸ δείκνυσθαι δέον αἰτήσει. τοῦτο δ' ἐπ' αὐτοῦ μὲν οὐ
ῥᾴδιον λανθάνειν, ἐν δὲ τοῖς συνωνύμοις, καὶ ἐν
163 a ὅσοις τὸ ὄνομα καὶ ὁ λόγος τὸ αὐτὸ σημαίνει,
μᾶλλον. δεύτερον δὲ ὅταν κατὰ μέρος δέον ἀπο-

---

in preference to several true arguments, if it destroys
some true proposition by means of premises which
are as generally accepted as possible. For an argument of this kind is a demonstration of other truths ;
for one of the premises ought not to find a place in
it at all, and so it will be a demonstration of this fact.
But if a true conclusion were to be reached from false
and entirely foolish premises, the argument would
be worse than many which argue to a false conclusion, and an argument leading to a false conclusion
might also be of this kind. It is, therefore, obvious *(c) Test-*
that the first thing to look for in an argument itself *questions*
is whether it reaches a conclusion ; the second thing, *detection.*
whether its conclusion is true or false ; and the third
thing, from what premises it is drawn. For if it is
reached from premises which are false but generally
accepted, it is a dialectical argument ; but if it is
reached from premises which are real but generally
rejected, it is bad ; whereas, if the premises are
both false and entirely rejected by general opinion,
it is obviously bad, either absolutely or with reference
to the subject in question.

XIII. How the questioner begs the original ques- *The begging*
tion and also begs contraries has been truly described *of ques-*
in the *Analytics* [a] ; it must now be described from the *ways of*
point of view of popular opinion. *doing this*
are dis-
There seem to be five ways in which people beg *tinguished.*
the original question. (1) The first and most obvious
way is when a man begs the very point which has
to be shown ; this does not easily escape detection
when the actual term is used, but is more liable to
do so where synonyms are used and the term and
the description signify the same thing. (2) A second
way is when a man begs something universally when

δεῖξαι καθόλου τις αἰτήσῃ, οἷον ἐπιχειρῶν ὅτι τῶν
ἐναντίων μία ἐπιστήμη, ὅλως τῶν ἀντικειμένων
ἀξιώσειε μίαν εἶναι· δοκεῖ γὰρ ὃ ἔδει καθ᾽ αὑτὸ
5 δεῖξαι μετ᾽ ἄλλων αἰτεῖσθαι πλειόνων. τρίτον εἴ
τις καθόλου δεῖξαι προκειμένου κατὰ μέρος αἰτήσειεν, οἷον εἰ πάντων τῶν ἐναντίων προκειμένου
τῶνδέ τινων ἀξιώσειε· δοκεῖ γὰρ καὶ οὗτος, ὃ
μετὰ πλειόνων ἔδει δεῖξαι, καθ᾽ αὑτὸ χωρὶς
αἰτεῖσθαι. πάλιν εἴ τις διελὼν αἰτεῖται τὸ προ-
10 βληθέν, οἷον εἰ δέον δεῖξαι τὴν ἰατρικὴν ὑγιεινοῦ
καὶ νοσώδους, χωρὶς ἑκάτερον ἀξιώσειεν. ἢ εἴ
τις τῶν ἑπομένων ἀλλήλοις ἐξ ἀνάγκης θάτερον
αἰτήσειεν, οἷον τὴν πλευρὰν ἀσύμμετρον τῇ δια-
μέτρῳ, δέον ἀποδεῖξαι ὅτι ἡ διάμετρος τῇ πλευρᾷ.

Ἰσαχῶς δὲ καὶ τἀναντία αἰτοῦνται τῷ ἐξ ἀρχῆς.
15 πρῶτον μὲν γὰρ εἴ τις τὰς ἀντικειμένας αἰτήσαιτο
φάσιν καὶ ἀπόφασιν, δεύτερον δὲ τἀναντία κατὰ
τὴν ἀντίθεσιν, οἷον ἀγαθὸν καὶ κακὸν ταὐτόν.
τρίτον εἴ τις τὸ καθόλου ἀξιώσας ἐπὶ μέρους
αἰτοῖτο τὴν ἀντίφασιν, οἷον εἰ λαβὼν τῶν ἐναντίων
μίαν ἐπιστήμην, ὑγιεινοῦ καὶ νοσώδους ἑτέραν
20 ἀξιώσειεν, ἢ τοῦτο αἰτησάμενος ἐπὶ τοῦ καθόλου

he ought to show it in a particular case ; for example, if, when he is endeavouring to show that there is one science of contraries, he were to claim that there is in general one science of opposites ; for then he is regarded as begging, among several other things, what he should have shown by itself. (3) A third way is when it is proposed to show something universally and he begs it in a particular case ; if, for example, when it is proposed to show that the science of contraries is always one, he begs it of a particular pair of contraries ; for he is also regarded as begging separately and by itself something which he ought to have shown in conjunction with a number of other cases. (4) Another way is when he divides the proposition up and begs its separate parts ; for example, if, when he has to show that medicine is the science of the healthy and of the diseased, he were to claim the two points separately ; or (5) if he were to beg one of two things which necessarily follow one another, for example, that the side is incommensurable with the diagonal when he has to show that the diagonal is incommensurable with the side.

There is the same number of ways of begging con-traries as of begging the original question. (1) The first way occurs if one were to beg the opposite affirmation and negation ; (2) the second, if he were to beg the contraries in an antithesis, saying, for example, that the same thing is good and bad ; (3) the third, if he were to claim something universally and beg the contradiction of it in a particular case, for example, if he were to secure an assumption that the knowledge of contraries is one and then claim that the knowledge of what is healthy and of what is diseased is different ; or (4) if, after begging this, The begging of con-traries : five ways of doing this are distin-guished.

731

τὴν ἀντίφασιν πειρῷτο λαμβάνειν. πάλιν ἐάν τις
αἰτήσῃ τὸ ἐναντίον τῷ ἐξ ἀνάγκης συμβαίνοντι
διὰ τῶν κειμένων, κἂν εἴ τις αὐτὰ μὲν μὴ λάβοι
τἀντικείμενα, τοιαῦτα δ᾿ αἰτήσαιτο δύο ἐξ ὧν
ἔσται ἡ ἀντικειμένη ἀντίφασις. διαφέρει δὲ τὸ
25 τἀναντία λαμβάνειν τοῦ ἐν ἀρχῇ ὅτι τοῦ μέν ἐστιν
ἡ ἁμαρτία πρὸς τὸ συμπέρασμα (πρὸς γὰρ ἐκεῖνο
βλέποντες τὸ ἐν ἀρχῇ λέγομεν αἰτεῖσθαι), τὰ δ᾿
ἐναντία ἐστὶν ἐν ταῖς προτάσεσι τῷ ἔχειν πως
ταύτας πρὸς ἀλλήλας.

XIV. Πρὸς δὲ γυμνασίαν καὶ μελέτην τῶν
30 τοιούτων λόγων πρῶτον μὲν ἀντιστρέφειν ἐθί-
ζεσθαι χρὴ τοὺς λόγους. οὕτως γὰρ πρός τε τὸ
λεγόμενον εὐπορώτερον ἕξομεν, καὶ ἐν ὀλίγοις πολλοὺς ἐξεπιστησόμεθα λόγους. τὸ γὰρ ἀντιστρέφειν ἐστὶ τὸ μεταλαβόντα τὸ συμπέρασμα μετὰ
τῶν λοιπῶν ἐρωτημάτων ἀνελεῖν ἓν τῶν δοθέν-
35 των· ἀνάγκη γάρ, εἰ τὸ συμπέρασμα μή ἐστι, μίαν
τινὰ ἀναιρεῖσθαι τῶν προτάσεων, εἴπερ πασῶν
τεθεισῶν ἀνάγκη ἦν τὸ συμπέρασμα εἶναι. πρὸς
ἅπασάν τε θέσιν, καὶ ὅτι οὕτως καὶ ὅτι οὐχ
163 b οὕτως, τὸ ἐπιχείρημα σκεπτέον, καὶ εὑρόντα τὴν
λύσιν εὐθὺς ζητητέον· οὕτω γὰρ ἅμα συμβήσεται
πρός τε τὸ ἐρωτᾶν καὶ πρὸς τὸ ἀποκρίνεσθαι
γεγυμνάσθαι. κἂν πρὸς μηδένα ἄλλον ἔχωμεν,
πρὸς αὑτούς. παράλληλά τε παραβάλλειν, ἐκλέ-
5 γοντα πρὸς τὴν αὐτὴν θέσιν[1] ἐπιχειρήματα· τοῦτο
γὰρ πρός τε τὸ βιάζεσθαι πολλὴν εὐπορίαν ποιεῖ

------

[1] Reading ἐκλέγοντα πρὸς τὴν αὐτὴν θέσιν with the best mss.

[a] Cf. An. Pr. 59 b 1 ff.

he were to try and secure the contradiction universally. (5) Another way occurs if he were to beg the contrary of that which necessarily follows from the premises, even without securing the assumption of actual opposites but merely begging two premises of such a kind that the opposite contradiction will result from them. The assumption of contraries differs from the begging of the original question, because in the latter case the error concerns the conclusion (for we are looking to this when we say that there is a begging of the original question), whereas the contraries are situated in the premises, namely, in the relation in which they stand to one another.

XIV. For training and practice in this kind of argument one should, in the first place, accustom oneself to converting arguments; for thus we shall be better provided for treating the subject under discussion and obtain by a quick method a thorough knowledge of a number of arguments. For conversion *a* is the reversing of the conclusion, together with the other questions raised, and the demolition of one of the points conceded; for of necessity, if the conclusion is not true, one of the premises must be demolished, since it was owing to the assumption of all of them that the conclusion necessarily followed. In dealing with any thesis we must examine the argument both for and against, and having discovered it we must immediately seek the solution; for the result will be that we shall have trained ourselves at the same time both for question and for answer. If we have no one else with whom to argue, we must do so with ourselves. Also one must choose arguments relating to the same thesis and compare them; for this procedure supplies an abundance of material

Various hints upon training and practice in dialectical arguments:
(a) The usefulness of converting arguments.

(b) The usefulness of scrutinizing the arguments pro and con.

ARISTOTLE

καὶ πρὸς τὸ ἐλέγχειν μεγάλην ἔχει βοήθειαν, ὅταν
εὐπορῇ τις καὶ ὅτι οὕτως καὶ ὅτι οὐχ οὕτως·
πρὸς τὰ ἐναντία γὰρ συμβαίνει ποιεῖσθαι τὴν
φυλακήν. πρός τε γνῶσιν καὶ τὴν κατὰ φιλοσοφίαν
10 φρόνησιν τὸ δύνασθαι συνορᾶν καὶ συνεωρακέναι
τὰ ἀφ' ἑκατέρας συμβαίνοντα τῆς ὑποθέσεως οὐ
μικρὸν ὄργανον· λοιπὸν γὰρ τούτων ὀρθῶς ἑλέσθαι
θάτερον. δεῖ δὲ πρὸς τὸ τοιοῦτο ὑπάρχειν εὐφυᾶ·
καὶ τοῦτ' ἔστιν ἡ κατ' ἀλήθειαν εὐφυΐα, τὸ δύνασθαι
15 καλῶς ἑλέσθαι τἀληθὲς καὶ φυγεῖν τὸ ψεῦδος·
ὅπερ οἱ πεφυκότες εὖ δύνανται ποιεῖν· εὖ γὰρ
φιλοῦντες καὶ μισοῦντες τὸ προσφερόμενον εὖ
κρίνουσι τὸ βέλτιστον.

Πρός τε τὰ πλειστάκις ἐμπίπτοντα τῶν προβλημάτων ἐξεπίστασθαι δεῖ λόγους, καὶ μάλιστα περὶ
τῶν πρώτων θέσεων· ἐν τούτοις γὰρ ἀποδυσ-
20 πετοῦσιν οἱ ἀποκρινόμενοι πολλάκις. ἔτι τε
ὅρων εὐπορεῖν δεῖ, καὶ τῶν ἐνδόξων τε καὶ τῶν
πρώτων ἔχειν προχείρους· διὰ γὰρ τούτων οἱ
συλλογισμοὶ γίνονται. πειρατέον δὲ καὶ εἰς ἃ
πλειστάκις ἐμπίπτουσιν οἱ ἄλλοι λόγοι κατέχειν.
25 ὥσπερ γὰρ ἐν γεωμετρίᾳ πρὸ ἔργου τὸ περὶ τὰ
στοιχεῖα γεγυμνάσθαι, καὶ ἐν ἀριθμοῖς τὸ περὶ
τοὺς κεφαλισμοὺς προχείρως ἔχειν μέγα διαφέρει
πρὸς τὸ καὶ τὸν ἄλλον ἀριθμὸν γινώσκειν πολλα-
πλασιούμενον, ὁμοίως καὶ ἐν τοῖς λόγοις τὸ
πρόχειρον εἶναι περὶ τὰς ἀρχὰς καὶ τὰς προτάσεις
ἀπὸ στόματος ἐξεπίστασθαι· καθάπερ γὰρ ἐν τῷ
30 μνημονικῷ μόνον οἱ τόποι τεθέντες εὐθὺς ποιοῦσιν
αὐτὰ μνημονεύειν, καὶ ταῦτα ποιήσει συλλογιστι-
κώτερον διὰ τὸ πρὸς ὡρισμένας αὐτὰς βλέπειν
734

for carrying the position by storm and is very helpful in refutation, when one has plenty of arguments both for and against; for the result is that one is put on one's guard against contrary arguments. Also to take and to have taken in at a glance the results of each of two hypotheses is no mean instrument for the cult of knowledge and philosophic wisdom; for then it only remains to make a correct choice of one of them. For such a process one must possess a certain natural ability, and real natural ability consists in being able correctly to choose the true and avoid the false. Men of natural ability can do this; for they judge correctly what is best by a correct feeling of love or hatred for what is set before them.

You ought thoroughly to learn arguments dealing with questions of frequent occurrence and especially primary propositions; for answerers often become discouraged in dealing with these. Moreover, you should have a good supply of definitions and have those of familiar and primary ideas ready to hand; for it is by means of these that reasonings are carried on. You should also try and grasp the categories into which the other arguments most often fall. For just as in geometry it is useful to have been trained in the elements, and in arithmetic to have a ready knowledge of the multiplication table up to ten times helps much to the recognition of other numbers which are the result of multiplication, so too in arguments it is important to be prompt about first principles and to know your premises by heart. For just as to a trained memory the mere reference to the places in which they occur causes the things themselves to be remembered, so the above rules will make a man a better reasoner, because he sees the premises

(c) The usefulness of a thorough knowledge of the most usual arguments.

κατ᾽ ἀριθμόν. πρότασίν τε κοινὴν μᾶλλον ἢ λόγον
εἰς μνήμην θετέον· ἀρχῆς γὰρ καὶ ὑποθέσεως εὐ-
πορῆσαι μετρίως χαλεπόν.

Ἔτι τὸν ἕνα λόγον πολλοὺς ποιεῖν ἐθιστέον, ὡς
35 ἀδηλότατα κρύπτοντας. εἴη δ᾽ ἂν τὸ τοιοῦτον,
εἴ τις ὅτι πλεῖστον ἀφισταίη τῆς συγγενείας περὶ
ὧν ὁ λόγος. ἔσονται δὲ δυνατοὶ τῶν λόγων οἱ
164 a μάλιστα καθόλου τοῦτο πάσχειν, οἷον ὅτι οὐκ ἔστι
μία πλειόνων ἐπιστήμη· οὕτω γὰρ καὶ ἐπὶ τῶν
πρός τι καὶ ἐπὶ τῶν ἐναντίων καὶ συστοίχων ἐστίν.

Δεῖ δὲ καὶ τὰς ἀπομνημονεύσεις καθόλου ποιεῖσθαι τῶν λόγων, κἂν ᾖ διειλεγμένος ἐπὶ μέρους·
5 οὕτω γὰρ καὶ πολλοὺς ἐξέσται τὸν ἕνα ποιεῖν.
ὁμοίως δὲ καὶ ἐν ῥητορικοῖς ἐπὶ τῶν ἐνθυμημάτων.
αὐτὸν δ᾽ ὅτι μάλιστα φεύγειν ἐπὶ τὸ καθόλου
φέρειν τοὺς συλλογισμούς. ἀεί τε δεῖ σκοπεῖν
τοὺς λόγους, εἰ ἐπὶ κοινῶν διαλέγονται· πάντες
γὰρ οἱ ἐν μέρει καὶ καθόλου διειλεγμένοι εἰσί, καὶ
10 ἔνεστιν ἐν τῇ τοῦ κατὰ μέρος ἢ τοῦ καθόλου
ἀπόδειξις διὰ τὸ μὴ εἶναι συλλογίσασθαι μηδὲν
ἄνευ τοῦ καθόλου.

Τὴν δὲ γυμνασίαν ἀποδοτέον τῶν μὲν ἐπακτικῶν
πρὸς νέον, τῶν δὲ συλλογιστικῶν πρὸς ἔμπειρον.
πειρατέον δὲ λαμβάνειν παρὰ μὲν τῶν συλλο-
15 γιστικῶν τὰς προτάσεις, παρὰ δὲ τῶν ἐπακτικῶν
τὰς παραβολάς· ἐν τούτοις γὰρ ἑκάτεροι γεγυμνα-
σμένοι εἰσίν. ὅλως δ᾽ ἐκ τοῦ γυμνάζεσθαι δια-

defined and numbered. A premiss of general application should be committed to memory rather than an argument, since it is pretty difficult to have a first principle or hypothesis ready to hand.

You must accustom yourself to making a single argument into many, keeping the process as secret as possible. This would be best achieved by avoiding as far as possible anything closely connected with the topic under discussion. Arguments which are entirely universal will be best suited to this treatment, for example, the argument that ' there is not one knowledge of more than one thing '; for this applies to relative terms, contraries and co-ordinates. *(d) An adversary's argument should be divided into many, and rendered as universal as possible.*

You should also make records of arguments in a universal form, even though the discussion has been concerned with a particular case; for thus it will be possible to make a single argument into many. (The same thing applies also to enthymemes in rhetoric.) You should, however, yourself avoid, as far as possible, directing discussions towards the universal. You should also always examine your arguments and see whether they are proceeding on the basis of principles of general application; for all particular arguments are also argued universally, and the demonstration of the universal is inherent in that of the particular, because it is impossible to reason at all without employing the universal.

Against a young man you should apply your training in inductive methods, against an expert your training in deductive methods. You should try to obtain premisses from those who employ deduction, and parallel instances from those who practise induction; for they have been trained in this or that branch respectively. In a word, as a result of *(e) Inductive arguments are most useful against the young, deductive against the expert.*

164 a

λεγόμενον πειρατέον ἀποφέρεσθαι ἢ συλλογισμὸν
περί τινος ἢ λύσιν ἢ πρότασιν ἢ ἔνστασιν, ἢ εἰ
ὀρθῶς τις ἤρετο ἢ εἰ μὴ ὀρθῶς, ἢ αὐτὸς ἢ ἕτερος,

164 b καὶ παρὰ τί ἑκάτερον. ἐκ τούτων γὰρ ἡ δύναμις,
τὸ δὲ γυμνάζεσθαι δυνάμεως χάριν, καὶ μάλιστα
περὶ τὰς προτάσεις καὶ ἐνστάσεις· ἔστι γὰρ ὡς
ἁπλῶς εἰπεῖν διαλεκτικὸς ὁ προτατικὸς καὶ ἐνστα-
τικός. ἔστι δὲ τὸ μὲν προτείνεσθαι ἓν ποιεῖν τὰ

5 πλείω (δεῖ γὰρ ἐν ὅλῳ ληφθῆναι πρὸς ὃ ὁ λόγος),
τὸ δ᾽ ἐνίστασθαι τὸ ἓν πολλά· ἢ γὰρ διαιρεῖ ἢ
ἀναιρεῖ, τὸ μὲν διδοὺς τὸ δ᾽ οὒ τῶν προτεινομέ-
νων.

Οὐχ ἅπαντι δὲ διαλεκτέον, οὐδὲ πρὸς τὸν τυχόντα γυμναστέον. ἀνάγκη γὰρ πρὸς ἐνίους φαύ-

10 λους γίνεσθαι τοὺς λόγους. πρὸς γὰρ τὸν πάντως
πειρώμενον φαίνεσθαι διαφεύγειν δίκαιον μὲν πάντως πειρᾶσθαι συλλογίσασθαι, οὐκ εὔσχημον δέ.
διόπερ οὐ δεῖ συνεστάναι εὐχερῶς πρὸς τοὺς τυ-
χόντας· ἀνάγκη γὰρ πονηρολογίαν συμβαίνειν· καὶ
γὰρ οἱ γυμναζόμενοι ἀδυνατοῦσιν ἀπέχεσθαι τοῦ

15 διαλέγεσθαι μὴ ἀγωνιστικῶς.

Δεῖ δὲ καὶ πεποιημένους ἔχειν λόγους πρὸς τὰ
τοιαῦτα τῶν προβλημάτων, ἐν οἷς ἐλαχίστων εὐ-
πορήσαντες πρὸς πλεῖστα χρησίμους ἕξομεν. οὗτοι
δ᾽ εἰσὶν οἱ καθόλου, καὶ πρὸς οὓς πορίζεσθαι χαλεπώτερον ἐκ τῶν παρὰ πόδας.

dialectical exercise you should try and achieve either
a syllogism on some subject, or a solution, or a proposition, or an objection, or a determination whether
a question has been put correctly or incorrectly either
by yourself or someone else, and the cause of its
being correctly or incorrectly put. These are the
sources of ability in discussion, and the purpose of
exercise is the acquisition of ability, particularly in
connexion with propositions and objections; for, to
put the matter simply, the man who can make propositions and objections is the skilled dialectician.
To make a proposition is to turn many things into
one (for the end to which the argument is directed
must be included in a single whole), while to make
an objection is to turn one thing into many; for the
objector distinguishes or demolishes, conceding one
proposition and refusing to concede another.

You ought not to discuss with everybody or (f) Do not
exercise yourself against any casual person; for argue with
against some people argument is sure to deteriorate; any casual
for with a man who tries every means to seem to person.
avoid defeat you are justified in using every means
to obtain your conclusion, but this is not a seemly
proceeding. You should not, therefore, readily join
issue with casual persons; this can only result in a
debased kind of discussion; for those who are practising cannot forbear from disputing contentiously.

Also you ought to have arguments already framed (g) Special
to deal with problems, where, though we are provided provision
with very few arguments, those which we have will made to deal
be useful on the greatest number of occasions. These with argu-
arguments are those which are universal and those universal
for which it is more difficult to provide material from application.
readily accessible sources.

INDICES

POSTERIOR ANALYTICS

Abstractions 81b3

Accident 73b4, 9, 75a18-22, 78a11, 83a27; topic of 97a27. See Attribute

Accidental knowledge 71b9, 28, 75b25, 76a2; a. events 73b11; a. predication 81b24 ff., 83a1-23, b11; a. connexion 99a3

Achilles 97b18

Activity 83a22, b17, 85b21

Affirmation 72a13, 86b35

Affirmative & negative demonstration I. xxv

Ajax 97b18

Alcibiades 97b18

Anacharsis 78b30

Analogy 76a38, 98a20, 99a15

Analysis 78a7, 88b18; analytical argument 84a8, b2

Angle, alternate 74a15; a. in a semicircle 94a28-34; right a. 96b18; exterior a.s 99a19. See Triangle

Appropriate principles 72a6, cf. 71b23, 76a6

Arithmetic 75a39, b3; & harmonics 75b16, 76a10, 24, 78b38, 87a34; & geometry 76b4, 7, 79a19, 87a35, 88b12

Arithmetician 72a22, 76b2, 93b24

Art, as mode of thought 89b8, 100a8

Astronomy 76b11, 78b39

Athens 94a37–b7

Atomic attribution I. xv, xvi. See Immediate

Attribute, *per se* or essential 73a34, 74b6, 75a28, 41, 76a7, b4, 6, 13, 82b37, 39, 83b19, 84a12, b16, 85b24, 90a11, 91a18, 97a24, b1; opposite a.s 73b19, 74b9, 97a14, 20; universal a.s 73b26—74b4, 96a26, b2, 99a33; necessary a.s 74b7, 12, cf. 89a34; accidental or non-essential a.s 74b11, 75a18, b11, 89a35, 90a11, cf. 92a32; non-universal a.s 75b25; order of a.s 97a25

Axiom 72a17, 75a41, 76b14, 77a31

741

Deciduous, see Leaf-shedding

Definition (ὁρισμός, ὅρος, λόγος, sts. τί ἐστι, τί ἦν εἶναι) defined 72a21 ; d. & demonstration 75b31, 89a18, II. iii-viii; d. not a hypothesis 76b35; d. assumed by mathematics 78a13 ; d. & essence 89a32, 90b3—91a1 ; d. by correlative 92a20 ; elements in d. 96a22, b2, 98b22 ; d.s of *infimae species* 96b17 ; d. by division 96b27—97b13 ; d. always universal 97b26 ; d. of particular & universal 97b28 ; middle term as d. 99a21 ; all sciences based on d. 99a22. See Essence, Formula

Deflection 76b9

Demonstration defined 71b17, *cf.* 85b23, 92a36 ; first principles of d. 71b20, 75b39, 84a30 ;)(syllogism 71b23 ; d. & knowledge 72a37, I. iii, 83b33, 90b9 ; circular, reciprocal d. 72b17 ; absolute d. 72b25, 76a14, *cf.* 74a37 ; d. & necessity 74b14 ; d. not transferable I. vii, 76a22 ; three factors in d. 75a39 ; no d. of non-eternal facts 75b24 ; d. & definition 75b31, 89a18, II. iii-viii ; d. & discourse 76b24 ; d. & Forms, universals 77a5, 81a40 ; d. & interrogation 77a33 ; d. & essential attributes 84a11 ; no d. without middle term 84b23 ; d. & intuition 85a1 ; universal)(particular d. I. xxiv ; affirmative)(negative d. I. xxv ; more than one d. of the same conclusion I. xxix ; hypothetical d. 92a6

Demonstrative knowledge 73a22 ; d. sciences 76a37

Diagonal incommensurable 71b26, 89a30

Dialectic 75a22, 77a29, b31, 78a12, 81b19 ; dialectical arguments 82b35, 84a7, b2, 86a22, 88a19

Difference in species 74a9, 22, 97a11, 98a29 ; in genus 88b26

Differentia 74a37, 83b1 ; division by d. 96b25—97b6 ; d. in definition 96b30—97b13

Discourse, external & internal 76b24

Divisibility 84a16, 95b30

Division (logical) II. v, 92a28 ; in systematization 96b15 ; in definition 96b27—97b13 ; in formulation of problems 98a1

Earth 89b30, 90a12, 93a31, 98b1, 18

Echo 98a27

Eclipse 90a7, 13, 93a23, 95a14 ; of moon 75b34, 88a1, 90a3, 15-30, 93a30, 98a37, b18 ; of sun 89b26

Effect, see Cause

Efficient cause 94a22, 36, b23

TOPICA

I. INDEX OF THE MORE IMPORTANT GREEK WORDS

Numbers refer to page, column and line in the Berlin edition, given in the left hand margin of the left page in this edition (but 100 has been subtracted from all page numbers). Lines are shorter in the Loeb edition than in the Berlin edition, so that the line numbers are only approximate. The symbol + means " and in the following lines."

ἀγαθός 7a6 +
ἀδύνατος 57b34 +
αἵρεσις 4b2
αἴσθησις 2a7, 4a17, 5a5, 28, b5
αἴτιον 16b1 +
ἀλήθεια 4b3, 5b30
ἅμα τῇ φύσει 31a17 +
ἀναγκαῖος 55b20, 29 +
ἀνάγκη 12b1 +, 25a34
τὰ Ἀναλυτικά 62a11, b 32
ἄνθρωπος (def.) 1b30
ἀντιδιῃρημένα 36b2 +, 42b7 +, 43a29 +
ἀντίθεσις 63a16
ἀντικατηγορεῖν 3b8 +
ἀντικείμενα 5b33, 35b8, 42a23 +, 47a29
ἀντιστρέφειν 9a10 +, 25a6, 49b12, 63a32
ἀντίφασις 6b13, 24b8
ἀπόδειξις (def.) 0a27, 5a8, 8b19, 41a30, 62a12
ἀπόκληρος 12b18
ἀπομνημόνευσις 64a3
ἀπόρημα 62a18

ἀπόφασις 36a6 +, 43b12
ἀριθμός 3a8 +
ἀρχή 8b28 +, 21b8, 58b5 +
ἄτομος 9b17 +, 20a35, 21a36, 21b19, 22b22, 44b2
αὐτοάνθρωπος 37b7, 48a18
αὐτοδόξα 62a30
αὐτοέκαστον 62a27
ἀφαίρεσις 19a25

γένεσις 14b16 +, 17b4 +, 46b13
γένος 1b17 +, 2a31 +, b27 +, 3a8 +, b5 +
γεωμετρία 1a7
γῆρας 17 a 28 +
γίνεσθαι 37a23 +
γνώριμος 0b23
γνωριμώτερος 11a8 +, 29b3 +, 31a3, 41a26 +, 59a11
γνῶσις 4b3
γονεύς 5a7, b23
γραμματική 2a20 +
γυμνασία 1a27 +, 59a25
γυμναστικός 5a9

751

INDICES

TOPICA

ENGLISH INDEX, INCLUDING ALL PROPER NAMES

Numbers refer to page, column and line in the Berlin edition, given in the left hand margin of the left page of this edition (but 100 has been subtracted from all page numbers). Lines are shorter in the Loeb edition than in the Berlin edition, so that the line numbers are only approximate. The symbol + means "and in the following lines."

INDICES